The Monster Book of
MANGA STEAMPUNK

The Monster Book of
MANGA STEAMPUNK

Edited by Jorge Balaguer

HARPER DESIGN
An Imprint of HarperCollinsPublishers

THE MONSTER BOOK OF MANGA STEAMPUNK

HarperCollins books may be purchased for educational, business, or sales promotional use. For information, please write: Special Markets Department, at SPsales@harpercollins.com.

First edition packaged in 2014 by:
LOFT Publications
Barcelona, Spain

First edition published in 2014 by:
Harper Design
An Imprint of HarperCollins*Publishers*
195 Broadway
New York, NY 10007
Tel.: (212) 207-7000
Fax: (212) 207-7654
harperdesign@harpercollins.com
www.harpercollins.com

Distributed throughout the world by:
HarperCollins*Publishers*
195 Broadway
New York, NY 10007
Fax: (212) 207-7654

Editorial coordination:
Claudia Martínez Alonso

Art direction:
Mireia Casanovas Soley

Ilustrations and texts:
Jorge Balaguer

Layout:
Sara Abril Abajo
Cristina Simó Perales

Translation:
textcase
www.textcase.nl

ISBN: 978-0-06-235199-9

Library of Congress Control Number: 2014942431

Printed in China
First printing, 2014

CONTENTS

6 INTRODUCTION
8 GALACTIC HERO
16 VICTORIAN LADY
24 NAVY SOLDIER
32 HUNTRESS
40 HORSE AND HORSEMAN
48 ENGINE DRIVER
56 AIRWOMAN
64 SPACE SOLDIER
72 VICTORIAN GENTLEMAN
80 FEMALE OUTLAW
88 PIRATE
96 SWORDSMAN
104 MERCENARY
112 ROBOT
120 FEMALE WARRIOR
128 MARSHAL
136 VAMPIRE
144 DETECTIVE
152 FEMALE MECHANIC
160 FEMALE VAMPIRE
168 WITCH
176 SCUBA DIVER
184 MEDIEVAL KNIGHT
192 FAIRY
200 FEMALE INVENTOR
208 SUBMARINE CAPTAIN
216 MONSTER HUNTER
224 LUMBERJACK
232 FLYING MAN
240 HAWKER
248 ARTIST
256 OCCULTIST
264 FORTUNE-TELLER
272 NINJA
280 DOCTOR TERROR
288 DYNAMITER
296 FIREMAN
304 SPY
312 TIME TRAVELER

INTRODUCTION

When my editor and friend Paco Asensio first intimated the idea of working on a manga steampunk book, I was more than pleasantly surprised. As an artist and illustrator of books and comics, I've been working in this field for a long time. Moreover, steampunk is a style that continues to grow everyday, not only through the majestic clothes adorning the mechanical princes and courtiers from a fantastical medieval epoch but rather as an essence that is filtered, like a perfume, through the pores of each person that idolizes this genre.

But what exactly is steampunk? What do we know about it? Where was it born? I don't have all of the answers, but I will try to approach it as narrowly as I can...

Everything has its origin—a spark that lights the match of collective memory and becomes engrained in our mind. For me, the start to everything was a film that debuted in 1960—*The Time Machine*—based on the novel by H.G. Wells. Seeing it as a child opened me up to a world that immediately fascinated me and to which I would later return as an adult time and time again. Later, exposure to science fiction through reading Jules Verne continued to increase my passion exponentially for this dark, romantic type of setting.

Building off of this base, but with echoes of the future, steampunk has its common denominator in the magnificent Victorian era in London in the second half of the nineteenth century. Specifically, there is a single feature of retrofuture technology that defines steampunk: steam. The combustion of coal and steam mechanisms have increased in complexity, manifesting the industrial progress in a world of gears and bits fastened by screws and nuts. This is, my friends, steampunk at its purest: to which we have dedicated this book. As you will see, there are several characters that perfectly embody this aesthetic form and this world.

Currently, as with any great trend, steampunk has become divided into subgenres that maintain the general essence but also test new waters.

The following are some subgenres that have emerged:

SteamGoth
This style portrays the Victorian era under the cloak of horror and supernatural fantasy. The film *Van Helsing* (2004) is an example of this subgenre.

Gaslamp Fantasy
Also known as *gaslight fantasy* or *gaslight romance*, it is an offshoot of steampunk. This variation tends to show a much more fantastical scene within the Victorian era, without putting special emphasis on technology or the industrial revolution.

Weird West
This subgenre mixes classic westerns with other genres like horror, fantasy and science fiction. Films like *Wild Wild West* and *Jonah Hex* (1999 and 2010, respectively) belong to this re-invented Wild West.

It's incredible, right? In addition to this, there are the literary and film cultures within steampunk, with an infinite assortment of novels and films that belong to the genre.

Personally, I would like to add that I have dedicated significant time to choosing the references that gave me the adequate design for the characters presented in this book. It is not my style to repeat myself, so I have opted to create something that is as varied as possible within an ample spectrum as unfathomably expansive as steampunk. Prepare for an experience! It is something you won't forget...

Sincerely,
Jorge Balaguer

GALACTIC HERO

Sun Rocket is without doubt one of the best astronauts, perhaps because he has adventure in his blood. Hardened by a thousand battles in space, he is afraid of nothing. He just awaits the next task that will whisk him away to some far-flung corner of the galaxy.

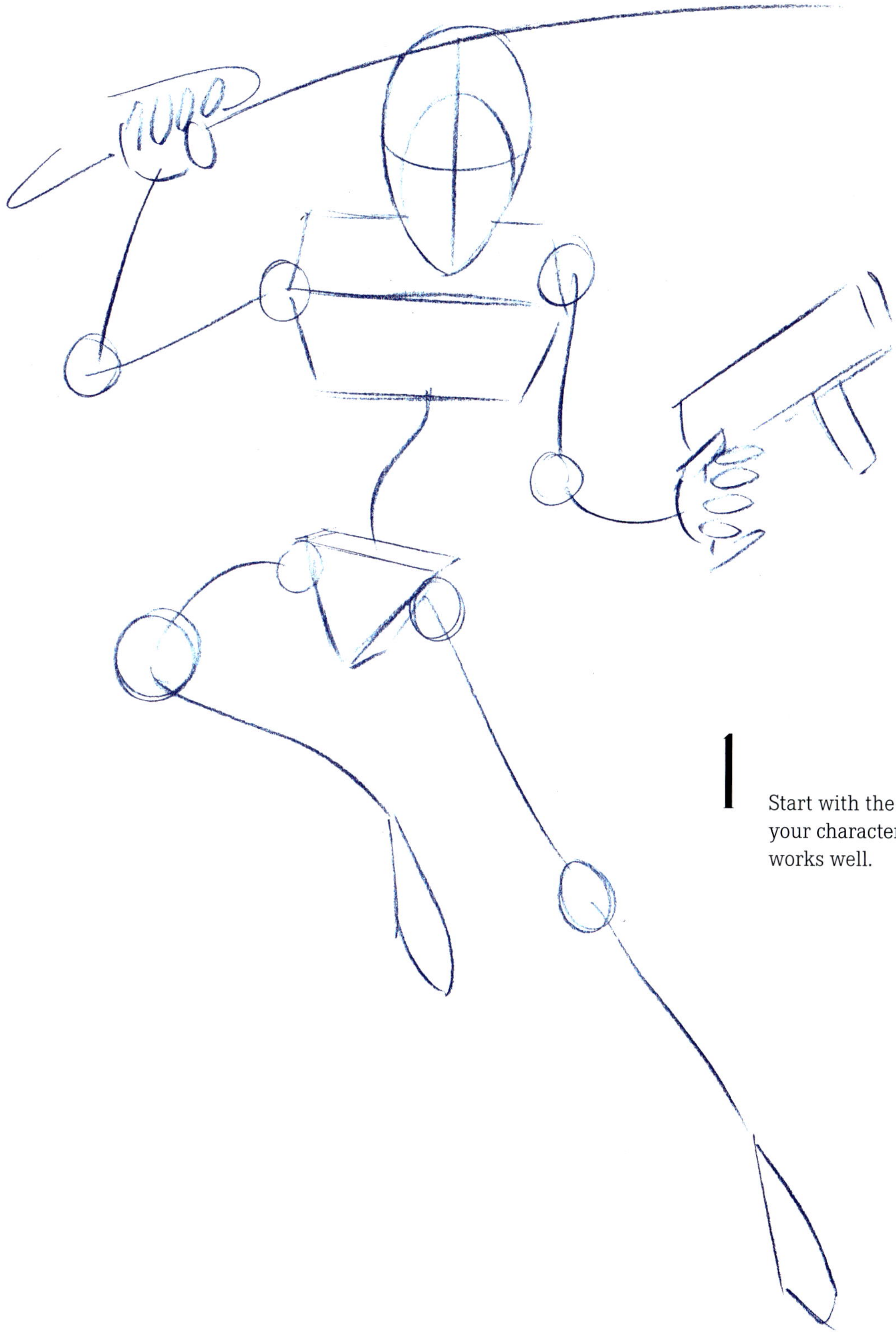

1

Start with the blue pencil base for your character: a jumping position works well.

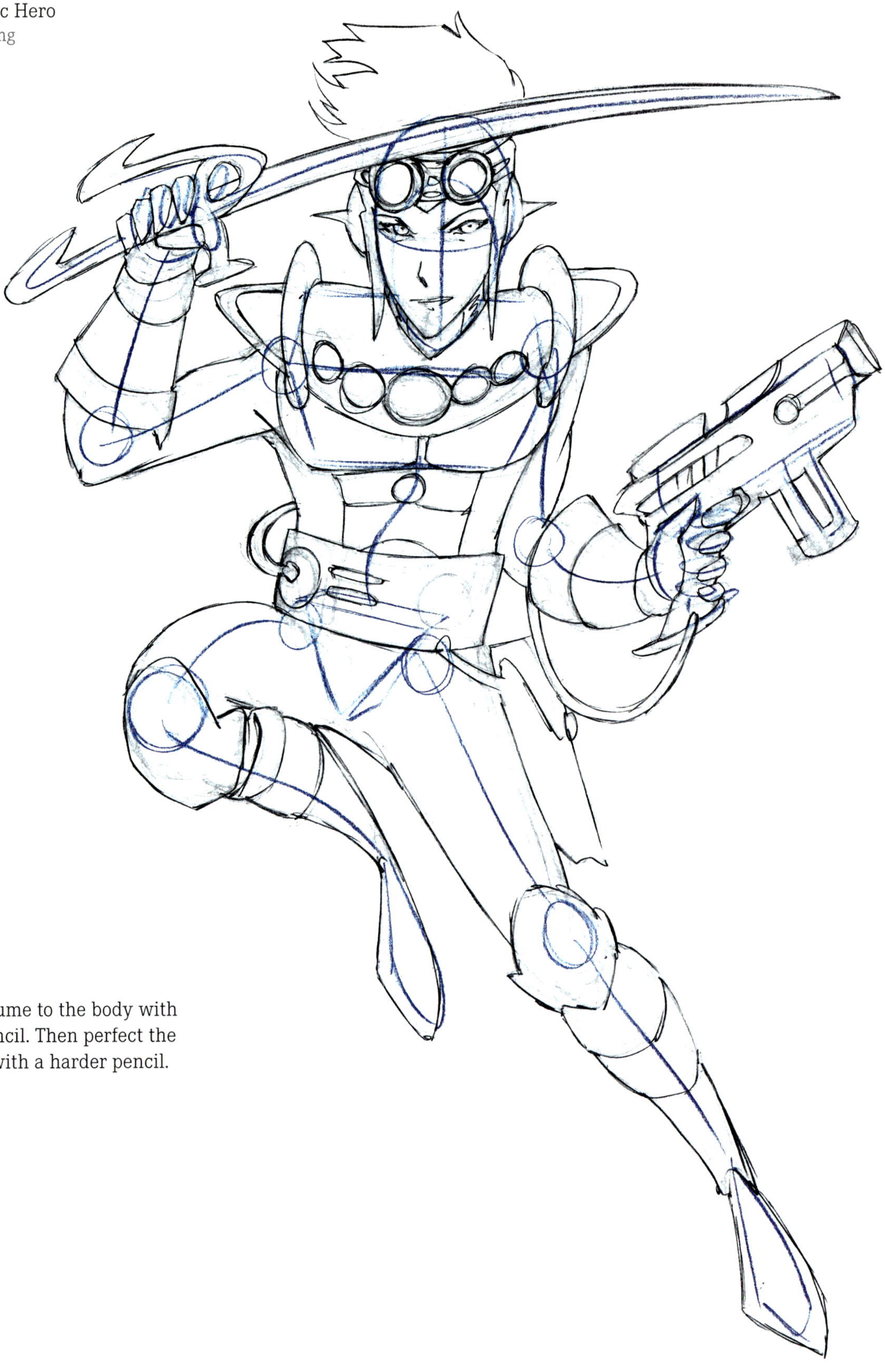

2

Add volume to the body with a 2H pencil. Then perfect the details with a harder pencil.

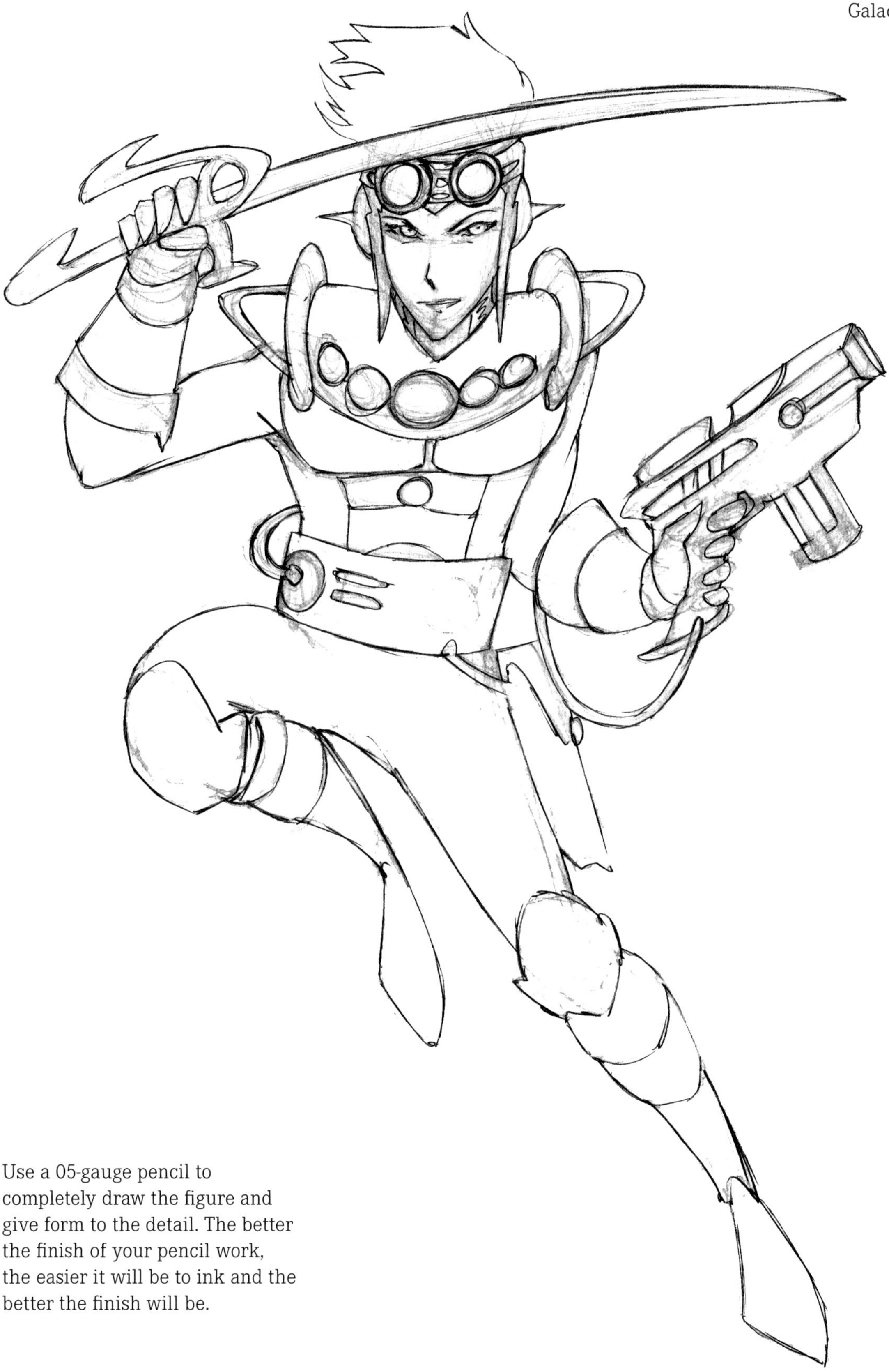

3

Use a 05-gauge pencil to completely draw the figure and give form to the detail. The better the finish of your pencil work, the easier it will be to ink and the better the finish will be.

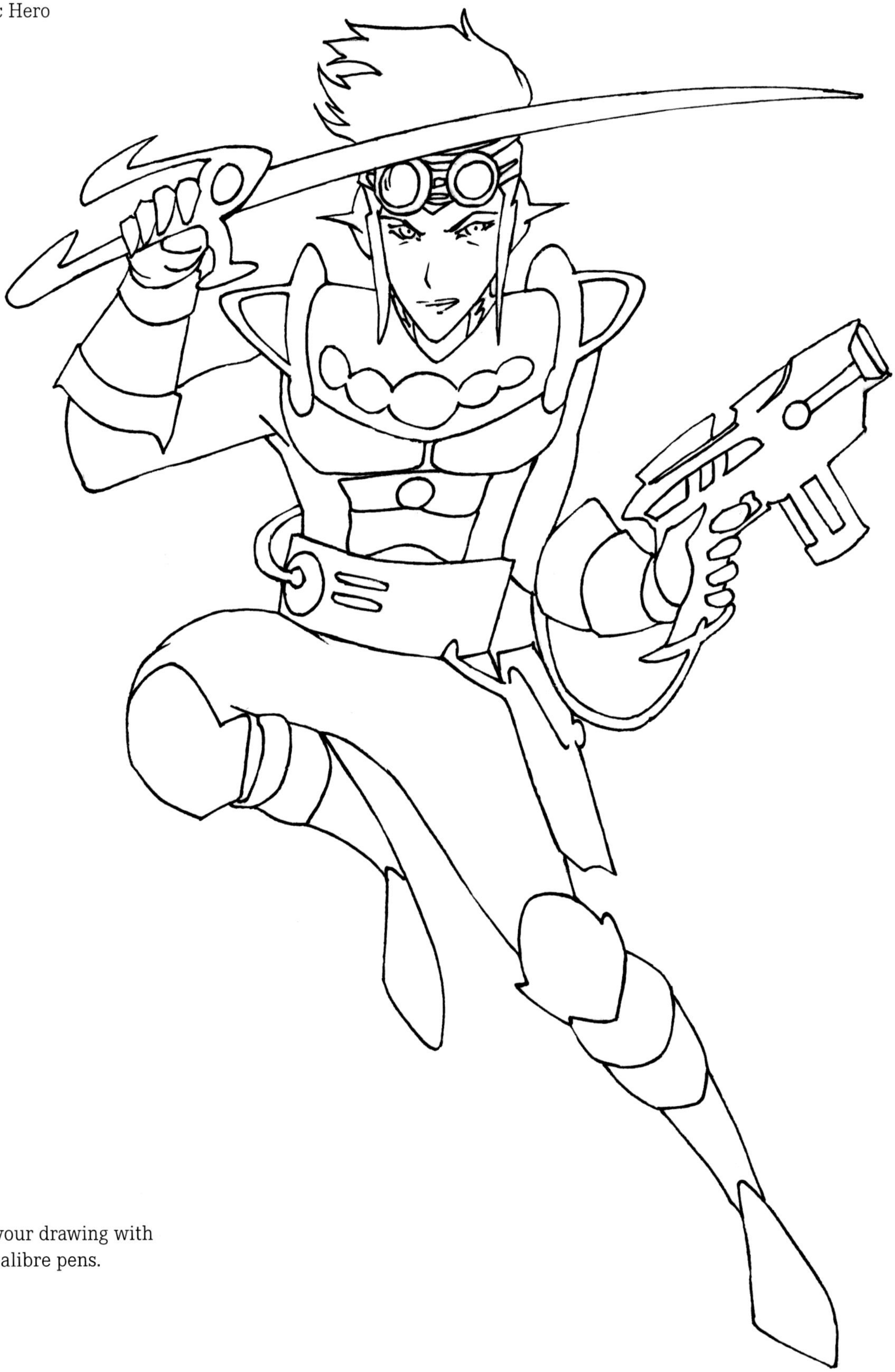

4

Go over your drawing with various calibre pens.

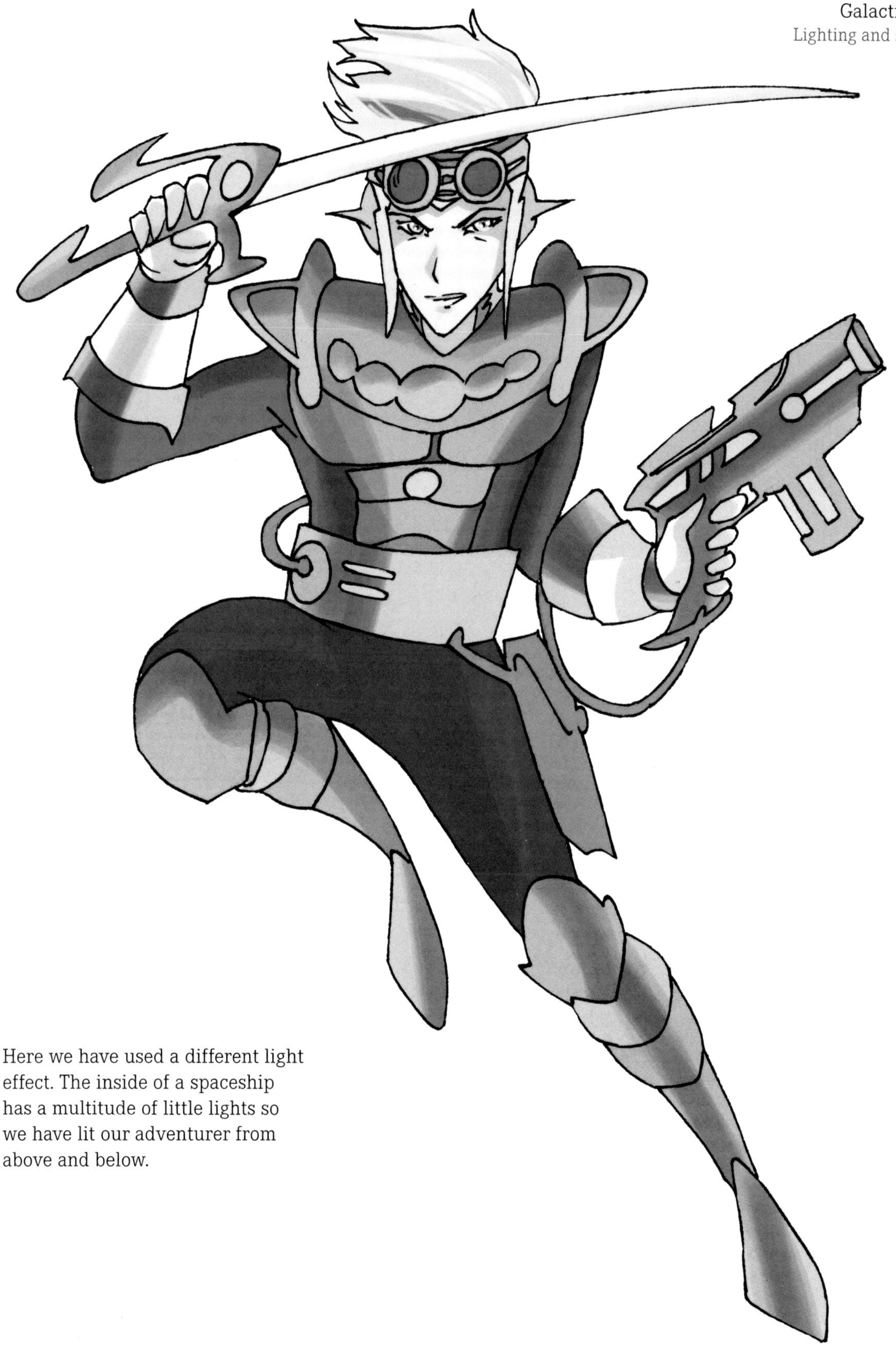

5

Here we have used a different light effect. The inside of a spaceship has a multitude of little lights so we have lit our adventurer from above and below.

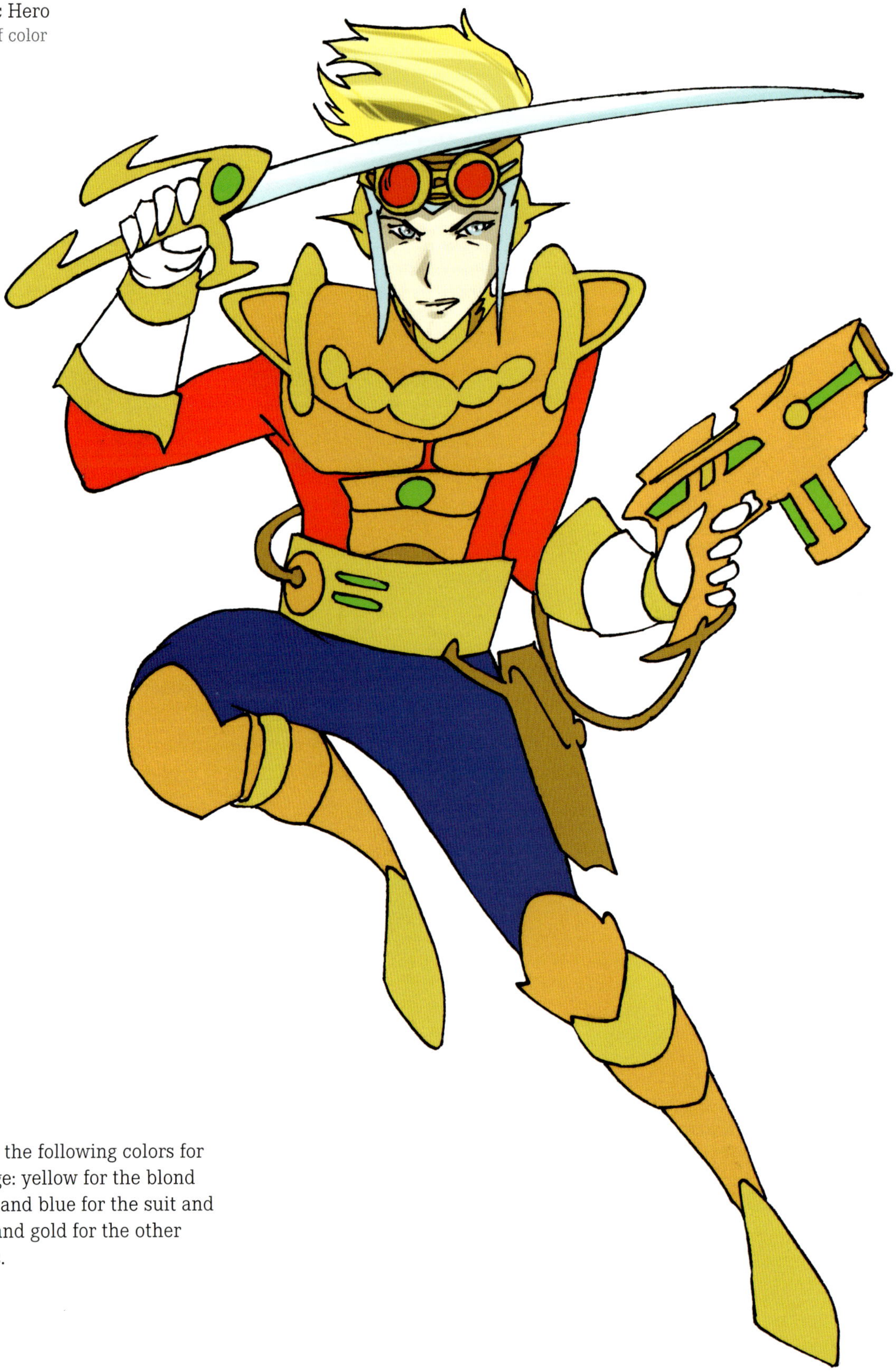

6

I've used the following colors for this image: yellow for the blond hair, red and blue for the suit and glasses, and gold for the other elements.

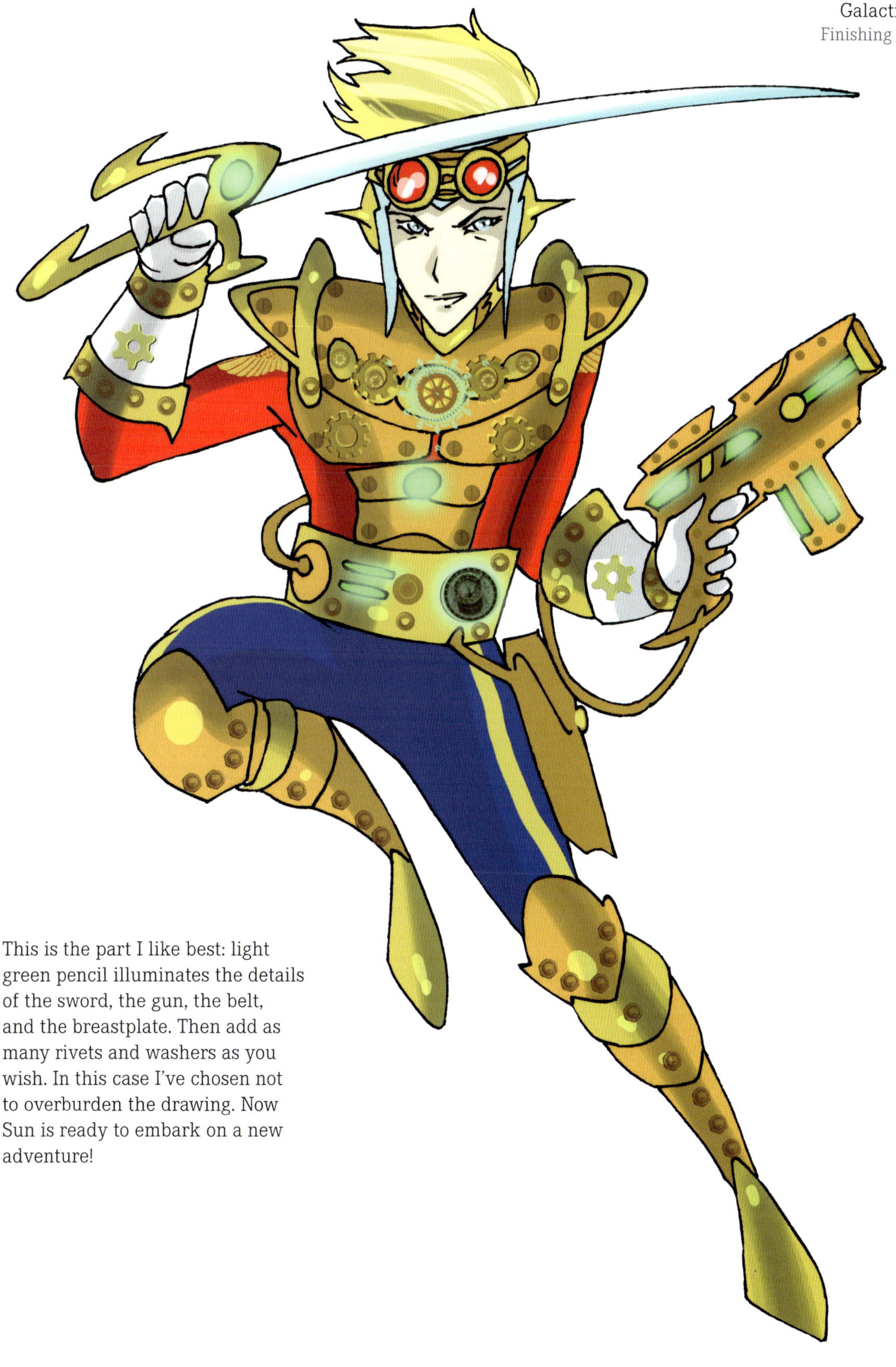

7

This is the part I like best: light green pencil illuminates the details of the sword, the gun, the belt, and the breastplate. Then add as many rivets and washers as you wish. In this case I've chosen not to overburden the drawing. Now Sun is ready to embark on a new adventure!

VICTORIAN LADY

Lady Margareth Ankor is a great lady, much respected in court and held in high esteem by the Queen of Needles. She is always seen at magnificent festivals and in the company of very powerful men ... of course it is rumored that she is working as a double agent for the country who pays her services. She certainly is a mysterious and attractive woman.

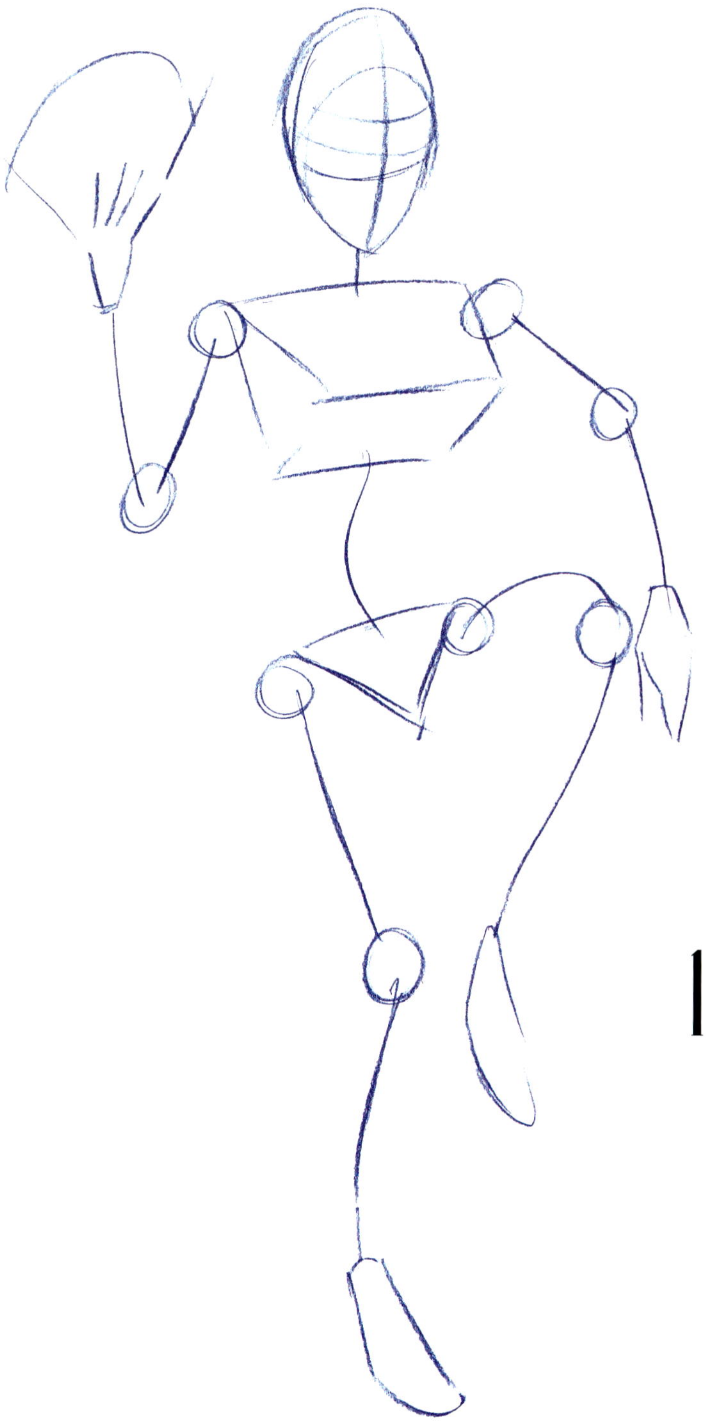

1

Use a blue pencil to draw what will be your lady, in a position as though she is hiding something beneath her skirt. With practice you should be able to draw this using a 2H pencil.

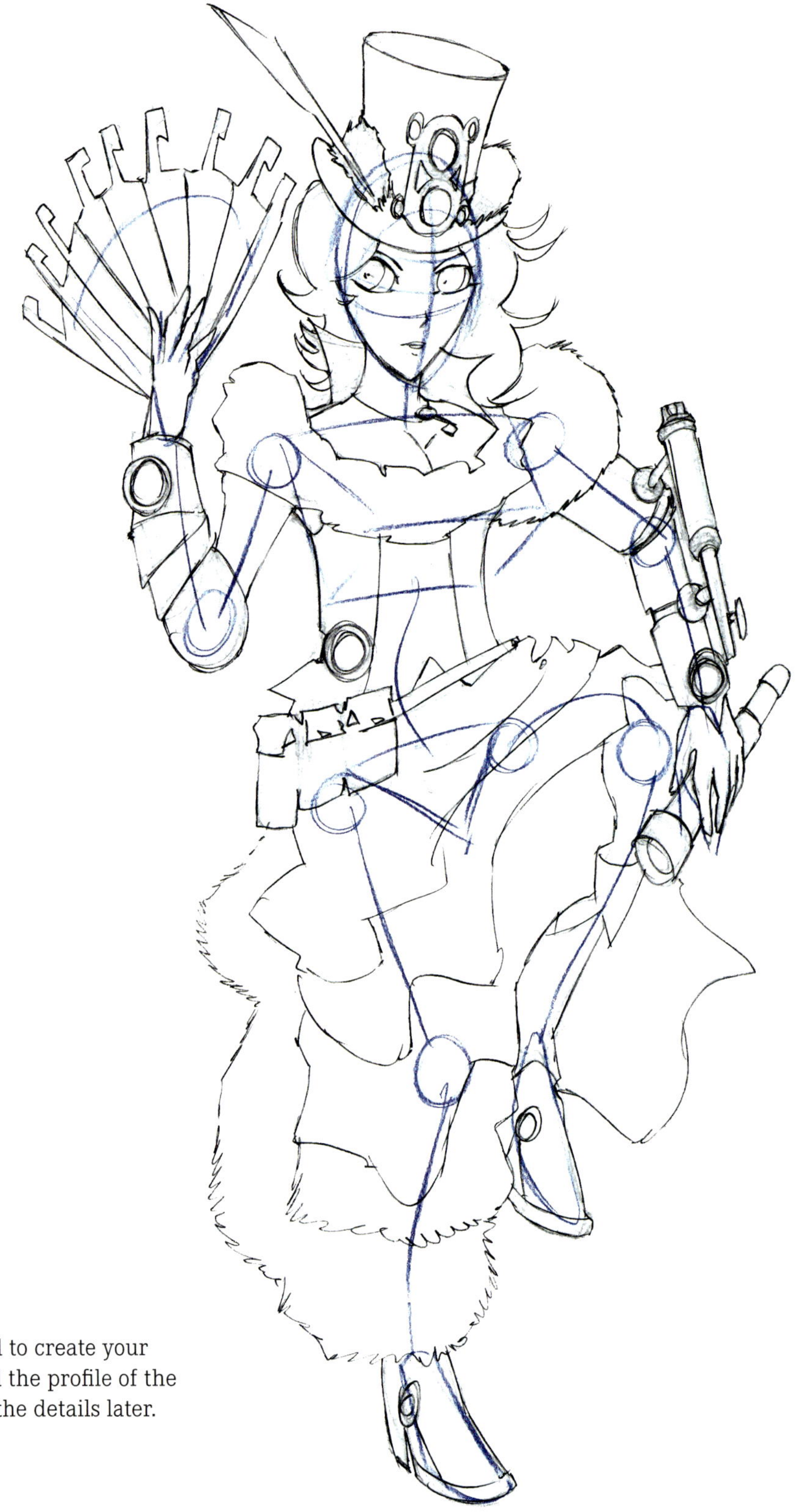

2

Use the 2H pencil to create your blue skeleton and the profile of the figure, adding in the details later.

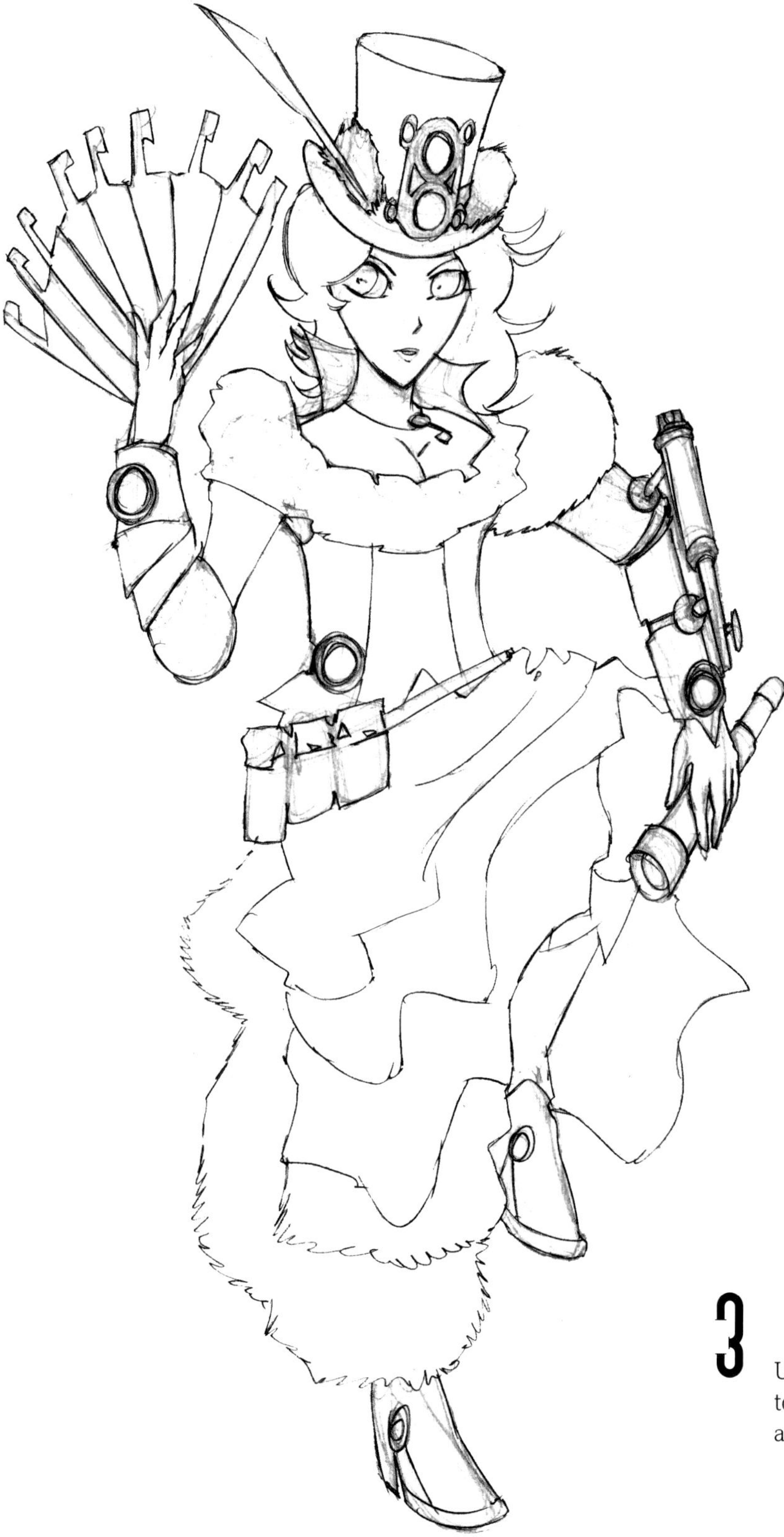

3

Use a 05-calibre mechanical pencil to sketch the figure, adding volume and detail.

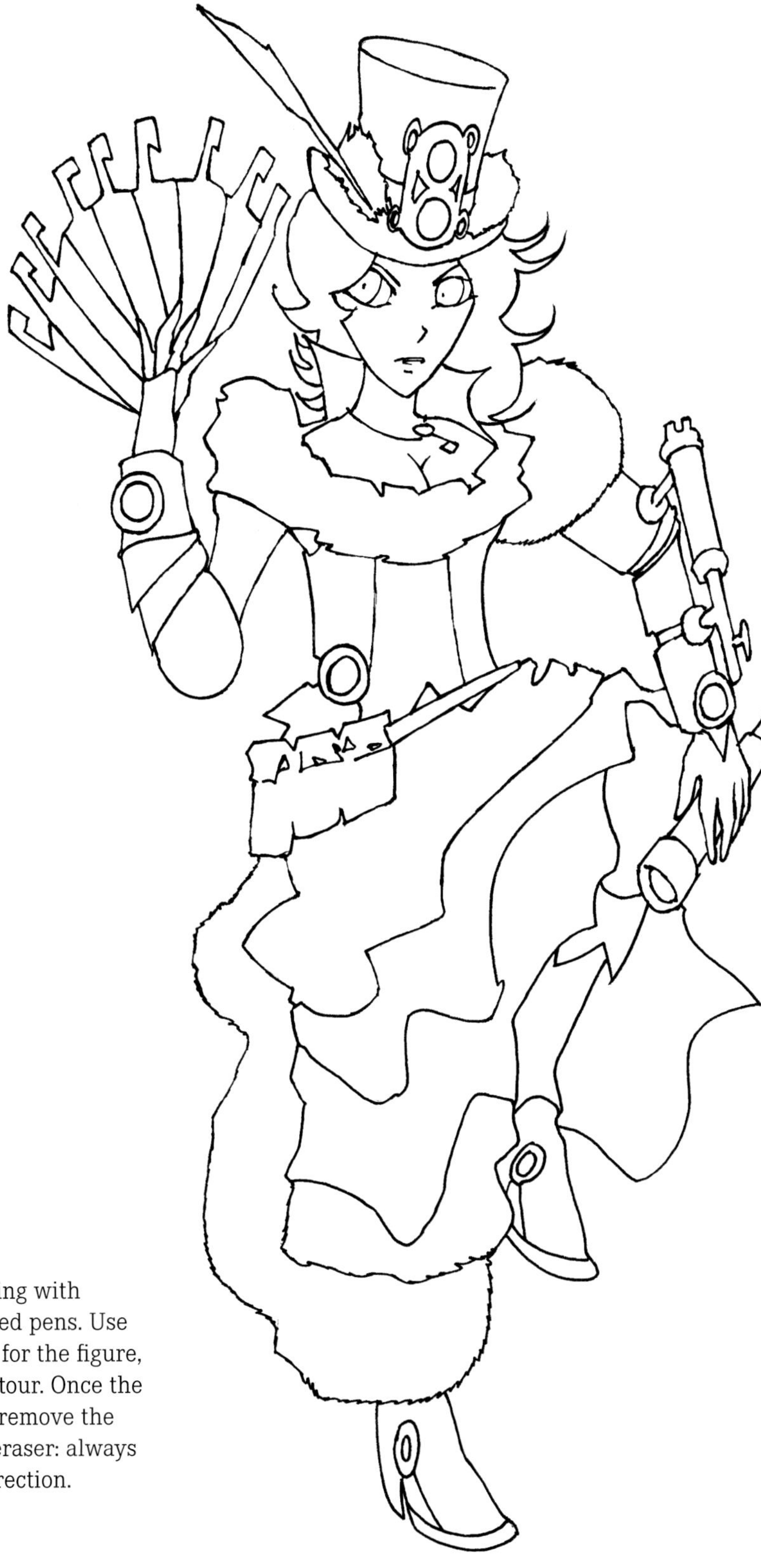

4

Go over your drawing with differently calibrated pens. Use a 0.2 for detail, 0.4 for the figure, and 0.8 for the contour. Once the ink is dry you can remove the pencil with a soft eraser: always rub in the same direction.

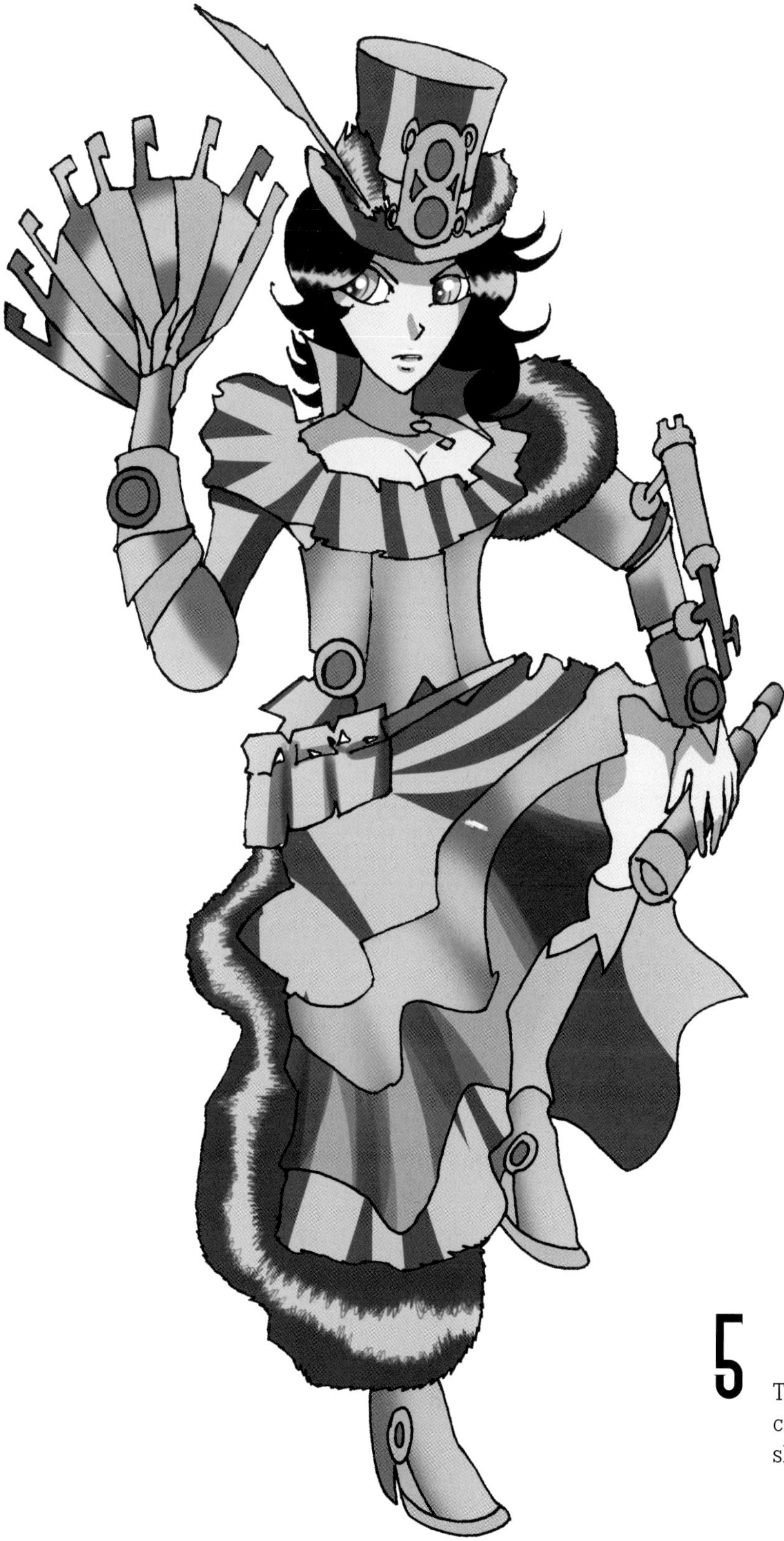

5

The light source for this lady comes from above, casting strange shadows on her face and figure.

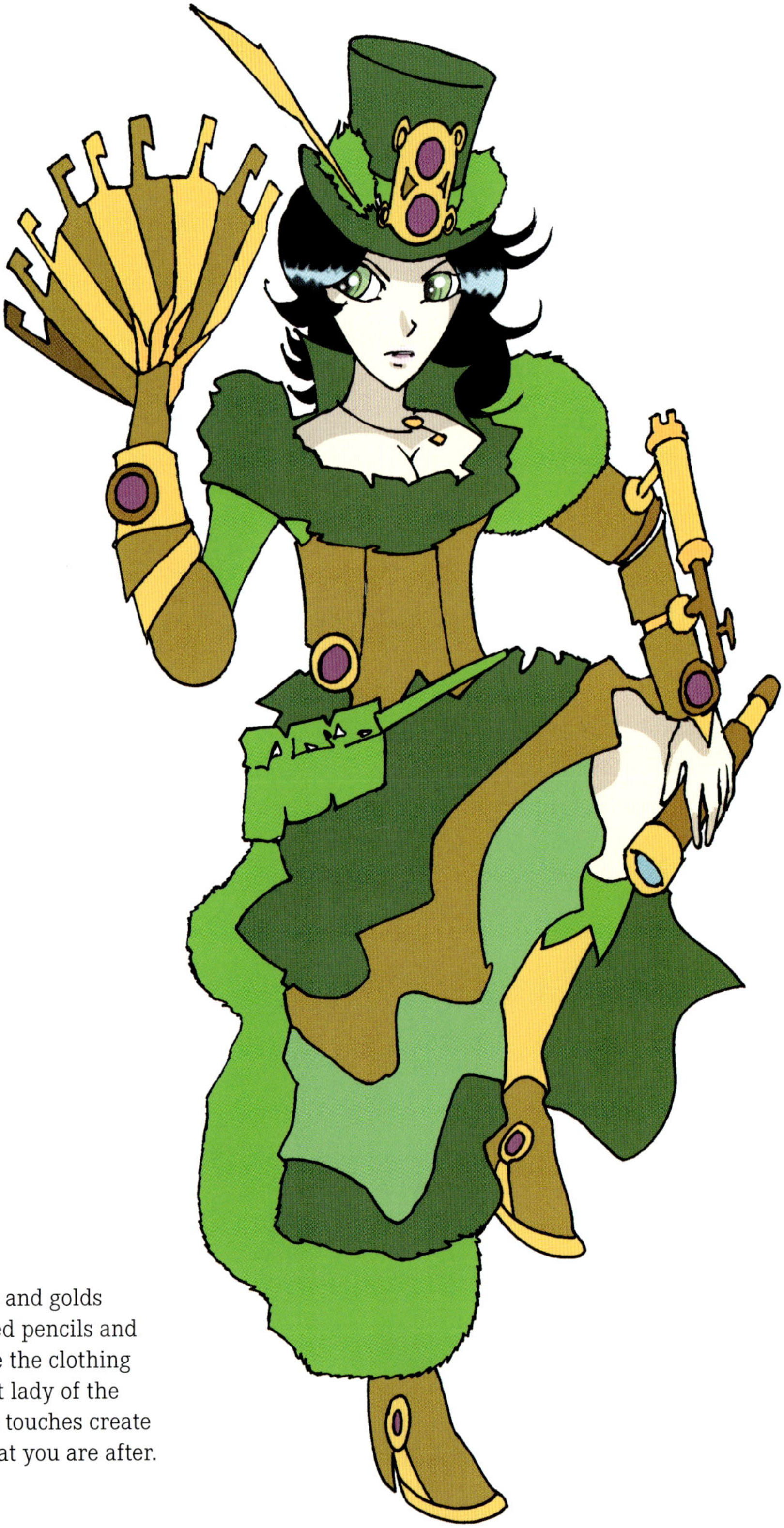

6

A variety of greens and golds applied with colored pencils and brush pens provide the clothing for this magnificent lady of the court. Some purple touches create the elegant look that you are after.

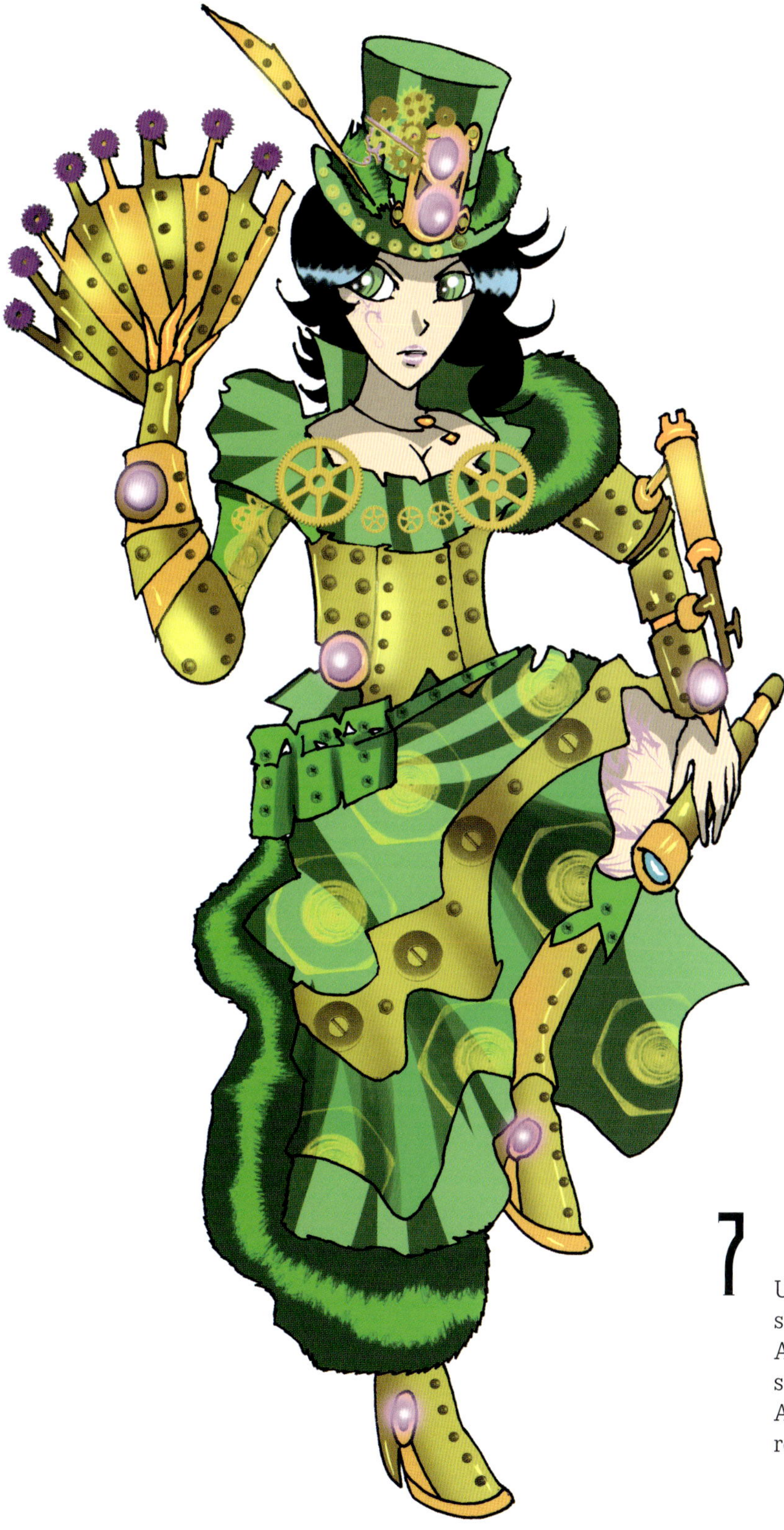

7

Use color pencils to add the final shine to the purples and golds. Add rivets to the dress and some screws with a gold pen. Fantastic! A mysterious and attractive woman ready to seduce...

NAVY SOLDIER

Rushell Monroe is the captain of the terrestrial army. Under his leadership, his battalion has won countless battles: he is a brilliant strategist and excels in finding his enemy's weak spot. Now he is preparing his maneuvers for taking over the northern lands.

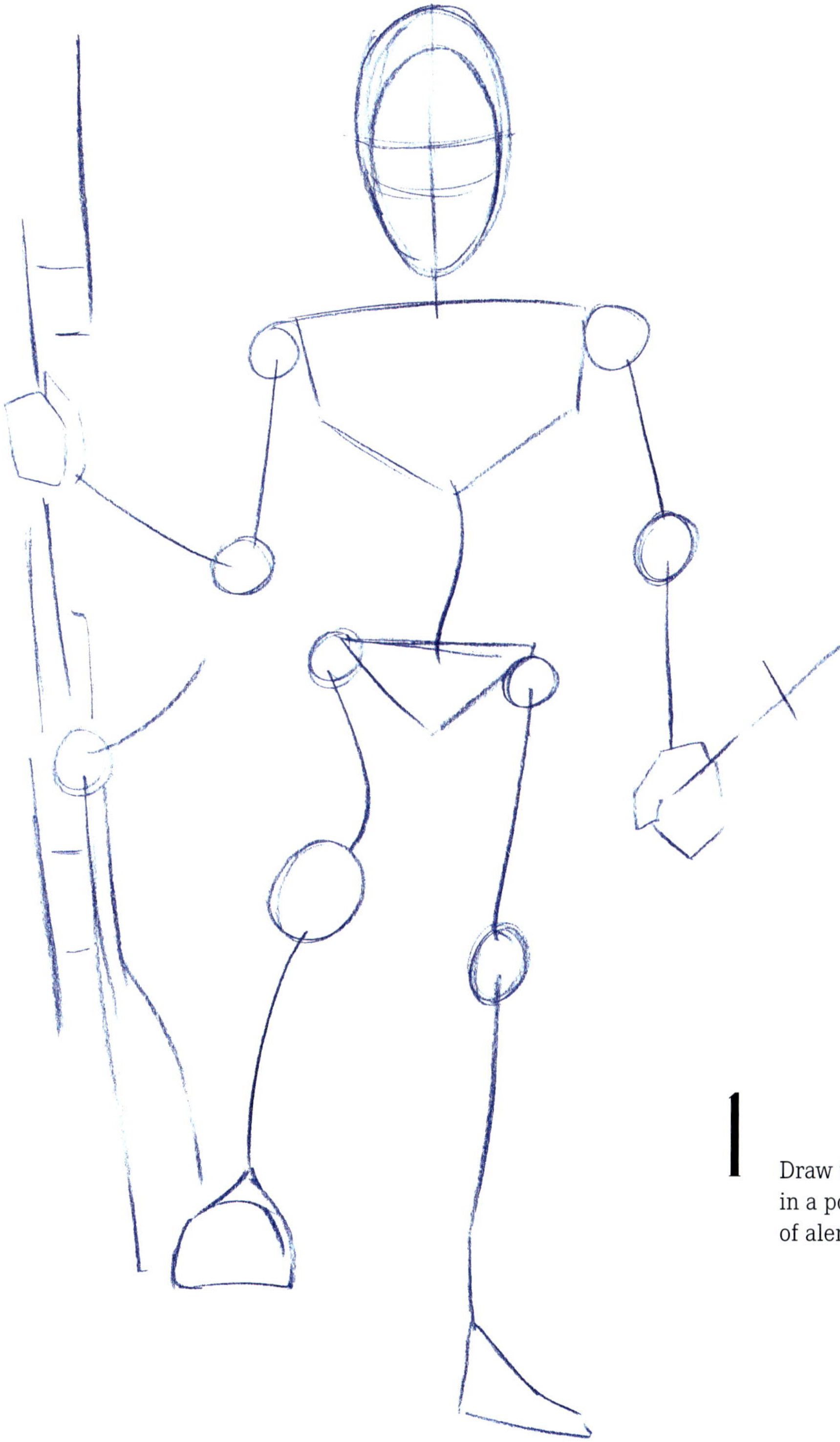

1

Draw the captain in blue pencil, in a pose that suggests a state of alertness.

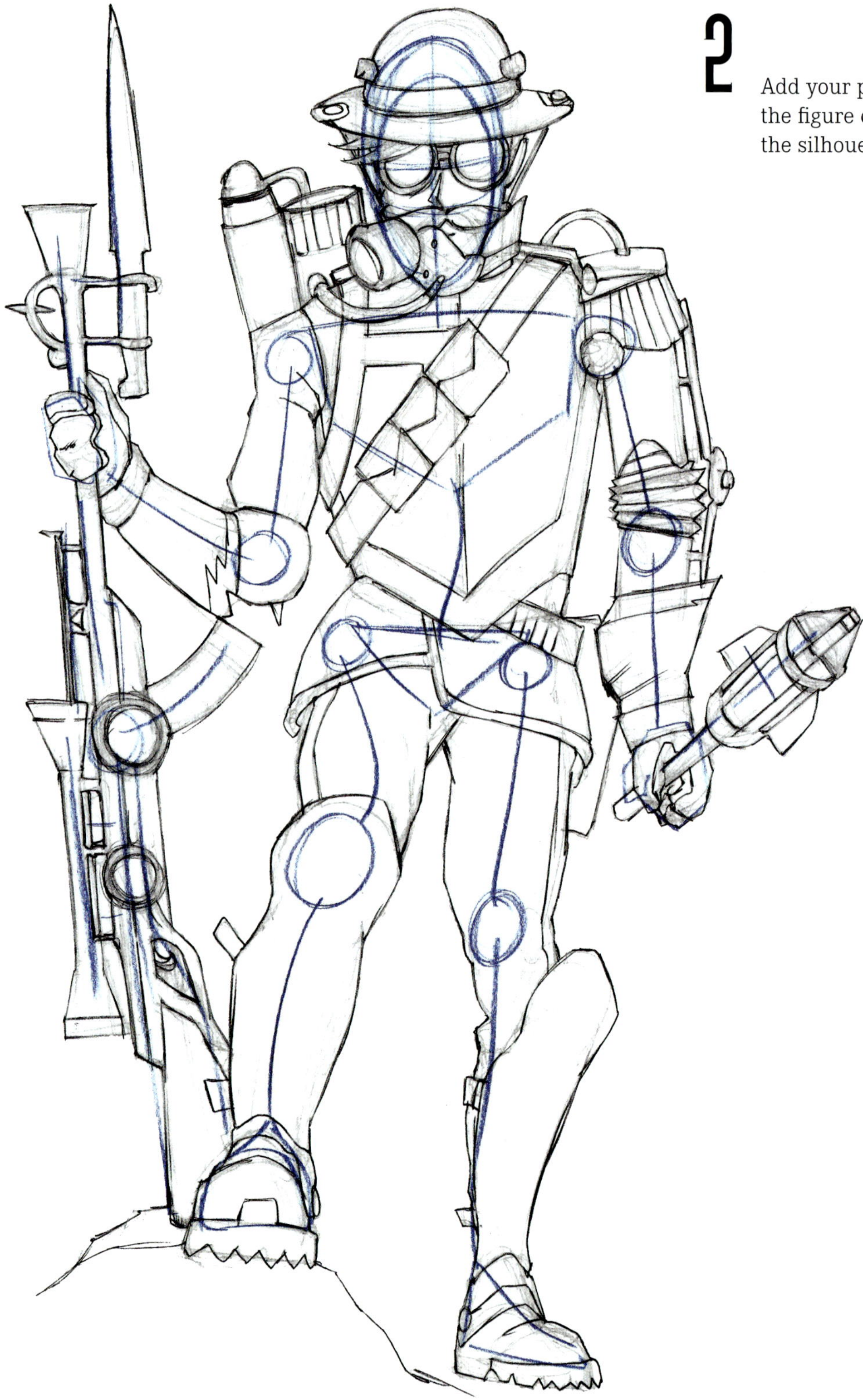

2

Add your pencil strokes to give the figure consistency and to shape the silhouette.

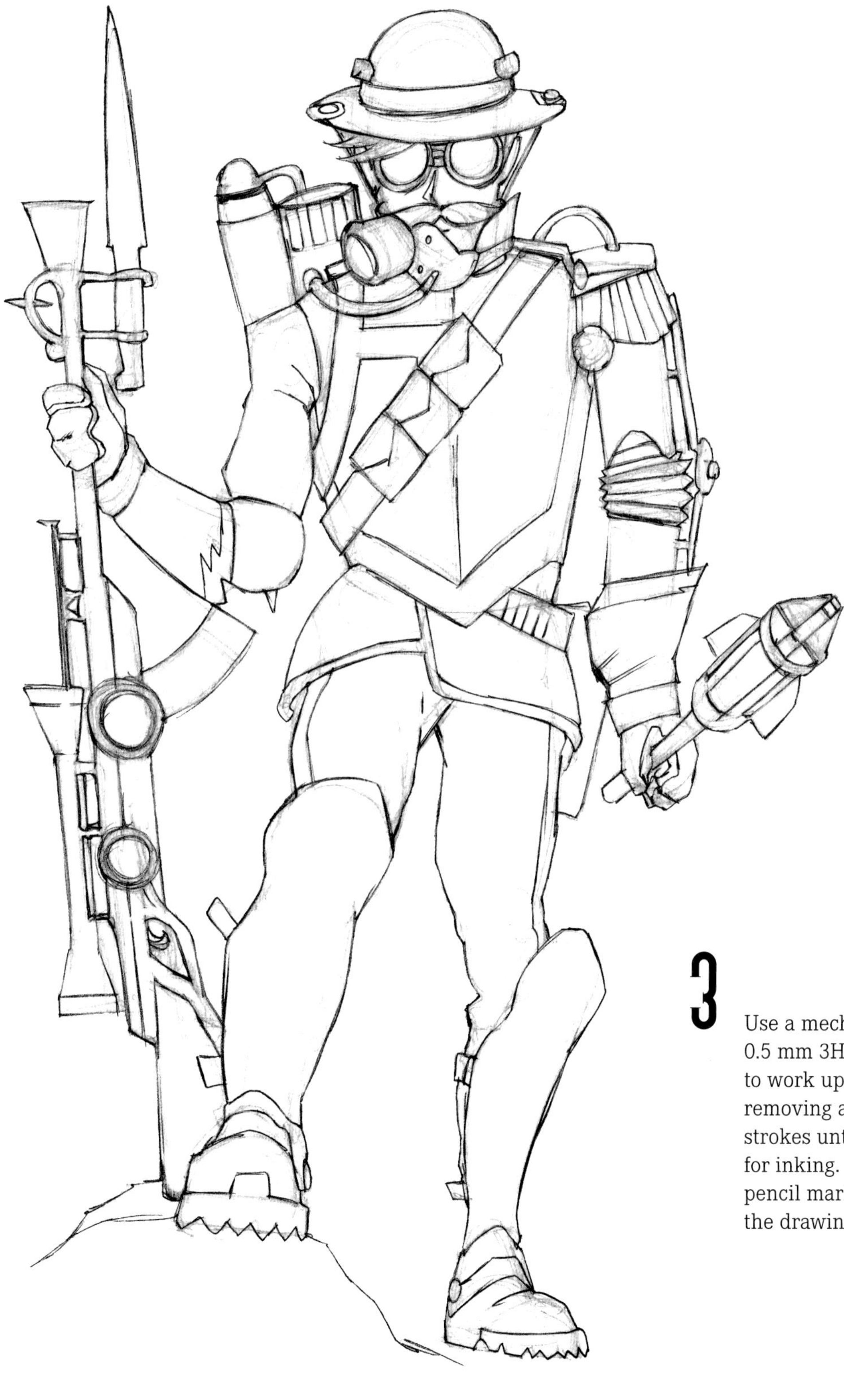

3

Use a mechanical pencil with a 0.5 mm 3H lead or an H3 pencil to work up the figure and details, removing and cleaning up leftover strokes until the design is ready for inking. The fewer unnecessary pencil marks you make, the better the drawing will ink.

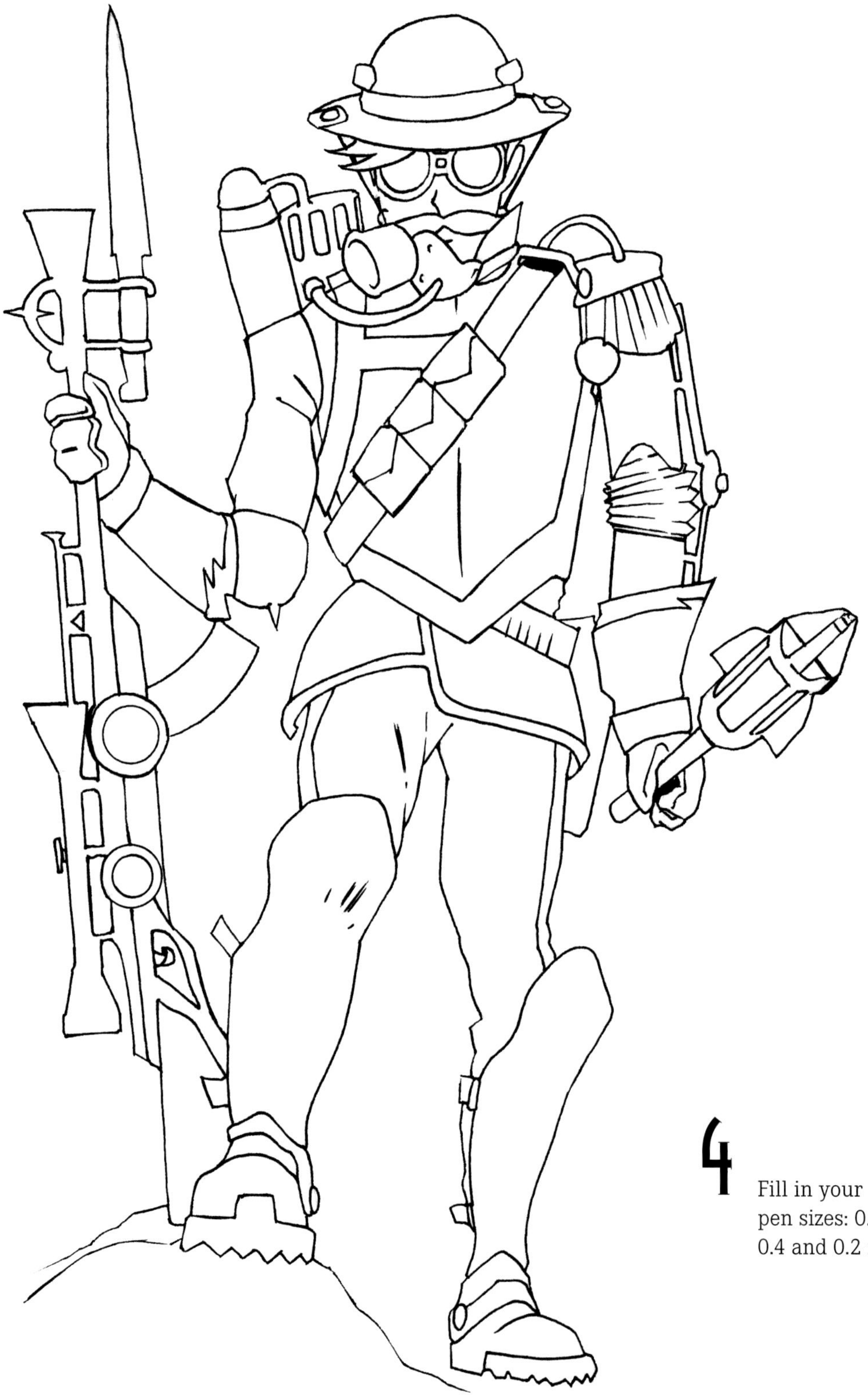

4

Fill in your captain using different pen sizes: 0.8 for the contour, 0.4 and 0.2 for the details.

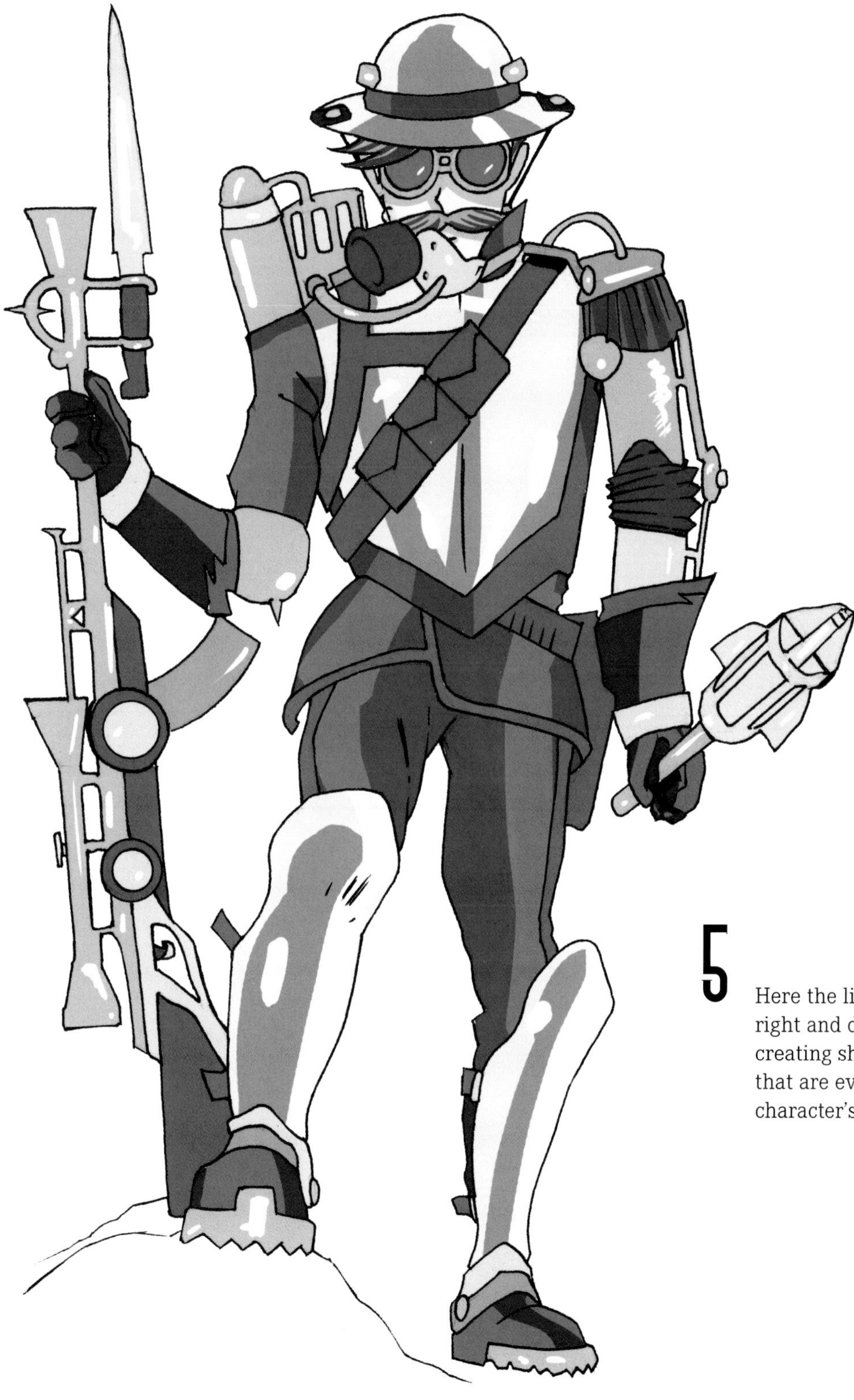

5

Here the light is coming from the right and diagonally from above, creating shapes and shadows that are evident throughout the character's entire suit.

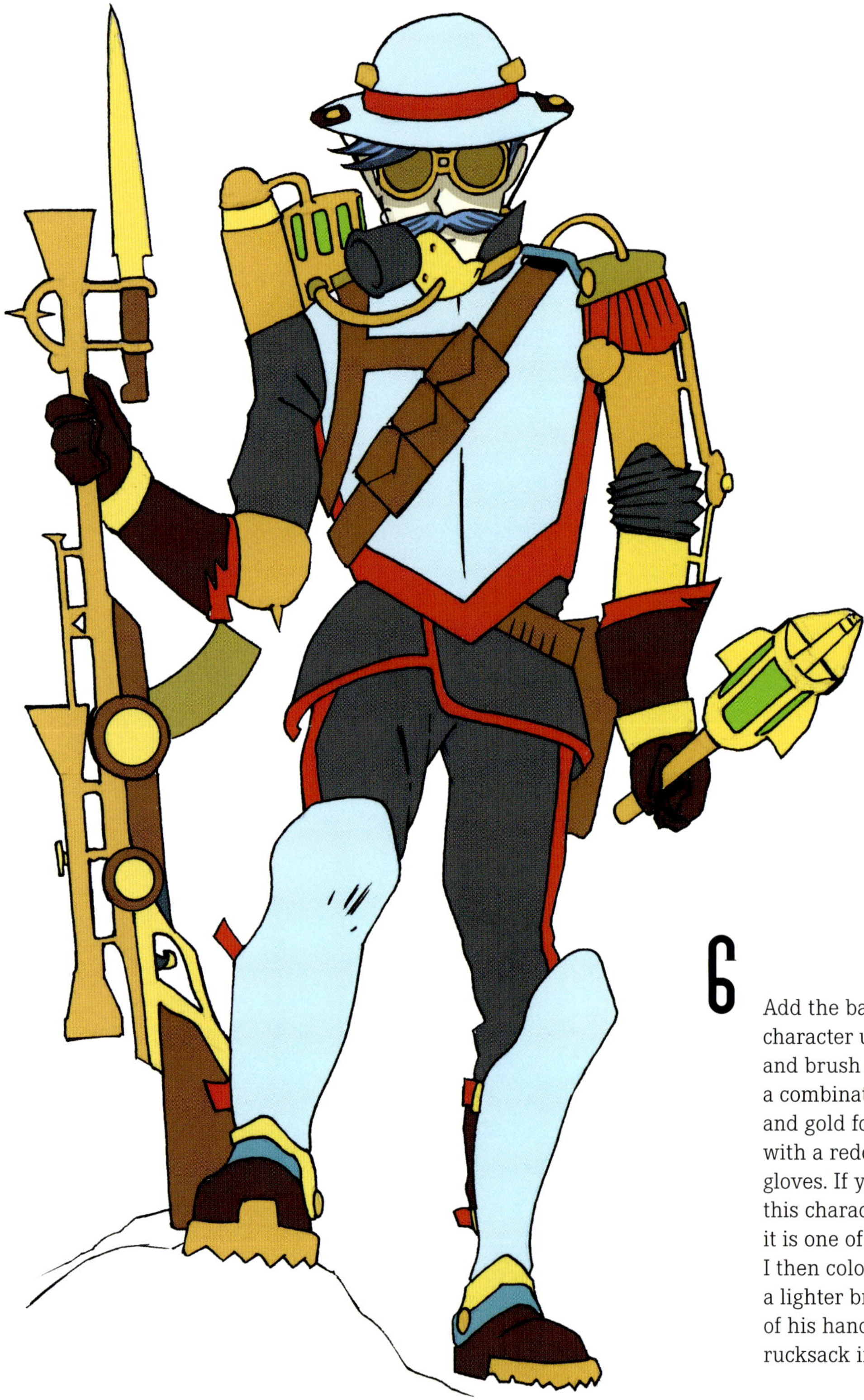

6

Add the base colors to your character using colored pencils and brush pens. I have chosen a combination of gray, blue, red, and gold for his clothing, along with a reddish brown for the gloves. If you decide to draw this character be patient: it is one of the most complex. I then color the cartridges in a lighter brown and the detail of his hand grenade and eons rucksack in green.

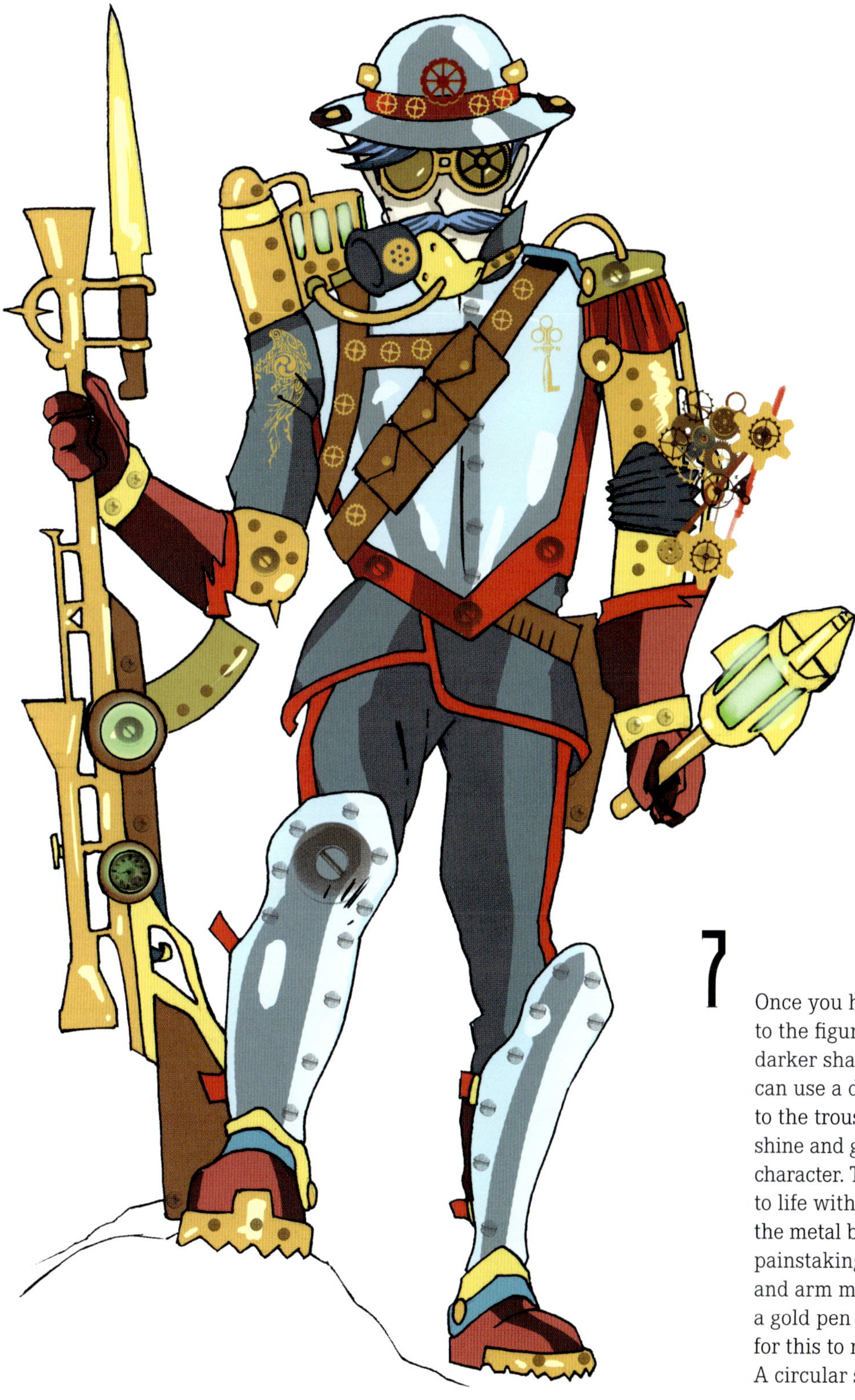

7

Once you have added volume to the figure with lighter or darker shades (for example, you can use a darker gray to add body to the trousers), you can add all the shine and golden touches to the character. Then bring the greens to life with white, add shine to the metal breastplate, and, finally, painstakingly add the washers and arm mechanism. You can use a gold pen or red and brown colors for this to make it more attractive. A circular stencil will do the job!

HUNTRESS

Lady Campbell is an extraordinary horsewoman and expert markswoman. She has won the state shooting championship several times and has an impeccable reputation among hunters. Hunting is her passion – whenever a major tournament is organized, everyone can count on her to attend.

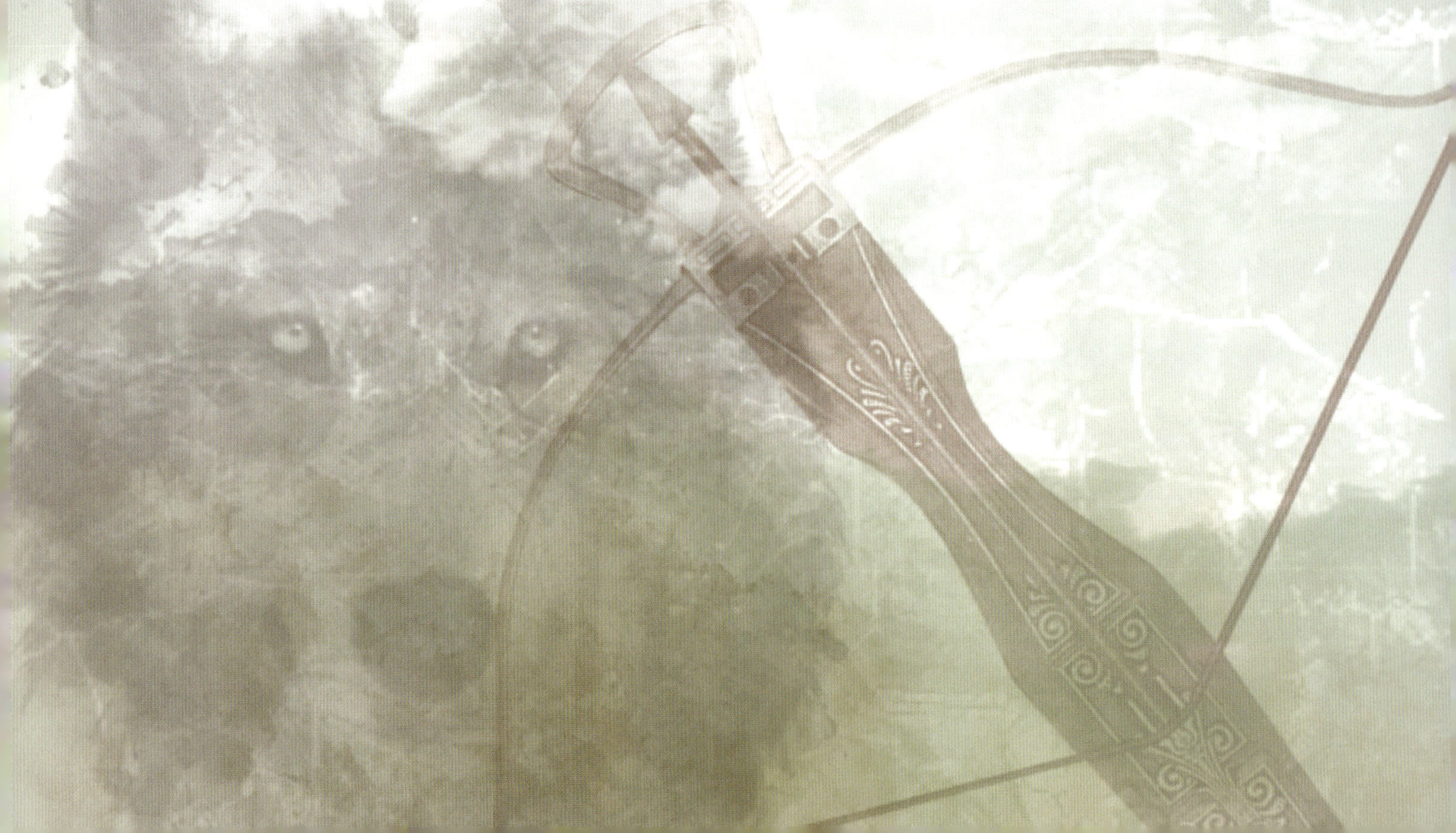

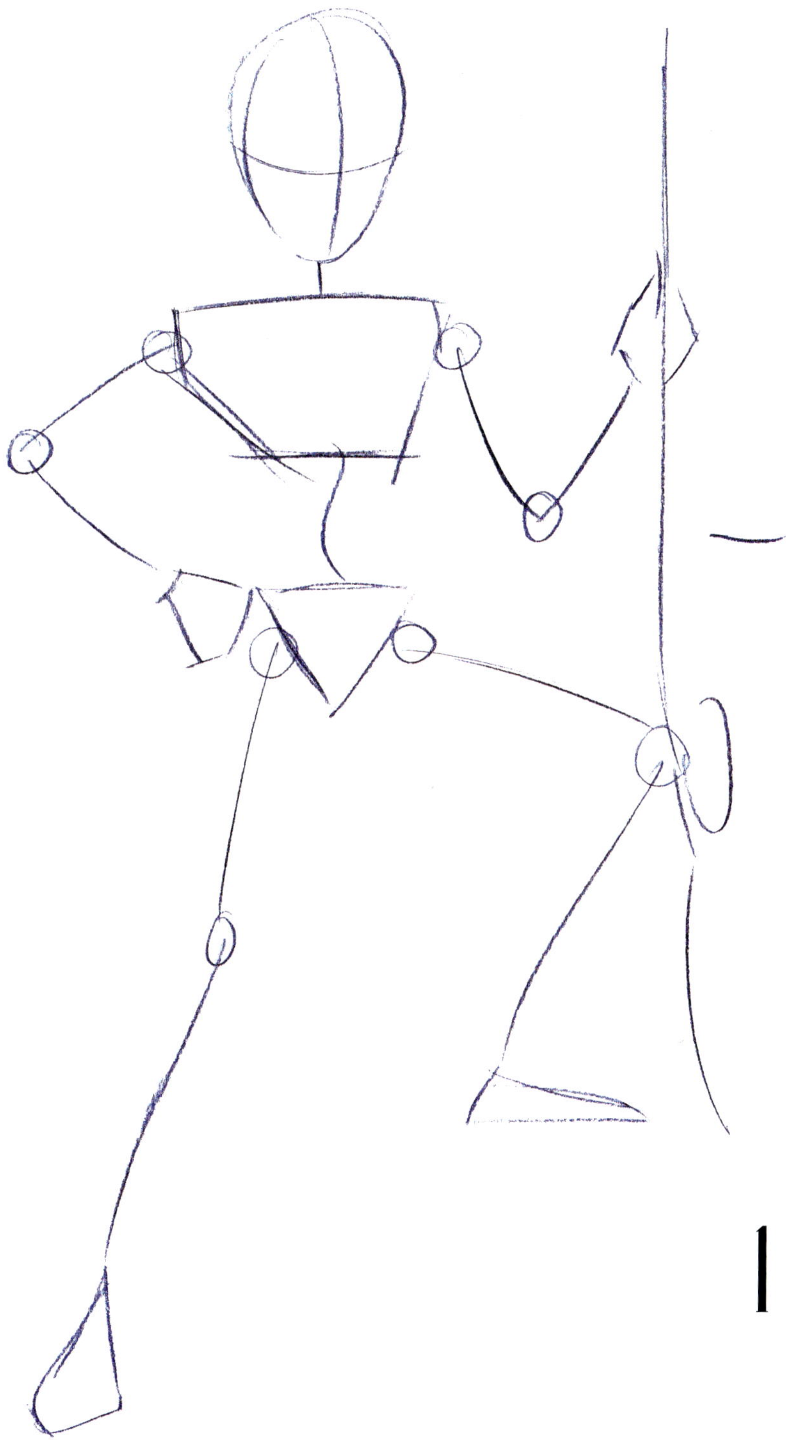

1

Start by drawing Lady Campbell's base in blue pencil, in a posture that is commensurate with her rank.

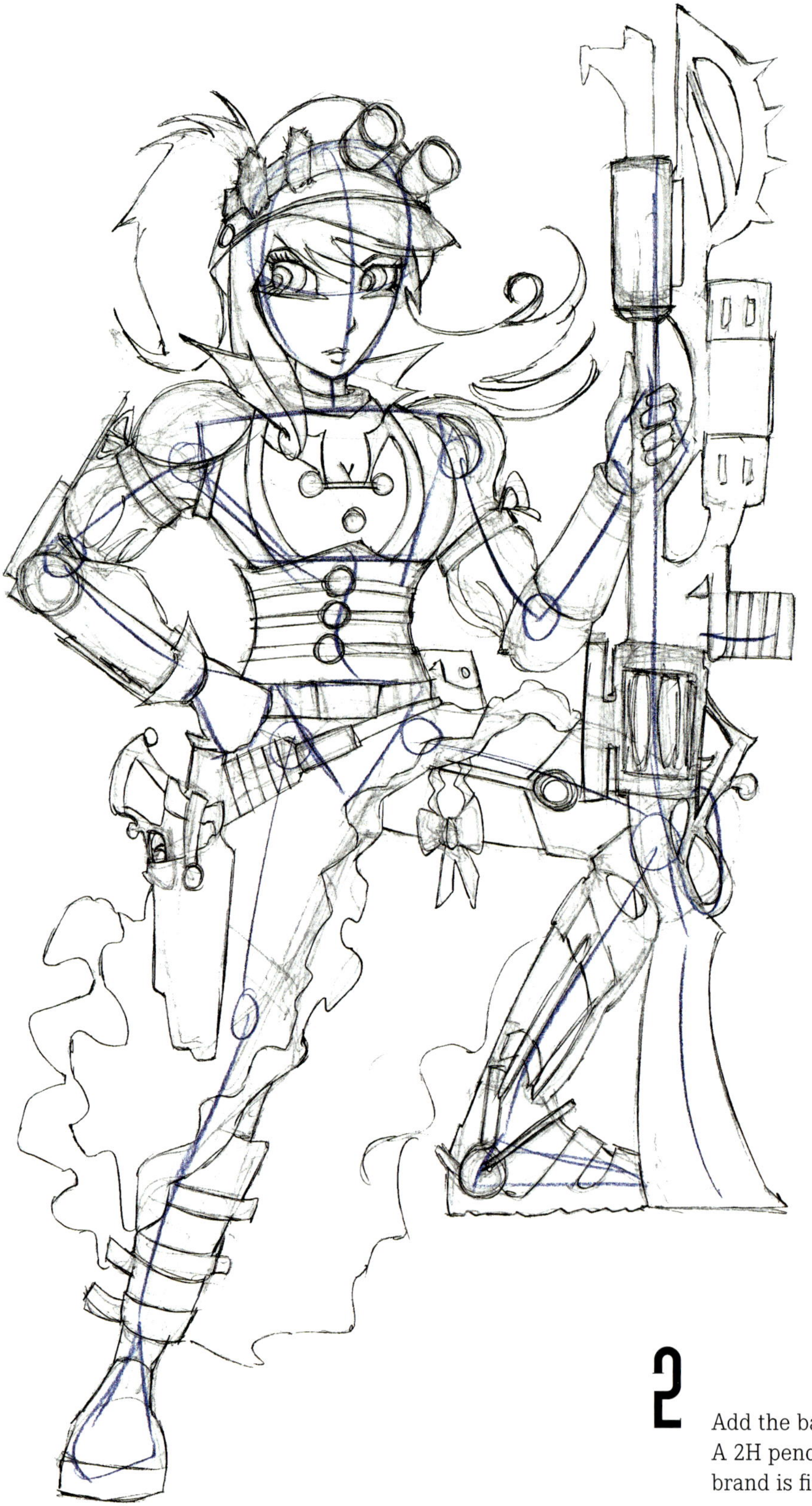

2

Add the base contour to the figure. A 2H pencil is best for this – any brand is fine.

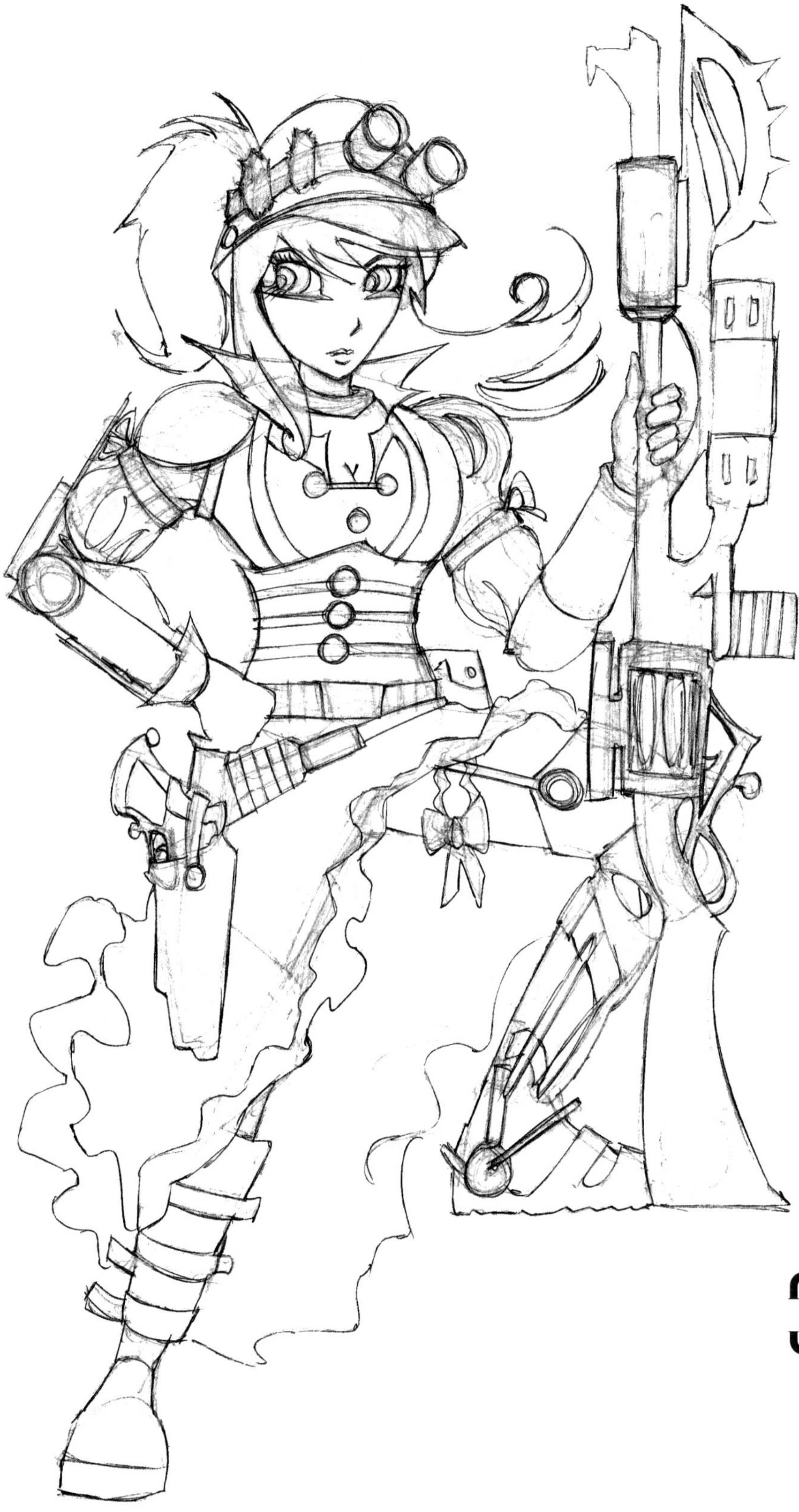

3

Work up the image with your pencil. Use a 05-calibre mechanical pencil to trace over the figure, giving it volume and adding in detail. Add volume and shape to the character.

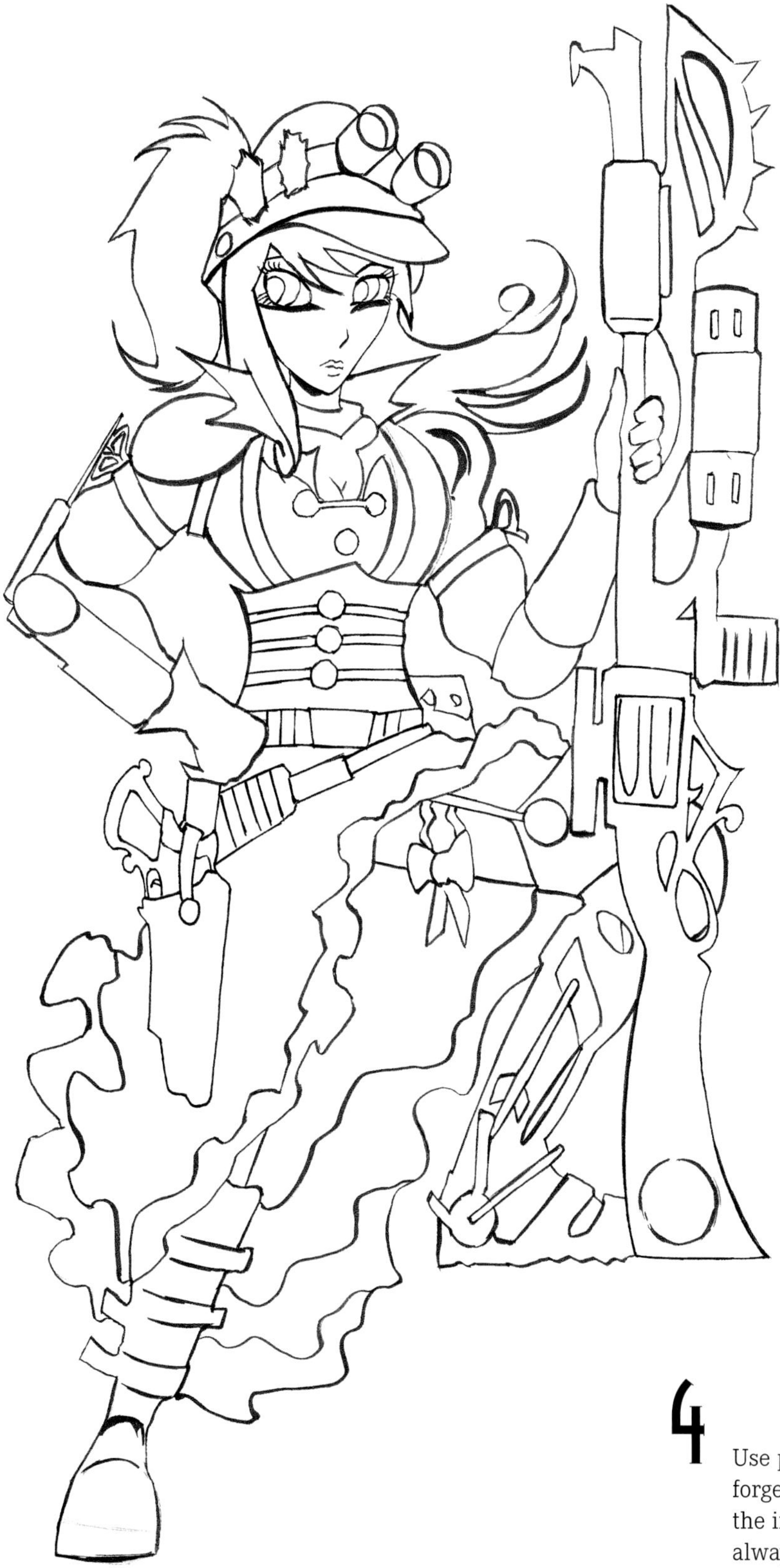

4

Use pens to ink the drawing. Don't forget to remove the pencil once the ink is dry: use a soft eraser and always rub in the same direction.

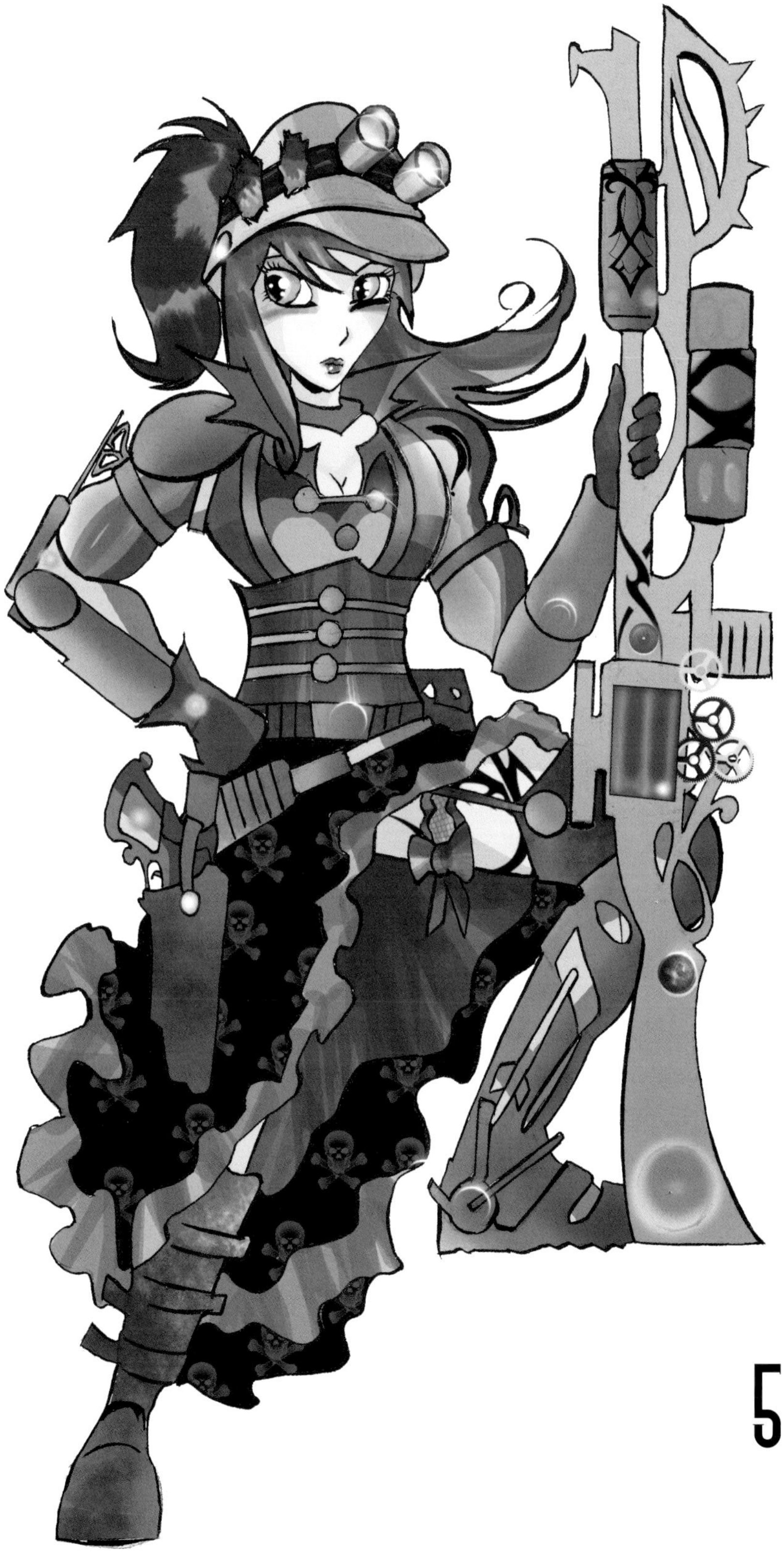

5

In this case the light is shining from above to below and diagonally from left to right.

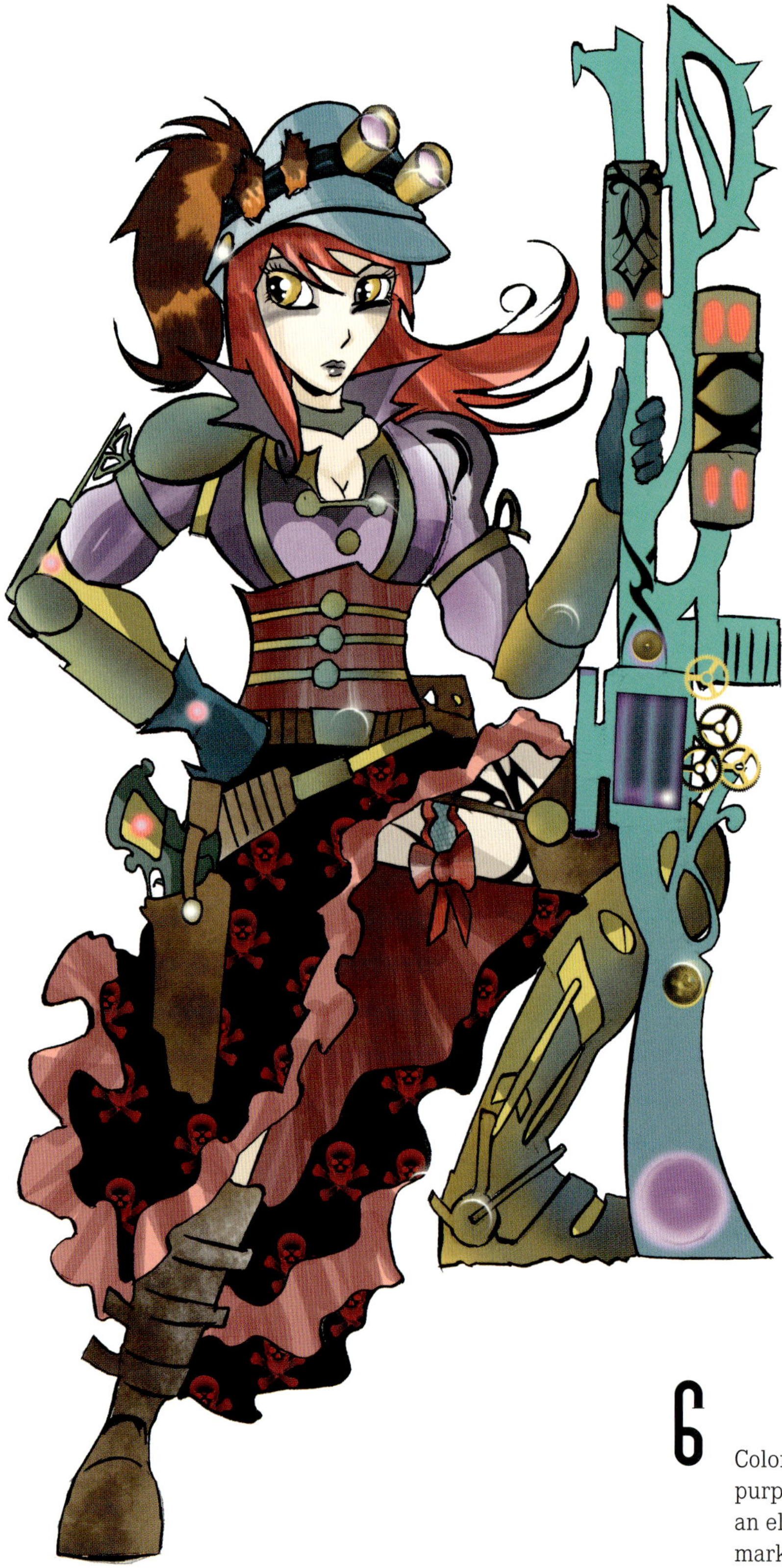

6

Color the character in blues, purples, reds, and metallic tones – an elegant combination for this fine markswoman.

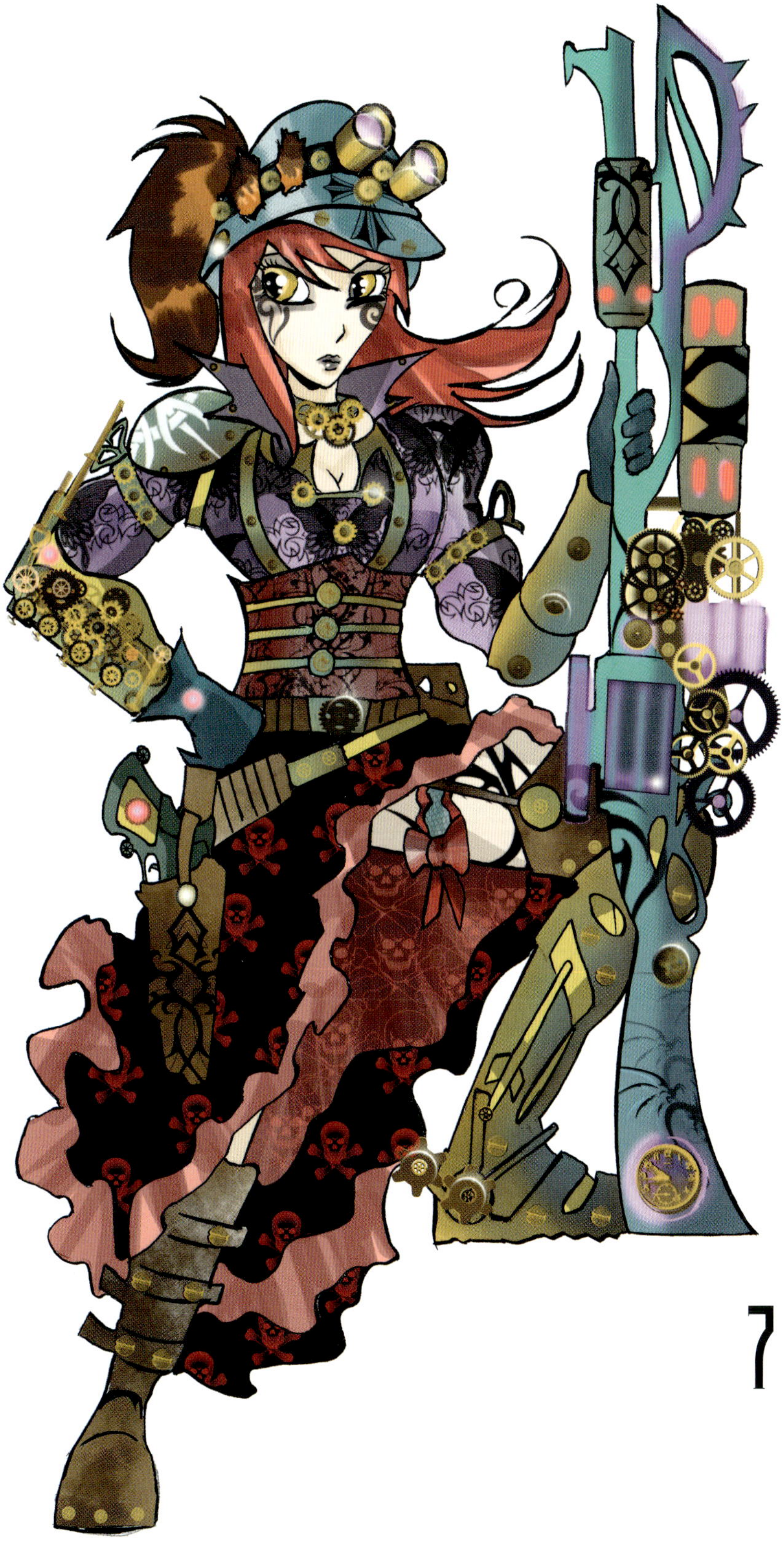

7

Finish by adding fine details to your character. Use gold markers for rivets or white pencil for highlights. With a little patience your character will be bursting with amazing details!

HORSE AND HORSEMAN

Lord August Montrooper is a tall knight of the mechanical horse cavalry. He is a great rider and is very effective in combat. His mechanical iron horse is the perfect companion for the battlefield. Together they create the ideal war machine to fulfill the orders of the Queen of Needles.

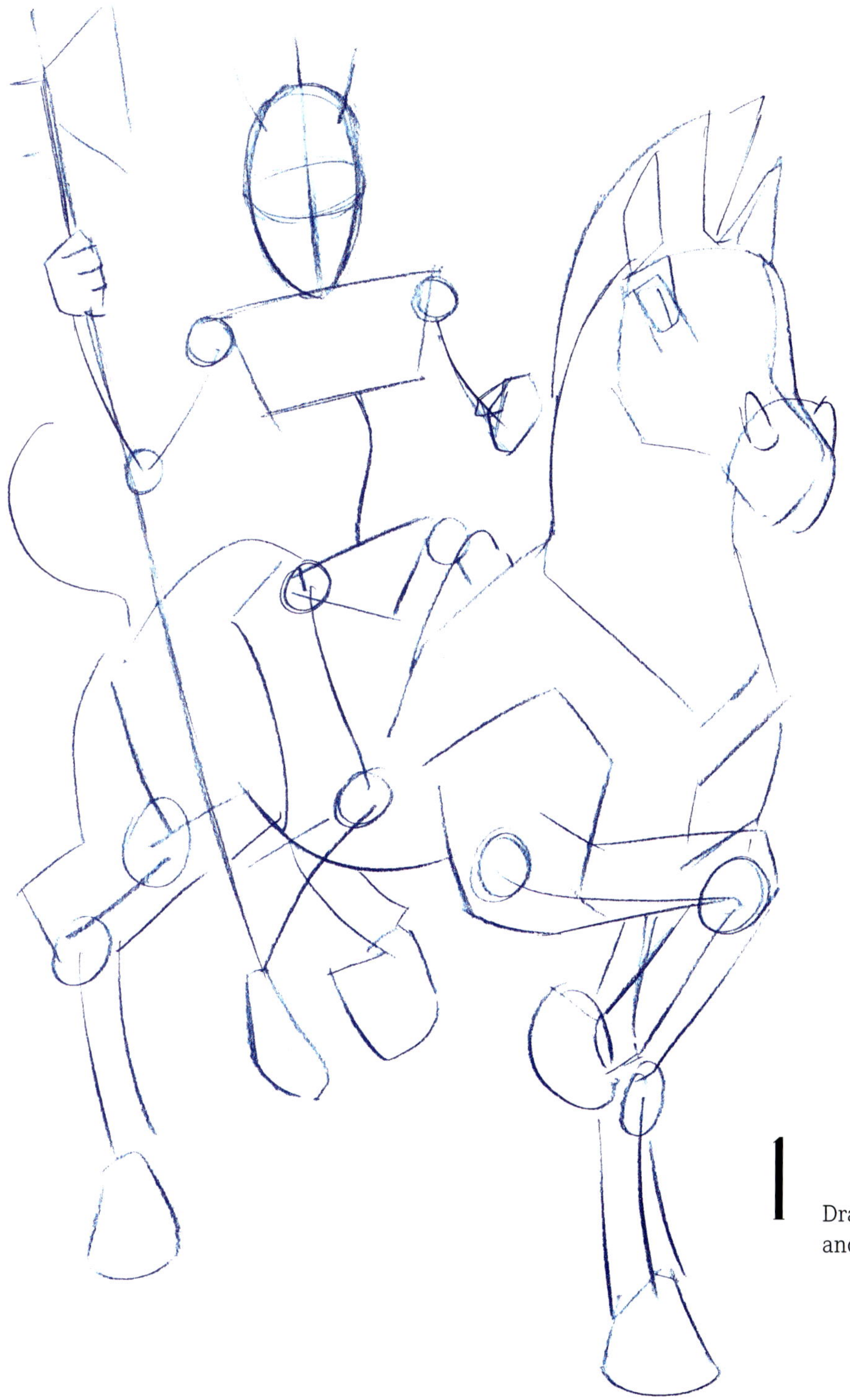

1

Draw the base shape of your rider and his mechanical horse in blue.

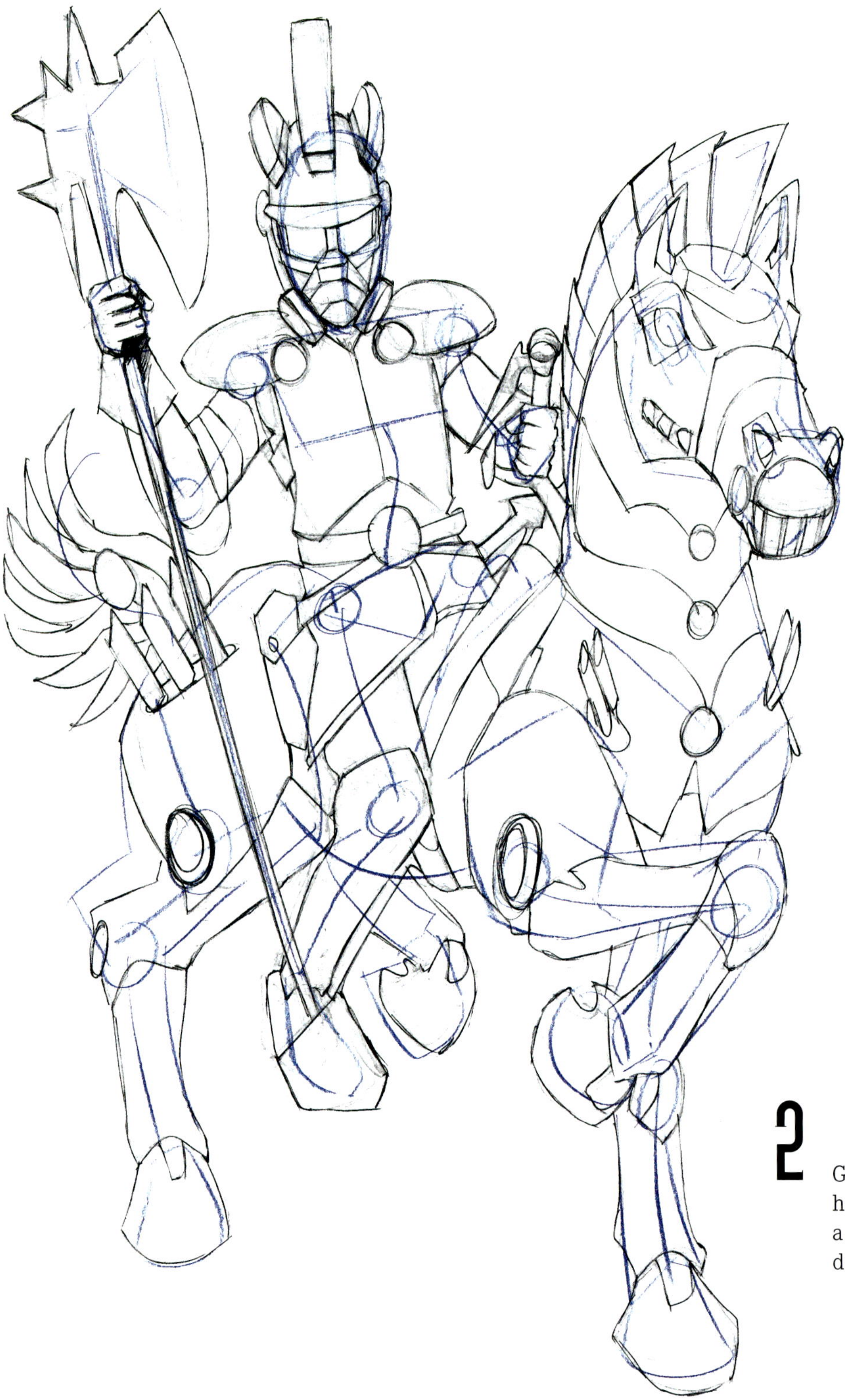

2

Give volume to the rider and his horse using a 2H pencil, then use a harder pencil to hone the finer details.

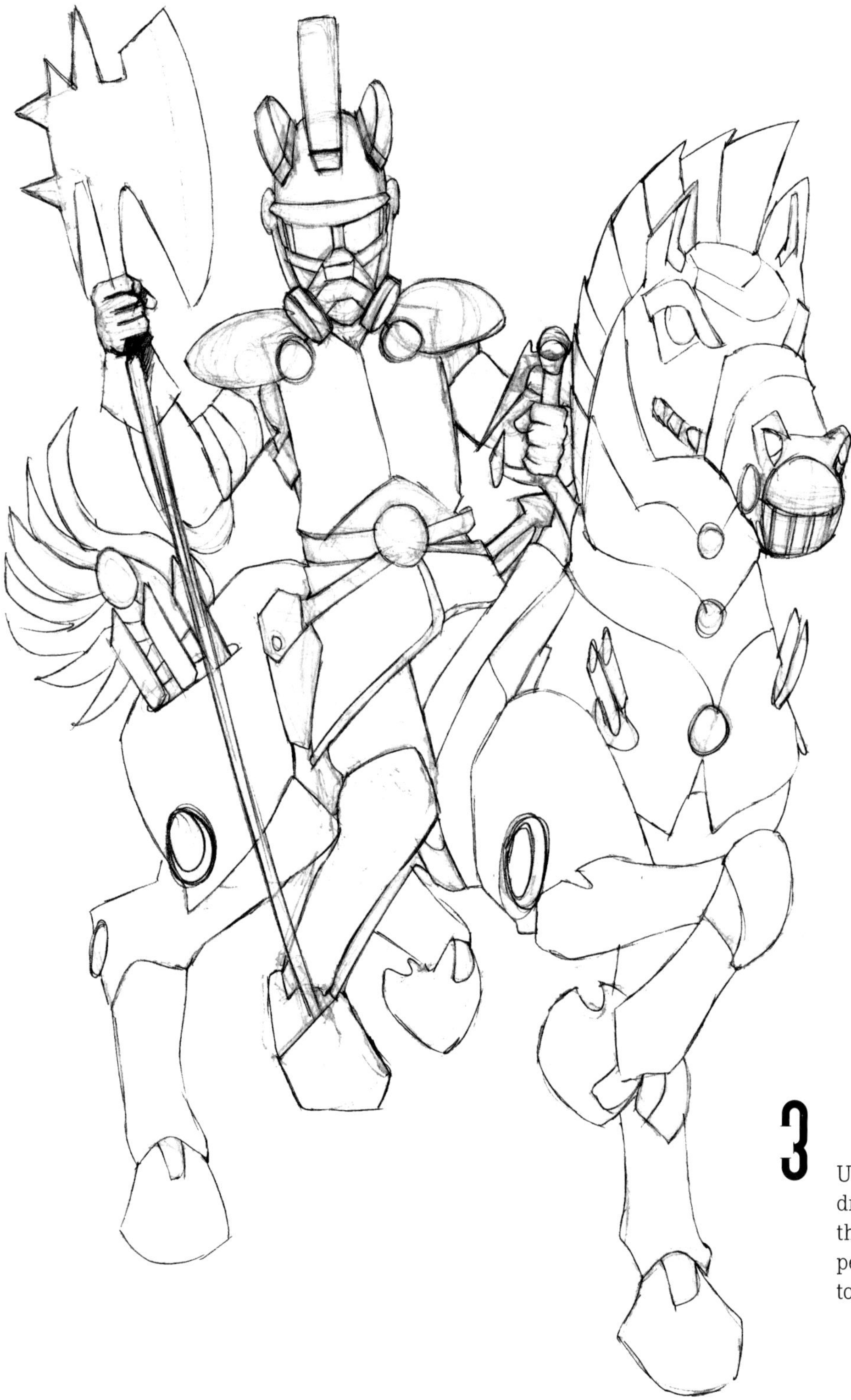

3

Use a 05-gauge pencil to completely draw the figure and give form to the detail: the more finished your pencil work is, the easier it will be to ink.

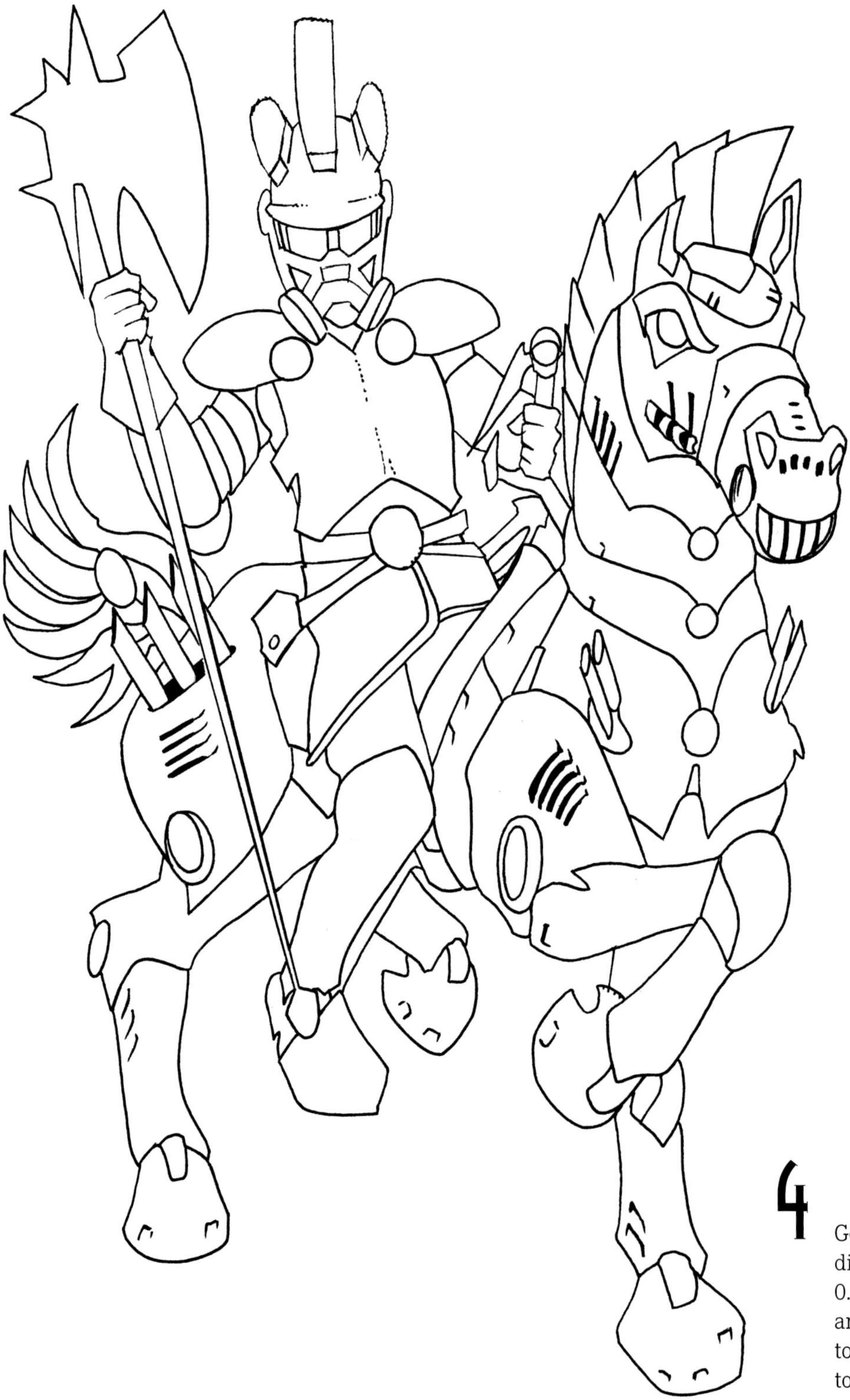

4

Go over your drawing with different-calibre pens. I use a 0.2 for detail, a 0.4 for the figure, and an 0.8 just for the contour and to highlight the lines that I want to stand out with more intensity.

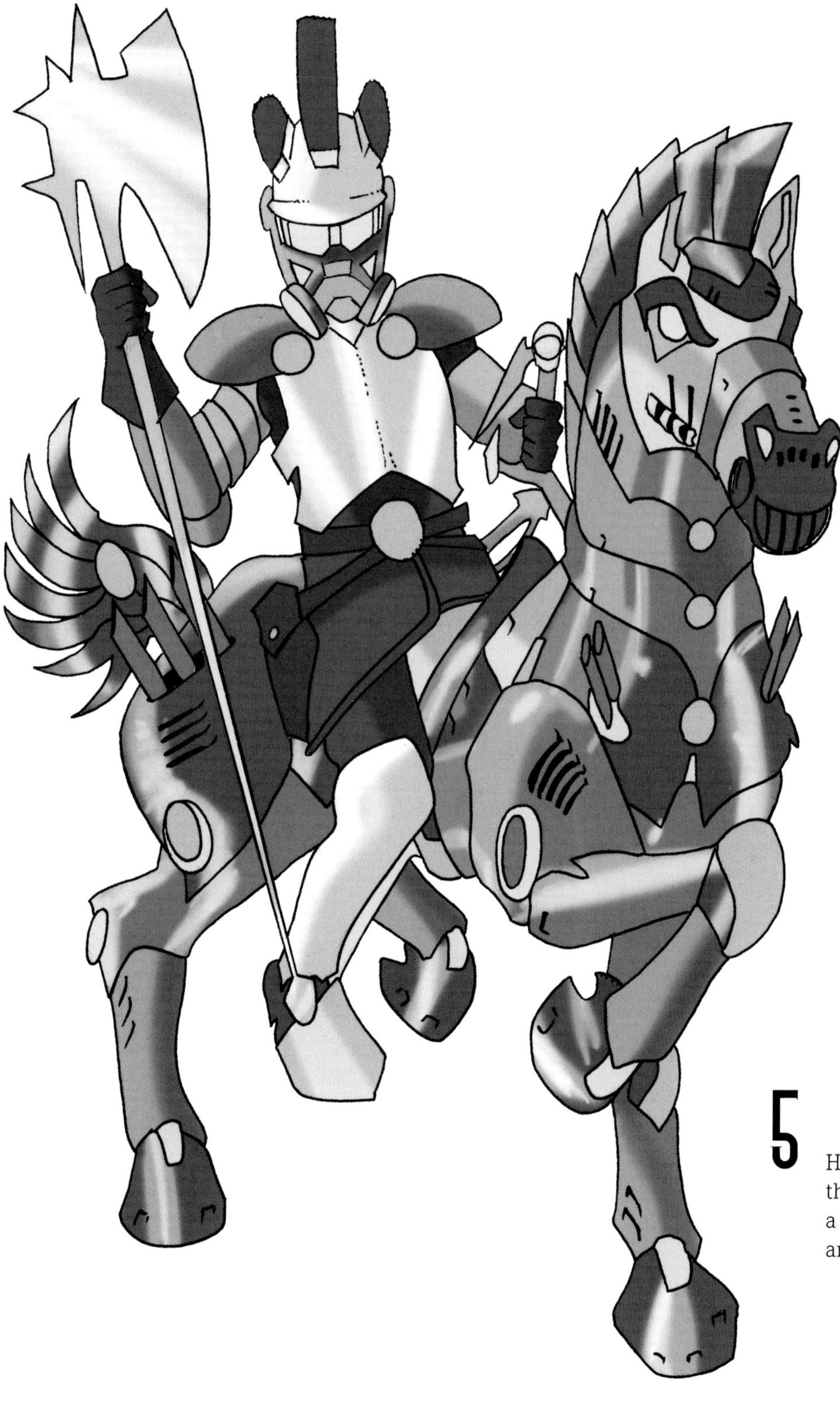

5

Here the light source is from the left of the character, adding a beautiful brilliance to his lance and volume to the entire design.

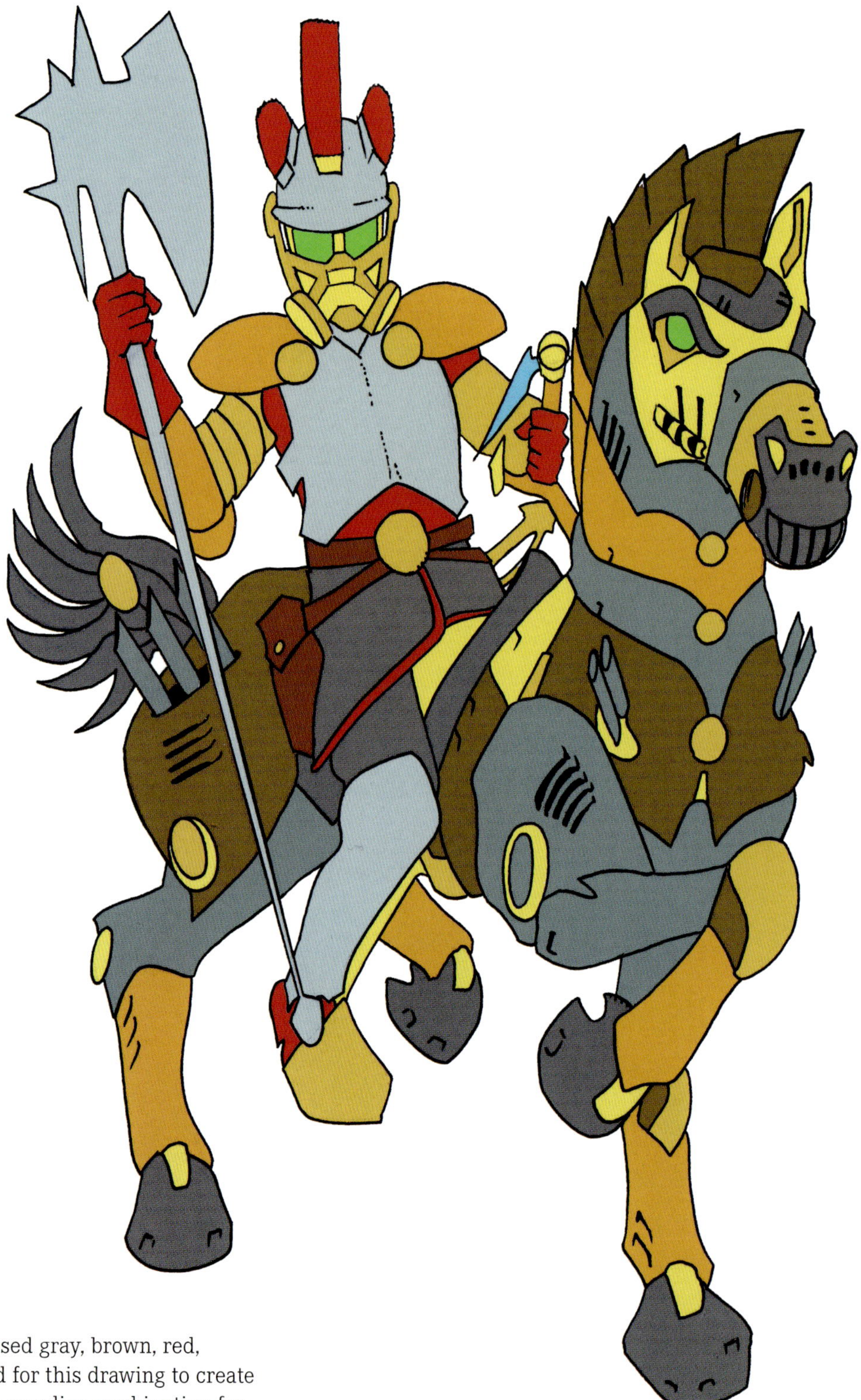

6

I have used gray, brown, red, and gold for this drawing to create a rather peculiar combination for this queen's horseman.

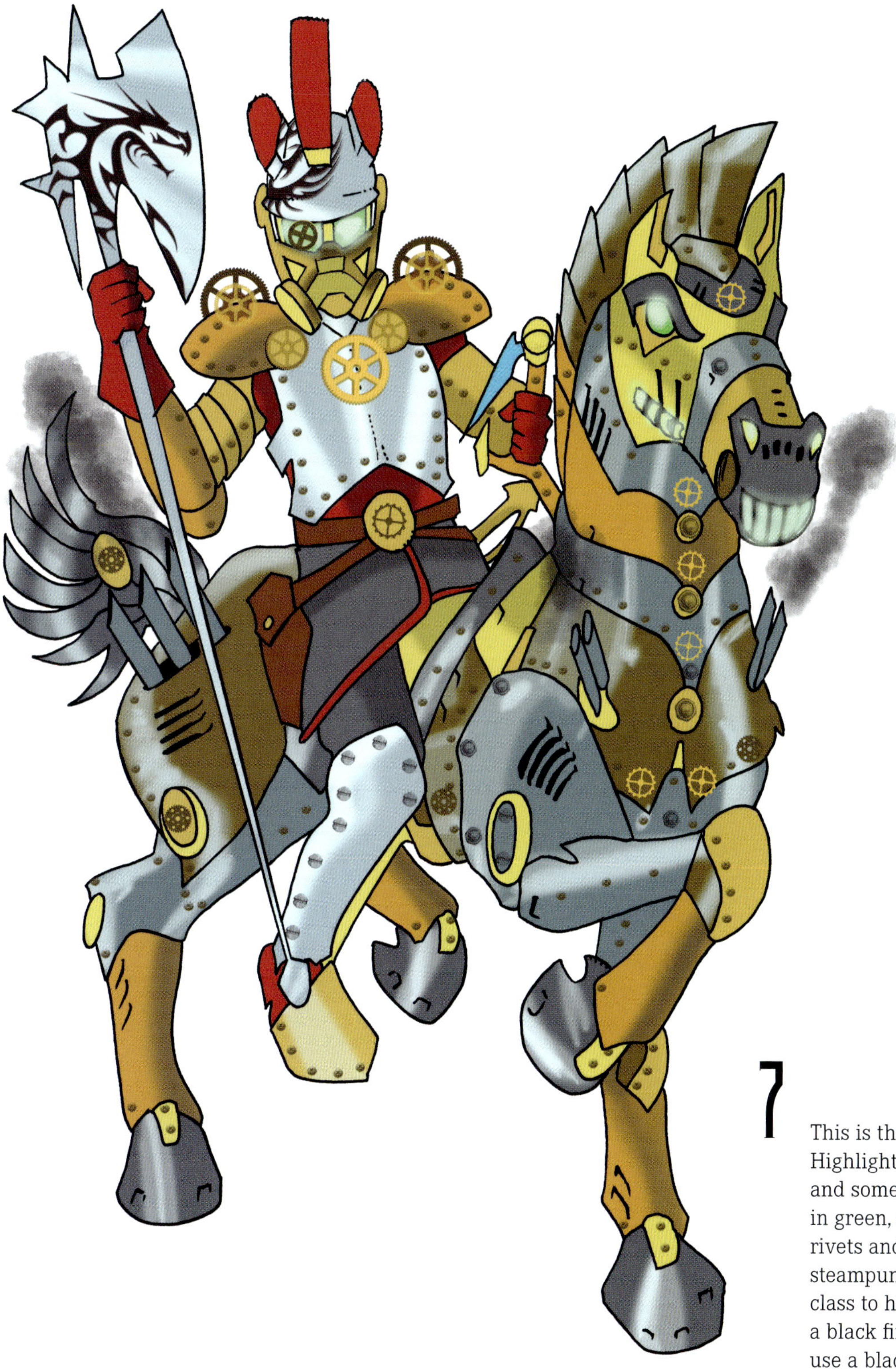

7

This is the part I like best. Highlight the horseman's glasses and some of the horse's detail in green, and then add all the rivets and washers worthy of this steampunk rider. Add a touch of class to his lance and helmet with a black fine-tip marker and, finally, use a black pen to add some smoke coming out of the horse. Sublime!

ENGINE DRIVER

Thork, the driver, is in charge of the train that travels from east to west through valleys and mountains, tunnels and lakes. He is of course an expert in mechanics. So much so, in fact, that when he lost his arm in a terrible accident, he made a new one for himself so that he could continue driving the train.

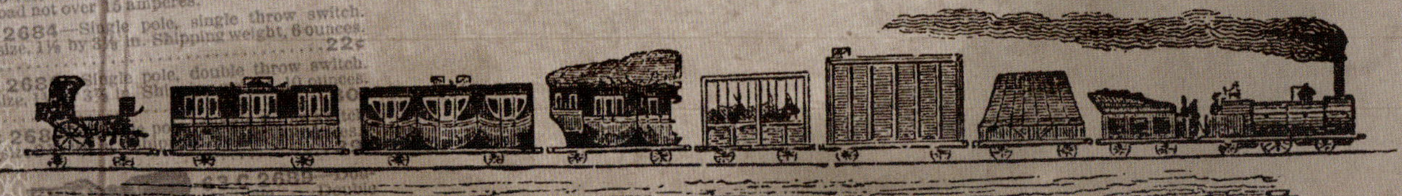

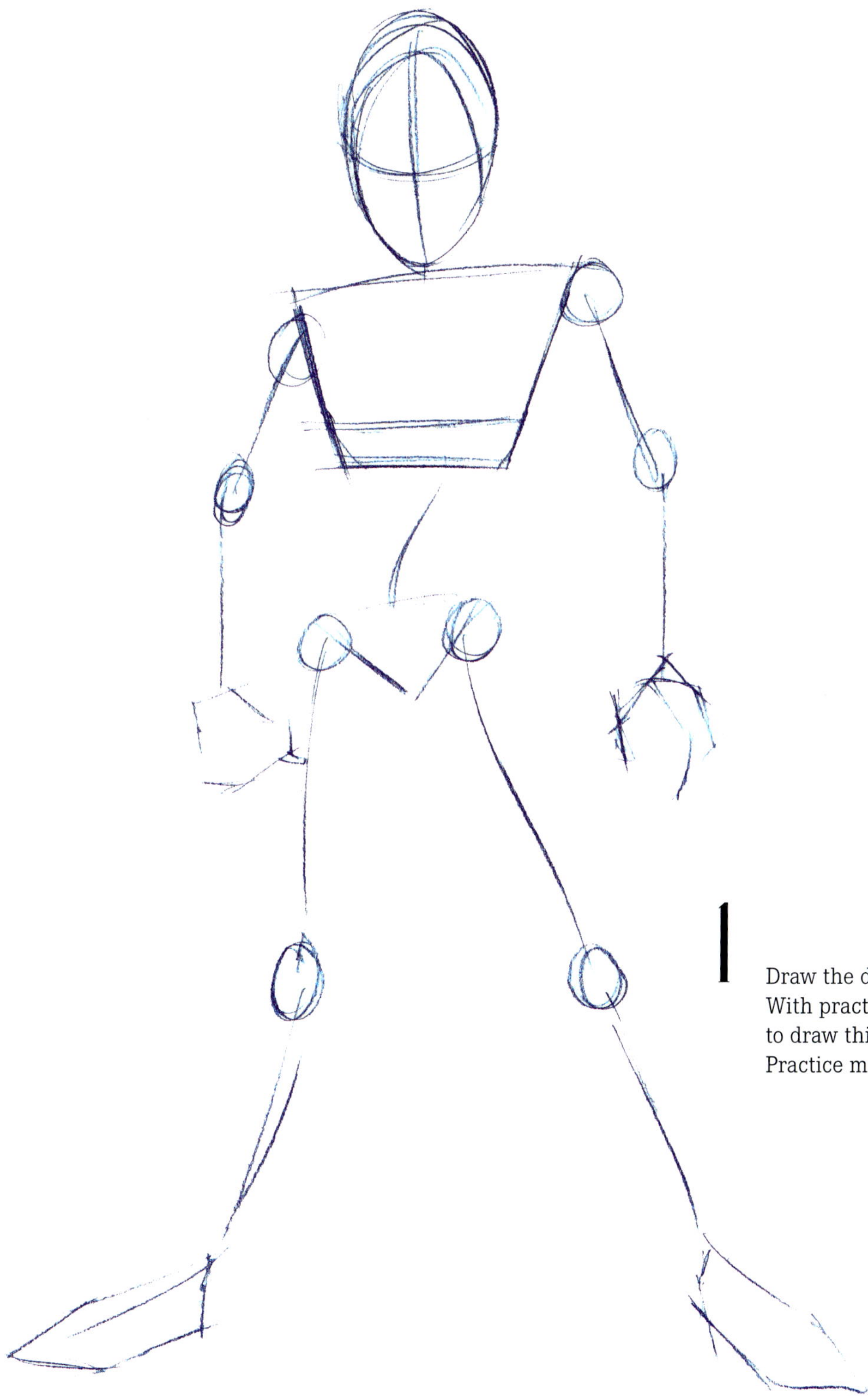

1

Draw the driver's blue pencil base. With practice you should be able to draw this using a 2H pencil. Practice makes perfect!

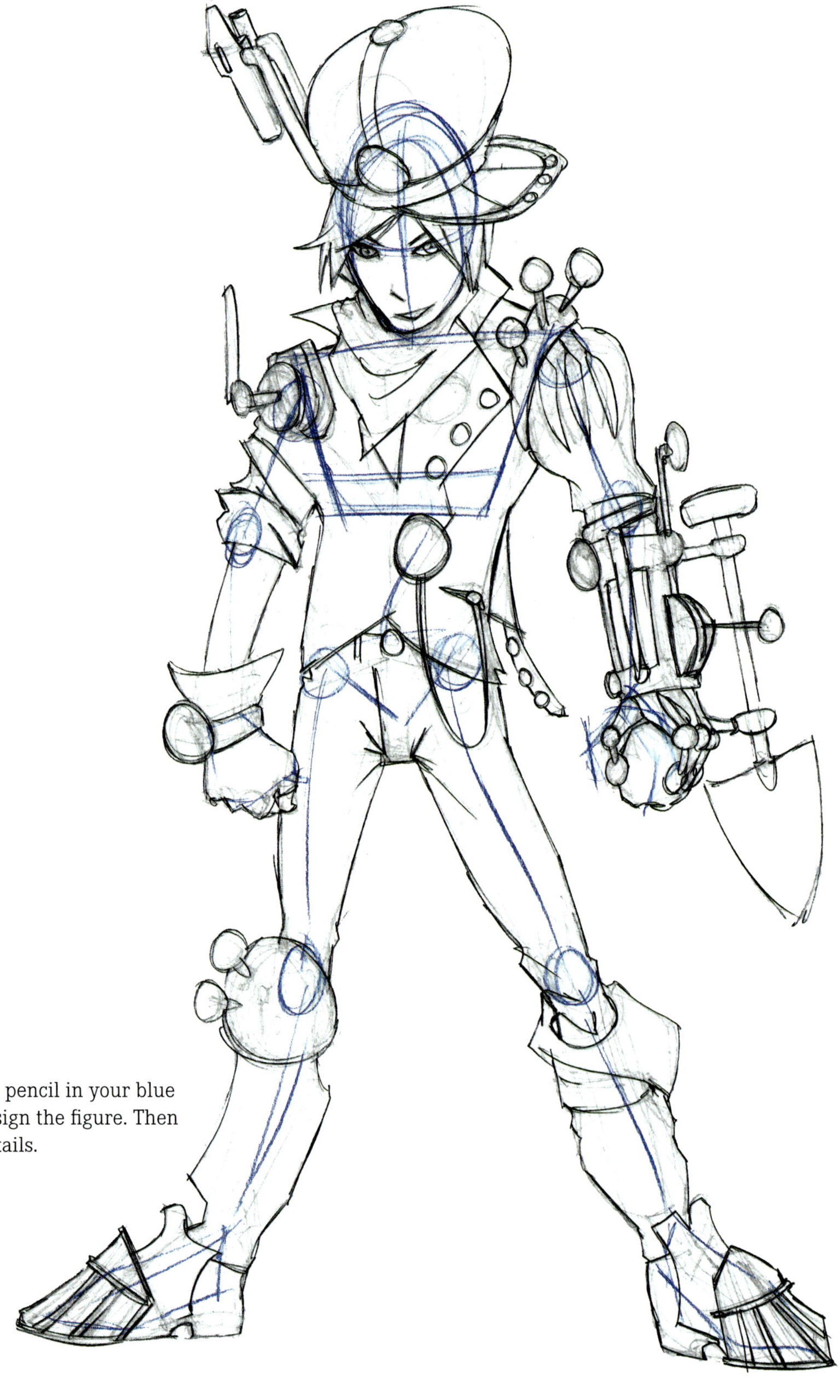

2

Use the 2H pencil in your blue draft to design the figure. Then add the details.

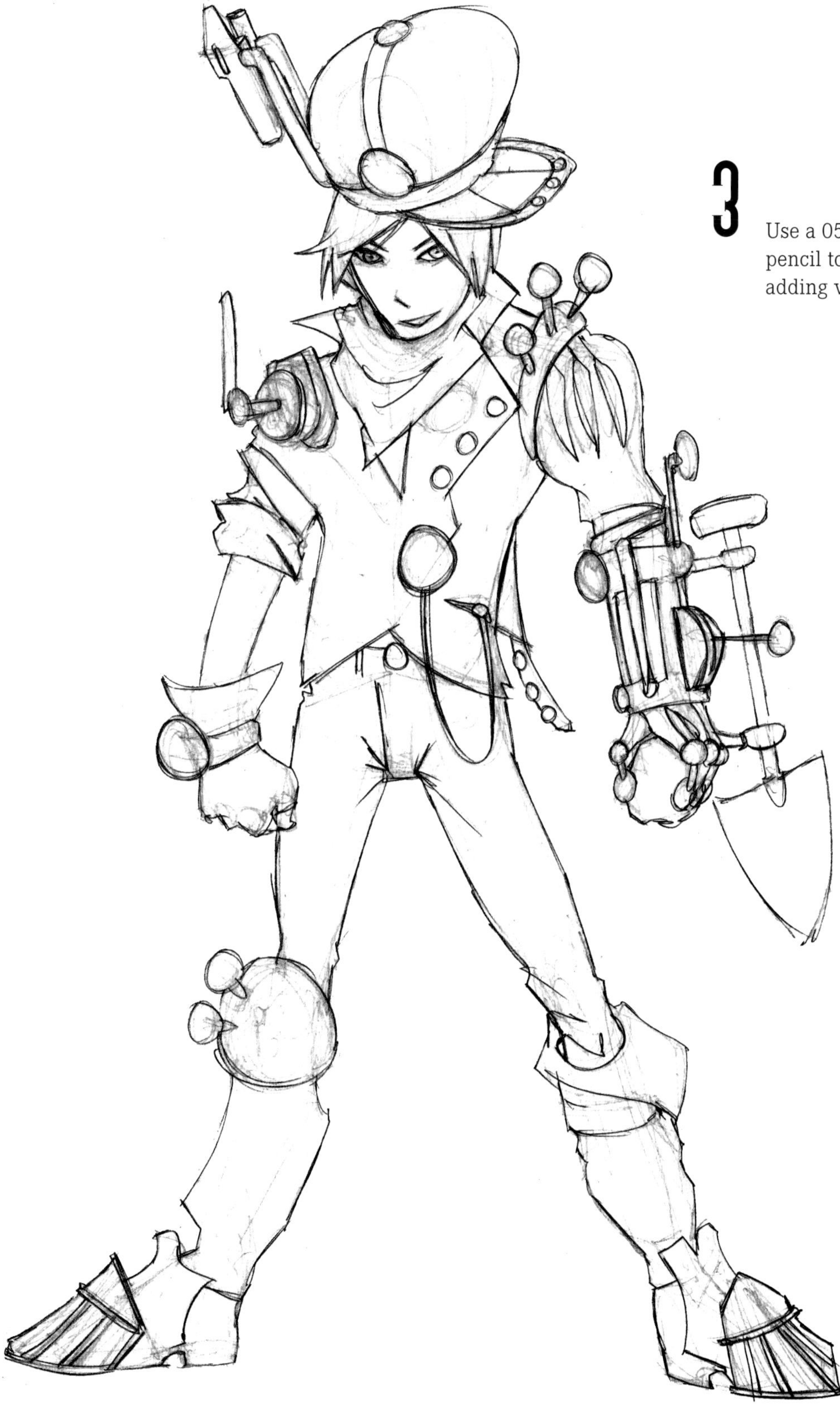

3

Use a 05-calibre mechanical pencil to sketch the figure, adding volume and detail.

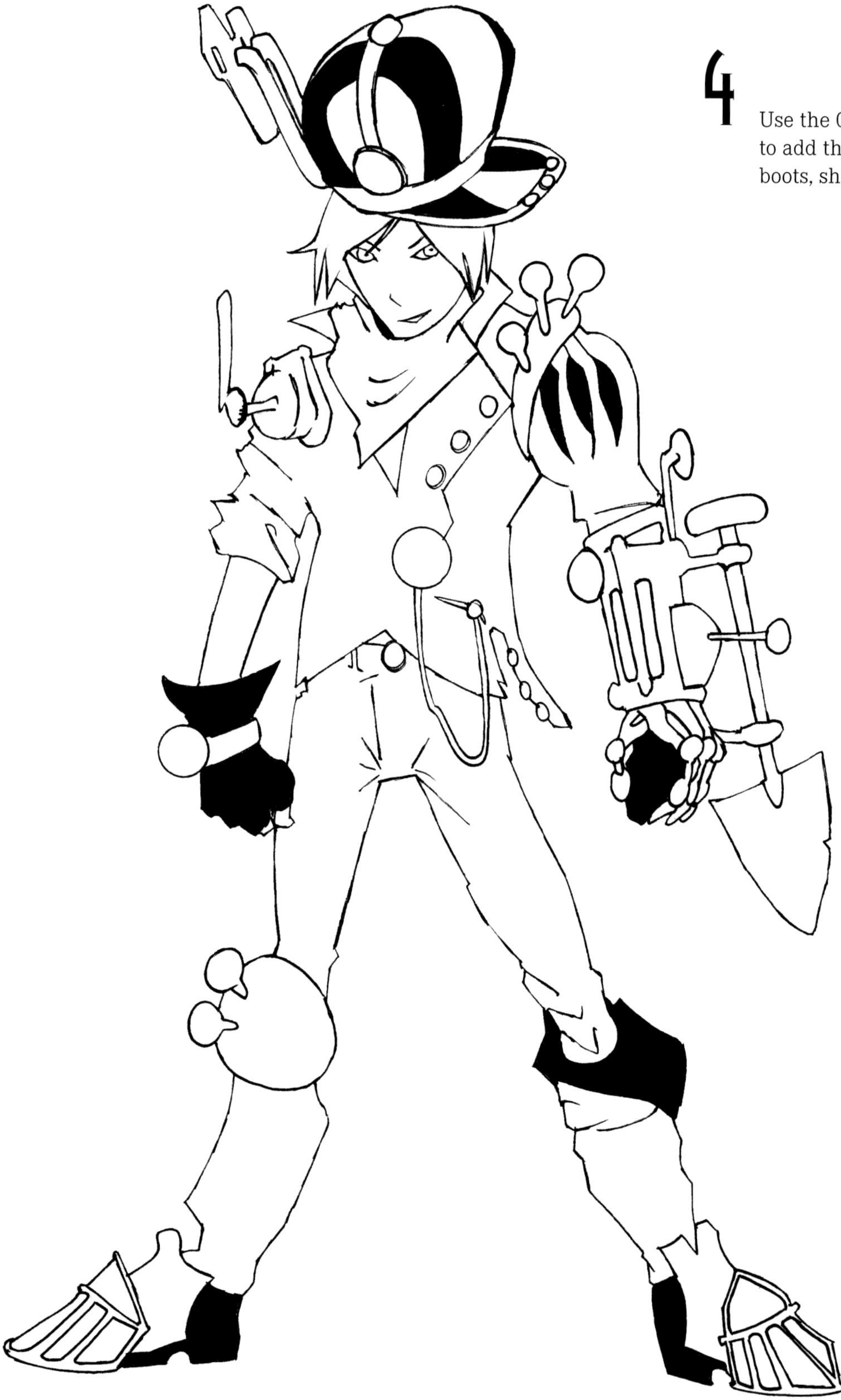

4

Use the 08 pen once more to add the black of the hat, boots, shirt ... and coal!

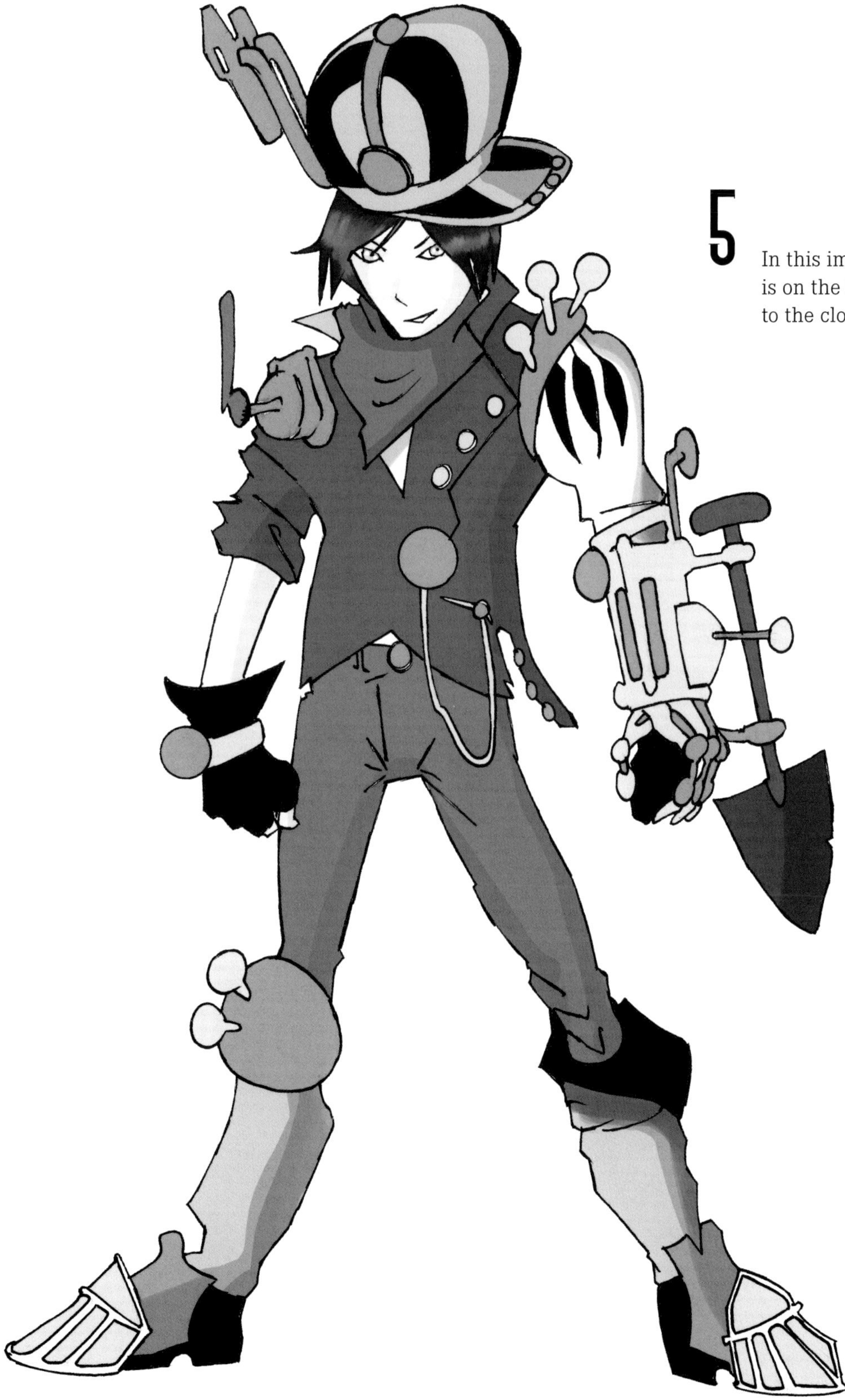

5

In this image the light source is on the left, adding volume to the clothing and accessories.

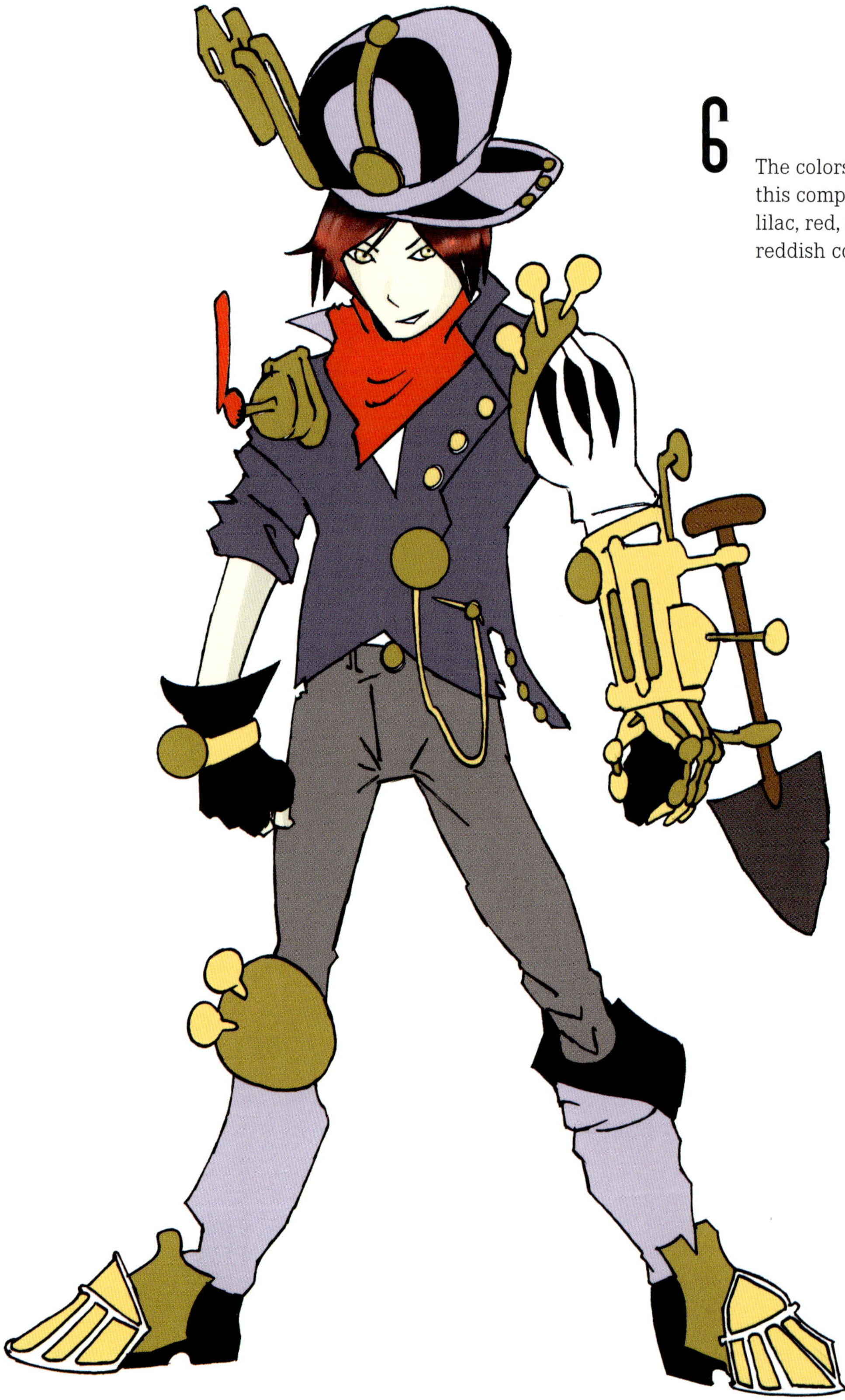

6

The colors I have chosen for this composition are purple, lilac, red, and gold, with another reddish color for the hair.

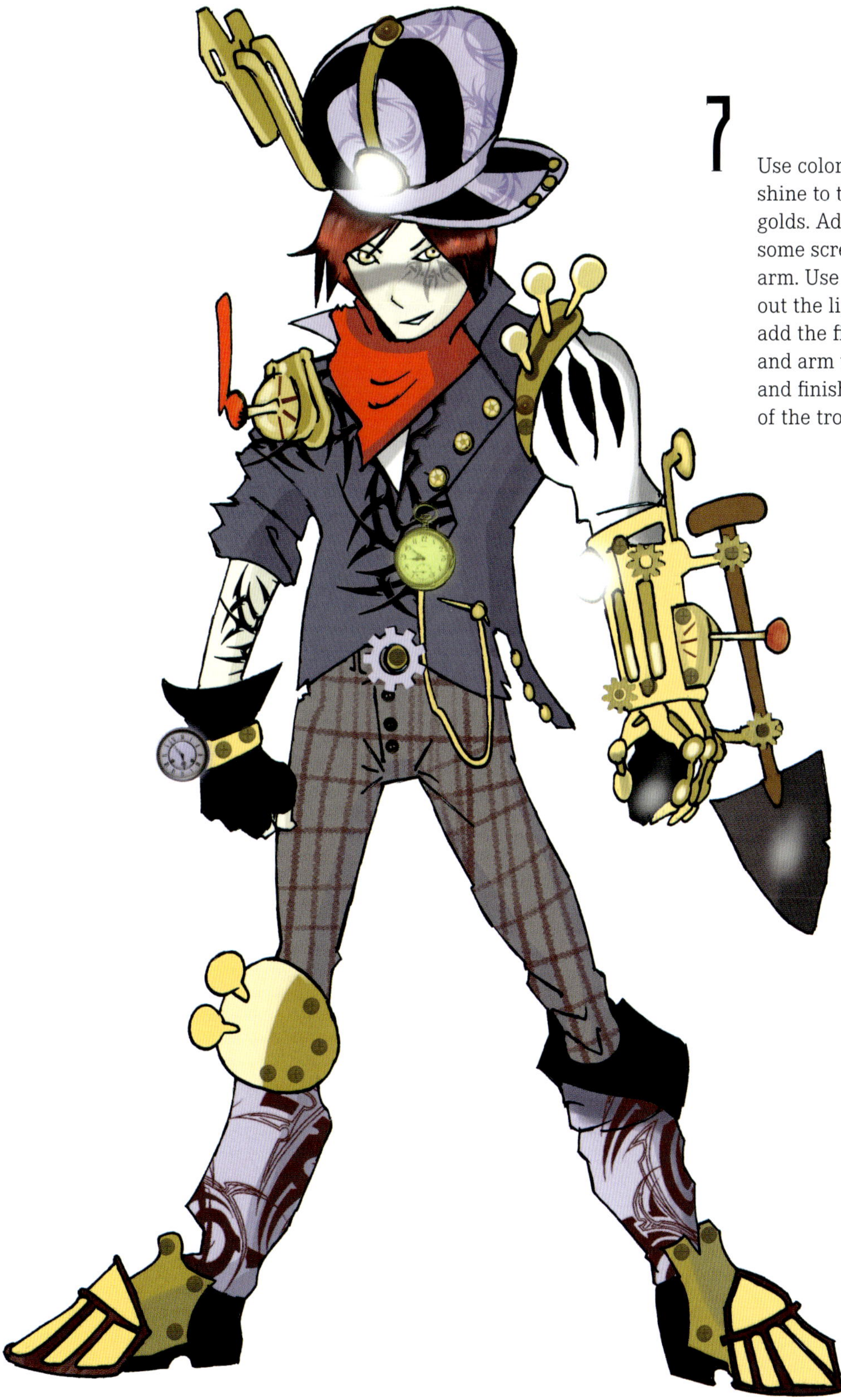

7

Use color pencils to add the final shine to the reds, purples, and golds. Add rivets to the coat and some screws to the mechanical arm. Use a white pencil to pick out the light on the hat and arm, add the final details to the vest and arm with a black 0.2 pen, and finish by drawing in the lines of the trousers with the red pen.

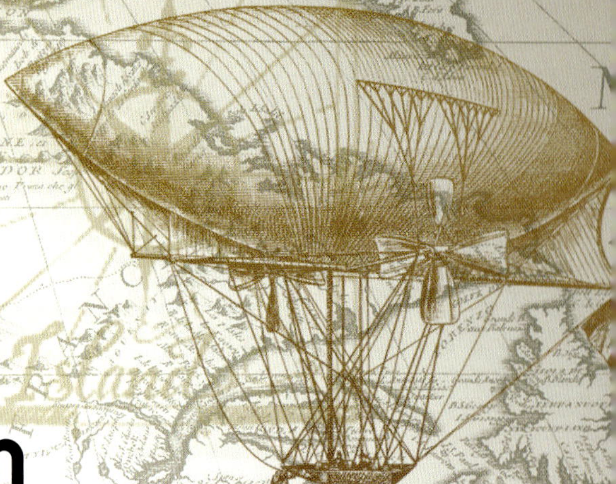

AIRWOMAN

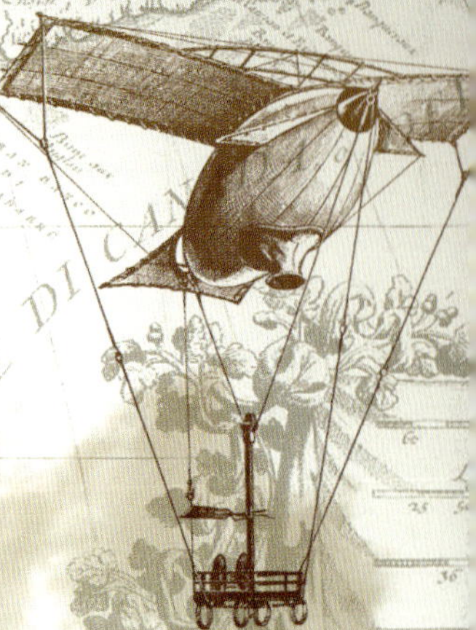

Krysa belongs to a highly original elite group of aviators: the human hawk squadron. This squadron, formed by the best, does not use planes but a sophisticated team of helices that enable its members to fly and carry out missions that others could only dream of.

1

Start by drawing the base of your character in blue pencil: this is so that you can see its proportions clearly. With practice you will be able to do this directly with black pencil.

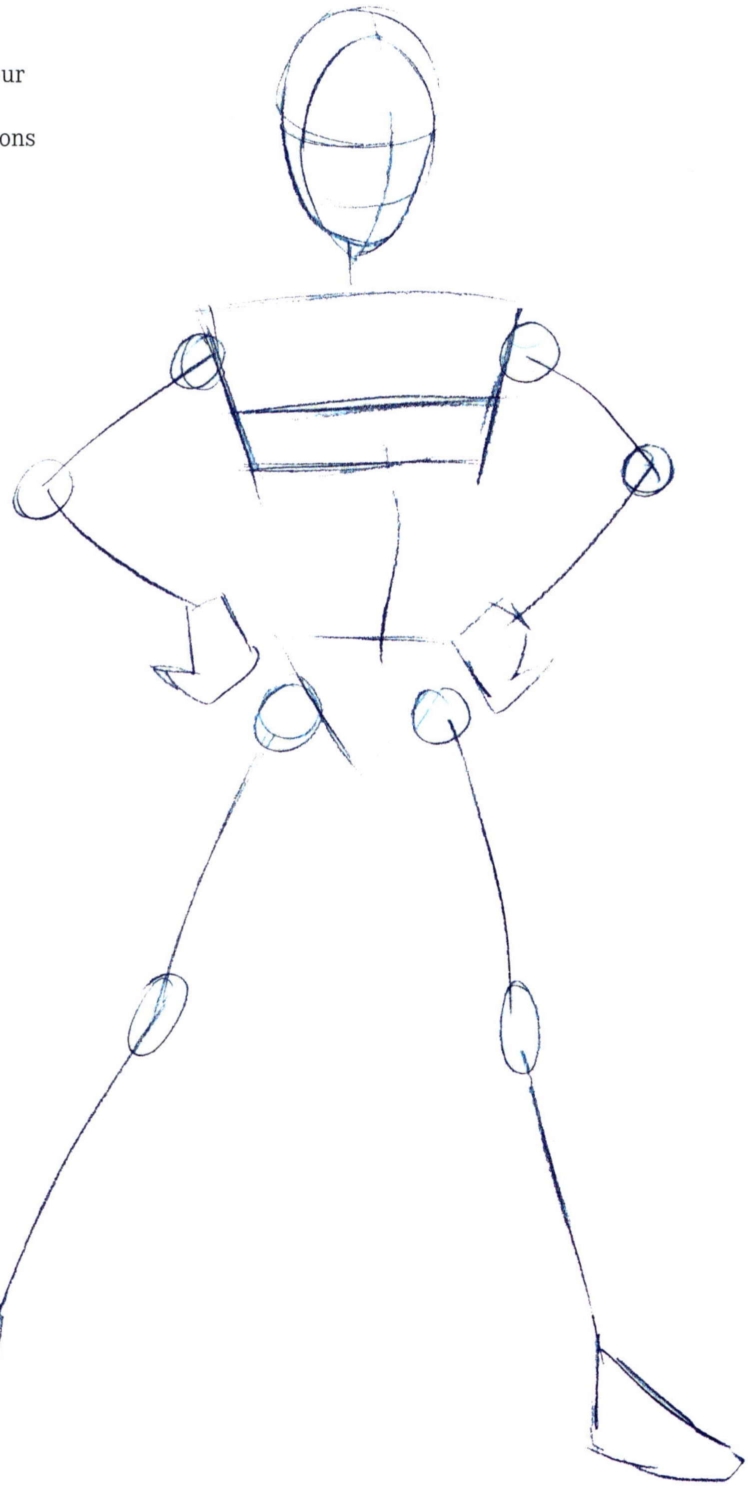

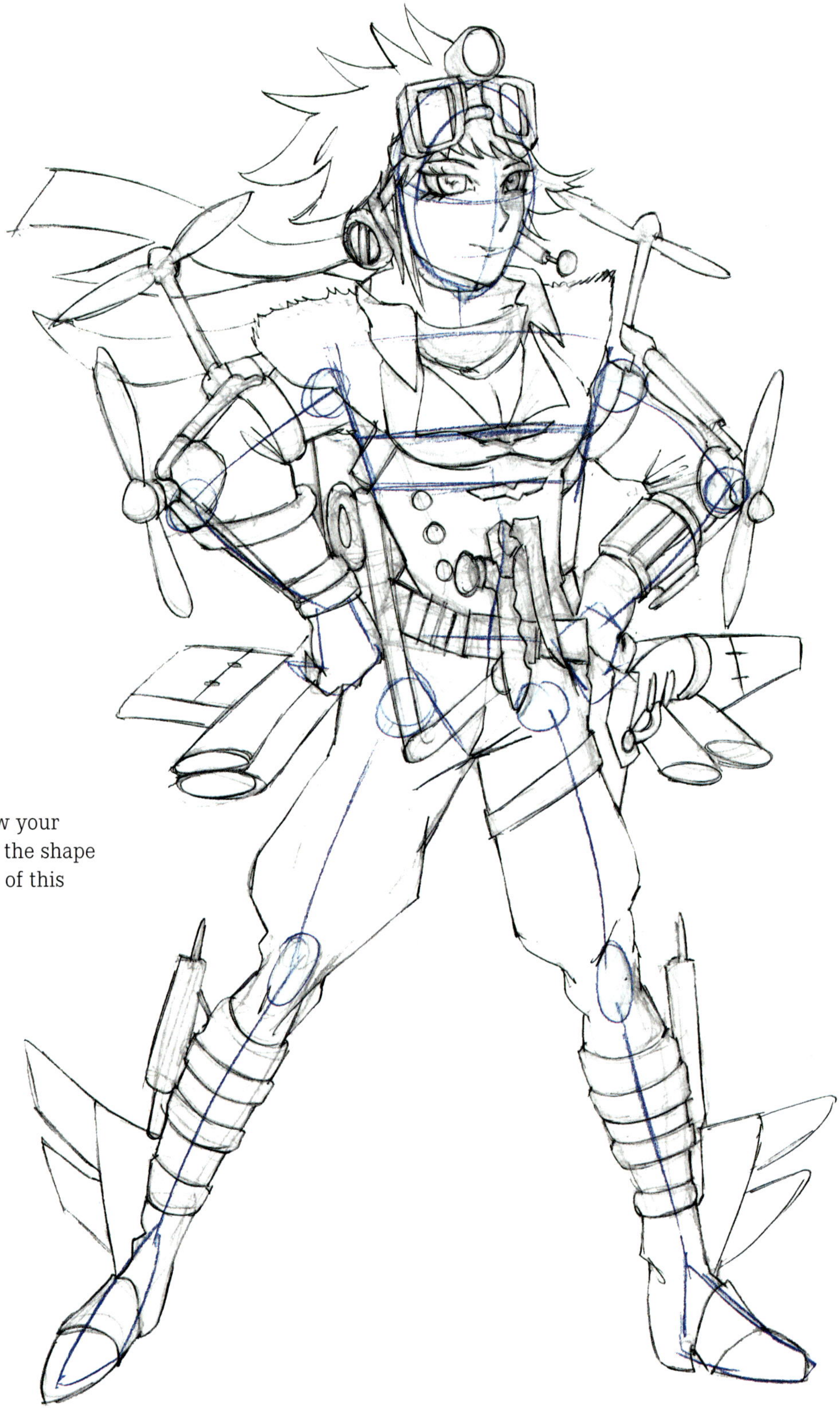

2

Use a 2H pencil to draw your character, highlighting the shape and the heroic bearing of this aviator.

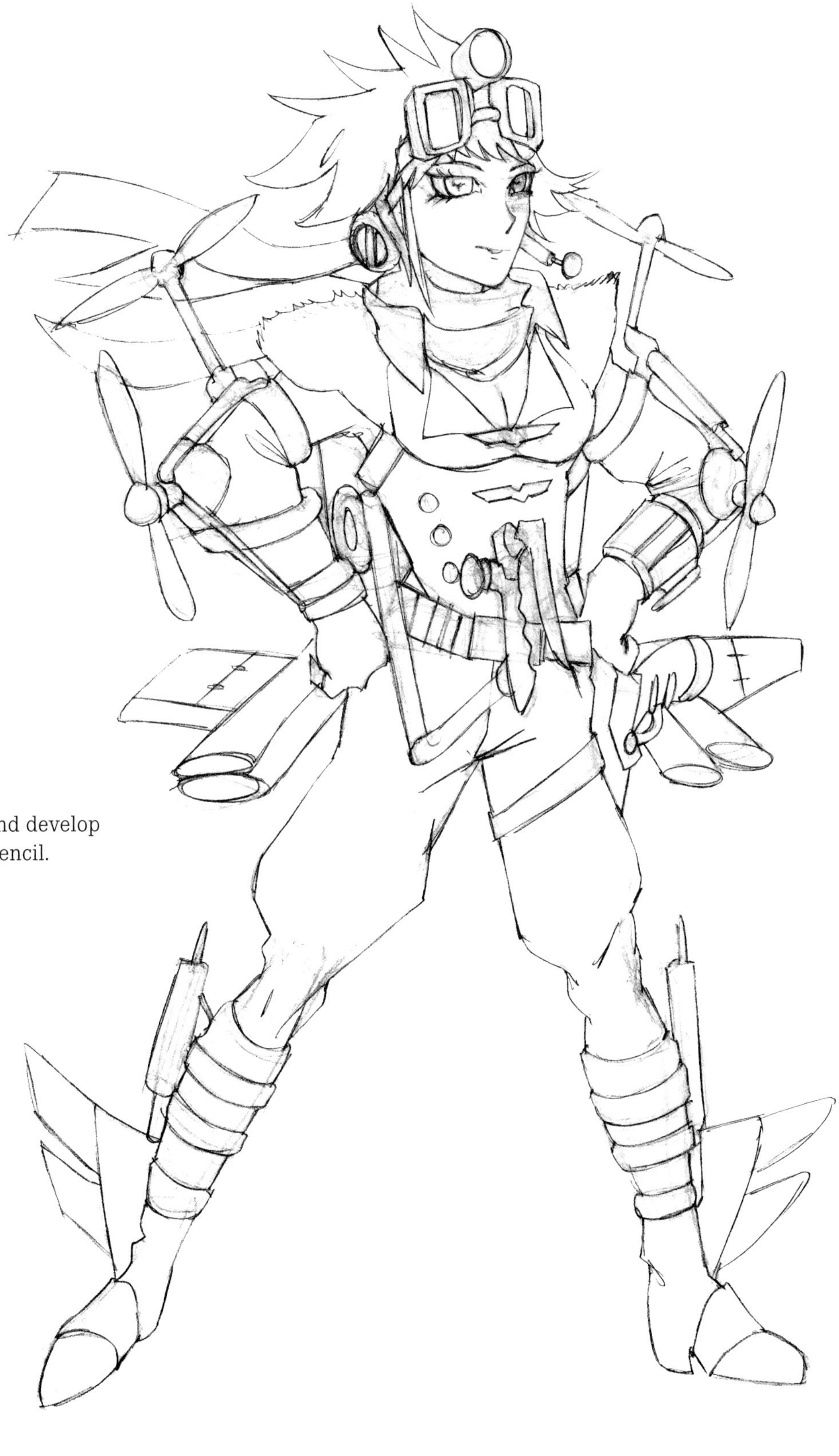

3

Outline the figure and develop details using a 2H pencil.

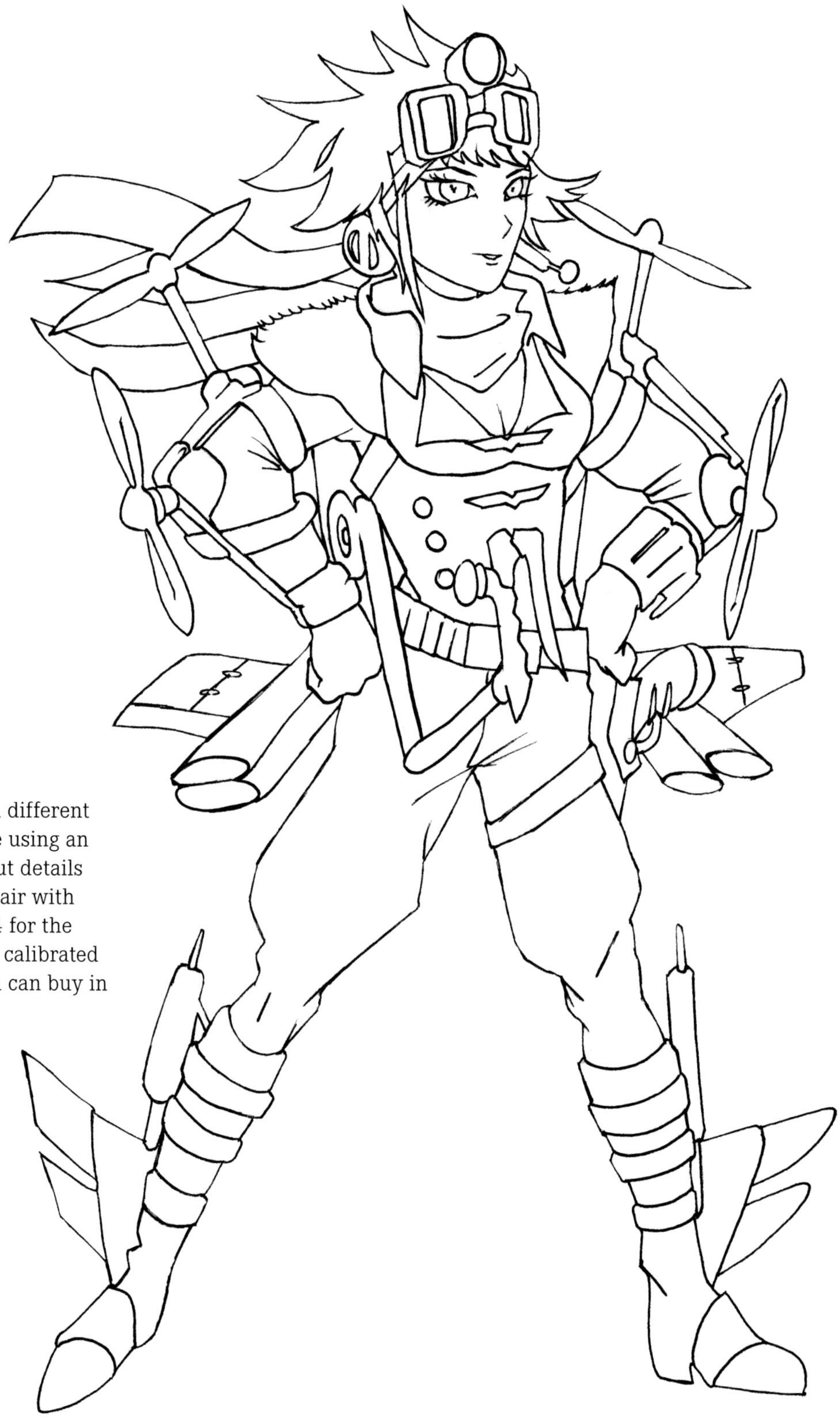

4

Ink the drawing. Give a different thickness to the outline using an 0.8-mm pen and pick out details such as eyes, nose, or hair with a 0.2-mm pen. Use a 0.4 for the remaining marks. I use calibrated felt tip pens, which you can buy in stationery stores.

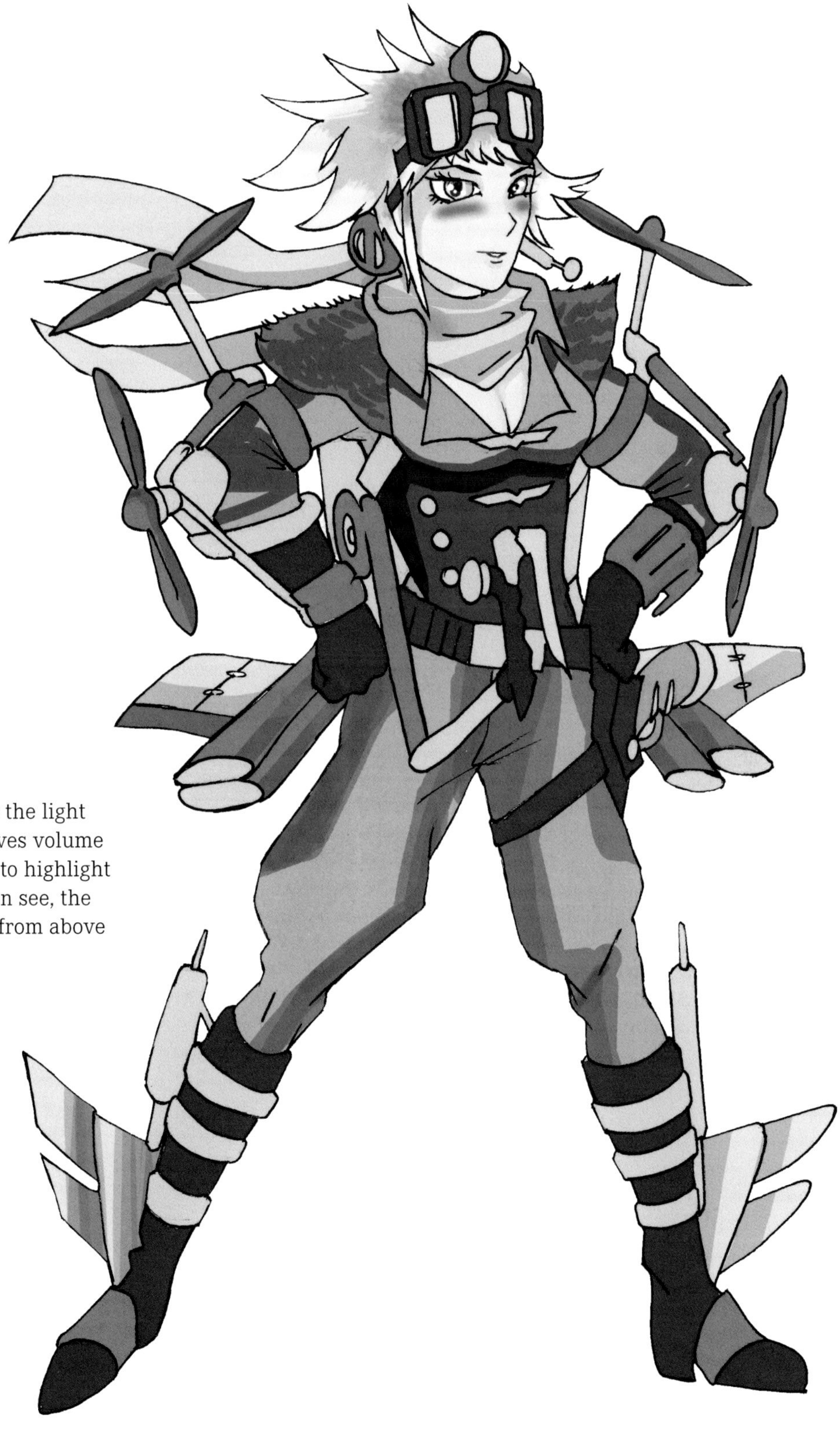

5

Now we will see where the light is coming from. This gives volume to the figure and helps to highlight more details. As you can see, the light source is directly from above the character.

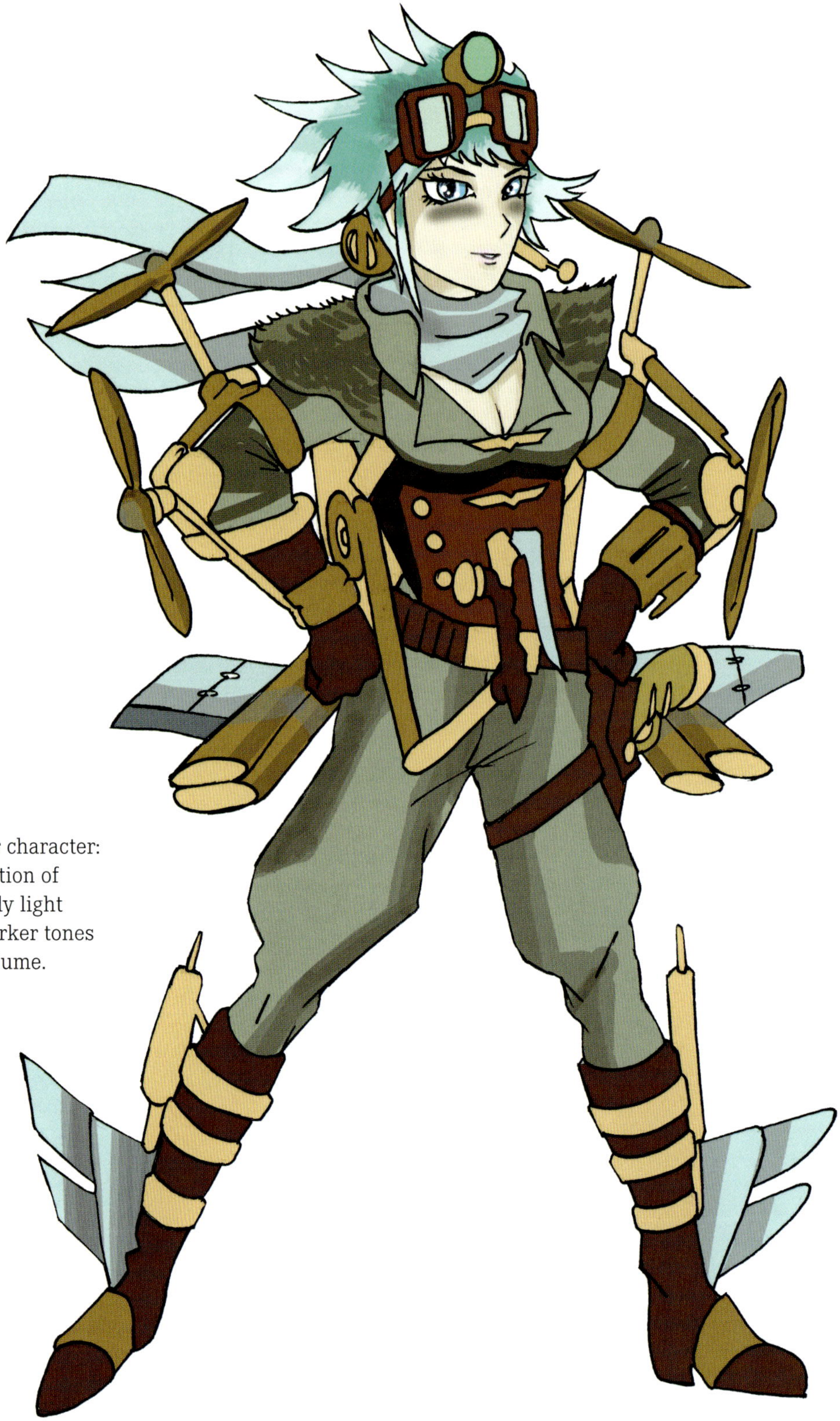

6

Add base colors to your character: I've gone for a combination of greens. It is best to apply light colors first, then use darker tones to add shadows and volume.

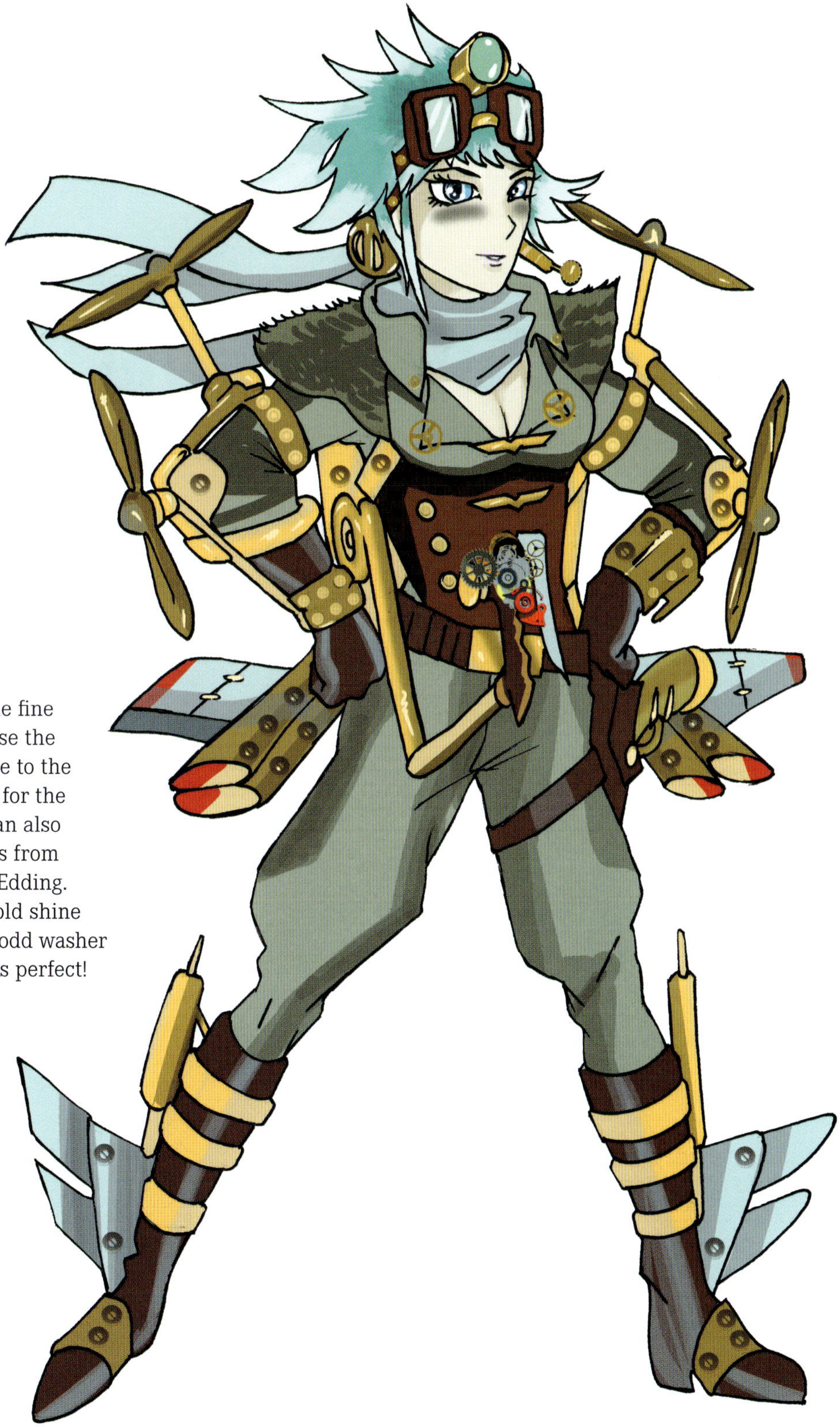

7

Now you need to add the fine detail to the drawing. Use the white pencil to add glare to the glasses and a light blue for the gloves and boots. You can also buy gold and silver pens from manufacturers such as Edding. You can use these for gold shine or even to highlight the odd washer or screw. Practice makes perfect!

SPACE SOLDIER

Logan Calanthir is a special soldier of the Space S-tiger order, a military elite trained in air combat. Propelled by their backpack rockets, the warriors of this battalion dominate the skies. After the wars, the order was vetoed and the soldiers dispersed. Now Logan is the last to remain in action. He is currently in the north where, allied with the rulers of those lands, he is training a new generation of Space S-tigers.

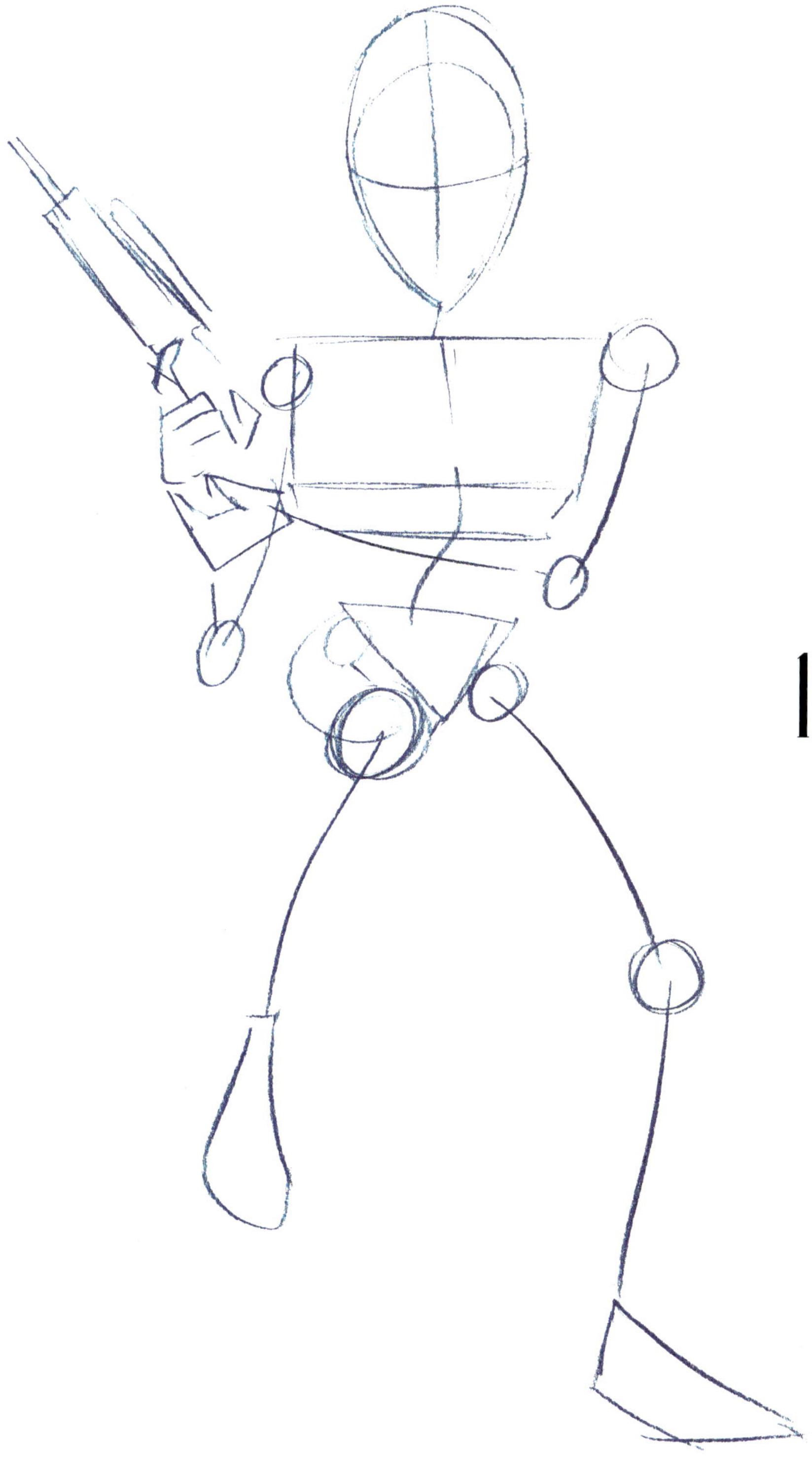

1

Begin by drawing Logan's base in blue pencil: he has a solemn posture in line with his rank and his discipline in the air.

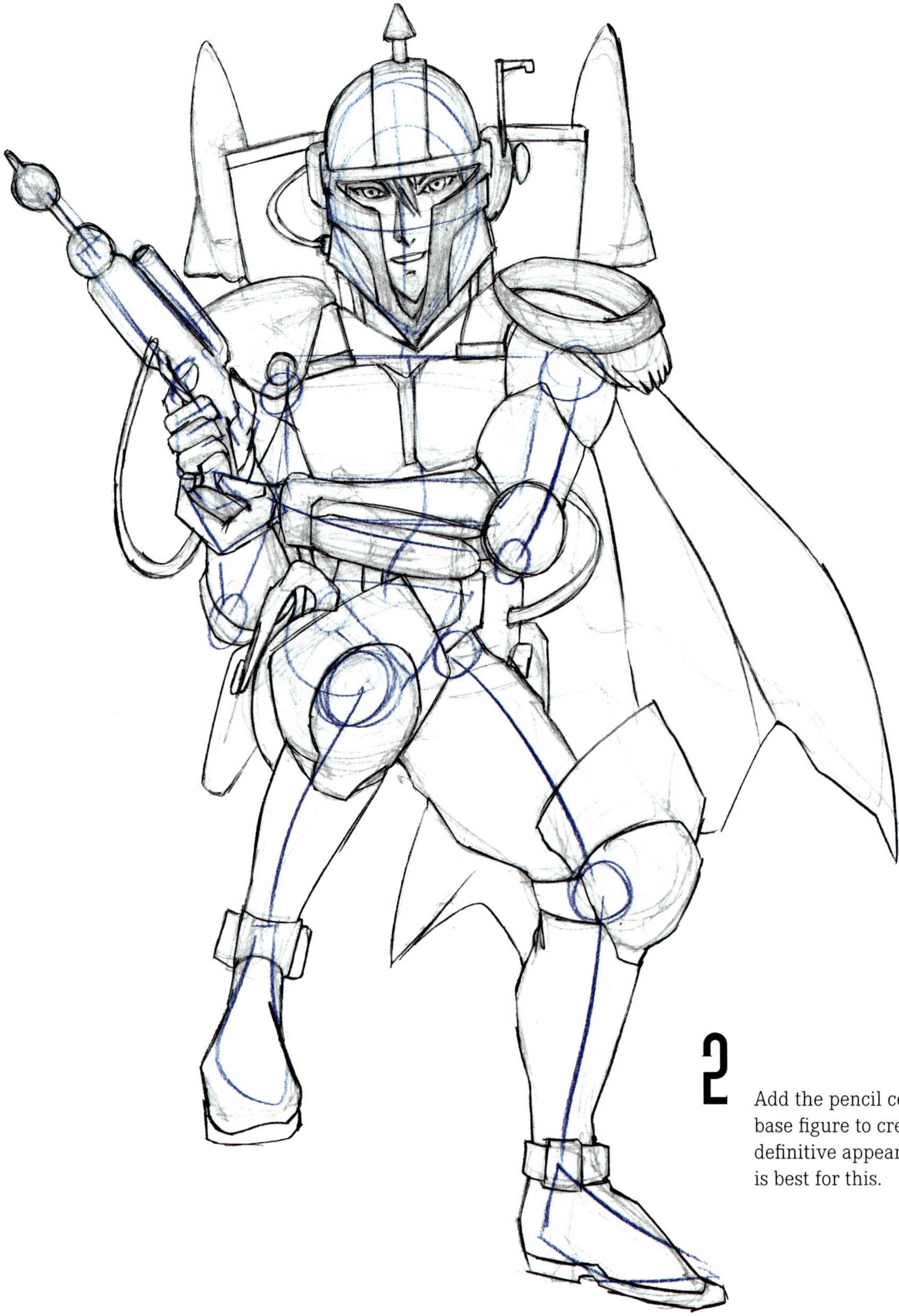

2

Add the pencil contour to the base figure to create volume and a definitive appearance. A 2H pencil is best for this.

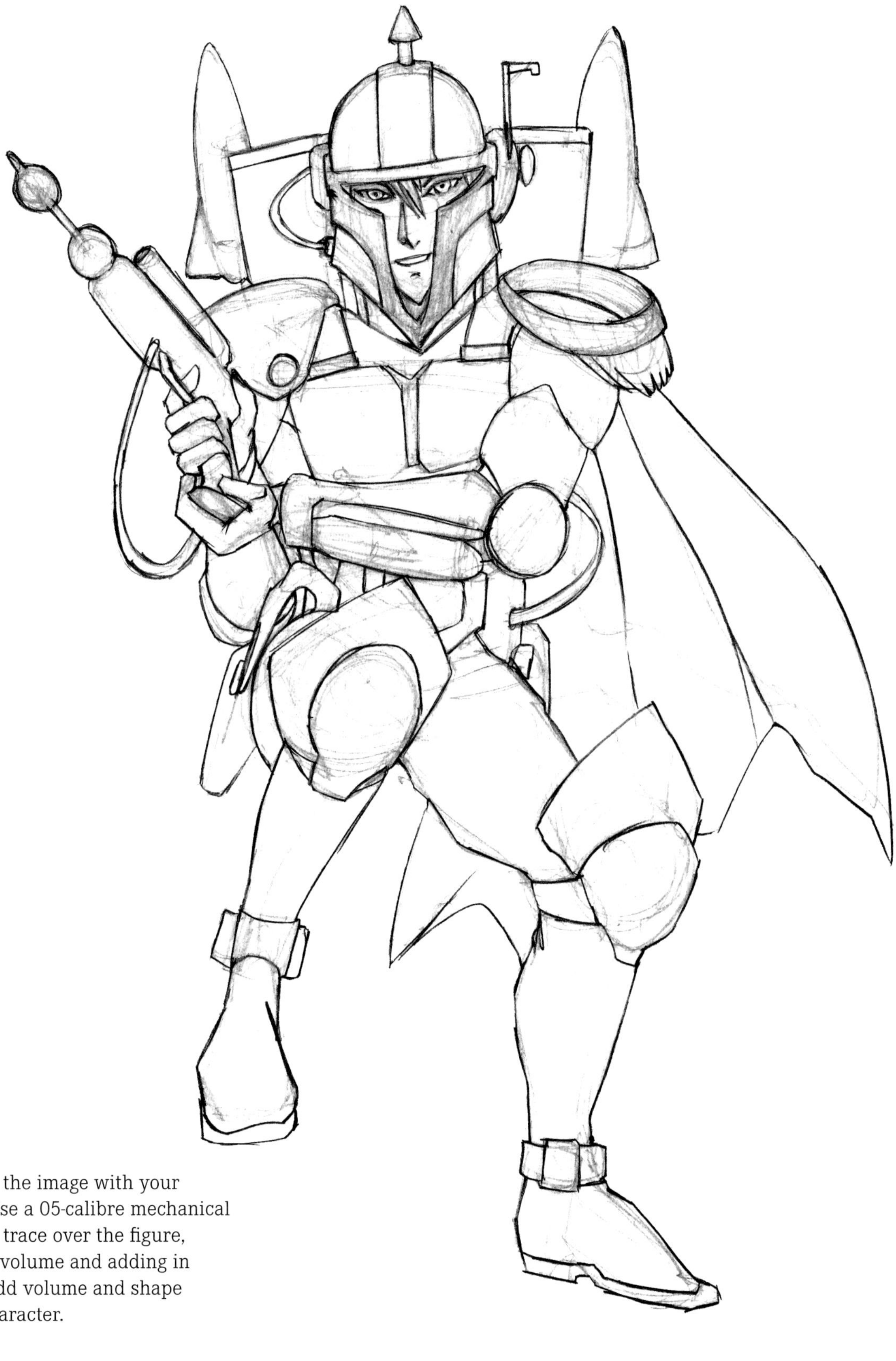

3

Work up the image with your pencil. Use a 05-calibre mechanical pencil to trace over the figure, giving it volume and adding in detail. Add volume and shape to the character.

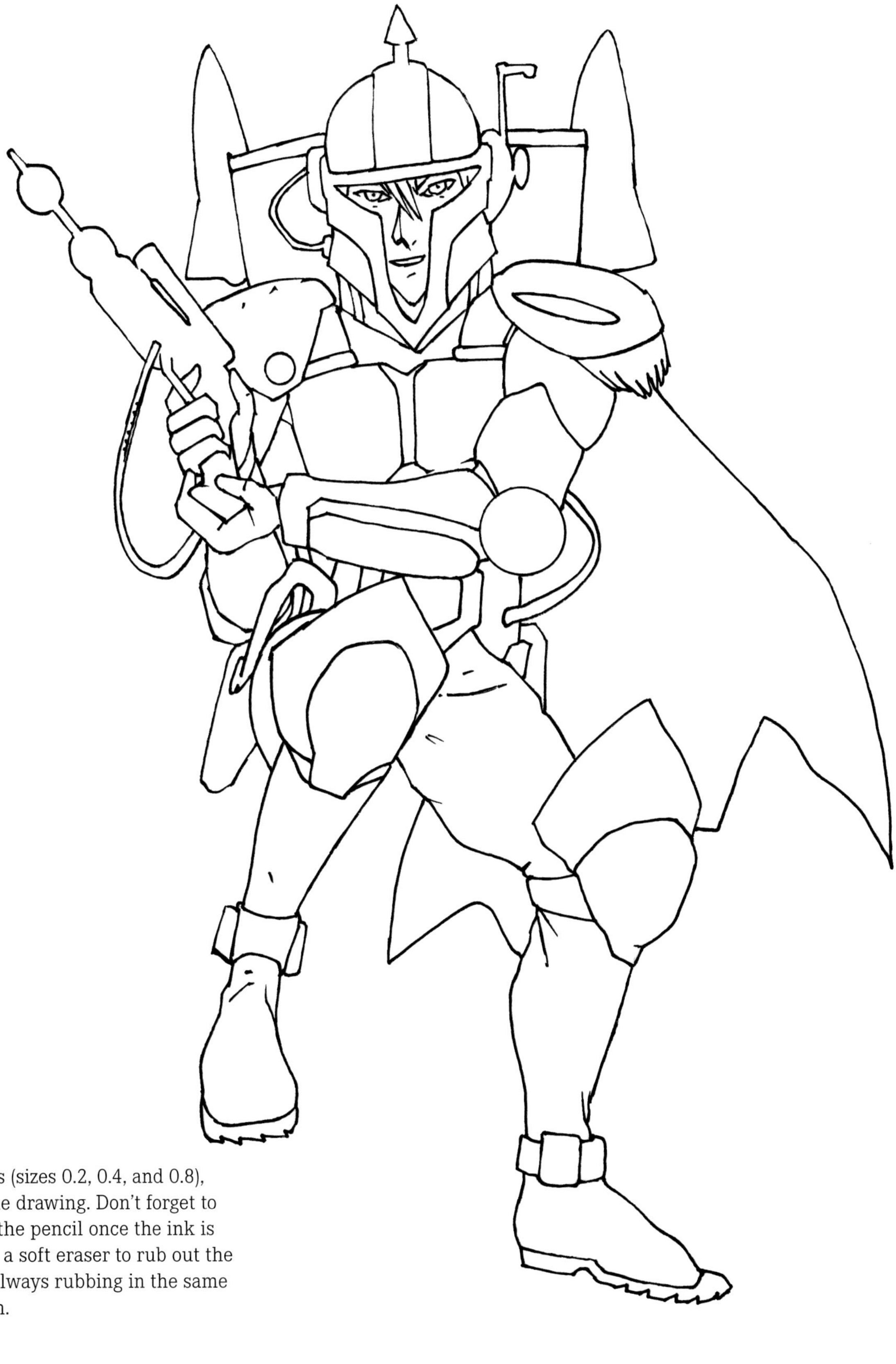

4

Use pens (sizes 0.2, 0.4, and 0.8), to ink the drawing. Don't forget to remove the pencil once the ink is dry. Use a soft eraser to rub out the pencil, always rubbing in the same direction.

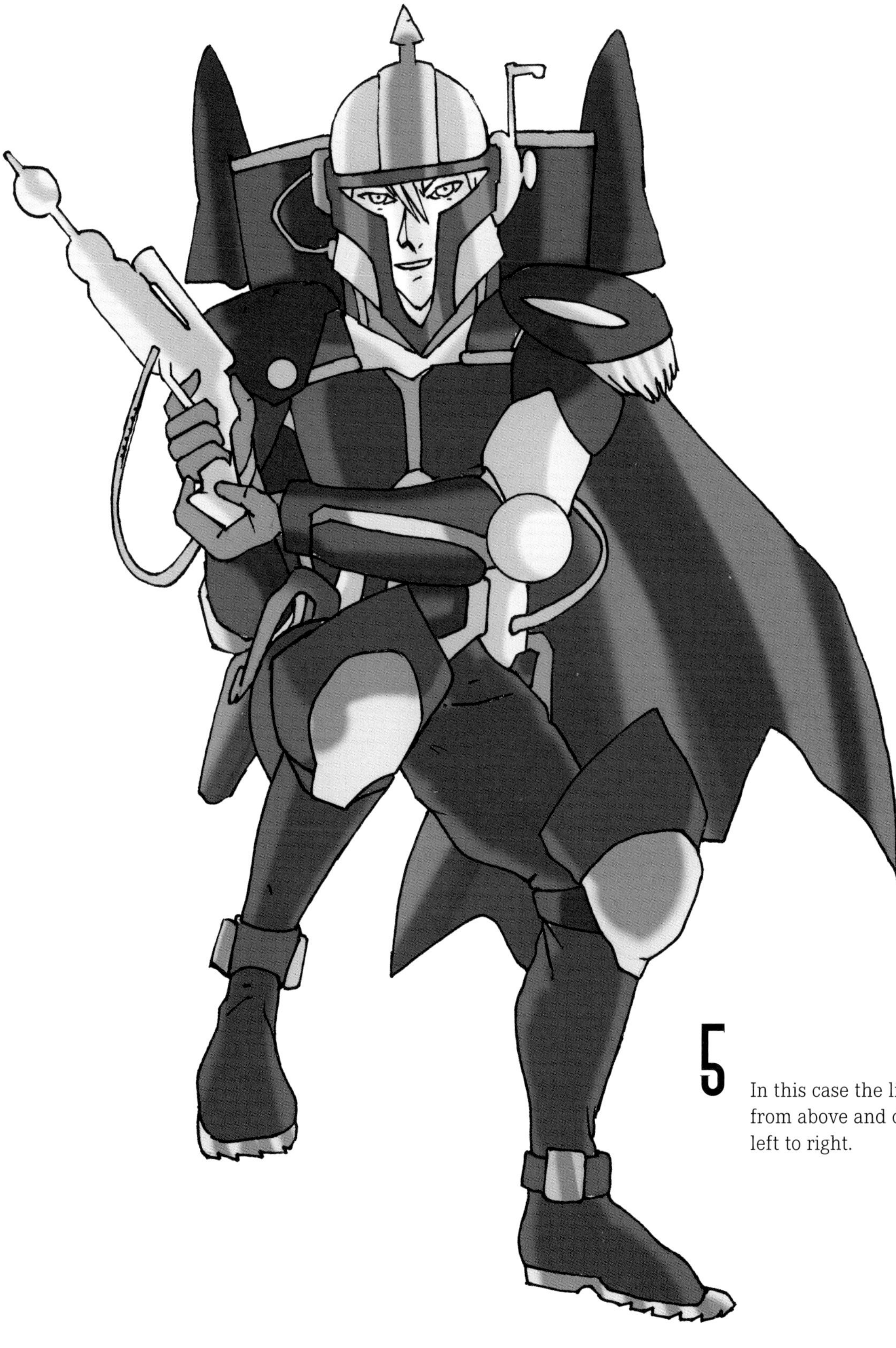

5

In this case the light is shining from above and diagonally from left to right.

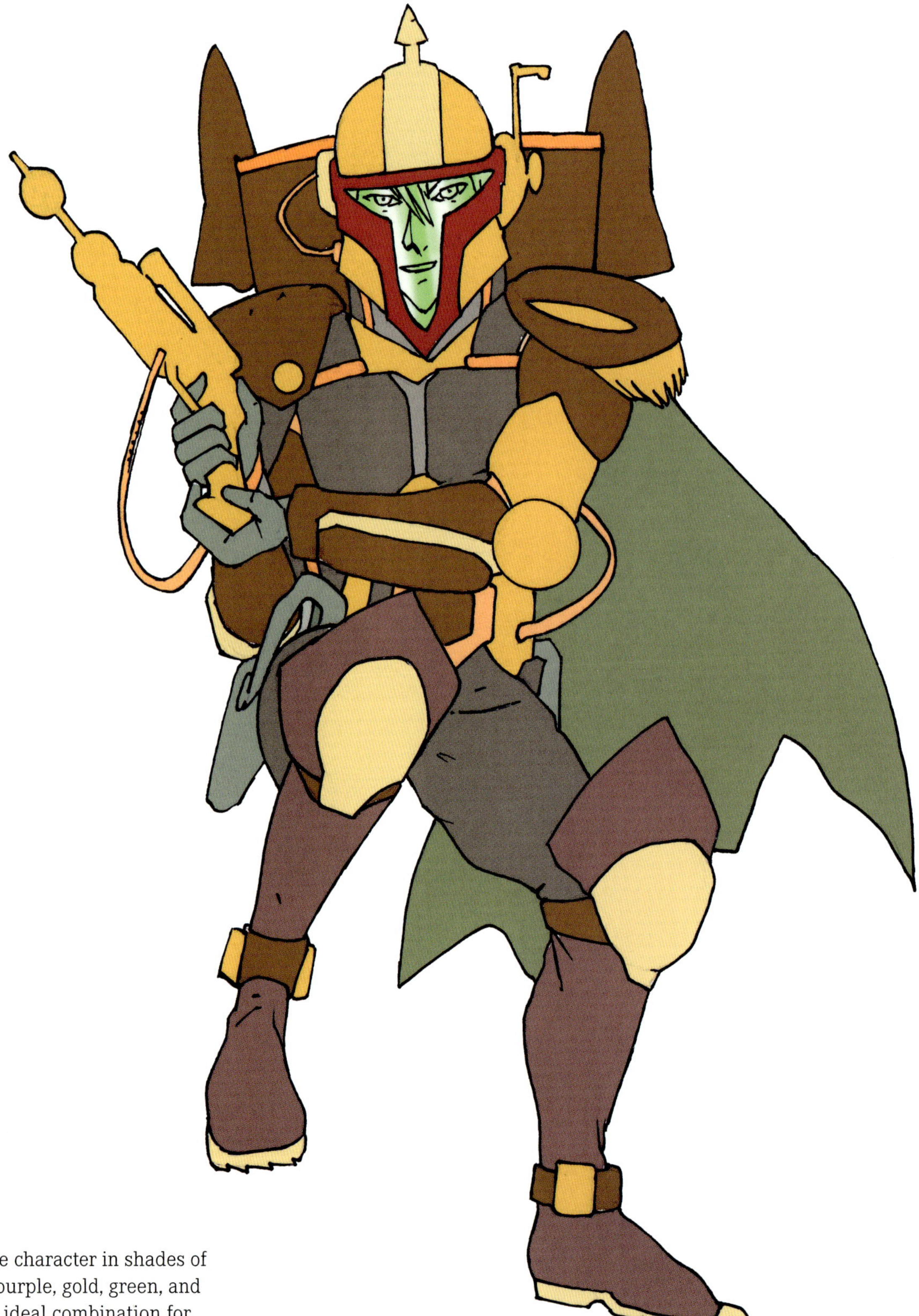

6

Color the character in shades of brown, purple, gold, green, and gray: an ideal combination for this flying ace.

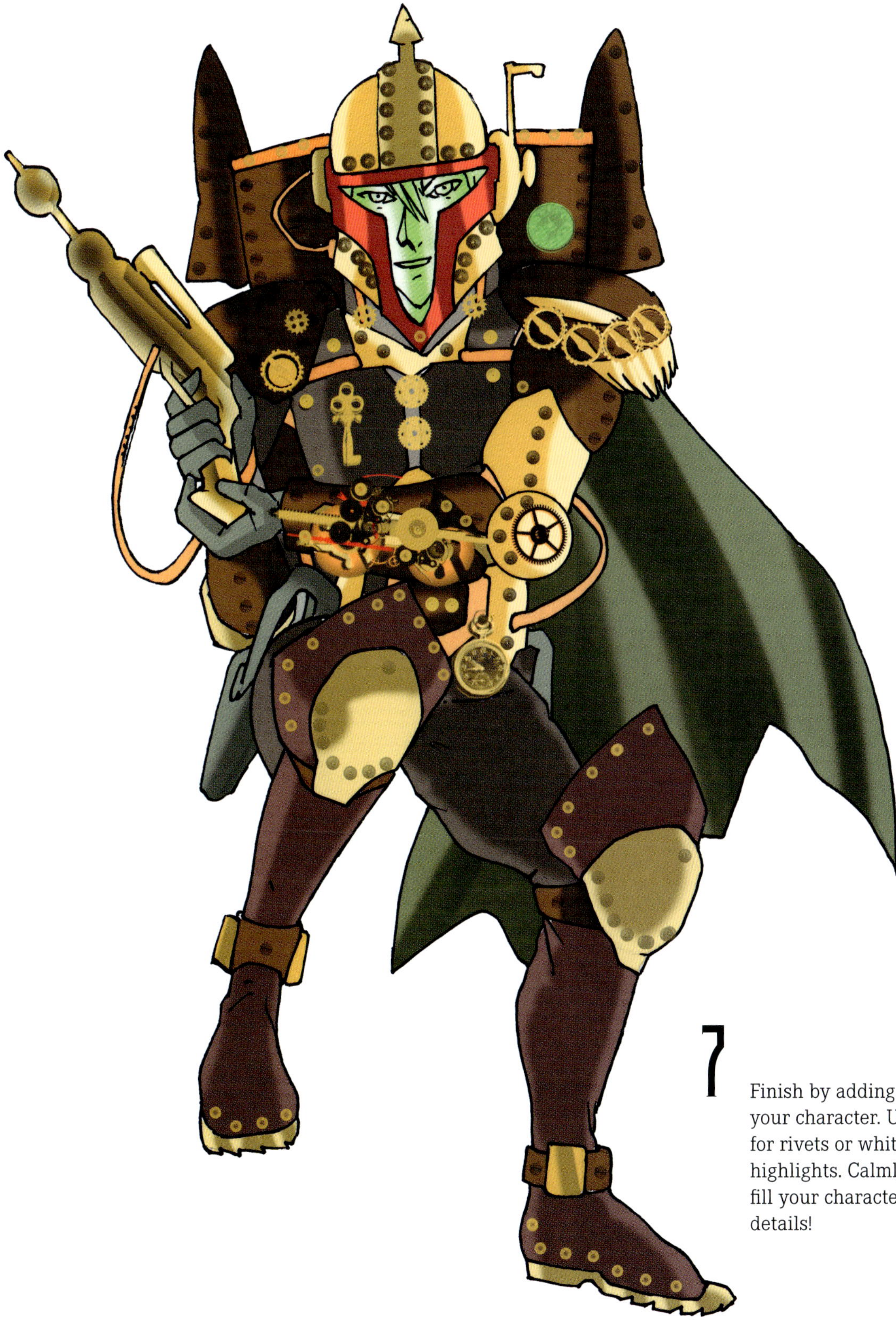

7

Finish by adding fine details to your character. Use gold markers for rivets or white pencil for highlights. Calmly and patiently fill your character in with amazing details!

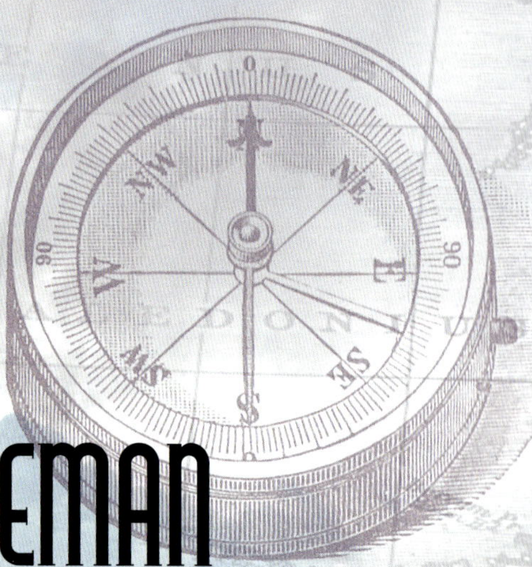

VICTORIAN GENTLEMAN

Sir Cooler Winds is a powerful knight, highly regarded in the royal court. He relishes adventure and major challenges – he is a great investigator and always helps out those in need. He is a great ally: if you come across him along the way, you are in luck!

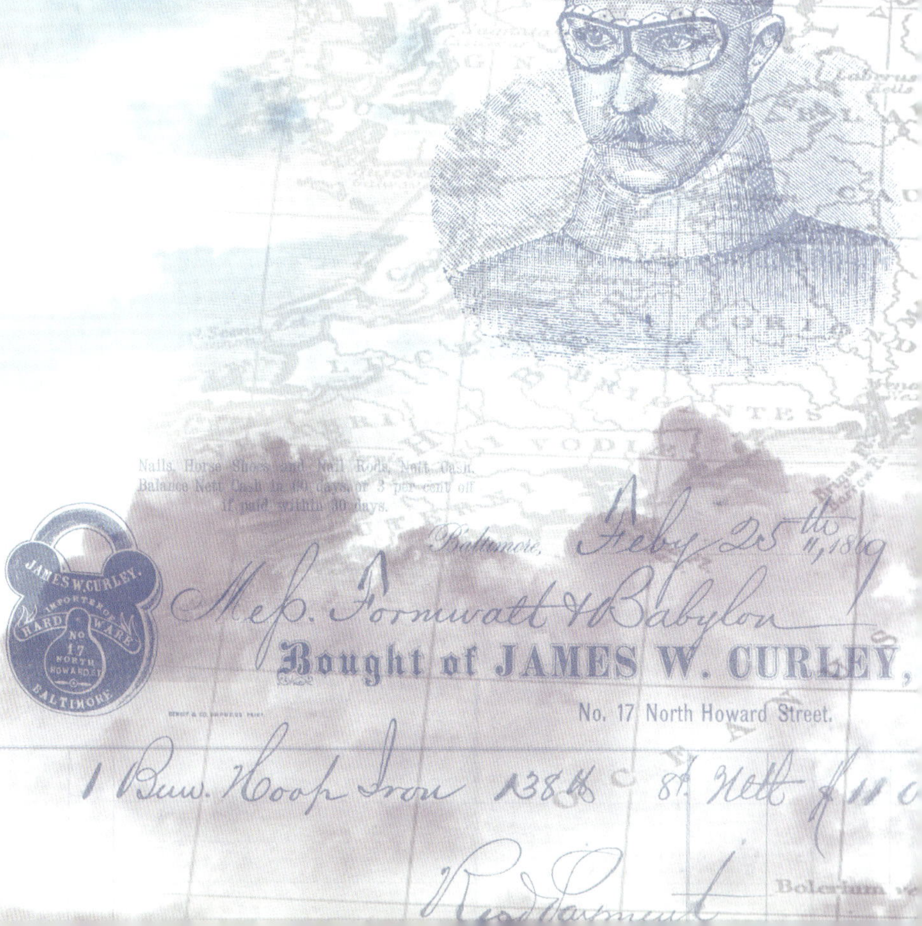

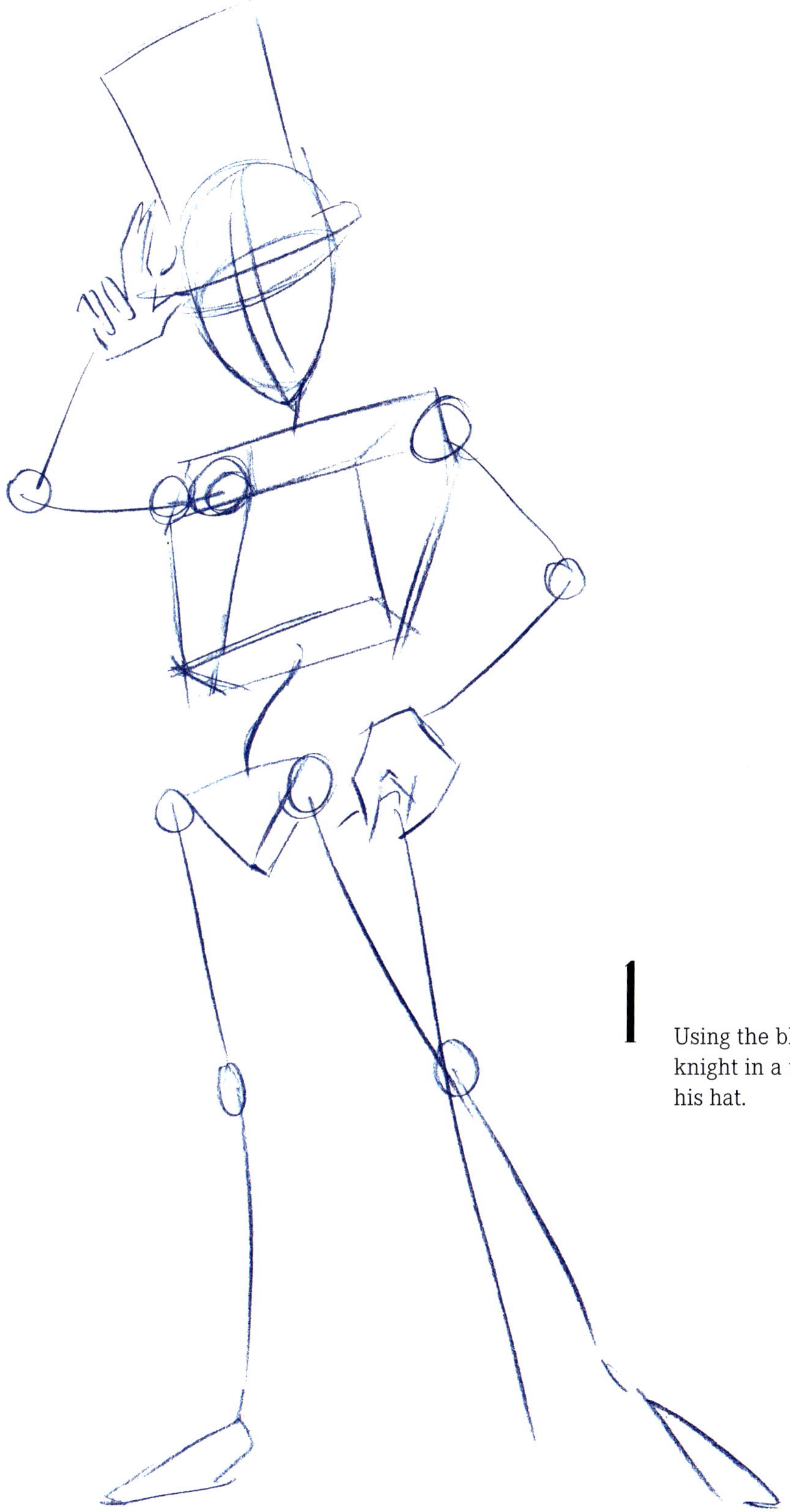

1

Using the blue pencil, draw a knight in a typical pose, waving his hat.

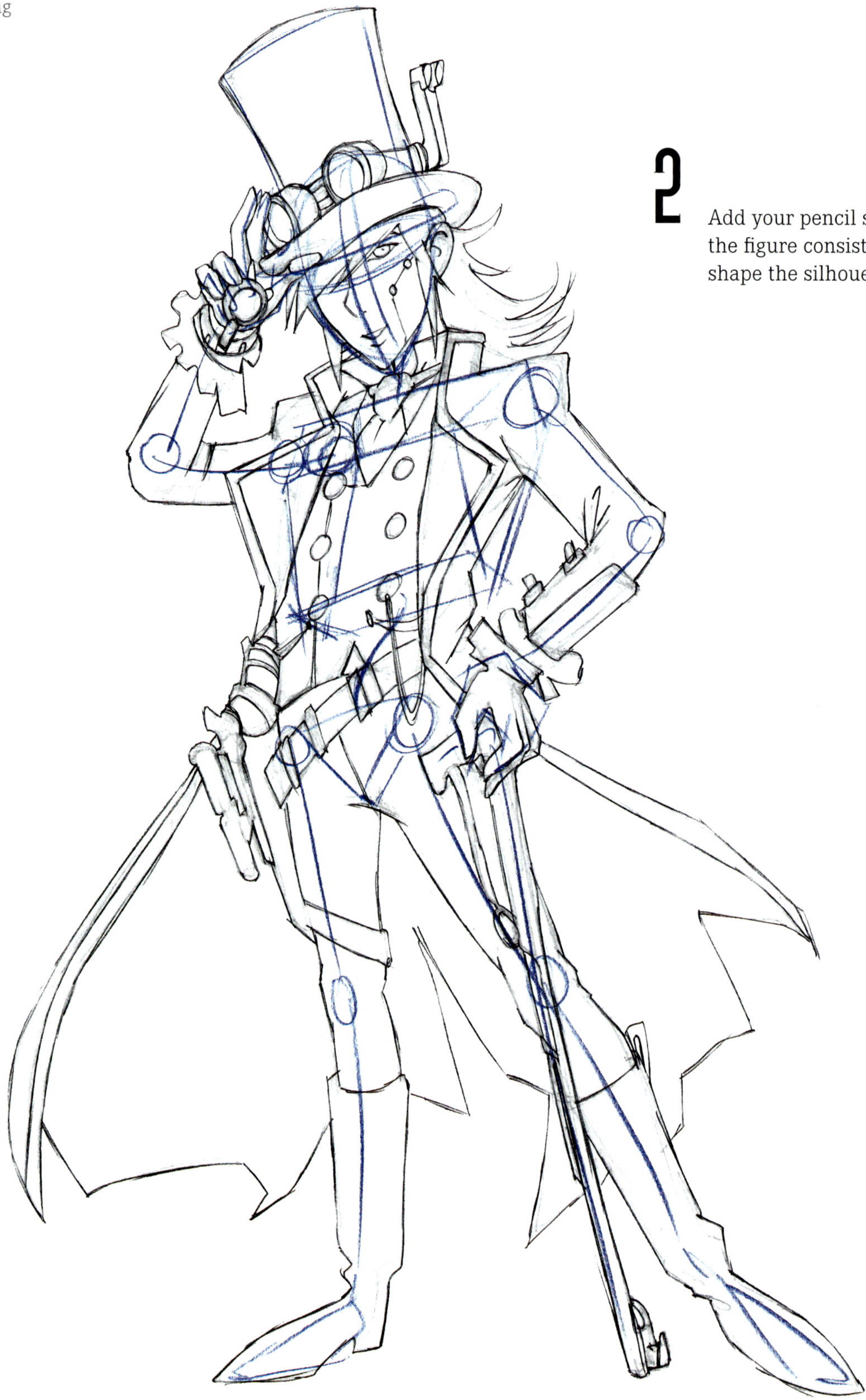

2

Add your pencil strokes to give the figure consistency and to shape the silhouette.

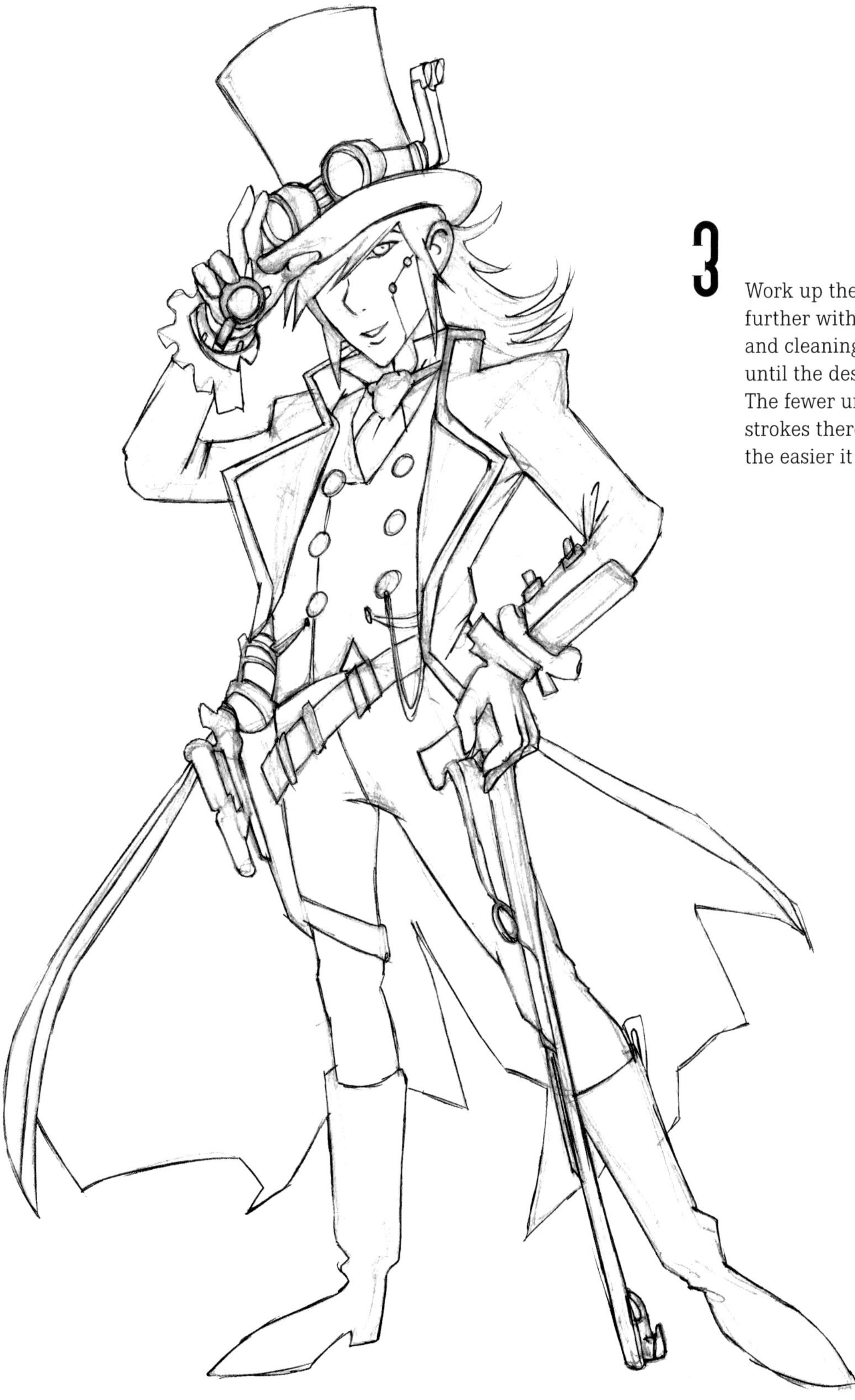

3

Work up the figure and details further with a pencil, removing and cleaning up leftover strokes until the design is ready for inking. The fewer unnecessary pencil strokes there are on the figure, the easier it will be to color.

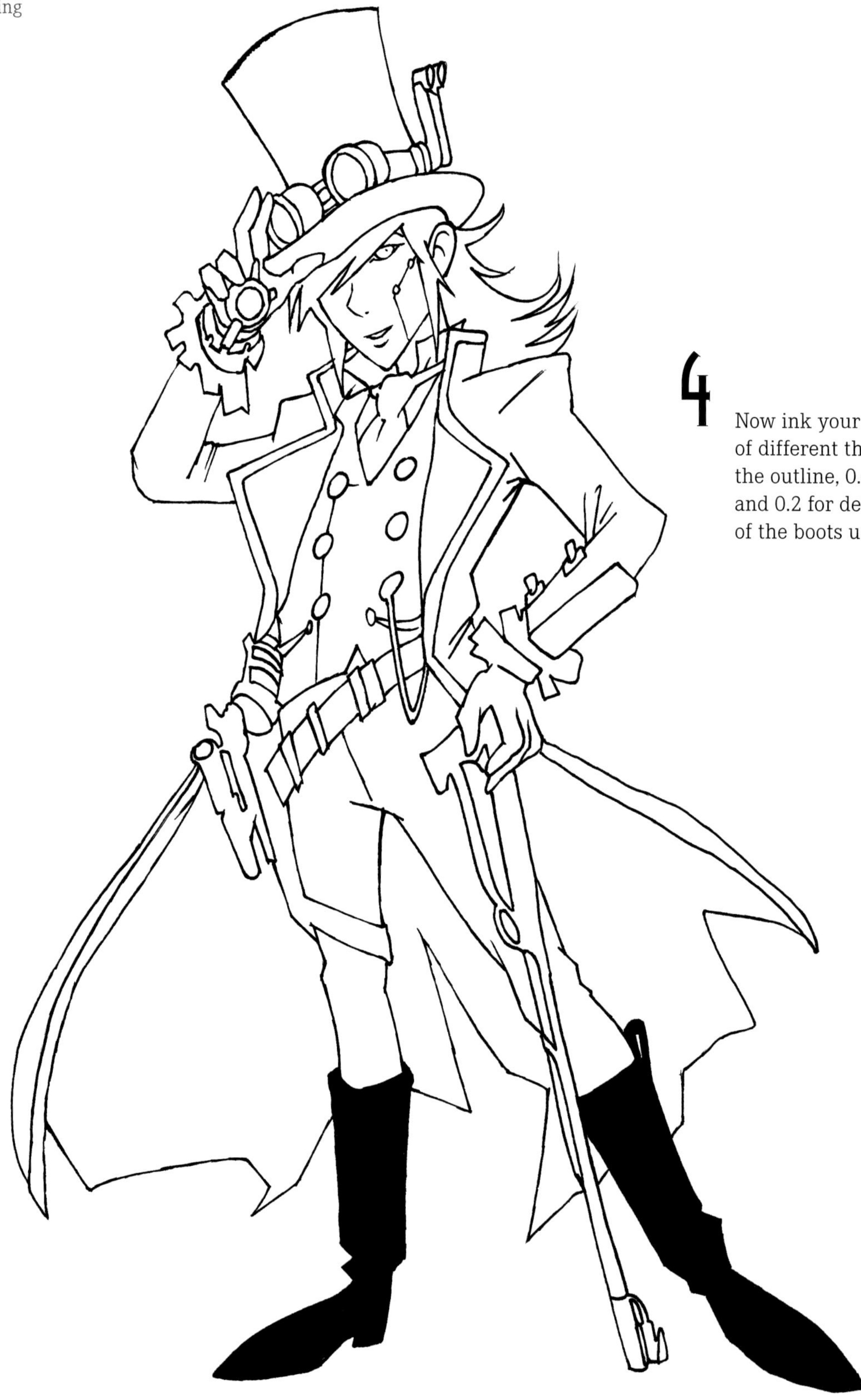

4

Now ink your knight using pens of different thicknesses: 0.8 for the outline, 0.4 for general color, and 0.2 for detail. Add the black of the boots using the 0.8-mm pen.

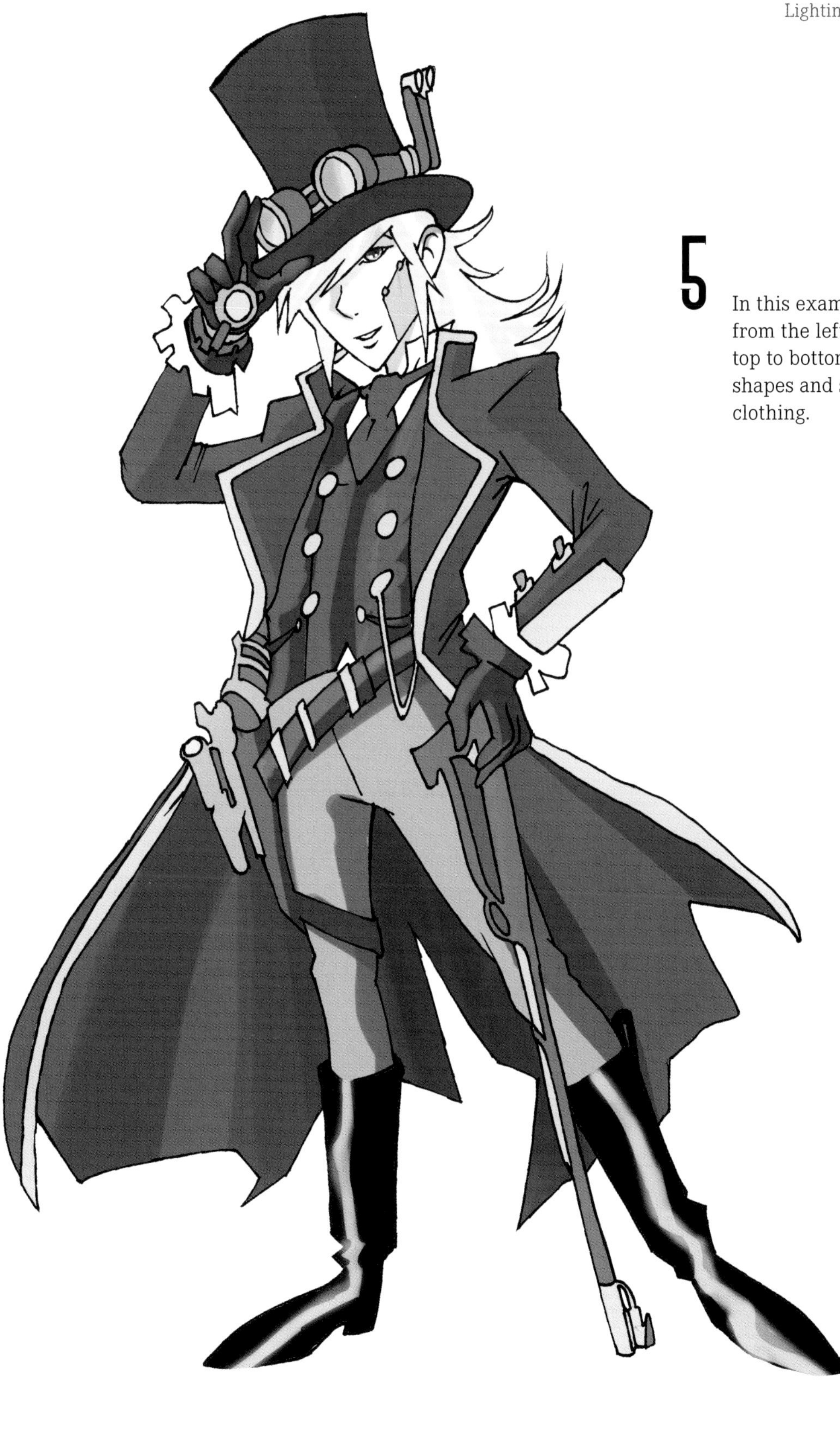

5

In this example the light is shining from the left and diagonally from top to bottom, creating interesting shapes and shadows in his clothing.

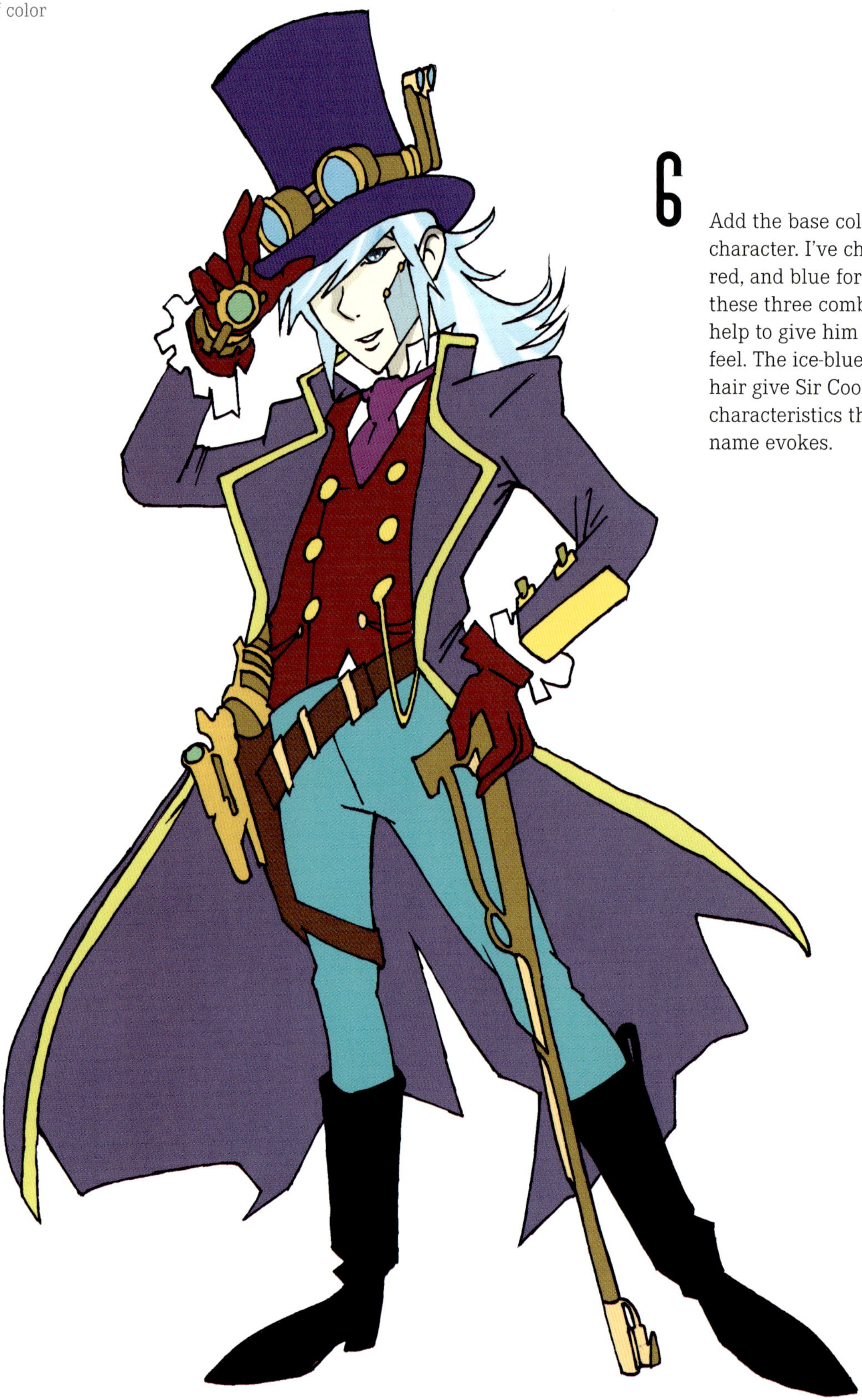

6

Add the base colors to your character. I've chosen purple, red, and blue for the clothing: these three combine well and help to give him an adventurous feel. The ice-blue eyes and white hair give Sir Cooler Winds the characteristics that his very name evokes.

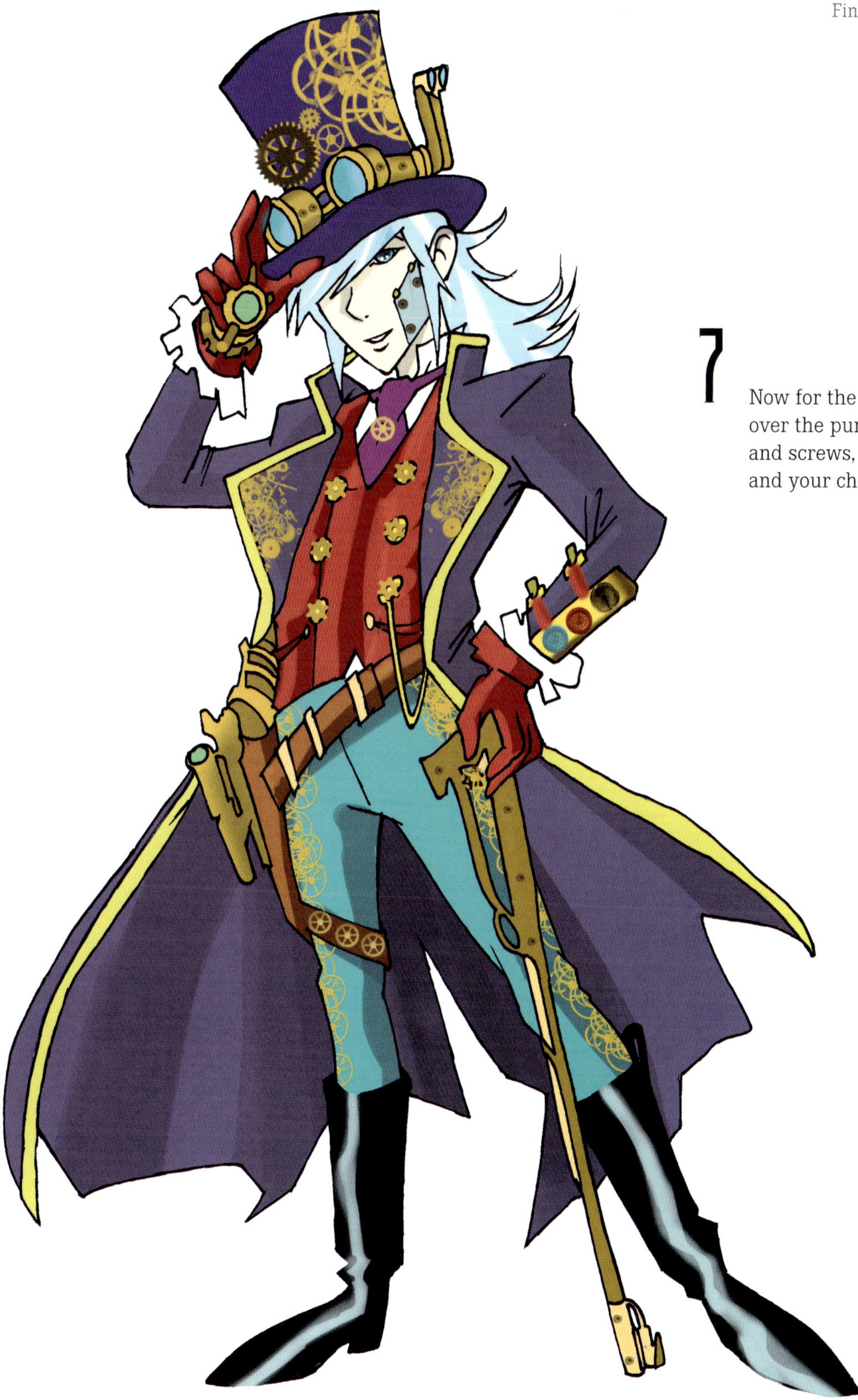

7

Now for the final details: gold over the purple, some washers and screws, watches on his wrist... and your character is done!

FEMALE OUTLAW

Laya West, adventurer, shooter, and robber of banks and stagecoaches, steals from the rich and shares all the booty with the poor. She and her band keep the banks of the west of the kingdom in check: you never know what her next target will be.

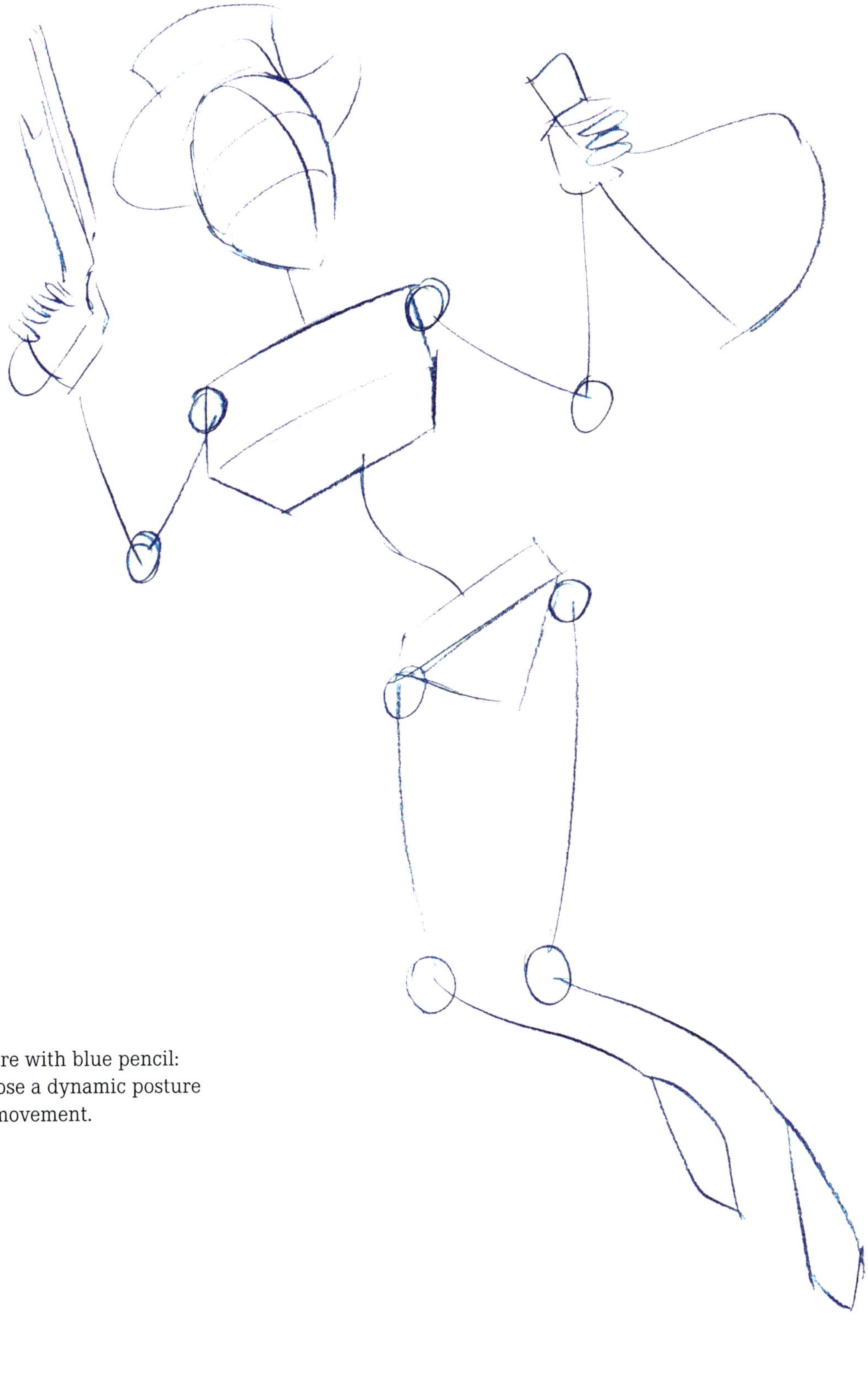

1

Draw the figure with blue pencil: this time choose a dynamic posture that implies movement.

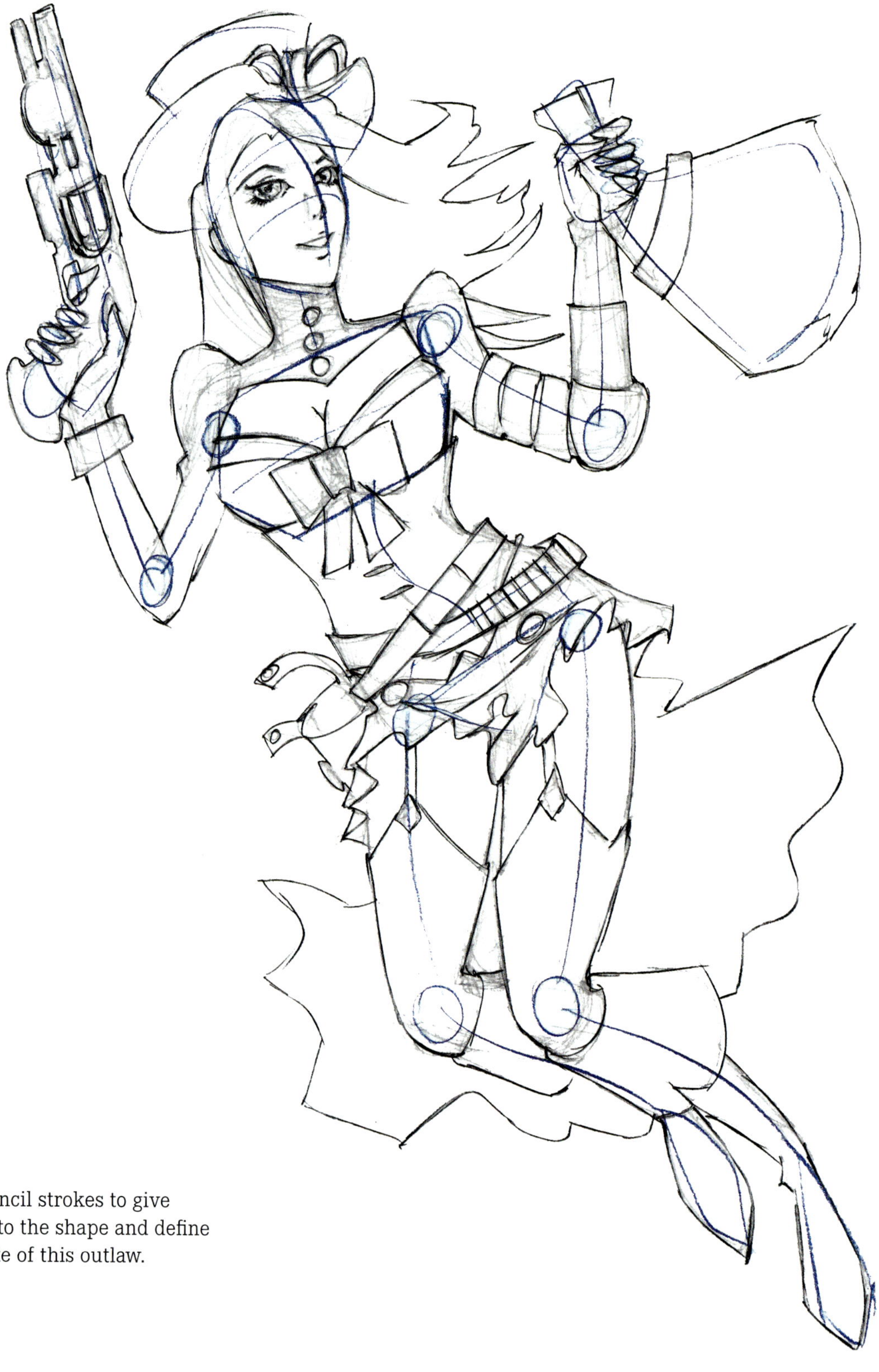

2

Add your pencil strokes to give consistency to the shape and define the silhouette of this outlaw.

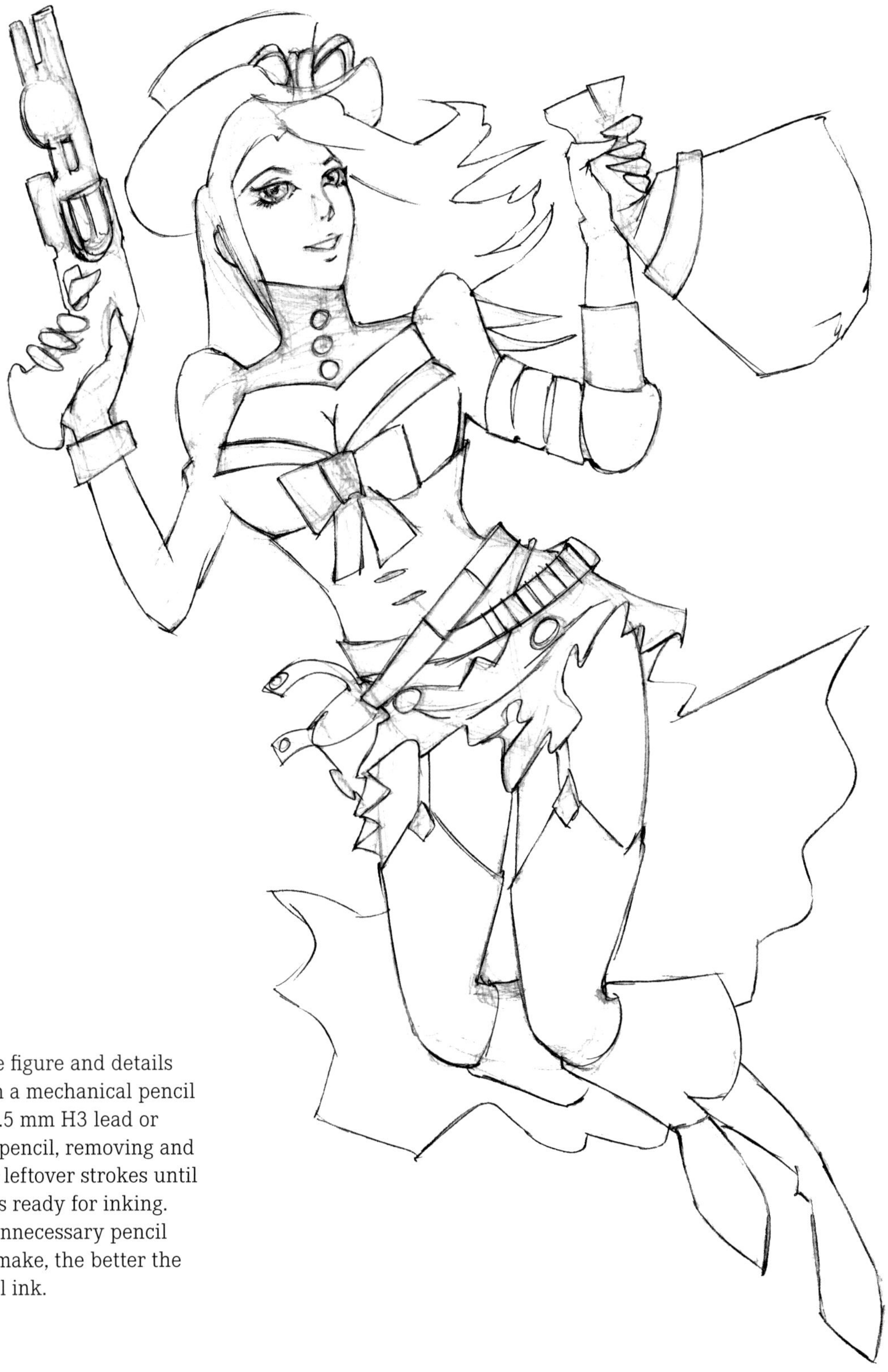

3

Work up the figure and details further with a mechanical pencil that has a 0.5 mm H3 lead or with an H3 pencil, removing and cleaning up leftover strokes until the design is ready for inking. The fewer unnecessary pencil marks you make, the better the drawing will ink.

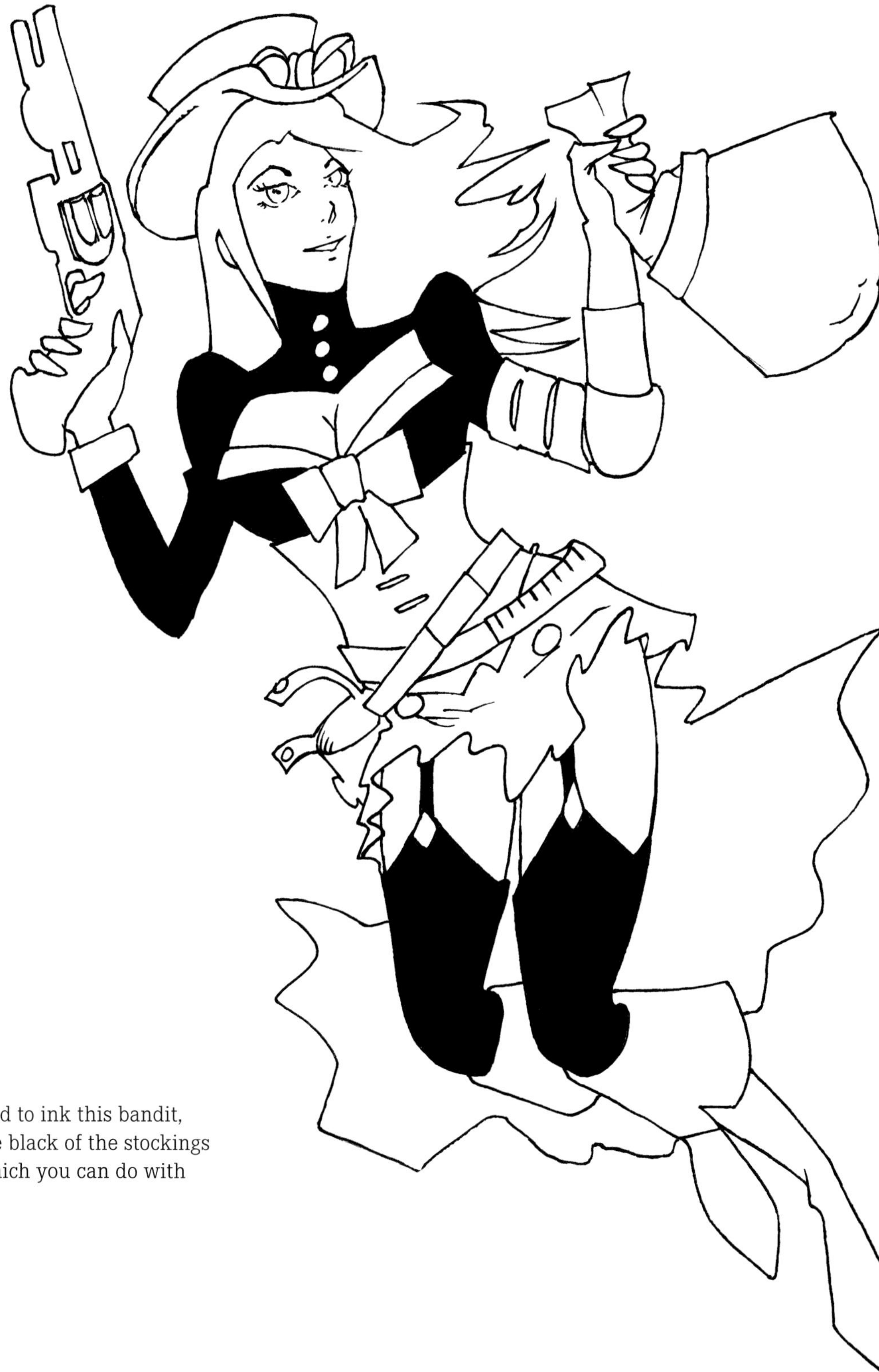

4

Now you need to ink this bandit, including the black of the stockings and shirt, which you can do with the 08 pen.

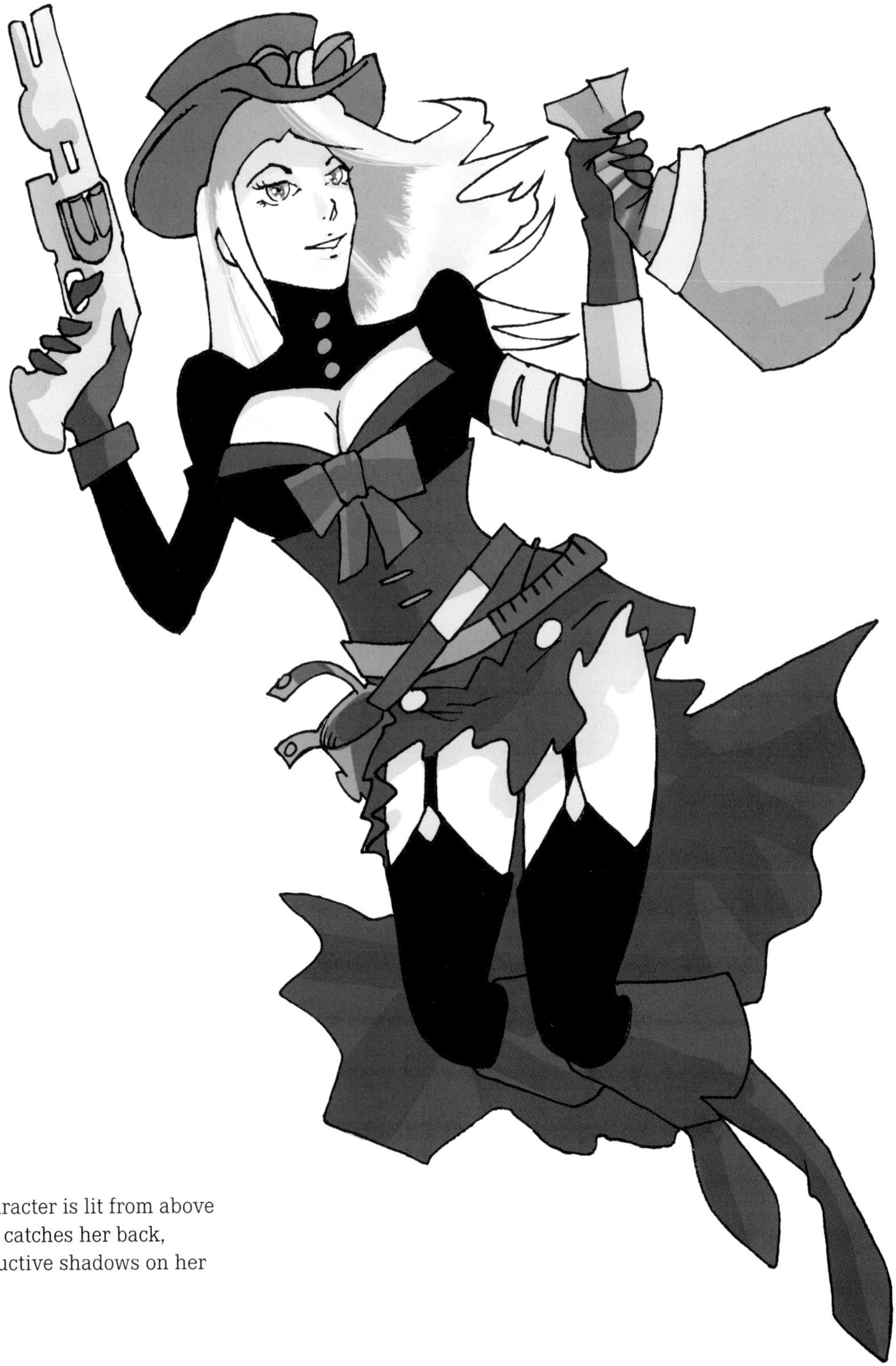

5

Here the character is lit from above but the light catches her back, creating seductive shadows on her dress.

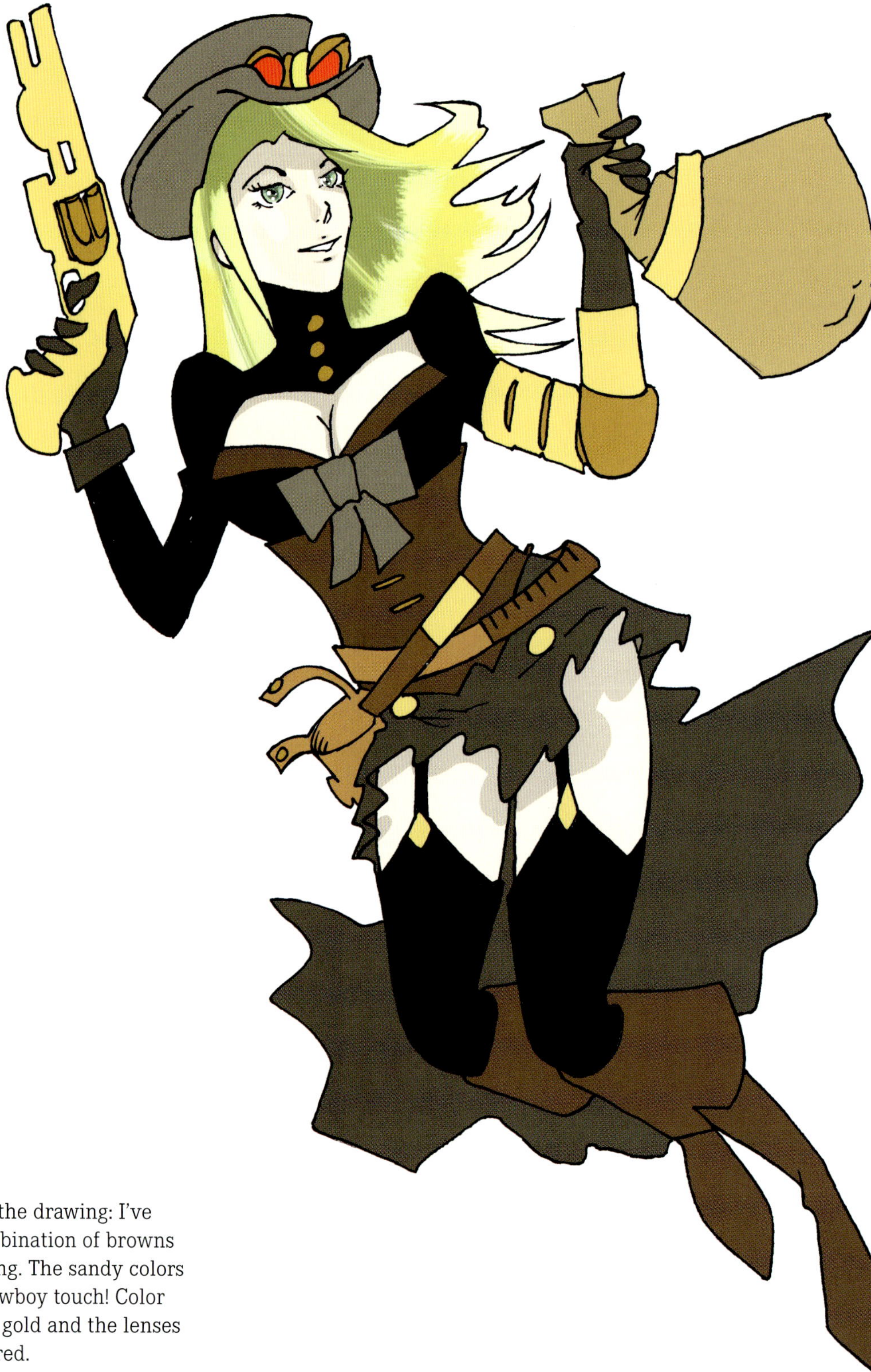

6

Now to color the drawing: I've chosen a combination of browns for the clothing. The sandy colors give a real cowboy touch! Color the details in gold and the lenses of the hat in red.

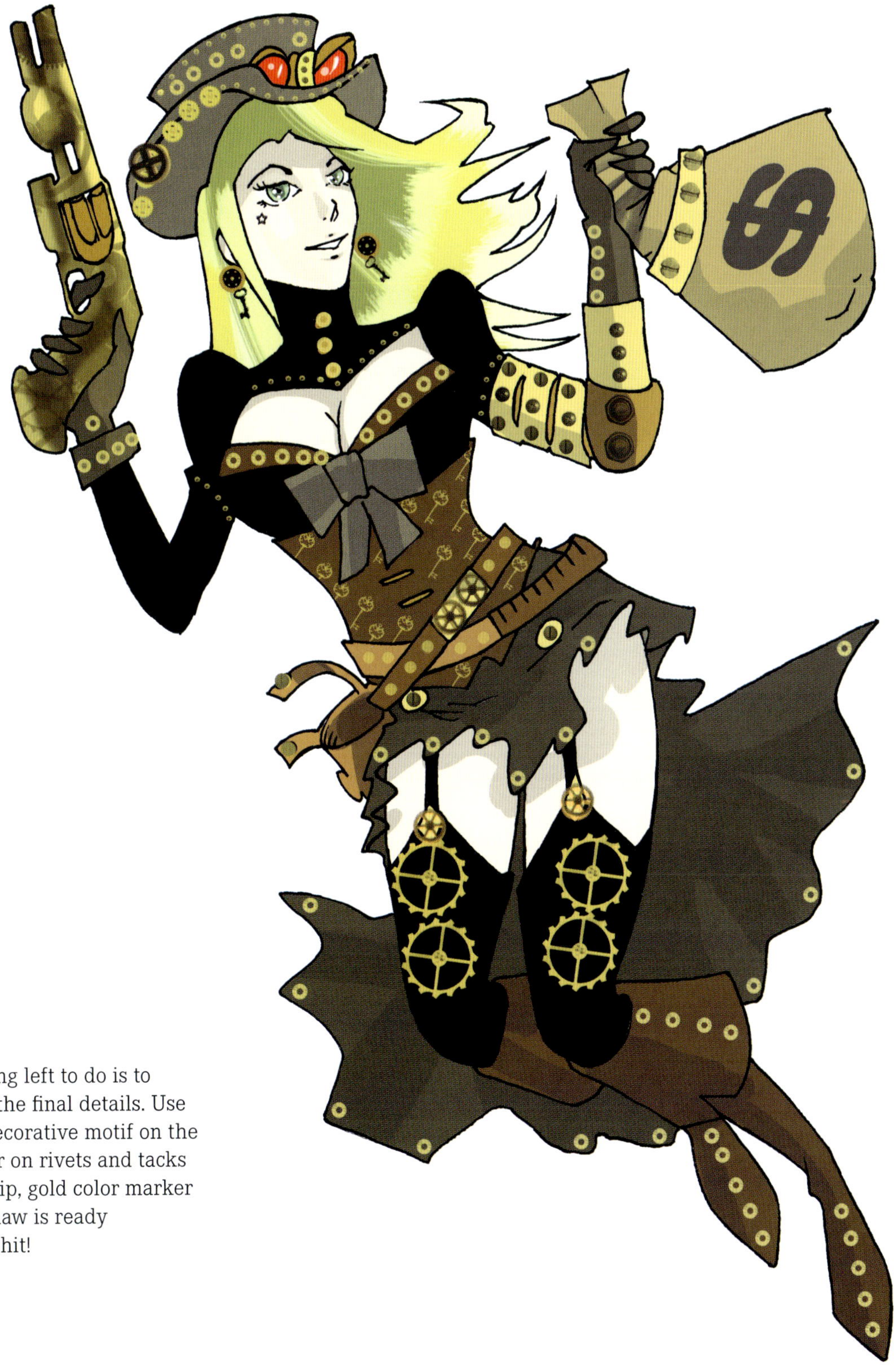

7

The only thing left to do is to incorporate the final details. Use a key as a decorative motif on the bodice. Color on rivets and tacks with a thin tip, gold color marker and this outlaw is ready for her next hit!

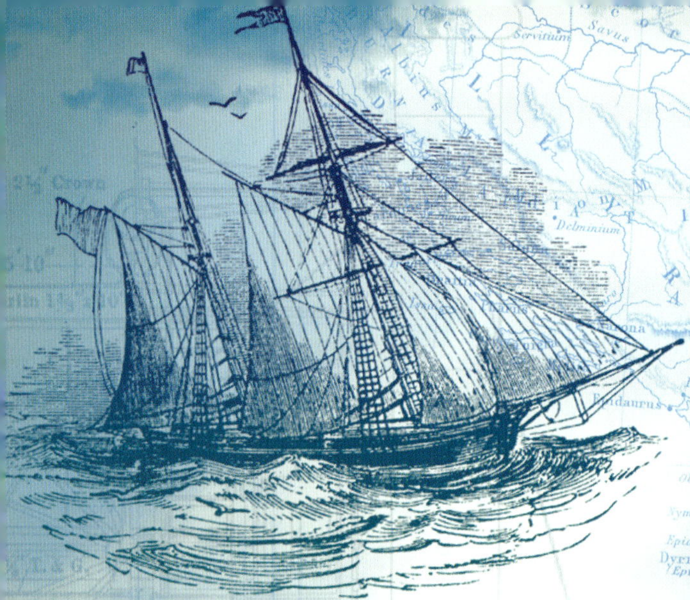

PIRATE

Carmina Burning Red is a pirate patron of the *Eternal Sea Married* and queen of contraband of the seven seas in this steampunk world. Carmina is the most feared person on the waves, where no other living being can overshadow her or her crew. There is no one braver or more courageous on any other pirate ship!

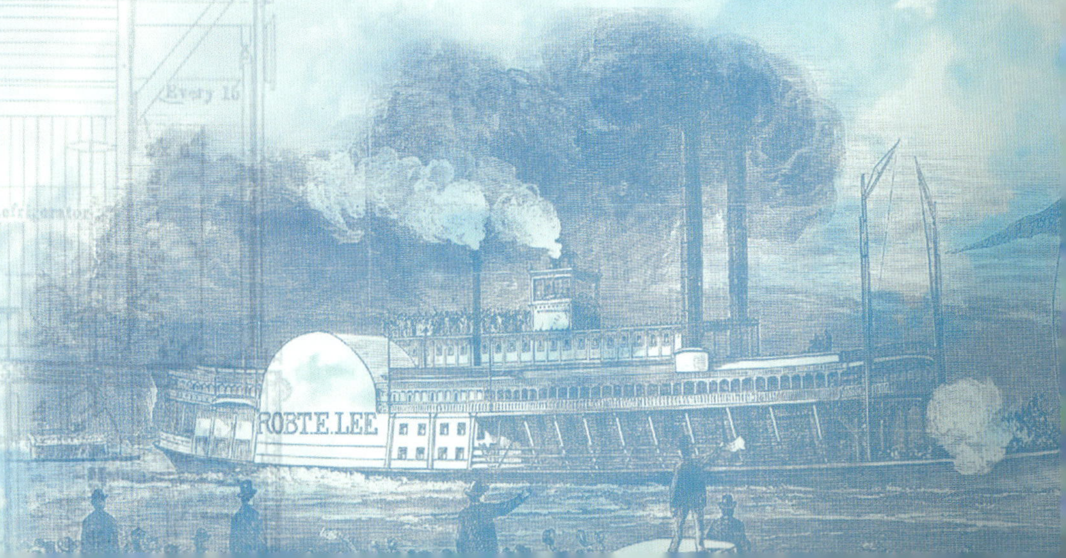

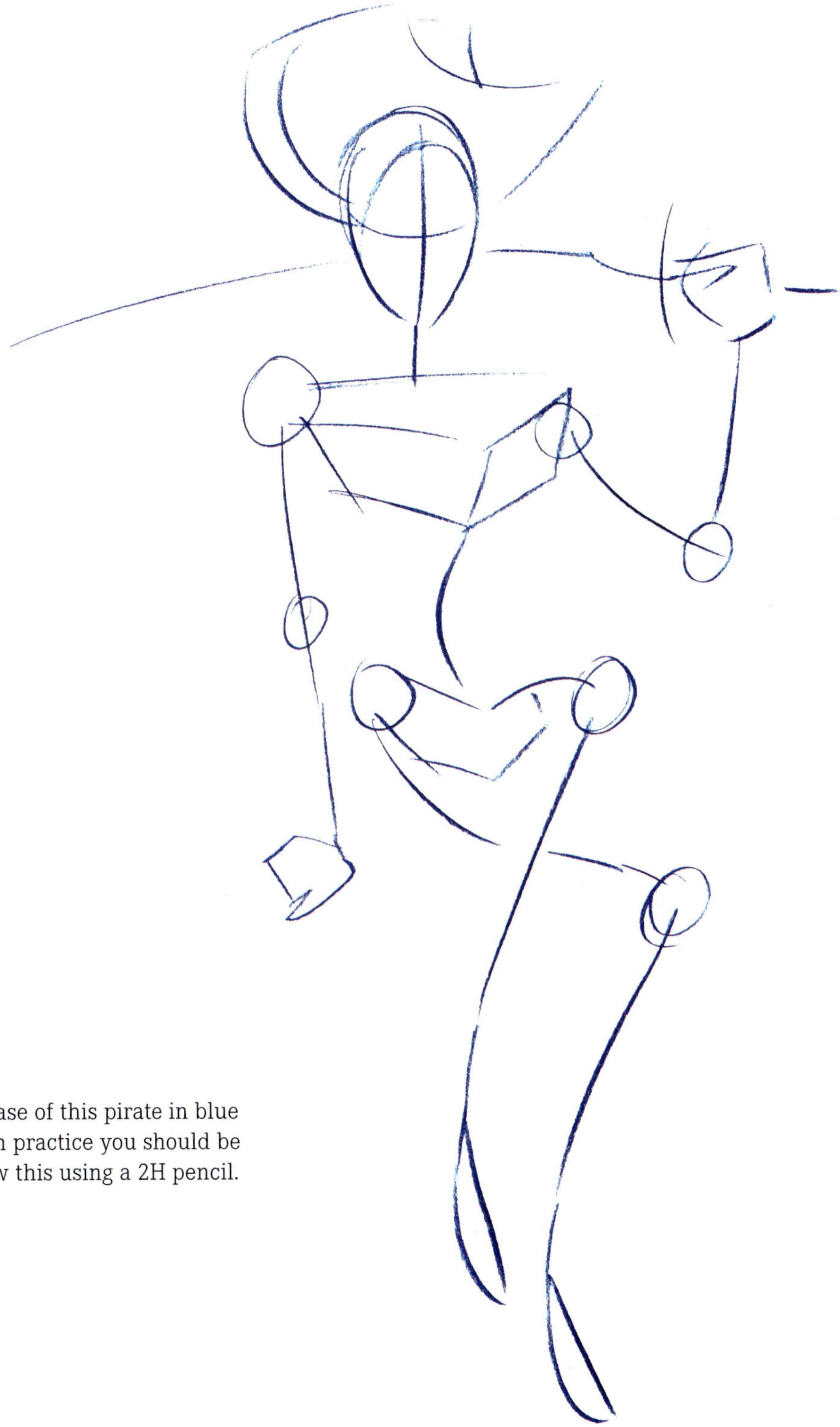

1

Draw the base of this pirate in blue pencil. With practice you should be able to draw this using a 2H pencil. Be patient!

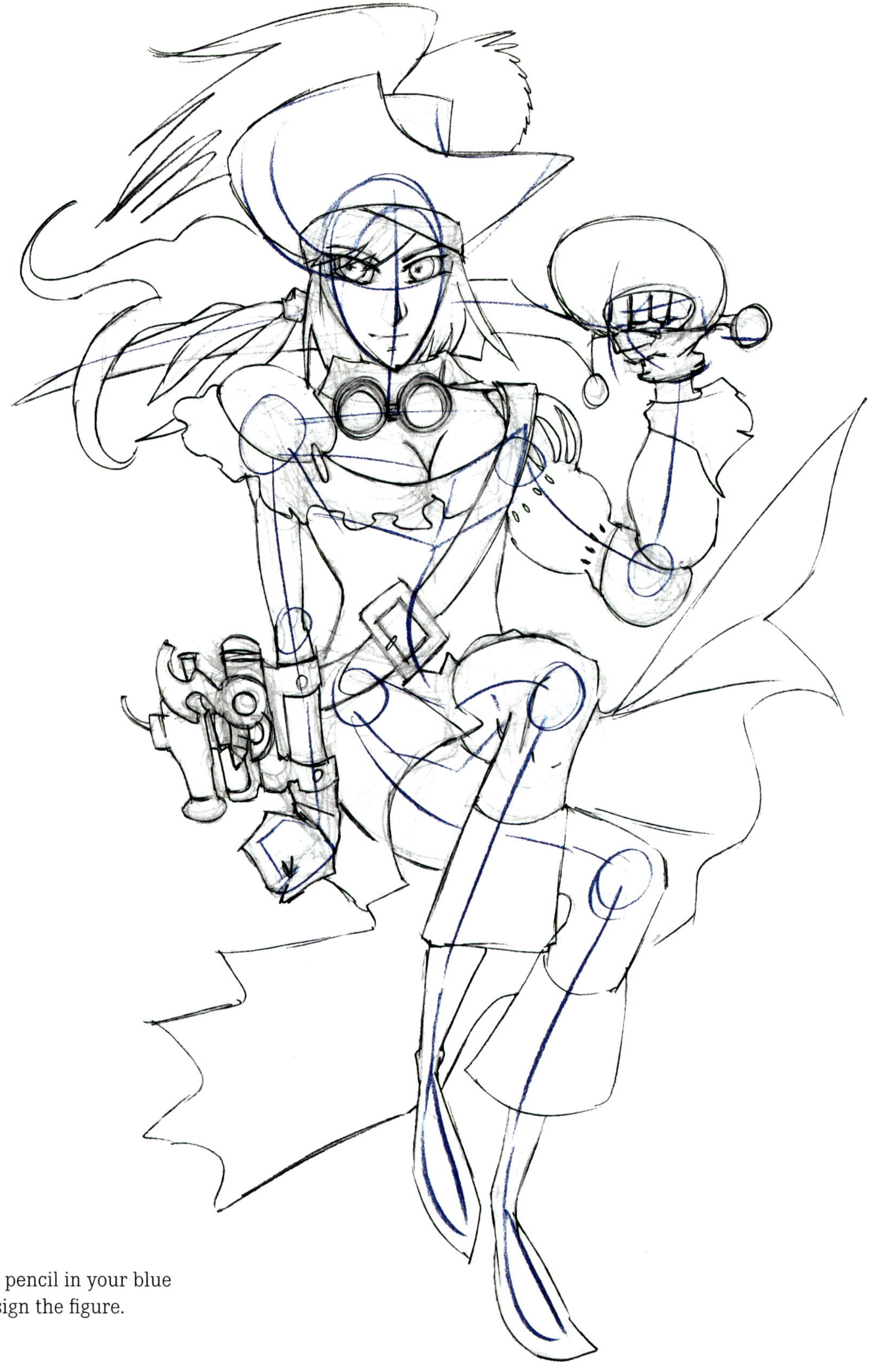

2

Use the 2H pencil in your blue draft to design the figure.

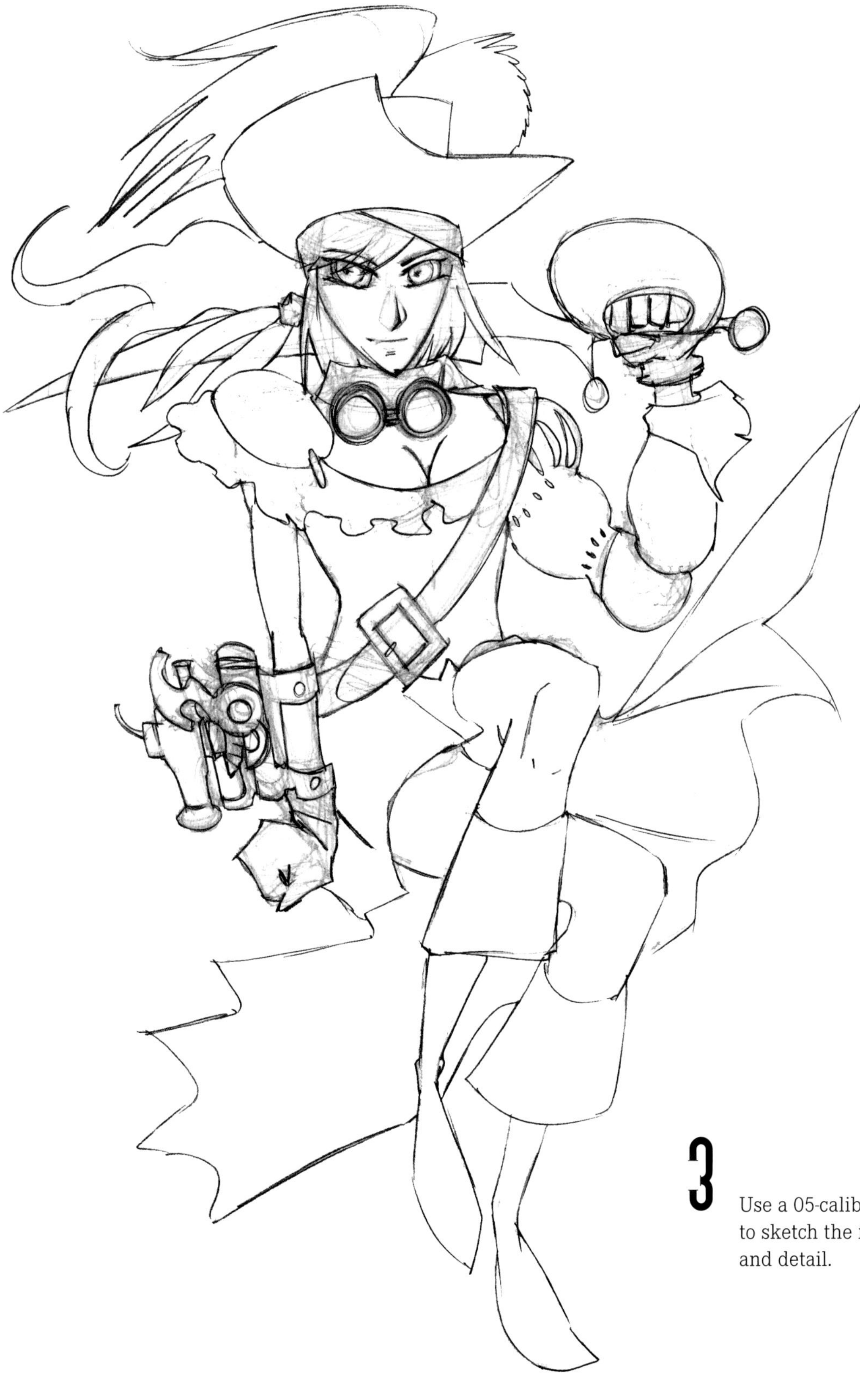

3

Use a 05-calibre mechanical pencil to sketch the figure, adding volume and detail.

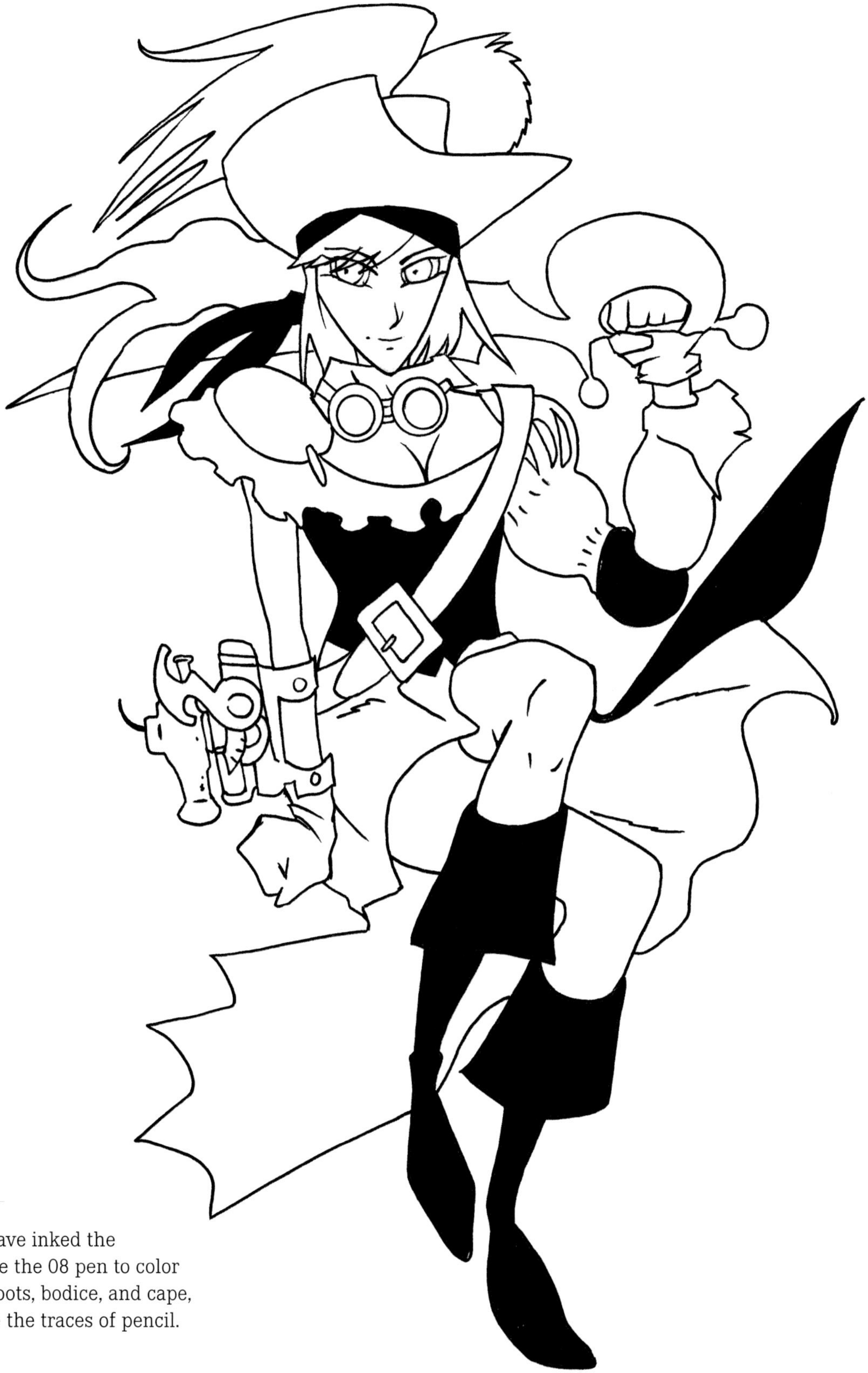

4

Once you have inked the drawing, use the 08 pen to color the scarf, boots, bodice, and cape, and remove the traces of pencil.

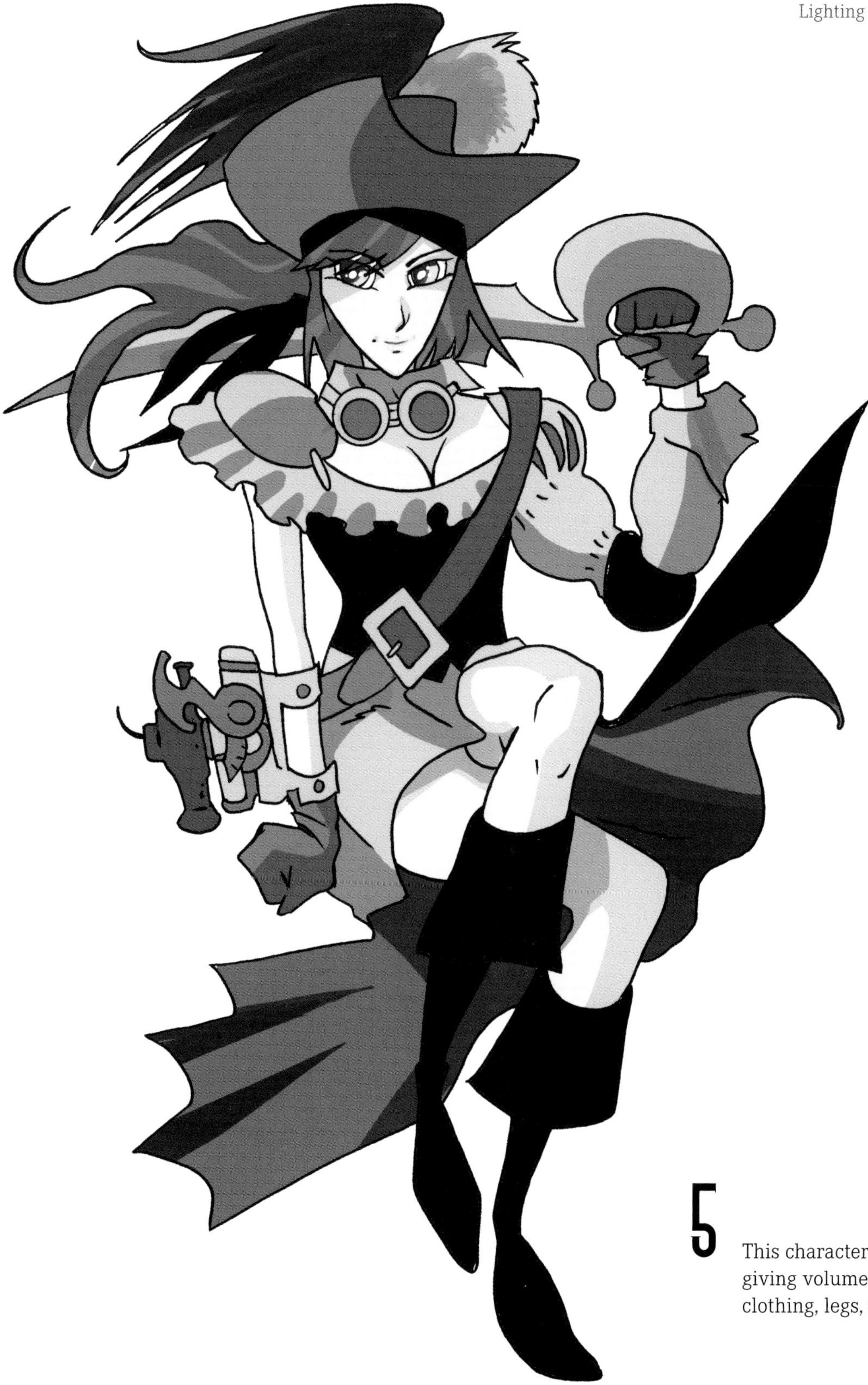

5

This character is lit from the left, giving volume to her sumptuous clothing, legs, and accessories.

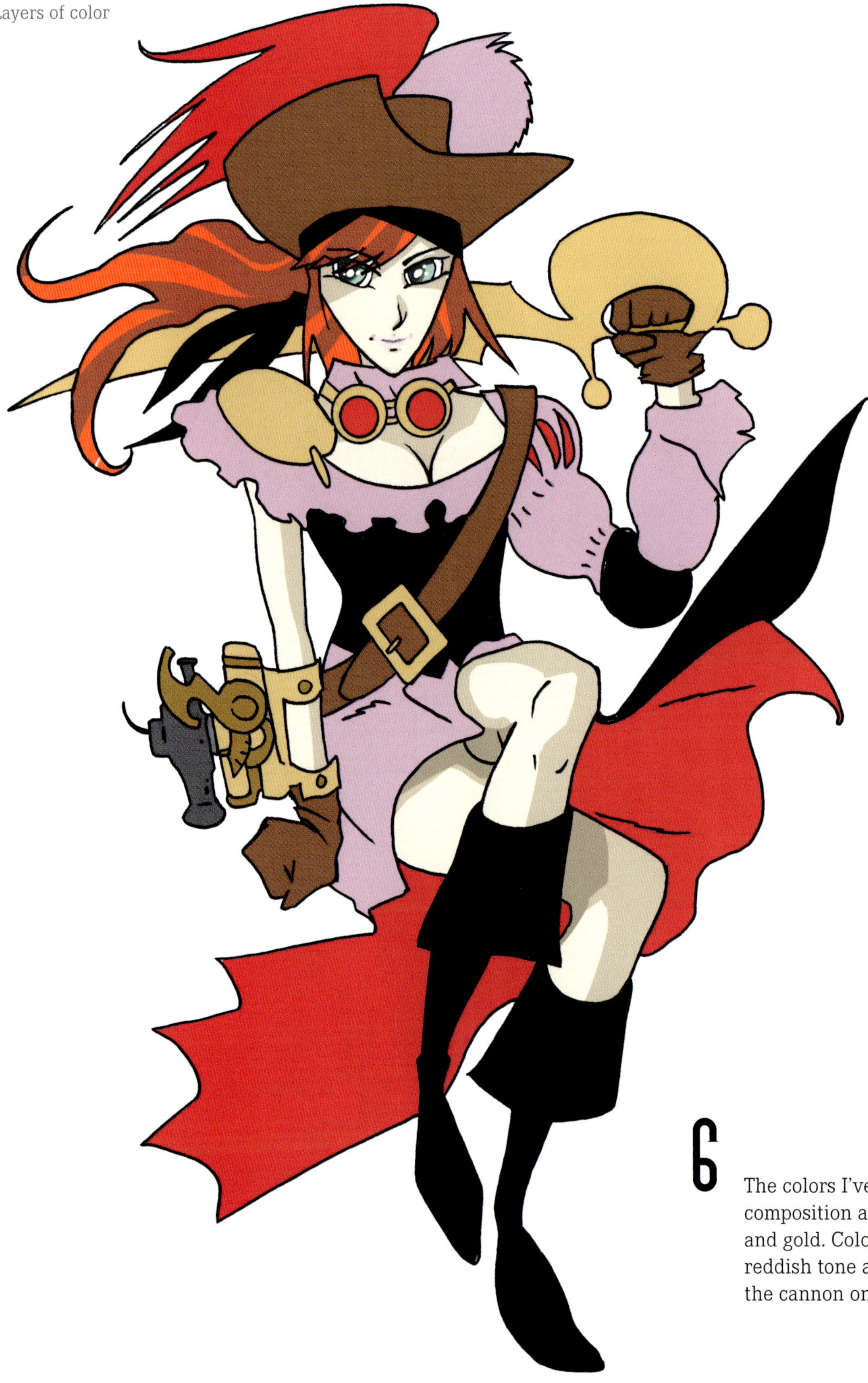

6

The colors I've chosen for this composition are pink, red, brown, and gold. Color the hair in a reddish tone and use the gray for the cannon on the wristband.

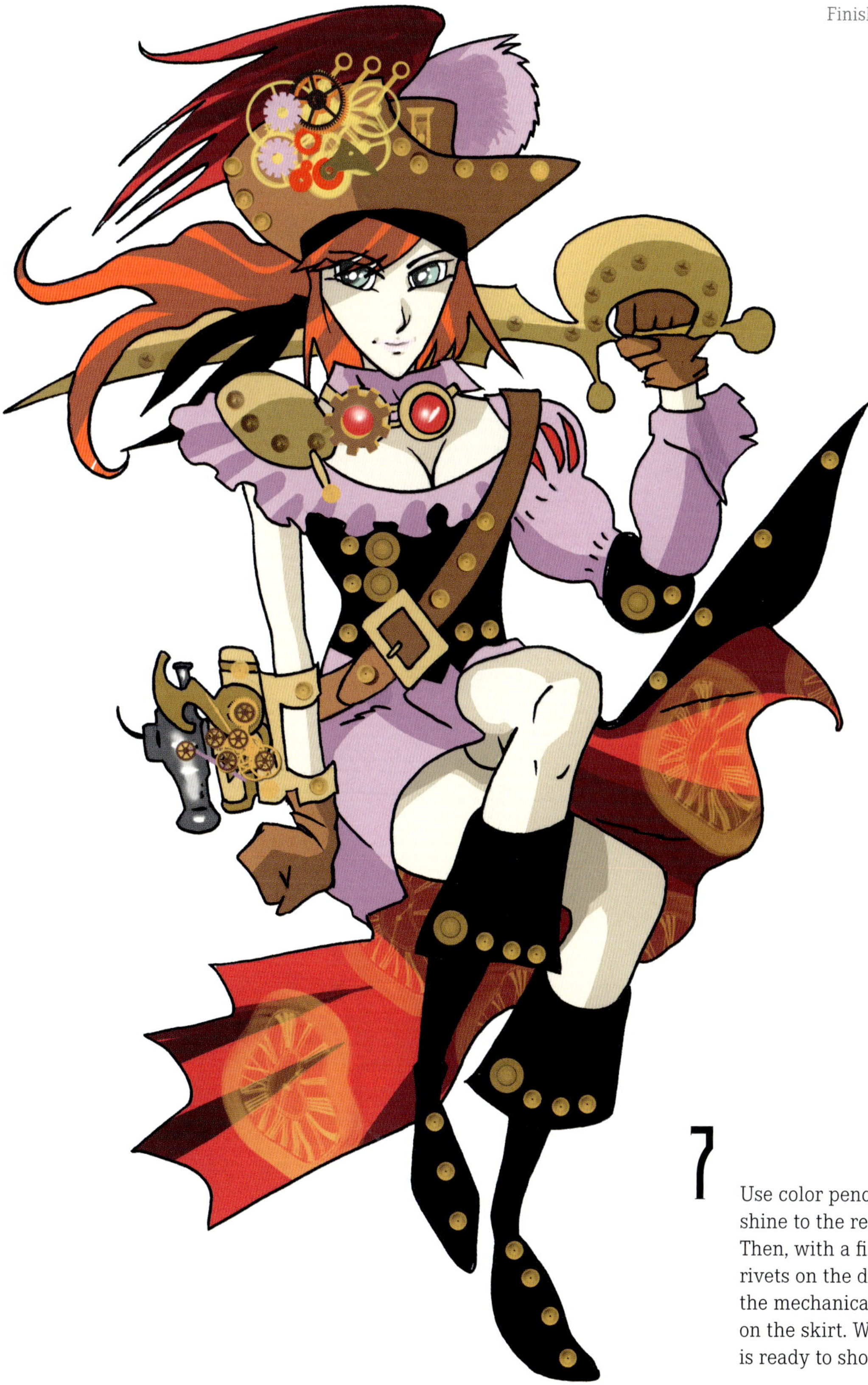

7

Use color pencils to add the final shine to the reds, pinks, and golds. Then, with a fine-tip gold pen, draw rivets on the dress, some screws on the mechanical cannon, and clocks on the skirt. With this, your pirate is ready to shout "All aboard"!

SWORDSMAN

Blackwell van Sant is an unparalleled swordsman and a relentless bounty hunter. He is also an expert in the art of escape and ambush, and a great marksman with any weapon. As long as he is paid, he accepts any assignment. So be careful with this warrior! His most unique attack, the Fire Thrust, is legendary.

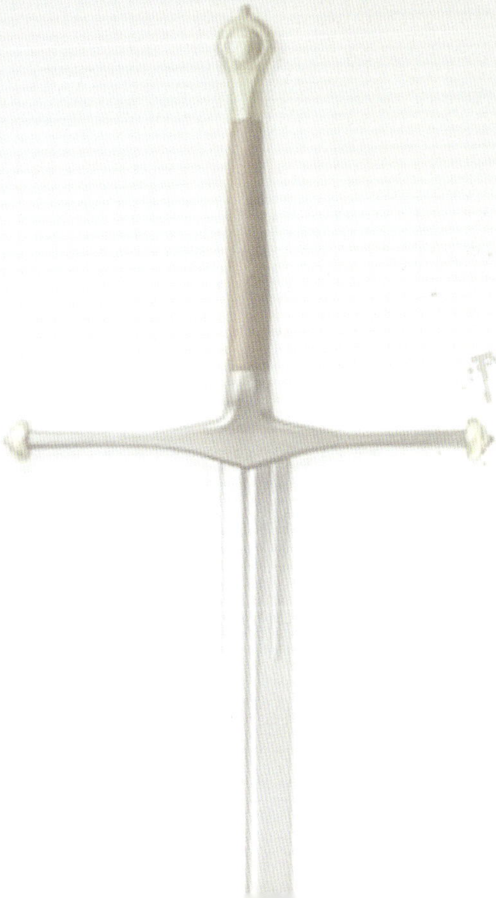

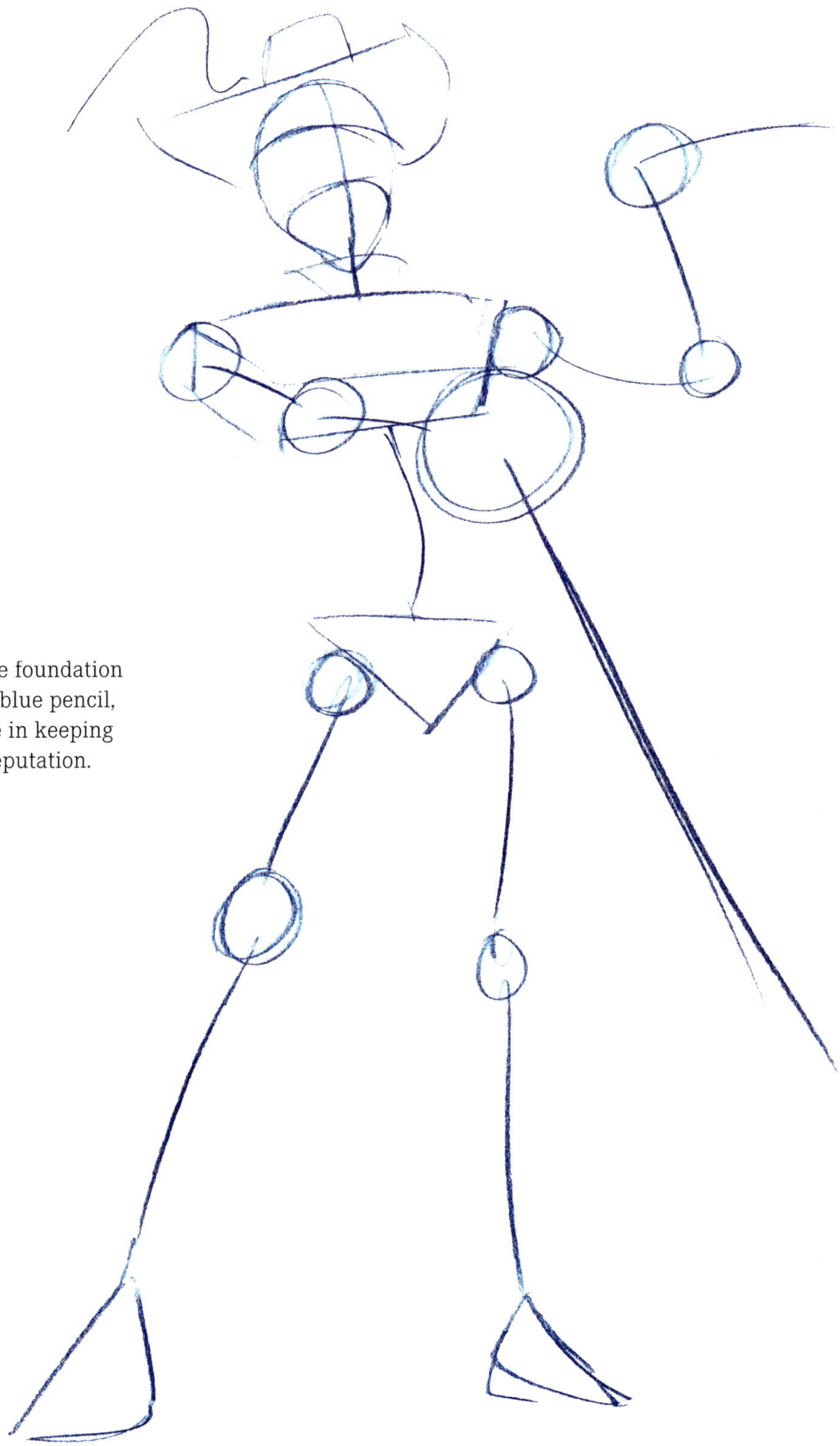

1

Begin by drawing the foundation of your character in blue pencil, giving him a posture in keeping with his infamous reputation.

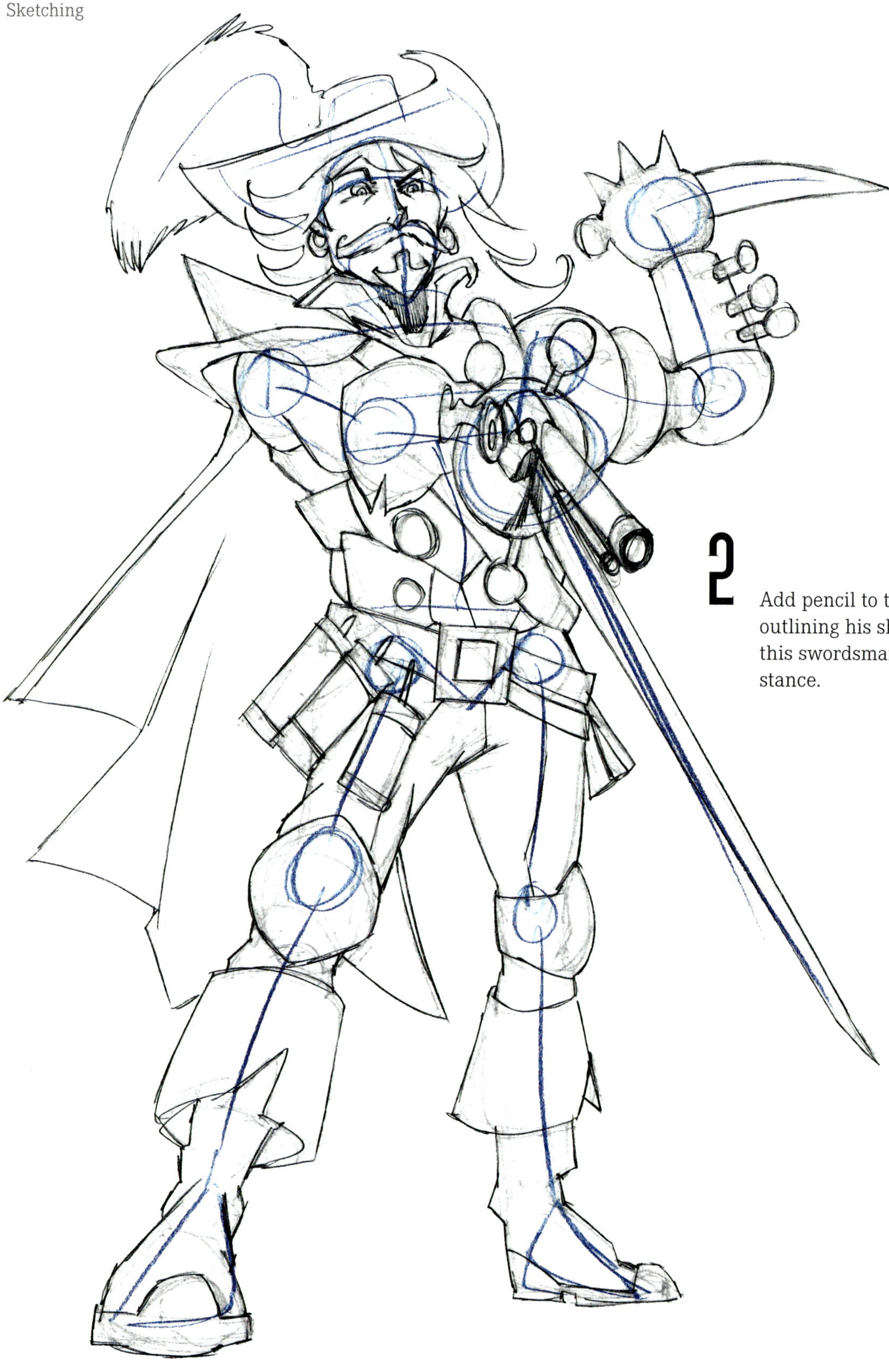

2

Add pencil to the character, outlining his shape and creating this swordsman's threatening stance.

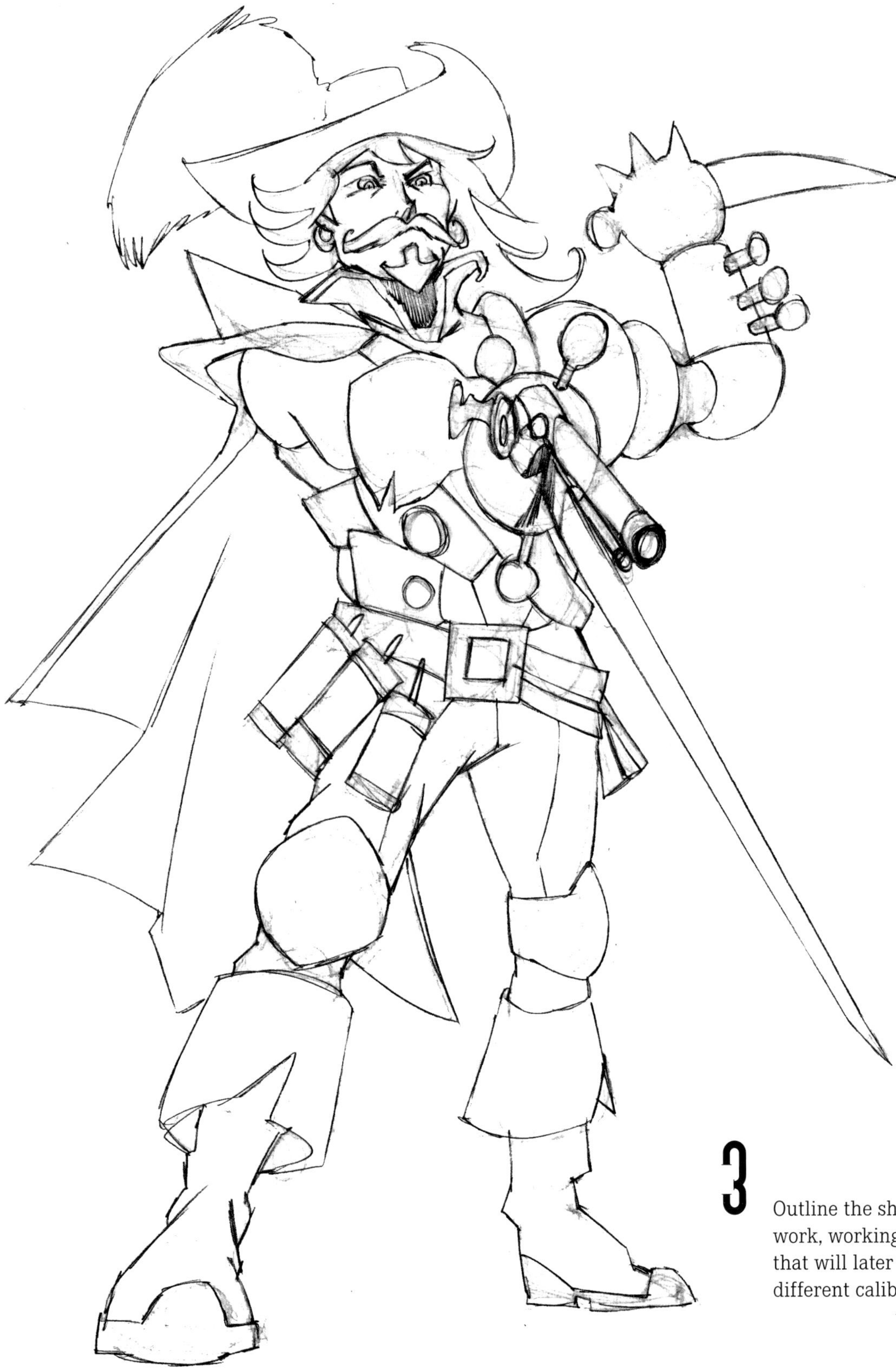

3

Outline the shape and the pencil work, working in the details that will later be inked with the different calibre pens.

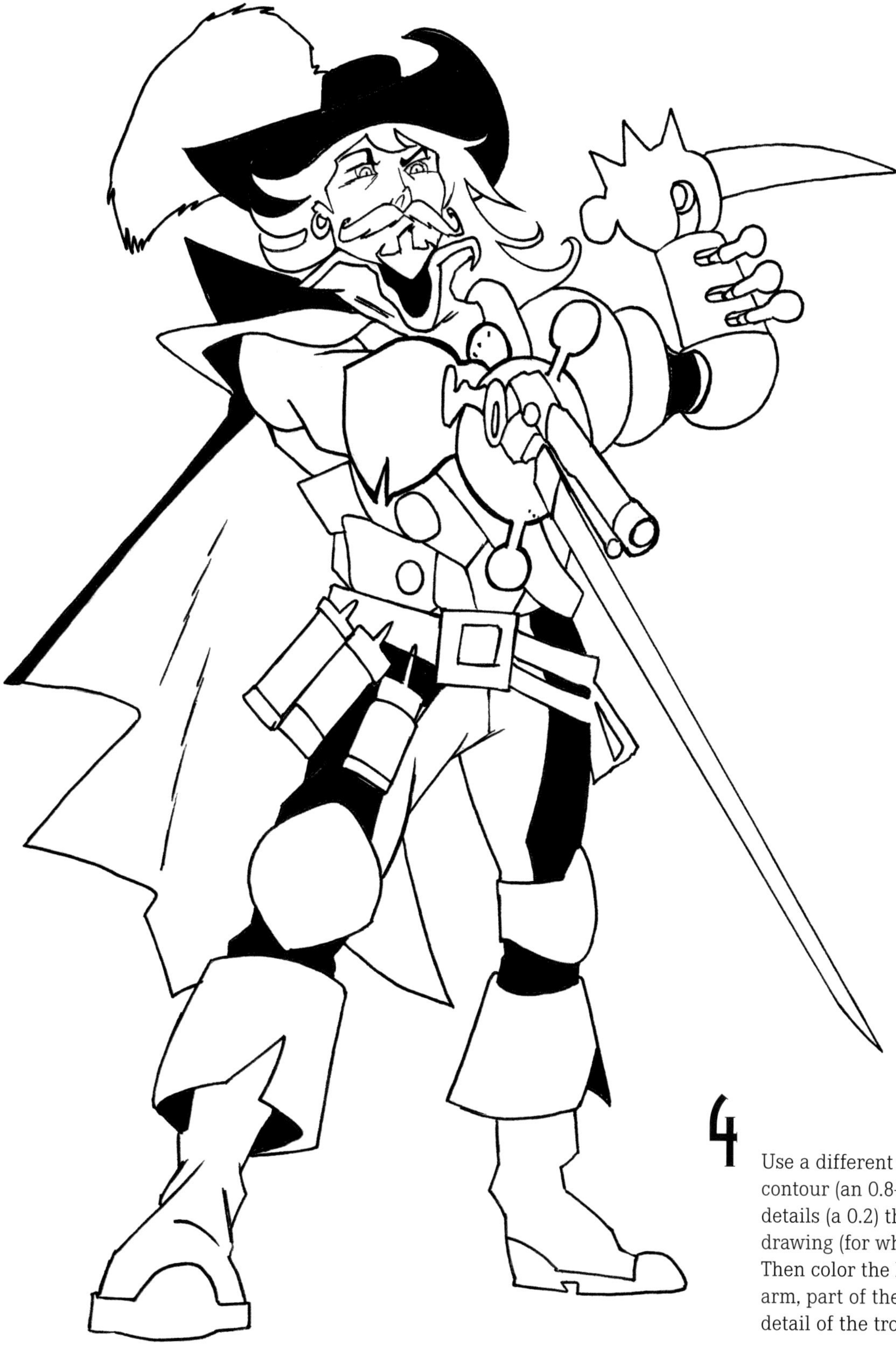

4

Use a different width for the contour (an 0.8-mm pen) and the details (a 0.2) than for the general drawing (for which we use a 0.4). Then color the hat, mechanical arm, part of the cape, and the detail of the trousers in black.

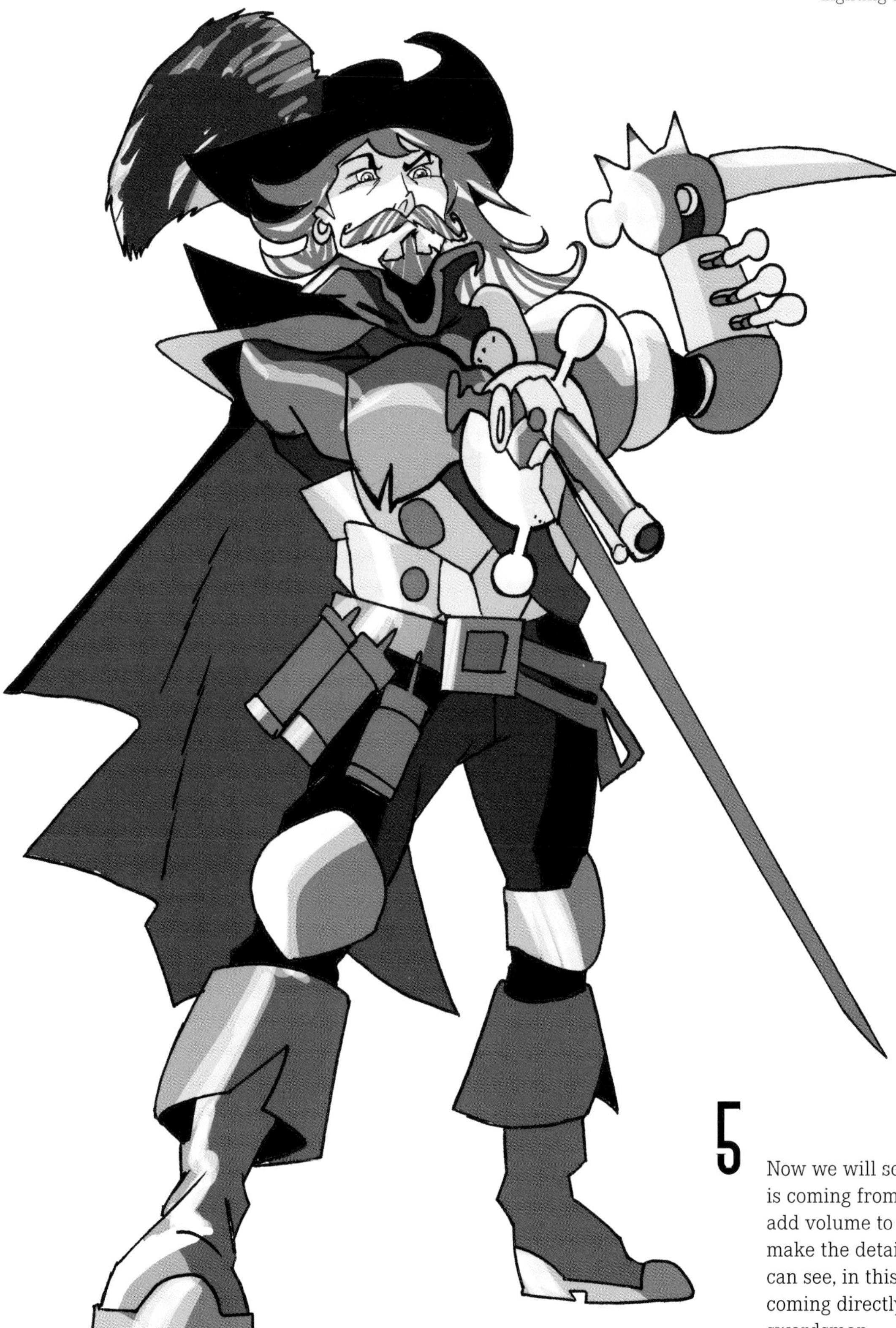

5

Now we will see where the light is coming from. This helps to add volume to the character and make the details stand out. As you can see, in this case the light is coming directly from the left of the swordsman.

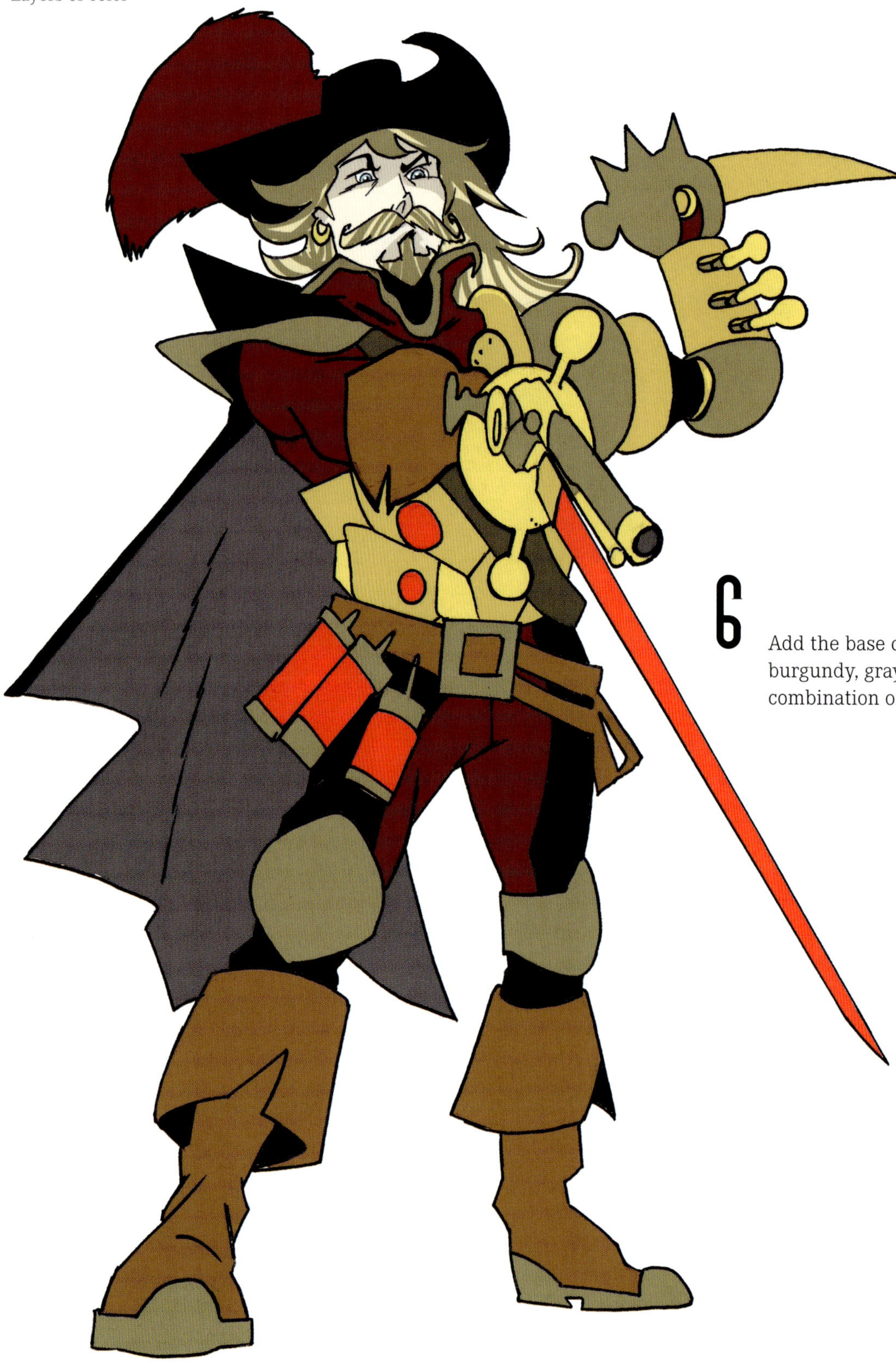

6

Add the base colors to the drawing: burgundy, gray for the cape, and a combination of golds.

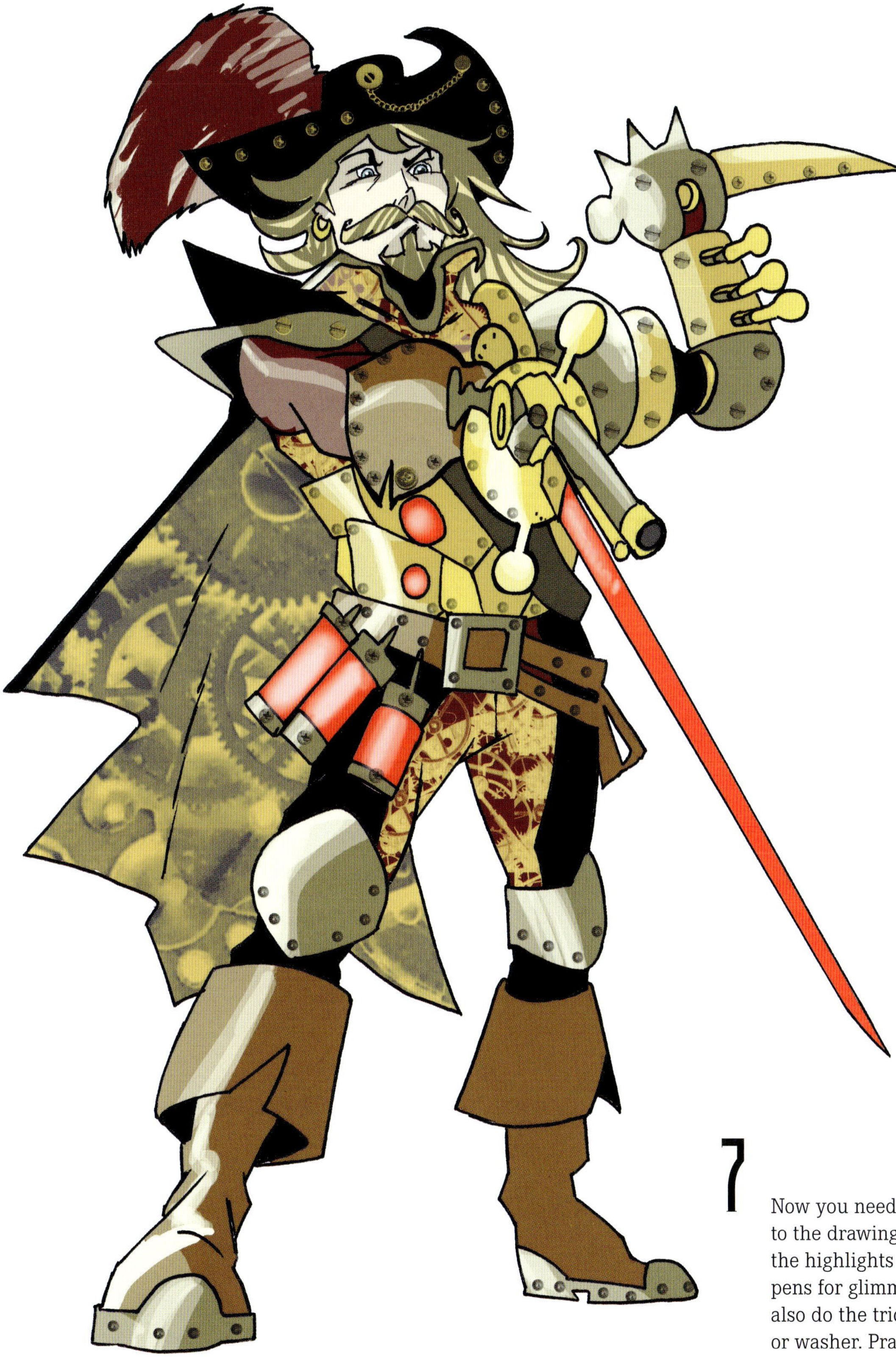

7

Now you need to add the details to the drawing: white pencil for the highlights and gold Edding pens for glimmer. These pens will also do the trick for the odd screw or washer. Practice makes perfect!

MERCENARY

Nicolaj Strogof: soldier of fortune, ex special forces, elite marksman, and master of body combat. A warrior who now, instead of pursuing the mission with which he has been charged, is on the trail of the man who hired him: the foolish man attempted to take him out. Now the only thing Nicolaj is interested in is finding him ... and settling the score!

1

Start by creating the base of your character in blue pencil. The best pose for Nicolaj is one that evokes him tracking his prey.

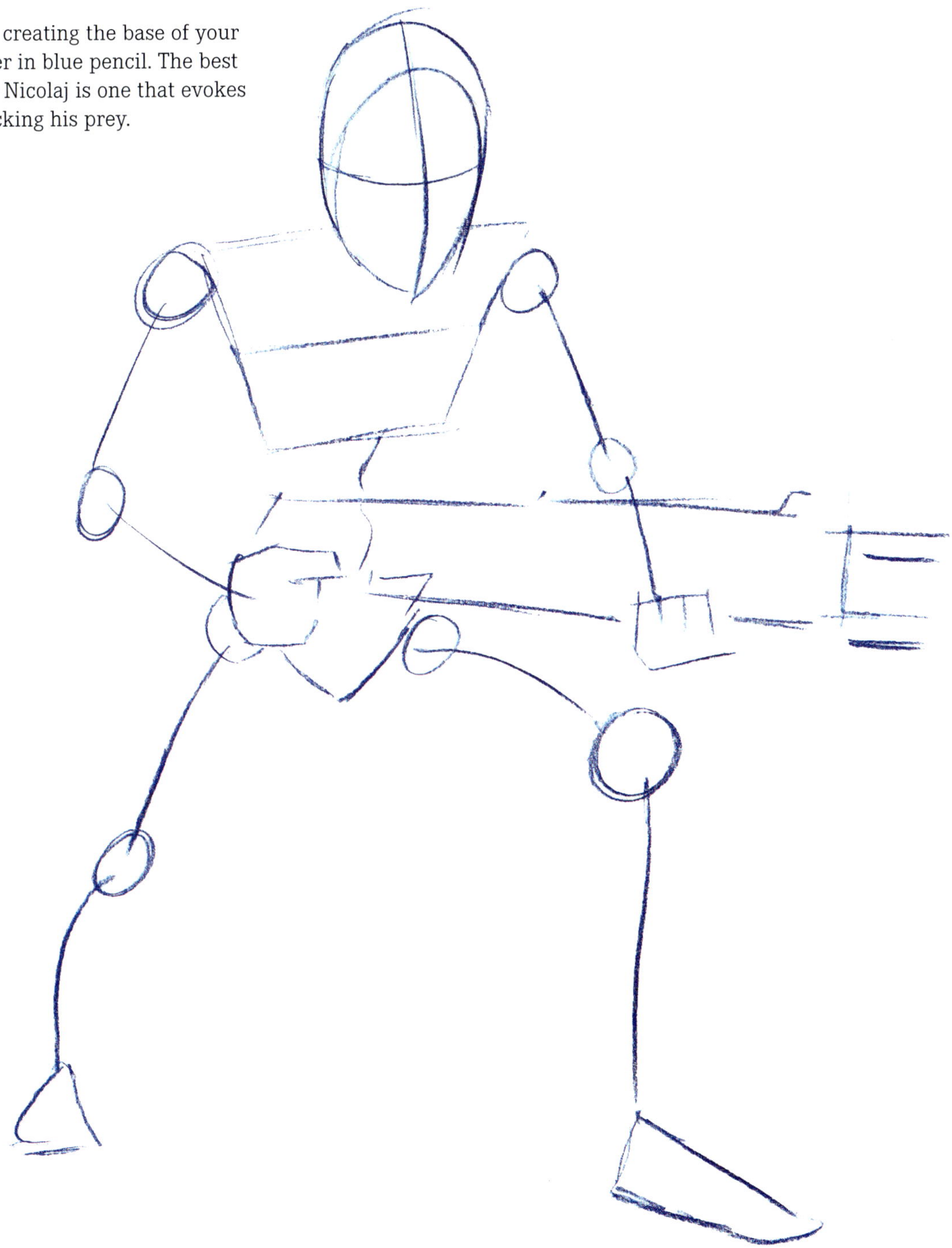

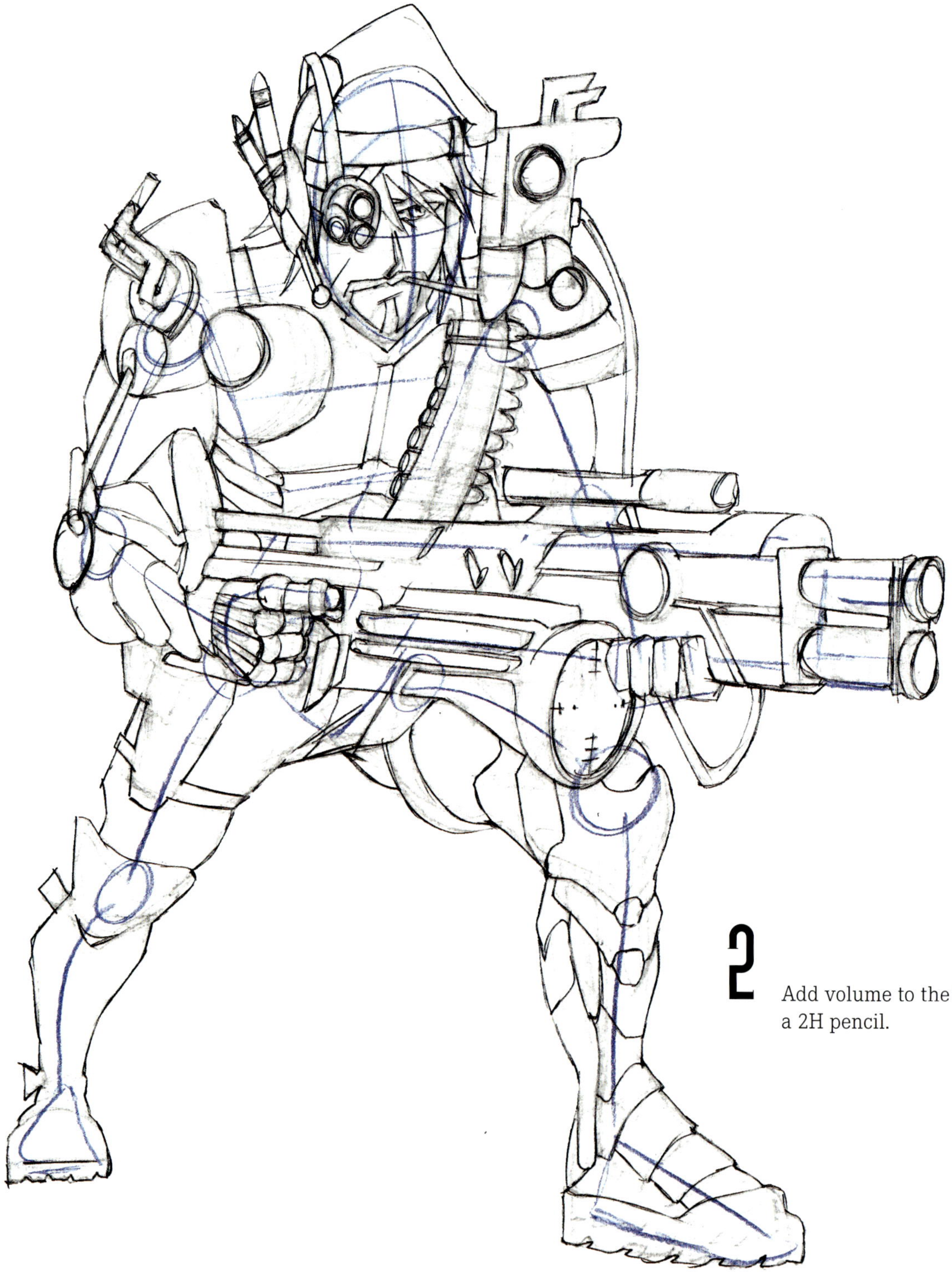

2

Add volume to the body with a 2H pencil.

3

Use a 05-gauge pencil to completely draw the figure and give form to the detail. The better the finish of your pencil work, the easier it will be to ink.

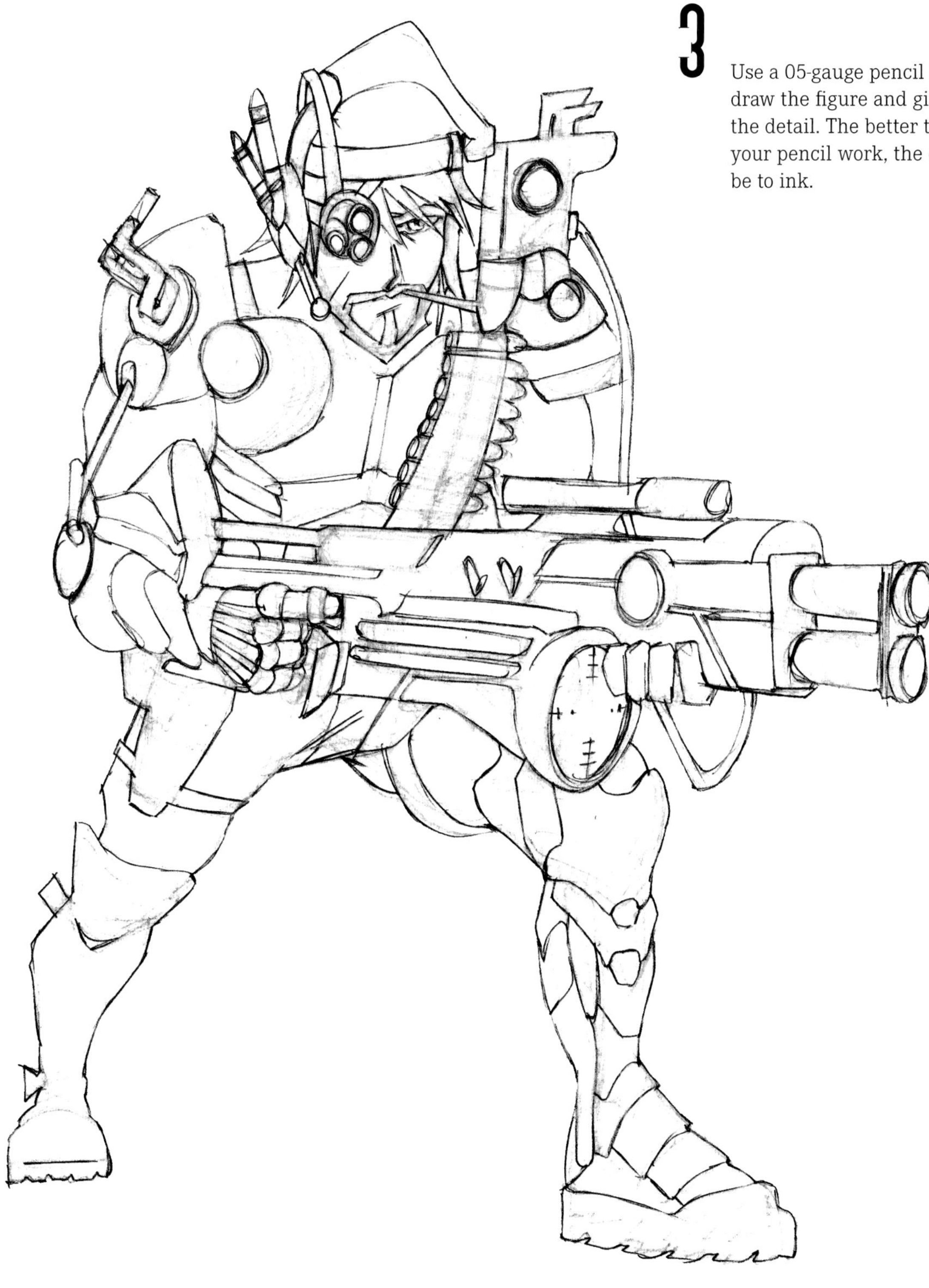

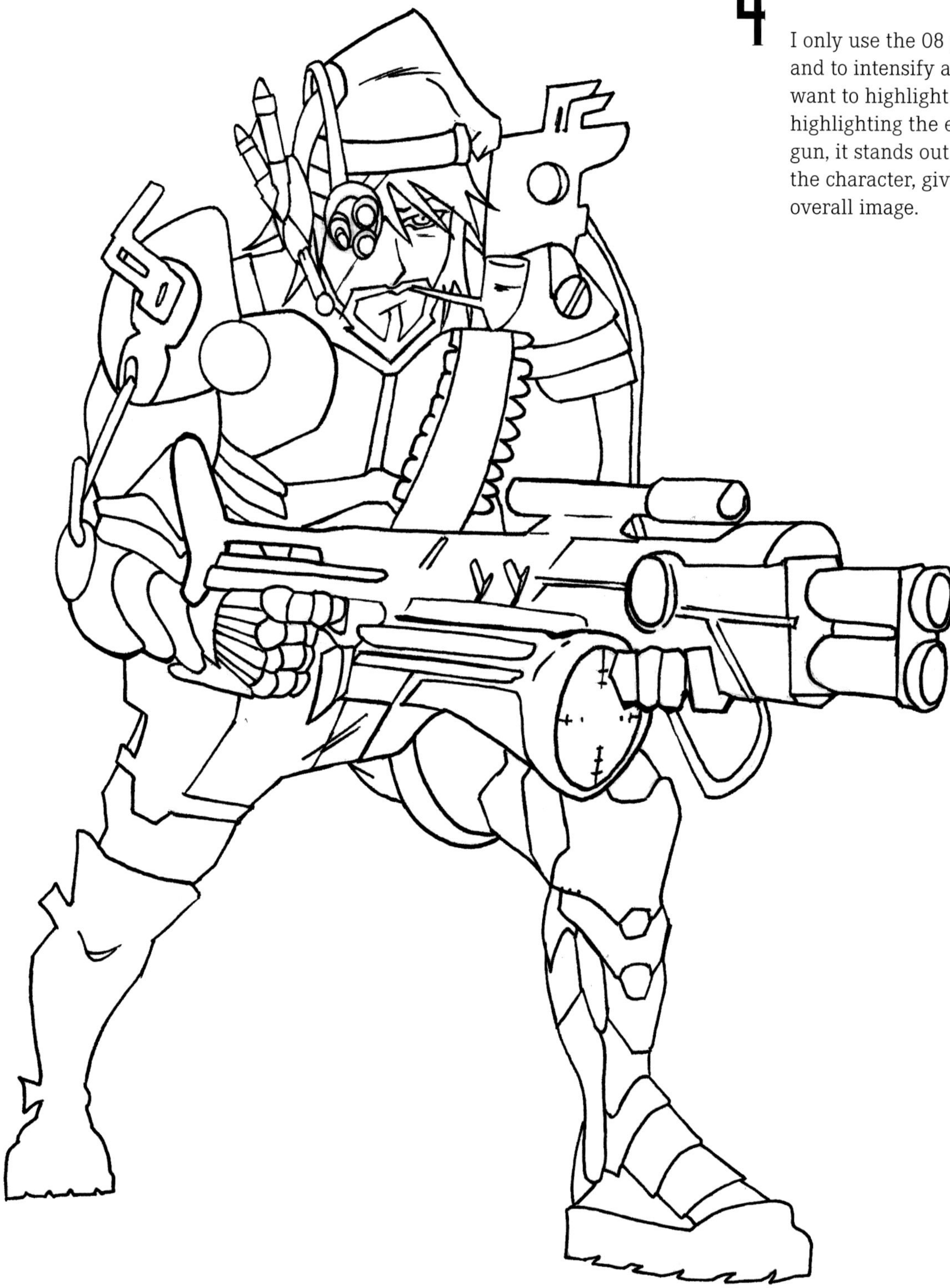

4

I only use the 08 pen for contour and to intensify any lines you want to highlight. For example, by highlighting the eons submachine gun, it stands out from the rest of the character, giving depth to the overall image.

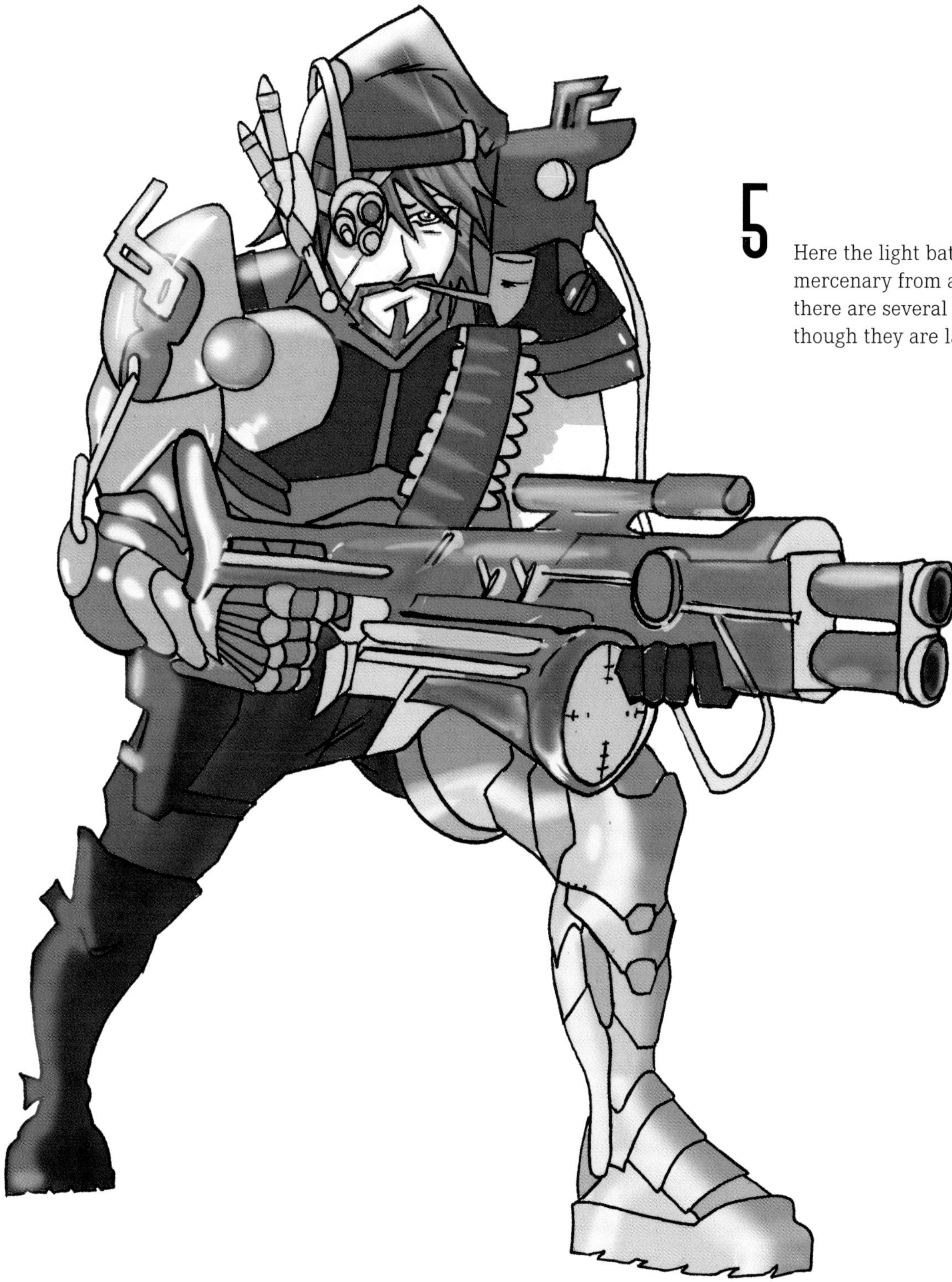

5

Here the light bathes our mercenary from above and right: there are several points of light, as though they are lanterns. Try it!

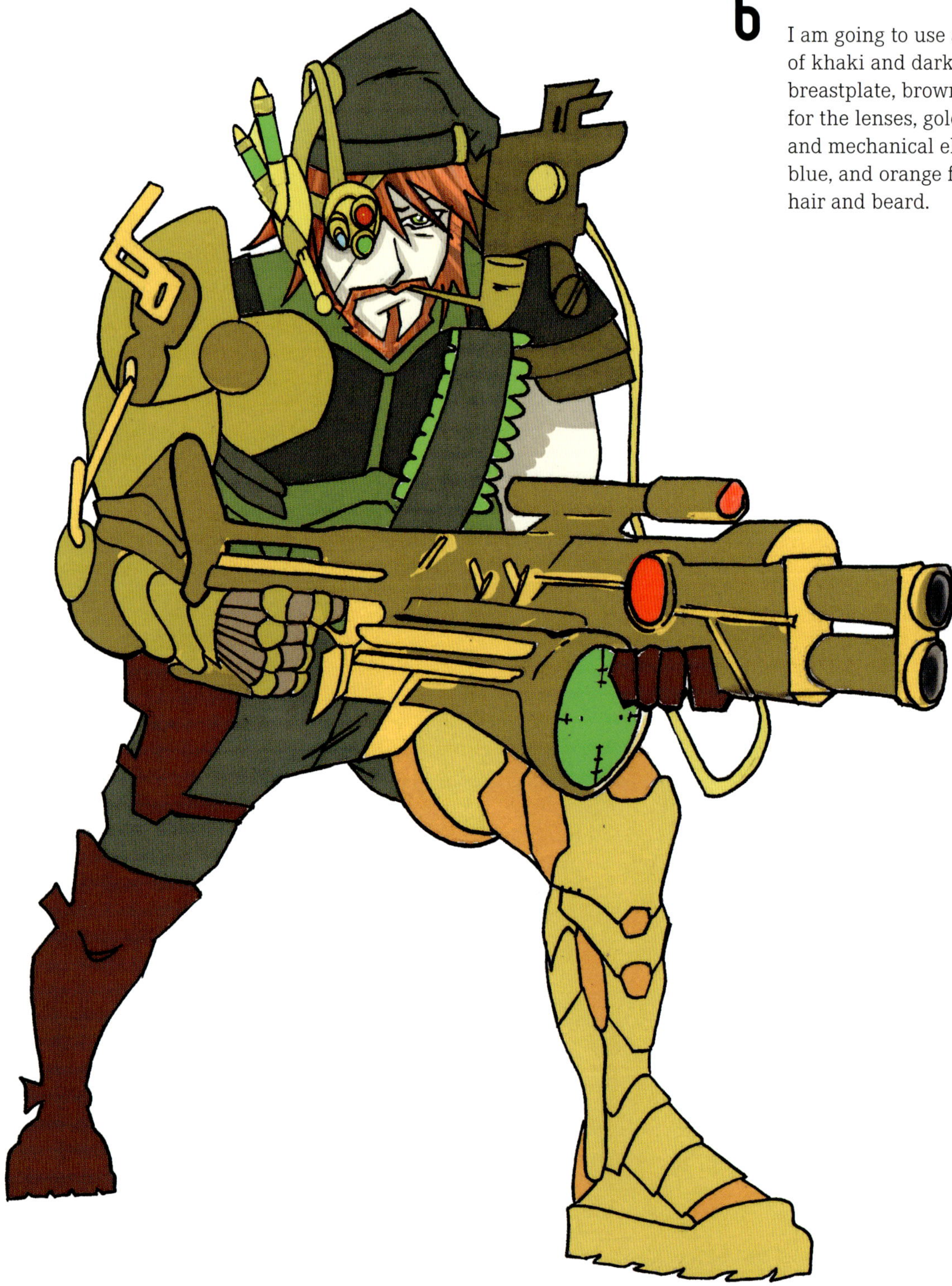

6

I am going to use a combination of khaki and dark green for the breastplate, brown and light green for the lenses, gold for the weapons and mechanical elements, and red, blue, and orange for the soldier's hair and beard.

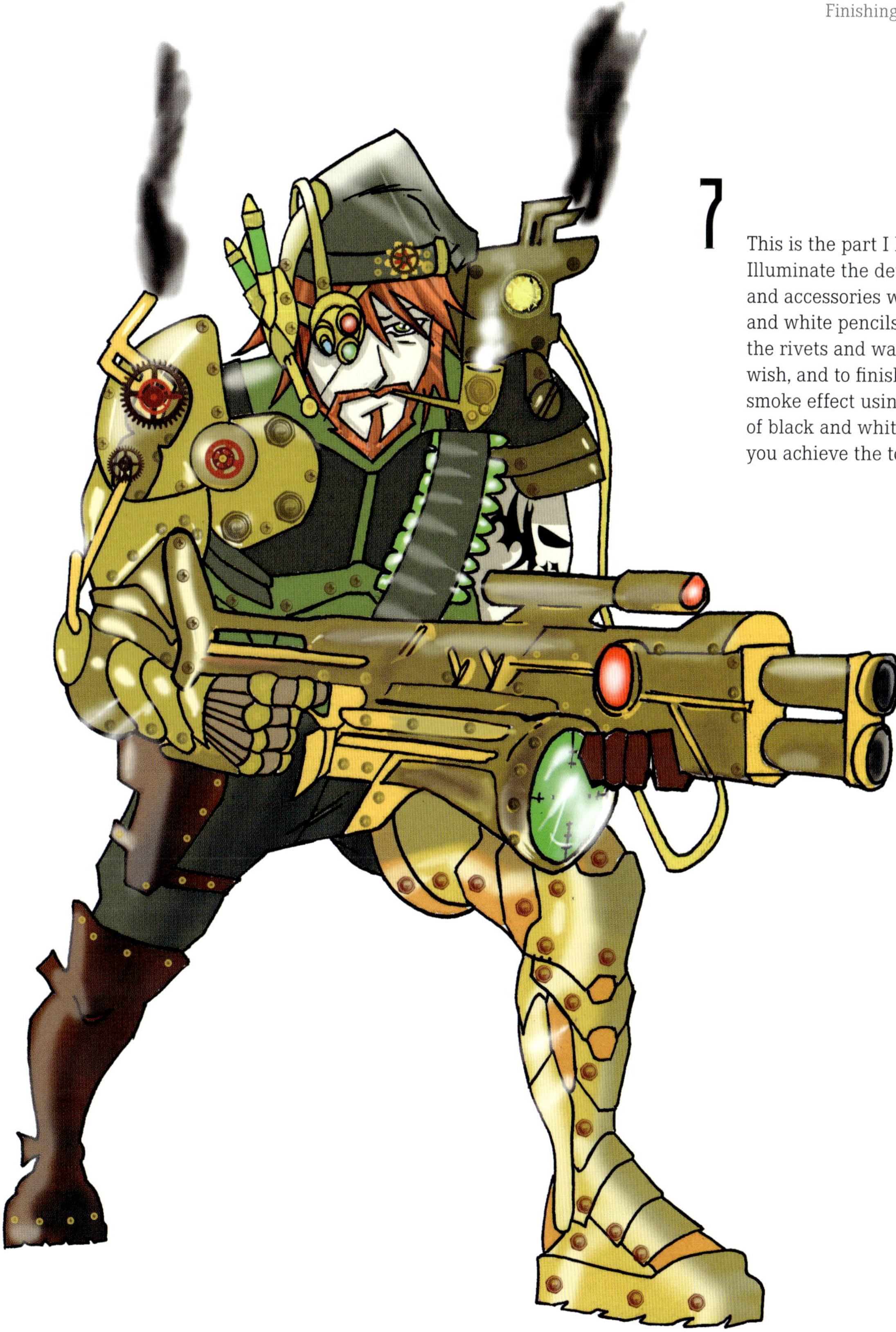

7

This is the part I like best. Illuminate the details of the rifle and accessories with light yellow and white pencils. Then add all the rivets and washers as you wish, and to finish up add the smoke effect using a mixture of black and white pencil until you achieve the tone you want.

ROBOT

Button is a robot herald to the royal court. Whenever the court hosts a celebration or event, he is in charge of making announcements to the attendees. Whenever he can, he accompanies his announcements with music and trumpets: after all, he does have a music box incorporated within his mechanism.

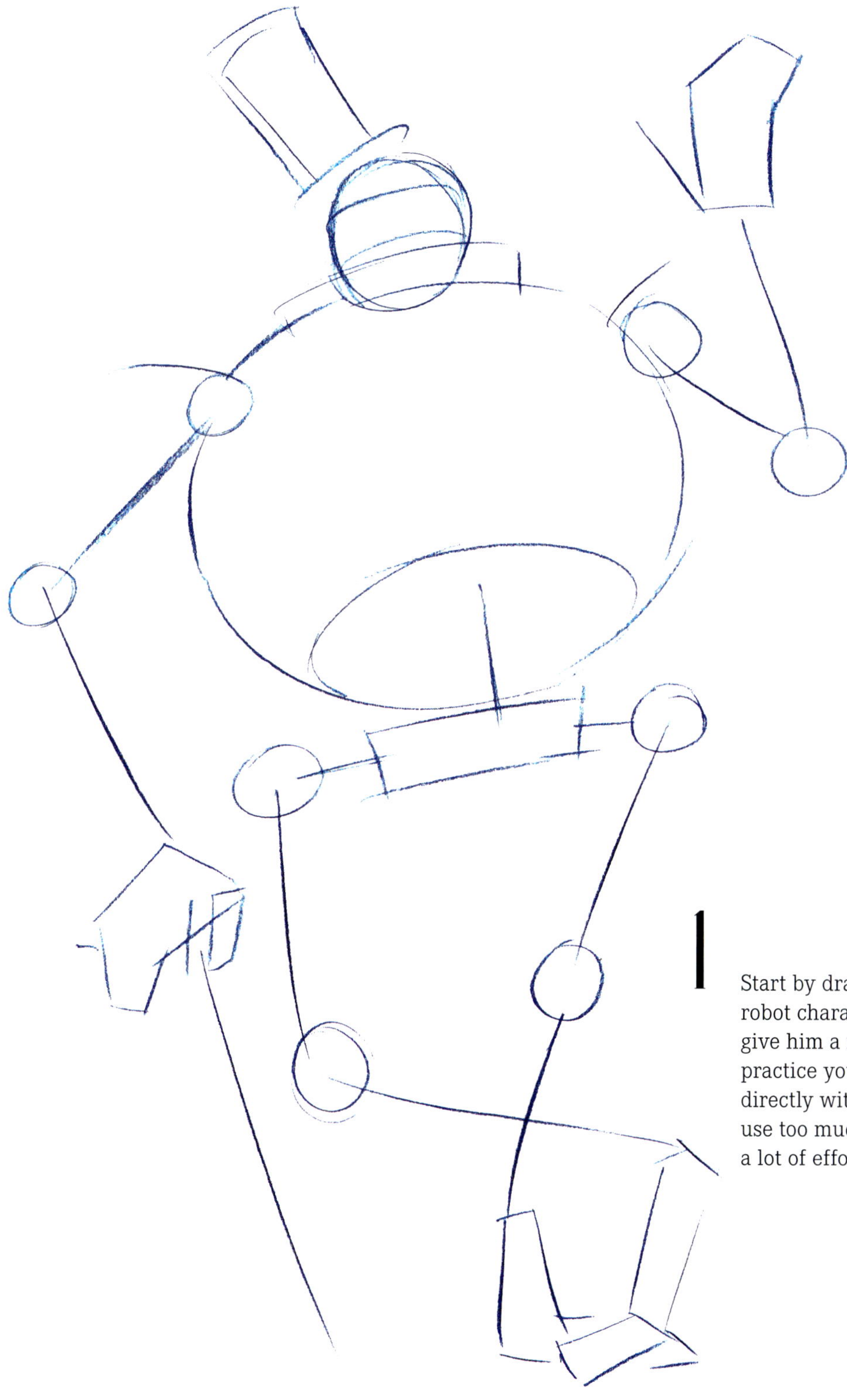

1

Start by drawing the base of your robot character in blue pencil: give him a relaxed posture. With practice you will be able to do this directly with black pencil. Don't use too much blue or it will take a lot of effort to rub out.

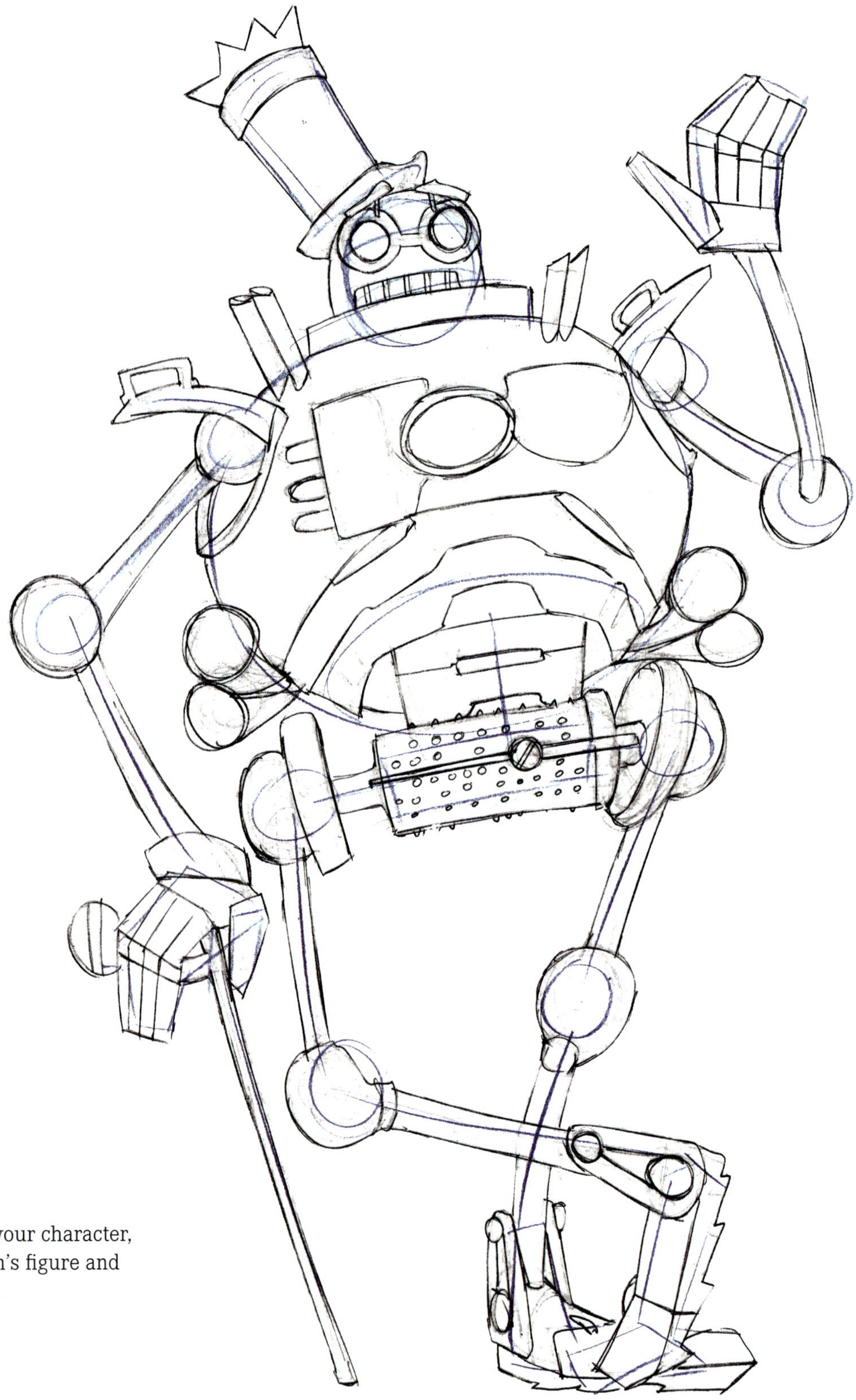

2

Add pencil to your character, defining Button's figure and elegant stance.

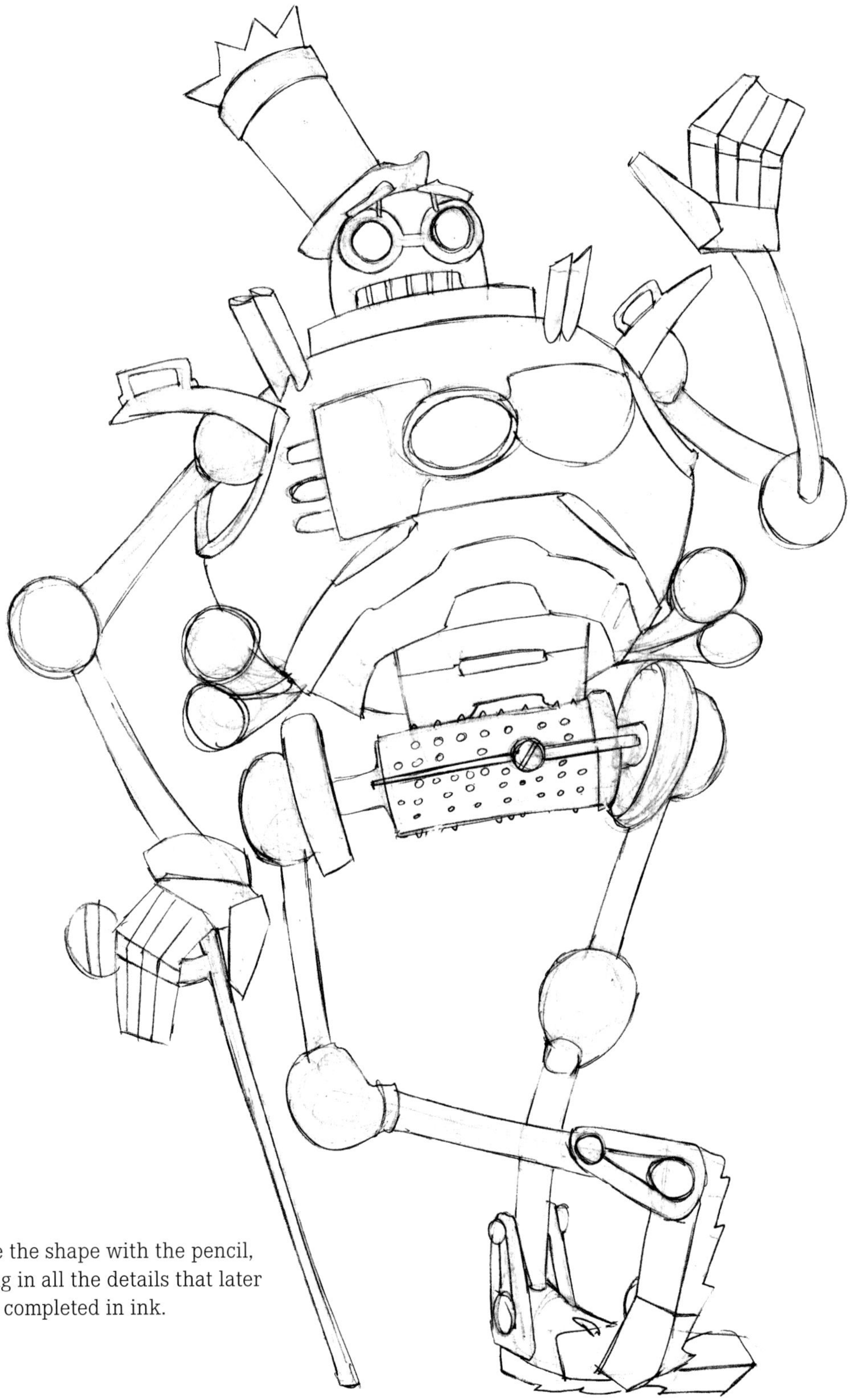

3

Outline the shape with the pencil, working in all the details that later will be completed in ink.

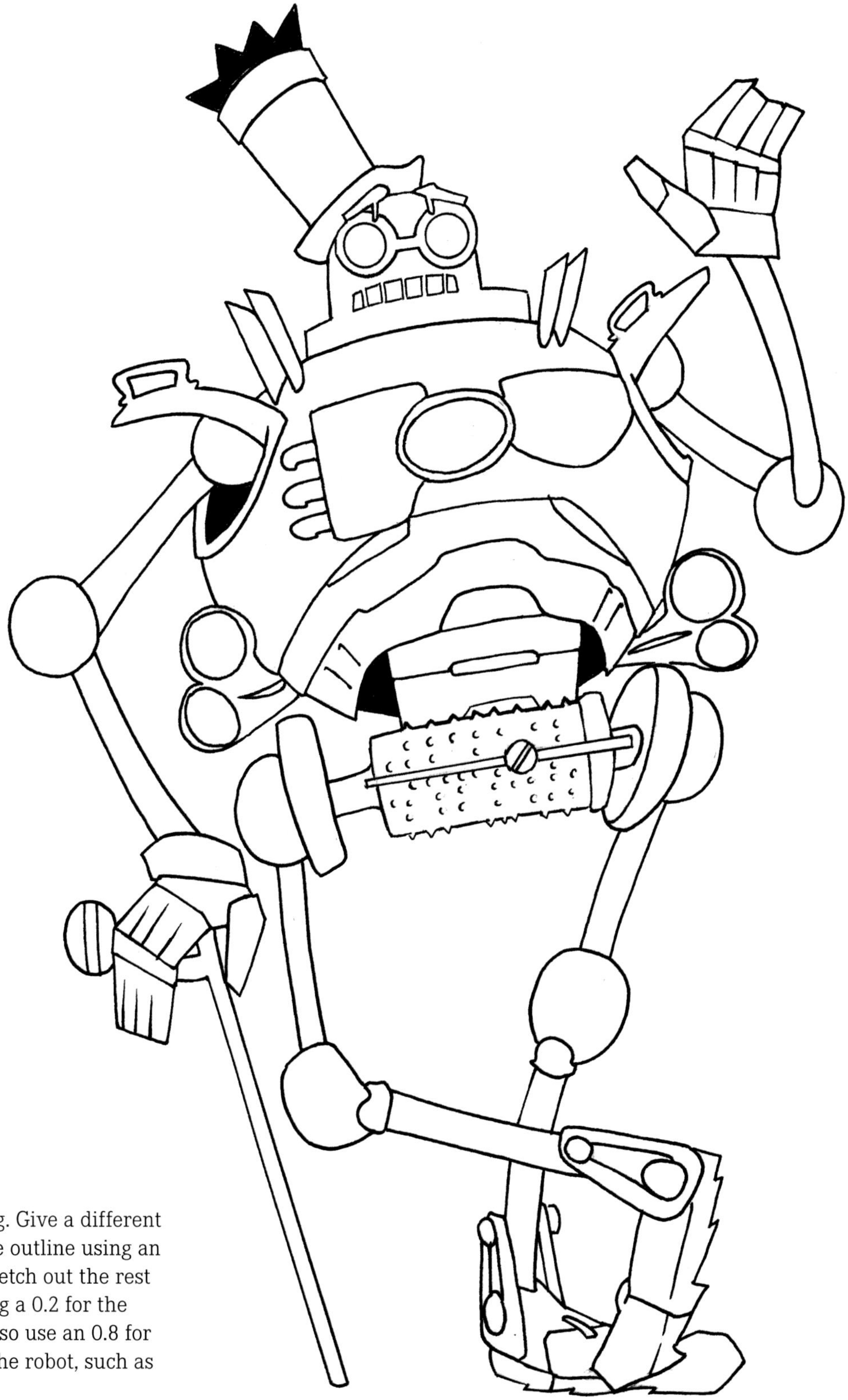

4

Ink the drawing. Give a different thickness to the outline using an 0.8-mm pen. Sketch out the rest with a 0.4, using a 0.2 for the finer details. Also use an 0.8 for the details on the robot, such as the vent.

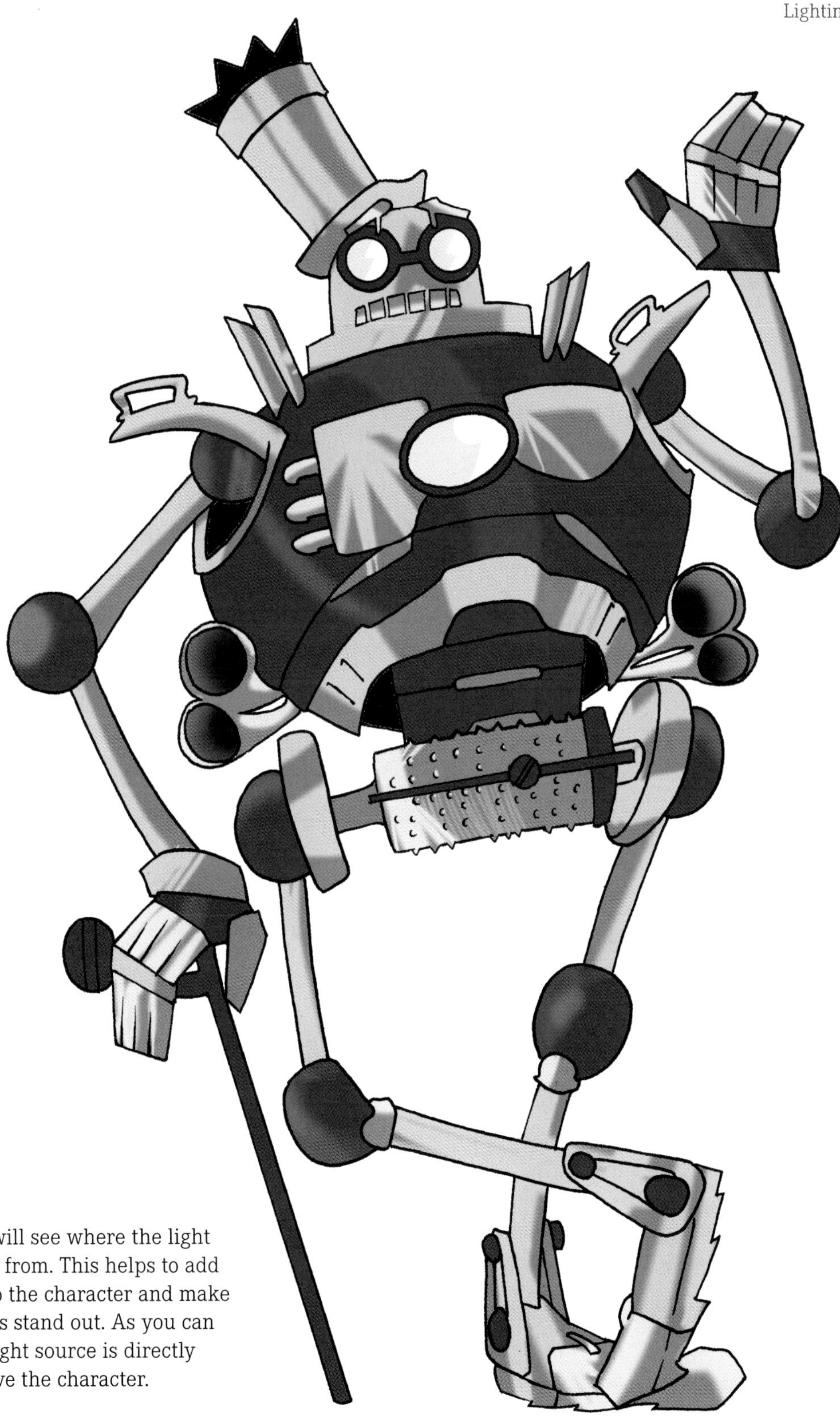

5

Now we will see where the light is coming from. This helps to add volume to the character and make the details stand out. As you can see, the light source is directly from above the character.

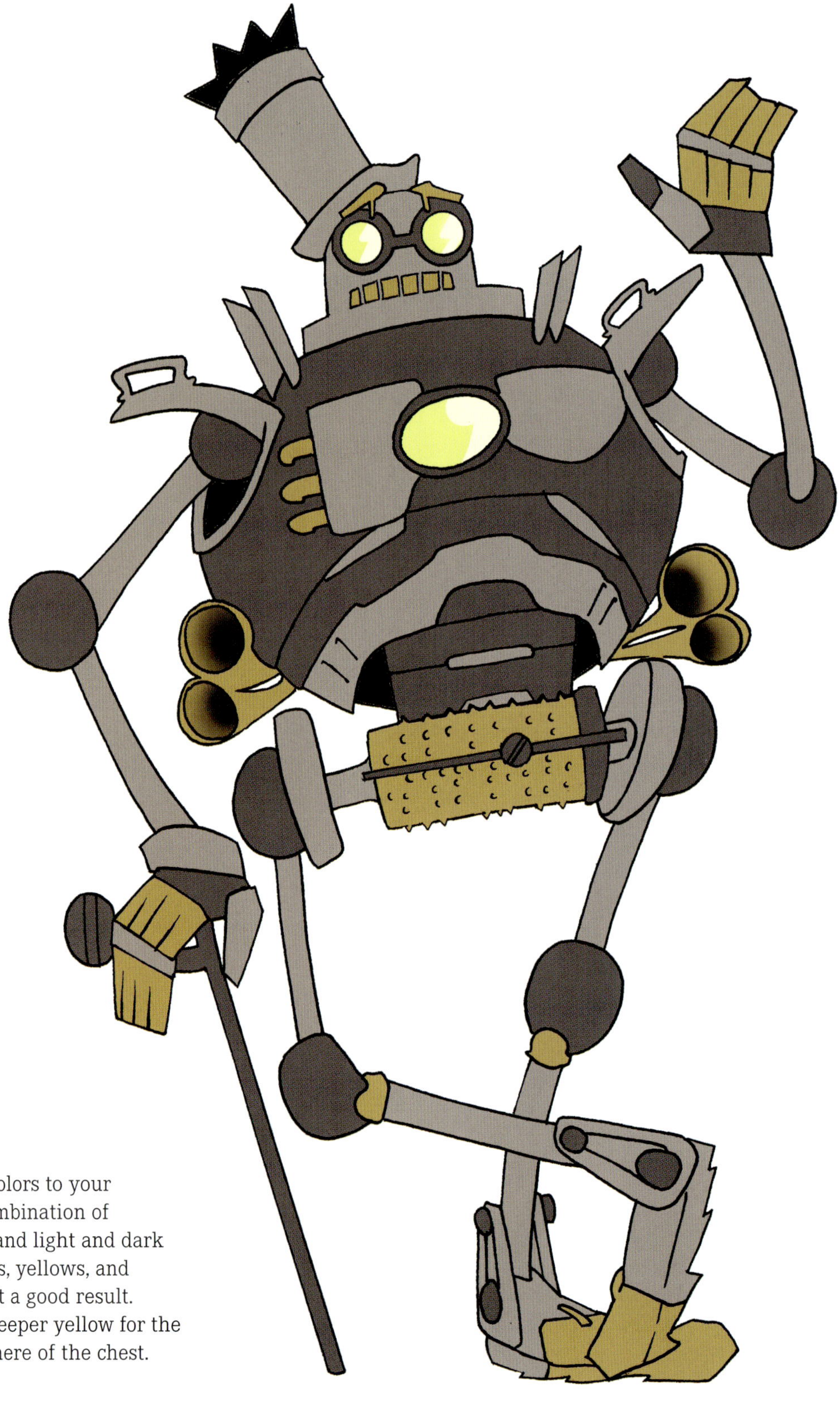

6

Add the base colors to your character, a combination of metallic tones and light and dark gray. Gold tones, yellows, and oranges will get a good result. Finally, use a deeper yellow for the glasses and sphere of the chest.

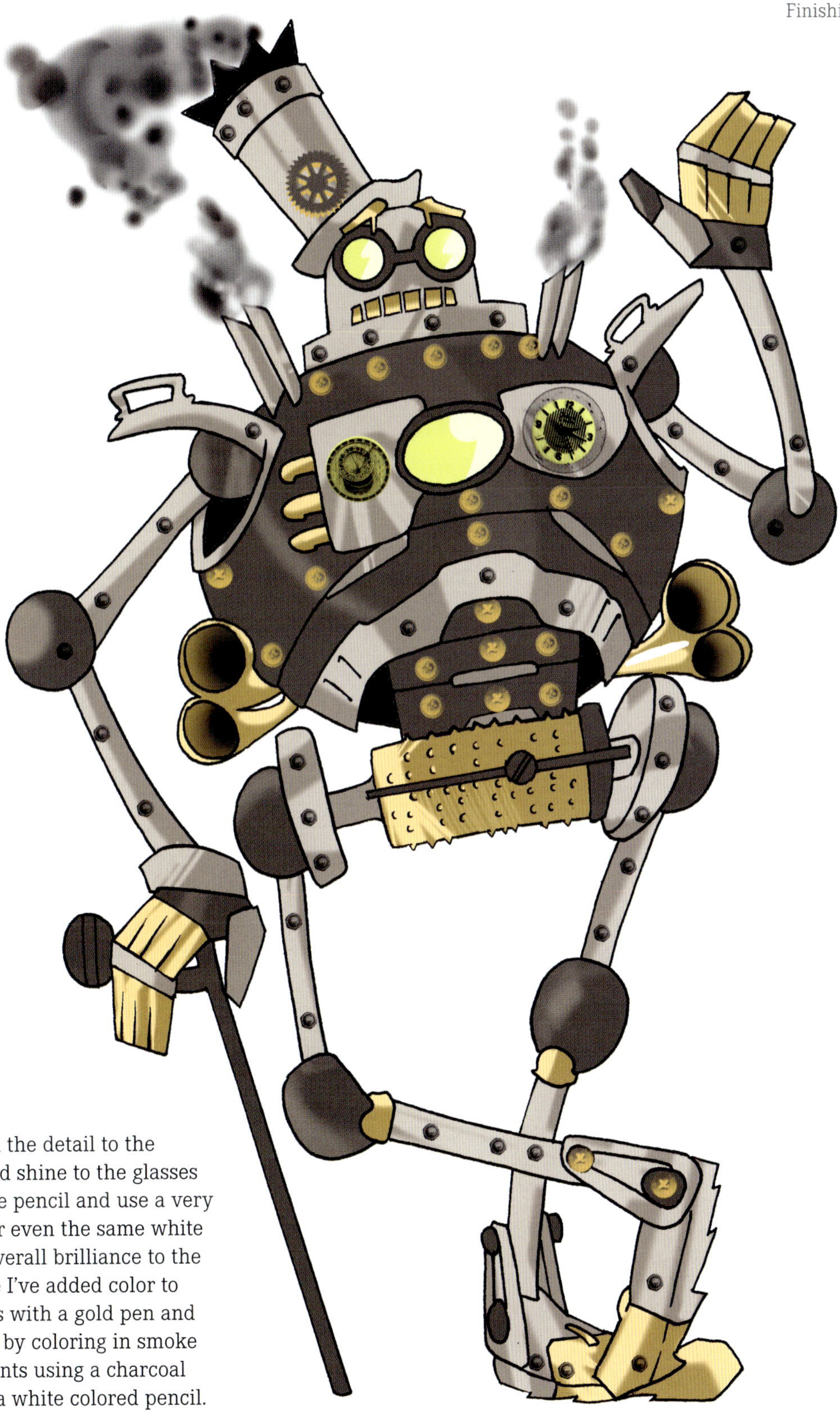

7

Now add all the detail to the drawing: add shine to the glasses with a white pencil and use a very light gray or even the same white to add an overall brilliance to the figure. Here I've added color to the washers with a gold pen and finished off by coloring in smoke from the vents using a charcoal pencil and a white colored pencil.

FEMALE WARRIOR

Lithlian "Stormrider" is captain of the northern horsewomen and, of course, a formidable warrior. Under the command of her army, she defends the borders and protects the frozen cities from the invading forces of the Queen of Needles.

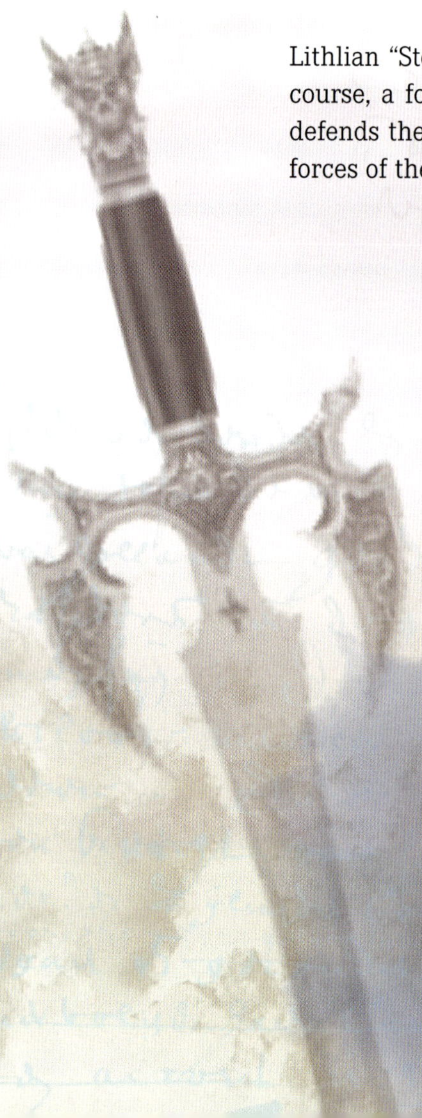

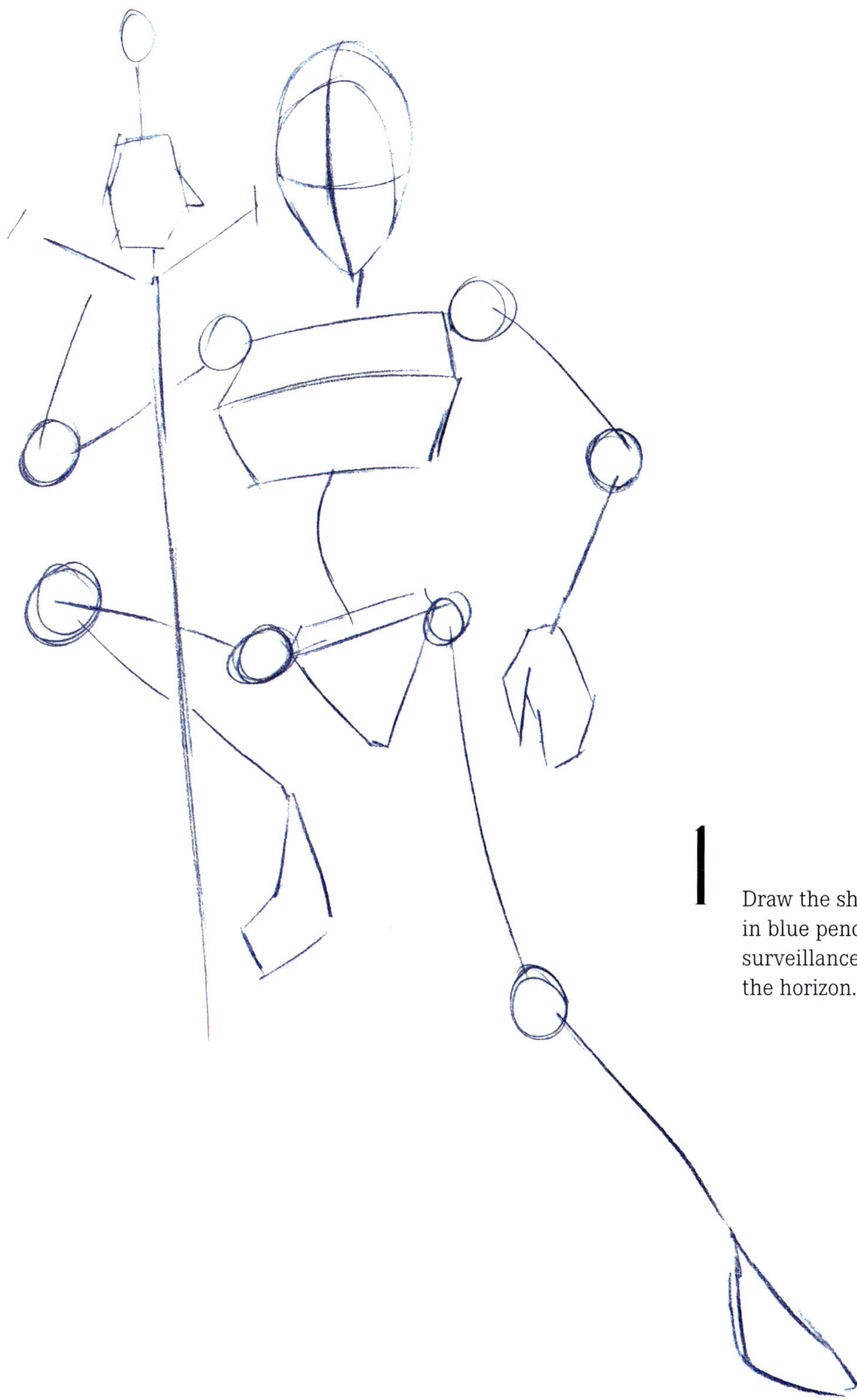

1

Draw the shape of your warrior in blue pencil, in a position of surveillance, as though scanning the horizon.

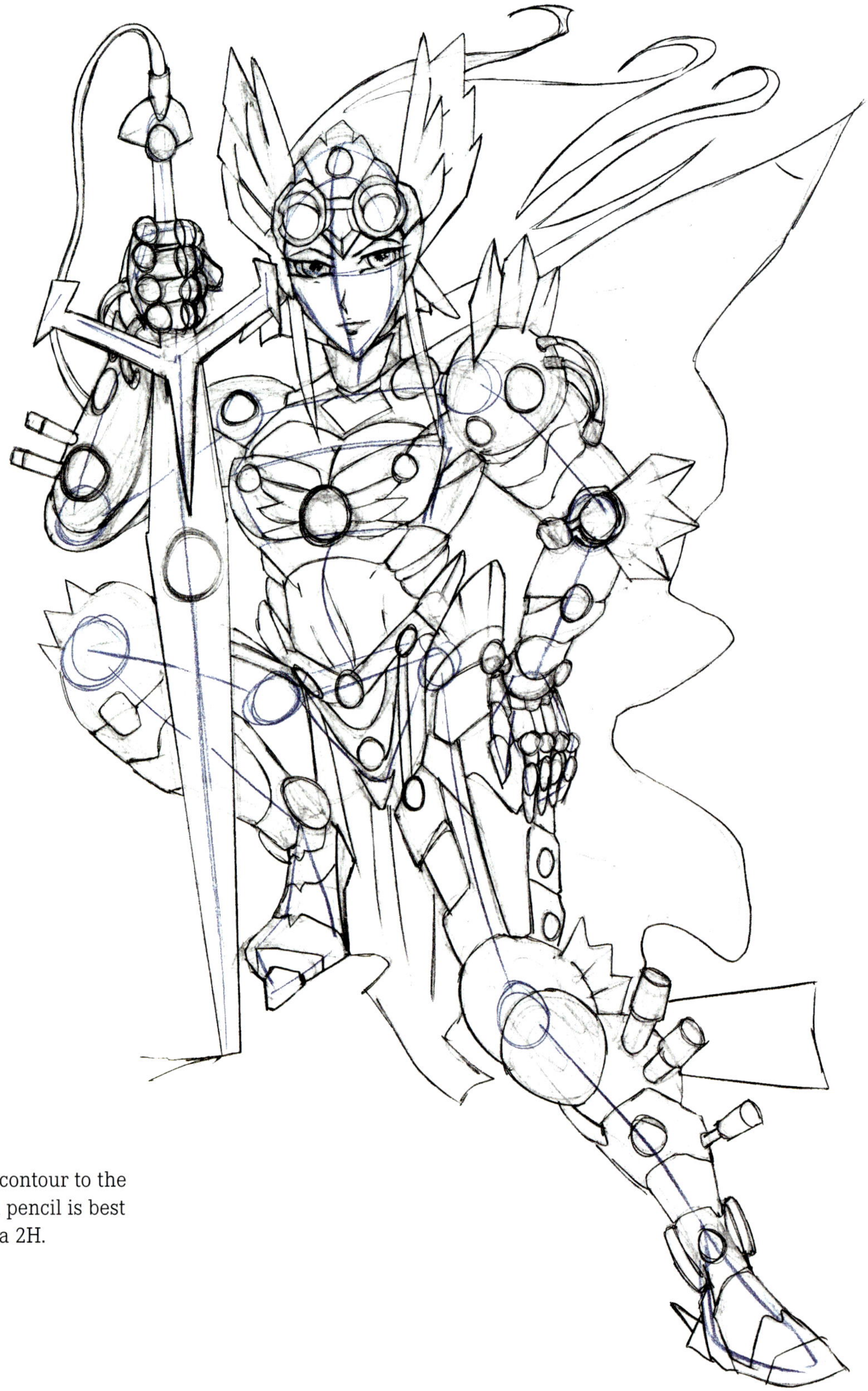

2

Add the base contour to the figure. A hard pencil is best for this. I use a 2H.

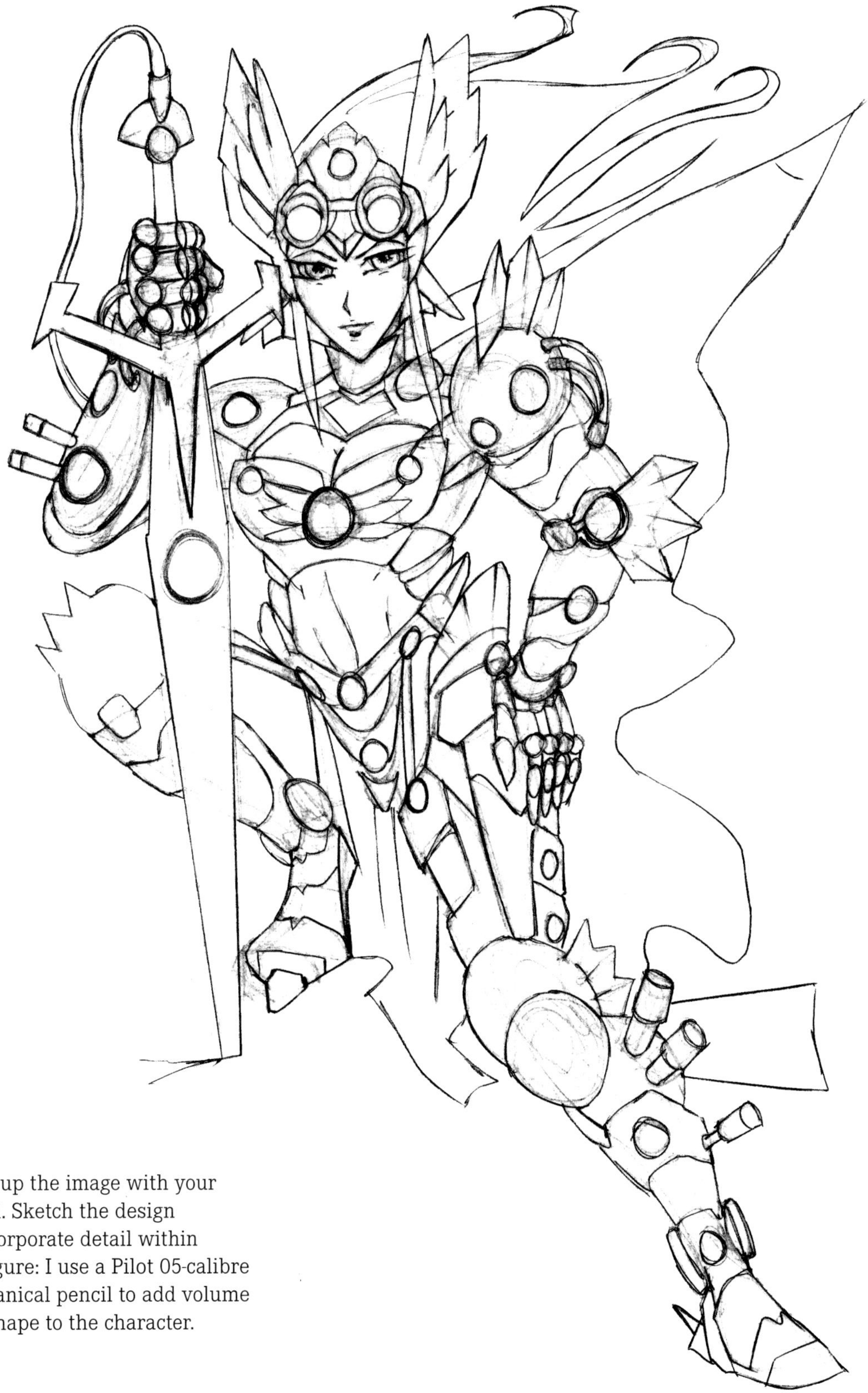

3

Work up the image with your pencil. Sketch the design to incorporate detail within the figure: I use a Pilot 05-calibre mechanical pencil to add volume and shape to the character.

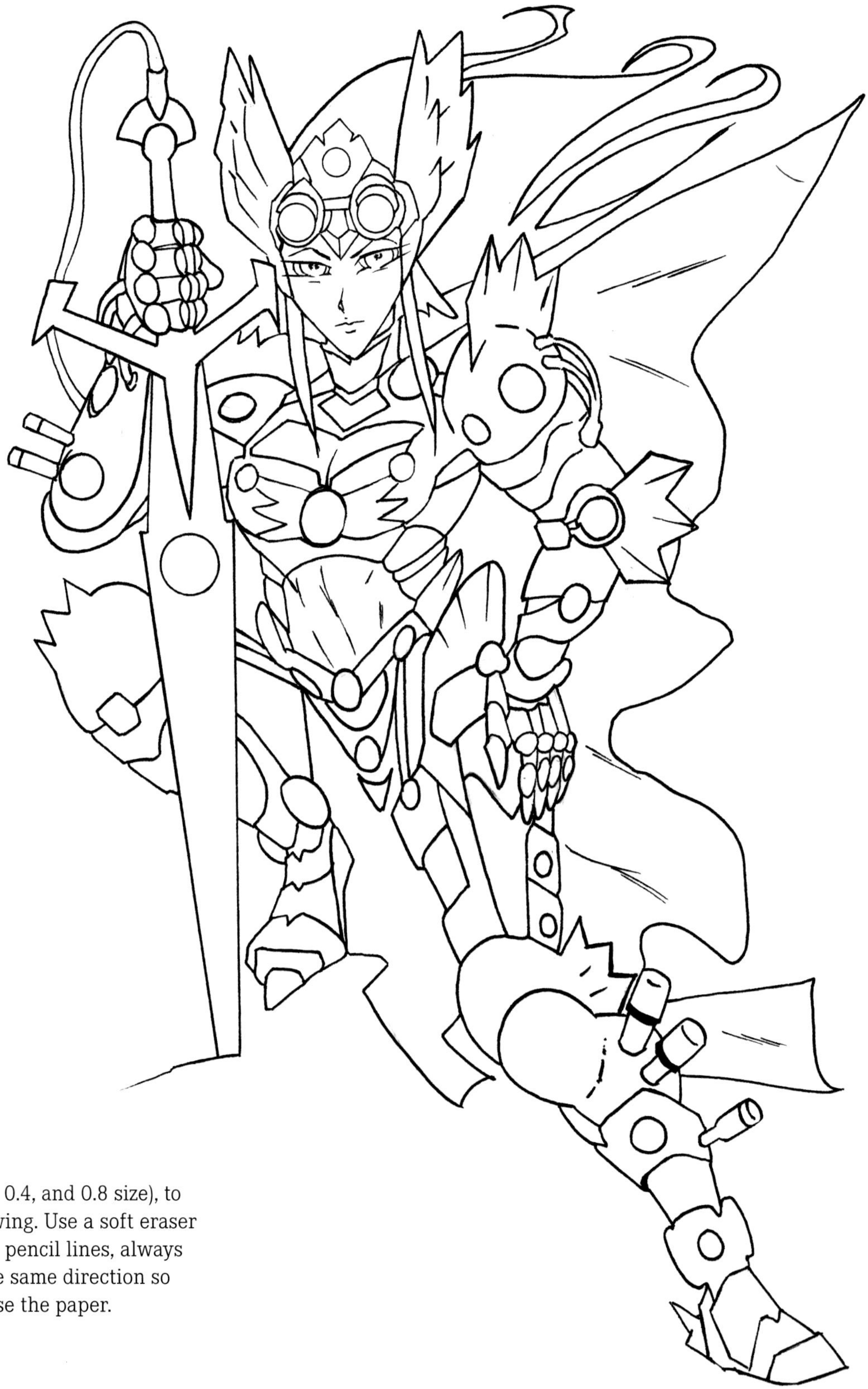

4

Use pens (0.2, 0.4, and 0.8 size), to color the drawing. Use a soft eraser to remove the pencil lines, always rubbing in the same direction so as not to crease the paper.

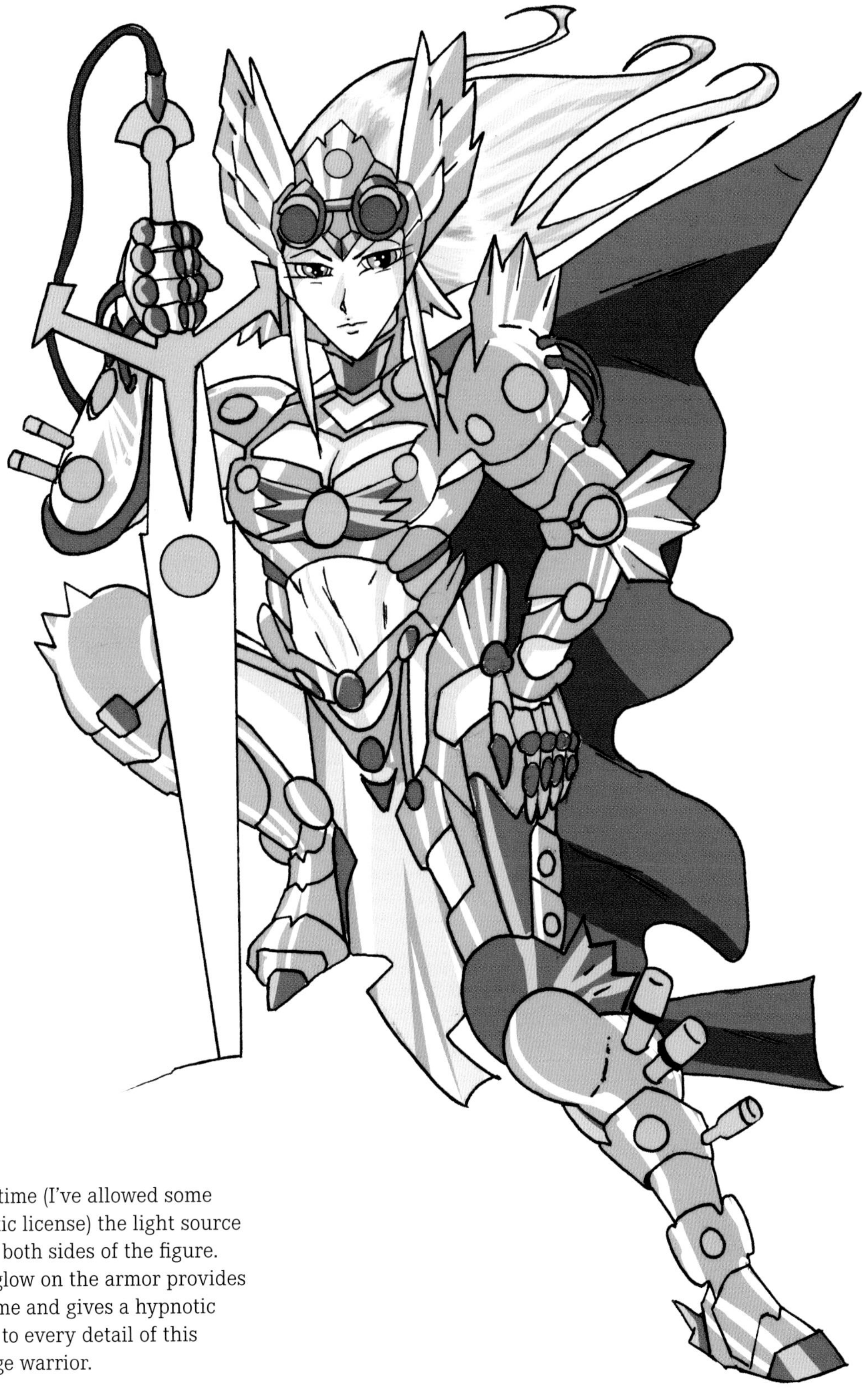

5

This time (I've allowed some artistic license) the light source is on both sides of the figure. The glow on the armor provides volume and gives a hypnotic glow to every detail of this savage warrior.

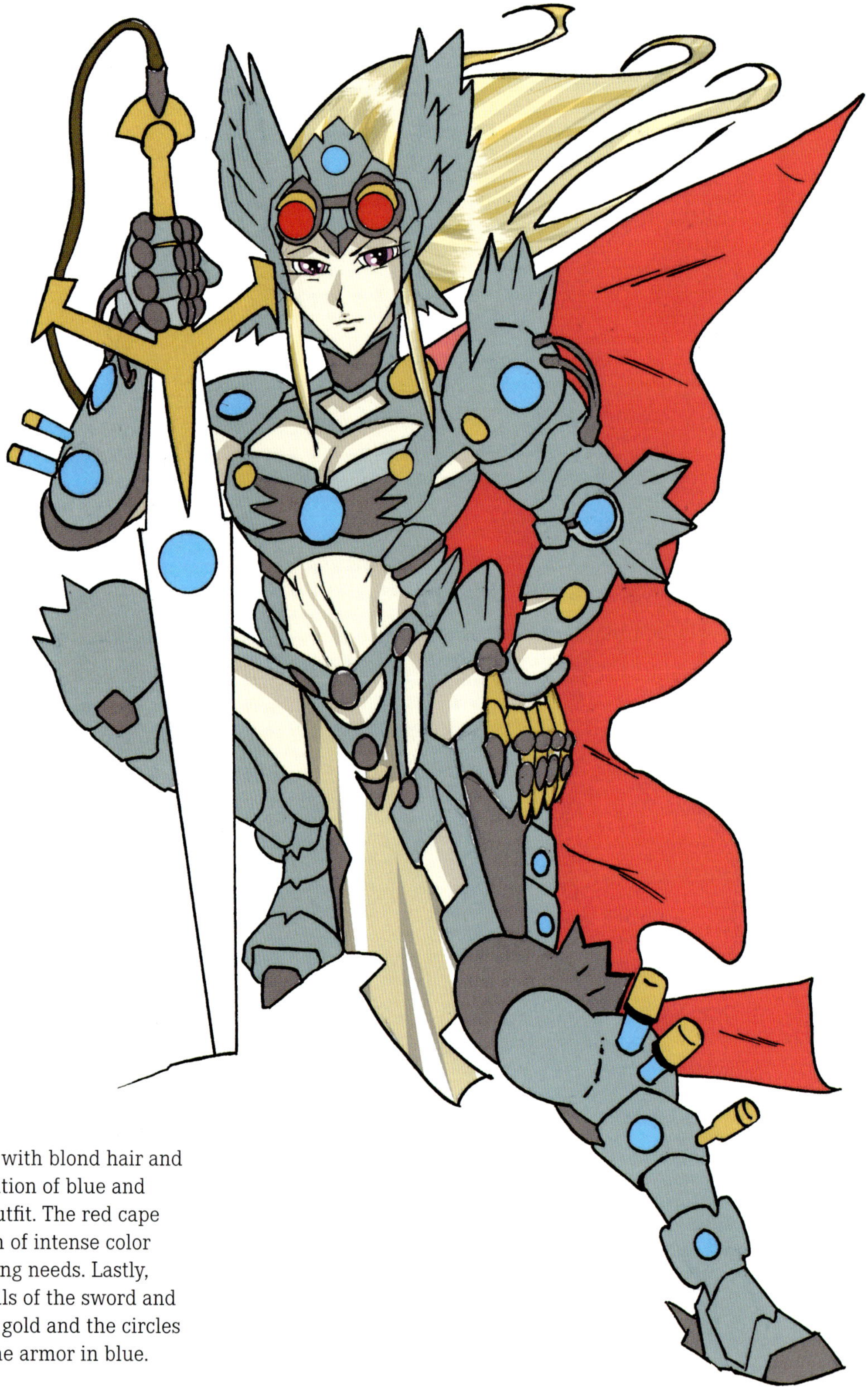

6

Color Lithlian with blond hair and use a combination of blue and gray for her outfit. The red cape adds the touch of intense color that the drawing needs. Lastly, color the details of the sword and accessories in gold and the circles of power on the armor in blue.

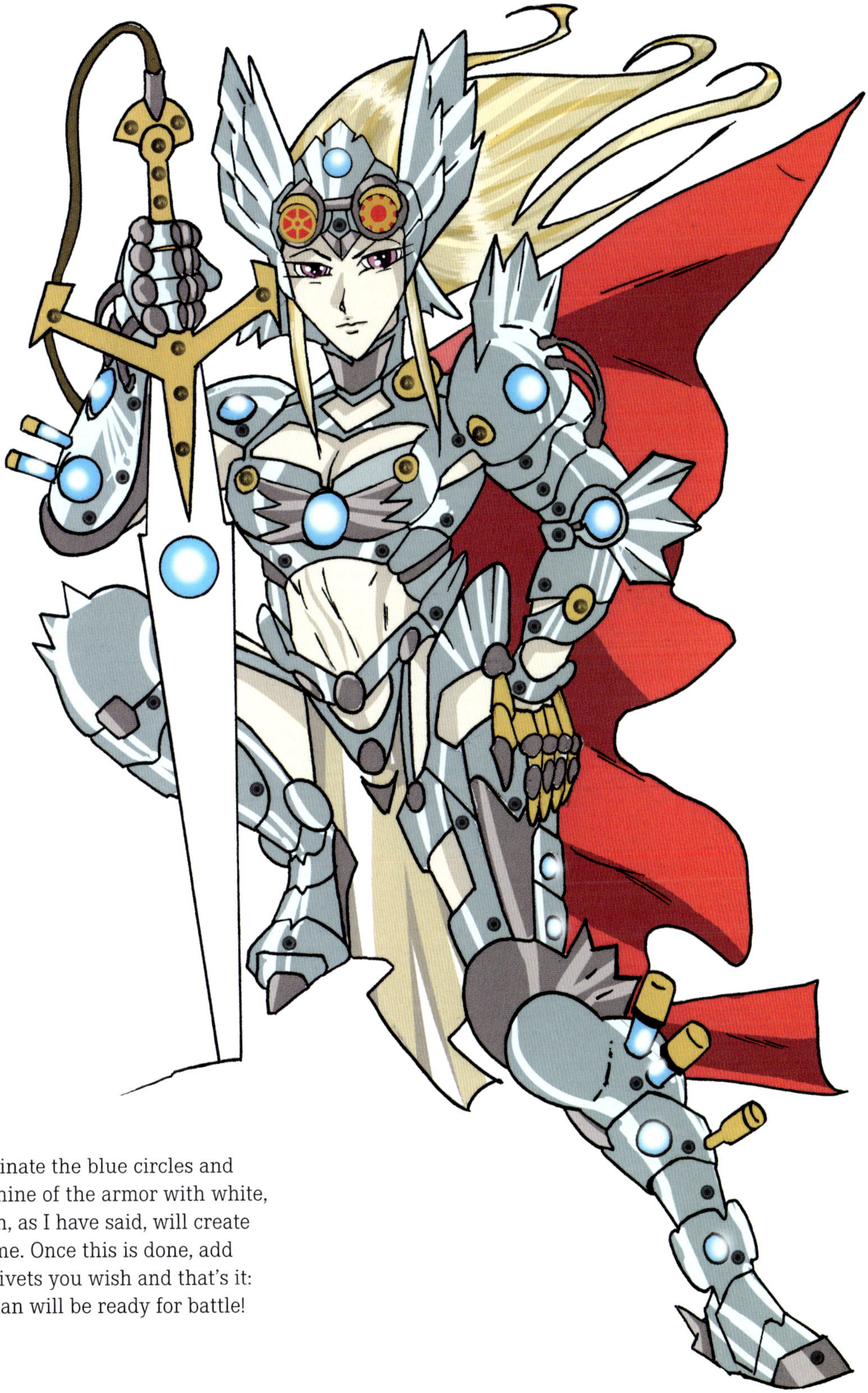

7

Illuminate the blue circles and the shine of the armor with white, which, as I have said, will create volume. Once this is done, add any rivets you wish and that's it: Lithlian will be ready for battle!

MARSHAL

Estwood Mcqueen is custodian and protector of Rangonash City. He is responsible for preventing chaos from spreading through the city. Now, with the announcement of a great poker game to take place shortly and a hefty prize for the winner, Estwood knows that it's only a matter of time before there is an attempted robbery. The bandits had better be prepared – they're going to have him to deal with!

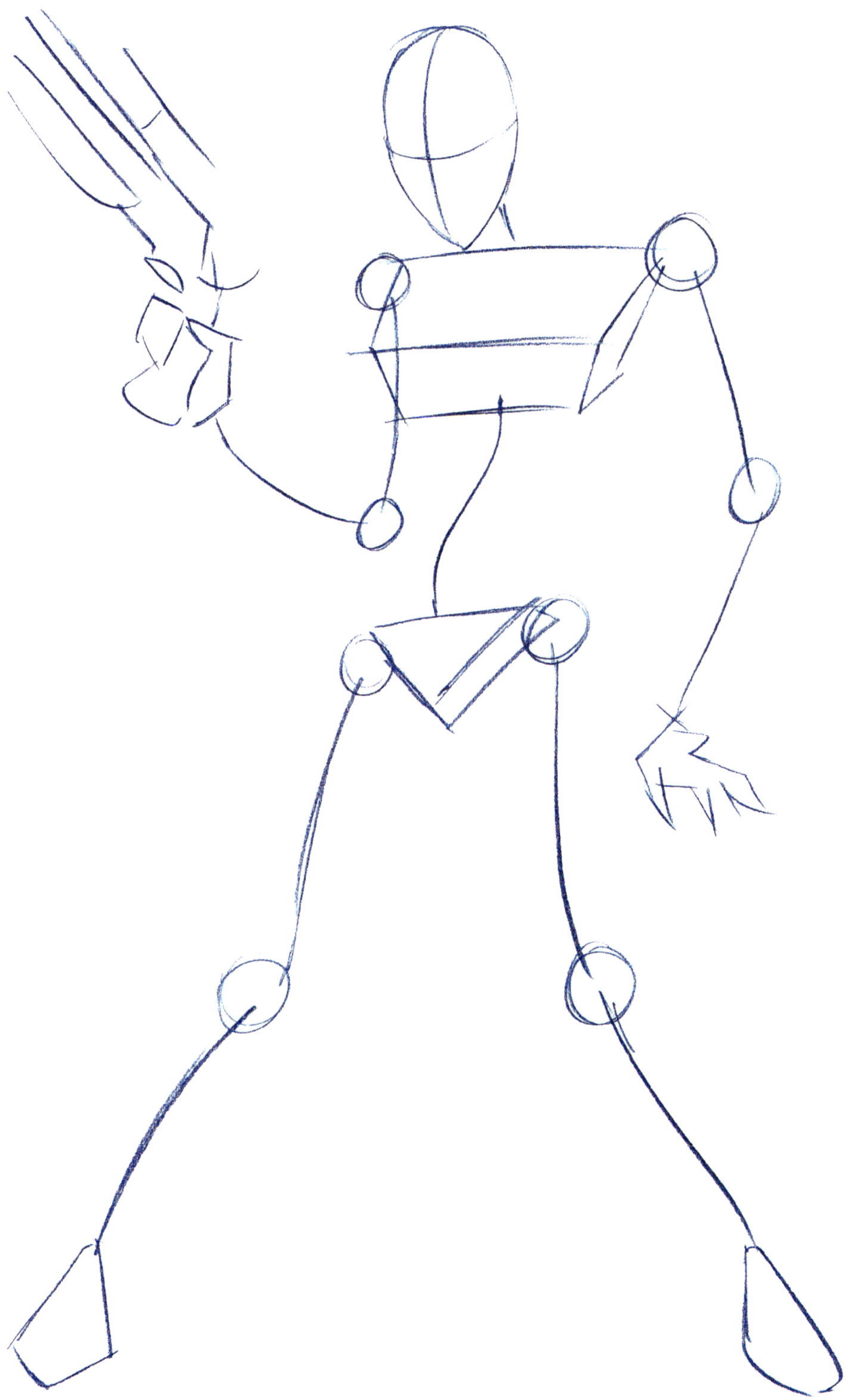

1

Draw the figure with blue pencil: this time choose a dynamic posture that implies movement.

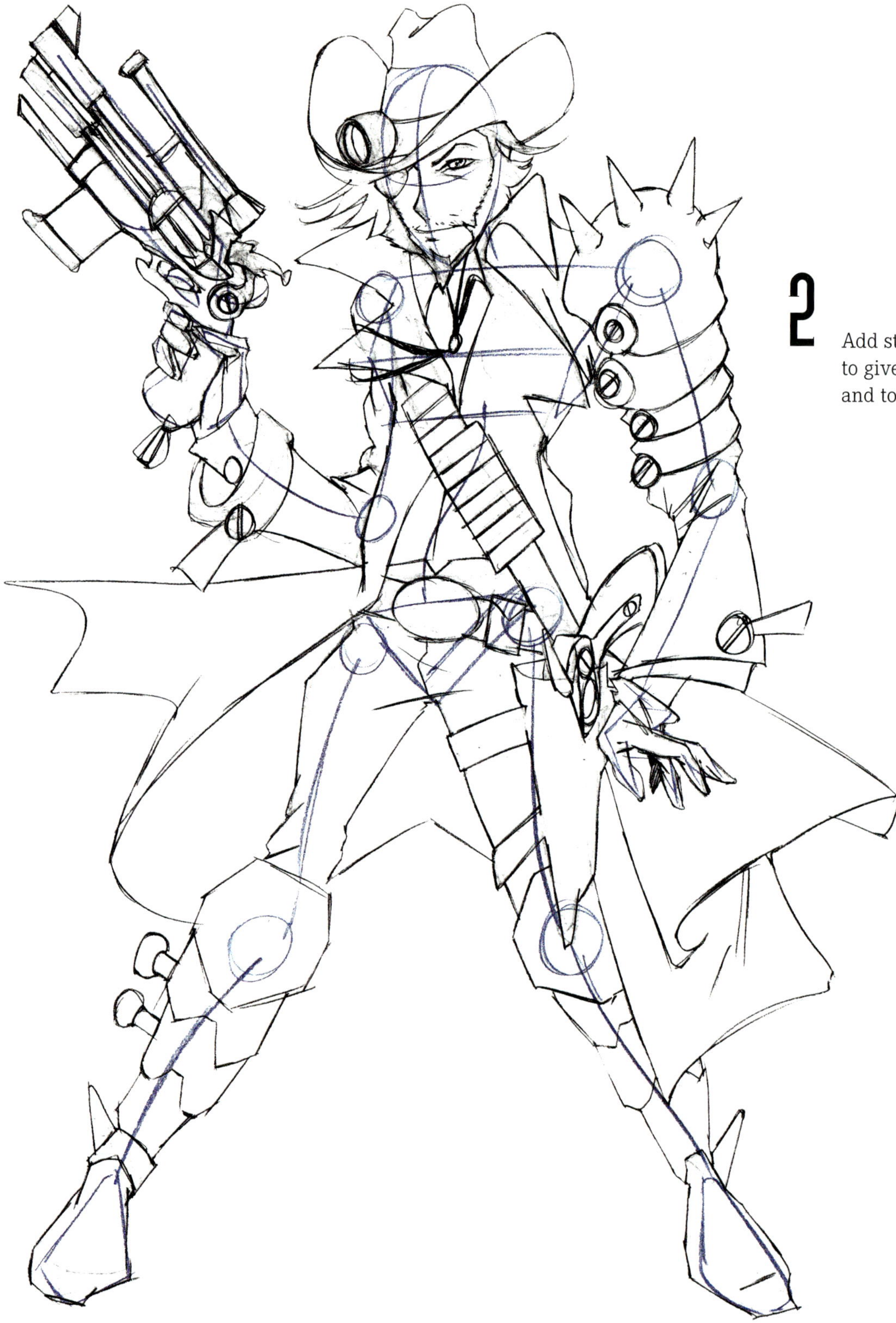

2

Add strokes using a 2H pencil to give the figure consistency and to shape the silhouette.

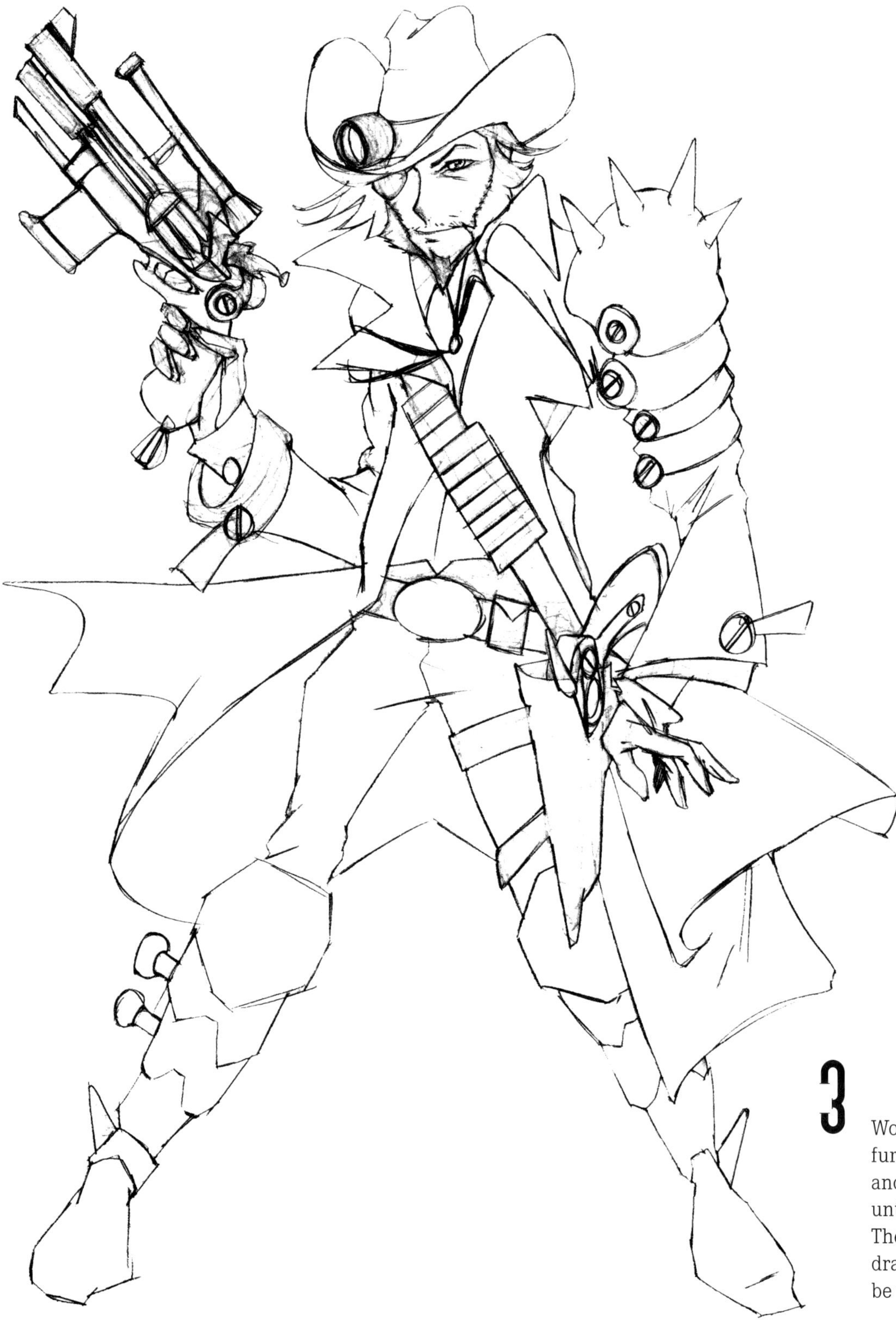

3

Work up the figure and details further with the pencil, removing and cleaning up leftover strokes until the design is ready for inking. The cleaner this stage of the drawing is, the easier it will be to color with your pens.

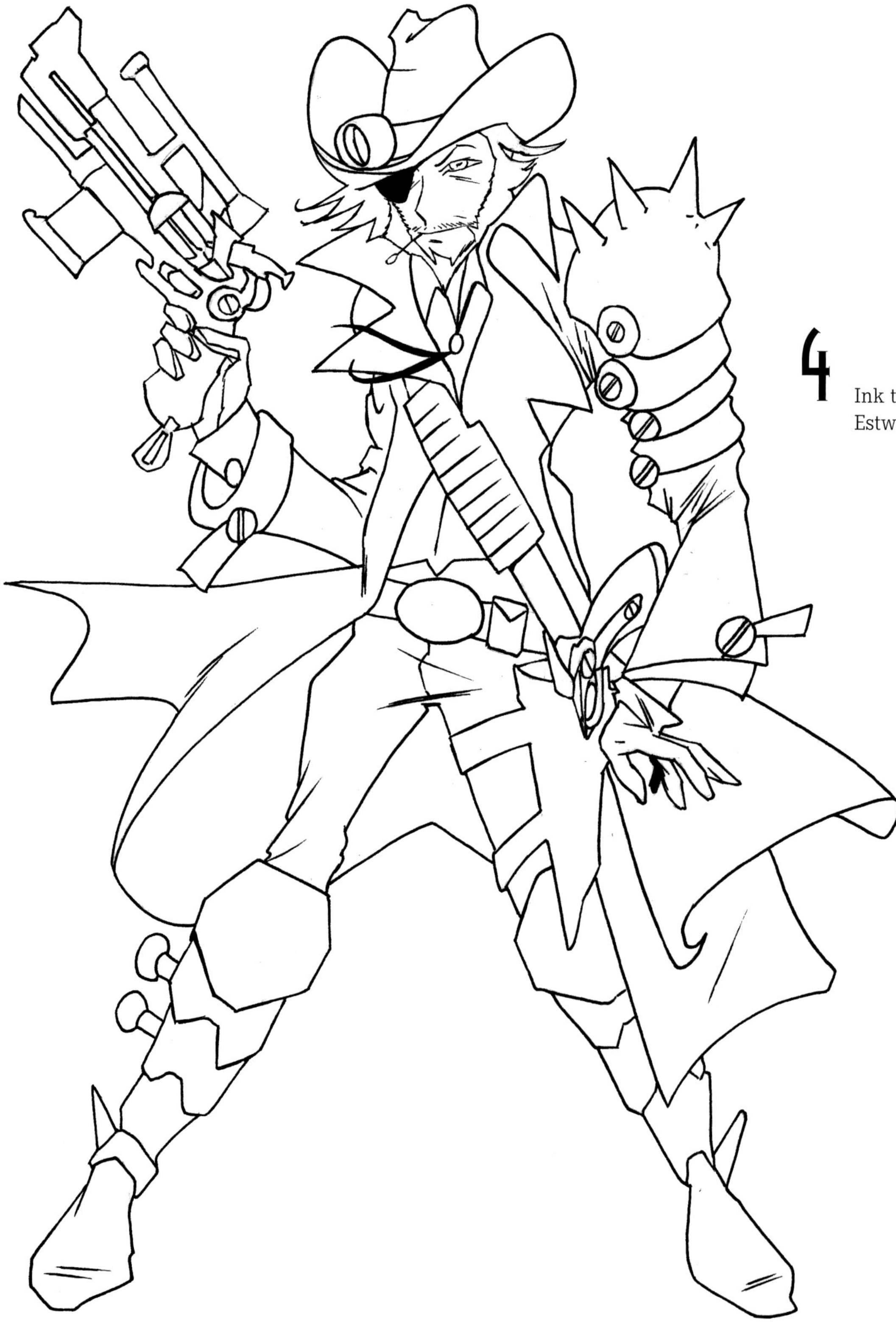

4

Ink the drawing and add Estwood's patch with the pen.

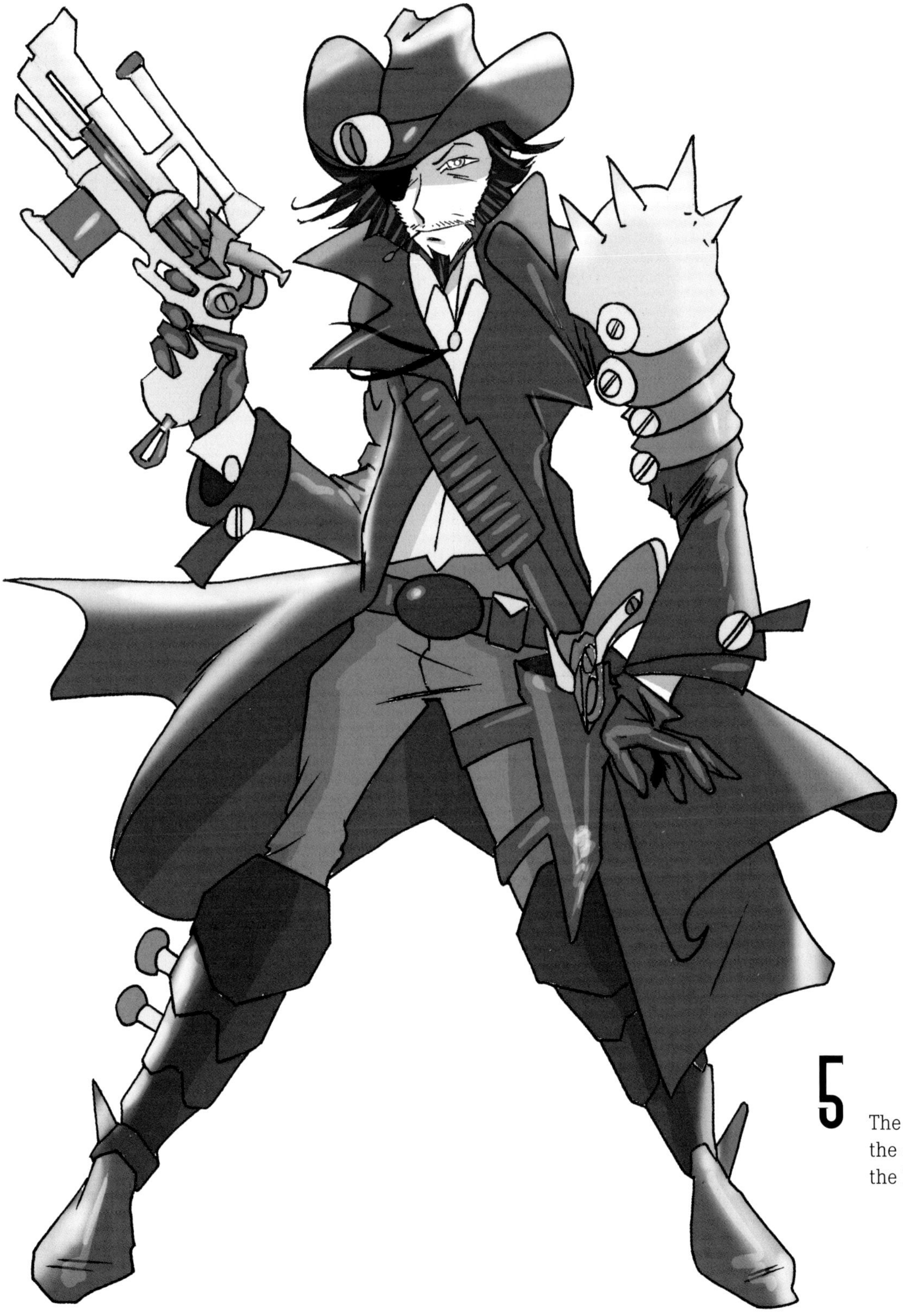

5 The light source is behind the character, filtering through the layers in his coat.

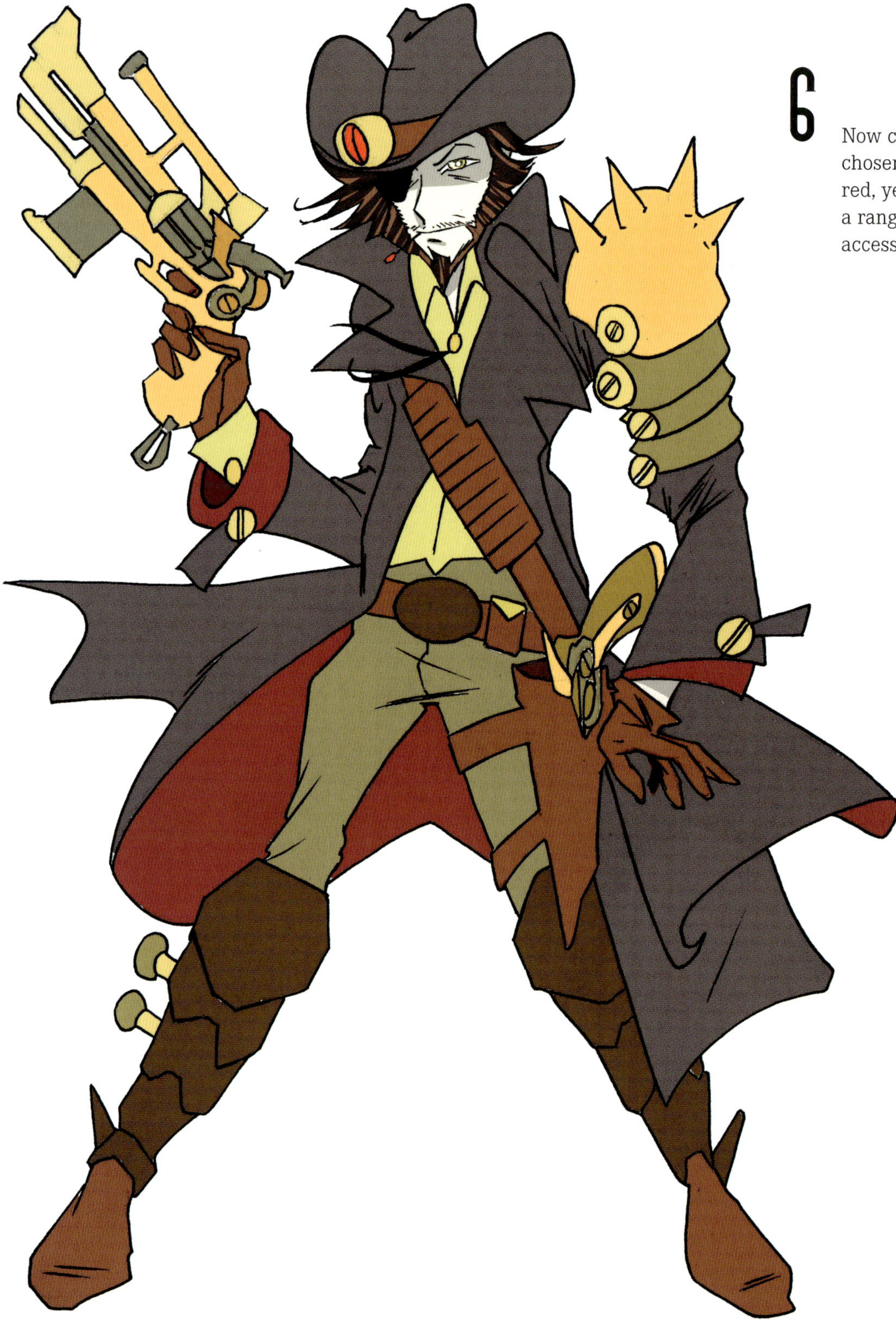

6

Now color the character: I've chosen a combination of gray, red, yellow, and gold, plus a range of browns for the accessories and boots.

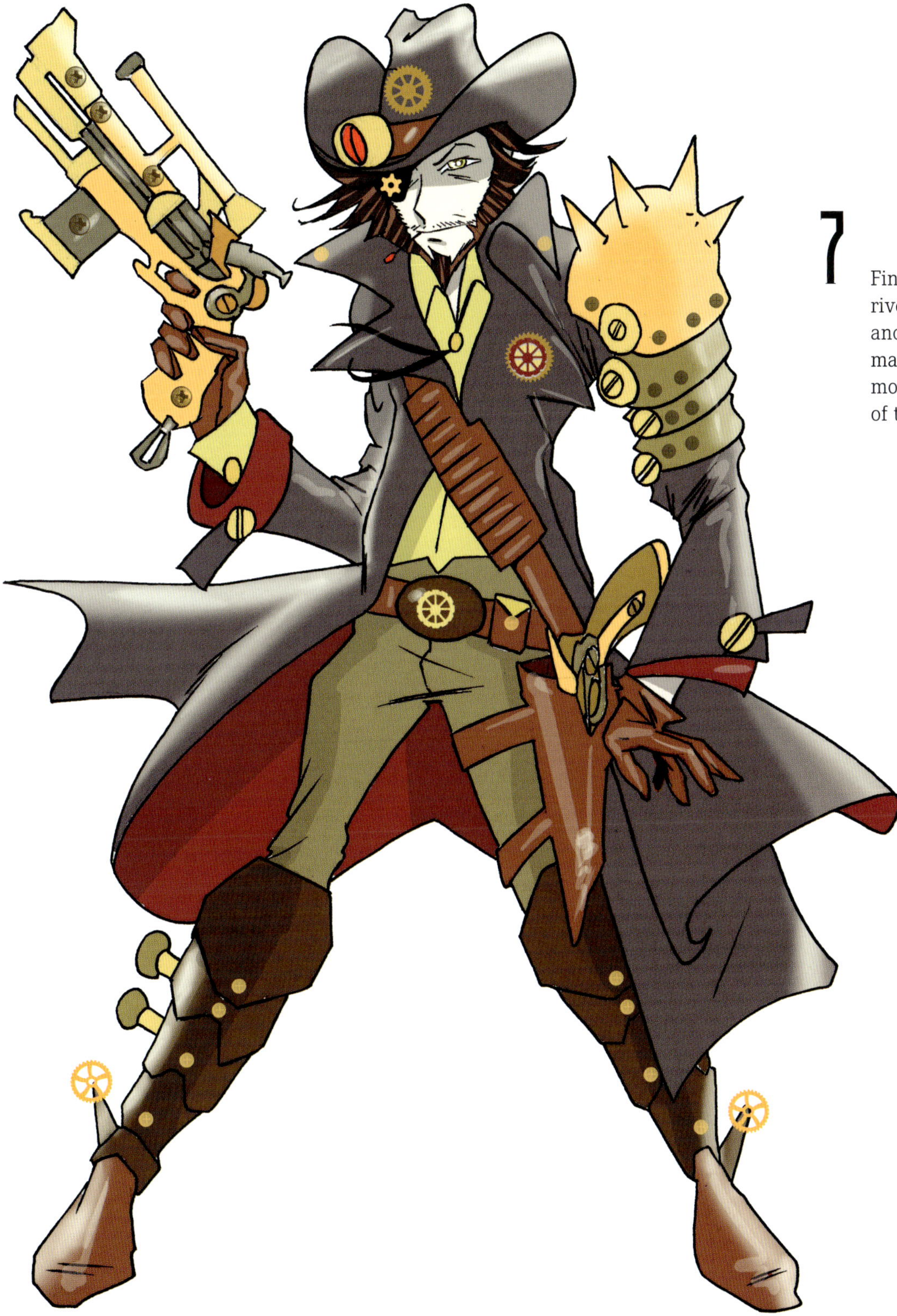

7

Finish by adding the details: rivets and bolts for the suit and some washers for the marshal's plate. Oh, and some more washers for the spurs of this unwavering sheriff.

VAMPIRE

Slovok Callhell was a magnificent alchemist engineer, devoted to finding a cure for his sick wife. However, an unexpected result with one of the drugs turned them both into different beings: they now have to renew their blood continuously, leading people to call them vampires. Slovok achieved immortality at a high price and now lives to find a cure that will restore his and his wife's mortality.

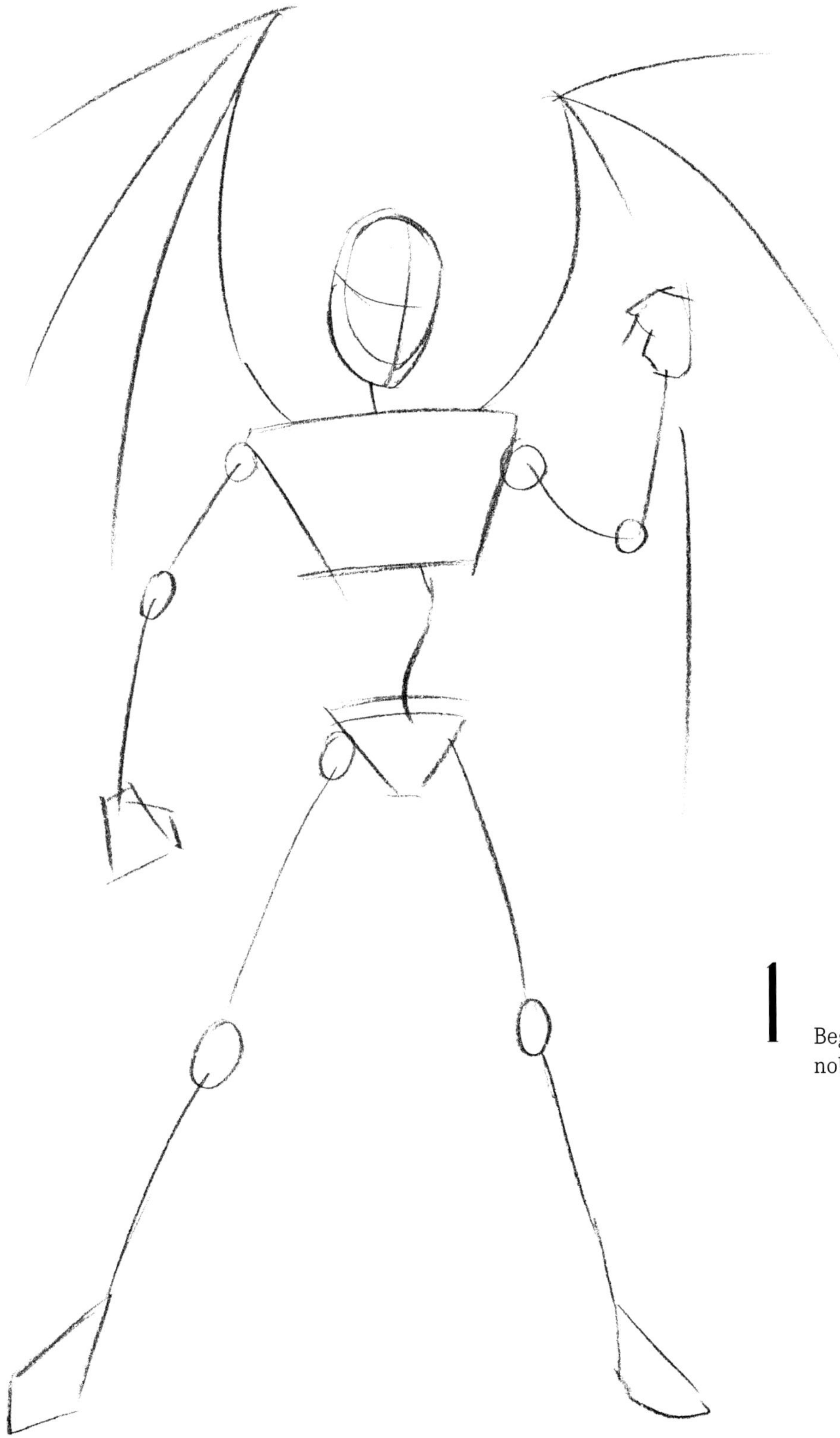

1

Begin by preparing the base of this noble character in blue pencil.

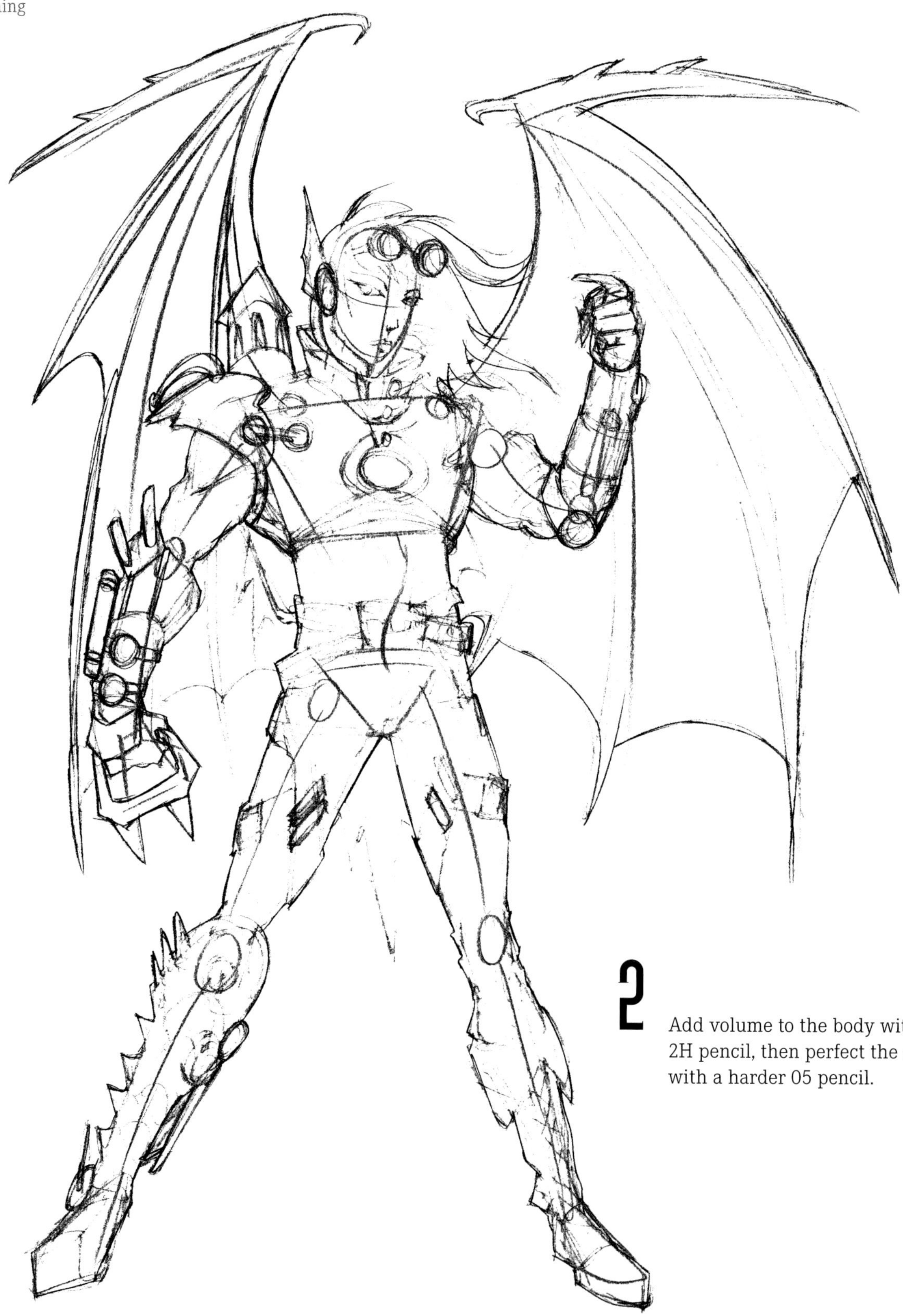

2

Add volume to the body with a 2H pencil, then perfect the details with a harder 05 pencil.

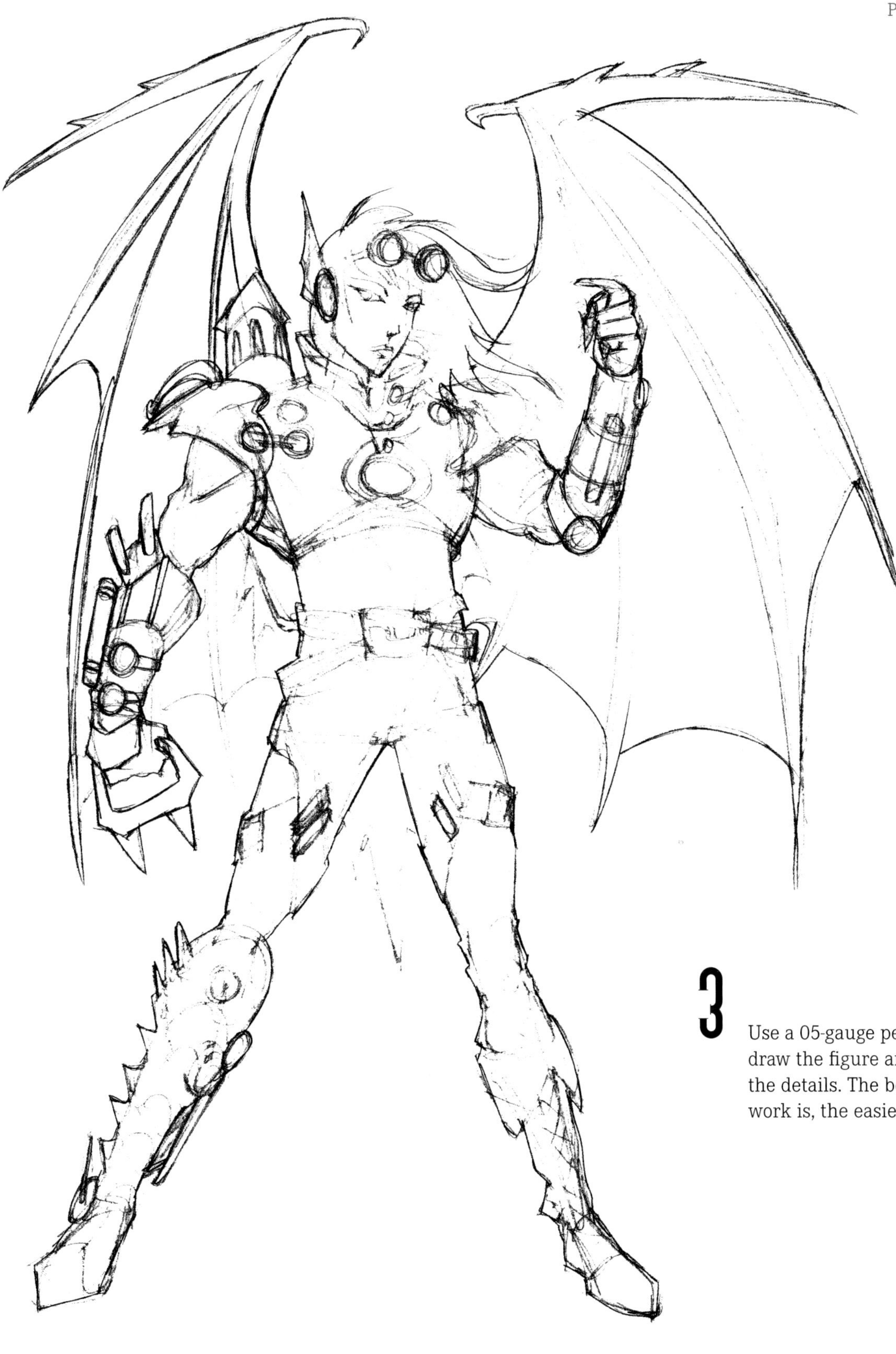

3

Use a 05-gauge pencil to completely draw the figure and give form to the details. The better your pencil work is, the easier it will be to ink.

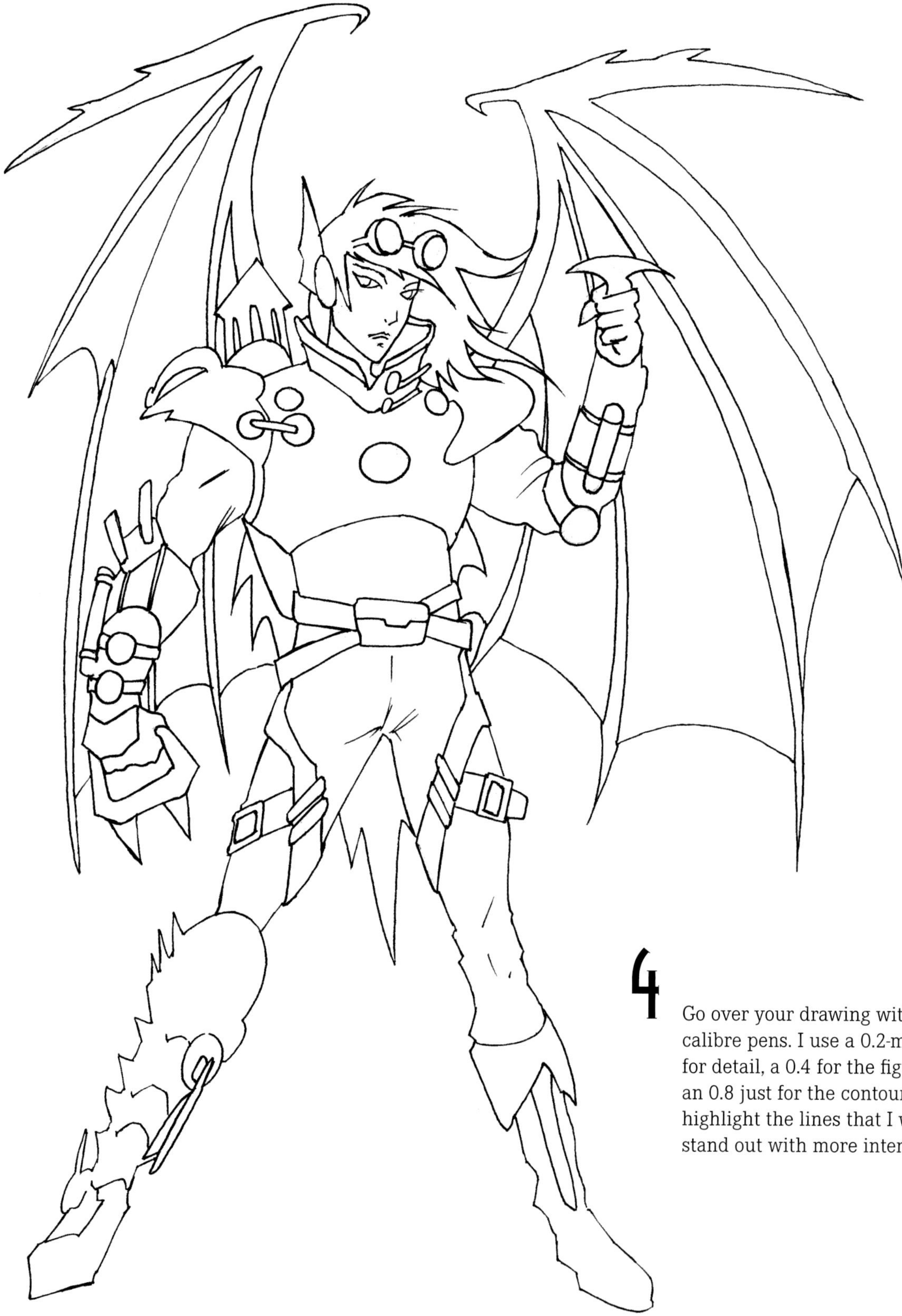

4

Go over your drawing with various calibre pens. I use a 0.2-mm pen for detail, a 0.4 for the figure, and an 0.8 just for the contour and to highlight the lines that I want to stand out with more intensity.

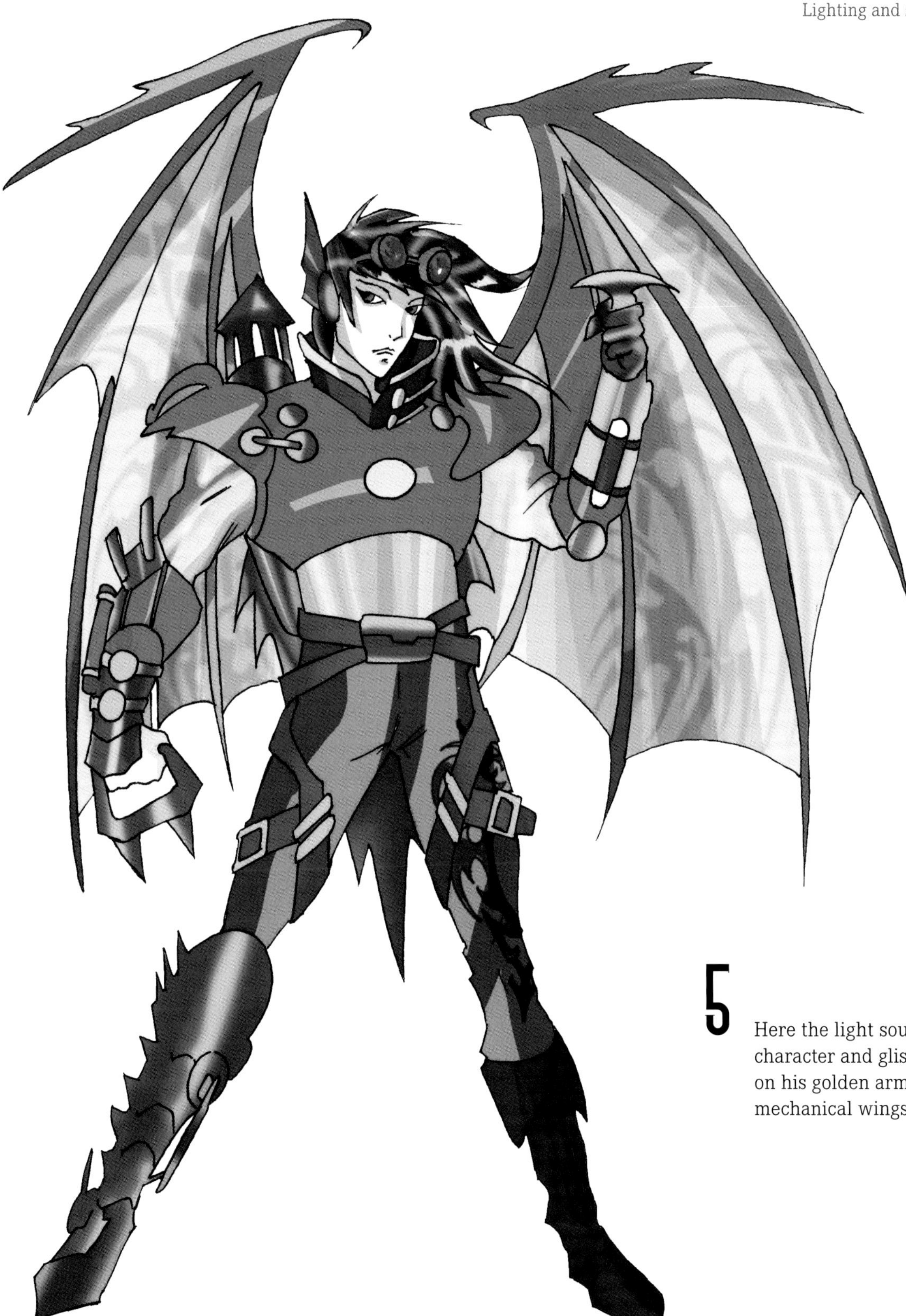

5

Here the light source is above the character and glistens beautifully on his golden armor and mechanical wings.

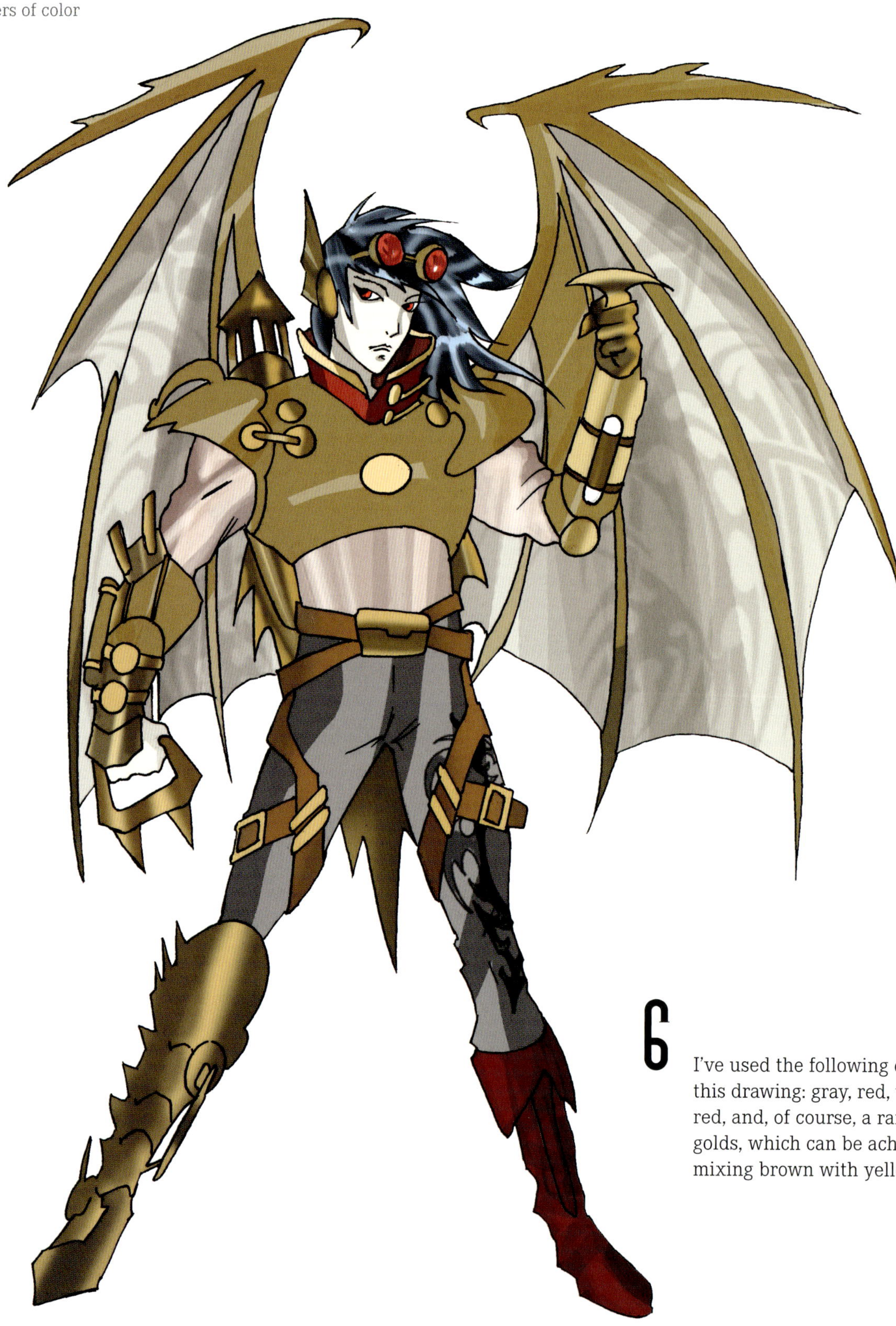

6

I've used the following colors for this drawing: gray, red, very light red, and, of course, a range of golds, which can be achieved by mixing brown with yellow.

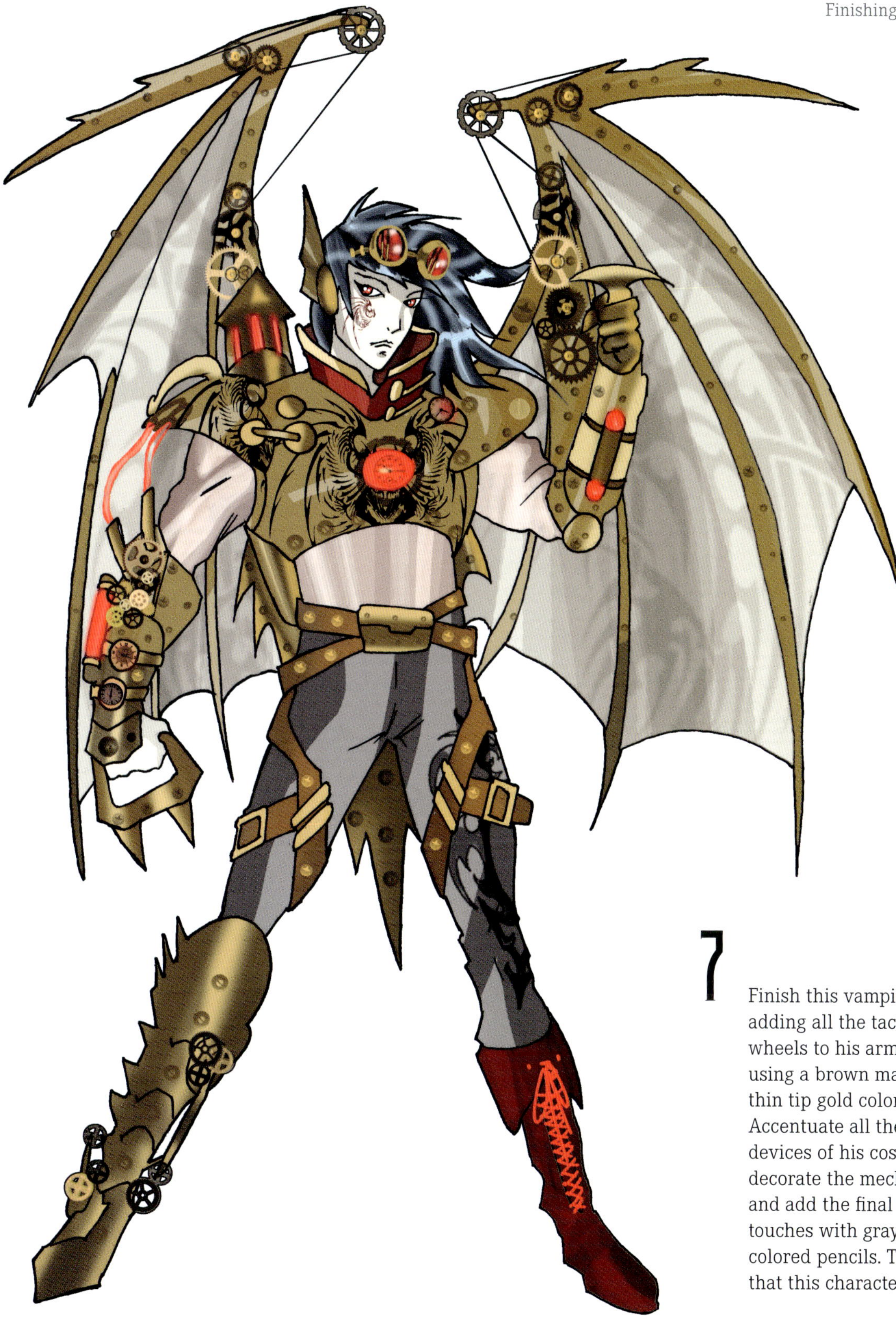

7

Finish this vampire figure by adding all the tacks and gear wheels to his armor and clothes using a brown marker and a thin tip gold color highlighter. Accentuate all the wires and devices of his costume in red, decorate the mechanical wings, and add the final highlights and touches with gray and white colored pencils. There is no doubt that this character looks stunning!

DETECTIVE

Ortiphus Corbin is the kingdom's incredible detective. Unmatched, he is the most effective of all the investigators in the service of the royal police. With his sophisticated testing equipment, Ortiphus can find any clue, no matter how small it may be.

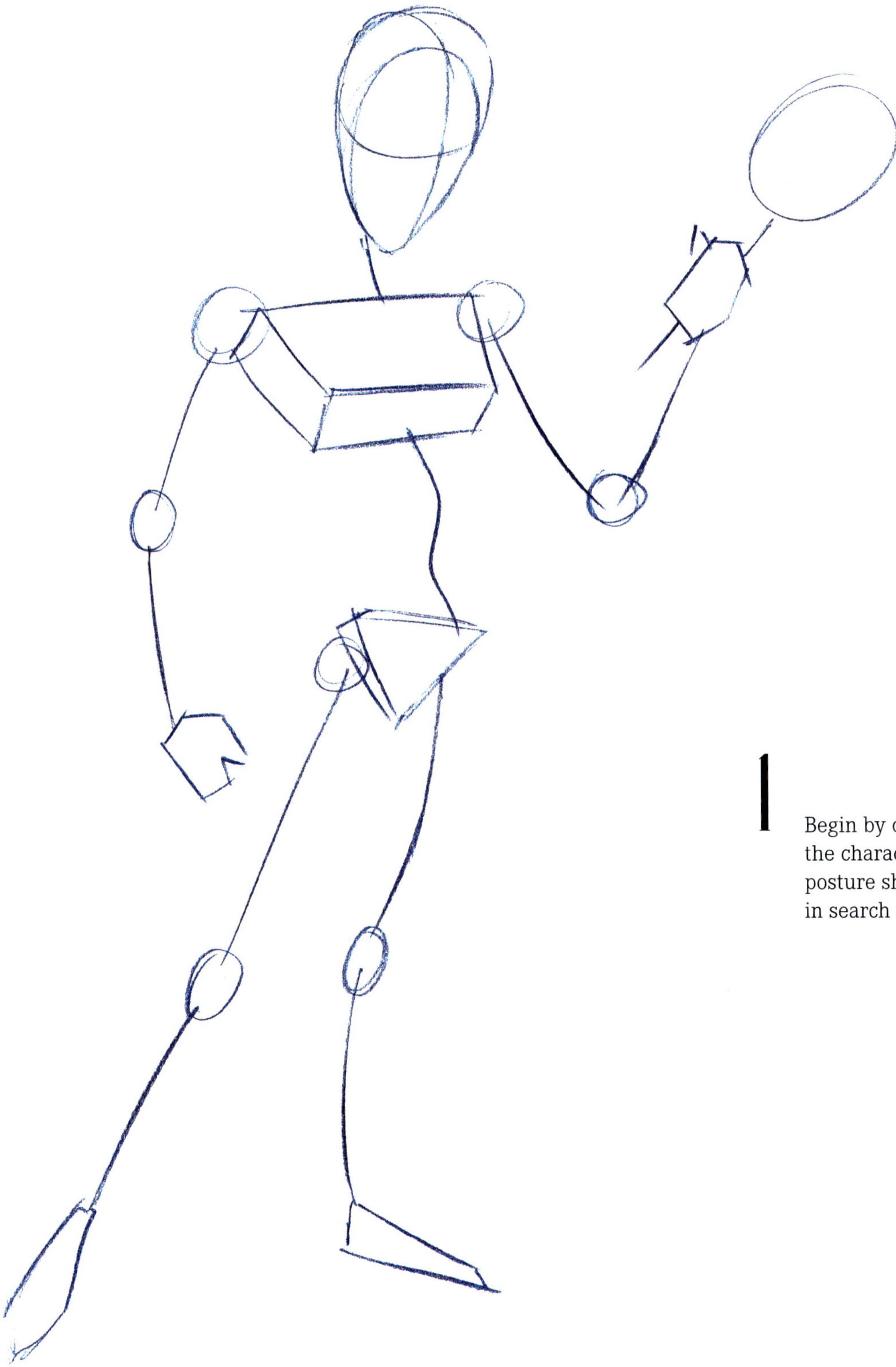

1

Begin by drawing the base of the character in blue pencil: this posture shows Ortiphus Corbin in search of evidence.

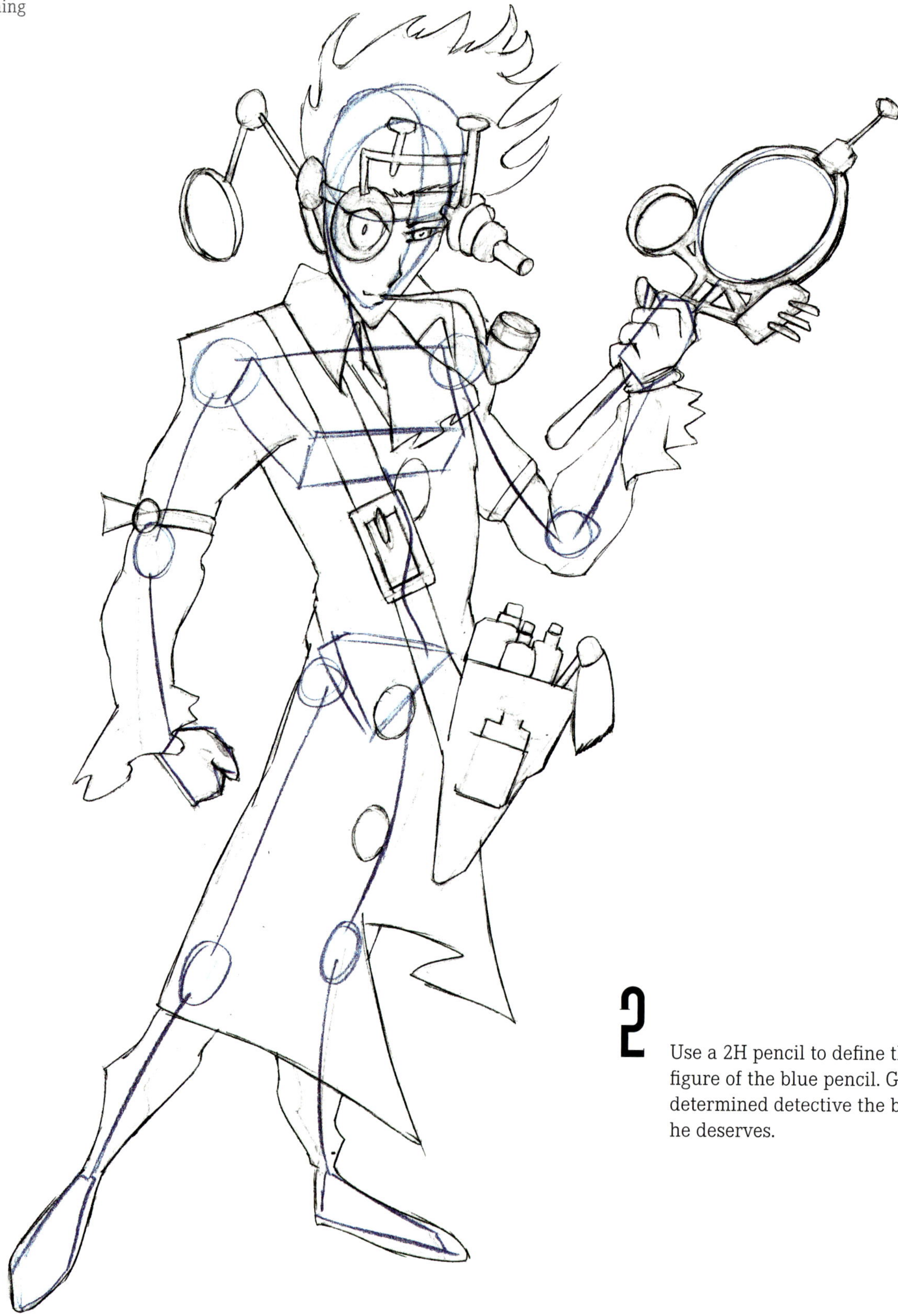

2

Use a 2H pencil to define the figure of the blue pencil. Give this determined detective the bearing he deserves.

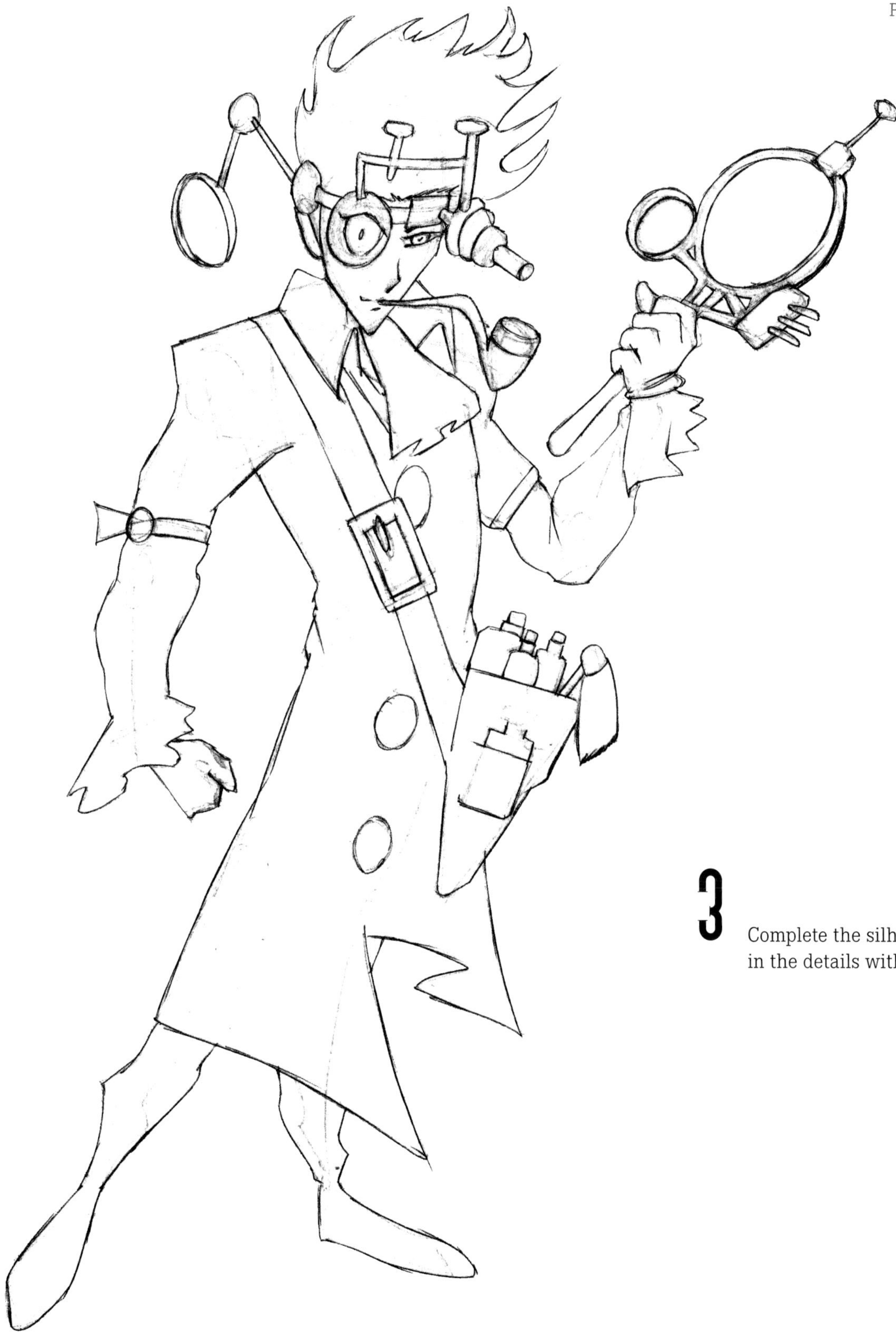

3

Complete the silhouette and work in the details with a 05 pencil.

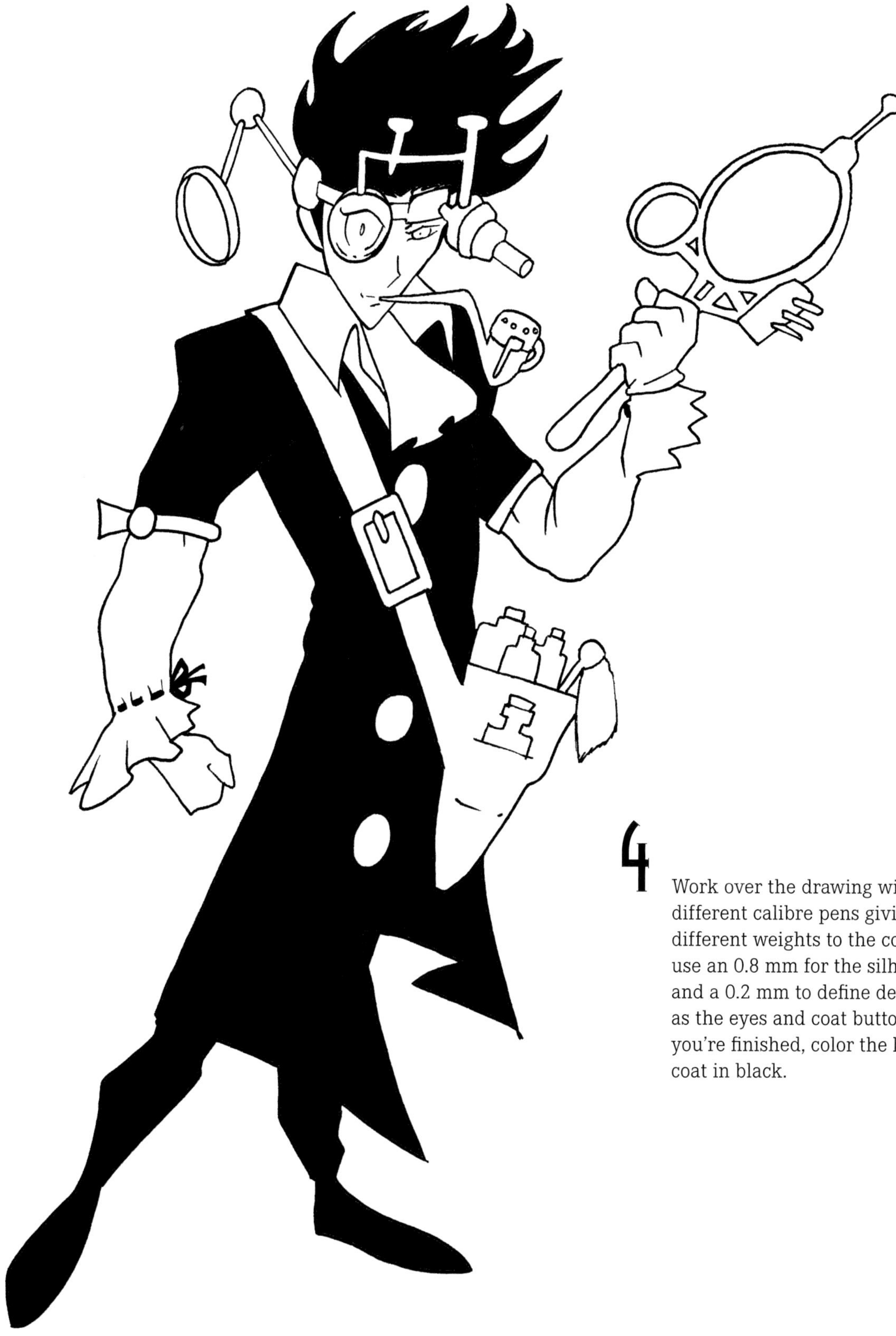

4

Work over the drawing with different calibre pens giving different weights to the contours: use an 0.8 mm for the silhouette, and a 0.2 mm to define details such as the eyes and coat buttons. When you're finished, color the hair and coat in black.

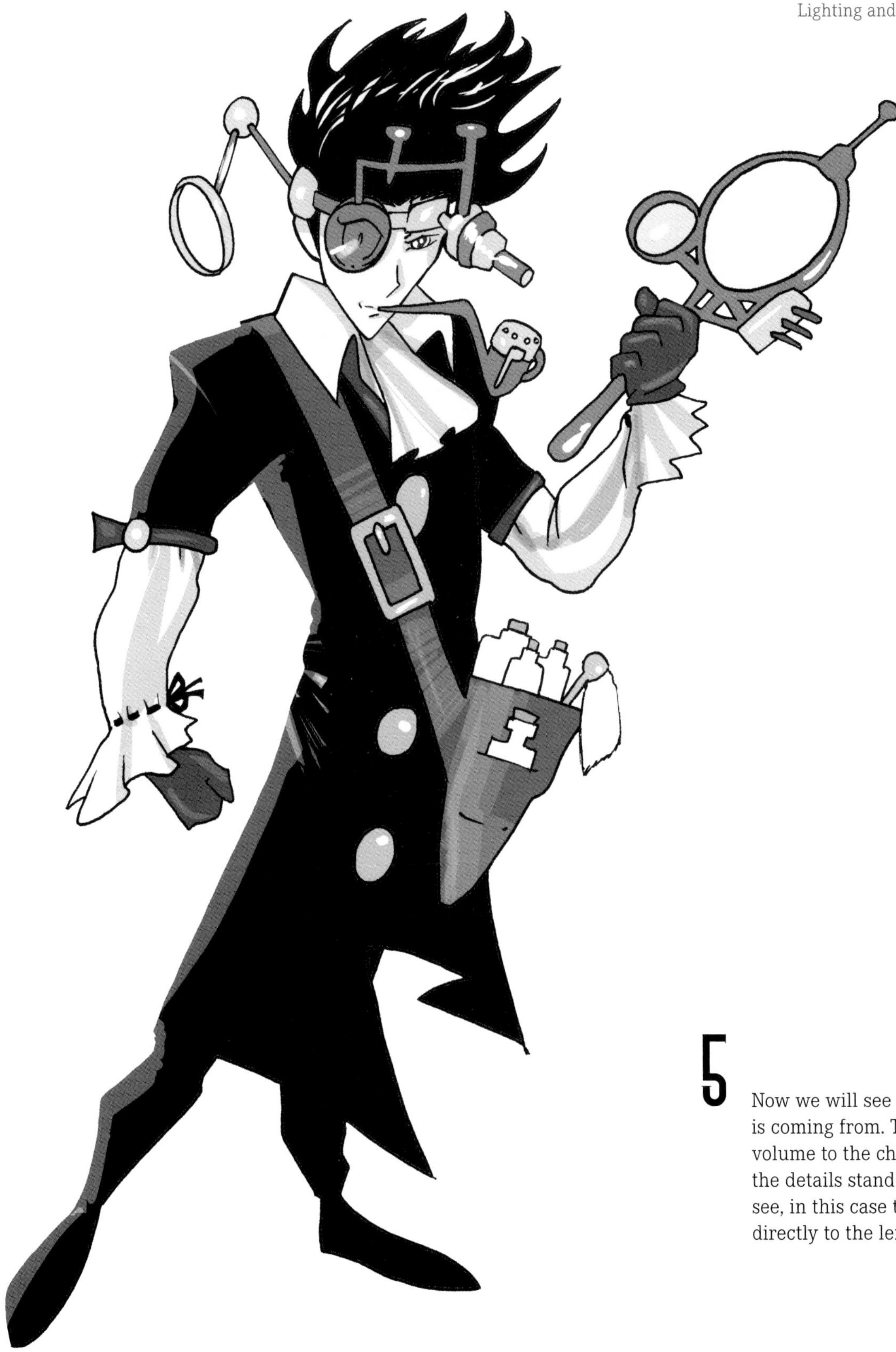

5

Now we will see where the light is coming from. This helps to add volume to the character and make the details stand out. As you can see, in this case the light source is directly to the left of the character.

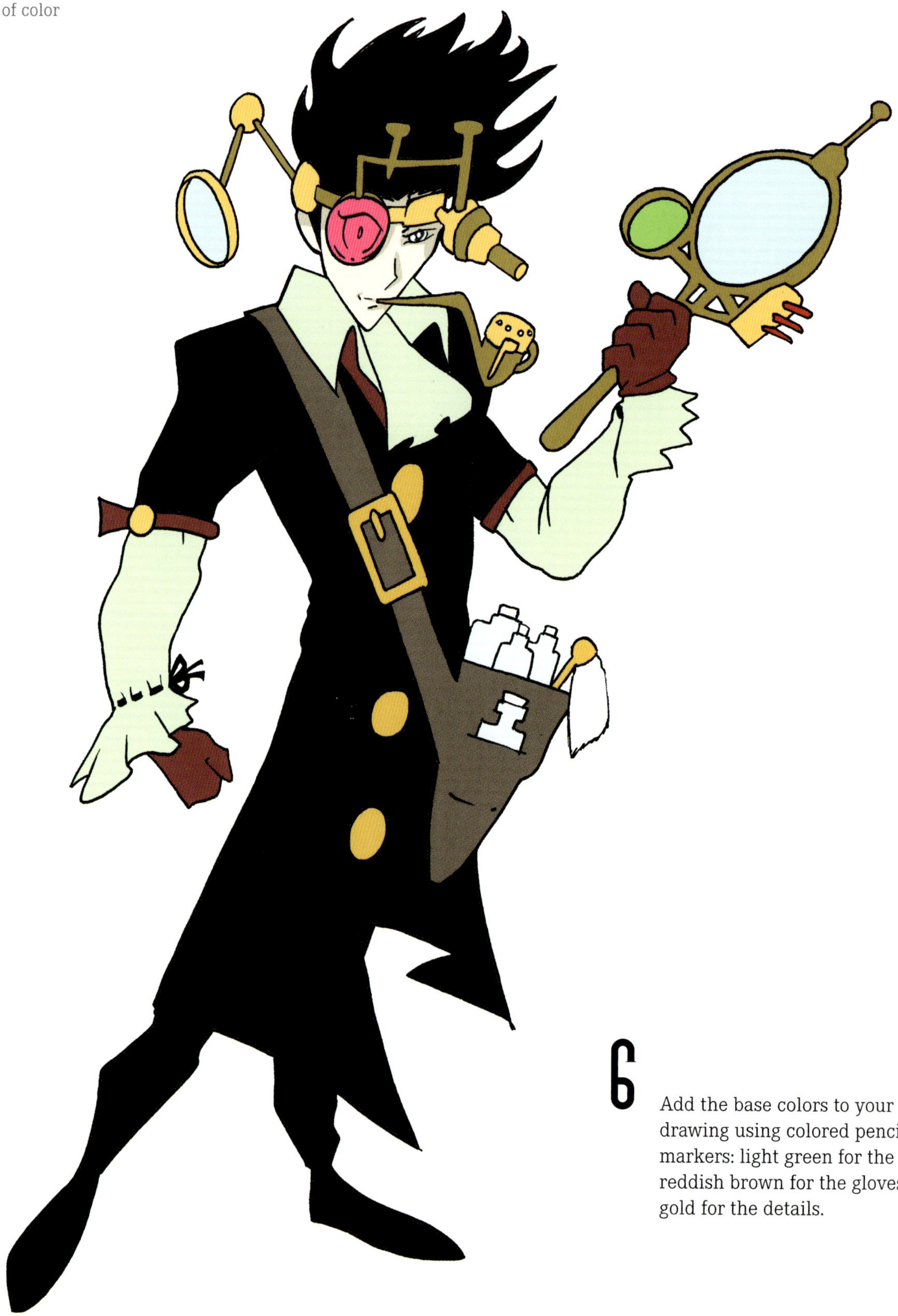

6

Add the base colors to your drawing using colored pencils and markers: light green for the shirt, reddish brown for the gloves, and gold for the details.

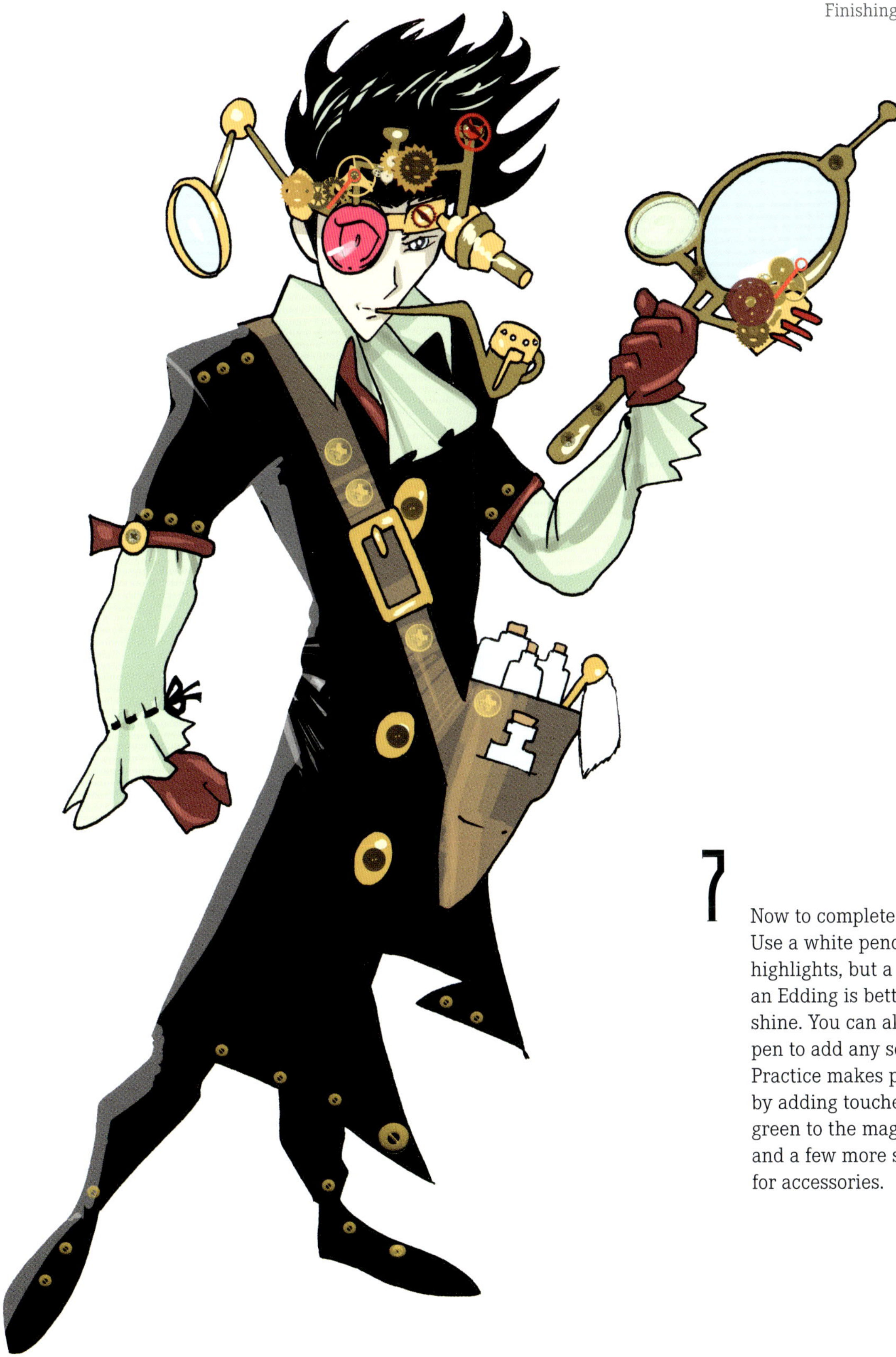

7

Now to complete the drawing. Use a white pencil for the general highlights, but a gold pen such as an Edding is better for the gold shine. You can also use this color pen to add any screws or washers. Practice makes perfect! Finish by adding touches of fuchsia and green to the magnifying glasses and a few more screws for accessories.

FEMALE MECHANIC

Tina Bolt works in a city workshop, the Grease Monkey. There is no mechanical device or robot that cannot be repaired in her beloved workshop. Tina is the best at fixing jet steam systems ... and knows how to leave things looking as though they've just come out of the factory!

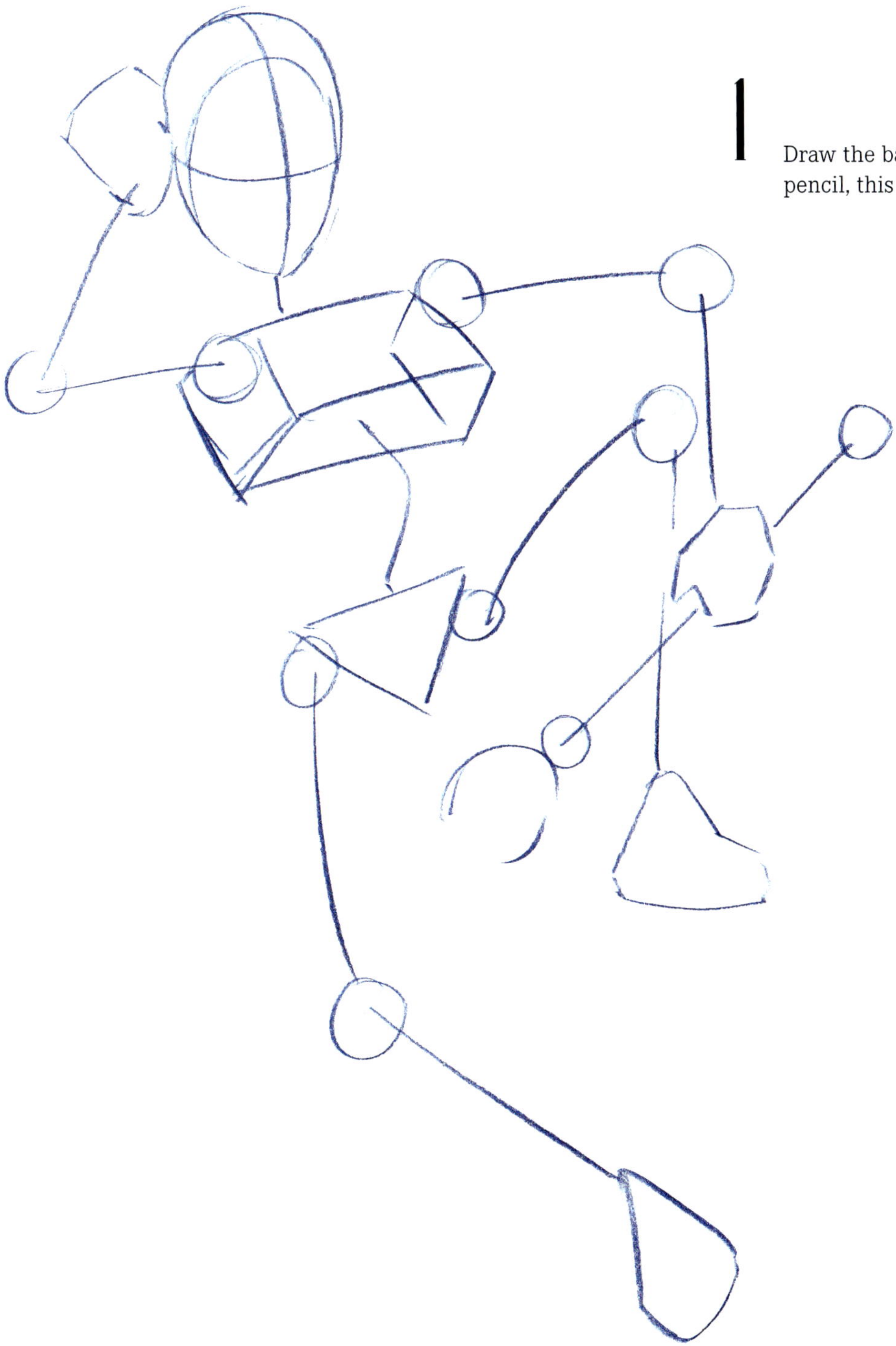

1

Draw the basis of your girl in blue pencil, this time in a relaxed pose.

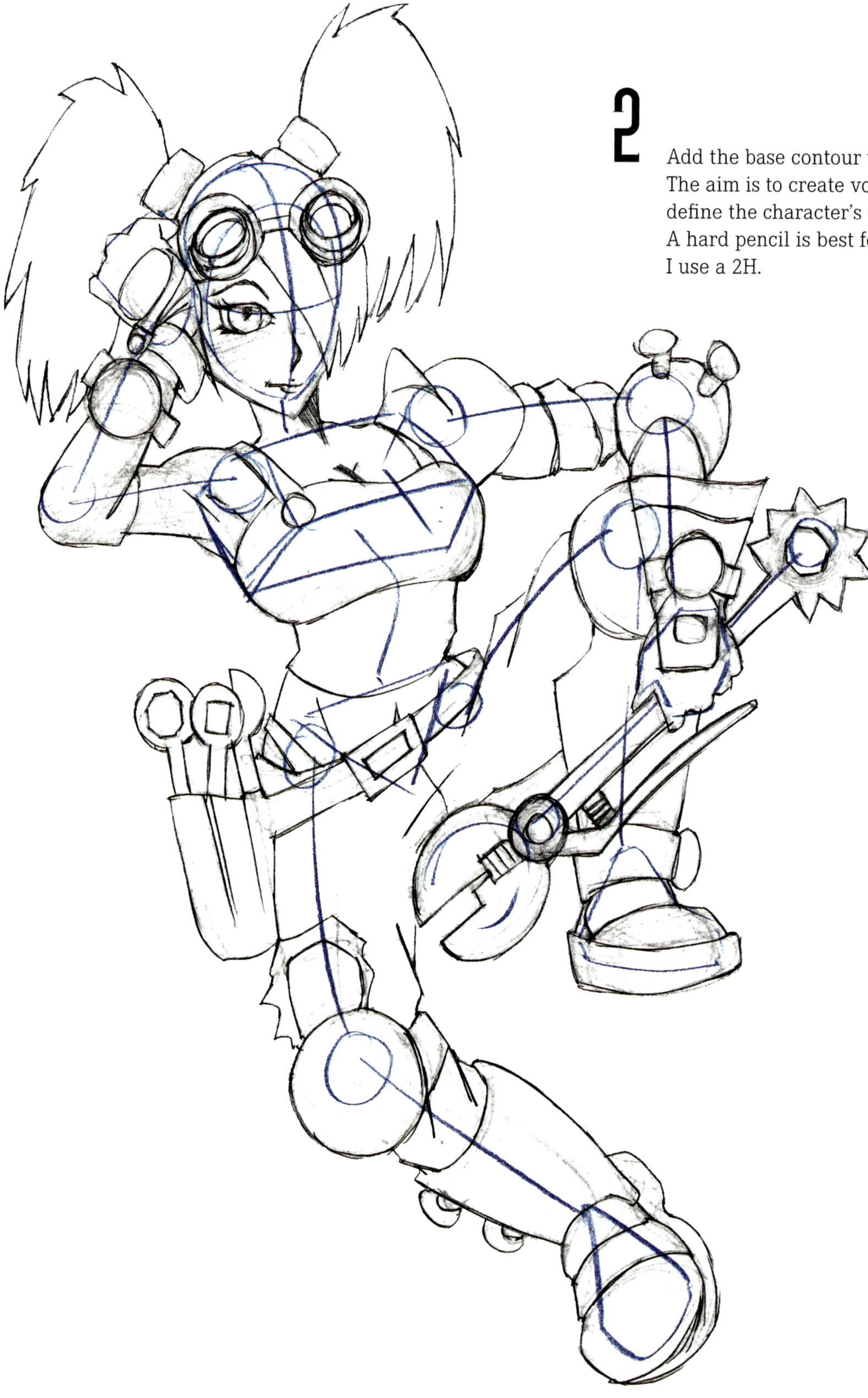

2

Add the base contour to the figure. The aim is to create volume and define the character's appearance. A hard pencil is best for this. I use a 2H.

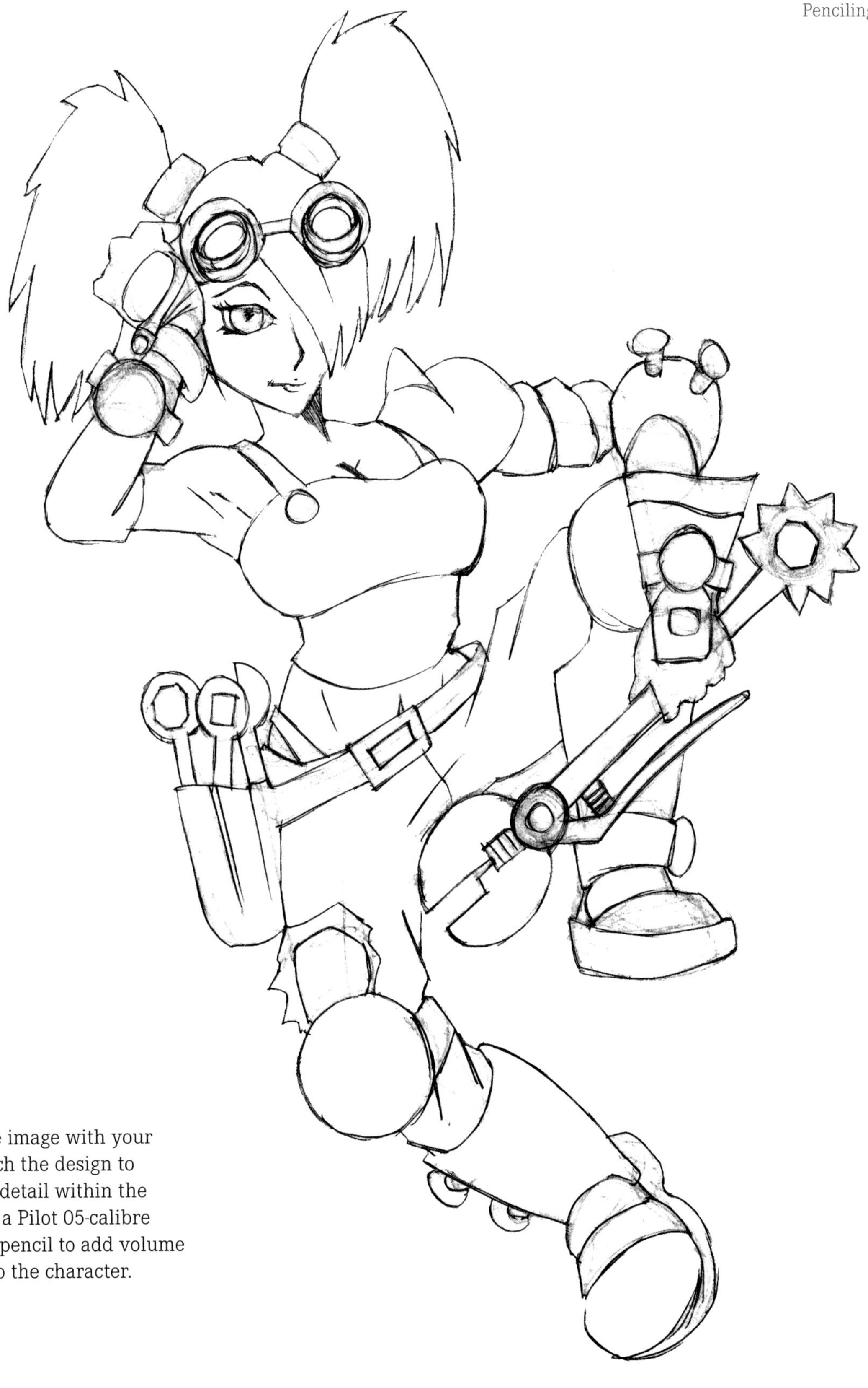

3

Work up the image with your pencil. Sketch the design to incorporate detail within the figure: I use a Pilot 05-calibre mechanical pencil to add volume and shape to the character.

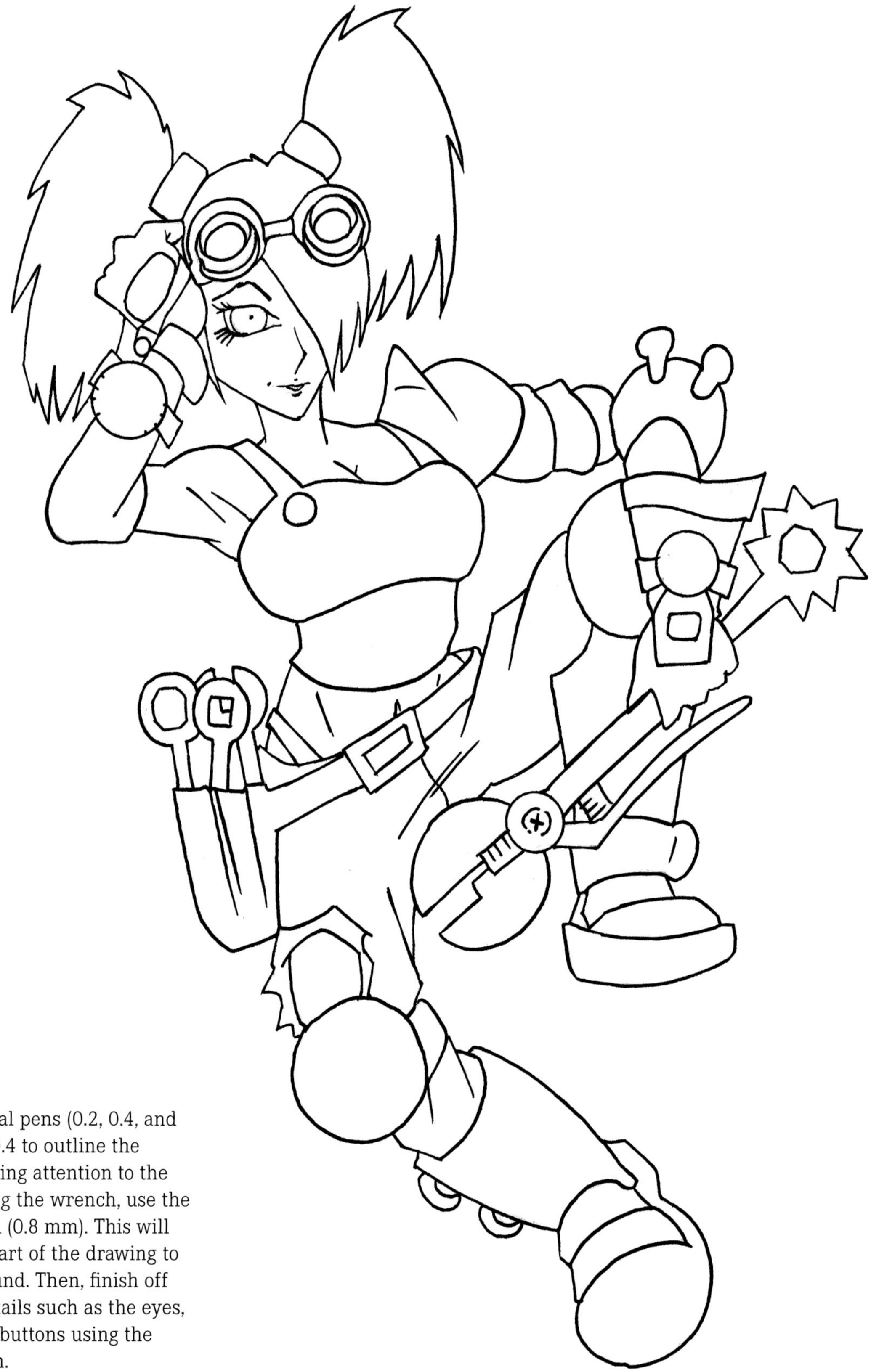

4

Use the usual pens (0.2, 0.4, and 0.8 mm): a 0.4 to outline the figure. To bring attention to the hand holding the wrench, use the thickest pen (0.8 mm). This will bring that part of the drawing to the foreground. Then, finish off with the details such as the eyes, mouth, and buttons using the thinnest pen.

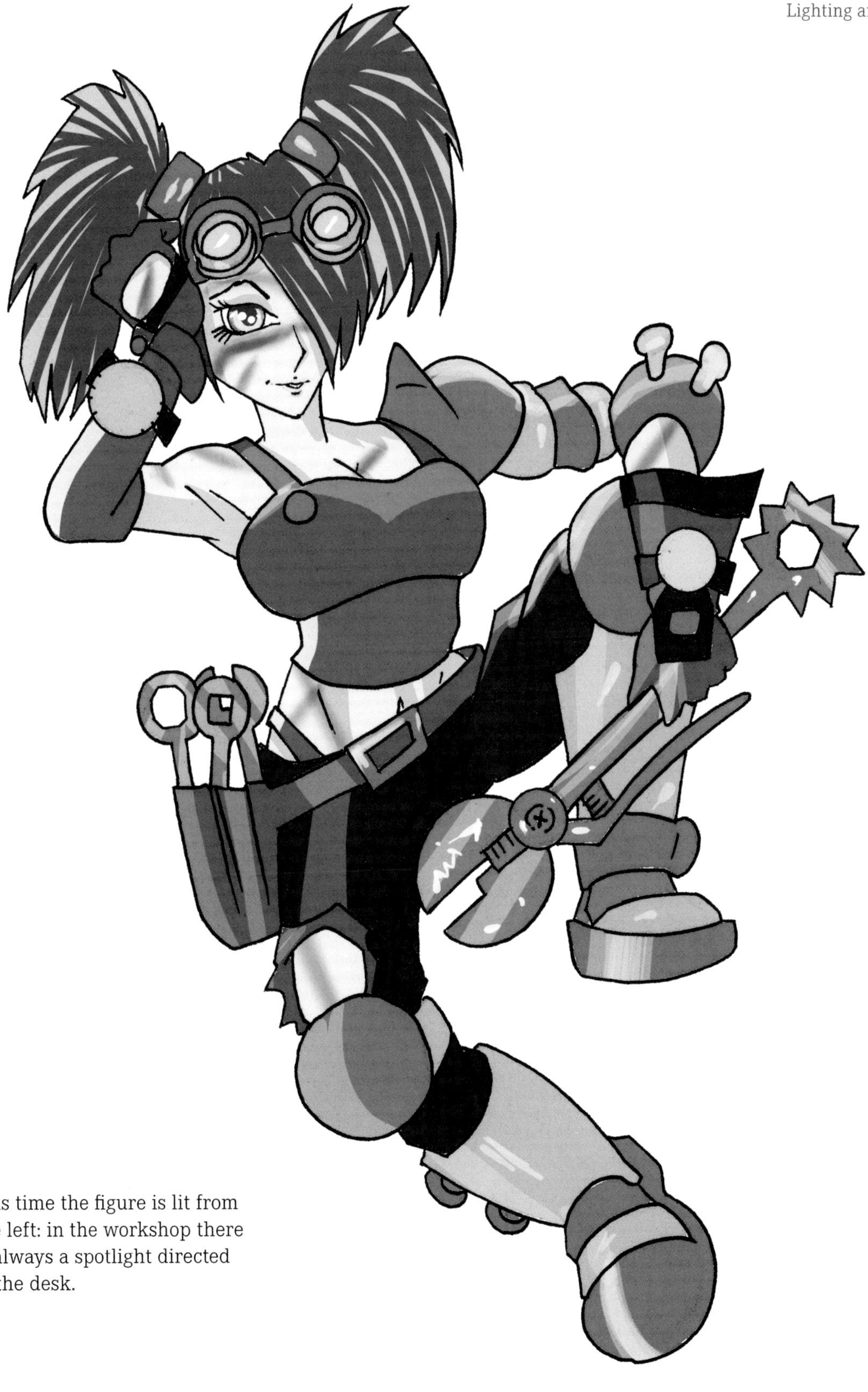

5

This time the figure is lit from the left: in the workshop there is always a spotlight directed at the desk.

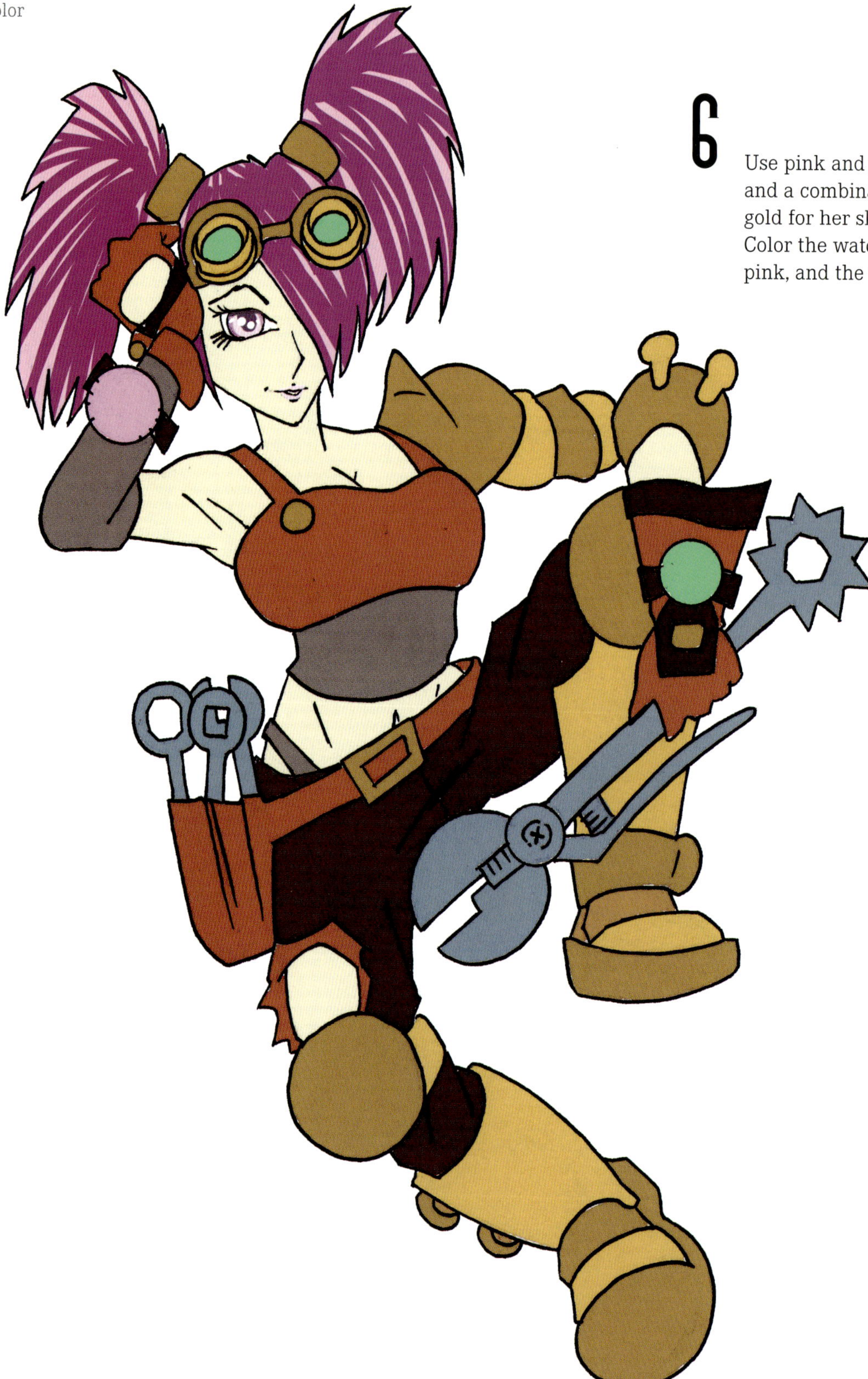

6

Use pink and purple for the hair, and a combination of orange and gold for her sleeve and boots. Color the watches in green and pink, and the wrenches in blue.

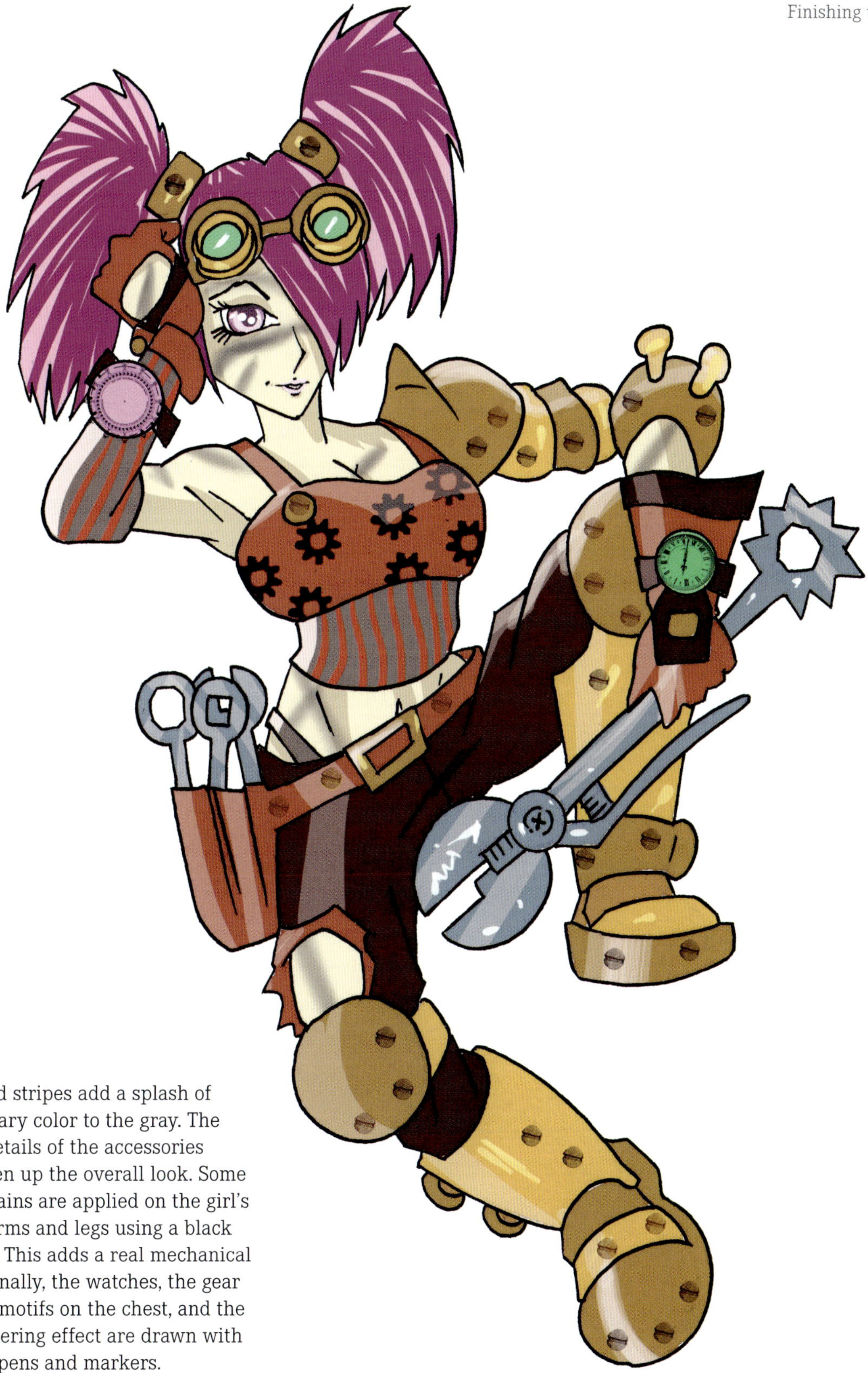

7

The red stripes add a splash of necessary color to the gray. The gold details of the accessories brighten up the overall look. Some soot stains are applied on the girl's face, arms and legs using a black pencil. This adds a real mechanical feel. Finally, the watches, the gear wheel motifs on the chest, and the shimmering effect are drawn with brush pens and markers.

FEMALE VAMPIRE

Lorna Callhell was certainly a brilliant woman in her time, a doctor and expert in vaccinations for all types of diseases ... all but one: her own. When she was young, she contracted a disease, which worsened over the years, slowly extinguishing her life ... until one day her husband, a great alchemist, developed a cure for it. The result was not as expected, however, and the drug transformed her into a vampire.

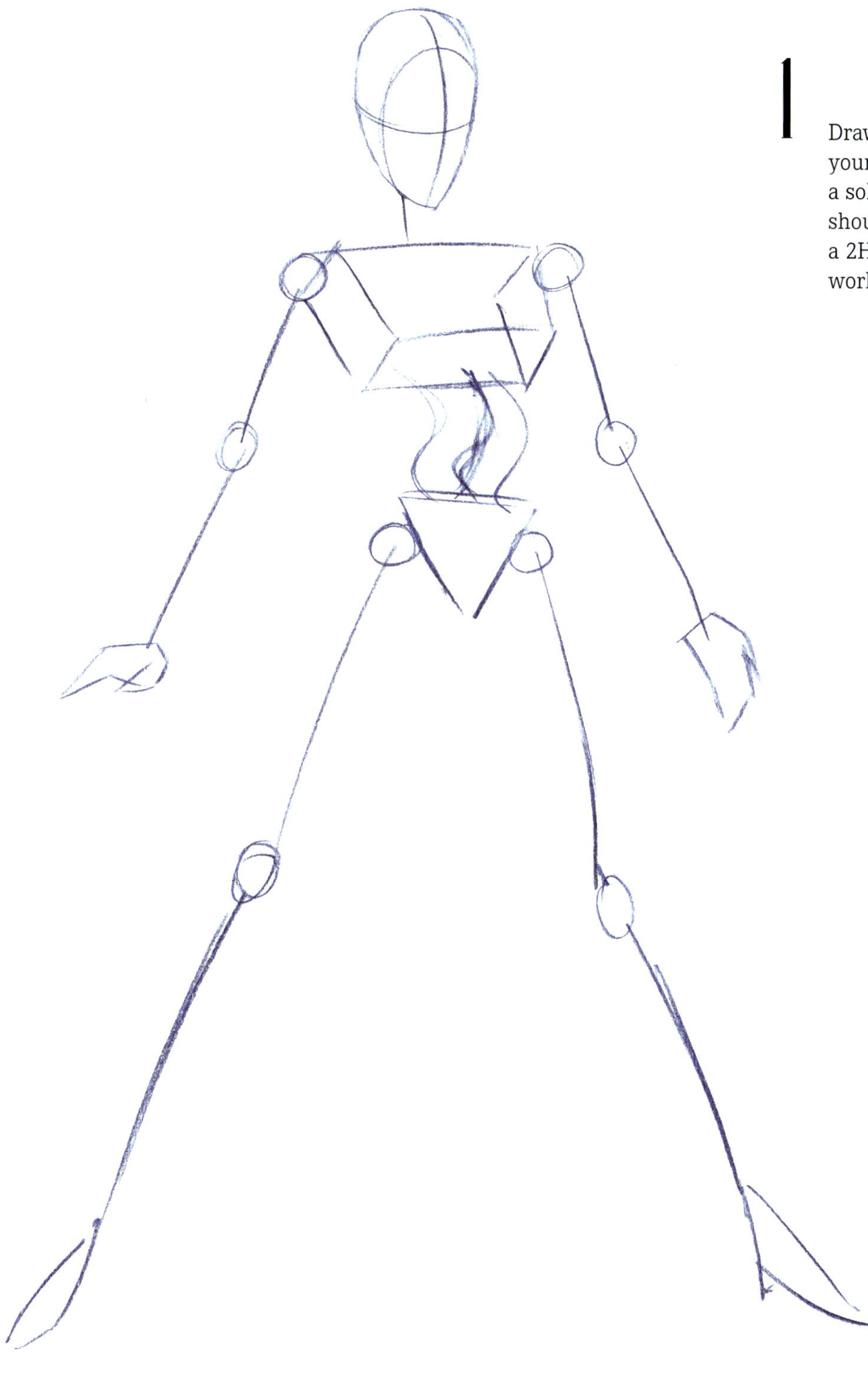

1

Draw the shape that will become your lady with a blue pencil, in a solemn pose. With practice you should be able to do this with a 2H pencil, but for the moment work with the blue.

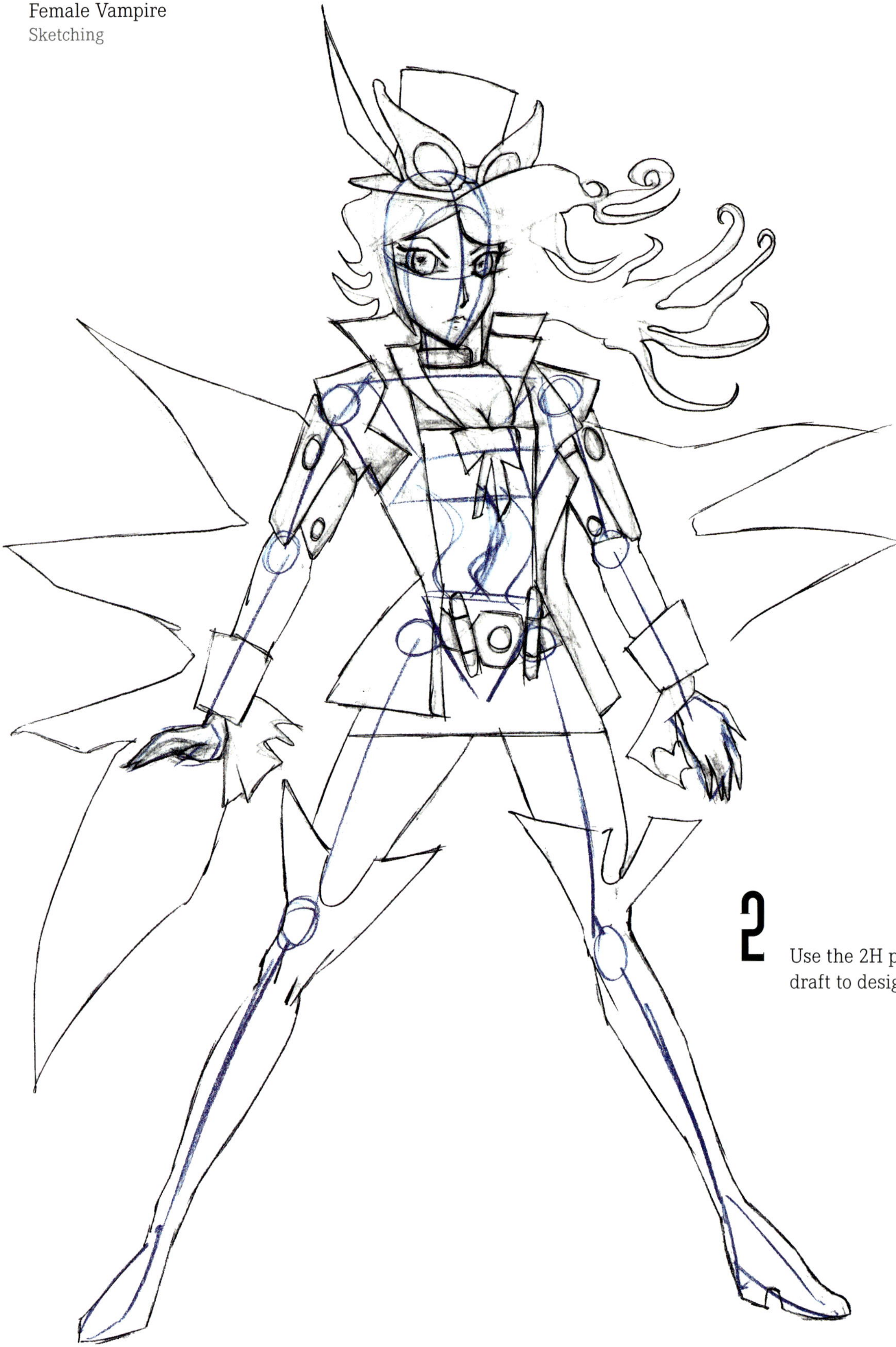

2 Use the 2H pencil in your blue draft to design the figure.

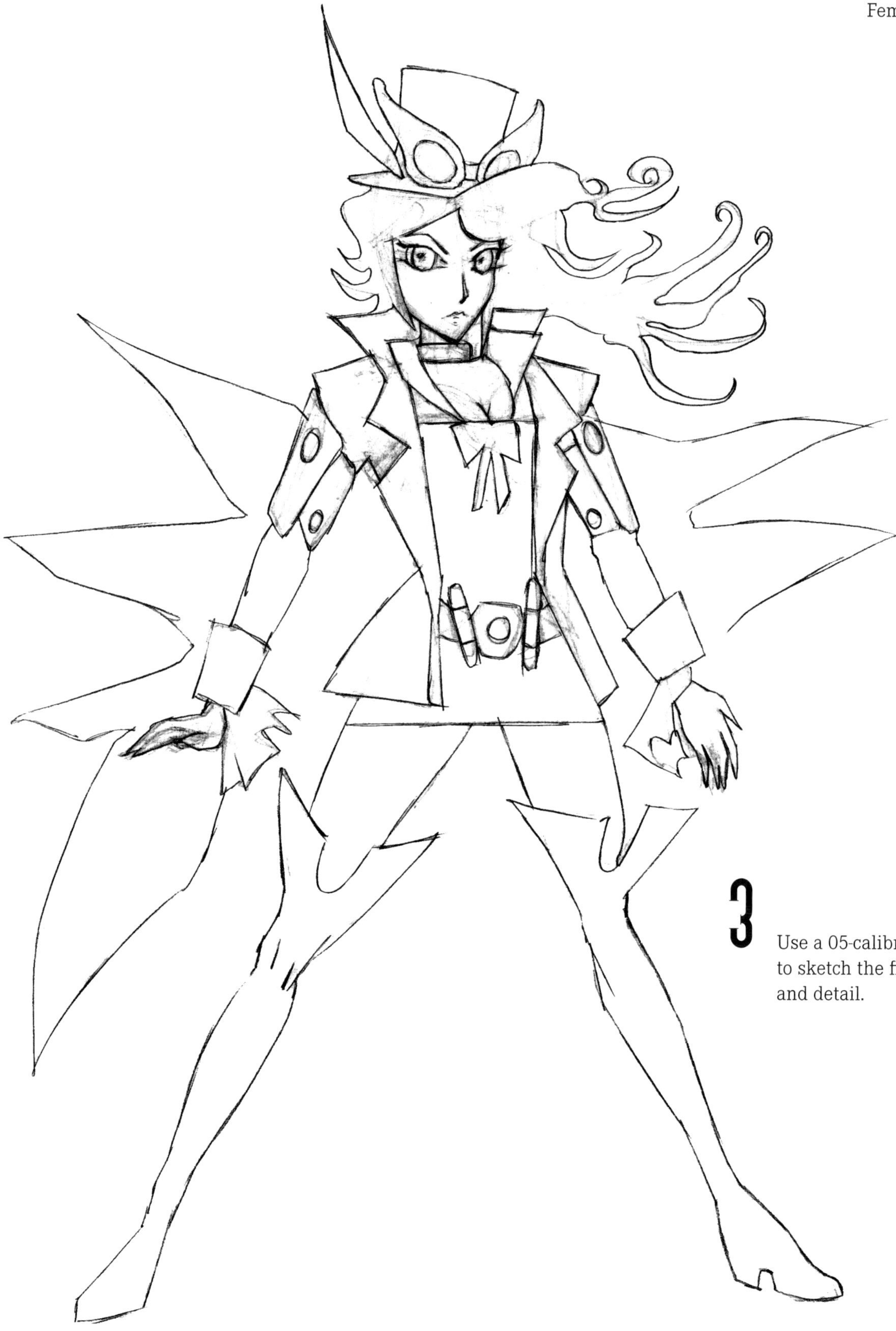

3

Use a 05-calibre mechanical pencil to sketch the figure, adding volume and detail.

4

Go over your drawing with various calibre pens. As I said before, use a 0.2 for the details, a 0.4 for the figure, and an 0.8 for the outline. Once the ink is dry, you can remove the pencil with a soft eraser: always rub in the same direction. Use the 0.8 also to draw the black of the vampire's hat, her hair, the wings of her outfit, and her high boots.

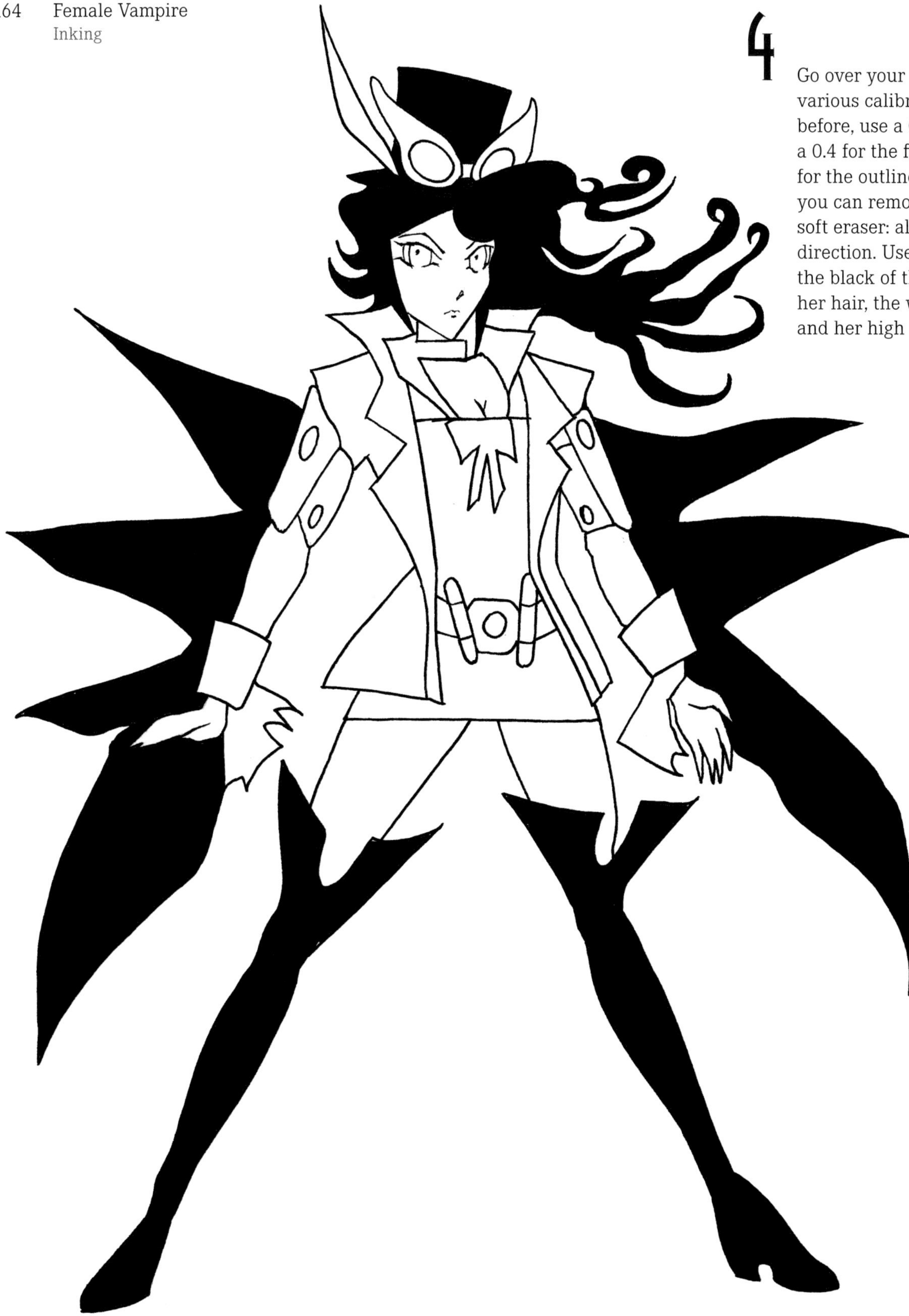

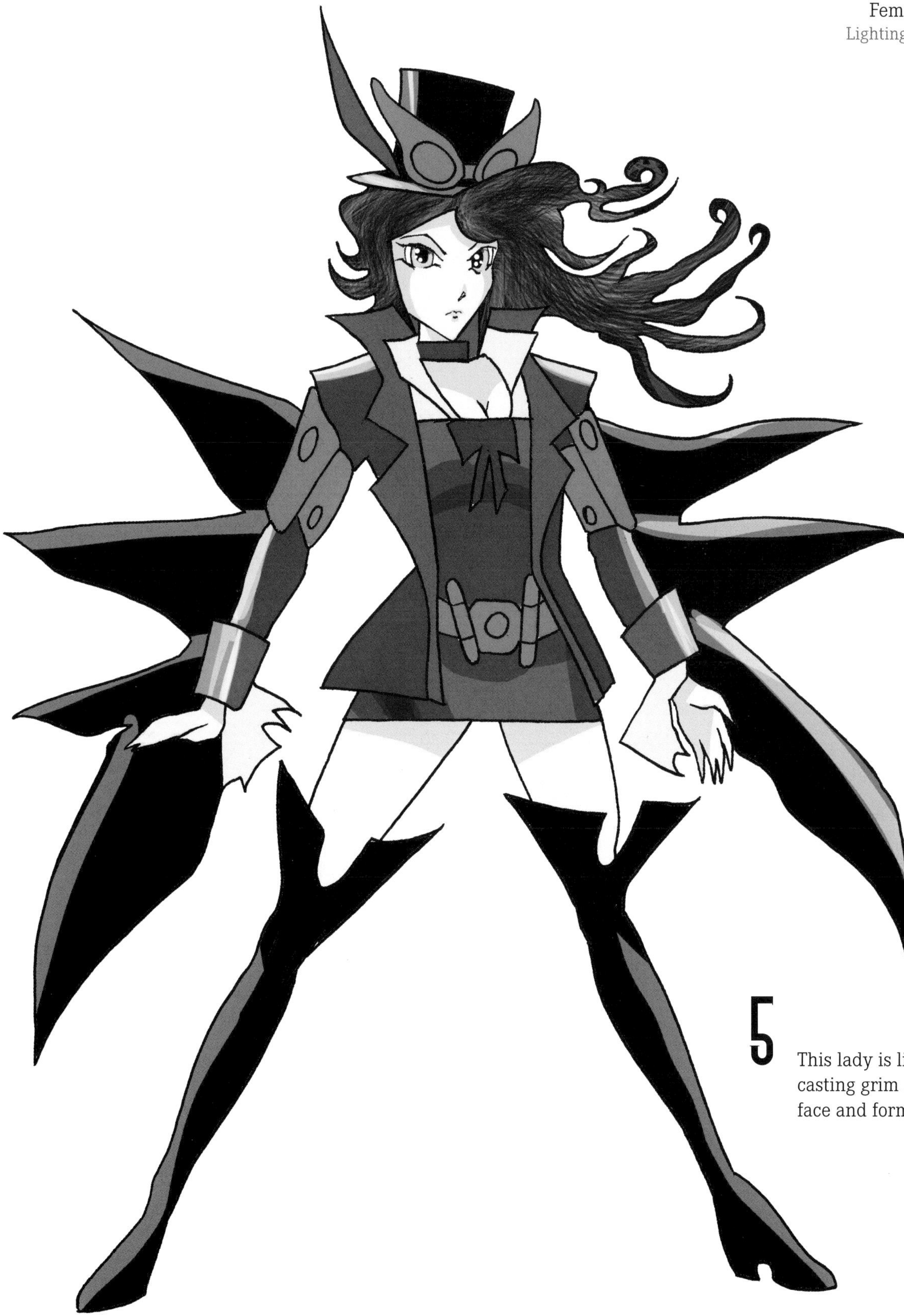

5

This lady is lit from above, casting grim shadows on her face and form.

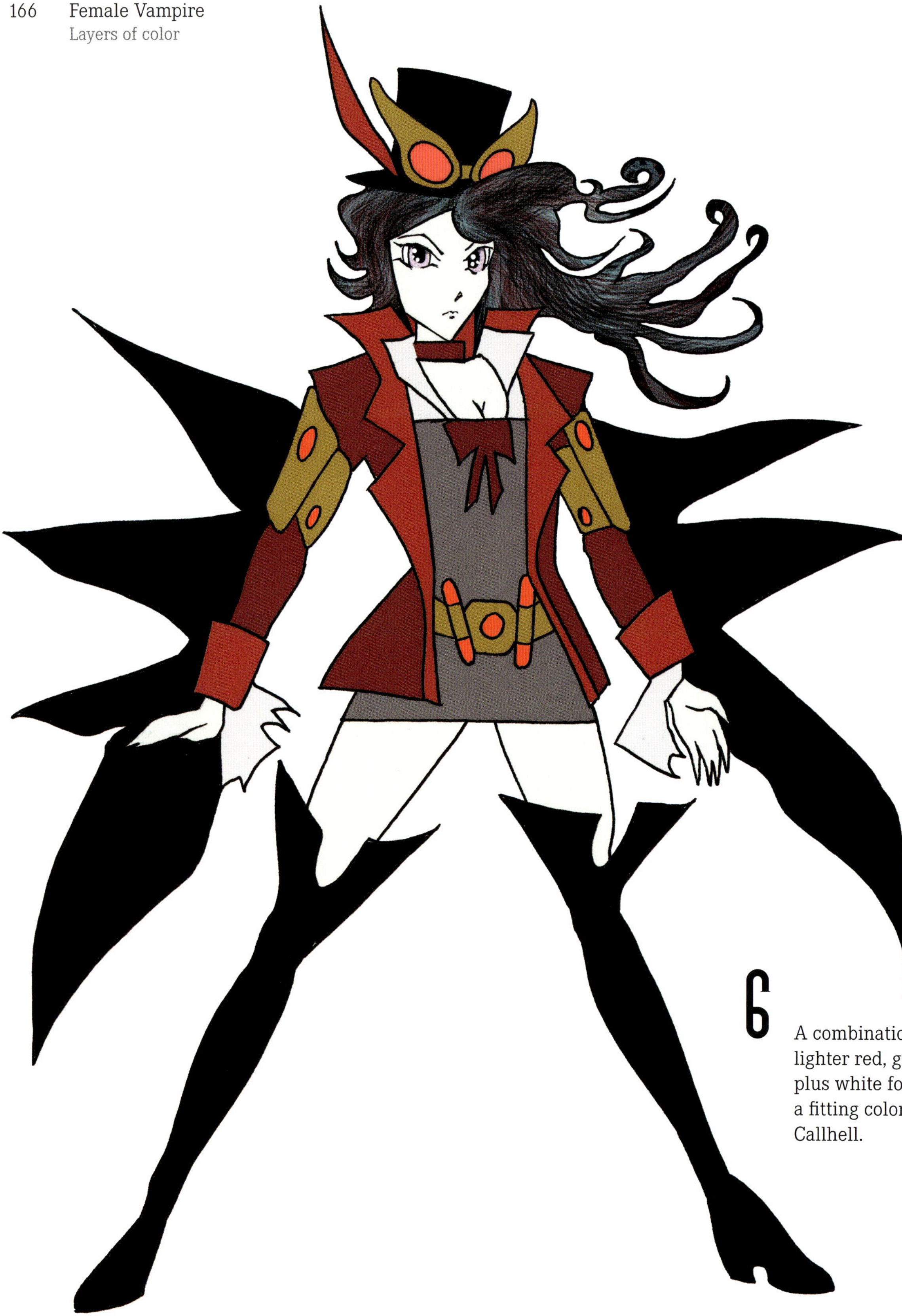

6

A combination of burgundy and lighter red, gray, and pastel tones, plus white for the shirt creates a fitting color scheme for Lorna Callhell.

7

Add the finishing touches of shine to the burgundy and black. A gold pen is perfect for drawing the rivets and decorative washers on her dress. Add some shine to her glasses ... and this vampire is ready to launch herself in search of blood!

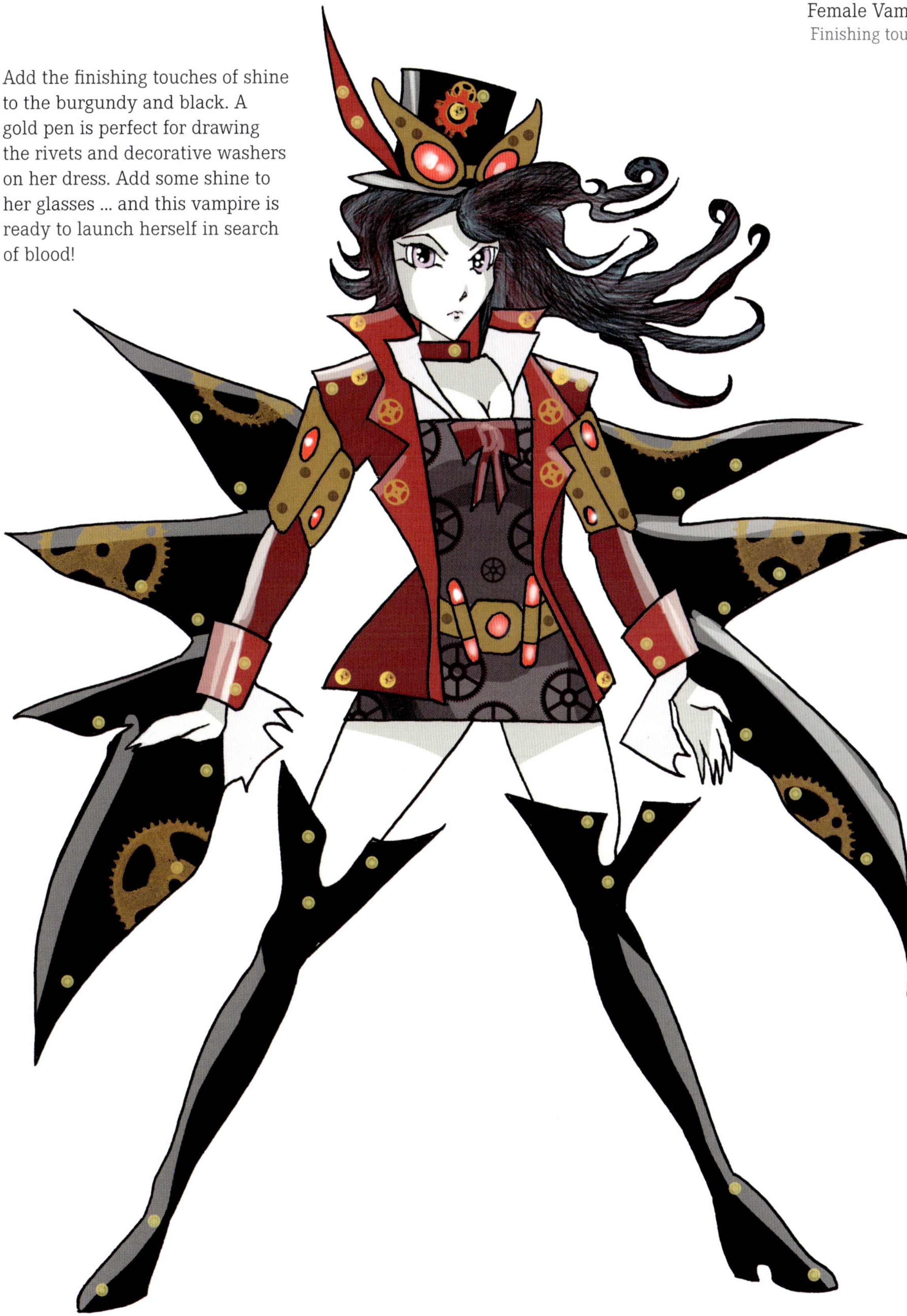

WITCH

Selina Monterrey is a great student of alchemy and the art of healing who is also interested in mechanics. By combining these she created a multifunction broom – it's non-polluting and helps with the housework as well. An enviable invention!

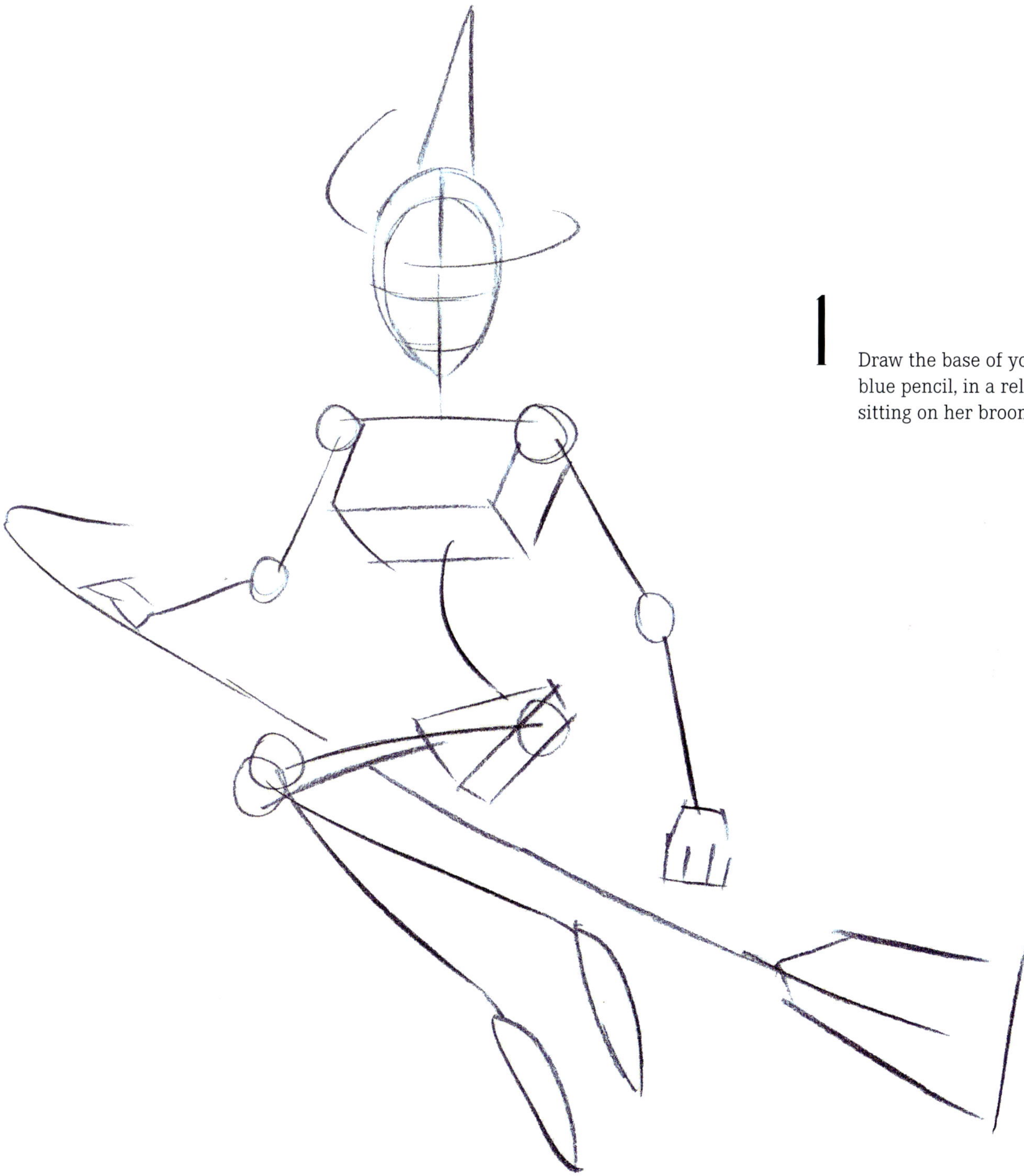

1

Draw the base of your witch in blue pencil, in a relaxed position sitting on her broom.

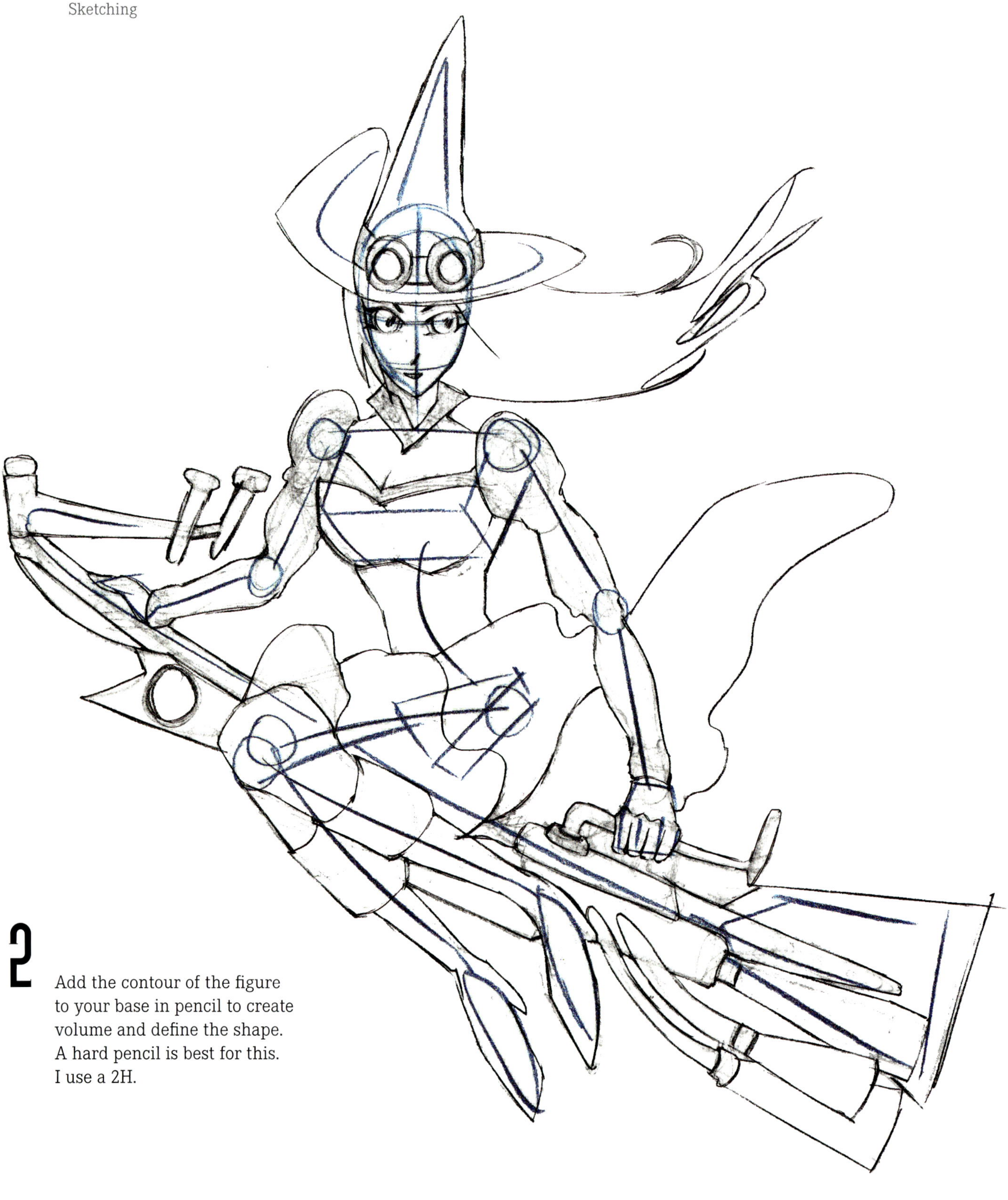

2

Add the contour of the figure to your base in pencil to create volume and define the shape. A hard pencil is best for this. I use a 2H.

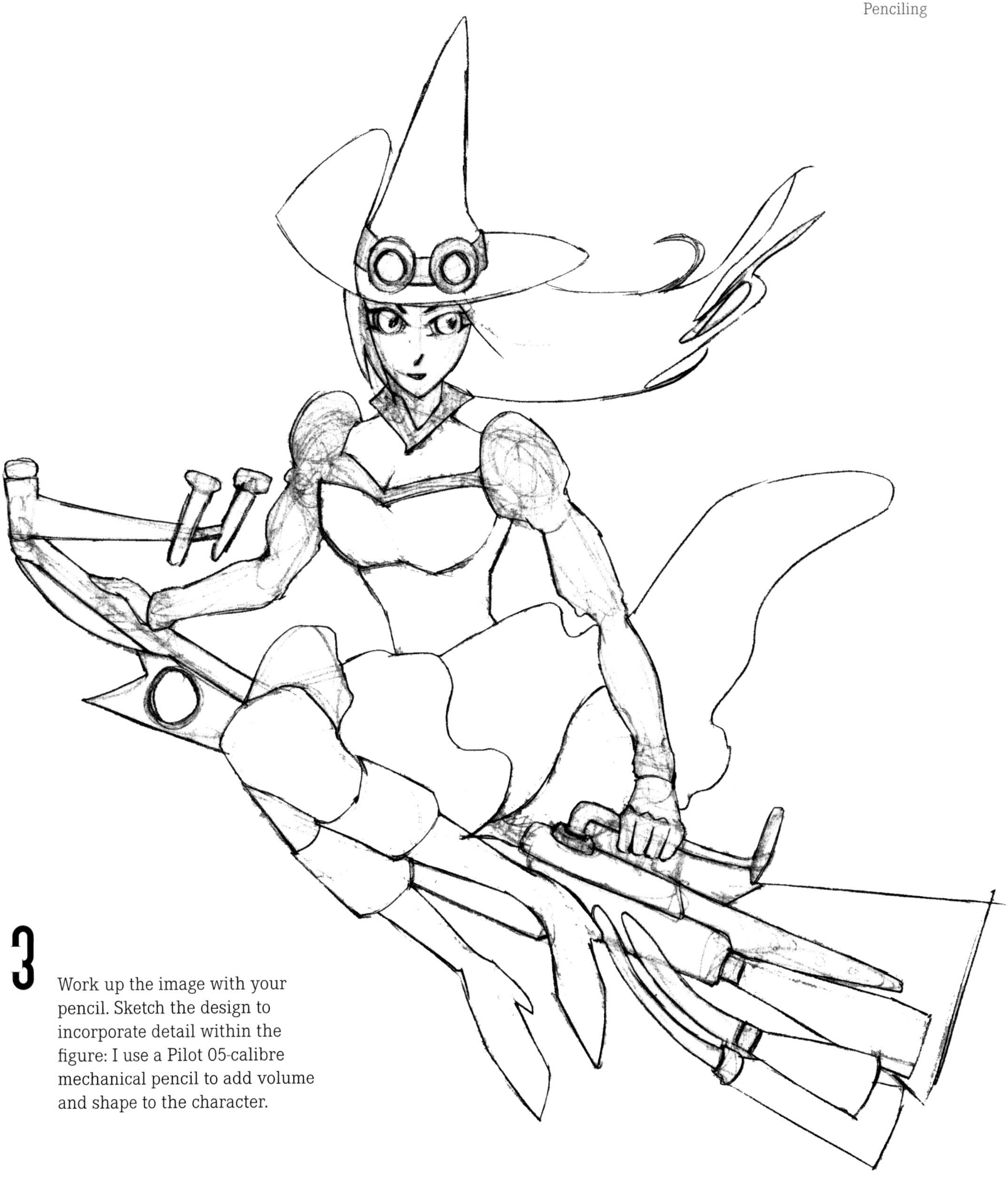

3

Work up the image with your pencil. Sketch the design to incorporate detail within the figure: I use a Pilot 05-calibre mechanical pencil to add volume and shape to the character.

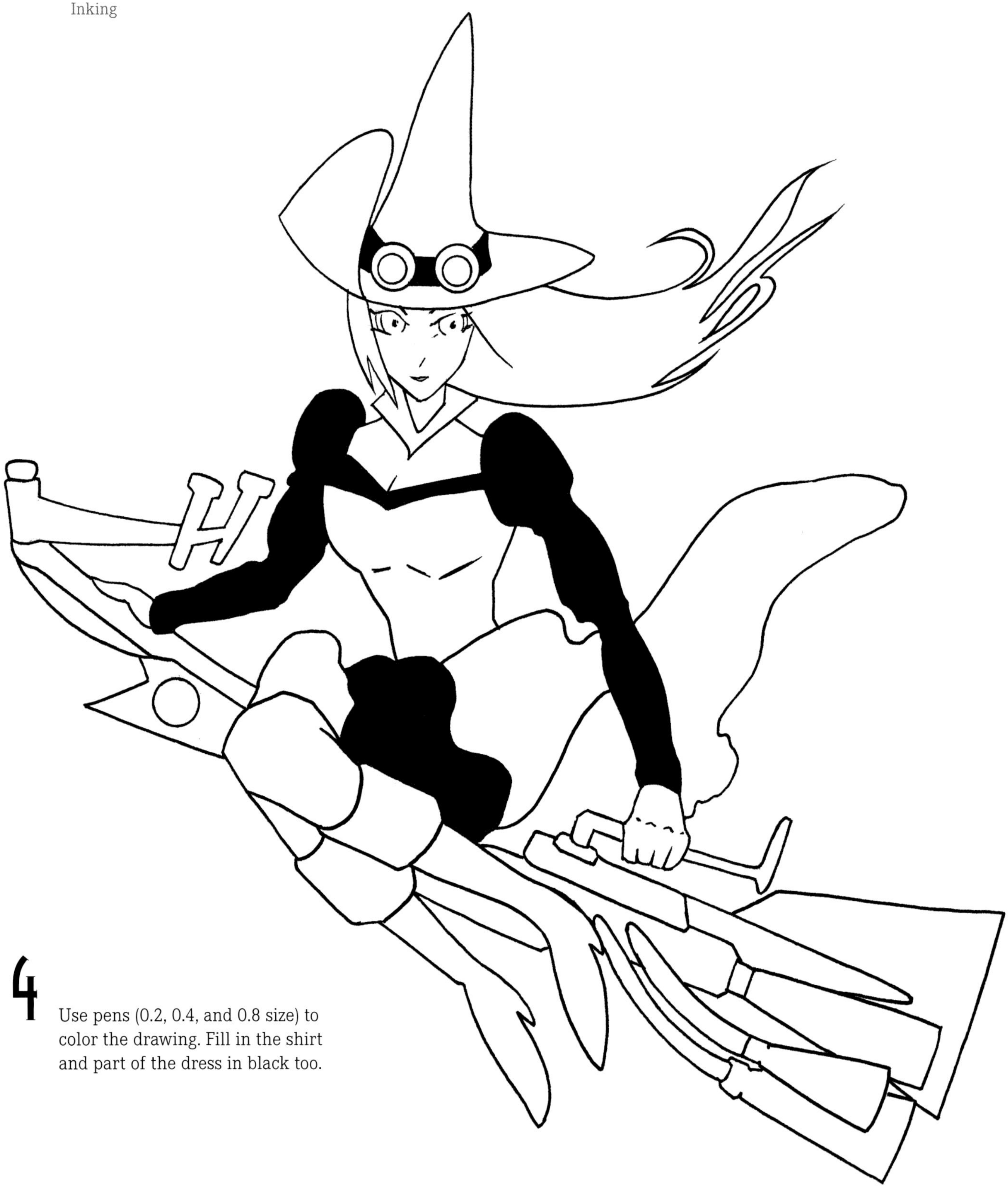

4 Use pens (0.2, 0.4, and 0.8 size) to color the drawing. Fill in the shirt and part of the dress in black too.

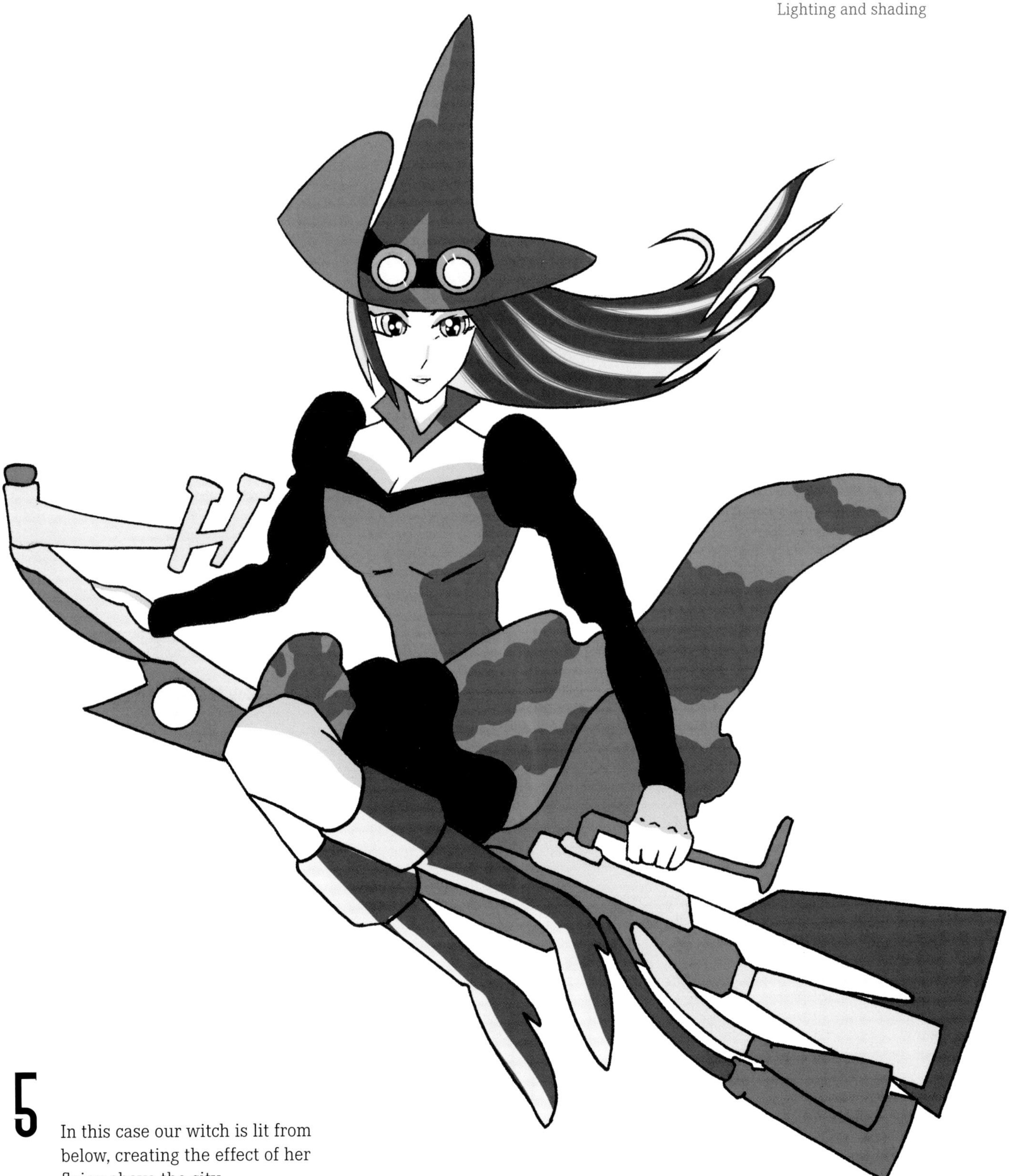

5

In this case our witch is lit from below, creating the effect of her flying above the city.

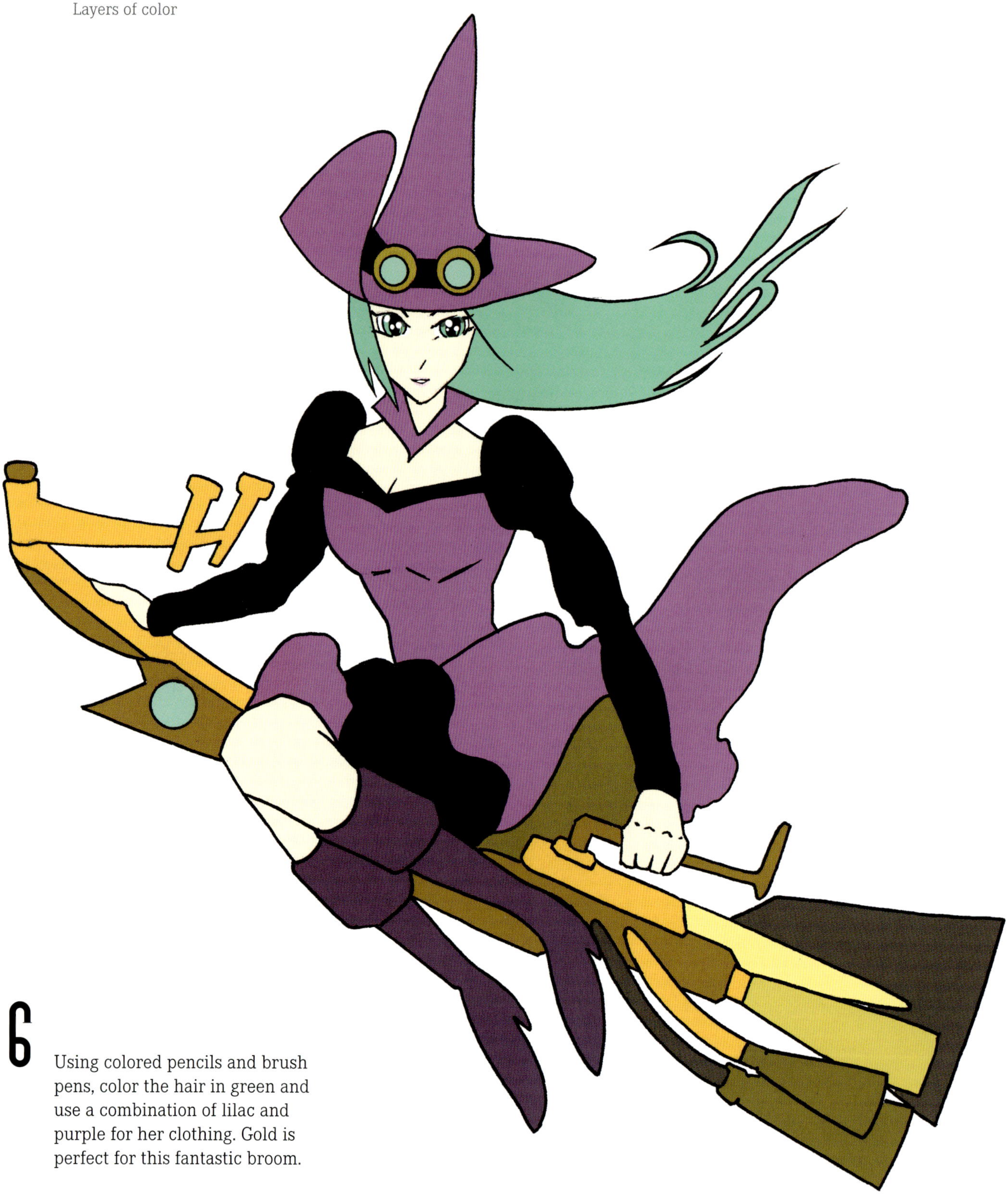

6

Using colored pencils and brush pens, color the hair in green and use a combination of lilac and purple for her clothing. Gold is perfect for this fantastic broom.

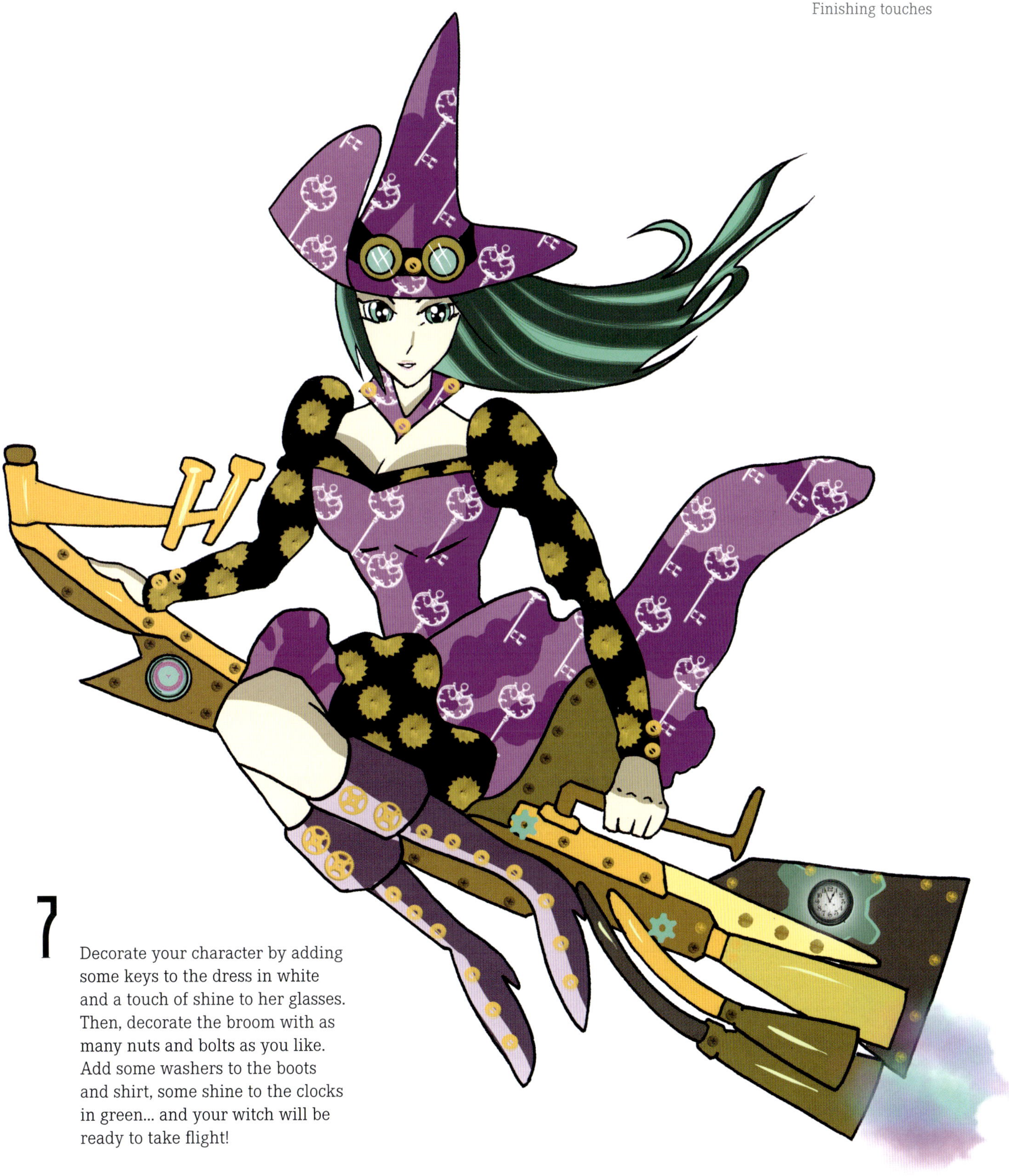

7

Decorate your character by adding some keys to the dress in white and a touch of shine to her glasses. Then, decorate the broom with as many nuts and bolts as you like. Add some washers to the boots and shirt, some shine to the clocks in green... and your witch will be ready to take flight!

SCUBA DIVER

Hal Morgan is an expert diver, always willing to take on a high-risk mission. He thrives at great depths and has taken part in searches for sunken treasures and the salvaging of ships. There is no one in the kingdom who can compete with his experience so he is always the first to be called upon when there is an underwater crisis.

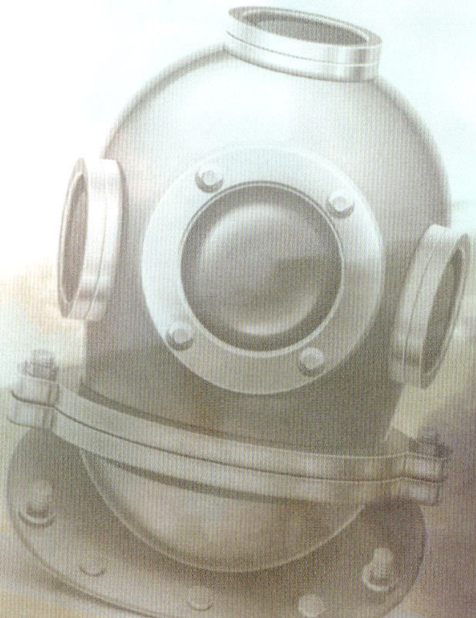

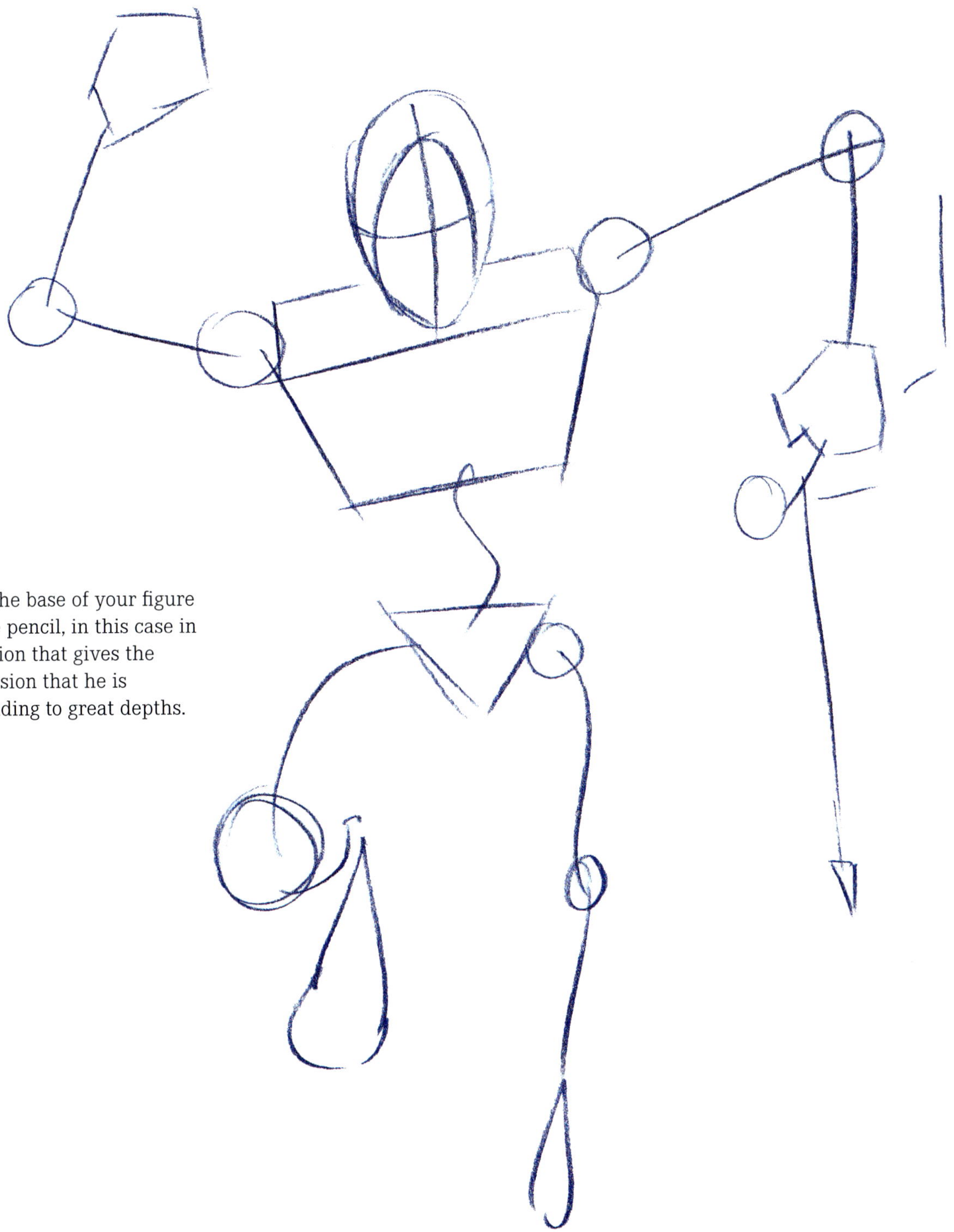

1

Draw the base of your figure in blue pencil, in this case in a position that gives the impression that he is descending to great depths.

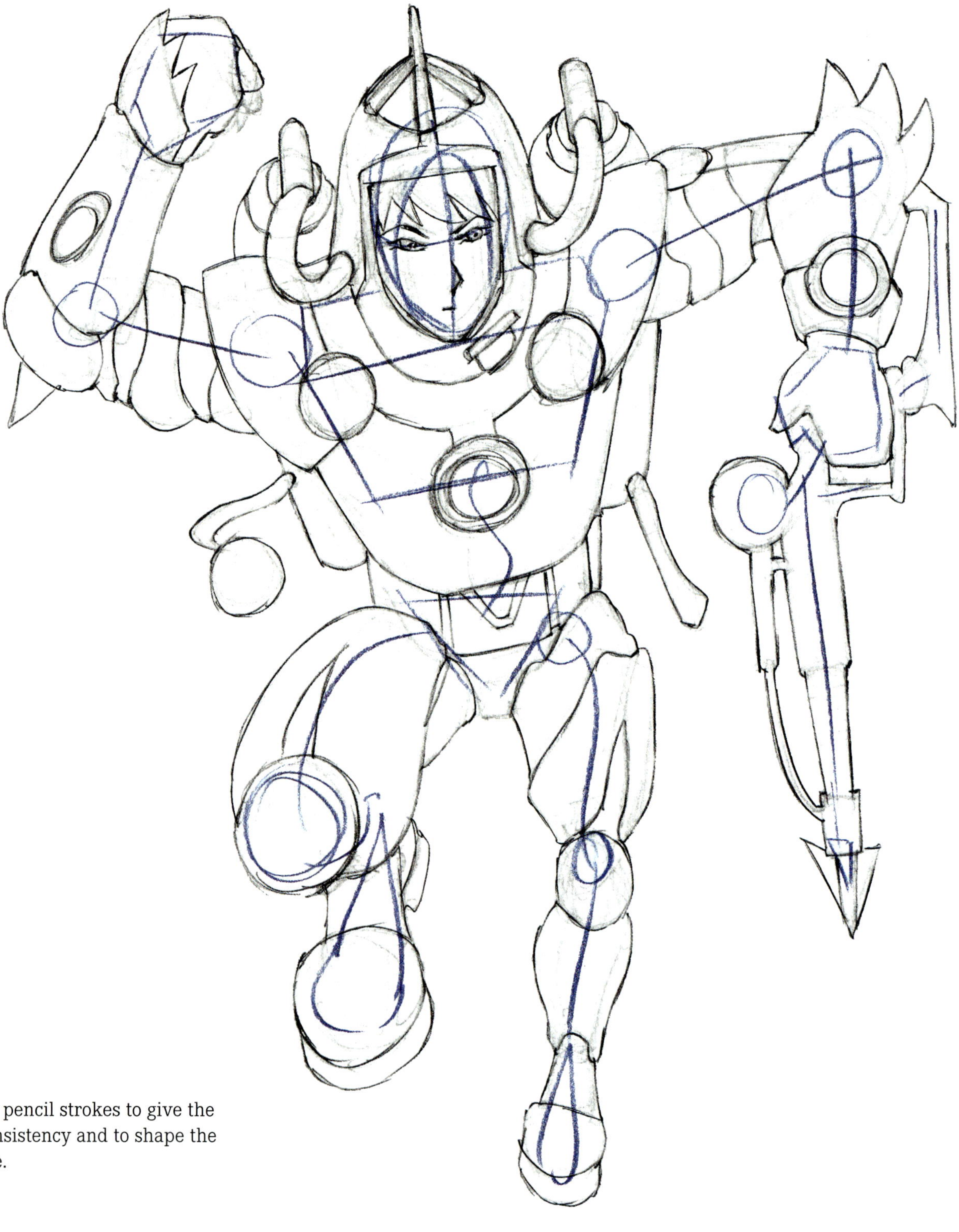

2

Add your pencil strokes to give the figure consistency and to shape the silhouette.

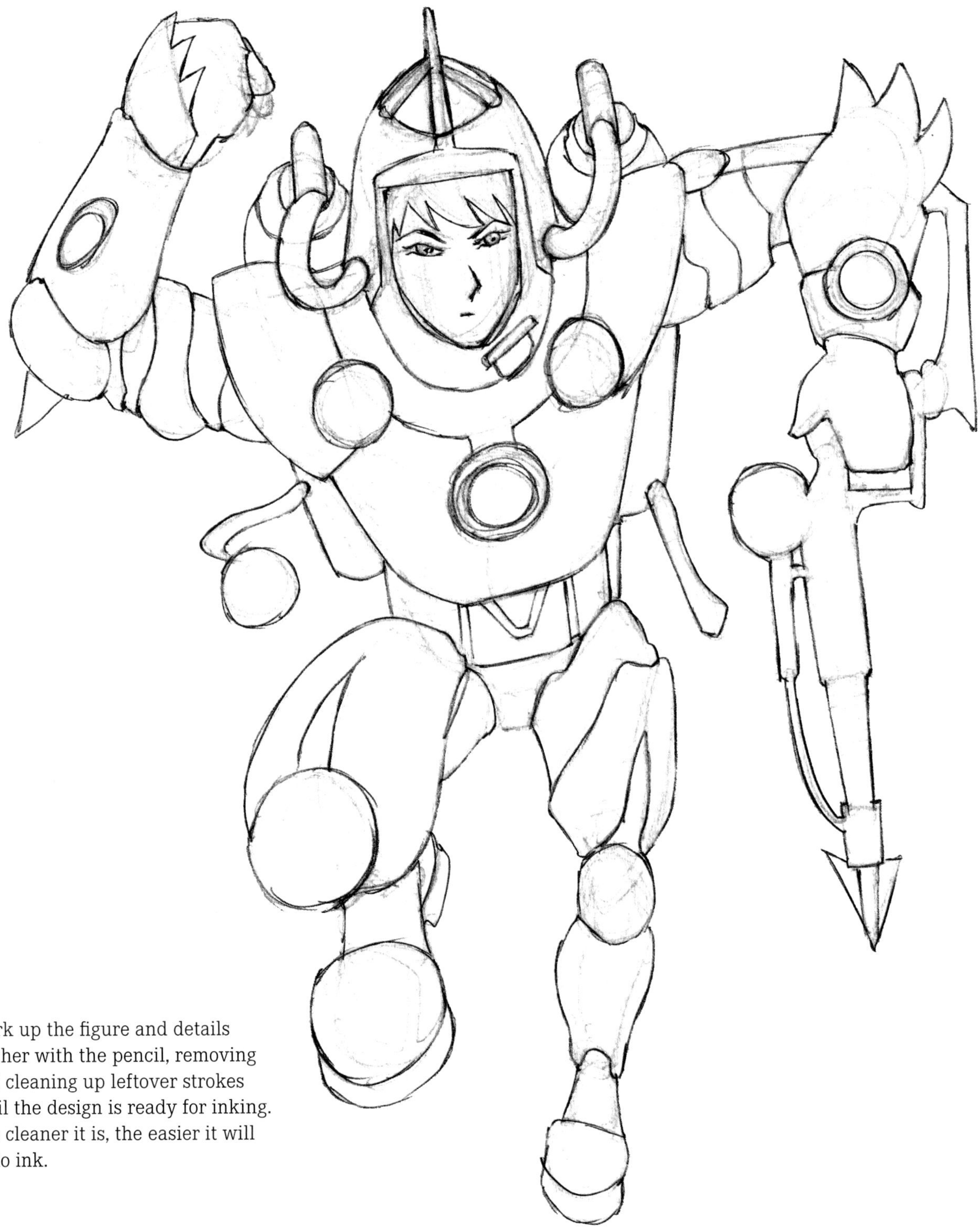

3

Work up the figure and details further with the pencil, removing and cleaning up leftover strokes until the design is ready for inking. The cleaner it is, the easier it will be to ink.

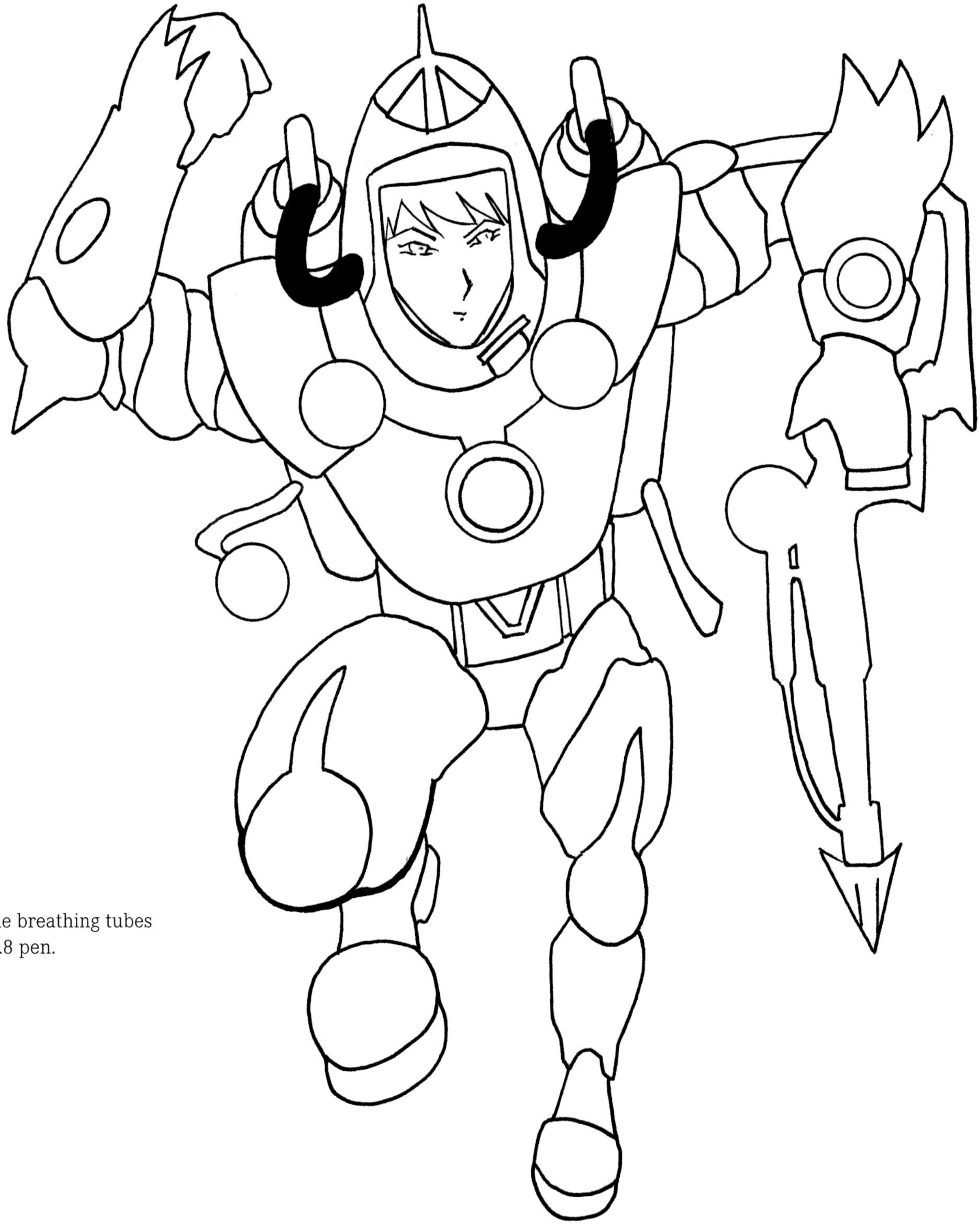

4

Add in the breathing tubes using a 0.8 pen.

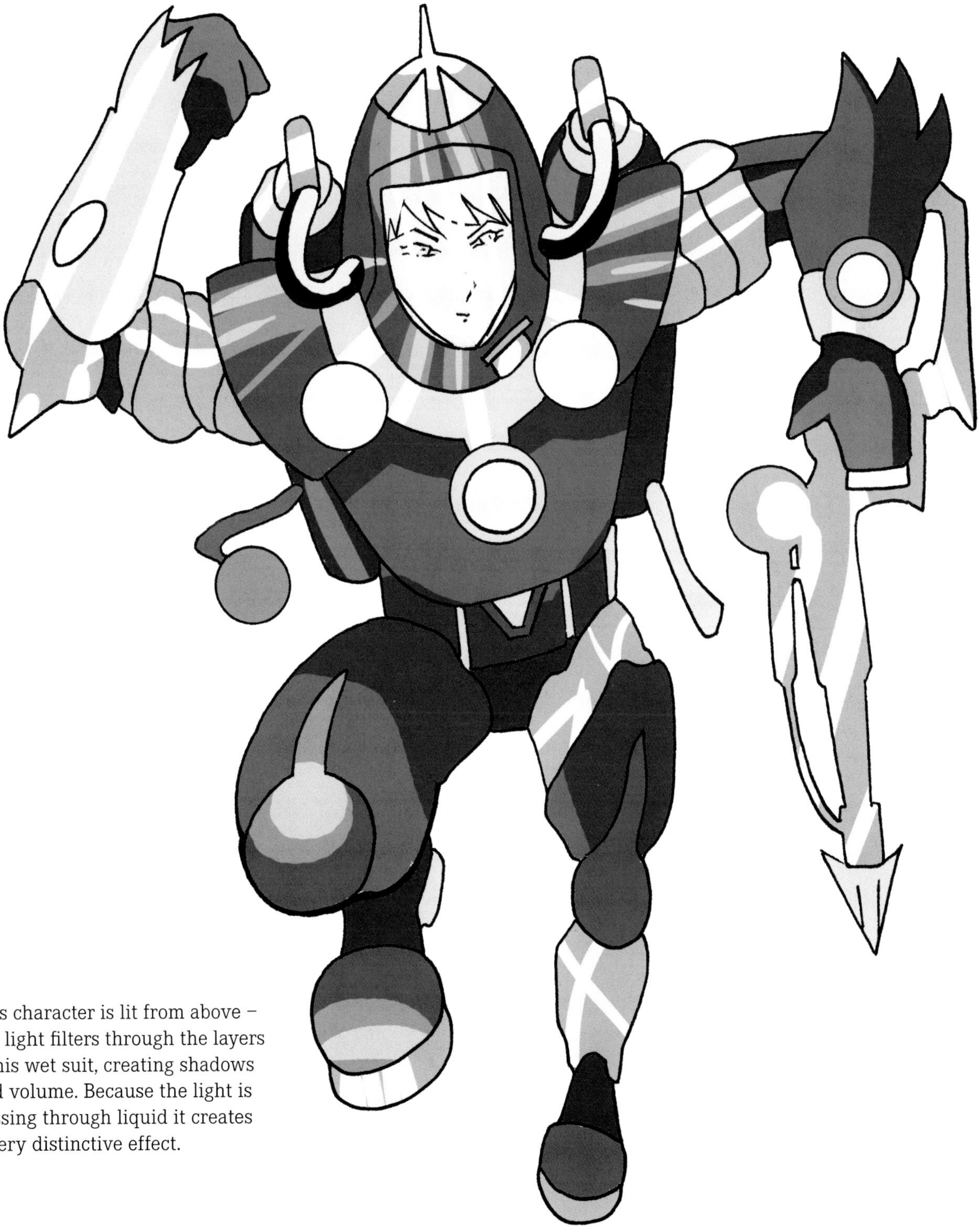

5

This character is lit from above – the light filters through the layers of his wet suit, creating shadows and volume. Because the light is passing through liquid it creates a very distinctive effect.

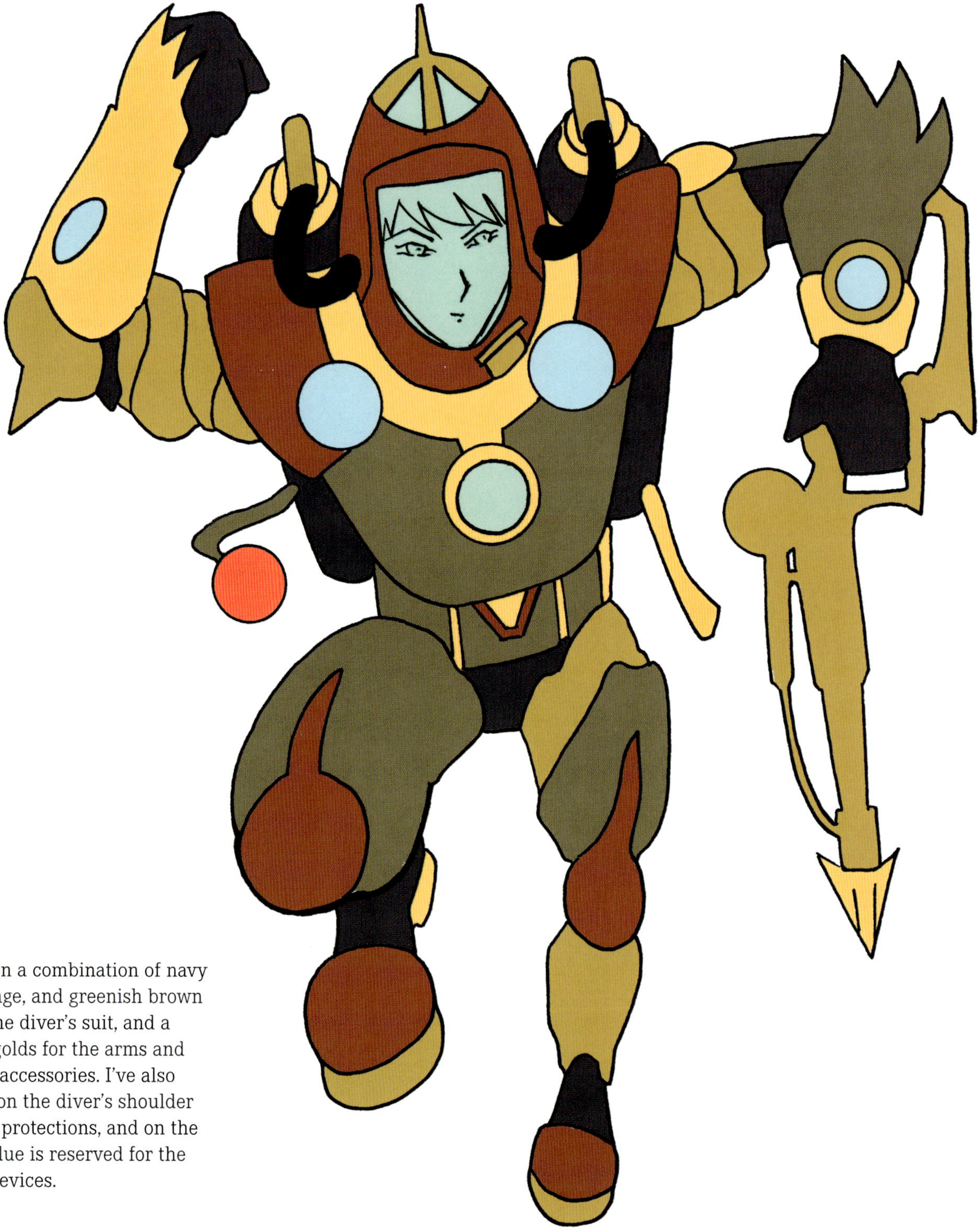

6

I've chosen a combination of navy blue, orange, and greenish brown to draw the diver's suit, and a range of golds for the arms and the suit's accessories. I've also used red on the diver's shoulder and knee protections, and on the helmet. Blue is reserved for the lighting devices.

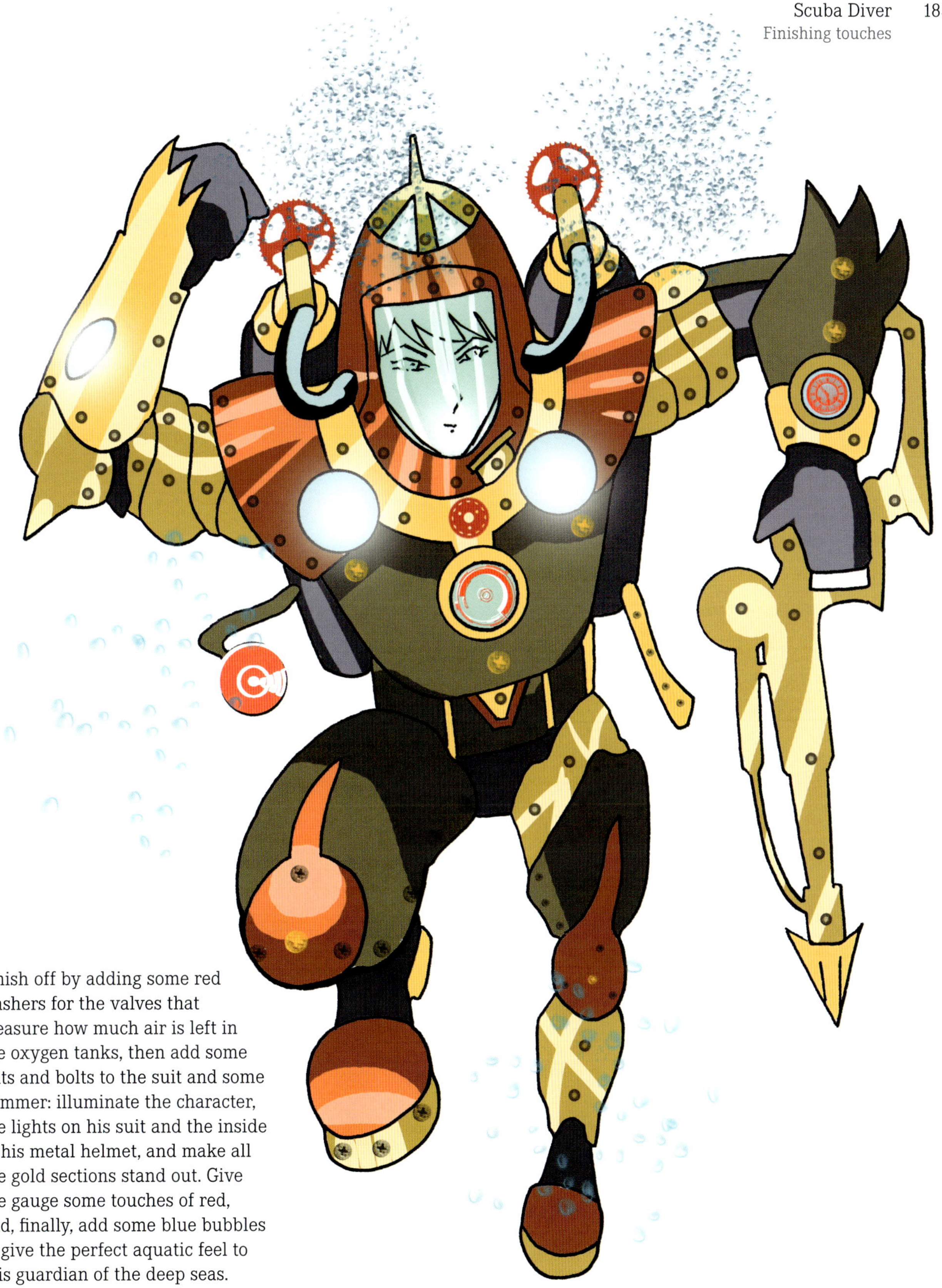

7

Finish off by adding some red washers for the valves that measure how much air is left in the oxygen tanks, then add some nuts and bolts to the suit and some glimmer: illuminate the character, the lights on his suit and the inside of his metal helmet, and make all the gold sections stand out. Give the gauge some touches of red, and, finally, add some blue bubbles to give the perfect aquatic feel to this guardian of the deep seas.

MEDIEVAL KNIGHT

Iskander Balgarian is Lieutenant Colonel of the famous and much-acclaimed Monster Steel Arrows, elite forces who unite in battle to break through enemy lines and defenses, bringing chaos and fear to the other side. His large hammer of blue eons ensures this character is unmatched in power and distinction as only a warrior who is both smart and strong can use it.

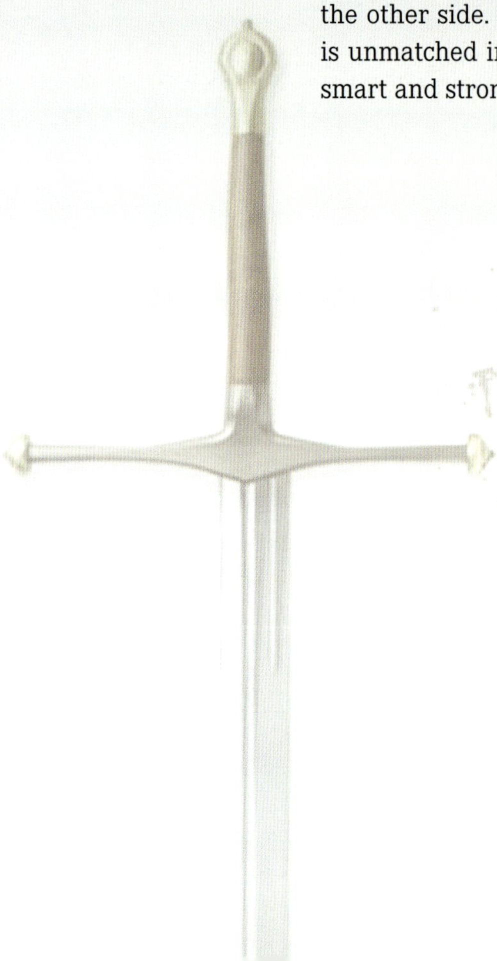

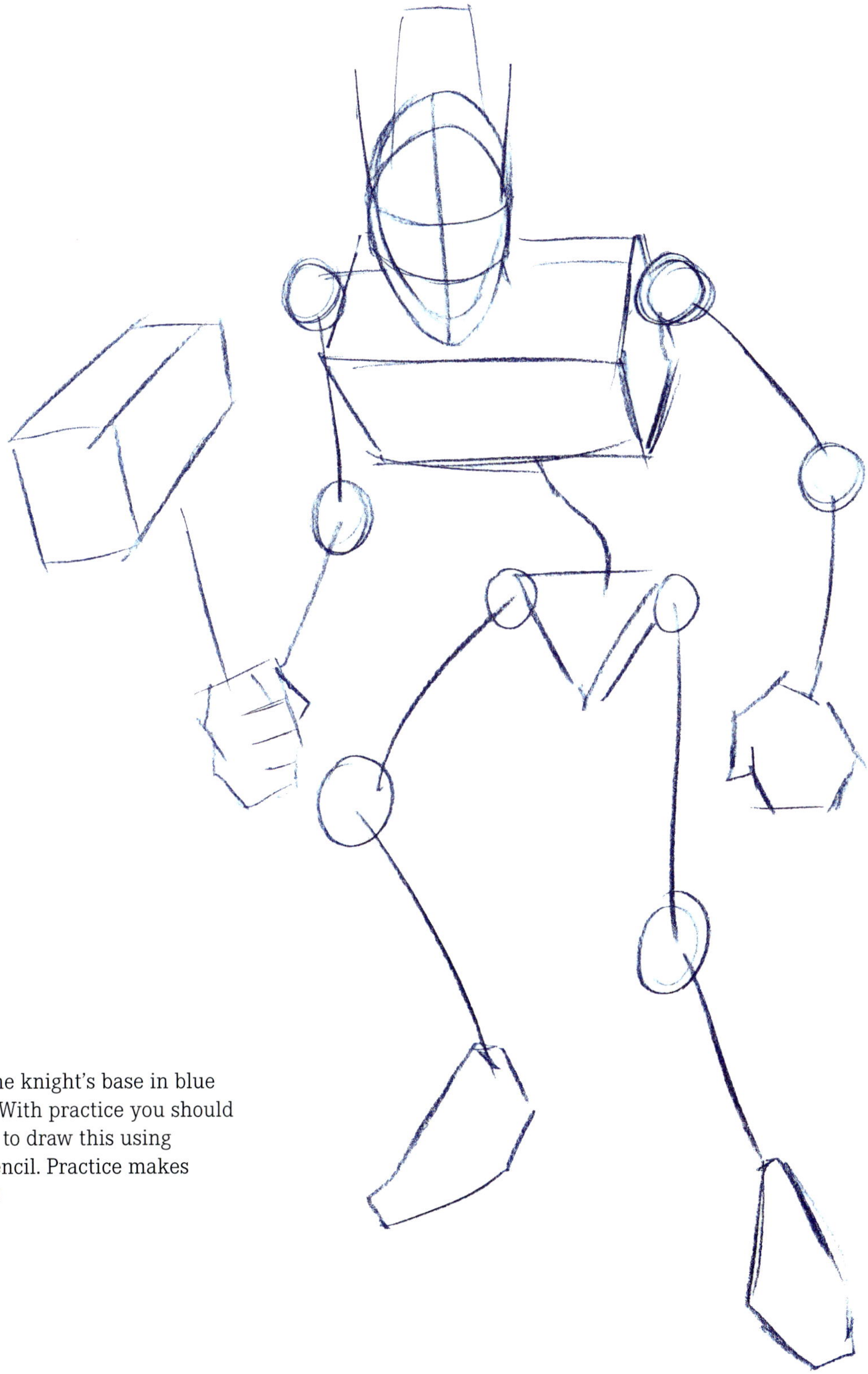

1

Draw the knight's base in blue pencil. With practice you should be able to draw this using a 2H pencil. Practice makes perfect!

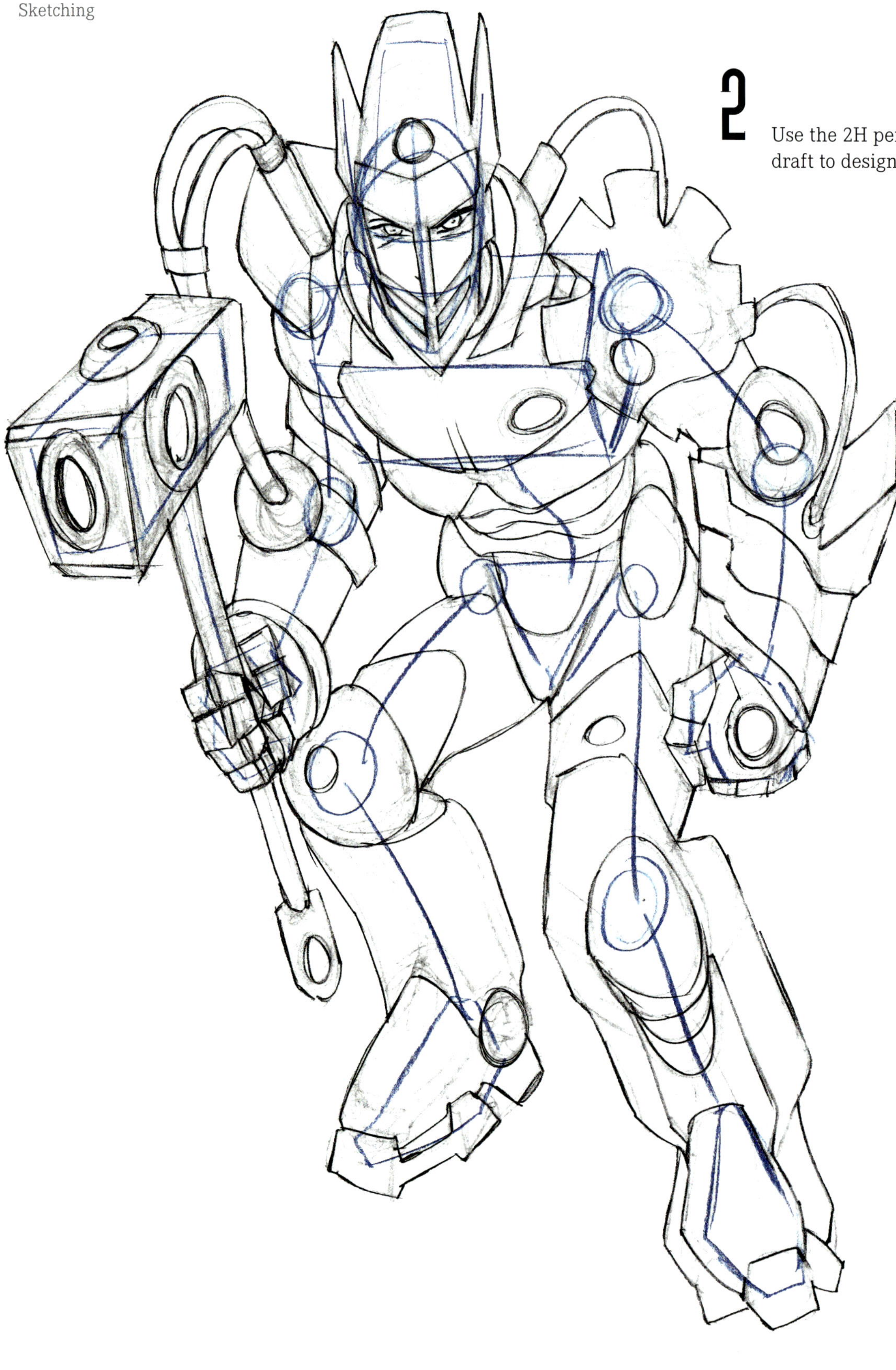

2 Use the 2H pencil in your blue draft to design the figure.

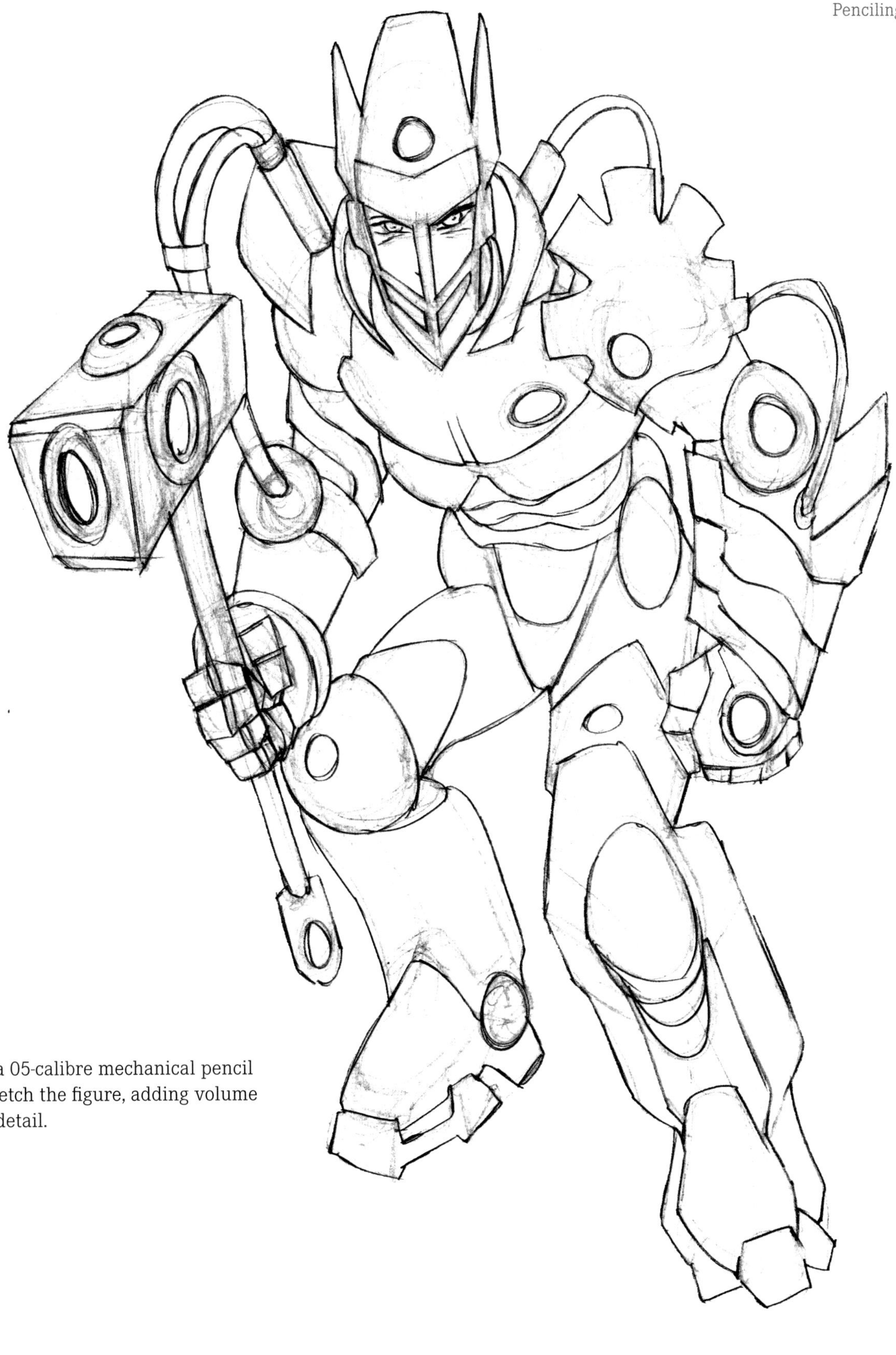

3

Use a 05-calibre mechanical pencil to sketch the figure, adding volume and detail.

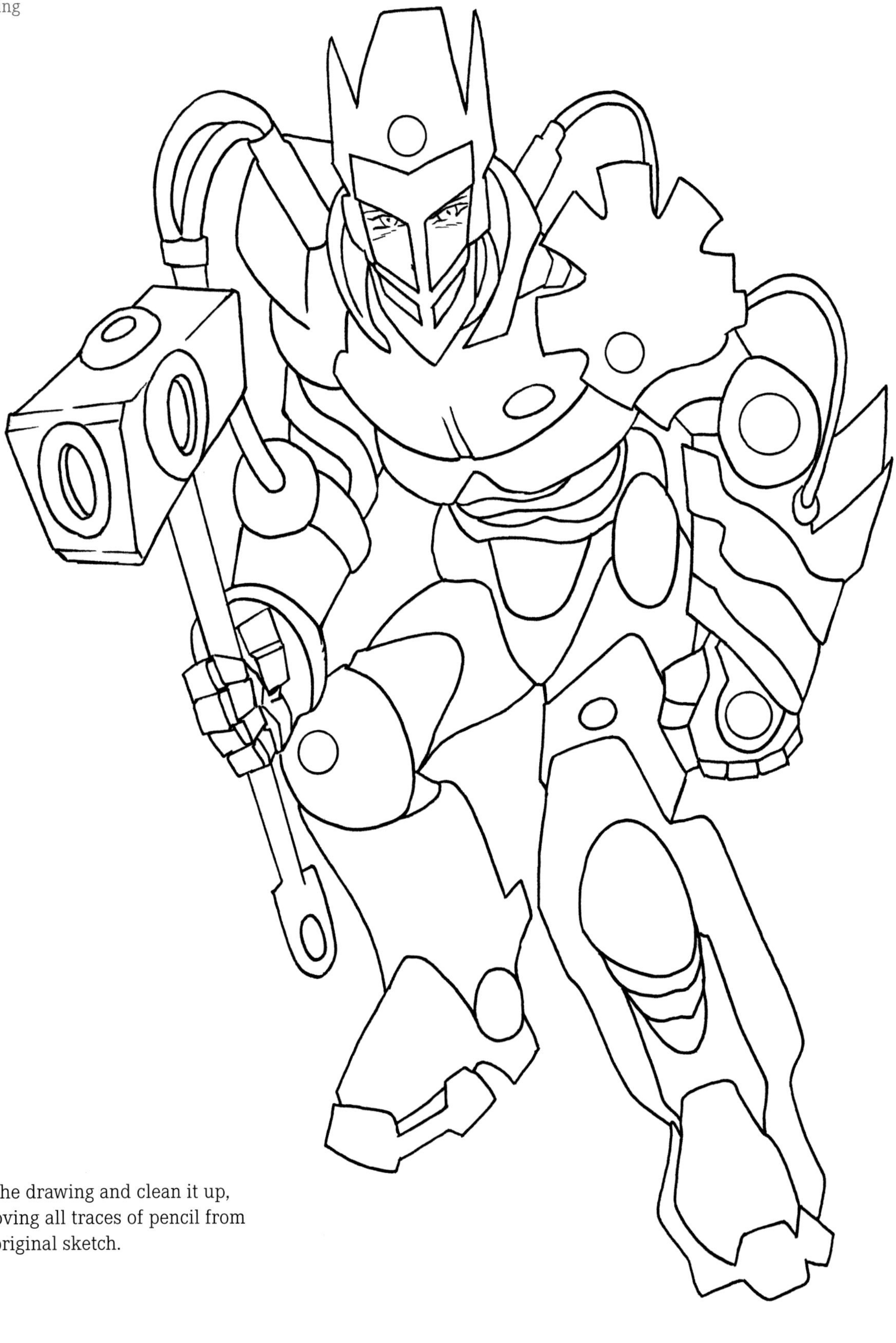

4

Ink the drawing and clean it up, removing all traces of pencil from the original sketch.

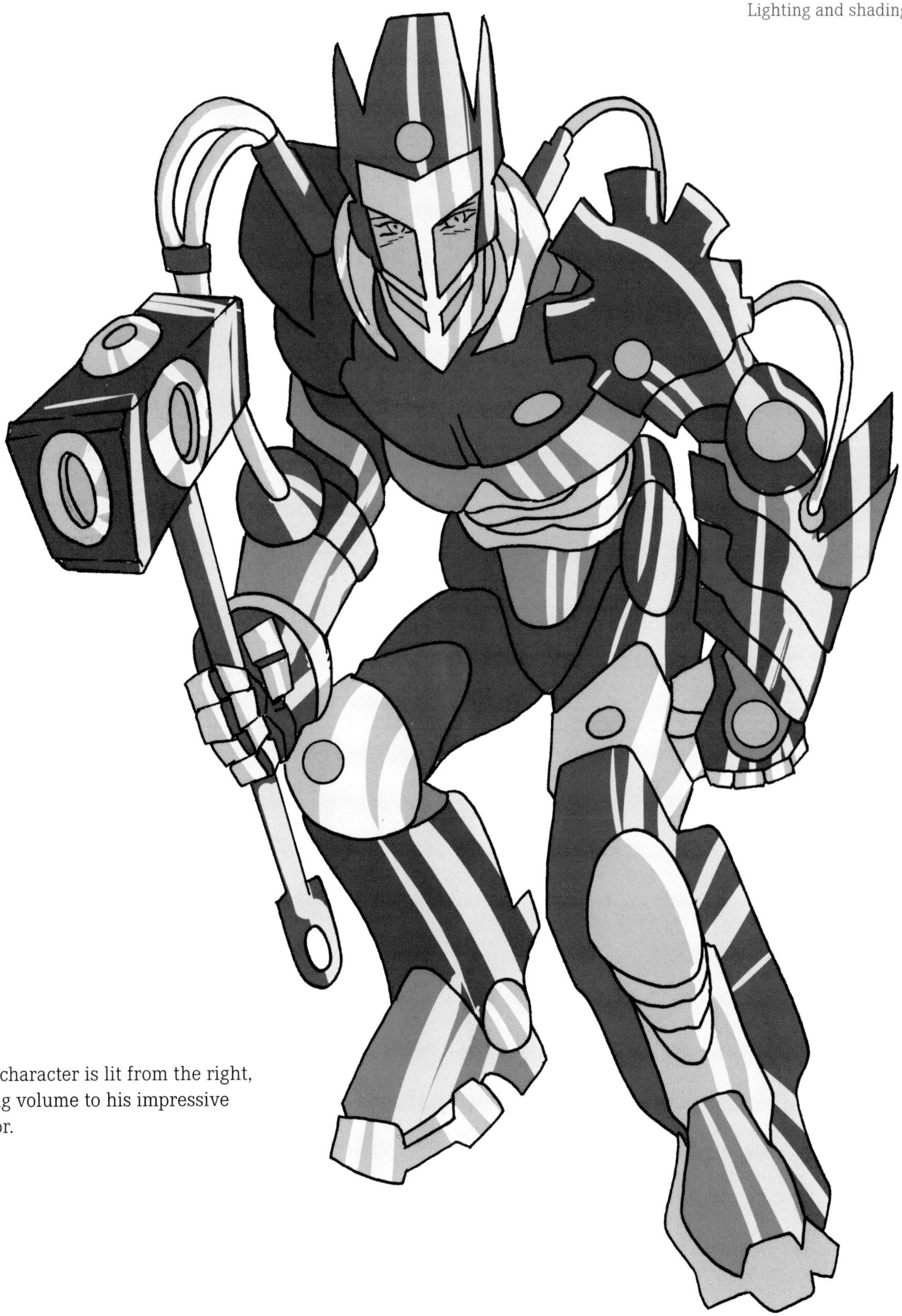

5

This character is lit from the right, giving volume to his impressive armor.

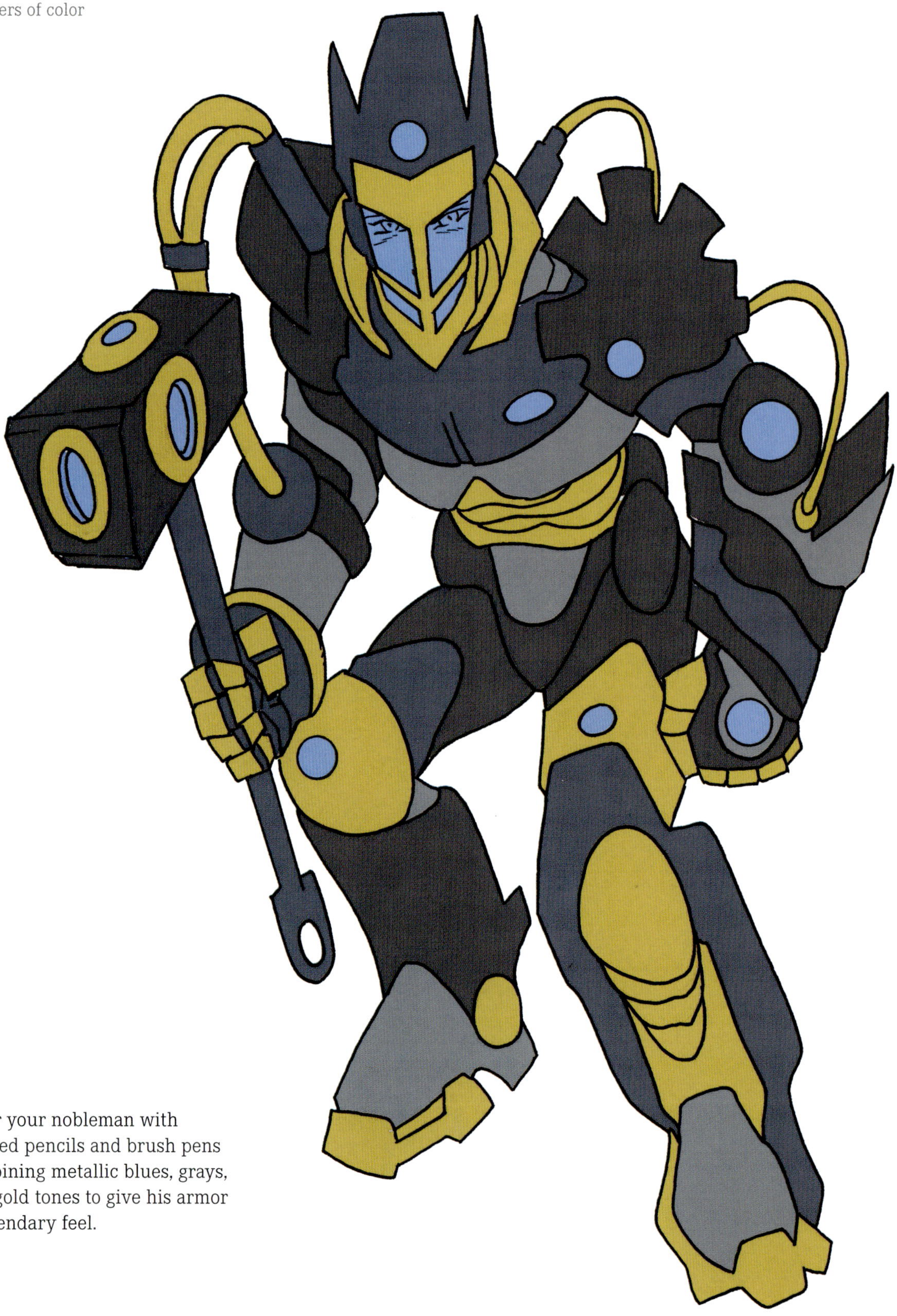

6

Color your nobleman with colored pencils and brush pens combining metallic blues, grays, and gold tones to give his armor a legendary feel.

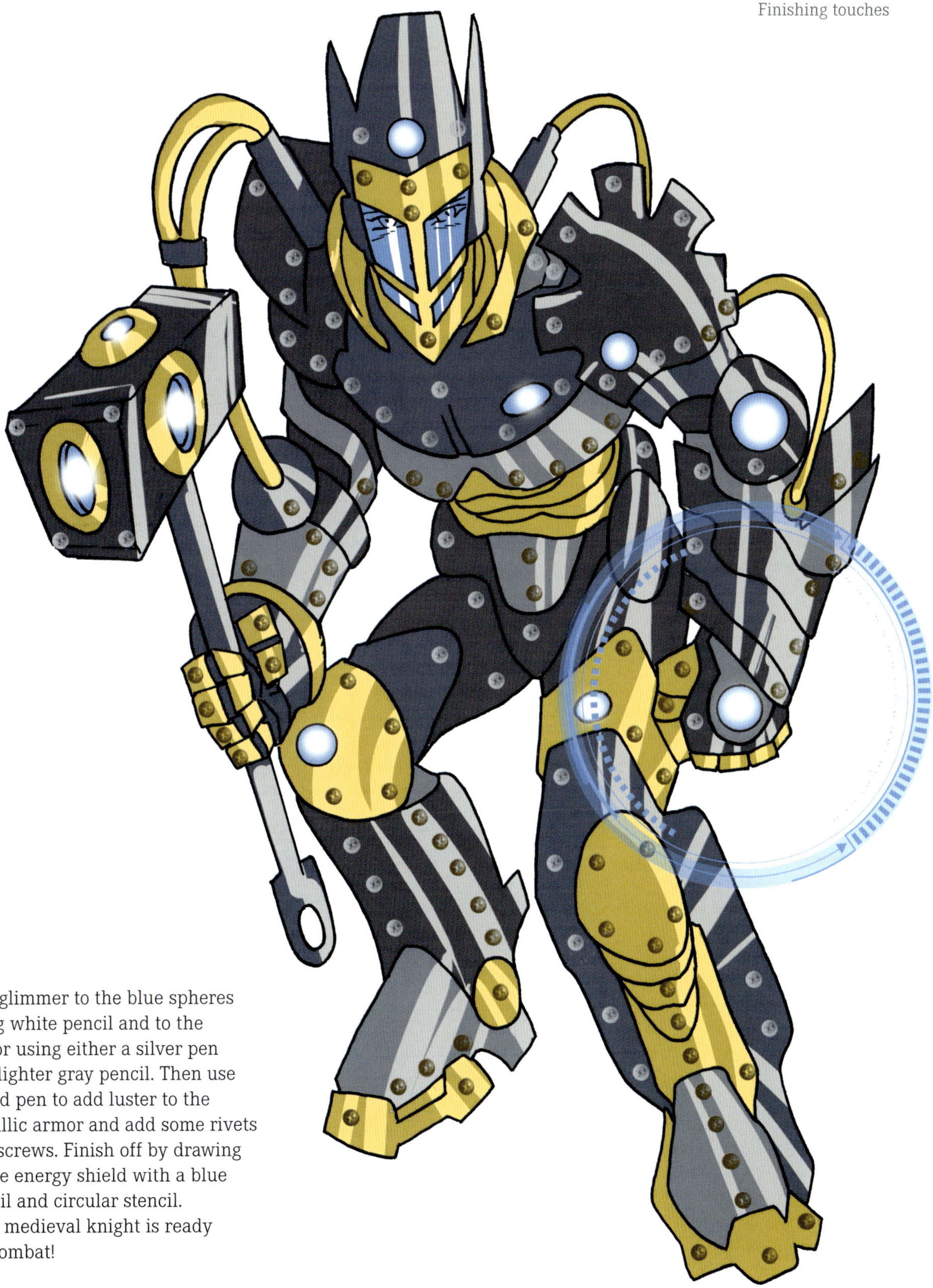

7

Add glimmer to the blue spheres using white pencil and to the armor using either a silver pen or a lighter gray pencil. Then use a gold pen to add luster to the metallic armor and add some rivets and screws. Finish off by drawing in the energy shield with a blue pencil and circular stencil. Your medieval knight is ready for combat!

FAIRY

Alina is a fairy elf: she is tiny and can go completely unnoticed when she wants to. Thanks to this gift she can sneak anywhere and eavesdrop on what the great men of the government are saying, then pass it on to those who know what to do with the information ... and can pay for it accordingly.

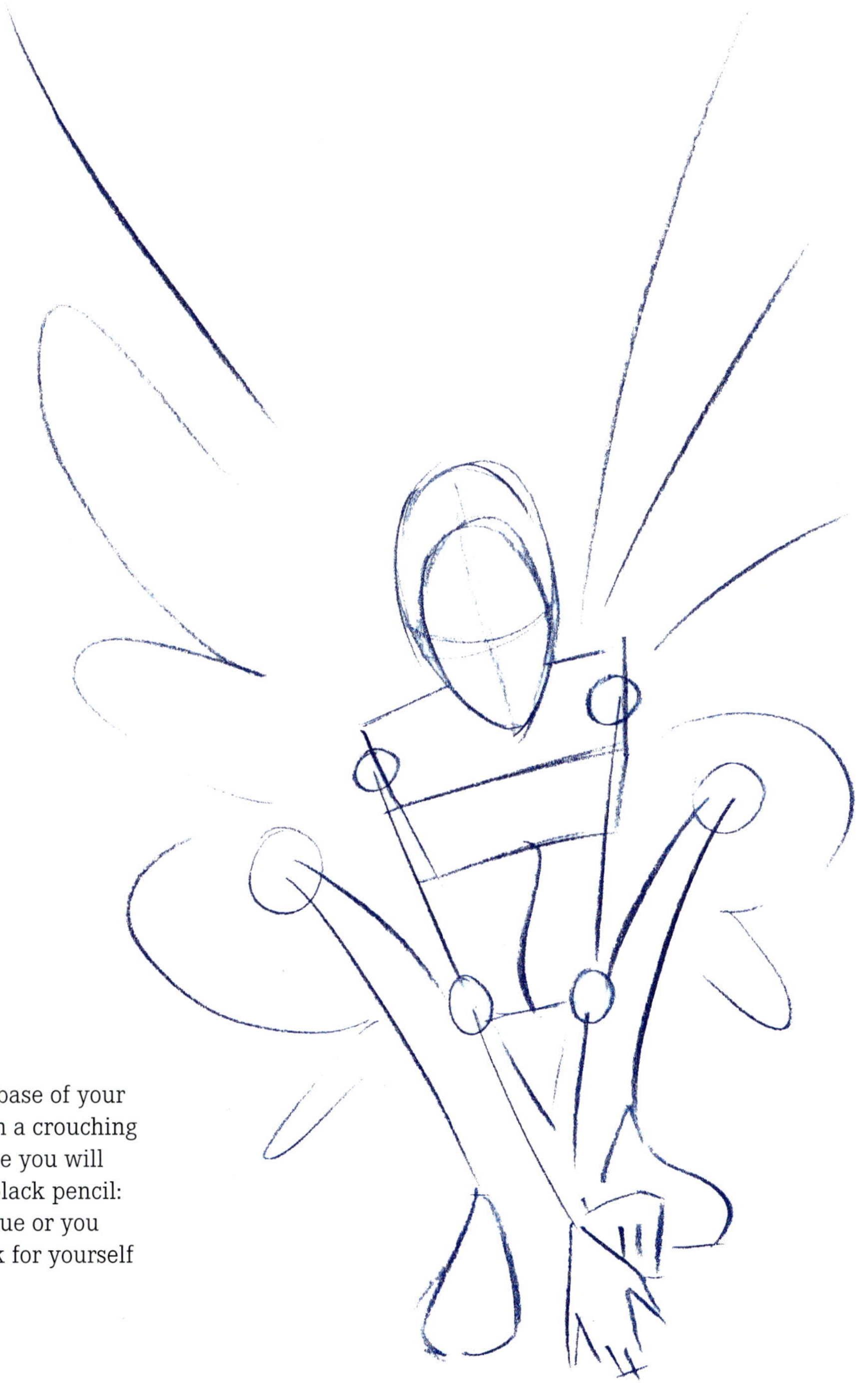

1

Start by drawing the base of your fairy in blue pencil, in a crouching position. With practice you will be able to do this in black pencil: don't use too much blue or you will create more work for yourself rubbing it out.

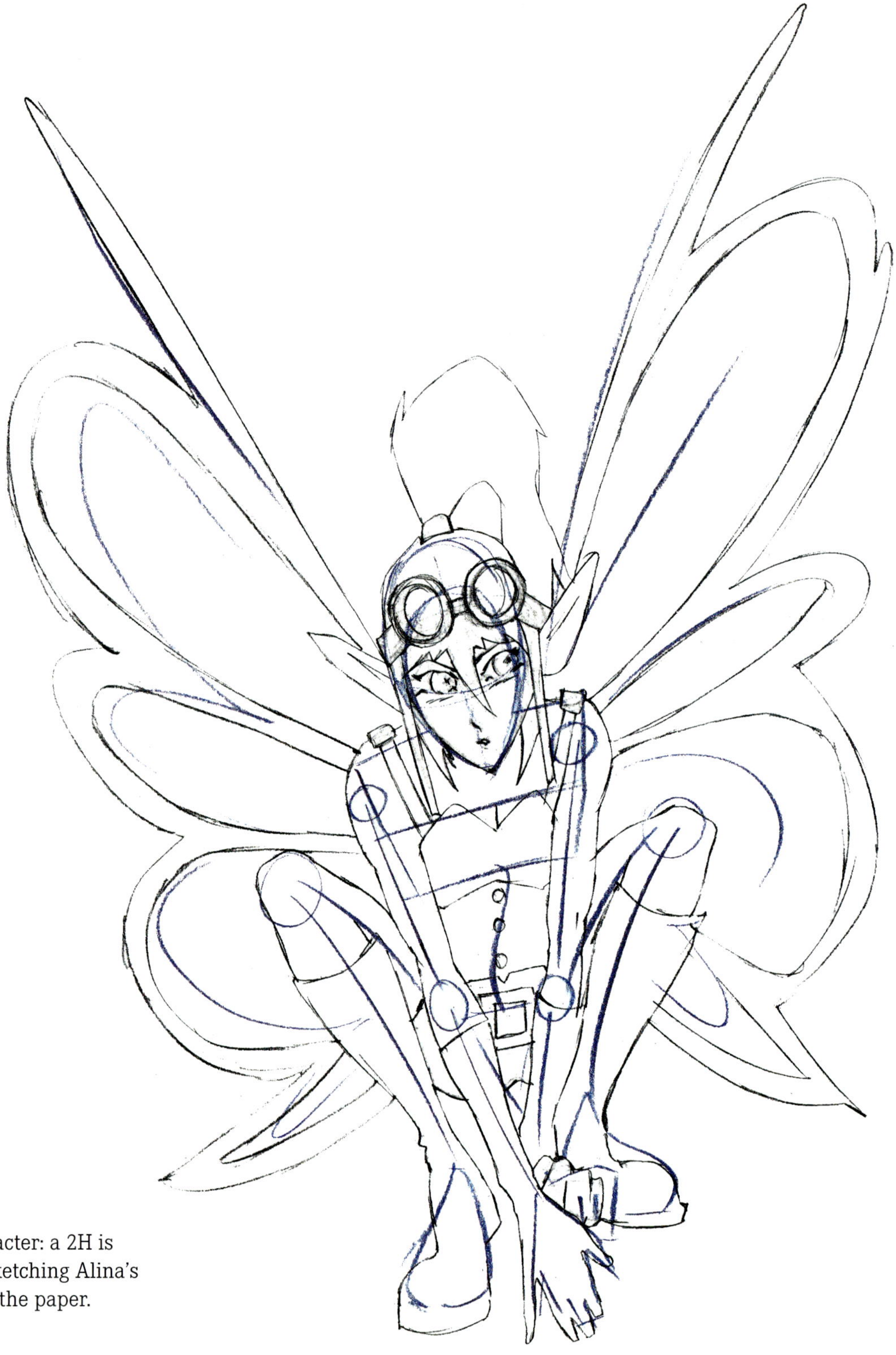

2

Pencil in your character: a 2H is perfect. Carry on sketching Alina's body and wings on the paper.

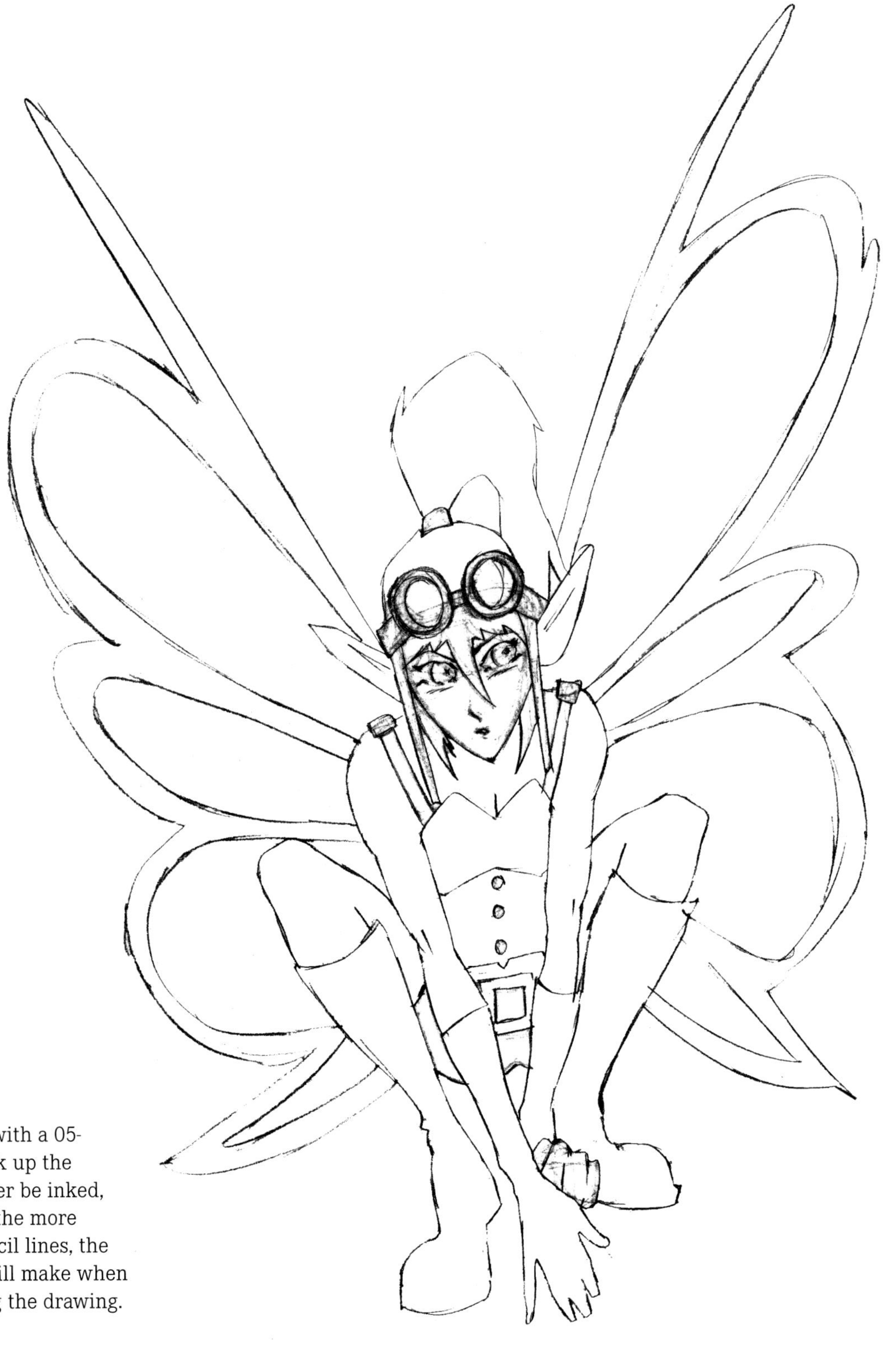

3

Outline the figure with a 05-calibre pencil. Work up the details that will later be inked, remembering that the more definitive your pencil lines, the fewer errors you will make when it comes to coloring the drawing.

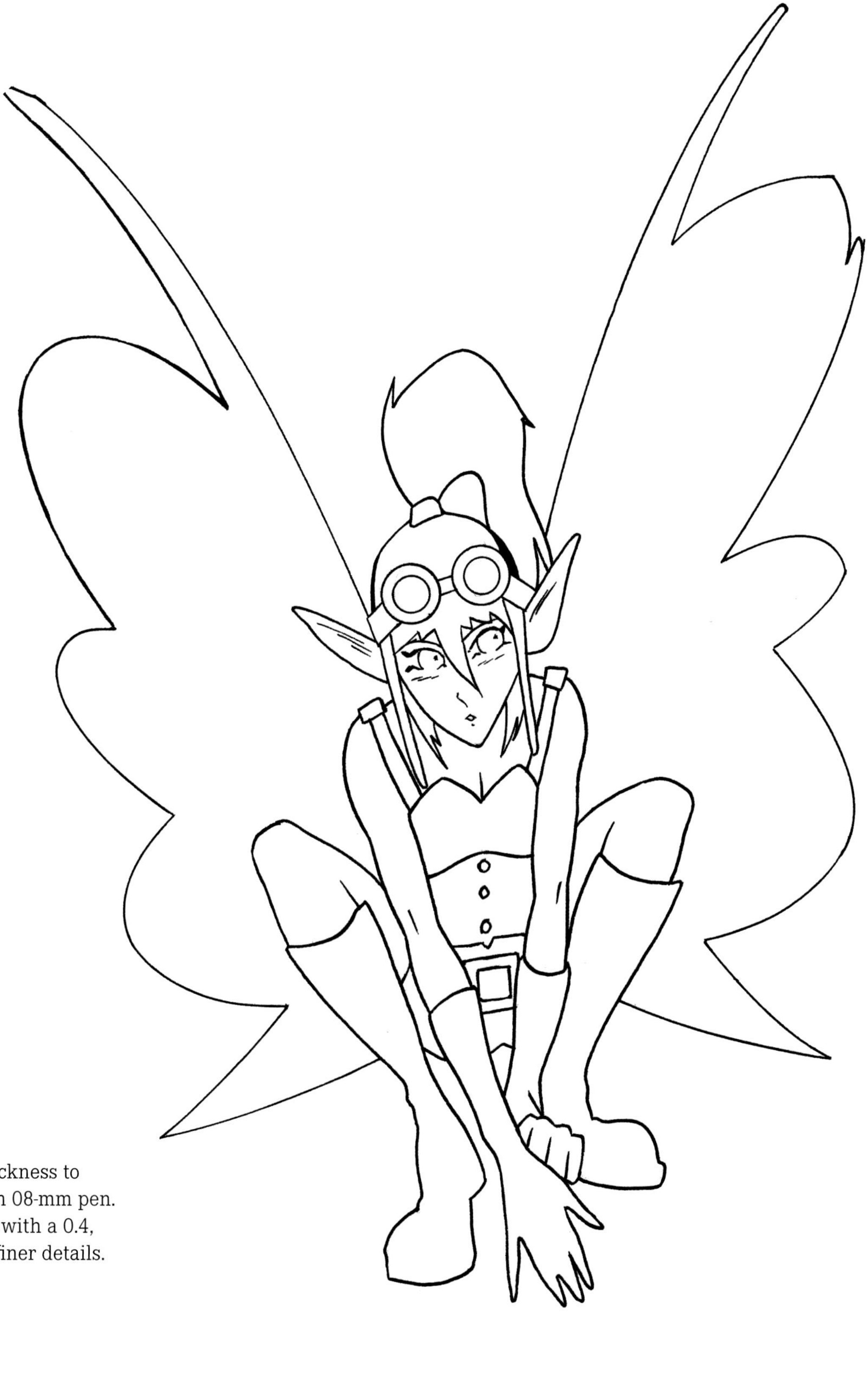

4

Give a different thickness to the outline using an 08-mm pen. Sketch out the rest with a 0.4, using a 0.2 for the finer details.

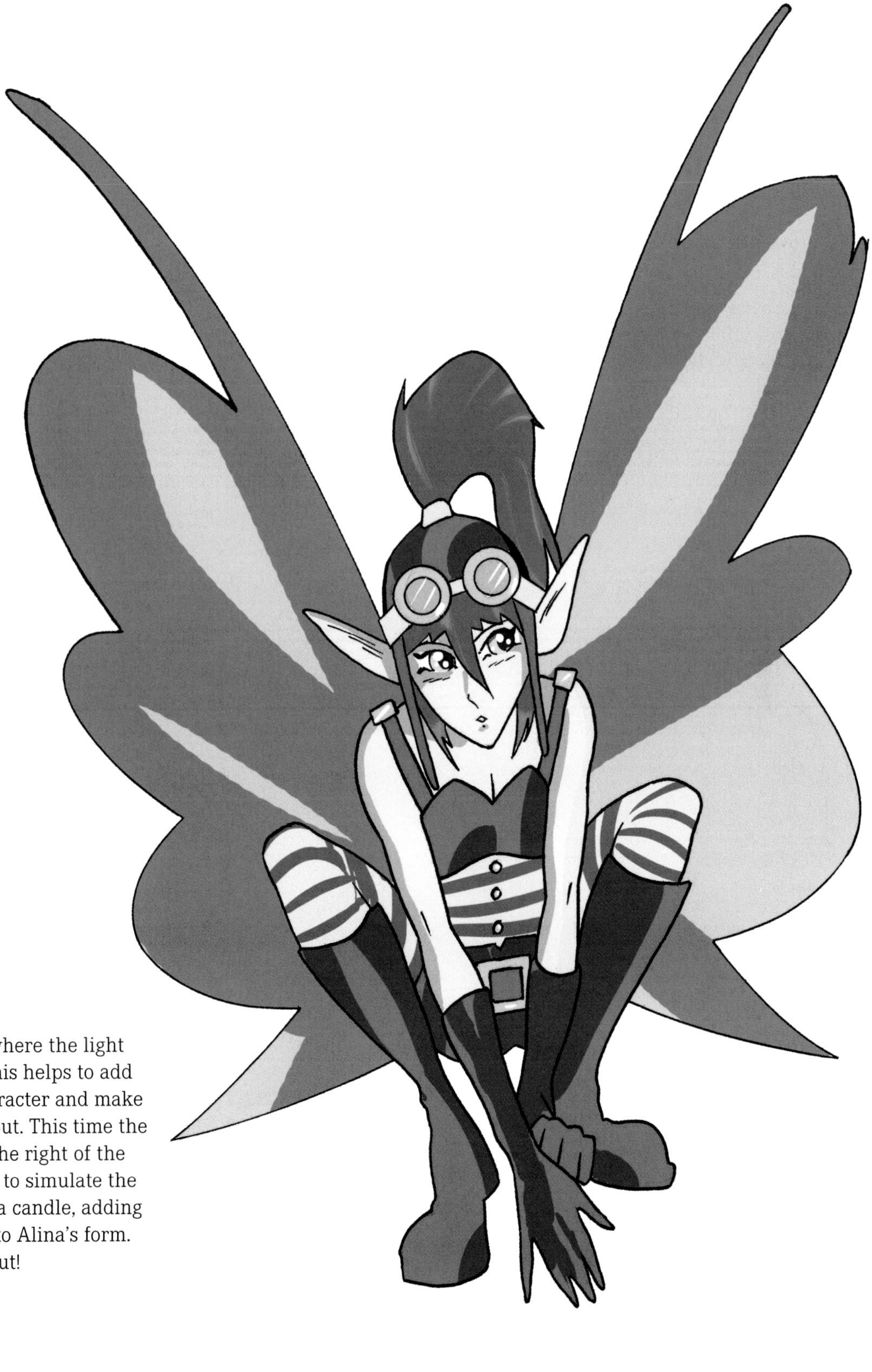

5

Now we will see where the light is coming from. This helps to add volume to the character and make the details stand out. This time the light source is to the right of the drawing. I wanted to simulate the flickering light of a candle, adding random shadows to Alina's form. Great fun. Try it out!

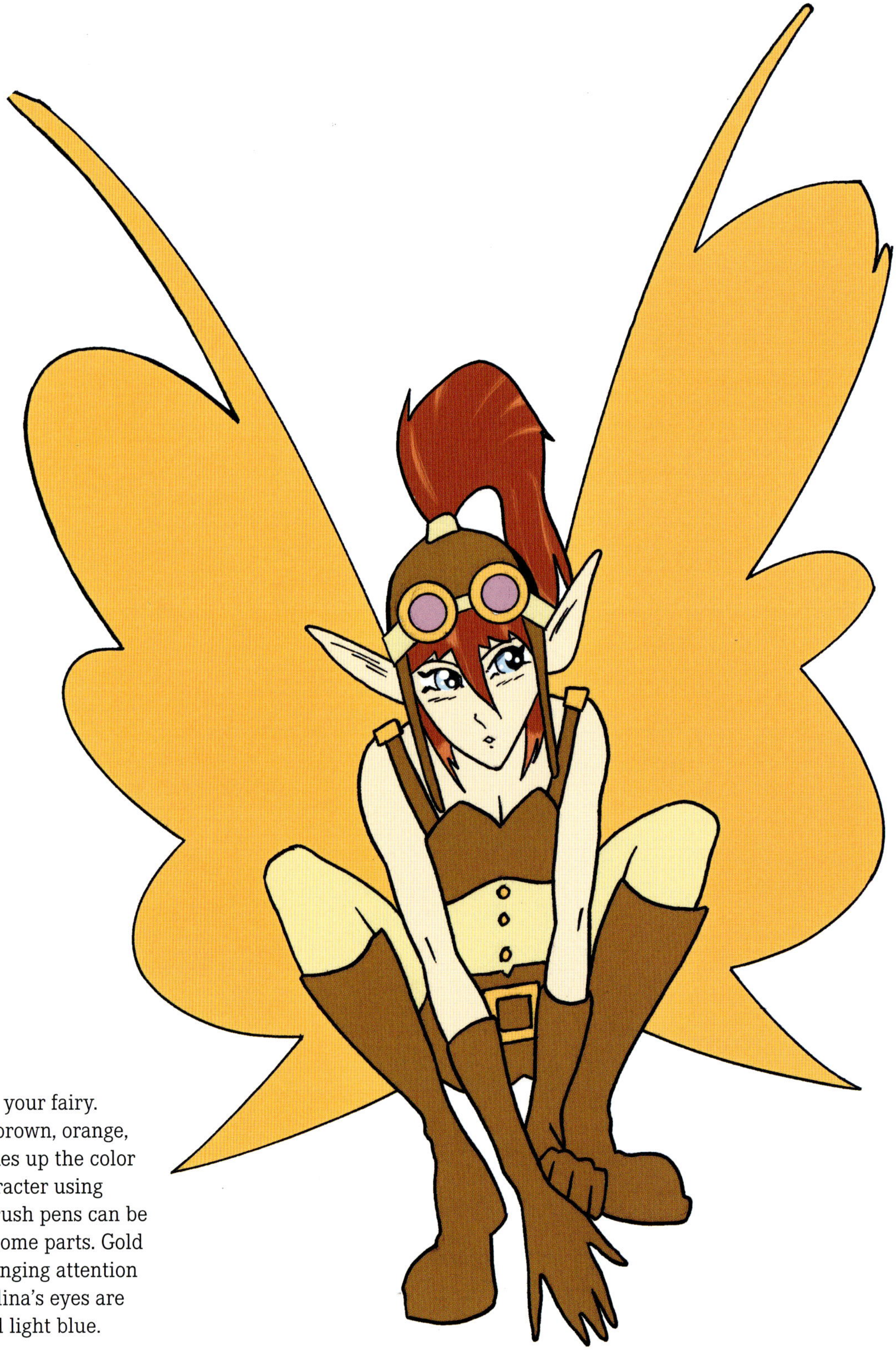

6

Add base colors to your fairy. A combination of brown, orange, and red tones makes up the color palette of this character using colored pencils. Brush pens can be used to highlight some parts. Gold is also used for bringing attention to details, while Alina's eyes are colored a beautiful light blue.

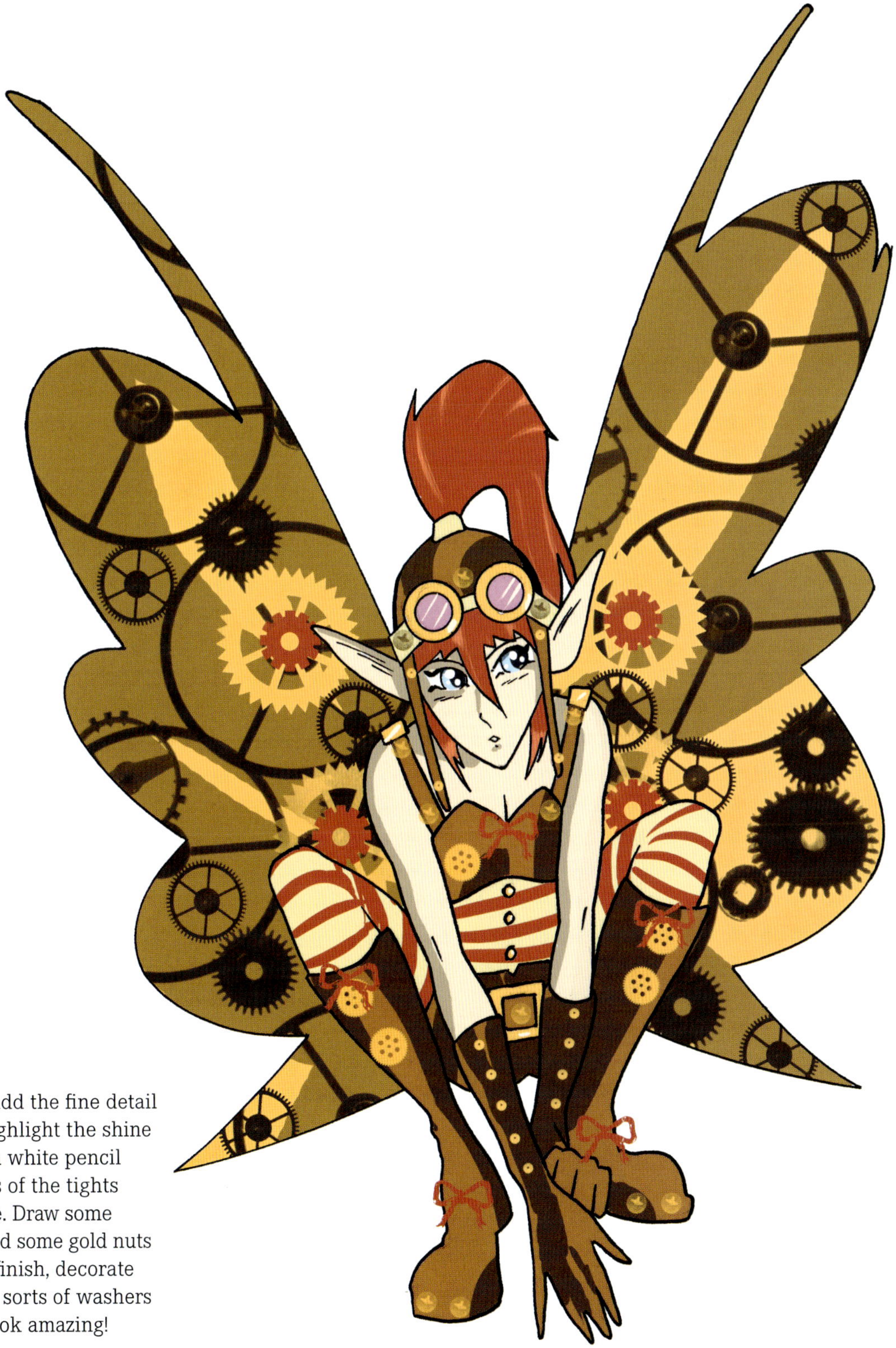

7

Now you need to add the fine detail to the drawing. Highlight the shine of the glasses with white pencil and color the lines of the tights and shirt in orange. Draw some orange washers and some gold nuts and bolts, and, to finish, decorate the wings with all sorts of washers and nuts. It will look amazing!

FEMALE INVENTOR

Marandra was not just any child: ever since she was small she was fascinated by engineering, so much so that as soon as she could she got a degree and set about building everything that came into her head. This was when she created her beloved Pinky Tool. Now she takes it with her everywhere and will certainly be taking it to the Genius Exhibition this year. Wouldn't you love to see their faces when it shows up?

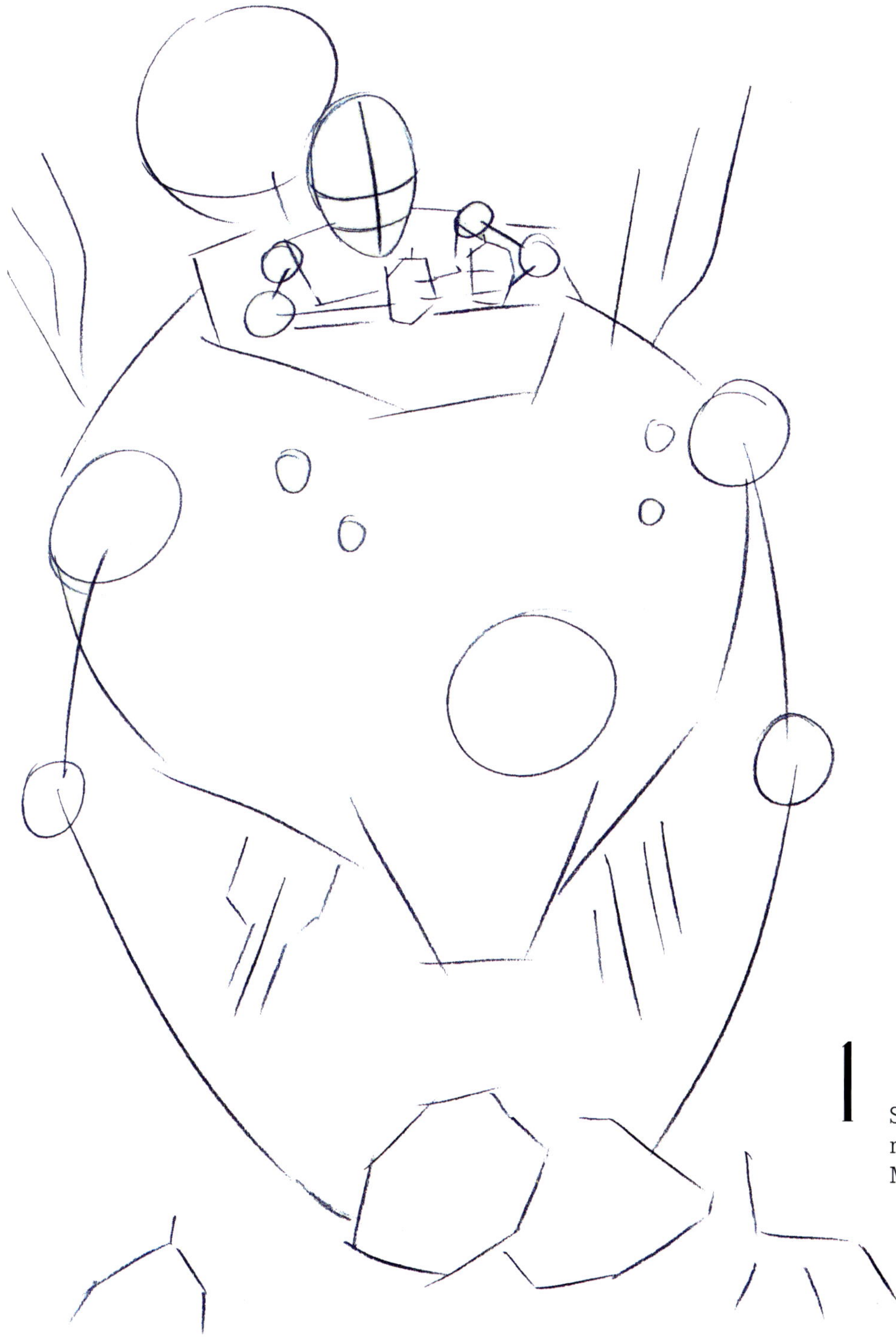

1

Start by drawing the base of the robot in blue pencil then add Marandra too.

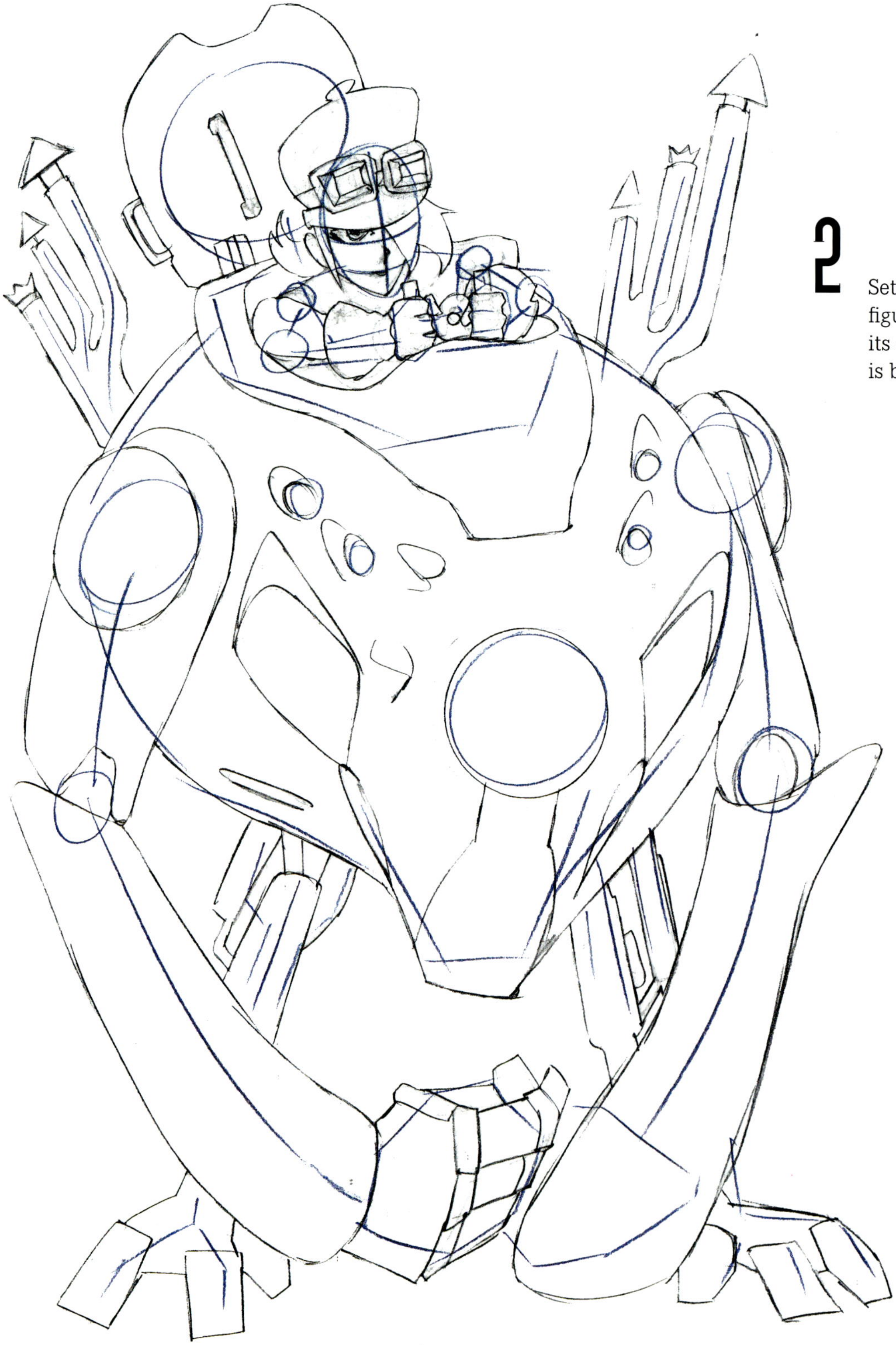

2

Set out the contour of the figure to add body and define its appearance. A hard pencil is best for this. I use a 2H.

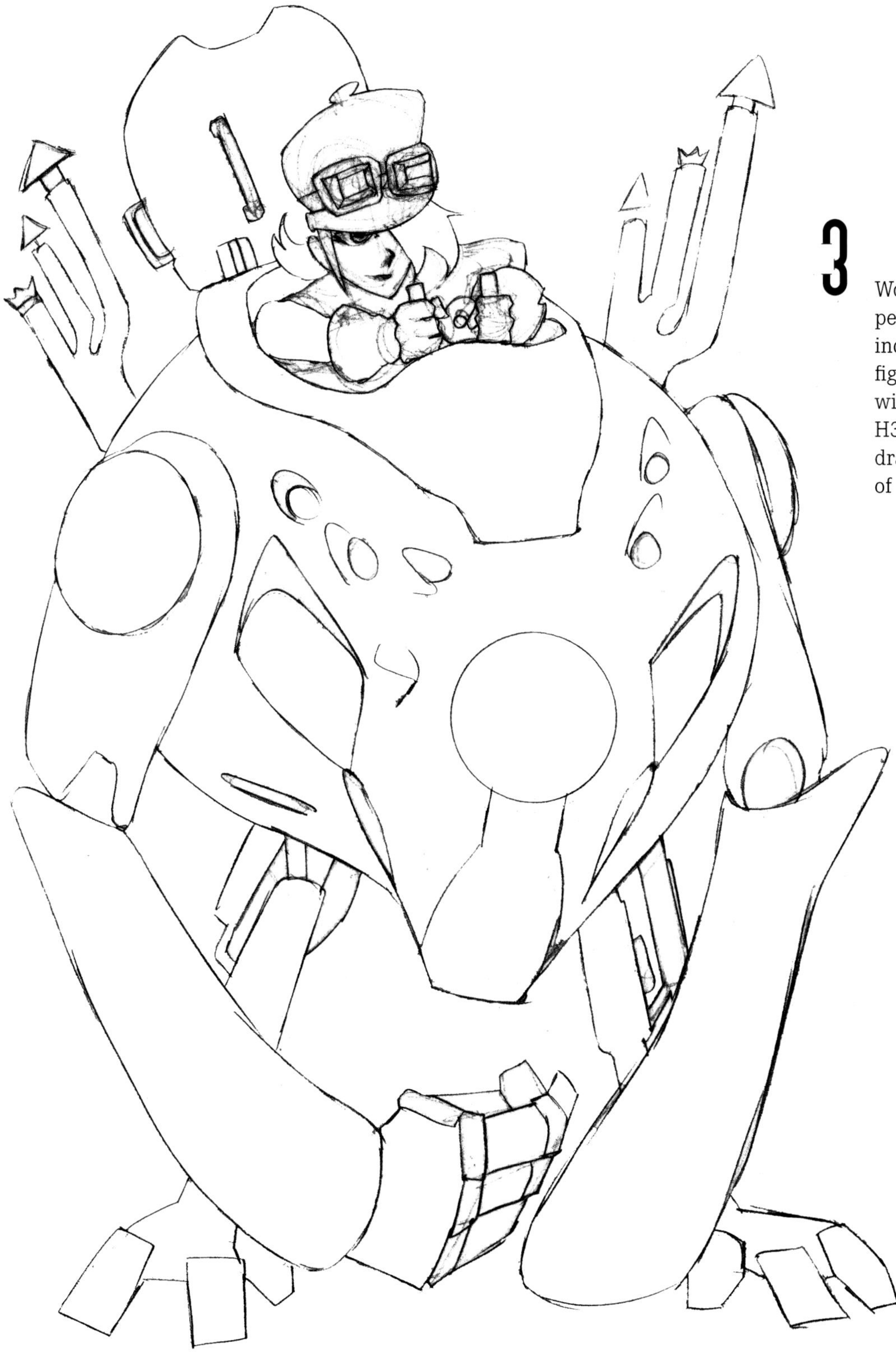

3

Work up the image with your pencil. Sketch the design to incorporate detail within the figure: I use a mechanical pencil with a 0.5 mm 3H lead or an H3 pencil to add volume to the drawing and complete the outline of the robot and the girl.

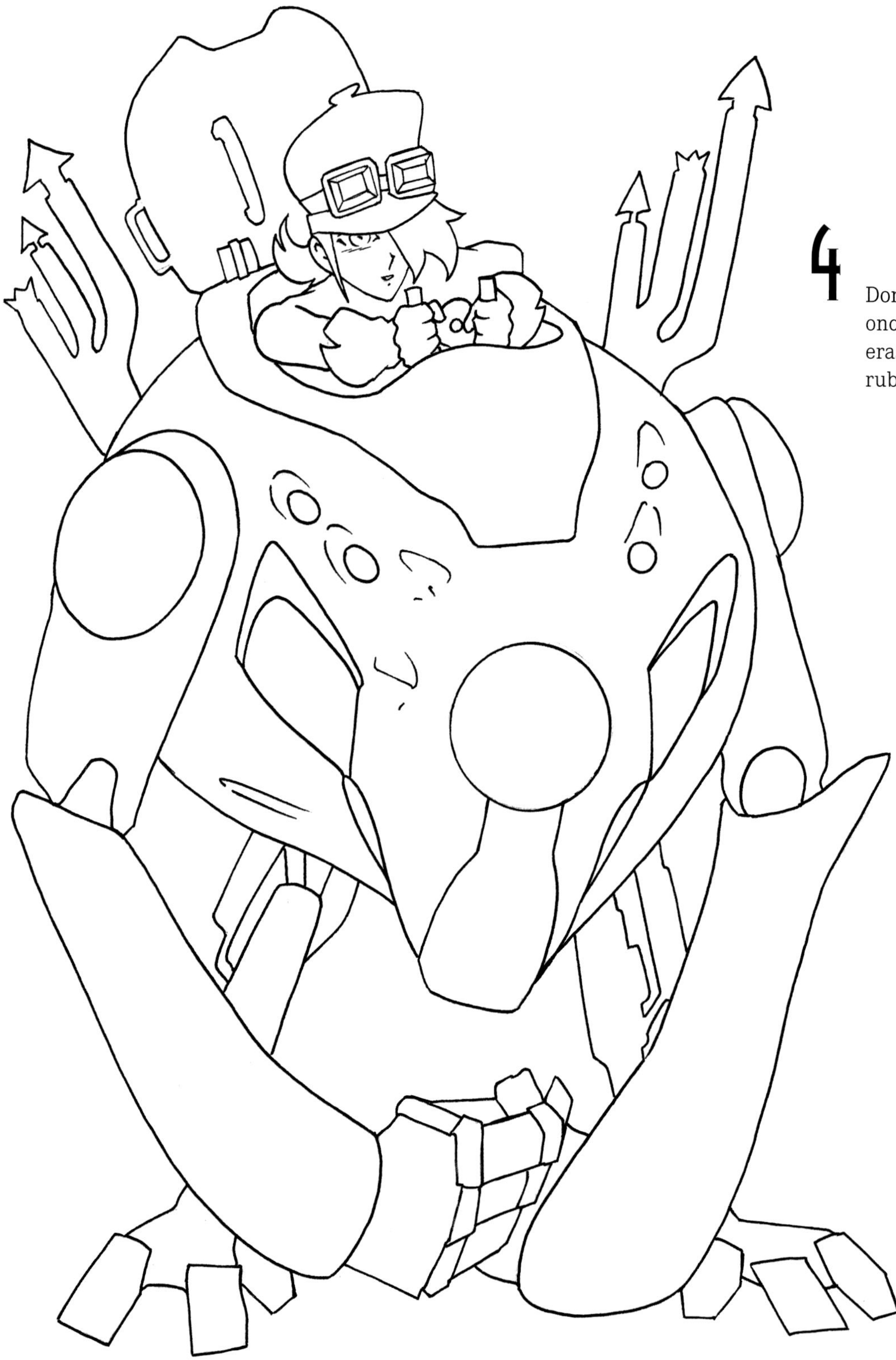

4

Don't forget to remove the pencil once the ink is dry. Use a soft eraser to rub out the pencil, always rubbing in the same direction.

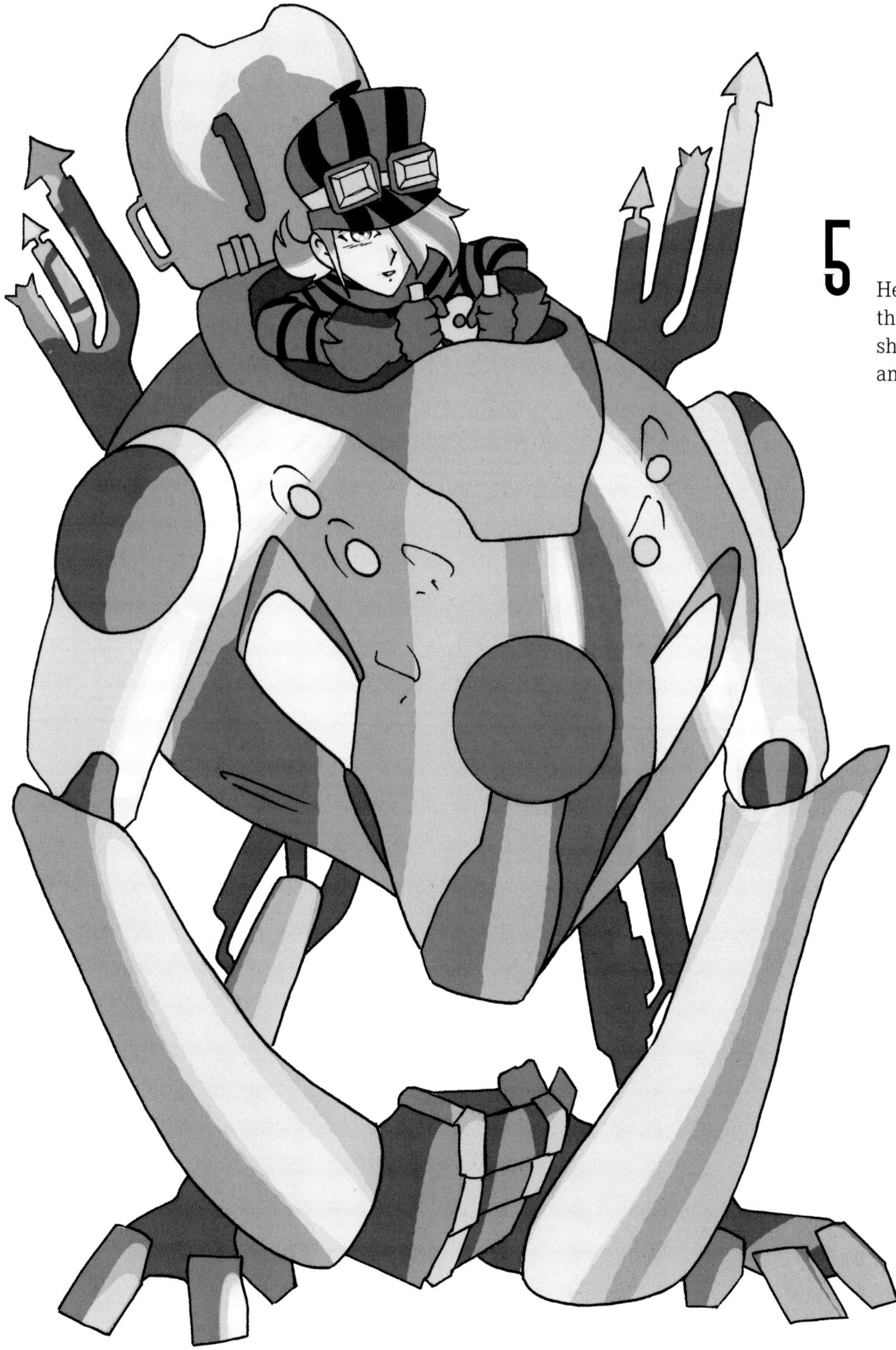

5 Here the light source is below the figures, creating comforting shadows around Marandra and her Pinky Tool robot.

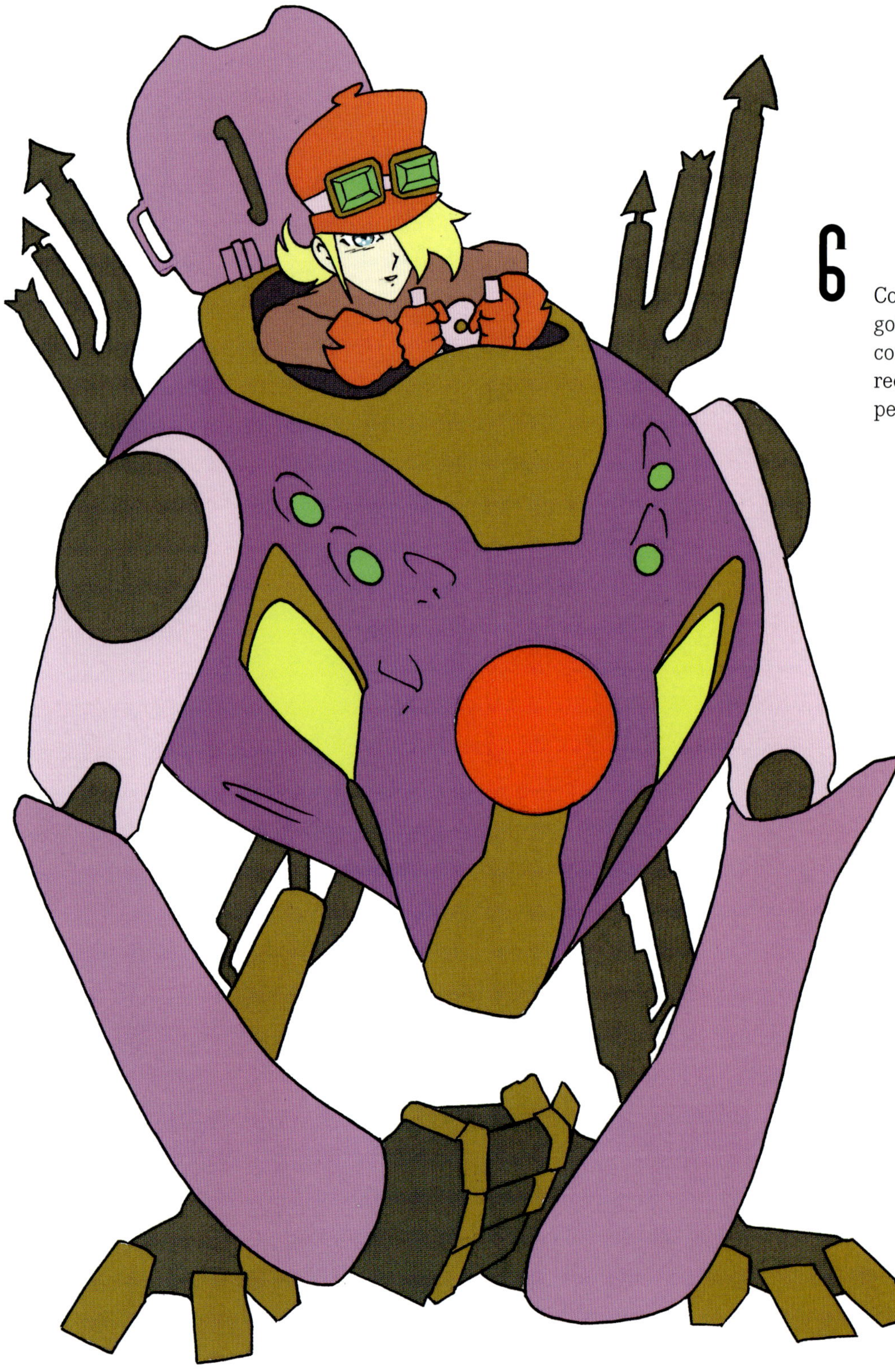

6

Color the robot in pinks, purples, gold, and gray, and choose a combination of light and dark reds for the girl using colored pencils and brush pens.

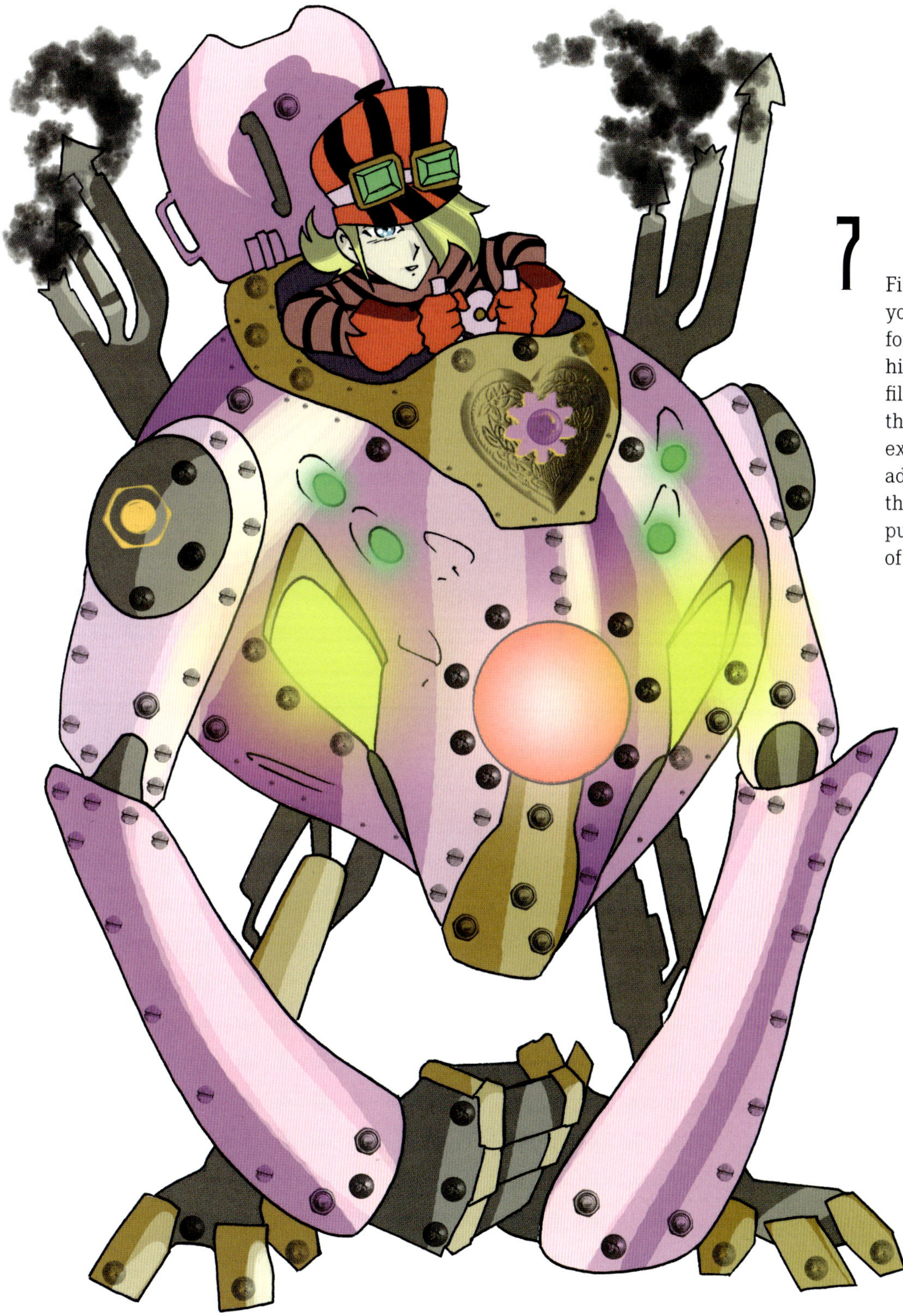

7

Finish by adding fine details to your character. Use gold markers for rivets or white pencil for highlights. Slowly and patiently fill your drawing with details that make it uniquely yours! For example, you can experiment by adding rivets in gray, illuminating the yellow and red lights or even putting smoke in the vents. Any of these ideas would work!

SUBMARINE CAPTAIN

Nacros Stanlak is captain of *El Demoledor*, a prodigious submarine with great maneuverability and immense firepower. In command of this formidable underwater weapon, Stanlak has launched a surprise attack on the enemy ships, spreading terror across the world's seas.

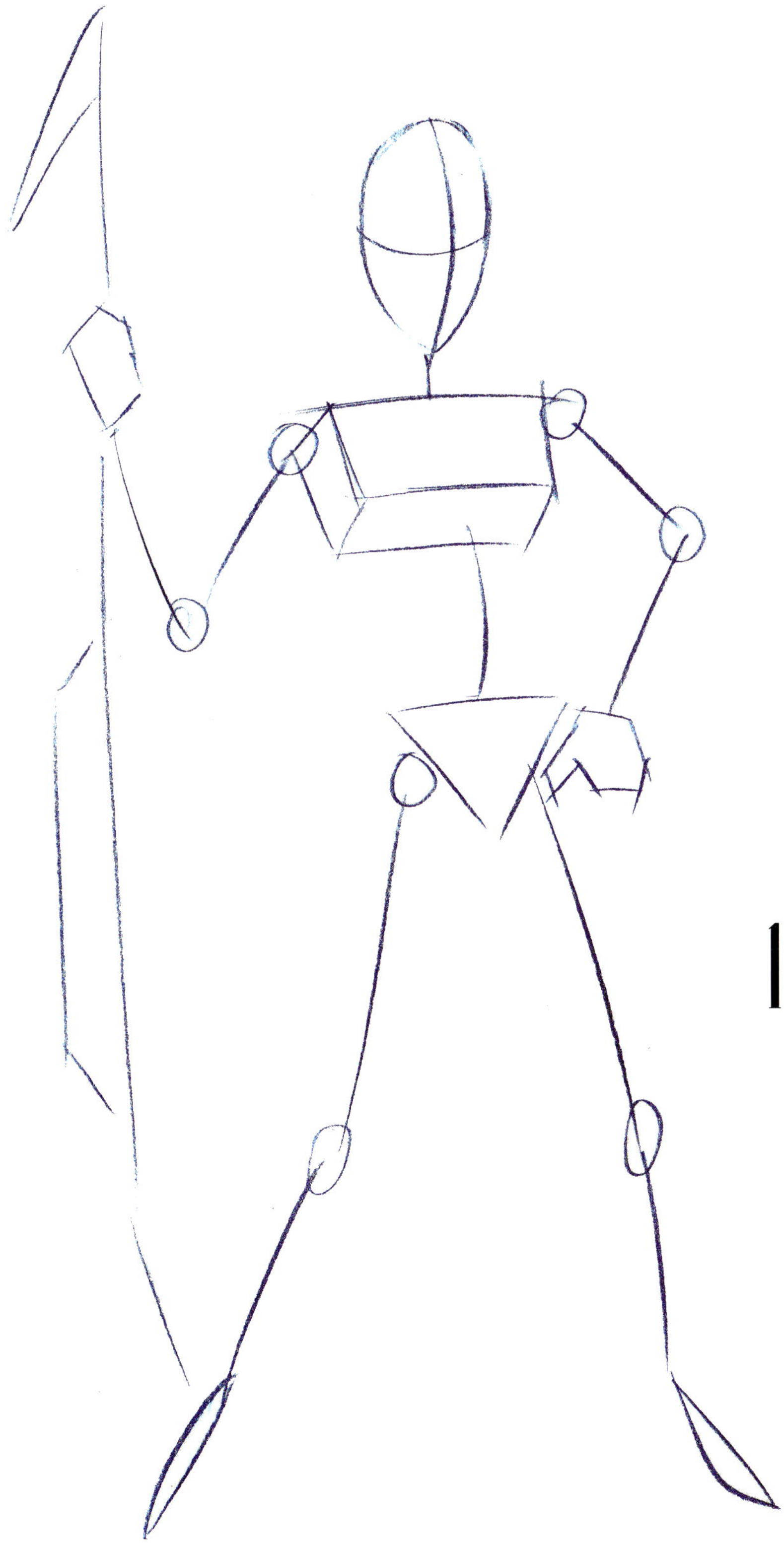

1

Begin by drawing the base of your character in blue pencil: a defiant pose.

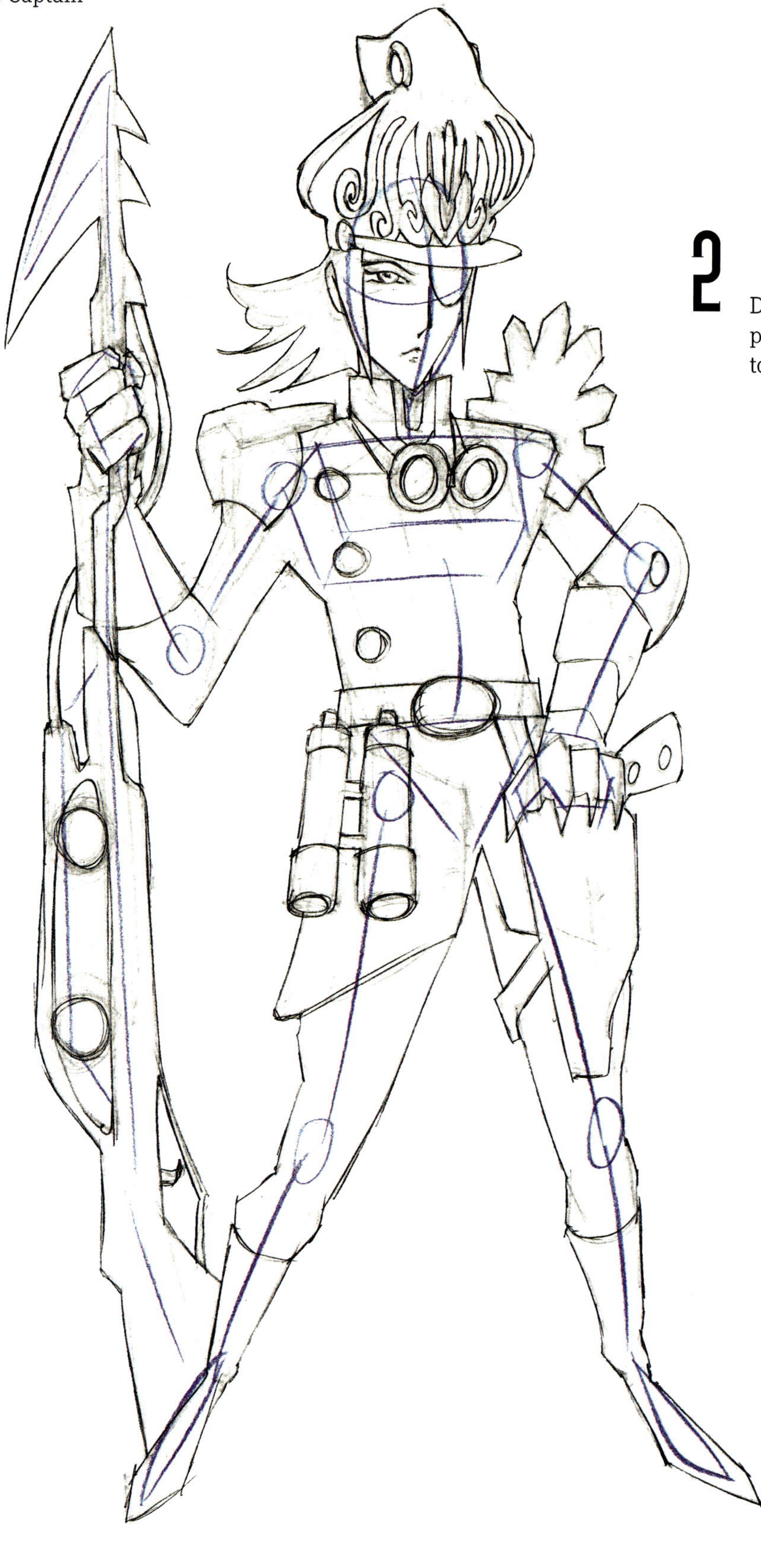

2

Define the figure over the blue pencil, and give shape and form to the captain using a 2H pencil.

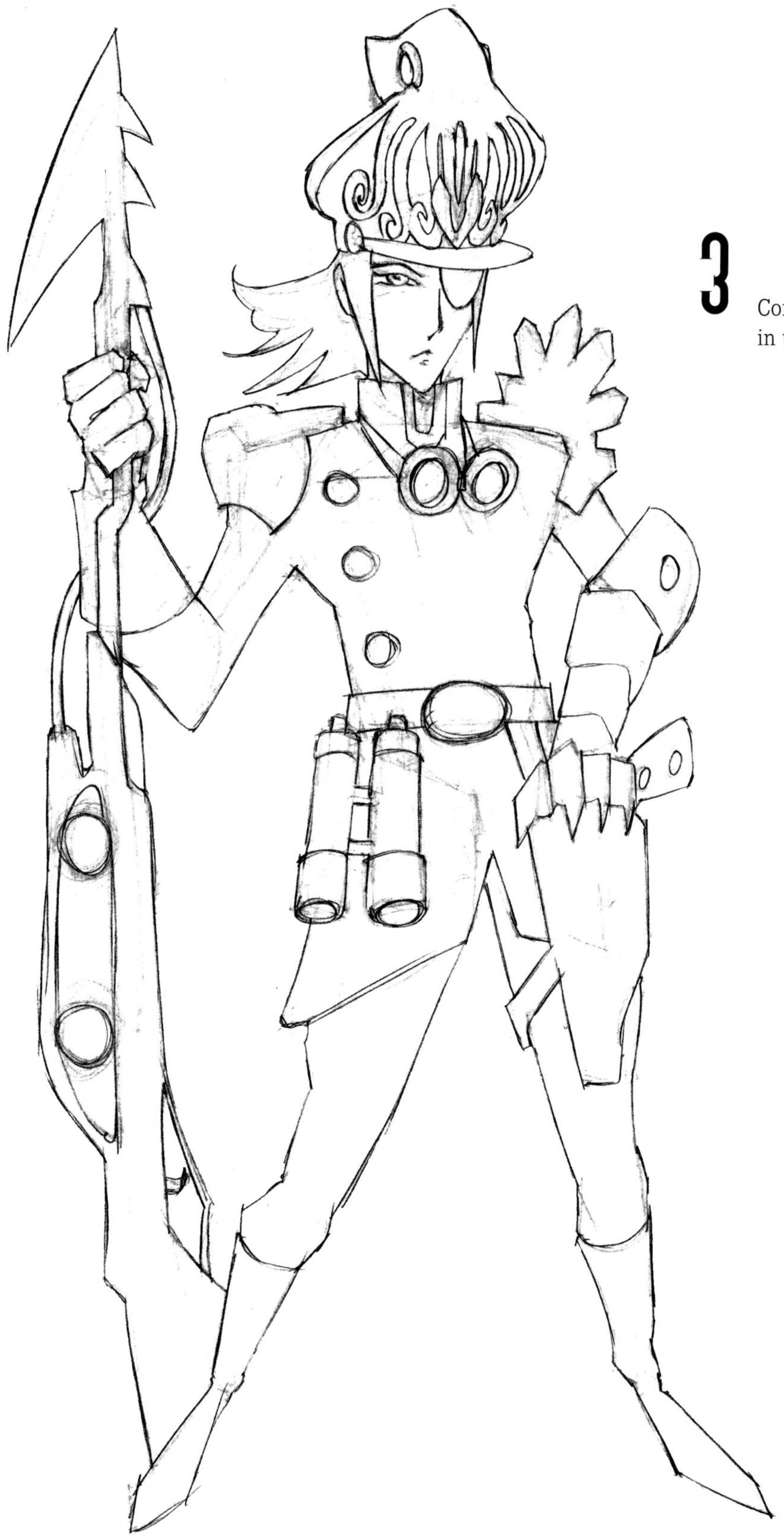

3

Complete the silhouette and work in the details with a 05 pencil.

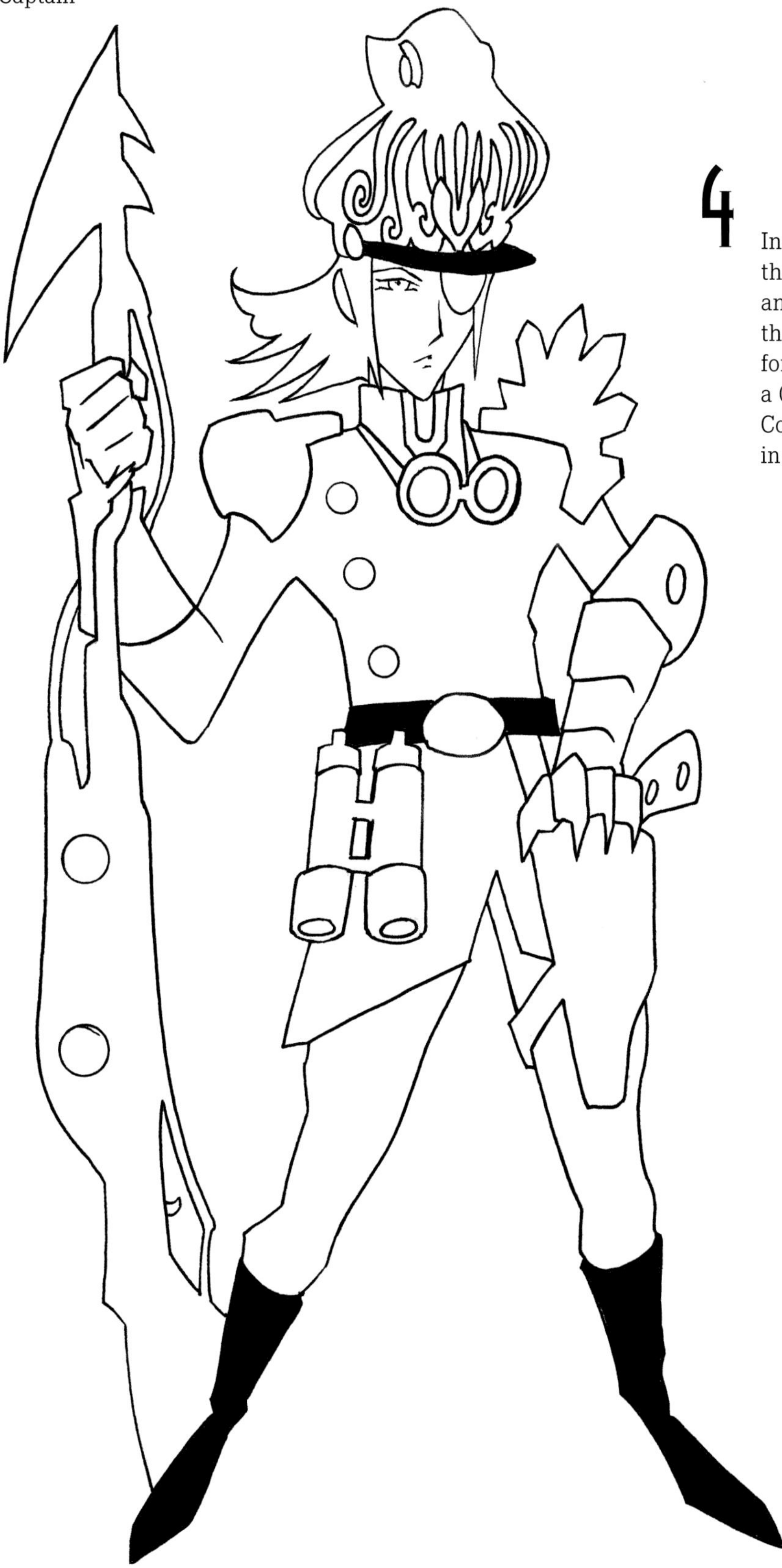

4

Ink the drawing. Give a different thickness to the outline using an 0.8-mm pen. Trace the rest of the lines with a 0.4-mm pen except for the finer detail, for which a 0.2-mm pen will do the job. Color the hat, belt, and boots in black too.

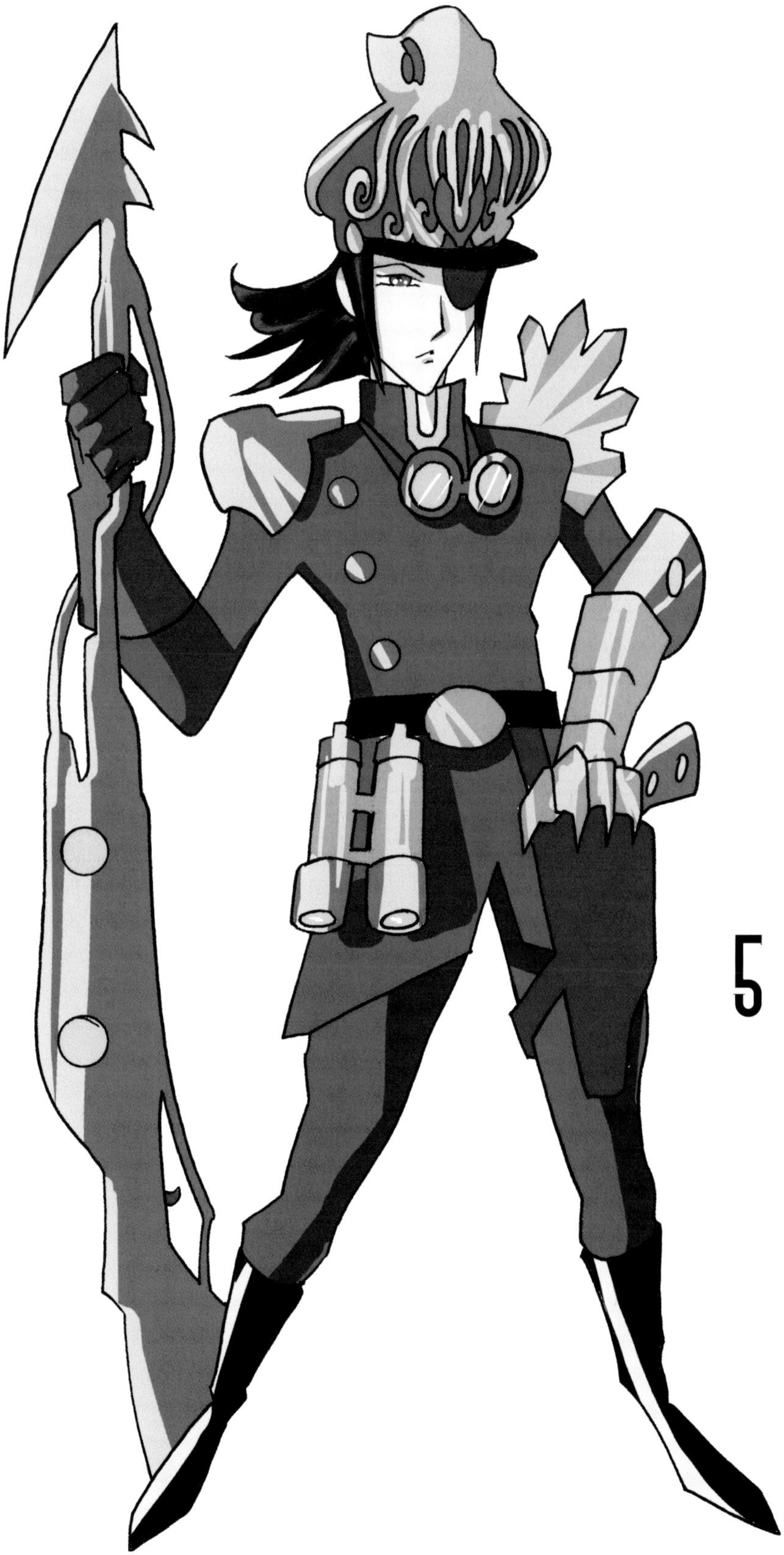

5

Now we will see where the light is coming from. This helps to add volume to the character and make the details stand out. As you can see, the light is coming directly from the character's left.

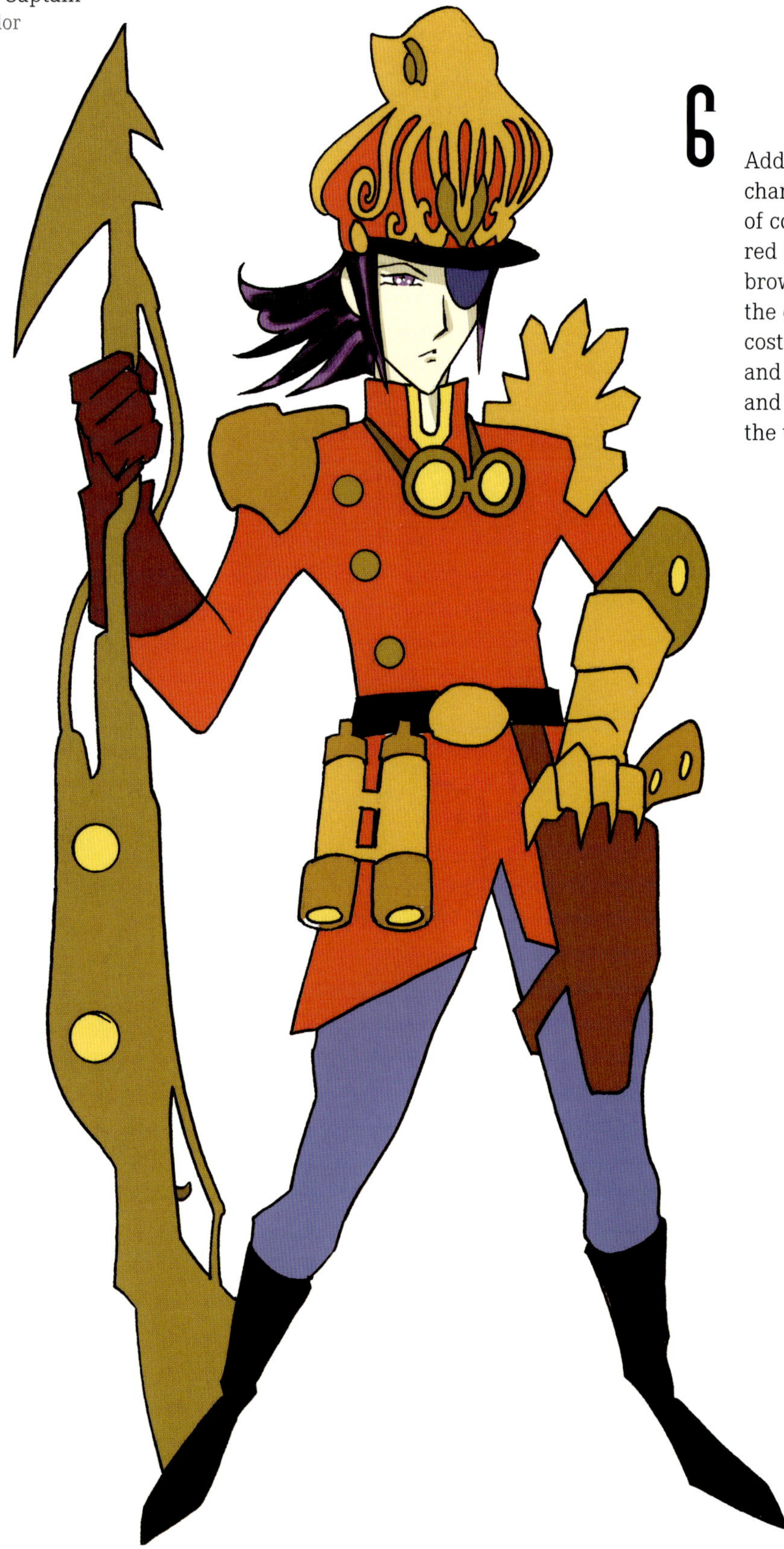

6

Add the base colors to your character using a combination of colored pencils and brush pens: red for the shirt and hat, reddish brown for the gloves, gold for the details and accessories of his costume, and blue for the trousers and patch. Color his hair purple and add touches of black to add the volume that you are after.

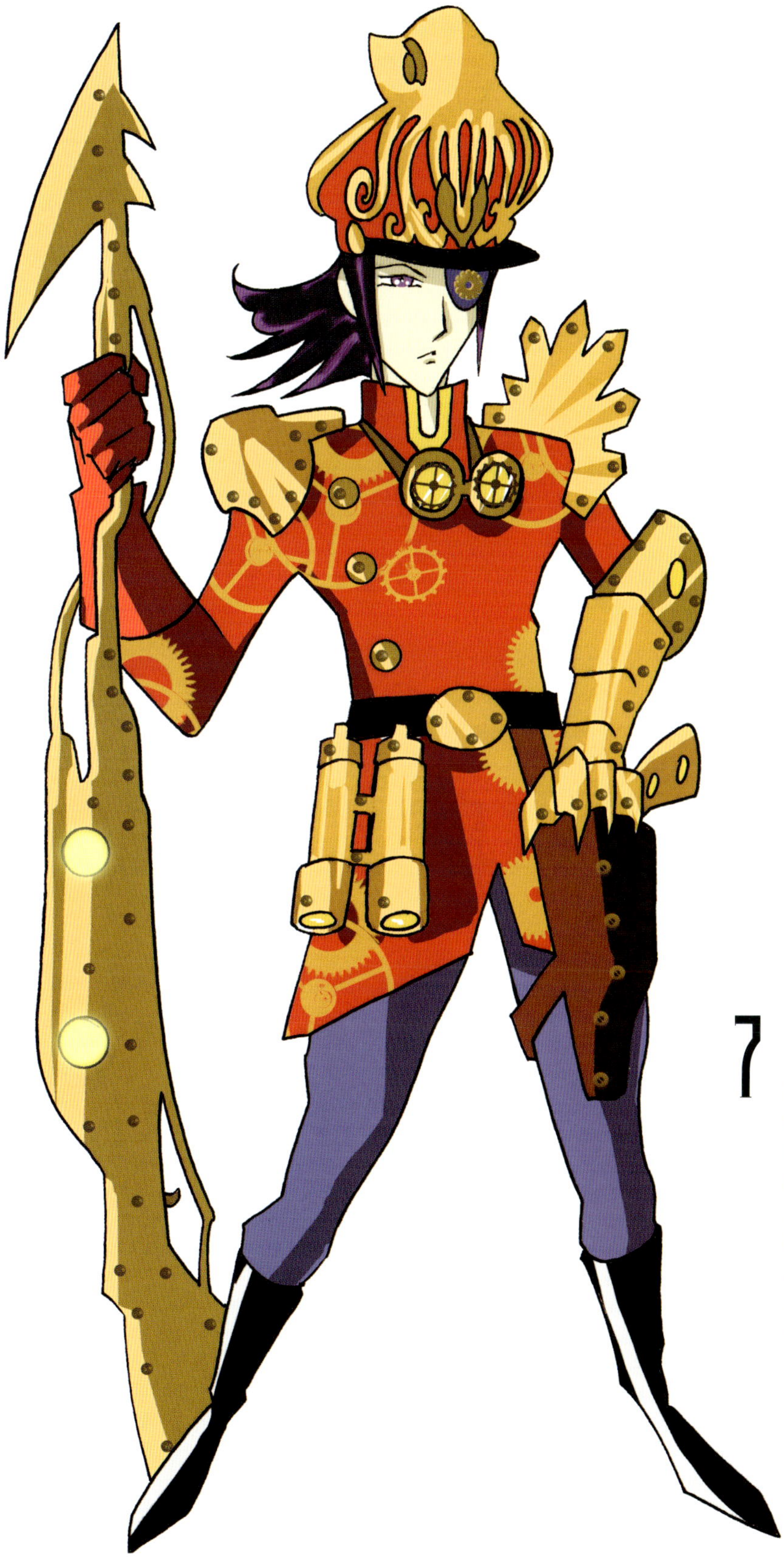

7

Now to incorporate detail into the drawing: white pencil for the highlights and gold Edding pen for the glistening metal, and any screws or washers you want to include. Practice makes perfect! Add some yellow touches to the glasses too, along with some screws and accessories such as the patch!

MONSTER HUNTER

Lugos Montecristy is descended from a family of monster hunters. His father and his grandfather before him devoted their lives to protecting the innocent from the evil creatures of the night. An expert in the use of the stake and in possession of an arsenal that includes silver daggers and a rifle of eons, this guy is a formidable monster hunter. What's more, he always has his magic monocle at the ready: an infallible detector of evil creatures!

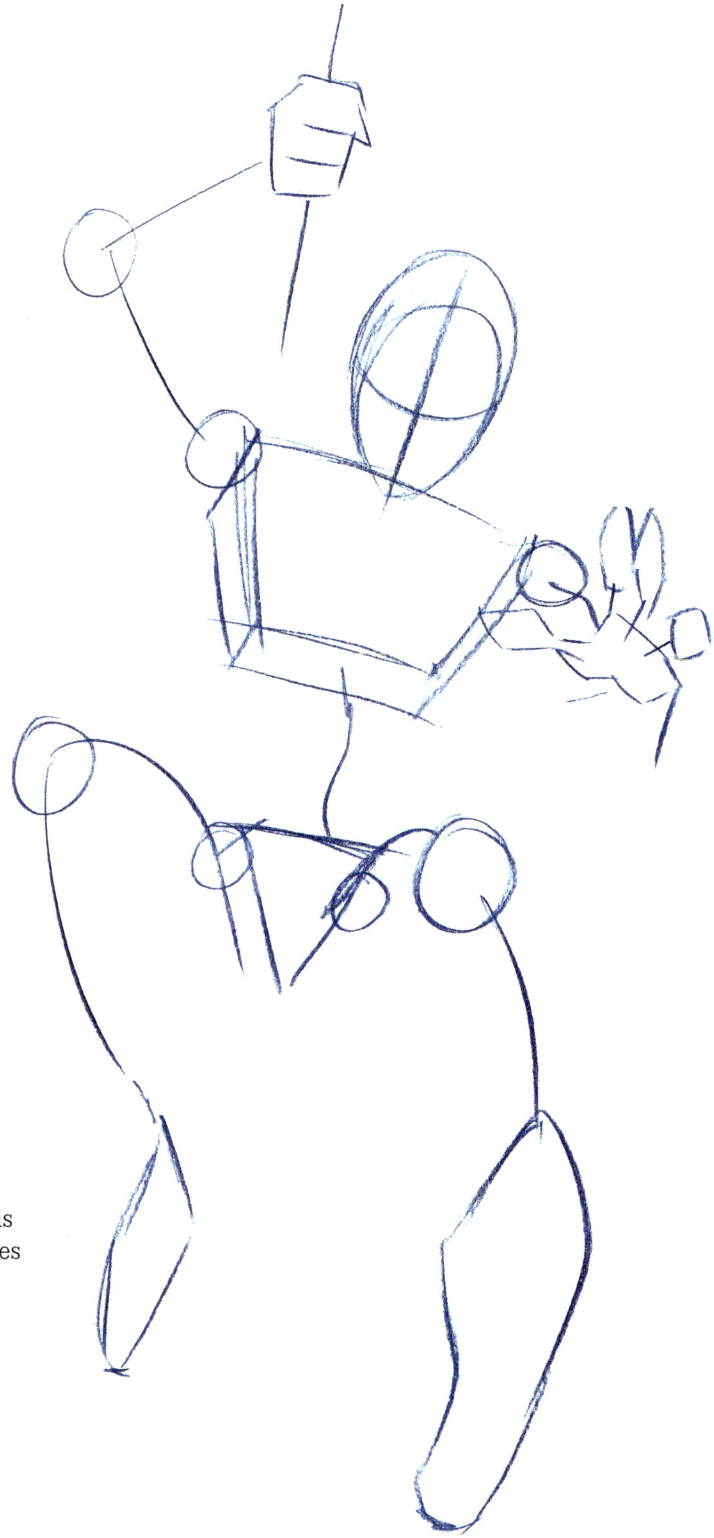

1

Draw the figure in blue pencil, using dynamic movement for this one: this is a stance that simulates a falling attack from the sky.

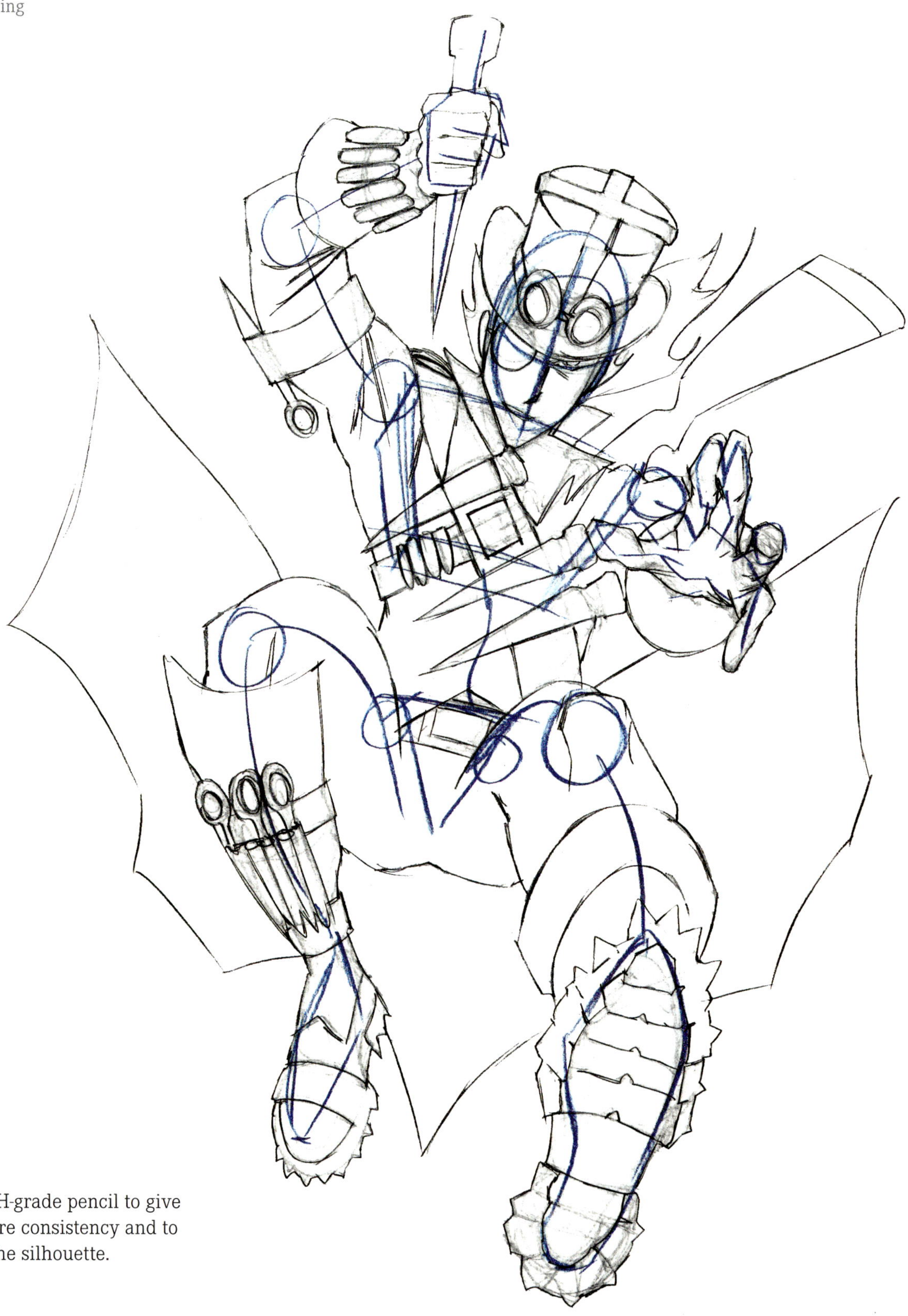

2

Use a 2H-grade pencil to give the figure consistency and to shape the silhouette.

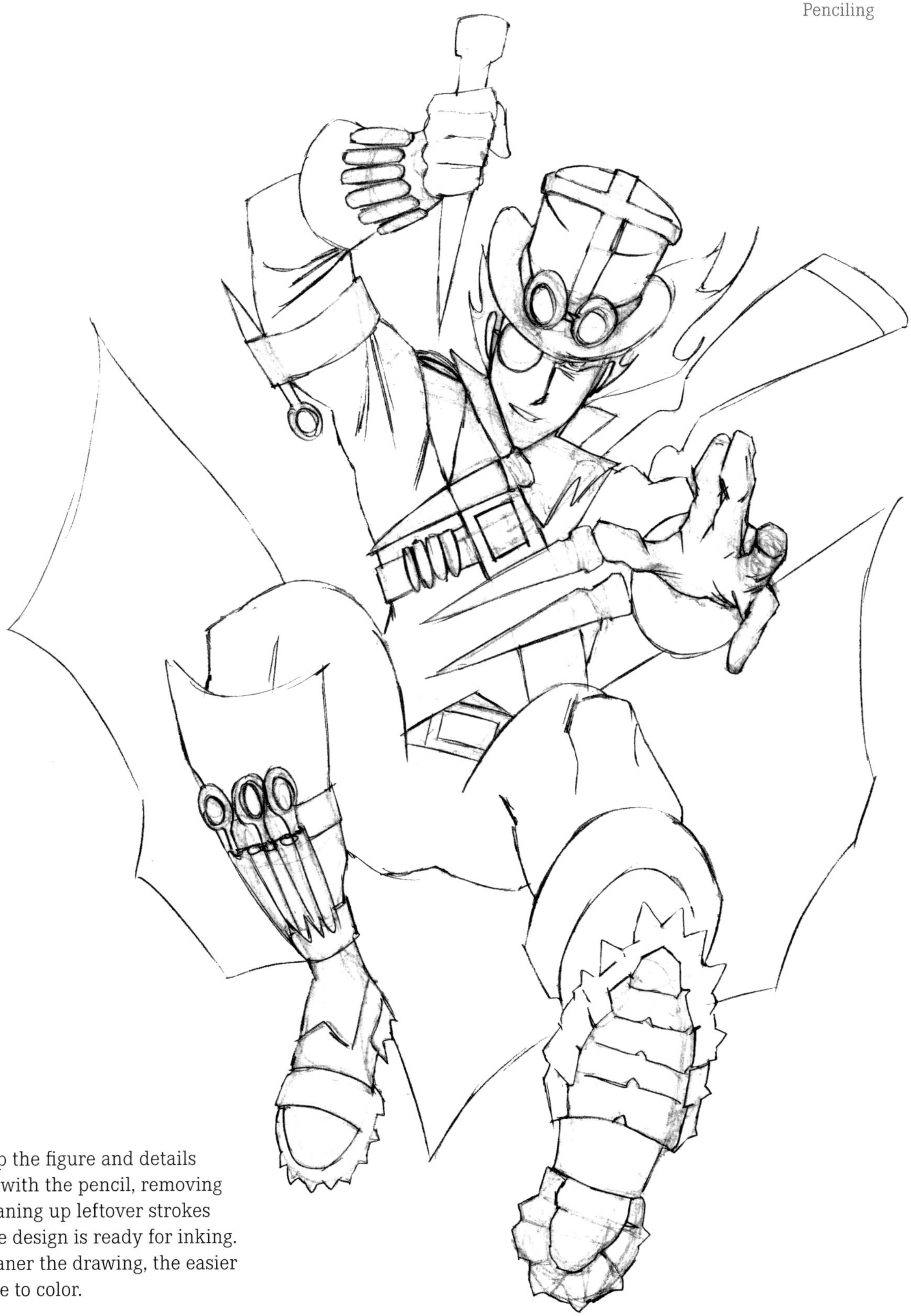

3

Work up the figure and details further with the pencil, removing and cleaning up leftover strokes until the design is ready for inking. The cleaner the drawing, the easier it will be to color.

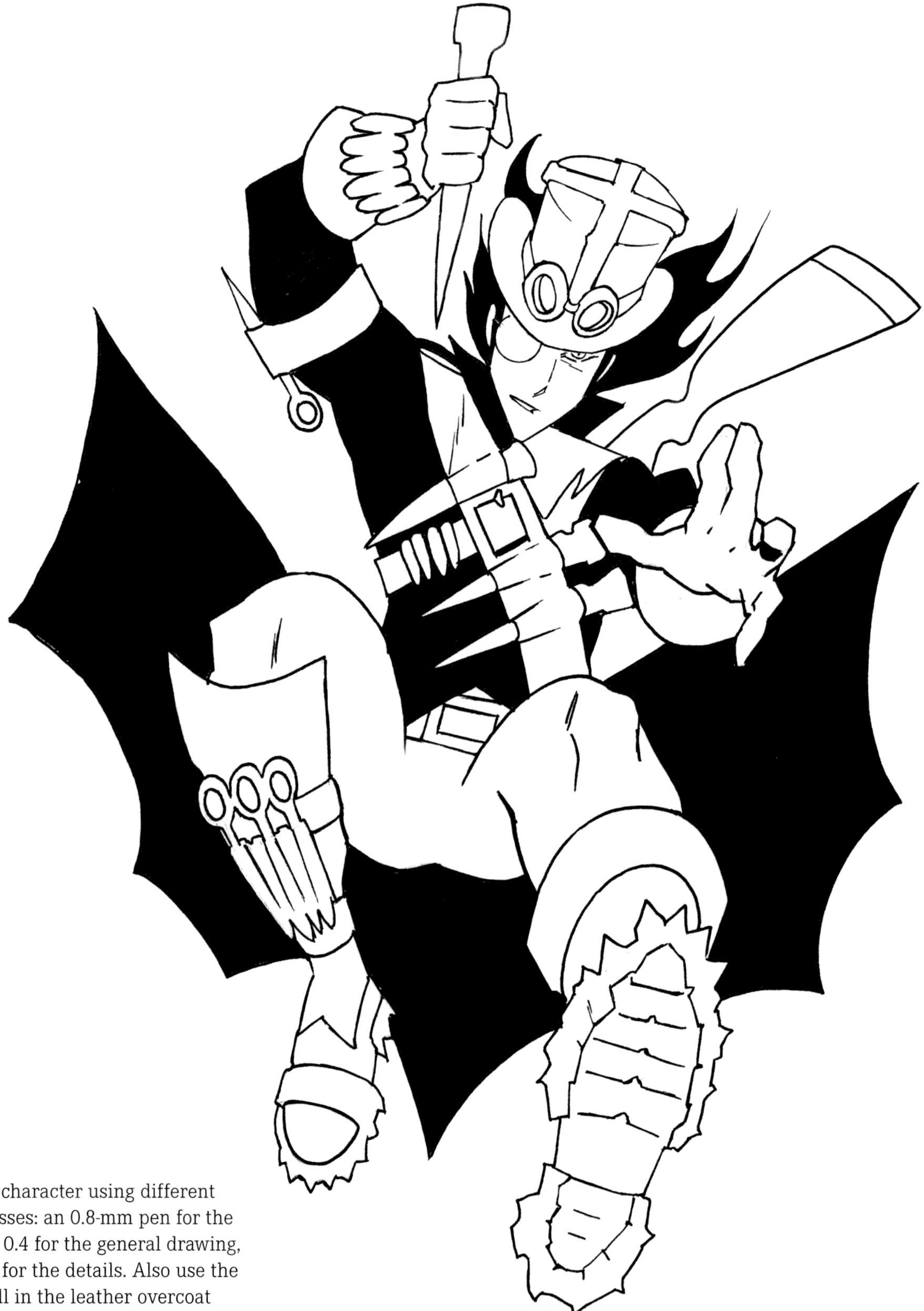

4

Ink the character using different thicknesses: an 0.8-mm pen for the outline, 0.4 for the general drawing, and 0.2 for the details. Also use the 0.8 to fill in the leather overcoat and the hair.

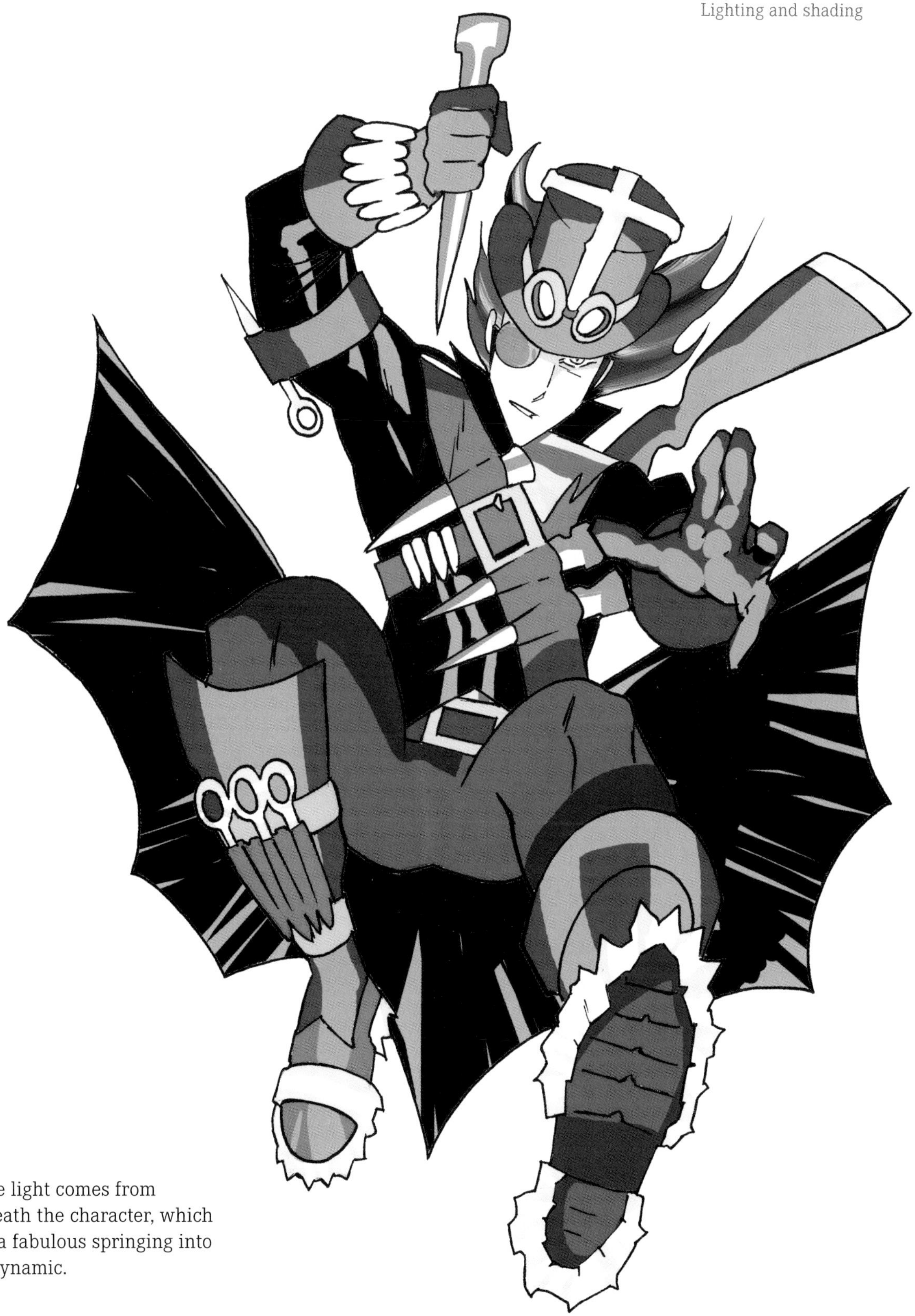

5

Here the light comes from underneath the character, which creates a fabulous springing into action dynamic.

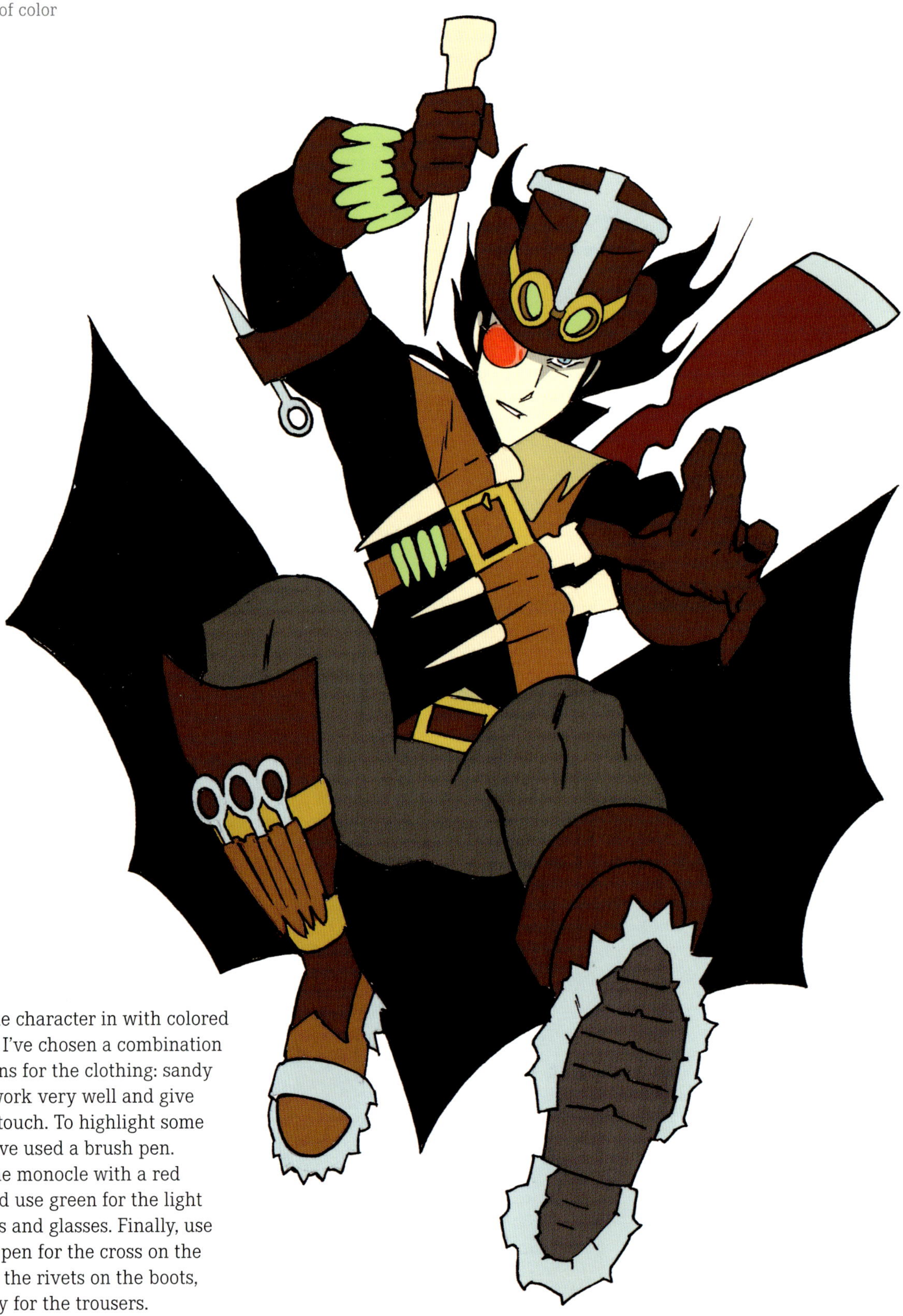

6

Color the character in with colored pencils. I've chosen a combination of browns for the clothing: sandy colors work very well and give a great touch. To highlight some areas, I've used a brush pen. Color the monocle with a red lens, and use green for the light capsules and glasses. Finally, use a silver pen for the cross on the hat and the rivets on the boots, and gray for the trousers.

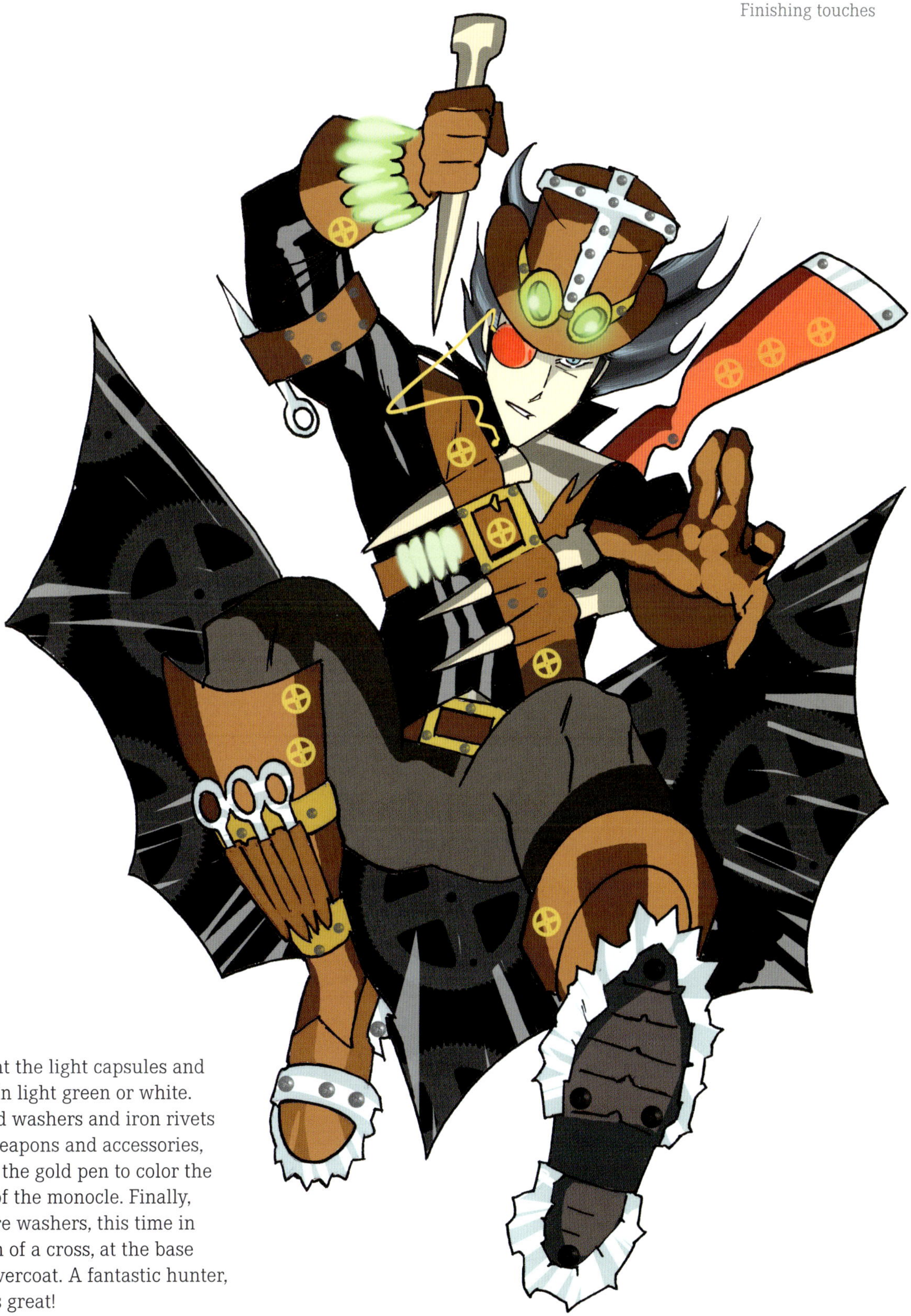

7

Highlight the light capsules and glasses in light green or white. Add gold washers and iron rivets to the weapons and accessories, and use the gold pen to color the thread of the monocle. Finally, add more washers, this time in the form of a cross, at the base of the overcoat. A fantastic hunter, he looks great!

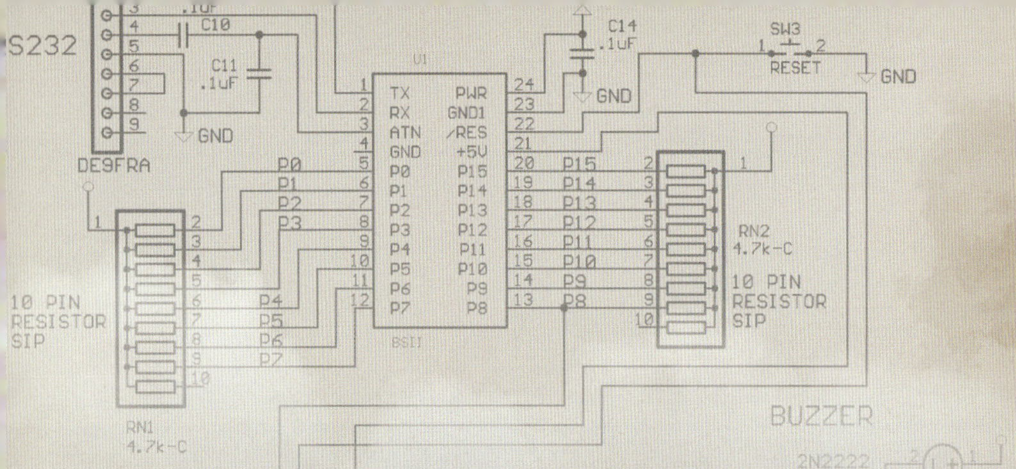

LUMBERJACK

After the first wars, giant robot soldiers were abandoned as scrap. They were mementos of darker times when nobody wanted them. Then one day somebody (some say it was a mechanic, some say it was a very young engineer, and others say it was both) picked up the pieces of these enormous robots to build something. At that time the forests of the kingdom were being plundered beyond control, but overnight the looters disappeared or fled and order was returned to the woods. Since then nothing has been taken other than the necessary firewood. Sometimes Lumberjack appears, as grandiose and solemn as the robots had once been, and kindly announces, "Hello, I am your ranger!"

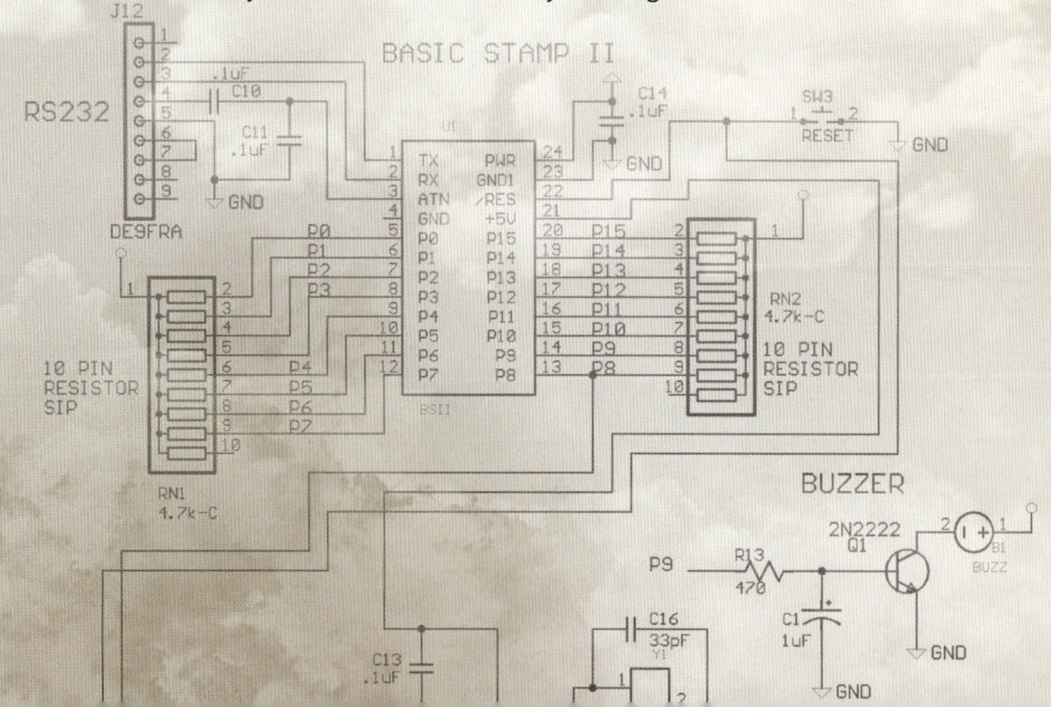

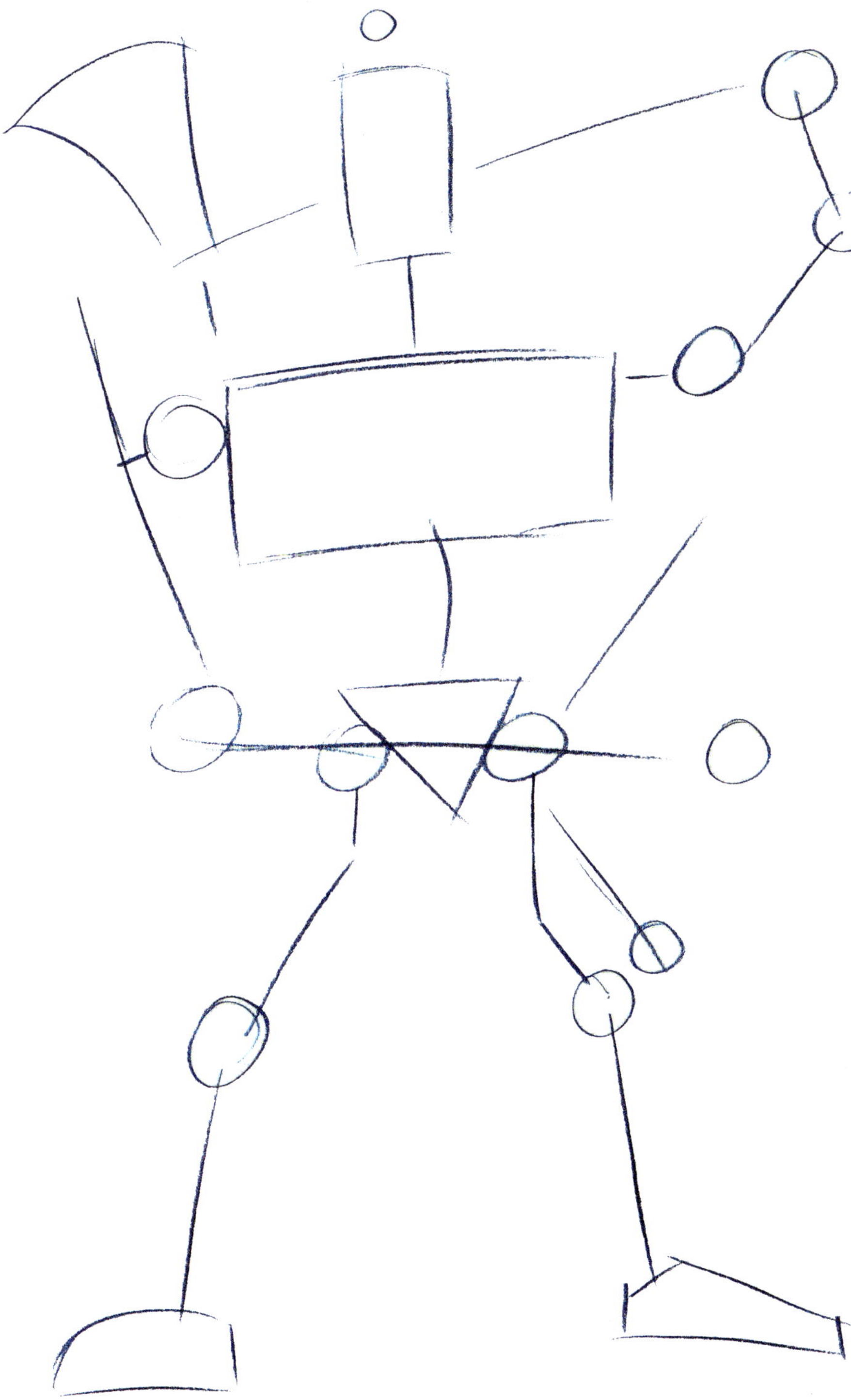

1

Start by drawing the foundation of your character in blue pencil, in a position as though he is working.

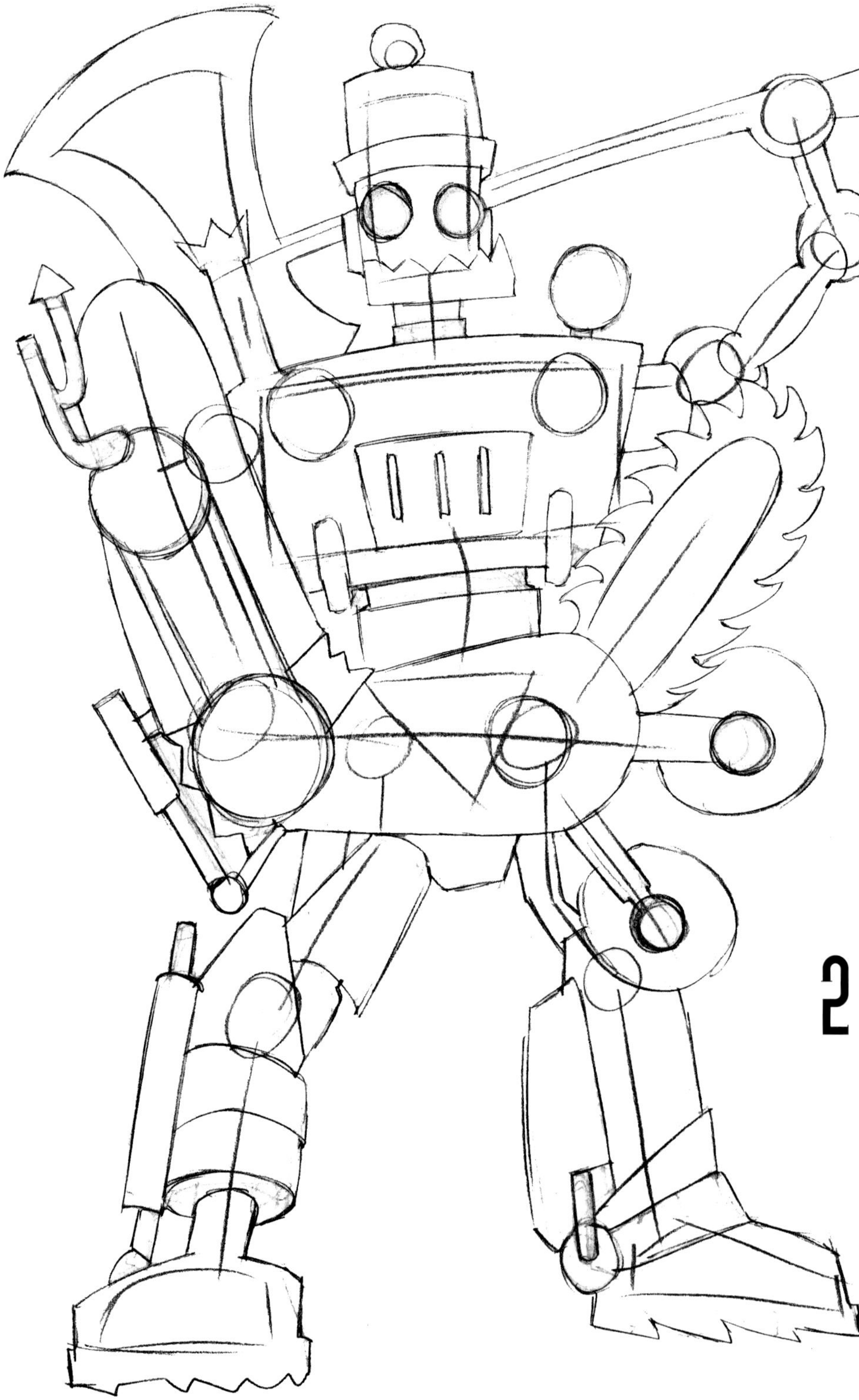

2

Draw in your character using a 2H-grade pencil, outlining his shape over the blue pencil and defining the stance of this great robot.

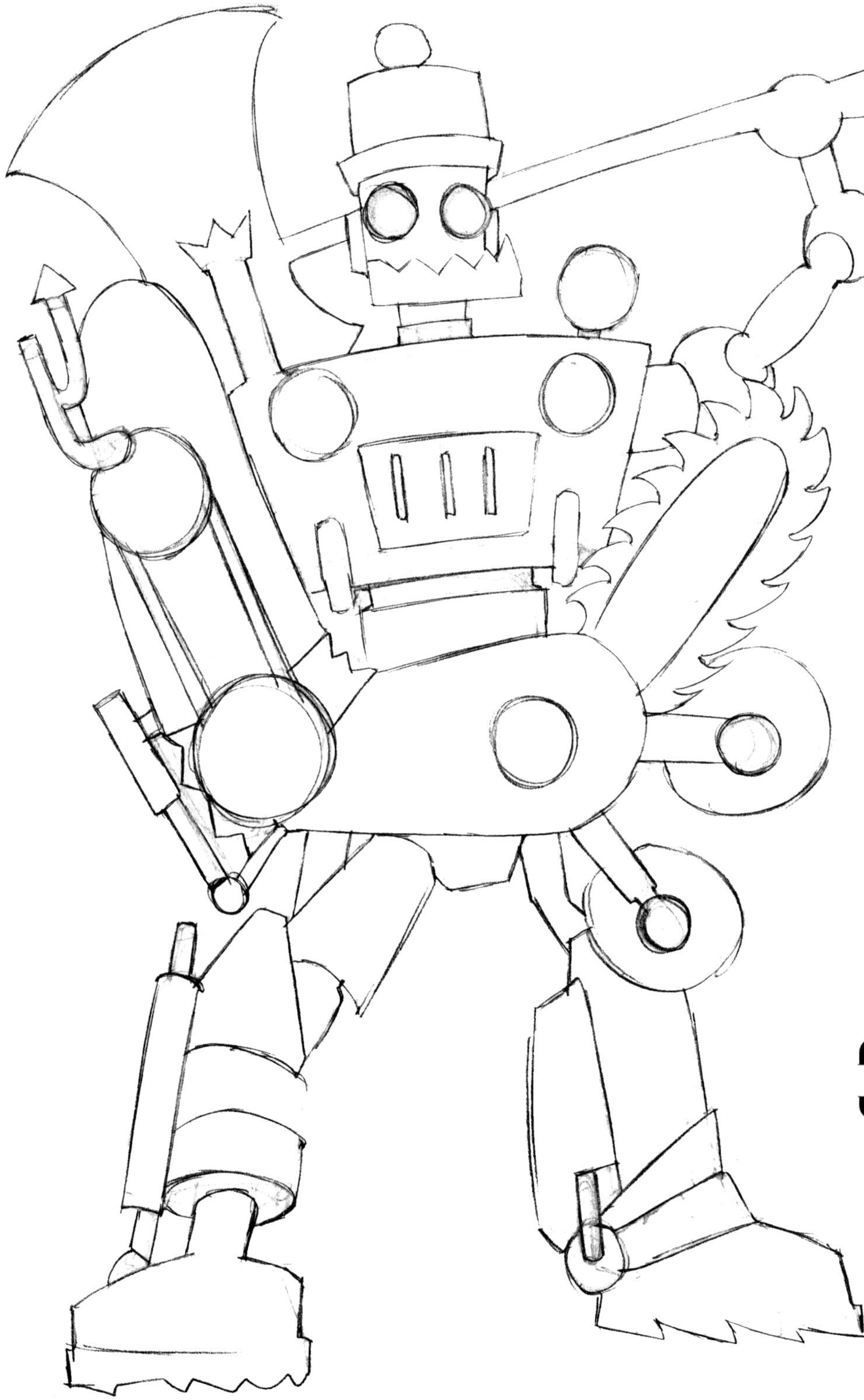

3

Complete the silhouette and work in the details with a 05 pencil.

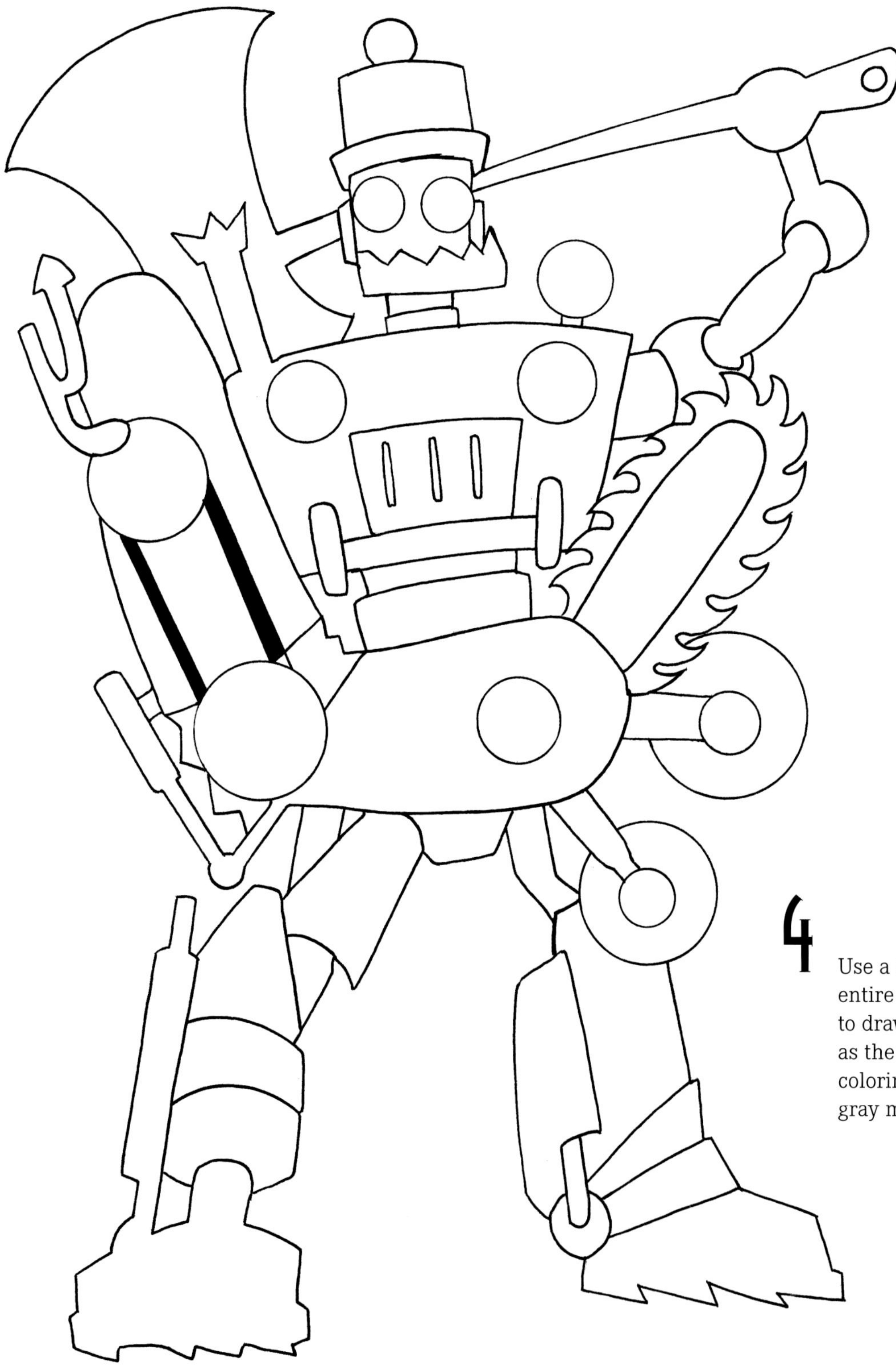

4

Use a 0.4-mm pen to define the entire robot. Then, use an 0.8 mm to draw attention to areas such as the chainsaw arm. Finish up by coloring the robot using black and gray markers.

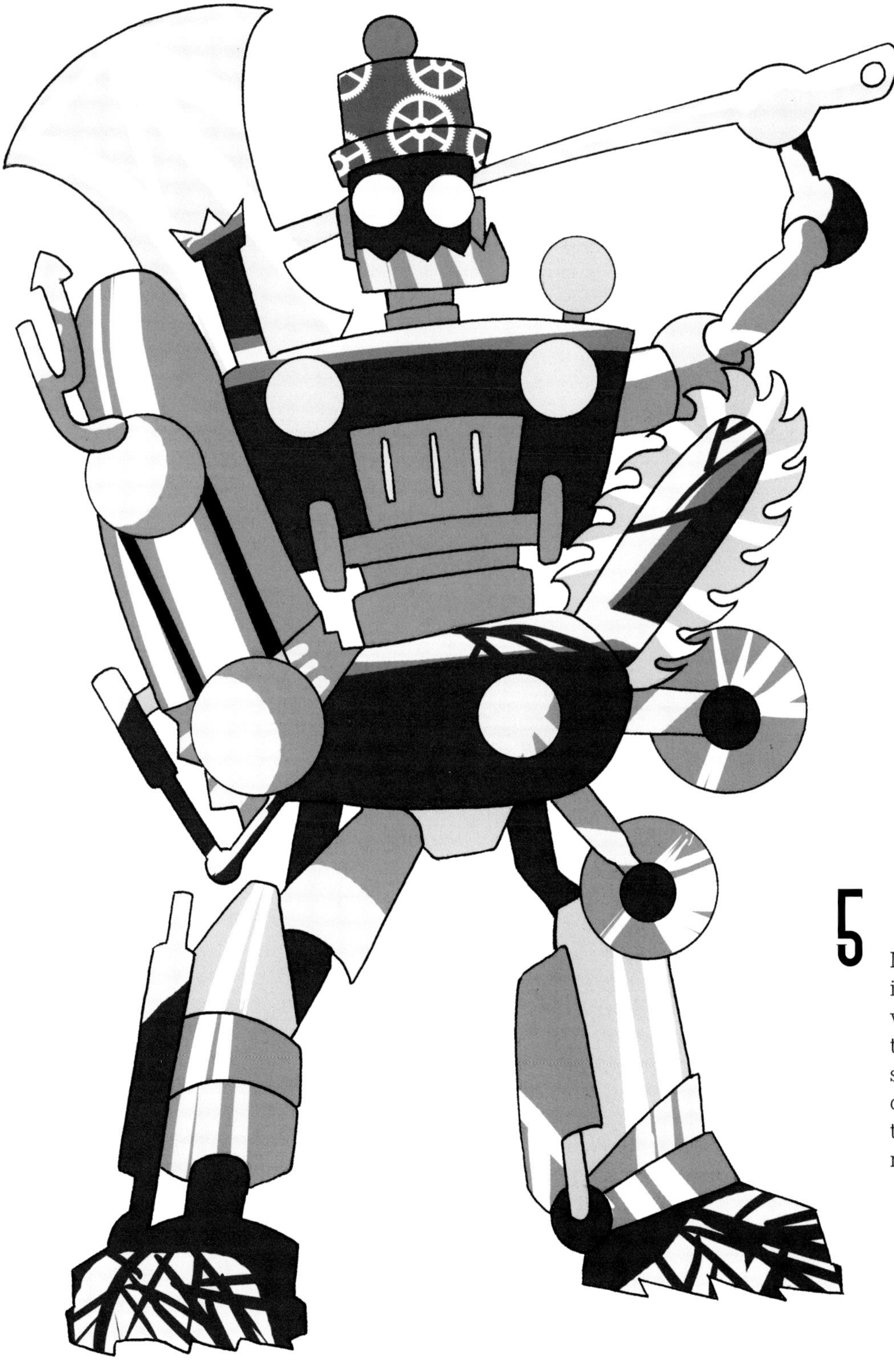

5

Now we will see where the light is coming from. This helps to add volume to the character and make the details stand out. As you can see, the light is directly overhead, creating shadows suggestive of tree branches at the feet of your ranger robot.

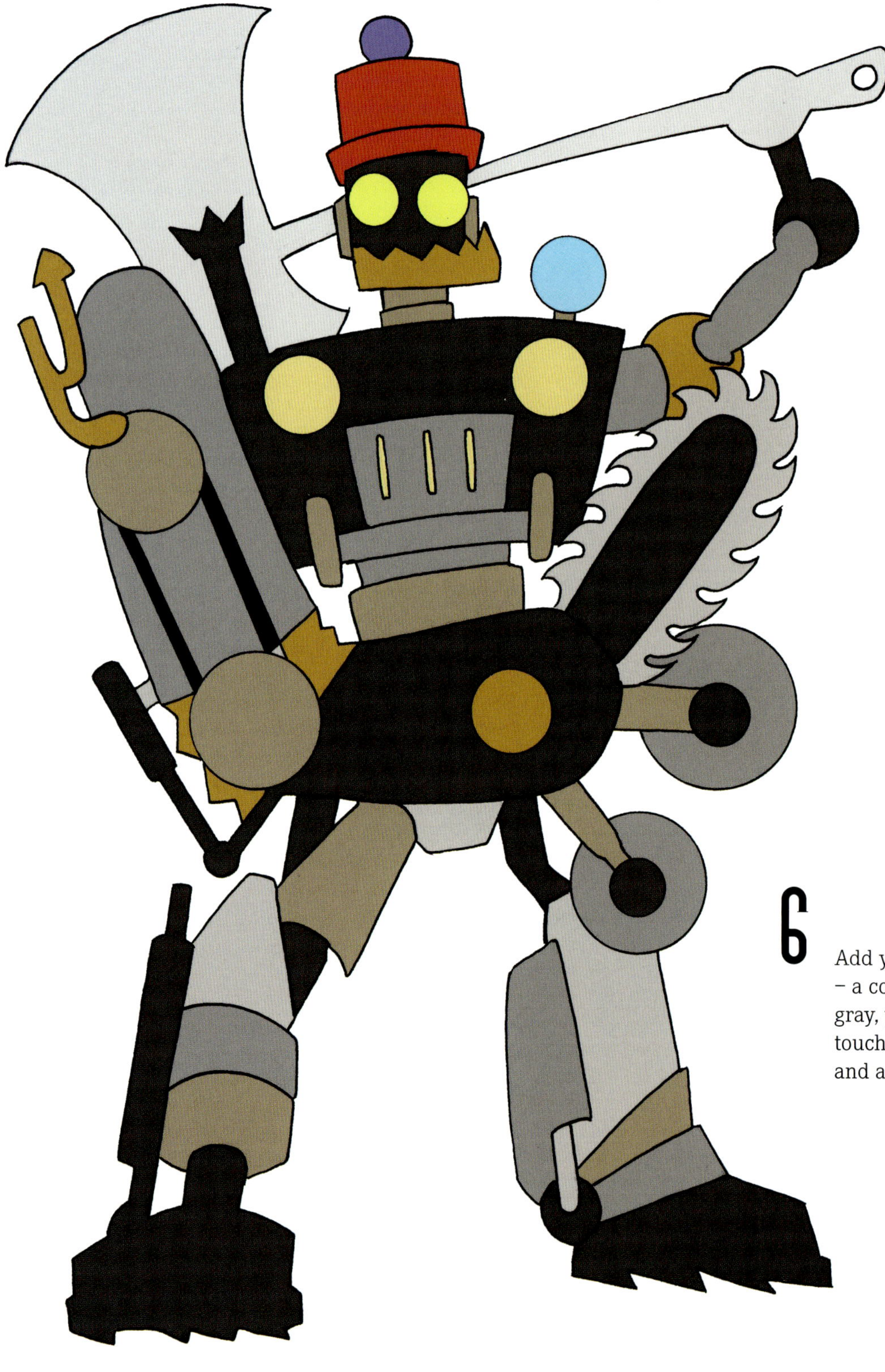

6

Add your character's base colors – a combination of brown, gold, gray, yellow, and blue. Color some touches in red, such as the hat, and add blue to the tassel.

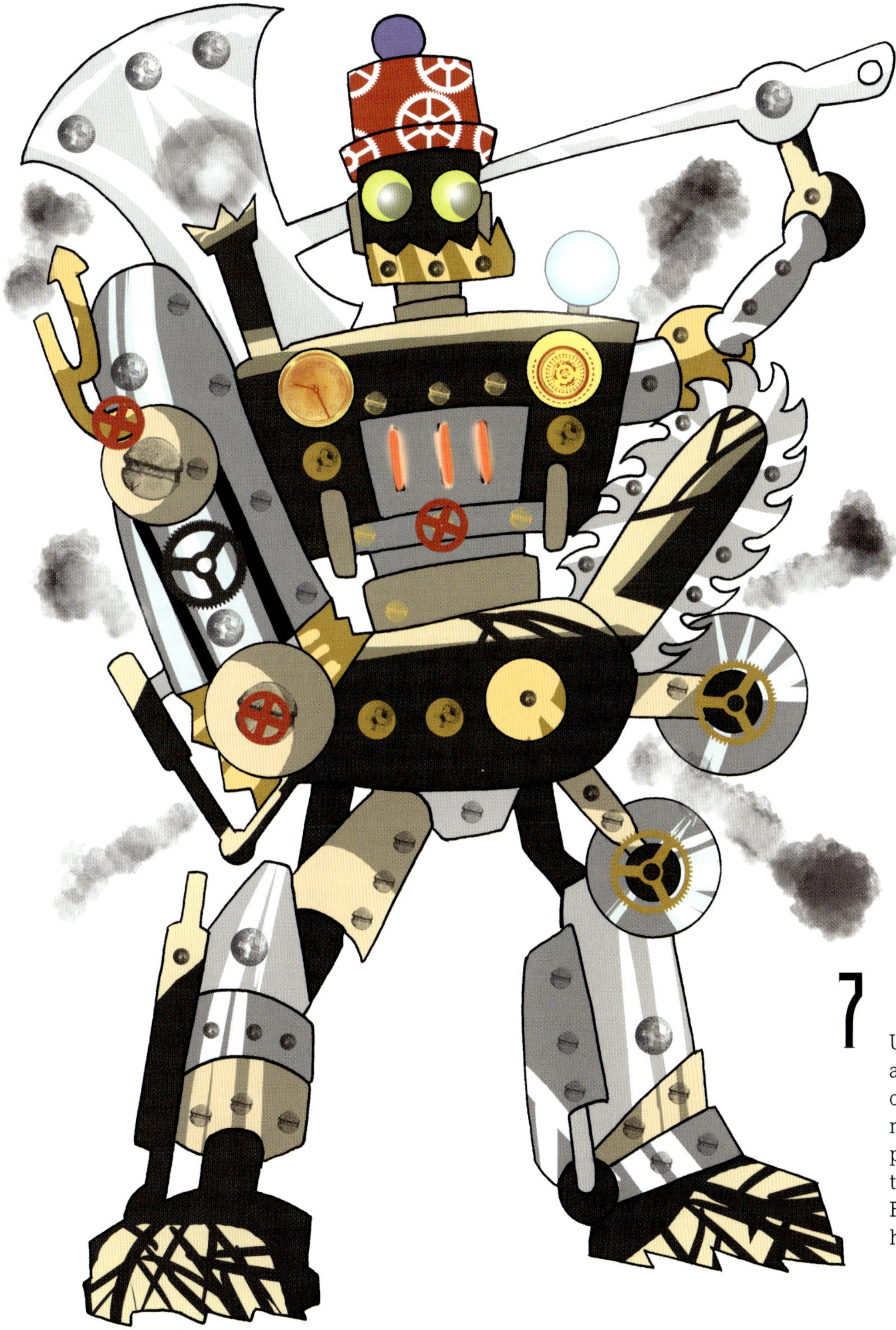

7

Use a gold or silver pen, such as an Edding, to add glimmers of gold or silver screws. Add washers, nuts, and bolts. Practice makes perfect! Use orange to pick up touches of light in the chest burner. Finally, decorate the lumberjack hat and you're done!

FLYING MAN

Marcus Wellson is the creator of the eons antigravity waves, an invention that can bring weightlessness to any device and enable you to fly if you know how to handle it. There is no doubt that Marcus is an expert in this method of wave flying: he has designed an entire birdman suit to show off his invention at the next Genius Exhibition.

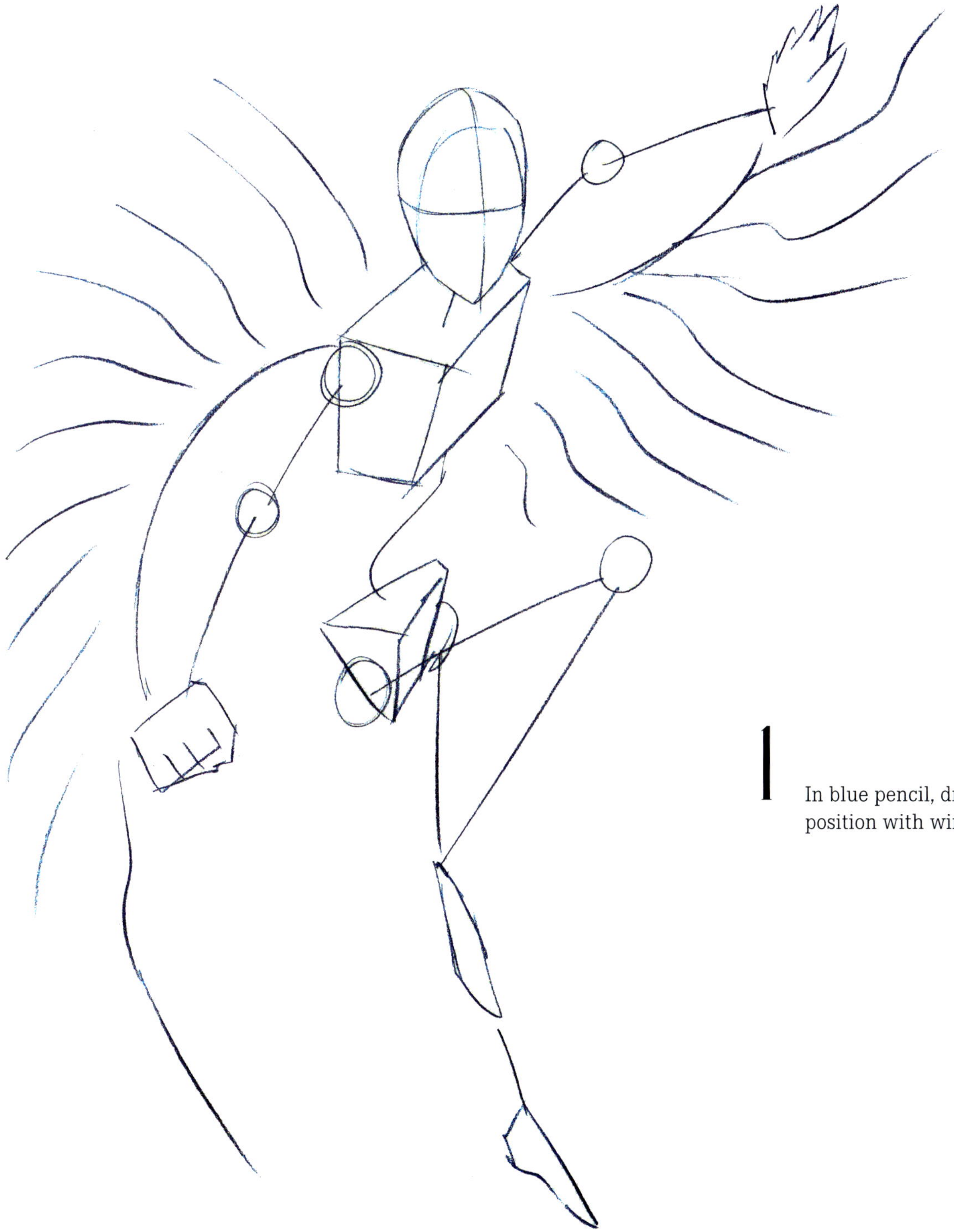

1

In blue pencil, draw a flight position with wings outstretched.

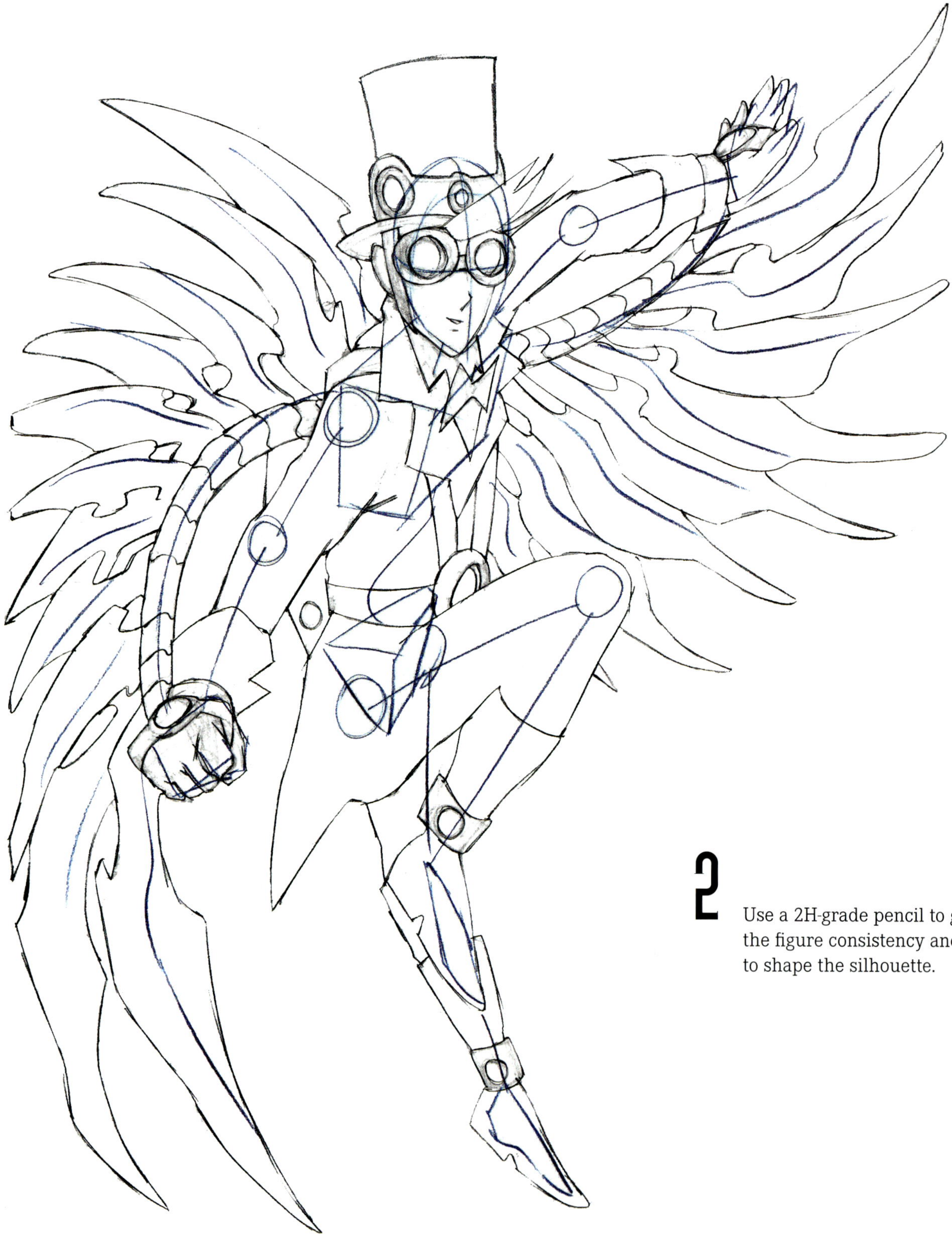

2

Use a 2H-grade pencil to give the figure consistency and to shape the silhouette.

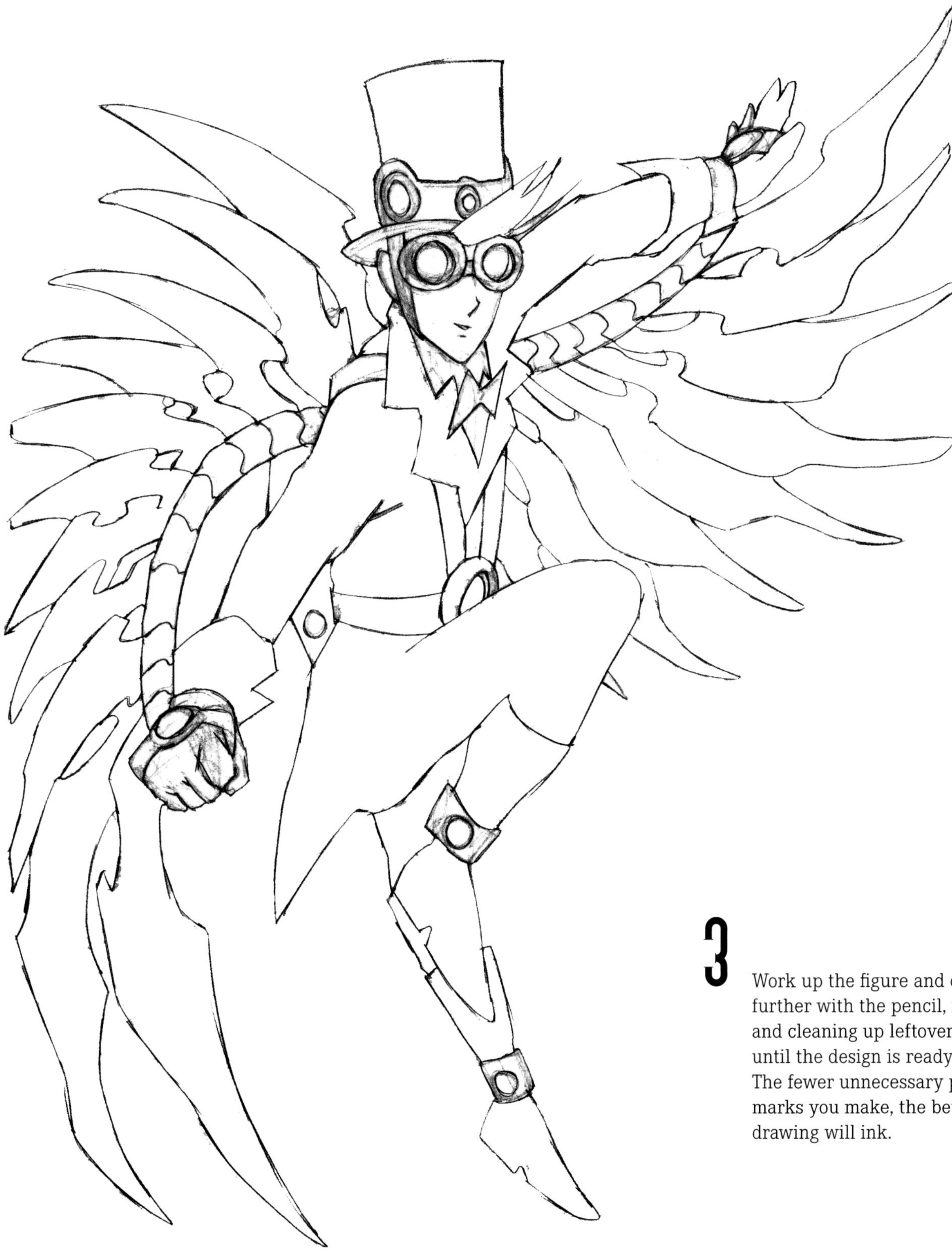

3

Work up the figure and details further with the pencil, removing and cleaning up leftover strokes until the design is ready for inking. The fewer unnecessary pencil marks you make, the better the drawing will ink.

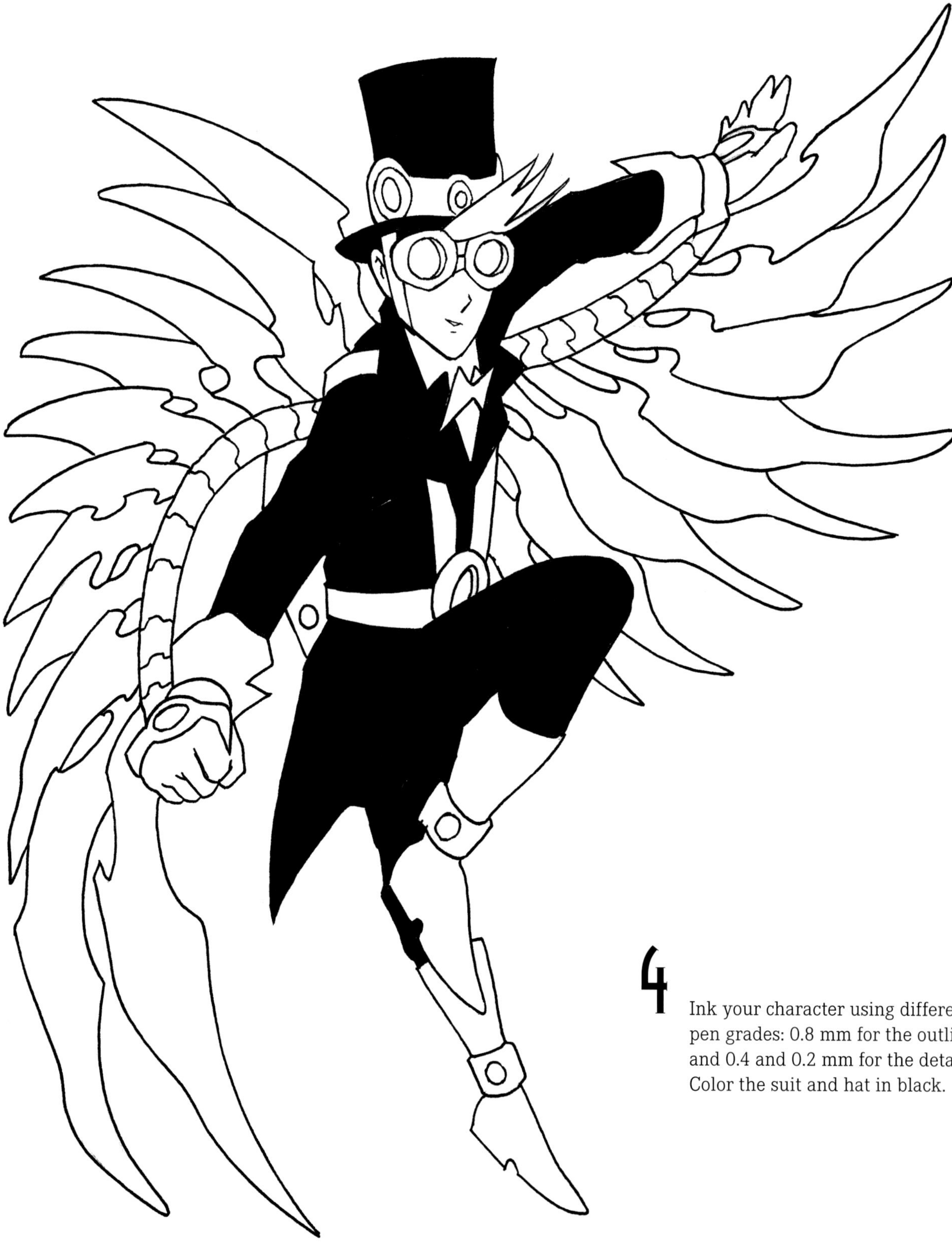

4

Ink your character using different pen grades: 0.8 mm for the outline, and 0.4 and 0.2 mm for the details. Color the suit and hat in black.

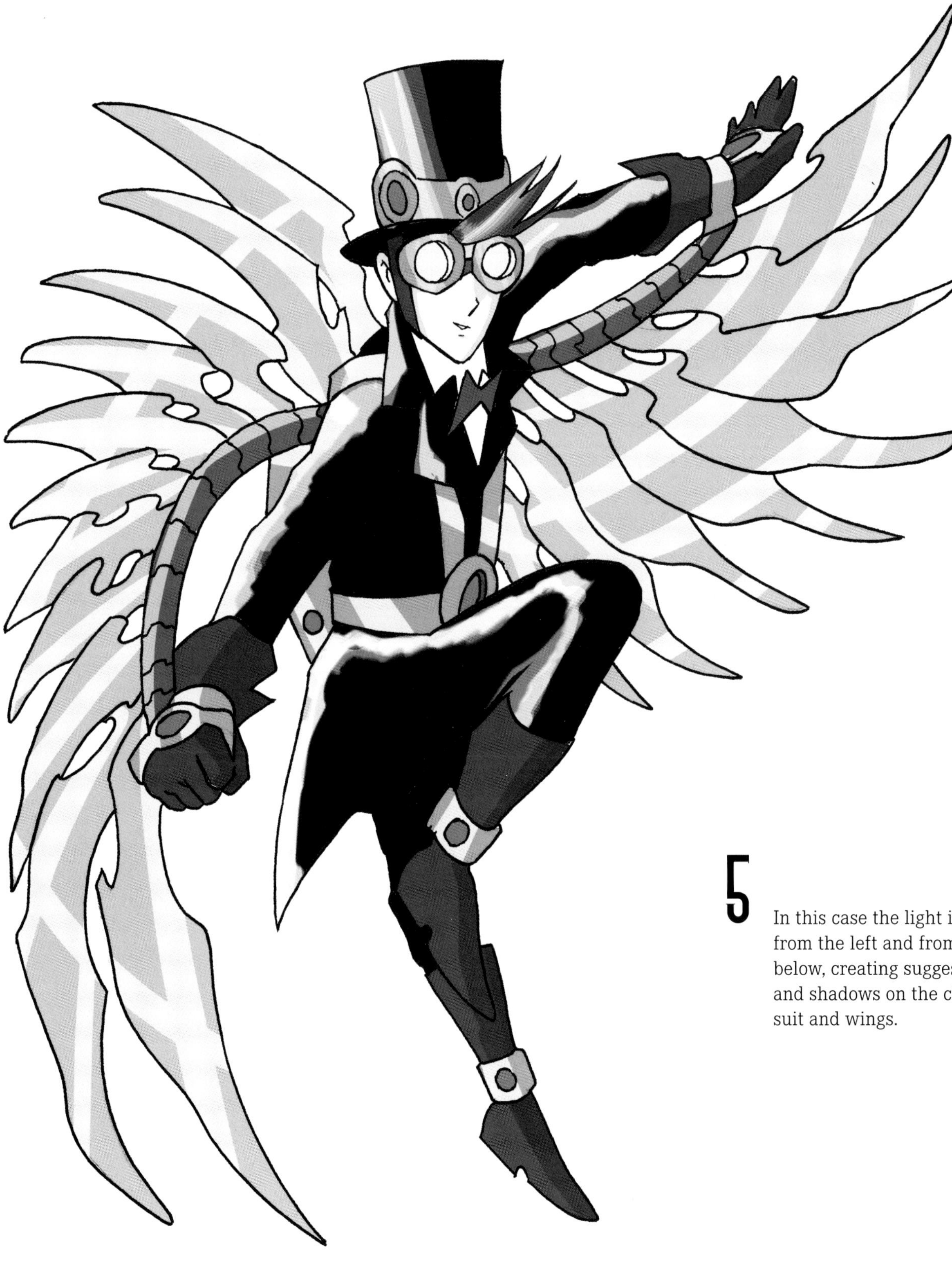

5

In this case the light is coming from the left and from above to below, creating suggestive forms and shadows on the character's suit and wings.

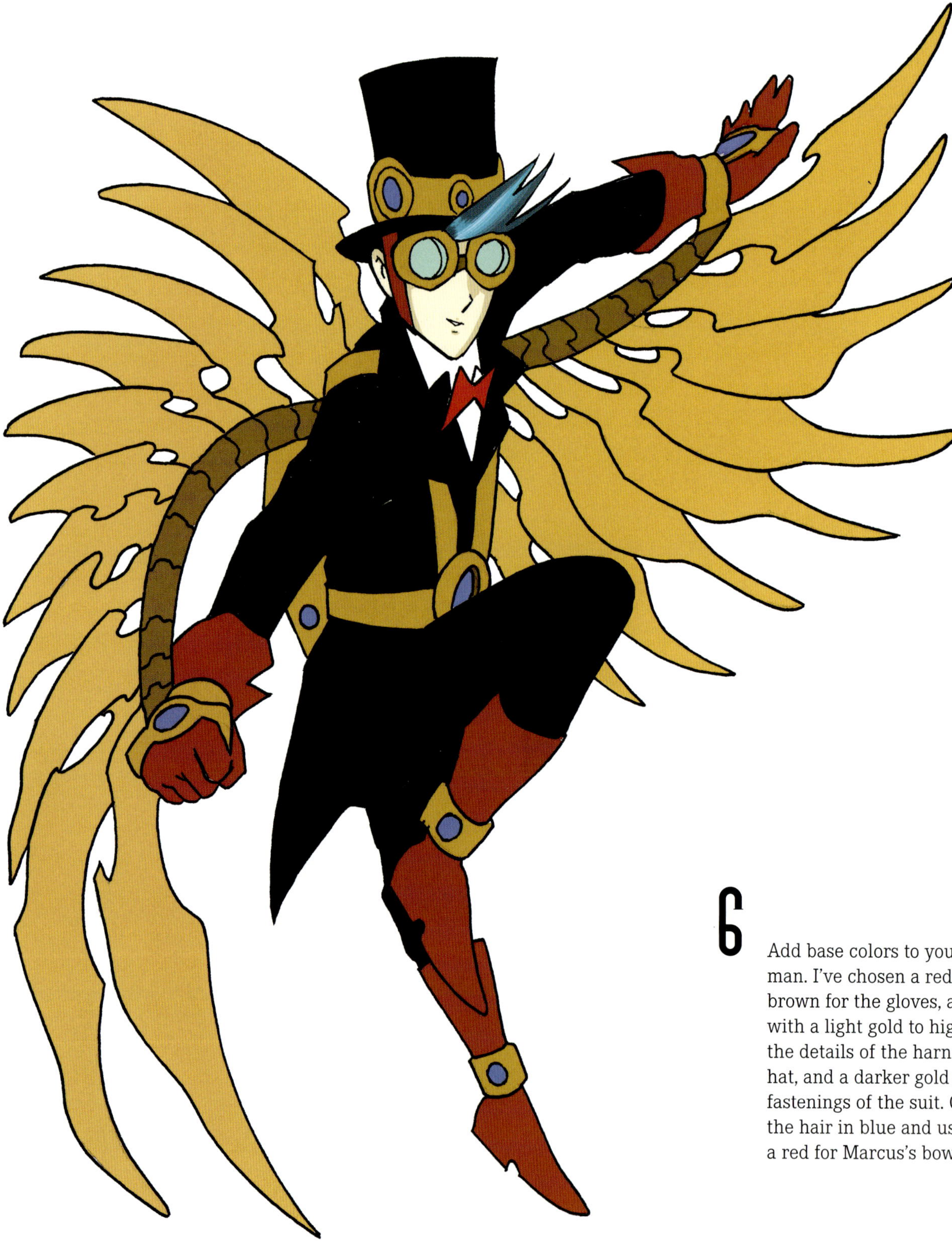

6

Add base colors to your flying man. I've chosen a reddish brown for the gloves, along with a light gold to highlight the details of the harness and hat, and a darker gold for the fastenings of the suit. Color the hair in blue and use a red for Marcus's bow tie.

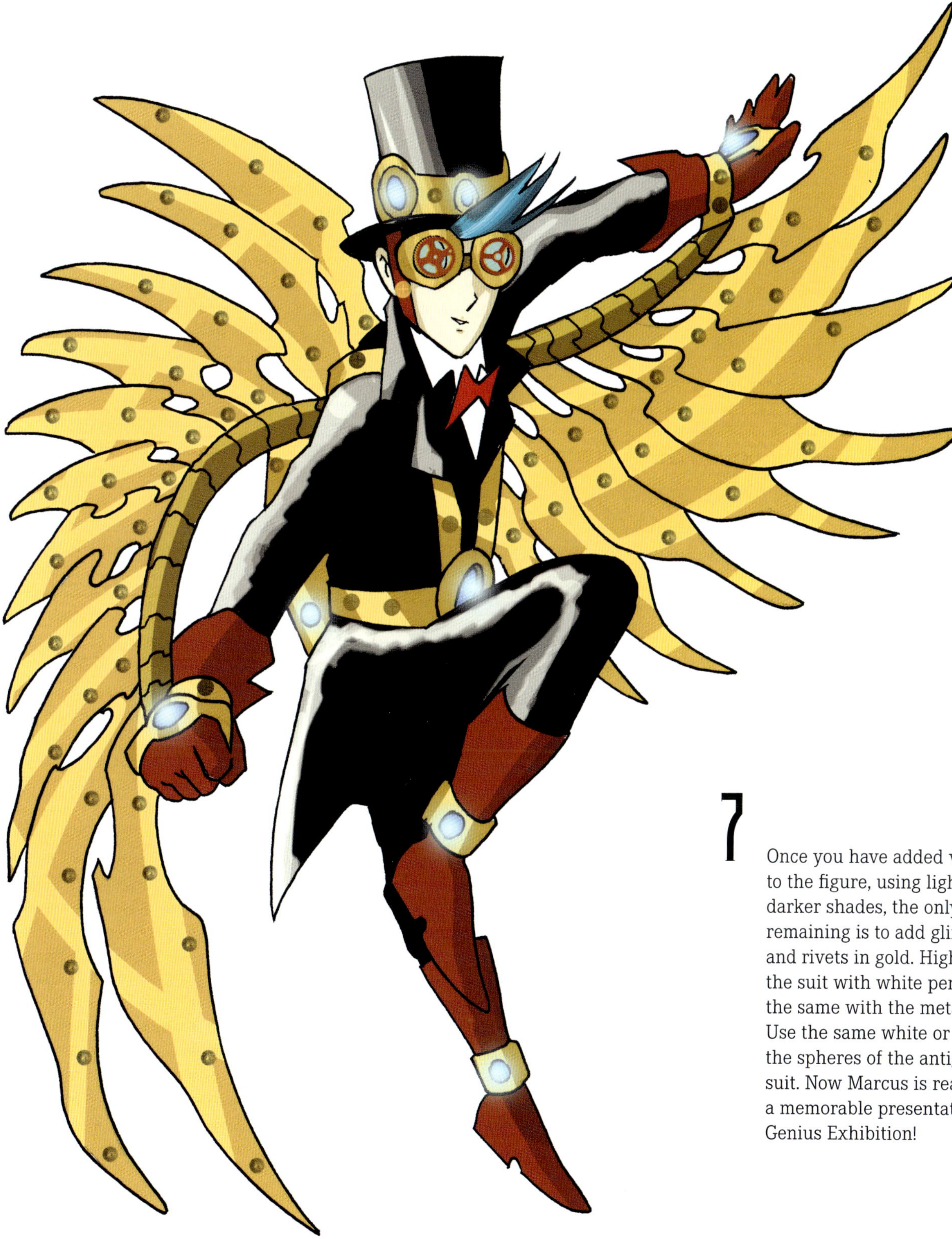

7

Once you have added volume to the figure, using lighter and darker shades, the only thing remaining is to add glimmer and rivets in gold. Highlight the suit with white pencil and do the same with the metal harness. Use the same white or a blue for the spheres of the antigravity suit. Now Marcus is ready to give a memorable presentation at the Genius Exhibition!

HAWKER

Charly Pagolix was a troubadour, but sadly he wasn't any good. His vague fame made things difficult when it came to finding another job, so he began collecting the junk that people threw in the garbage and bartered with any innocents who could be fooled. He succeeded in building a small collection of objects and now earns his living as a crafty trader. He is wanted by the law for being a swindler and a con man ... If you see him don't let yourself be had!

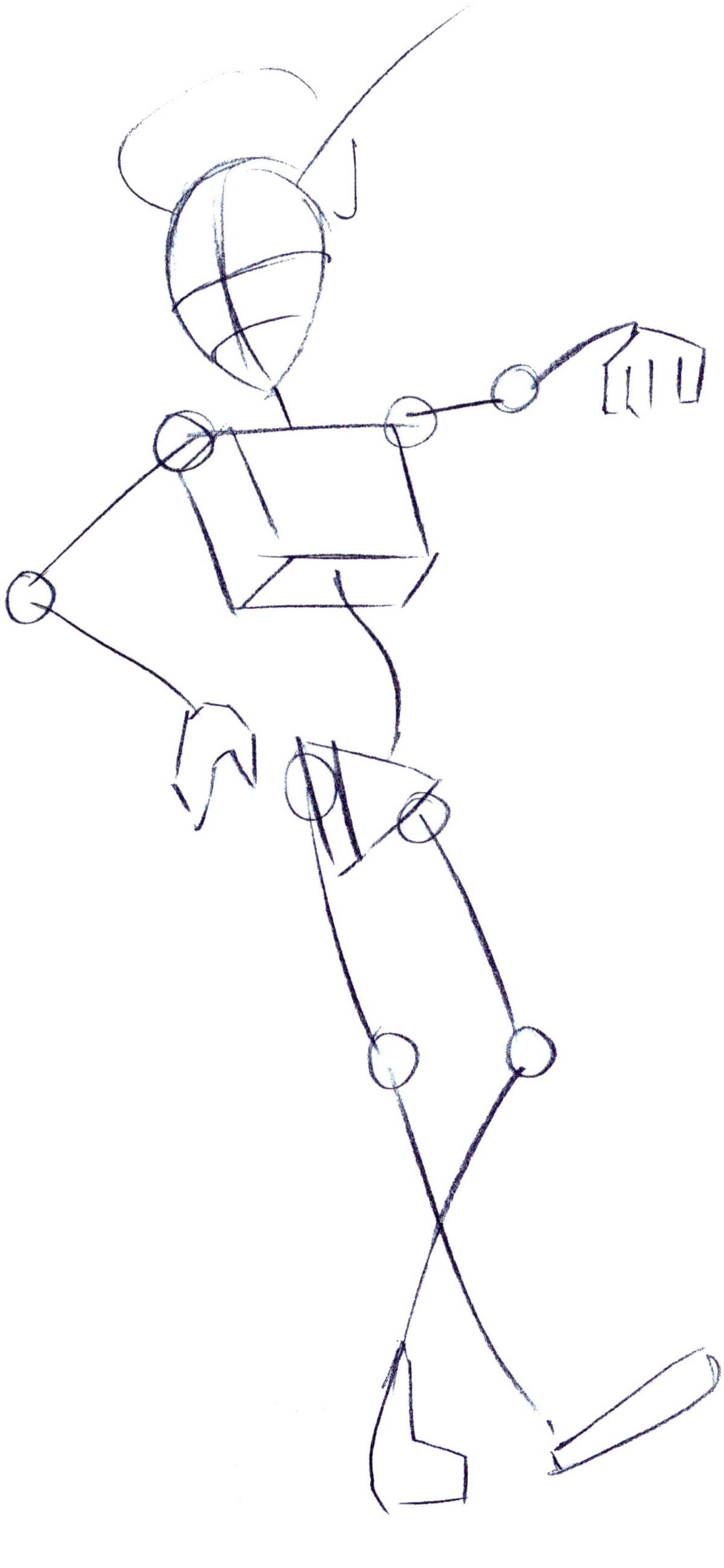

1

Begin by drawing the base of your character in blue, in full street-trading pose.

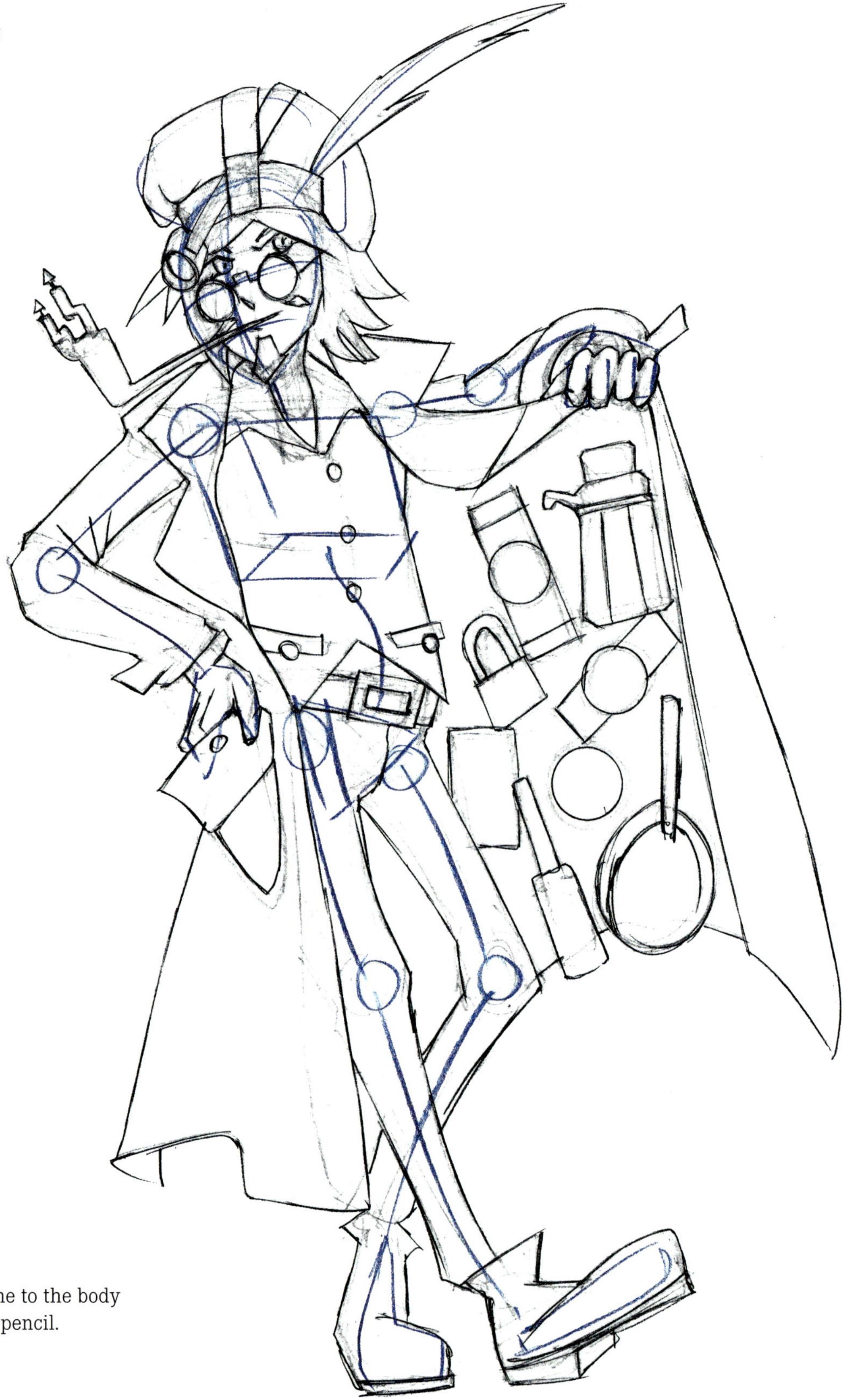

2

Add volume to the body with a 2H pencil.

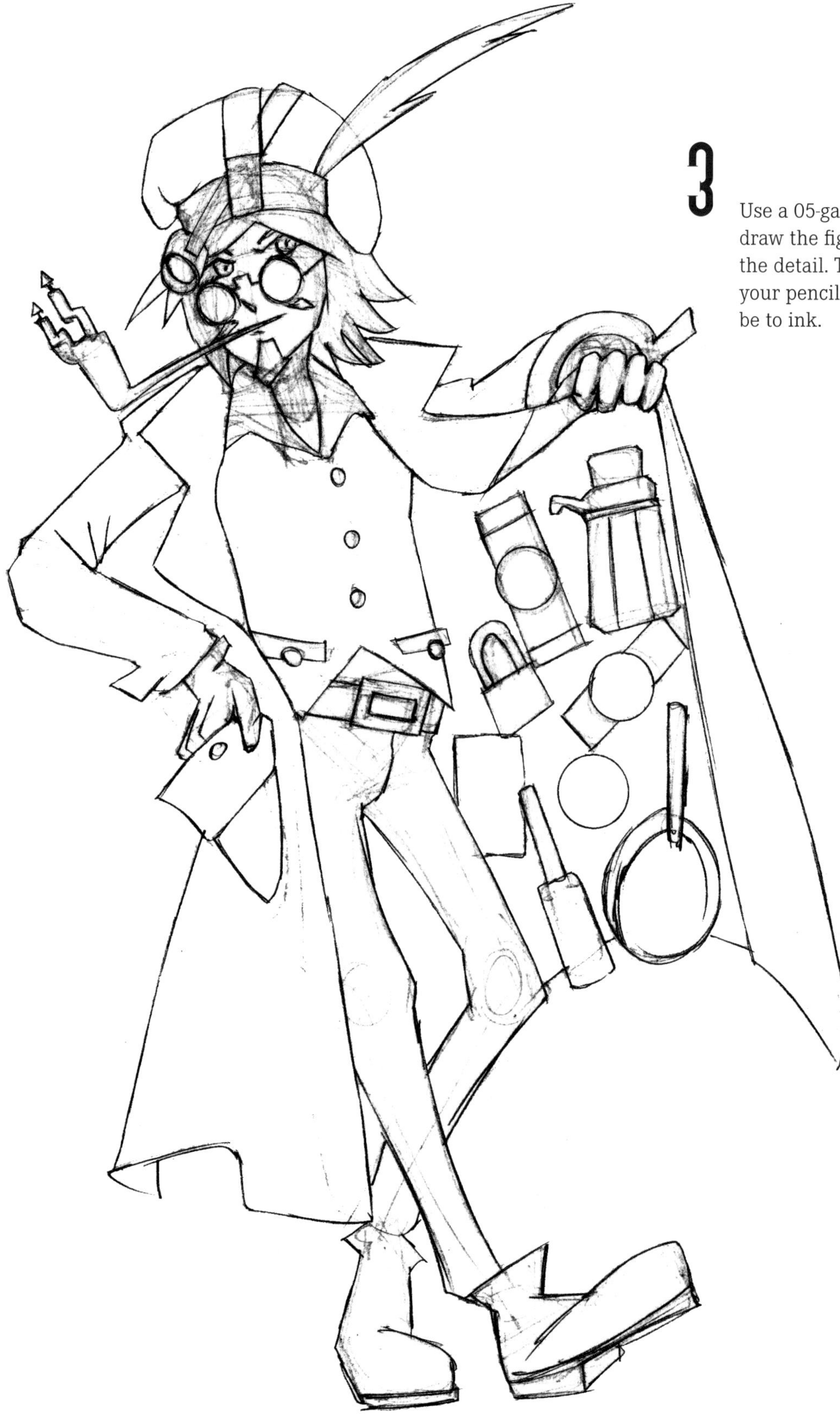

3

Use a 05-gauge pencil to completely draw the figure and give form to the detail. The better the finish of your pencil work, the easier it will be to ink.

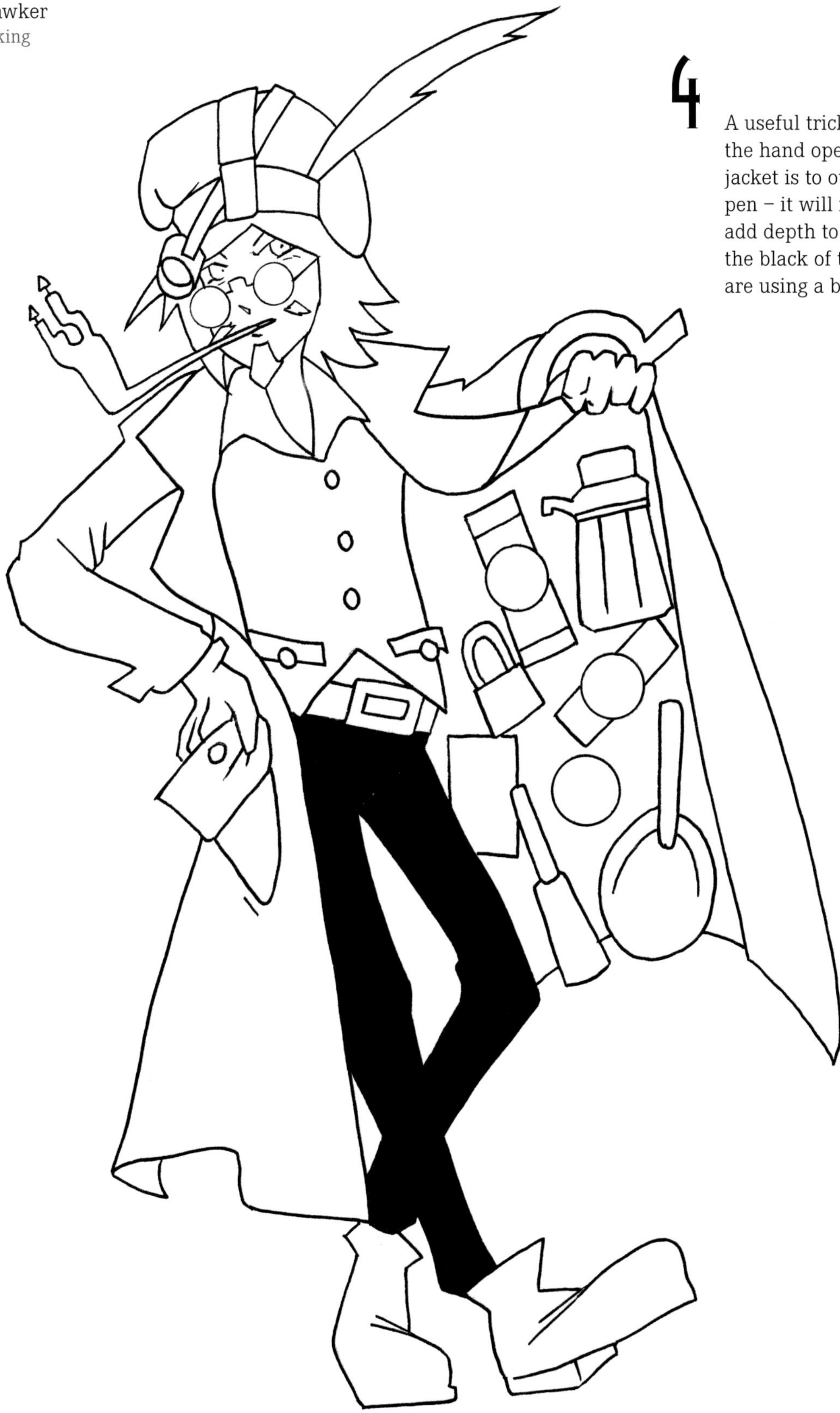

4

A useful trick that might help for the hand opening the peddler's jacket is to outline it with a 0.8-mm pen – it will make it stand out and add depth to the drawing. Color in the black of the trousers while you are using a black marker.

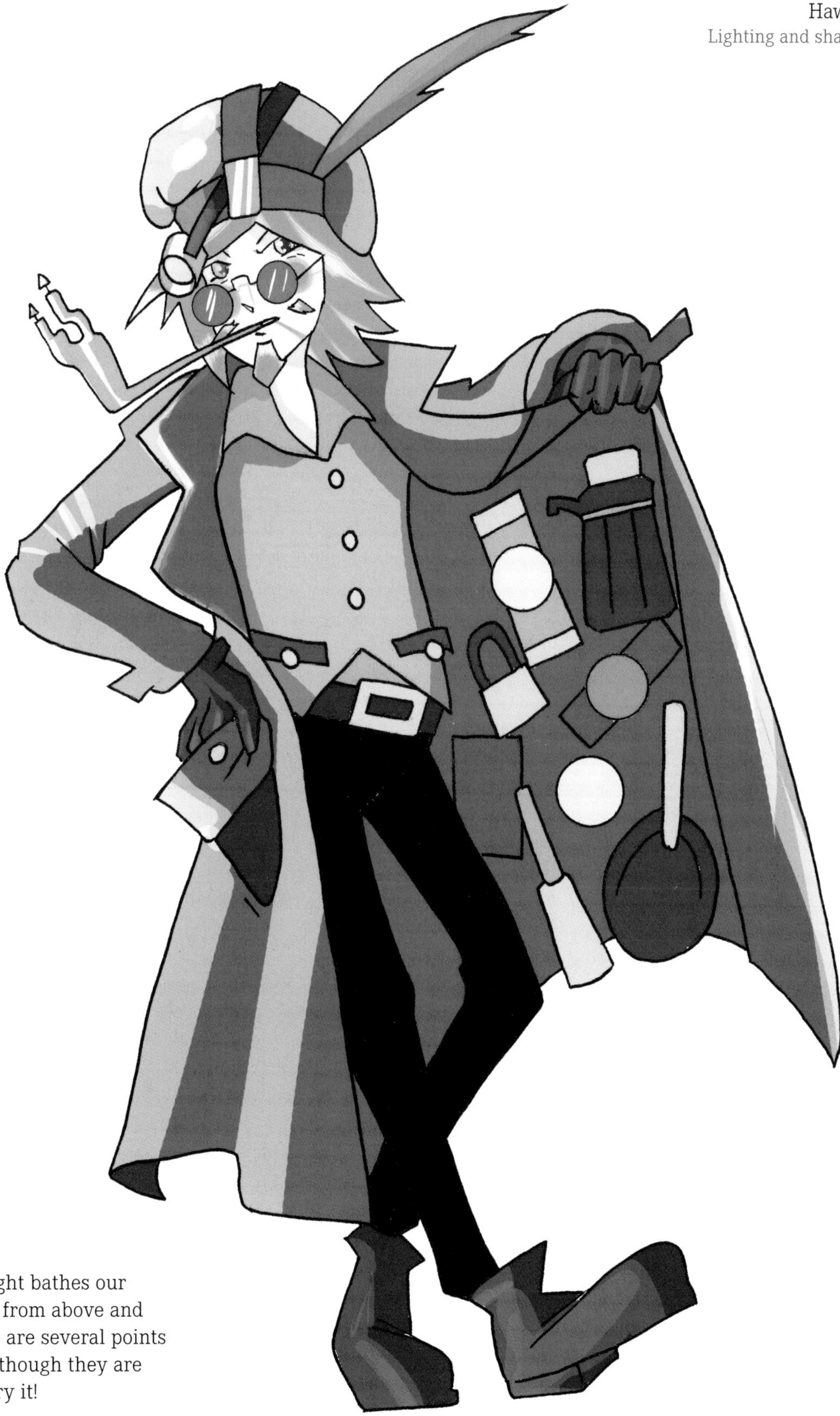

5

Here the light bathes our mercenary from above and right: there are several points of light, as though they are lanterns. Try it!

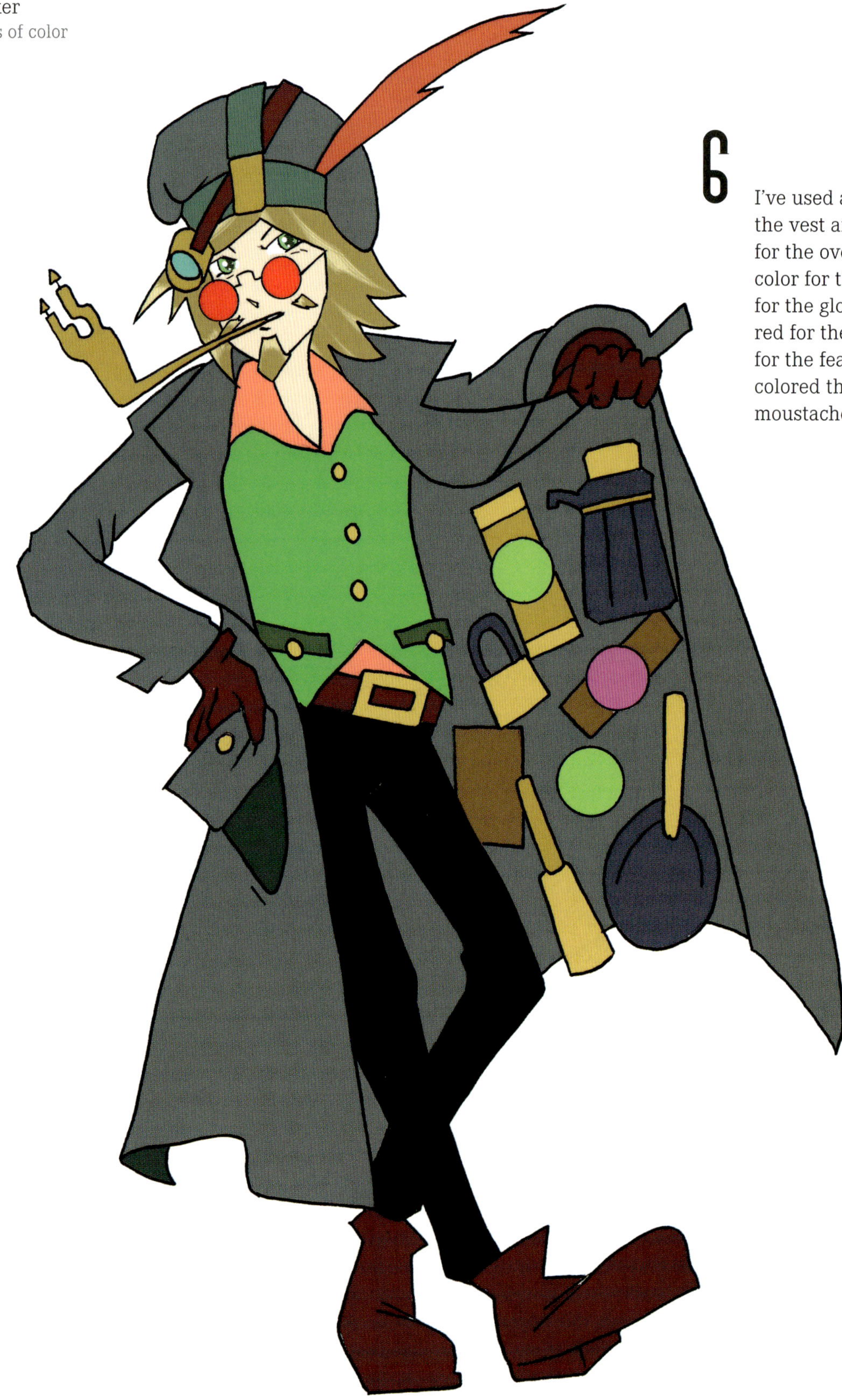

6

I've used a light green for the vest and a darker green for the overcoat. A golden color for the objects, brown for the gloves and shoes, red for the lenses, and orange for the feather. To finish I've colored this hustler's hair, moustache, and beard blond.

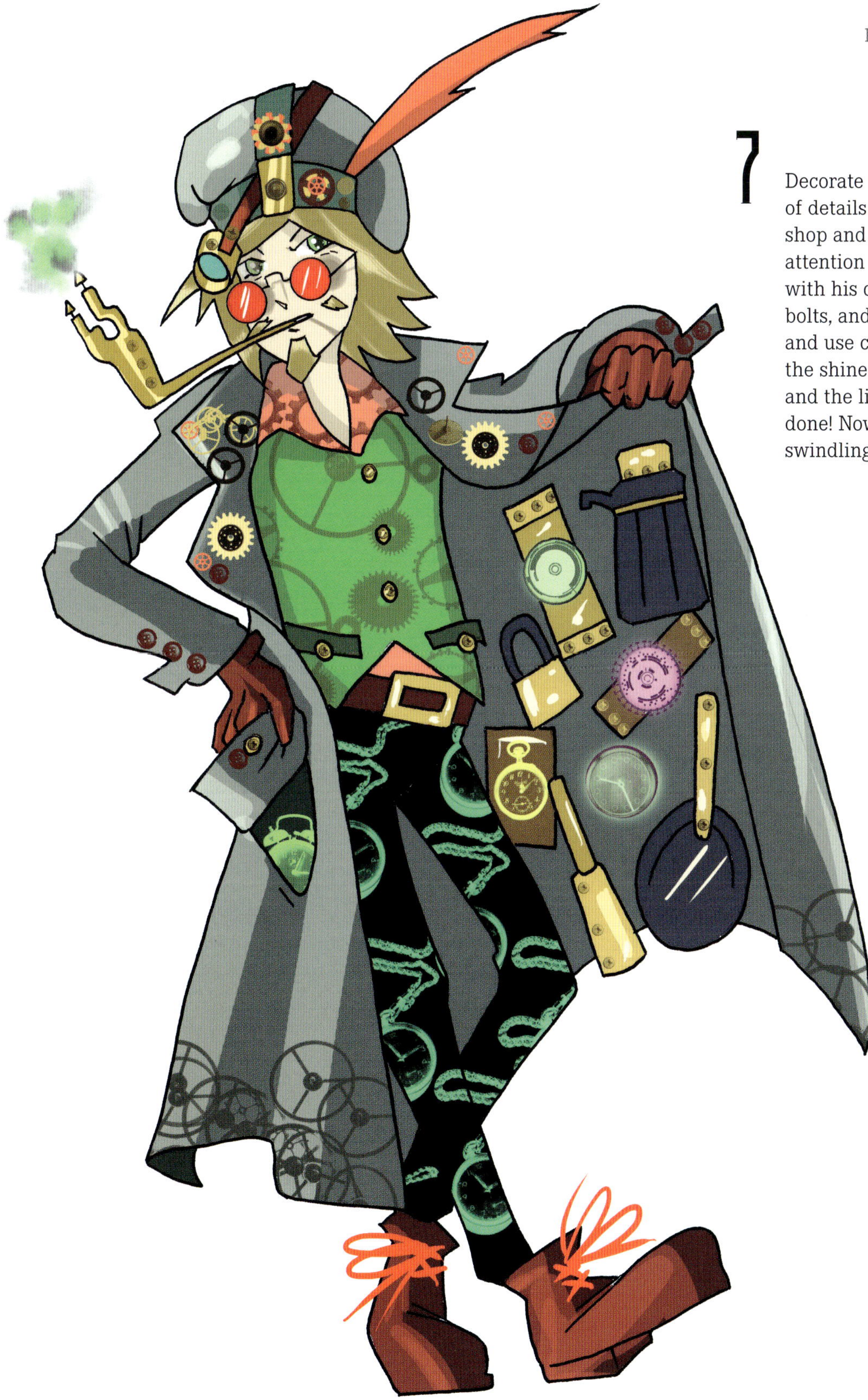

7

Decorate your peddler with plenty of details – he is like a walking shop and needs to capture the attention of unwary passersby with his objects. Add buttons, bolts, and washers to his clothing, and use color pencils to highlight the shine on the golden elements and the light on the watches. And done! Now let's get on with the swindling!

ARTIST

Goldyna Van Turnis is an artist of renown throughout the kingdom. Her beautiful works are displayed in exhibitions, halls, and museums. Whenever a new exhibition of her work is opened, all the great and good come to admire it.

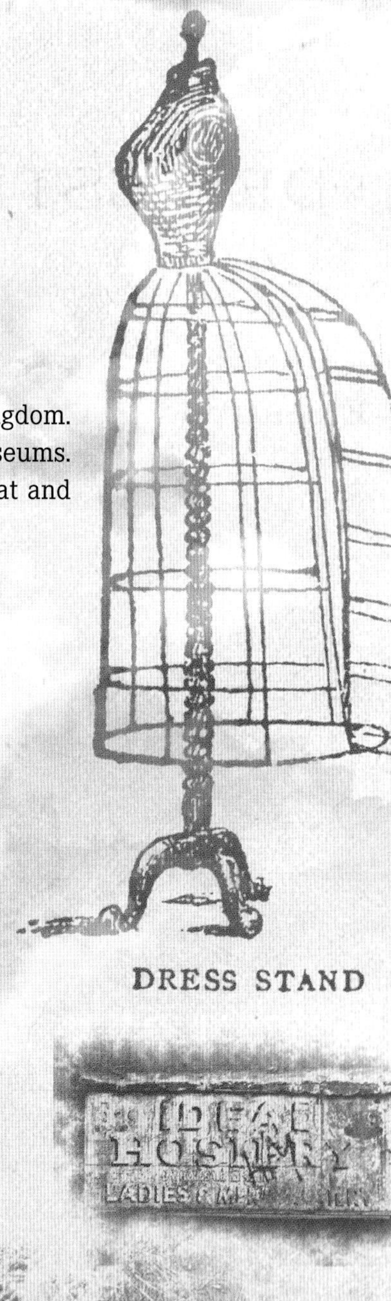

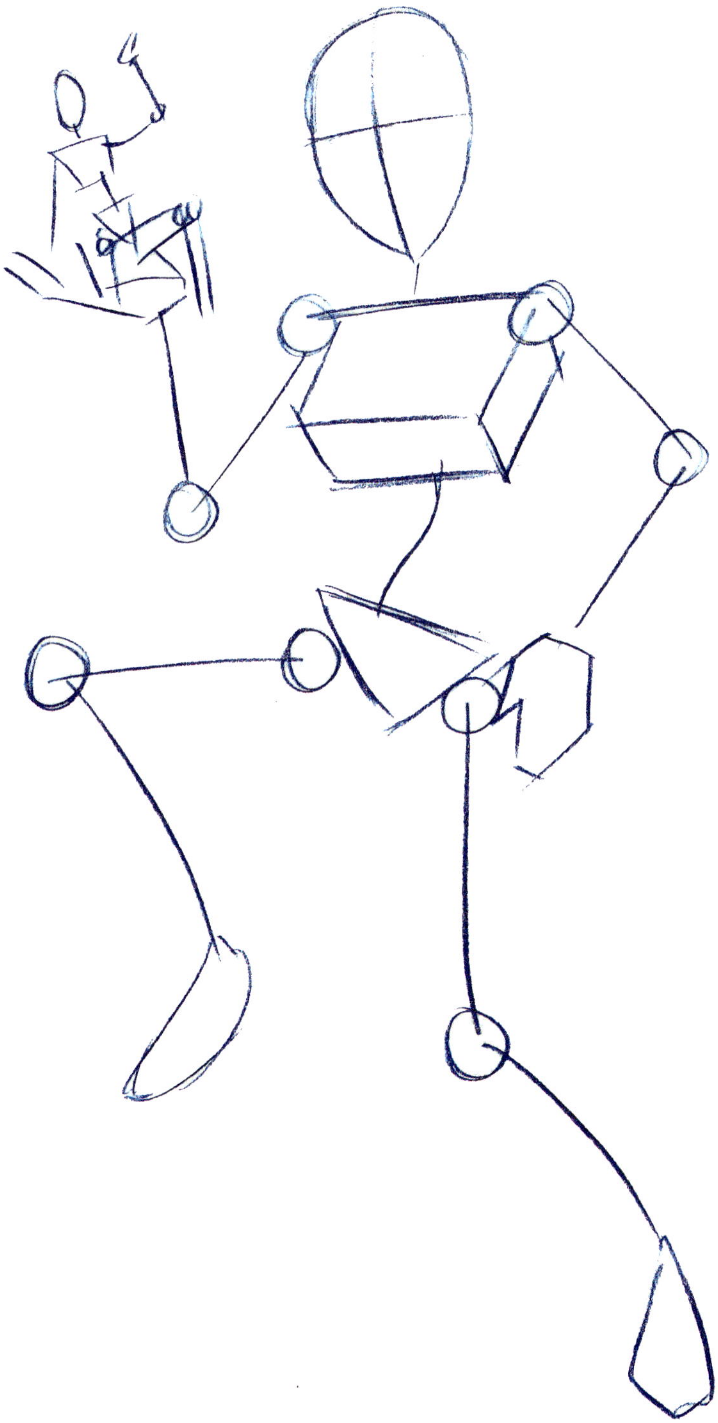

1

Begin by drawing the foundation of your character in blue pencil, giving her a pose that is fitting of an artist.

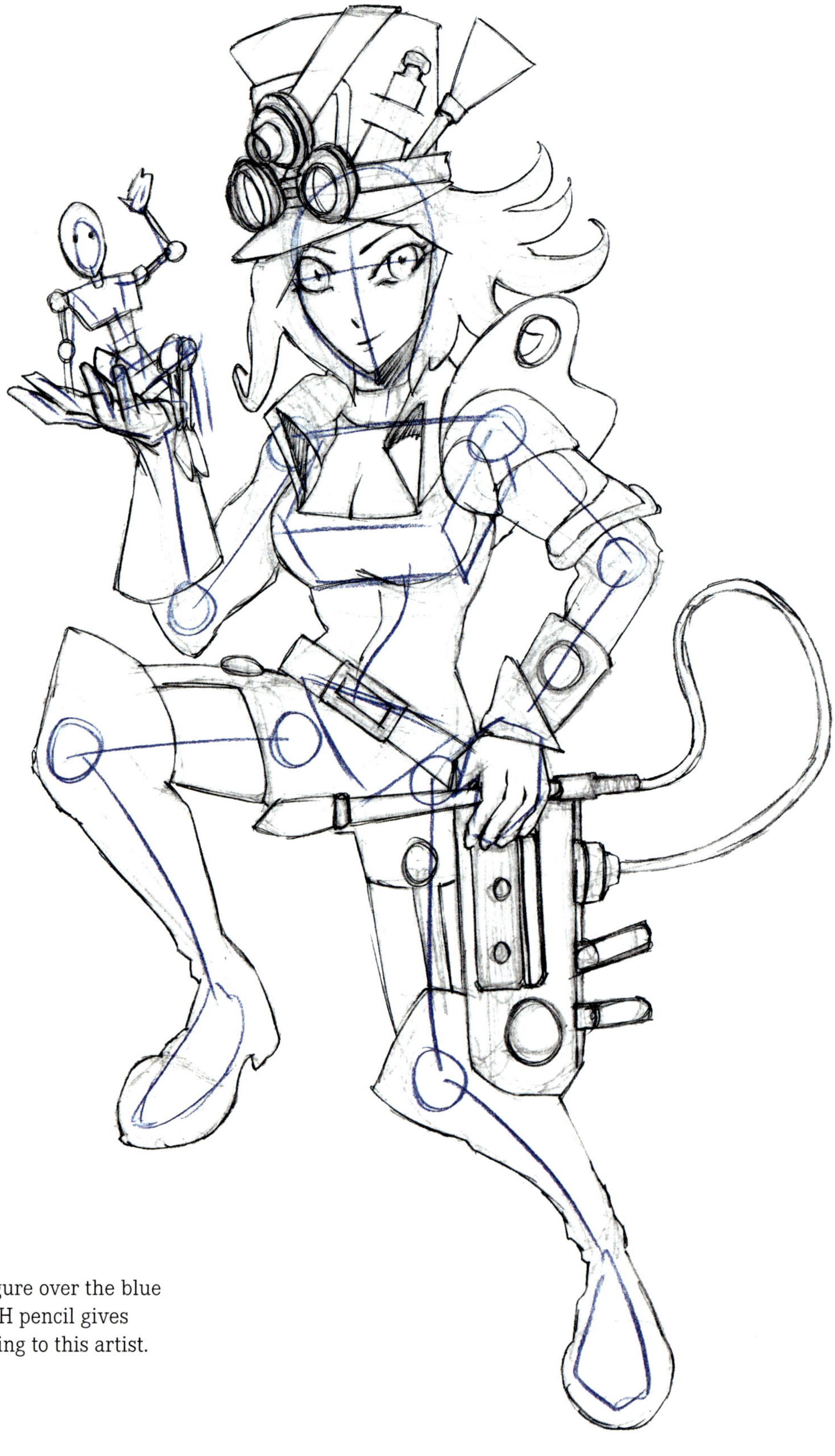

2

Defining the figure over the blue pencil with a 2H pencil gives a sublime bearing to this artist.

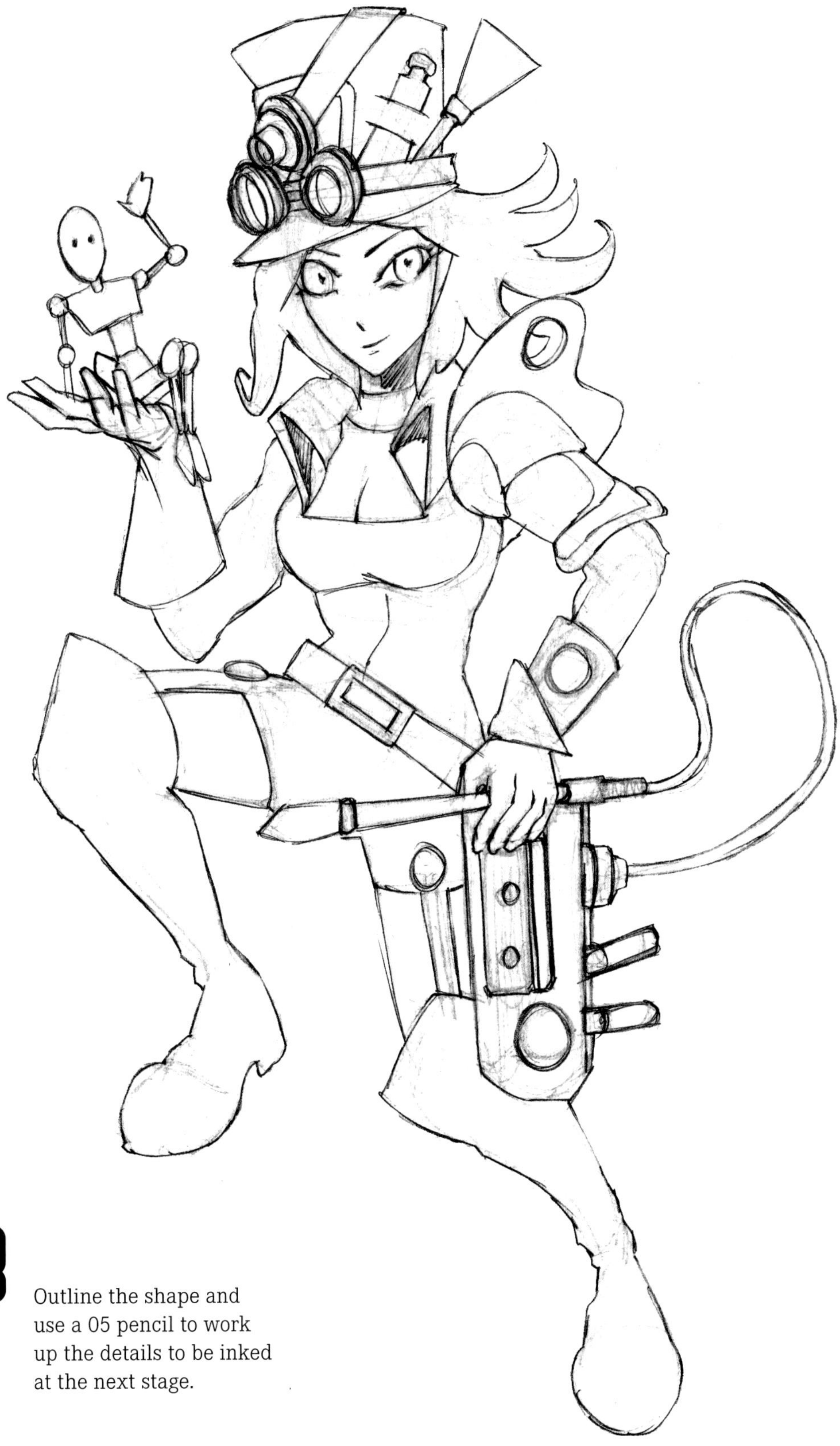

3

Outline the shape and use a 05 pencil to work up the details to be inked at the next stage.

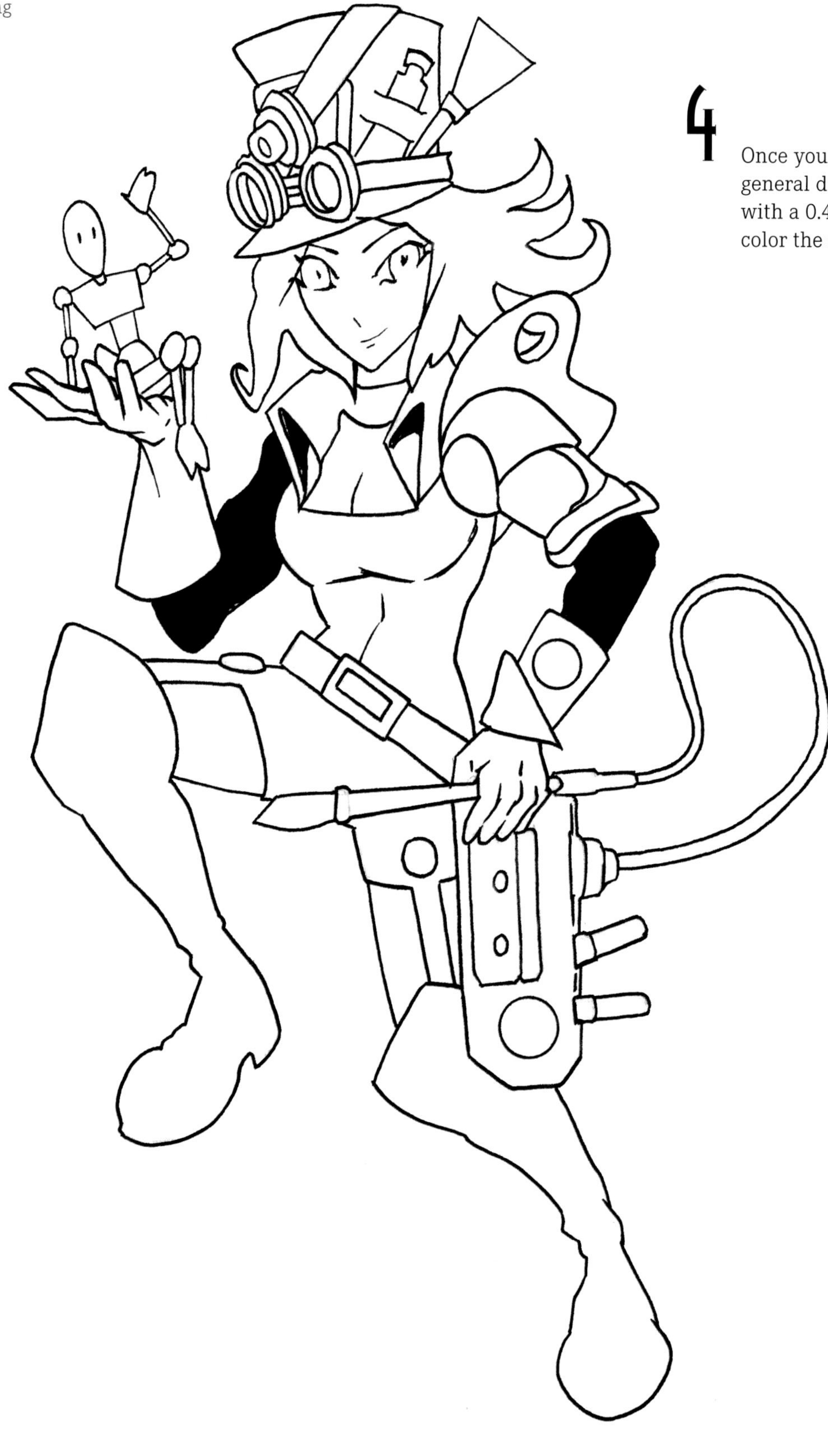

4

Once you have gone over the general drawing, go over the figure with a 0.4-mm pen. Finally we will color the shirt in black.

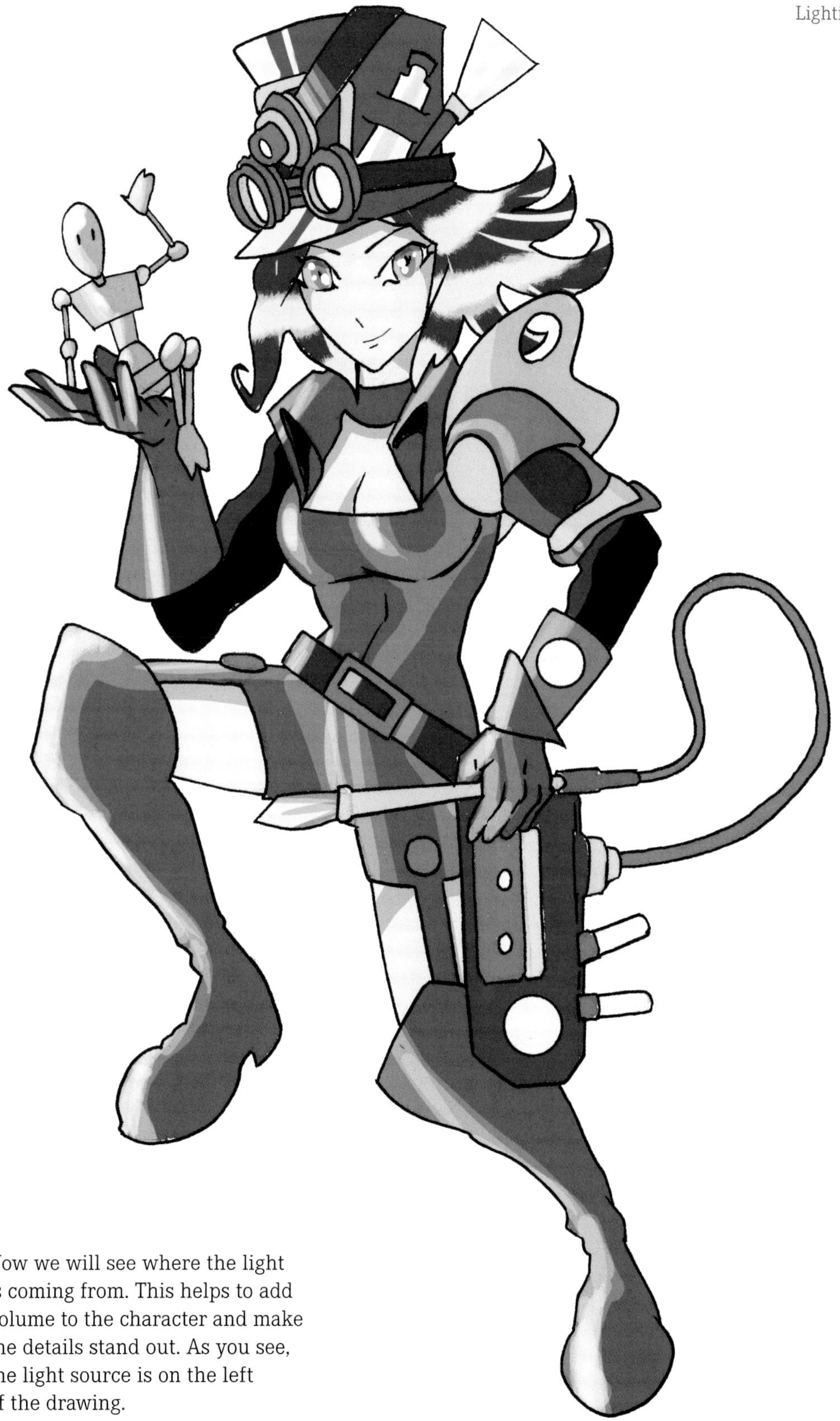

5

Now we will see where the light is coming from. This helps to add volume to the character and make the details stand out. As you see, the light source is on the left of the drawing.

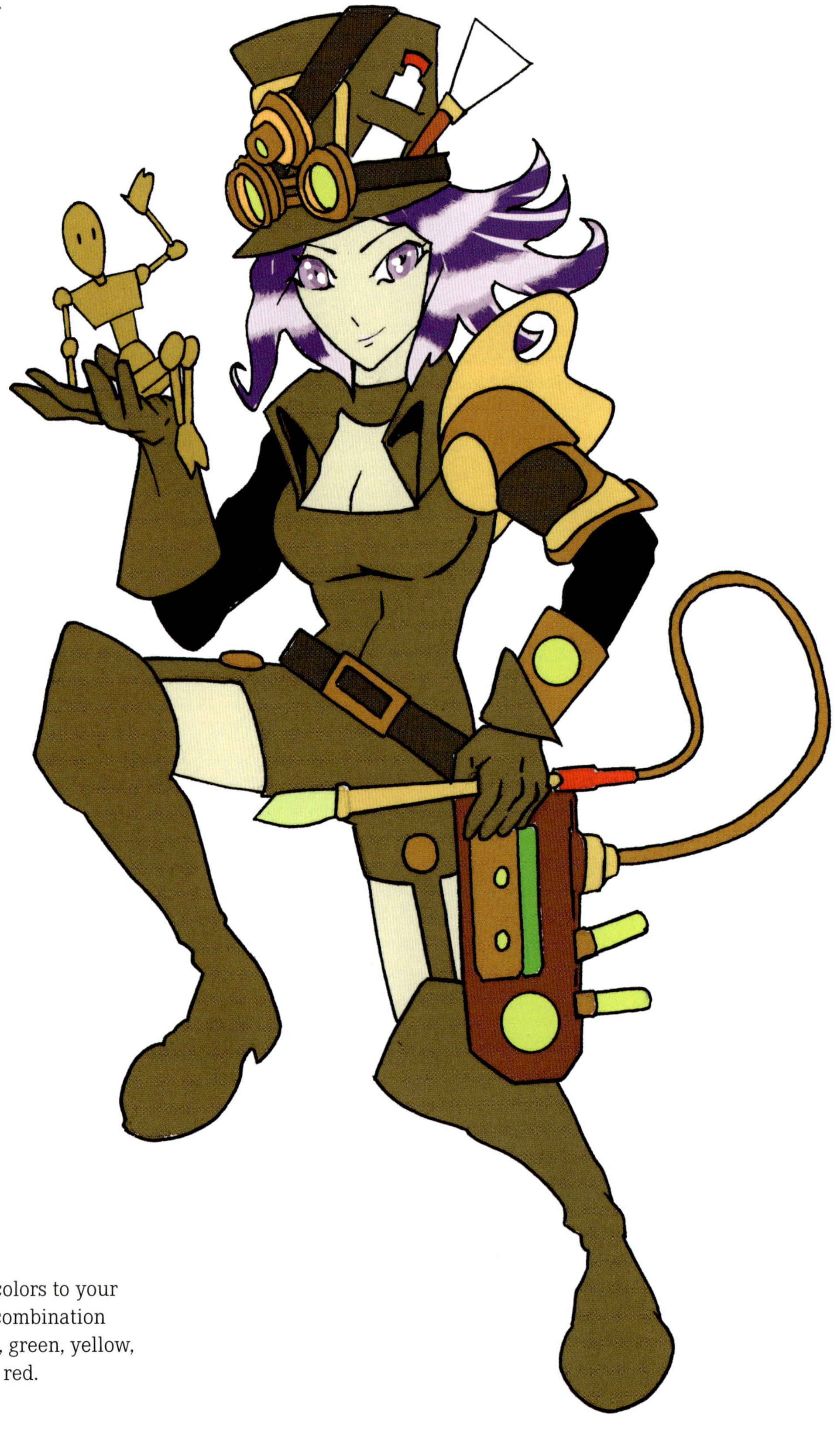

6

Add the base colors to your character – a combination of brown, gold, green, yellow, and a touch of red.

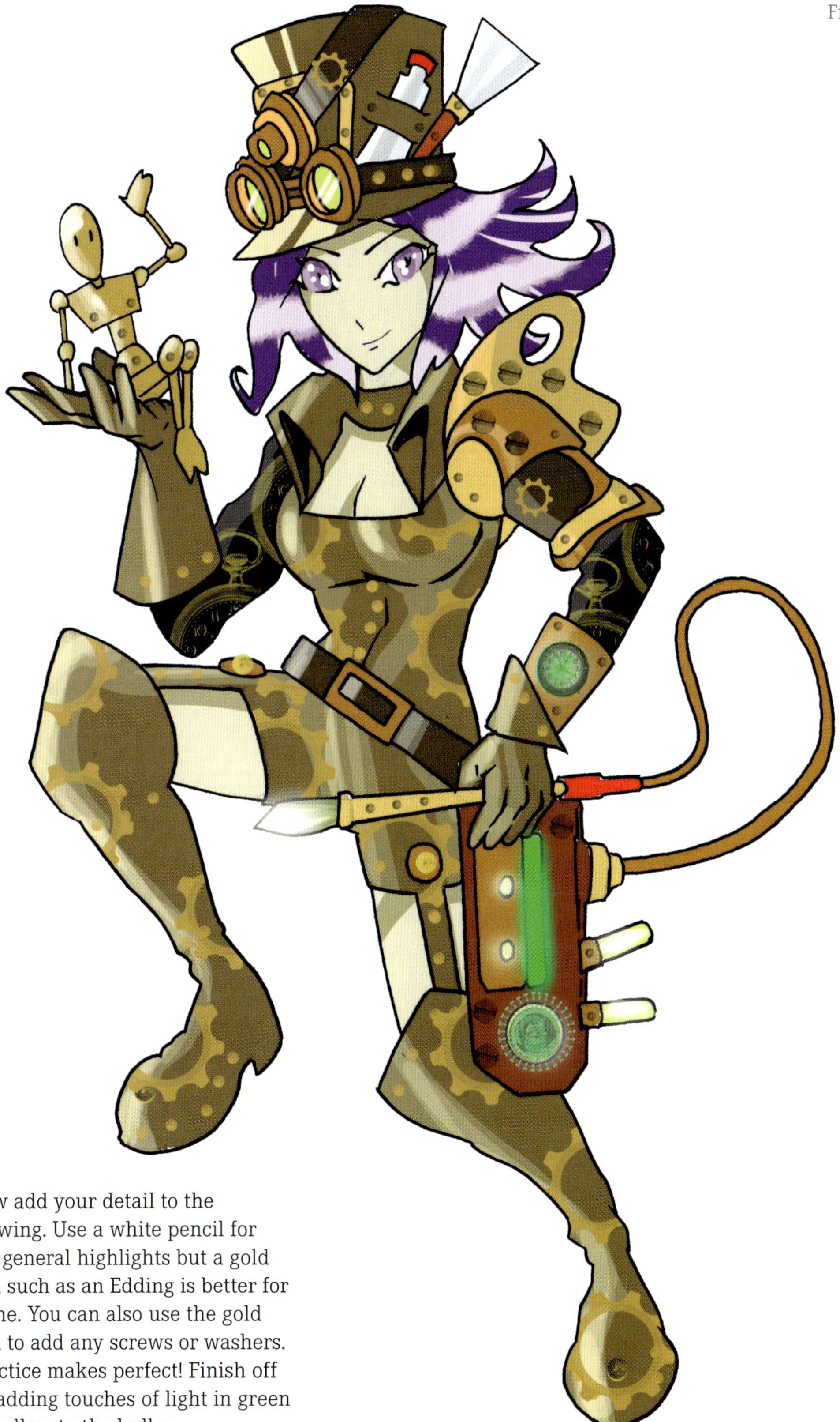

7

Now add your detail to the drawing. Use a white pencil for the general highlights but a gold pen such as an Edding is better for shine. You can also use the gold pen to add any screws or washers. Practice makes perfect! Finish off by adding touches of light in green or yellow to the bulbs.

OCCULTIST

Castelini Morgauss was always a great lover of the supernatural. This former student of the dark arts, who graduated with honor from the school of occultism, now guards the gates that connect this world to the world of the dead. The most rebellious and dangerous of the dead are far from happy about losing their life, so many of them try to return. Morgauss is one of only a few who can stop them.

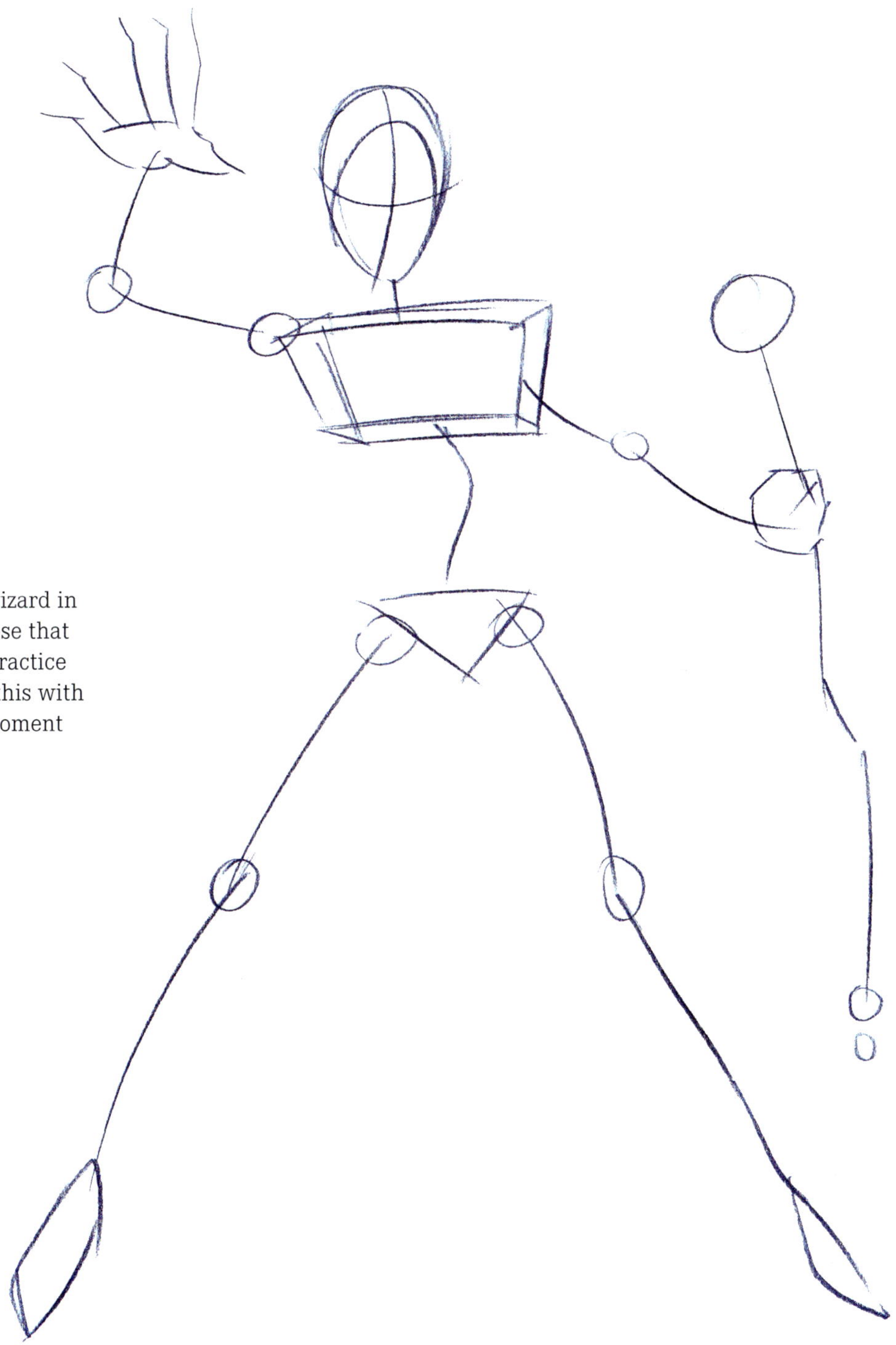

1

Draw the figure of your wizard in blue pencil: give him a pose that reflects his power. With practice you should be able to do this with a 2H pencil, but for the moment work with the blue.

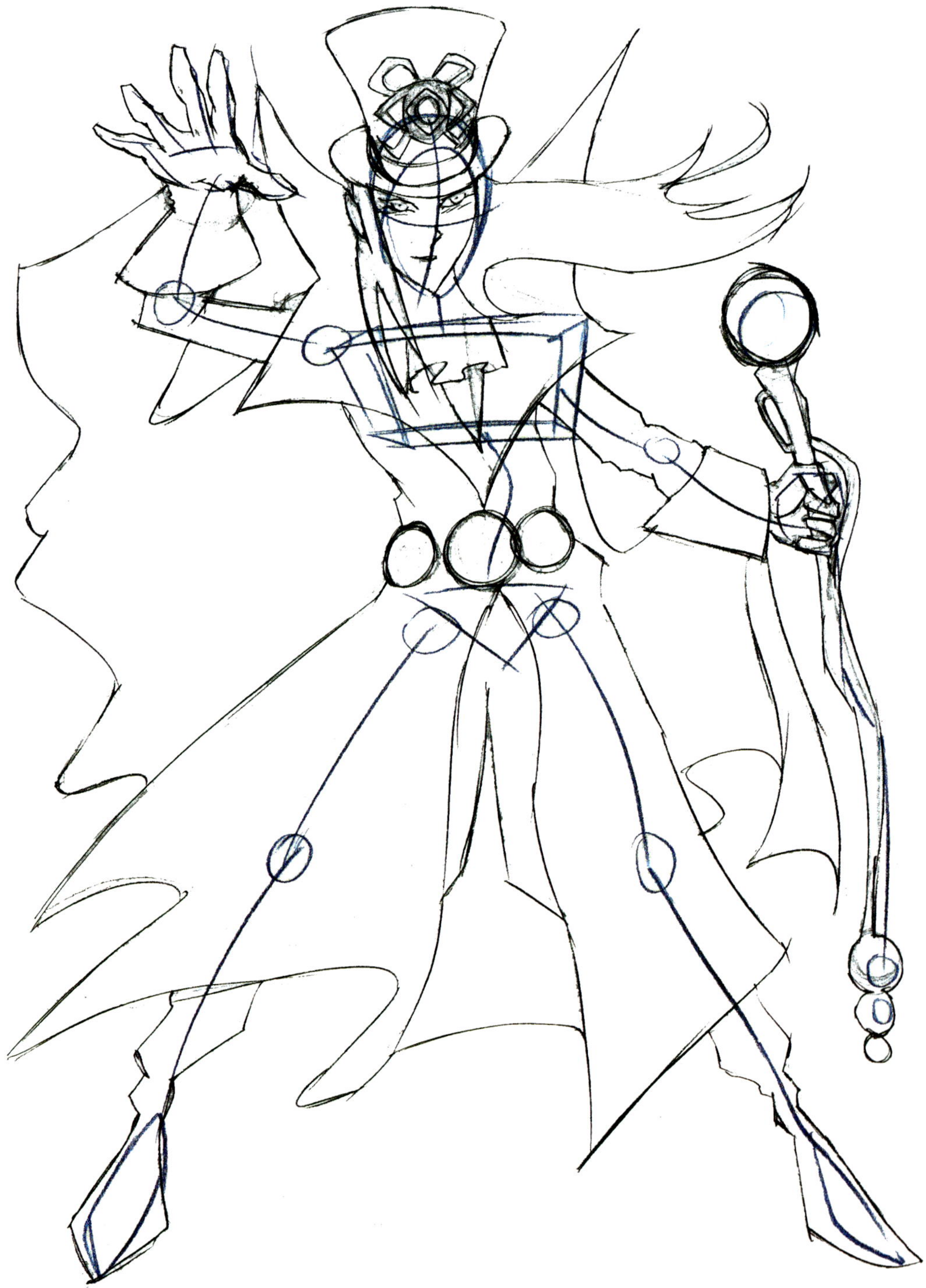

2

Use the 2H pencil in your blue draft to design the figure; you can add the details later.

3

Use a 05-calibre mechanical pencil to sketch the figure. Work on adding volume and any necessary details before beginning to ink the drawing.

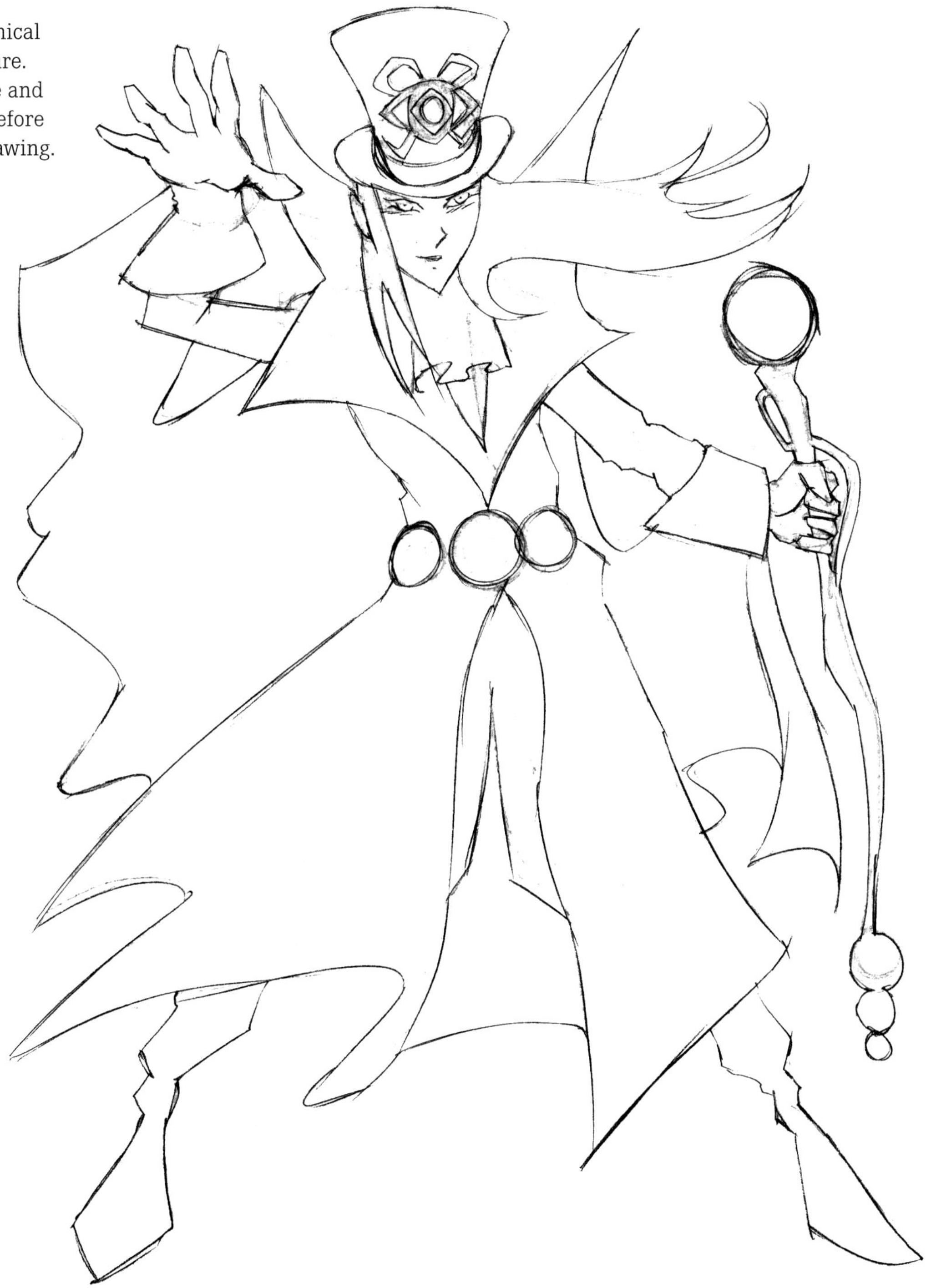

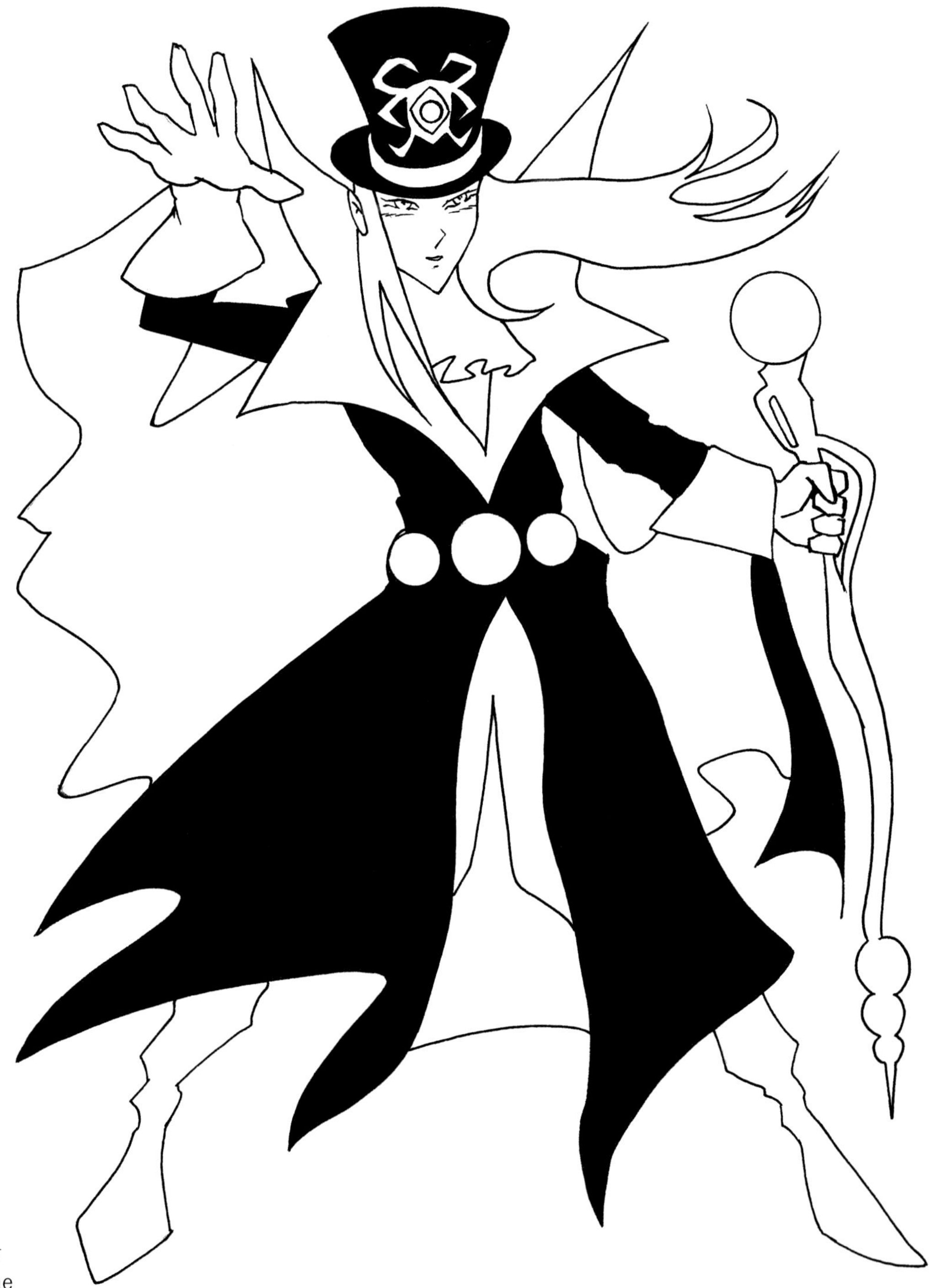

4

Outline your drawing. Once the ink is dry you can remove the pencil with a soft eraser. Finally use an 0.8-mm pen to color in the black of the hat, the suit, and part of the cape.

5

The light is directly upon this wizard, but look: the light is coming from the wizard himself – a magic spell that casts an unexpected glow from his cape. Try it out! Illuminate the character as though you had a light in the palm of your hand...

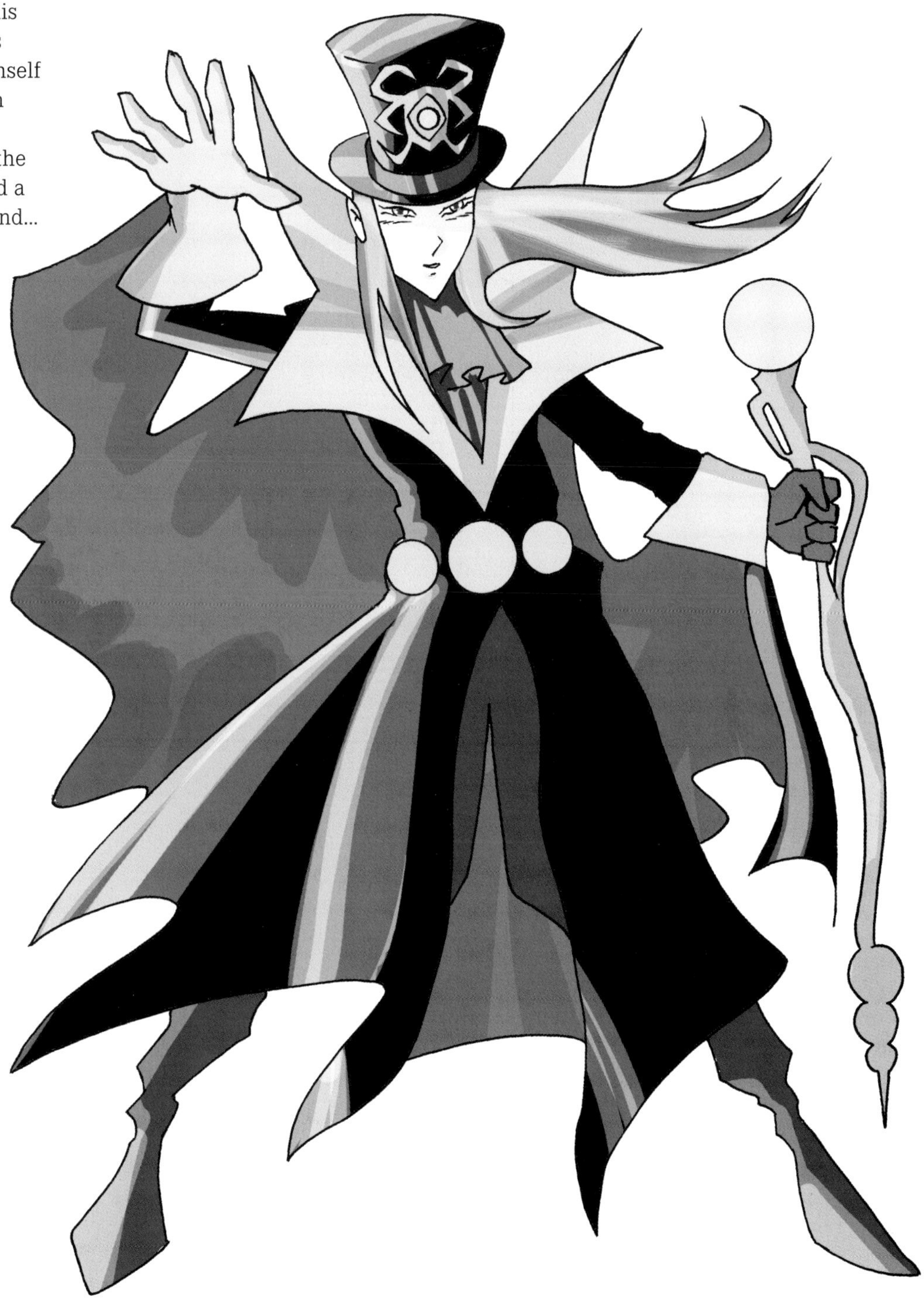

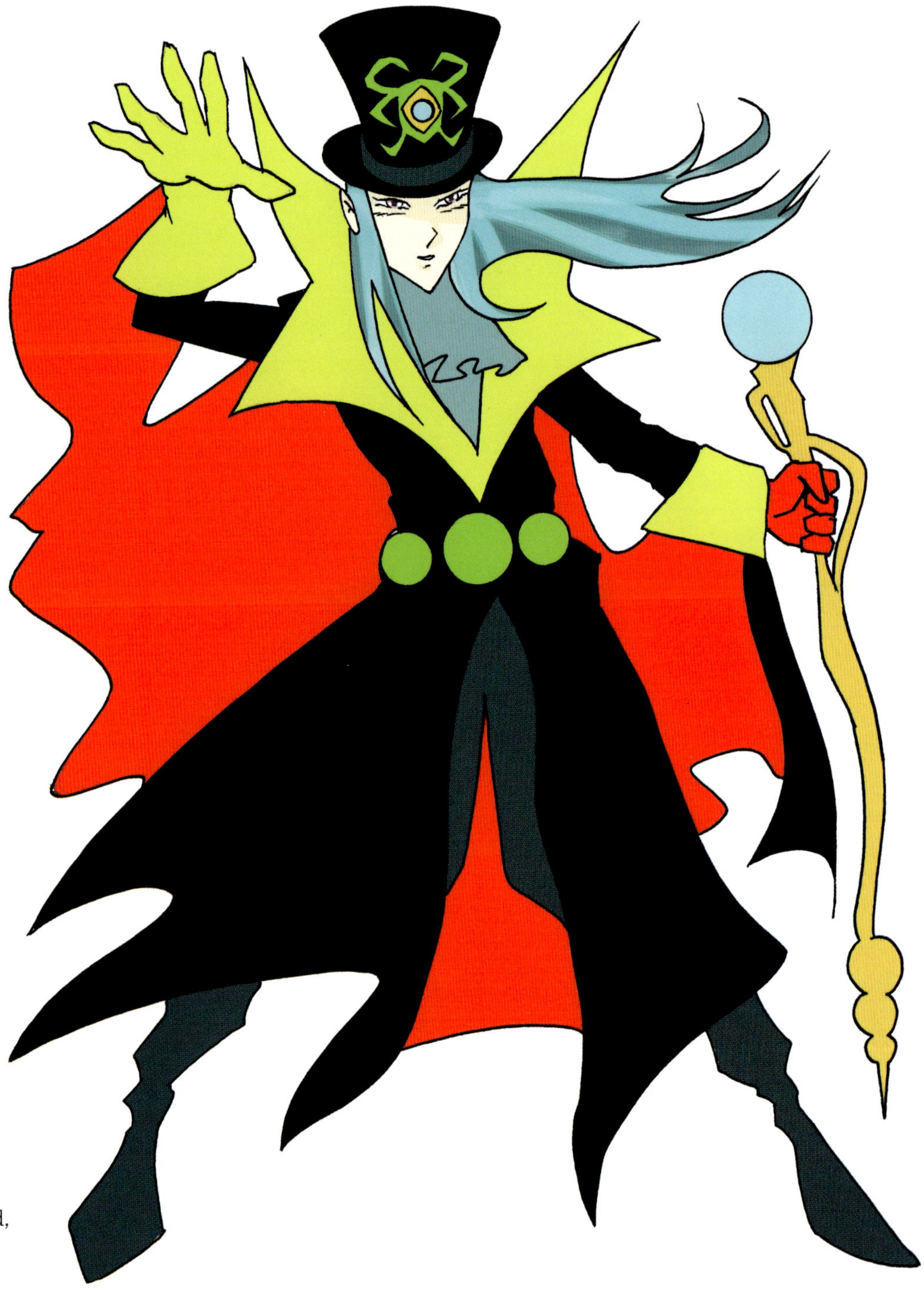

6

Color your wizard with a combination of red, yellow, blue, and green. Use gold for the wand, a greenish gray for the trousers, and a lighter green for the shirt.

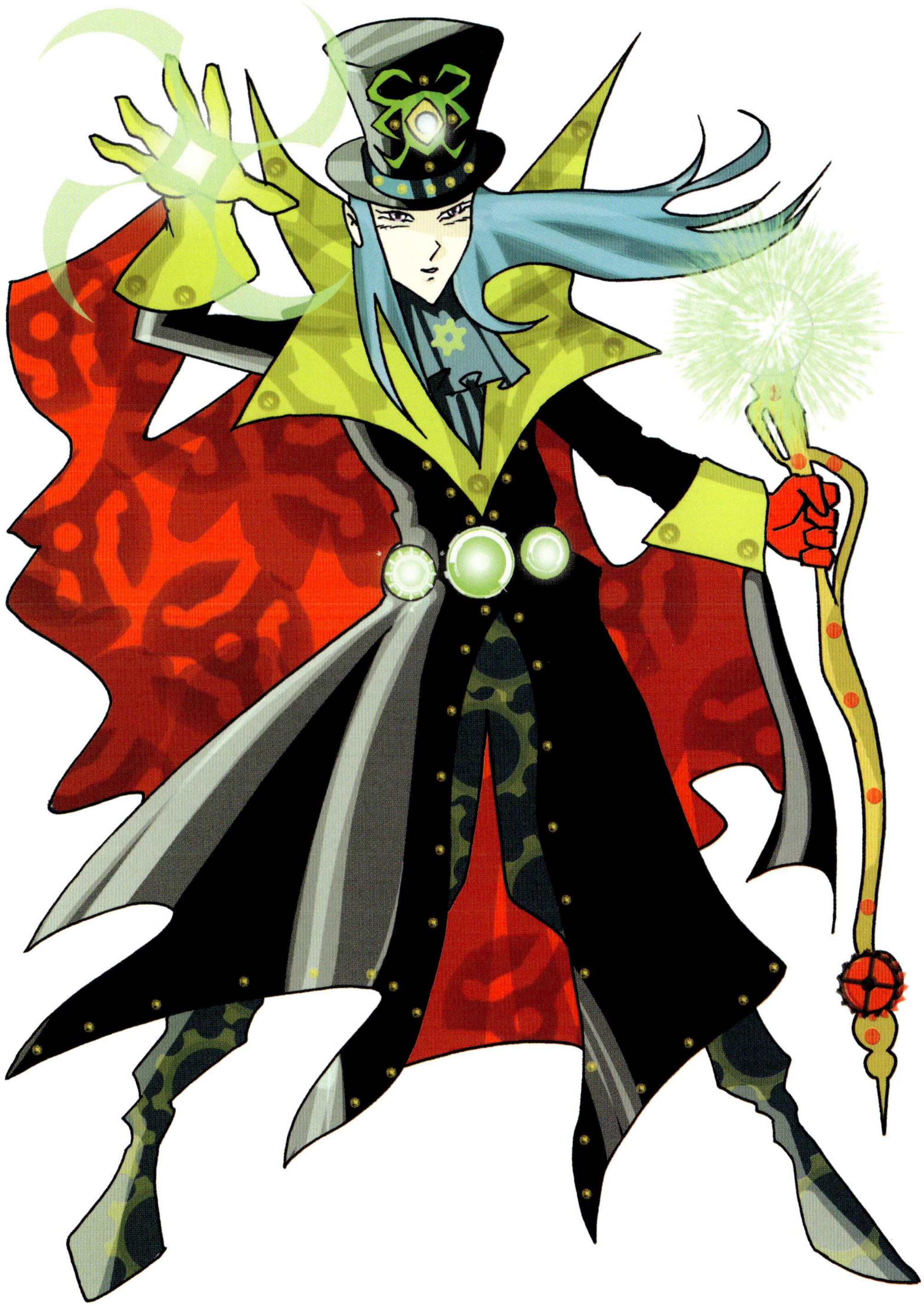

7

Illuminate every detail of this magical character with white. Add washers to his clothing and some red rivets to decorate the wand. Finally, use a darker red to decorate the bottom of the cape: my choice would be to add some magic symbols. It looks completely mystical!

FORTUNE-TELLER

Chantell the Gypsy is a fortune-teller and tarot card reader, student of white magic and expert in the technical arts of reading the future. Related to courtiers, she is often seen at parties in the company of high-ranking ladies. Of course she also has an office in the city, which I'm telling you just in case you want to have your fortune read...

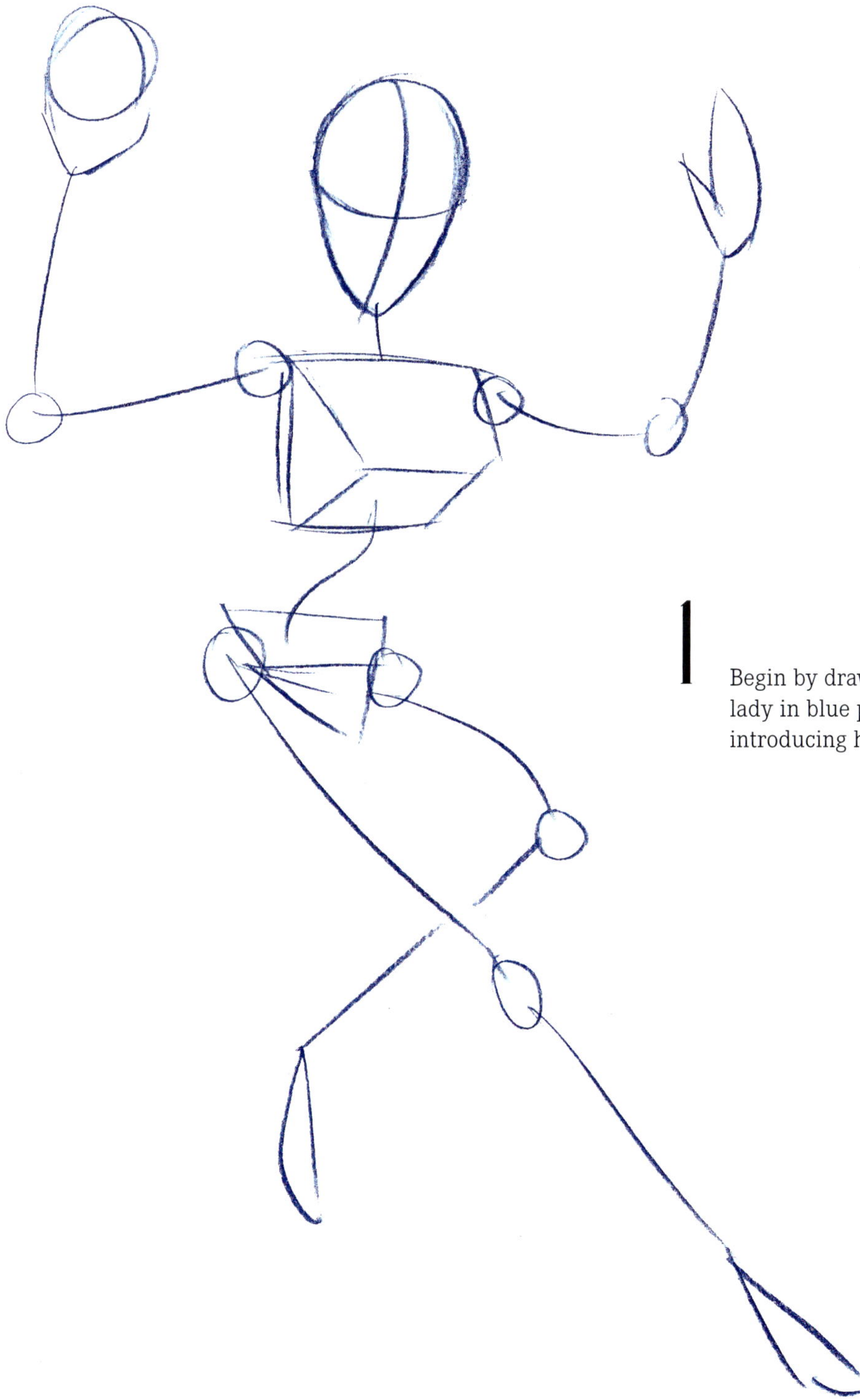

1

Begin by drawing the base of your lady in blue pencil – draw her introducing herself.

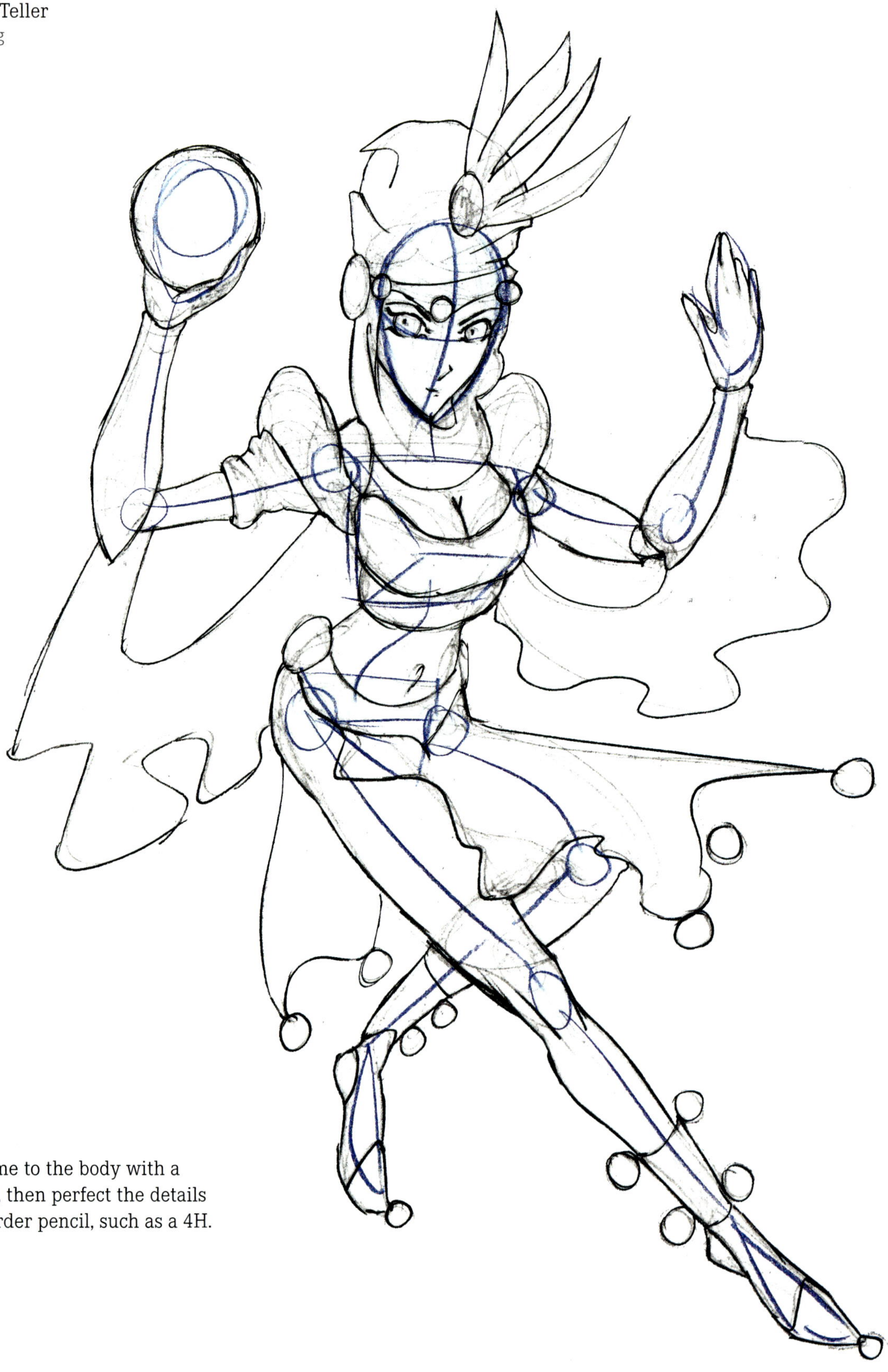

2

Add volume to the body with a 2H pencil, then perfect the details with a harder pencil, such as a 4H.

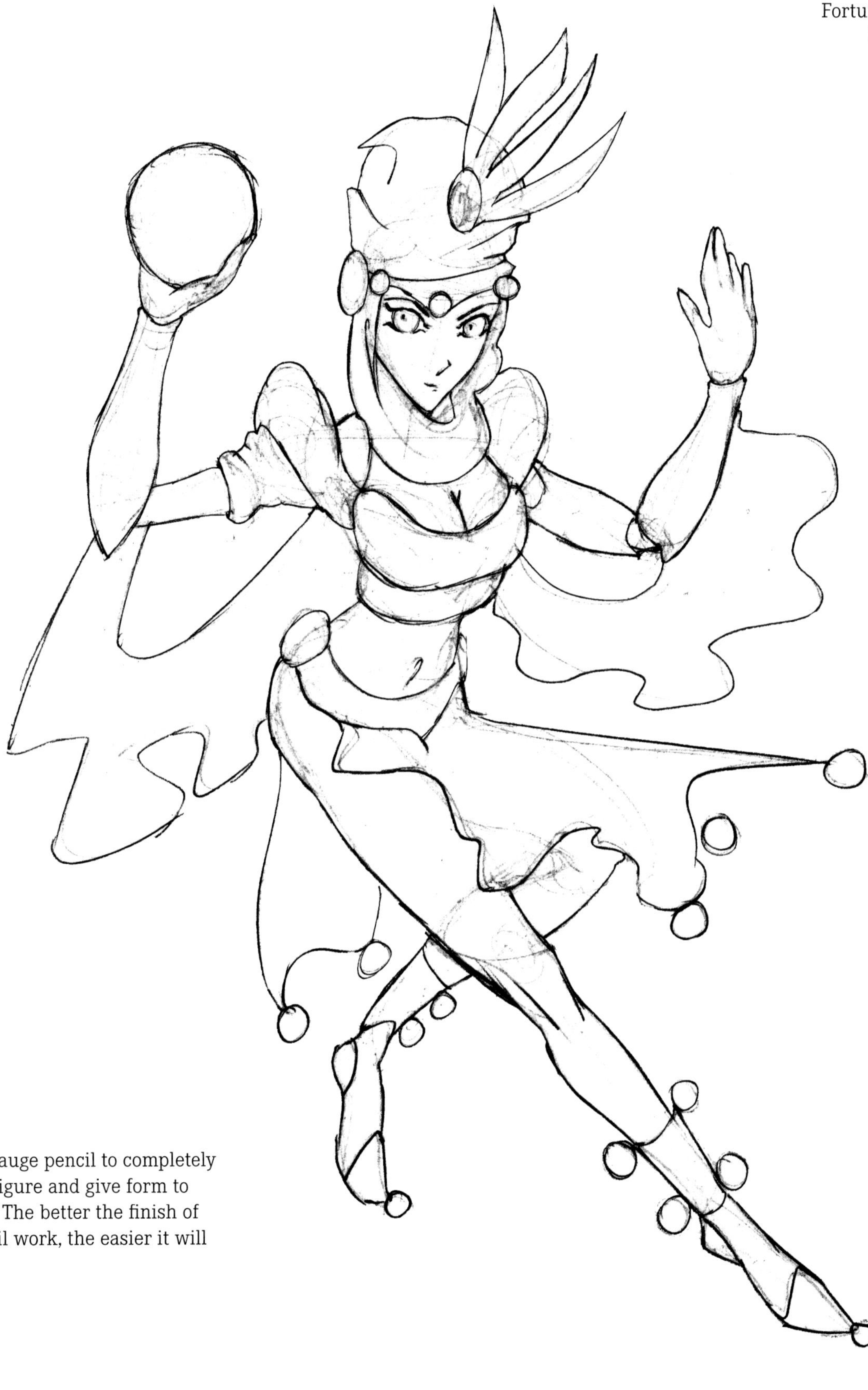

3

Use a 05-gauge pencil to completely draw the figure and give form to the detail. The better the finish of your pencil work, the easier it will be to ink.

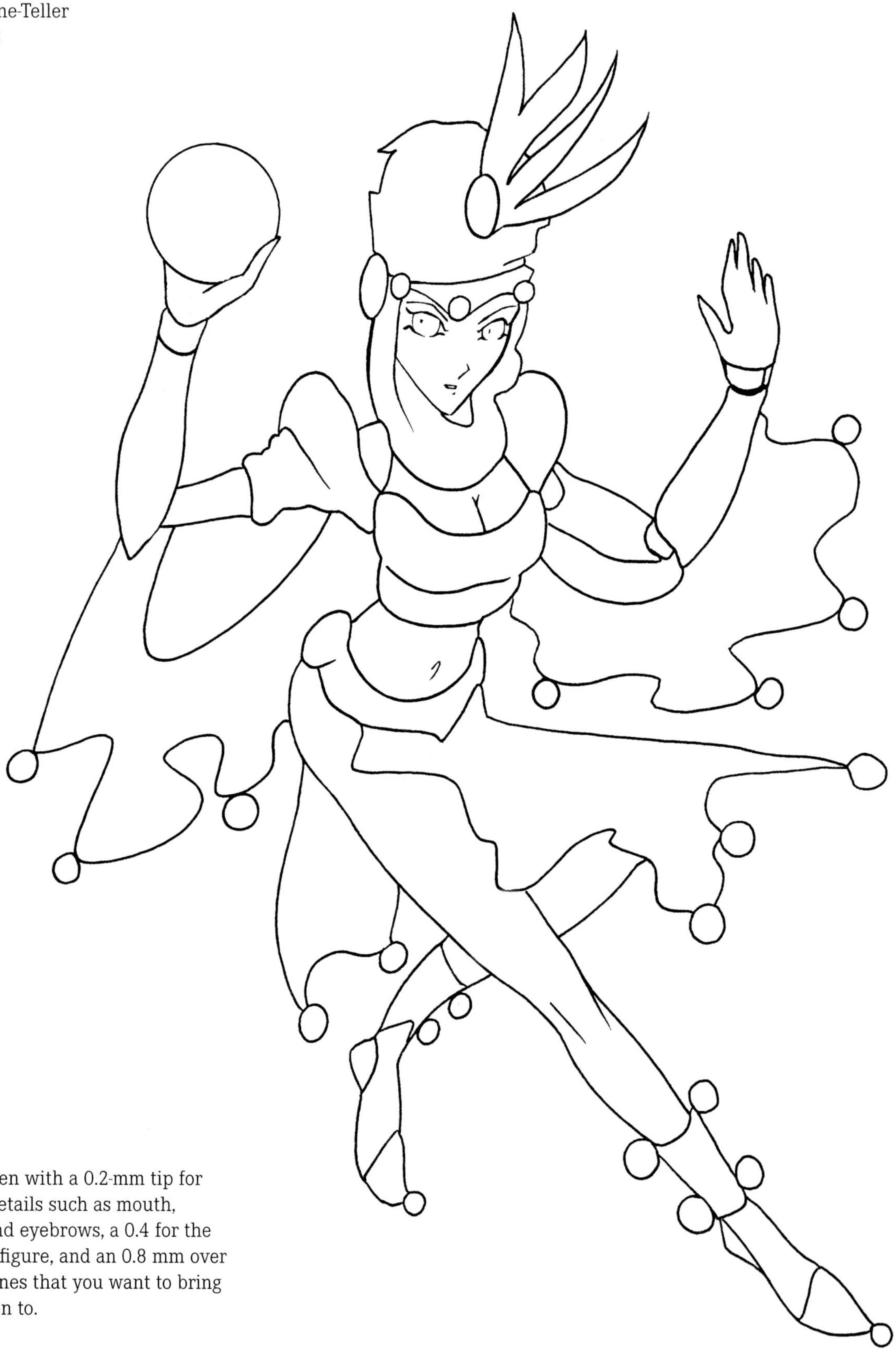

4

Use a pen with a 0.2-mm tip for small details such as mouth, eyes, and eyebrows, a 0.4 for the overall figure, and an 0.8 mm over those lines that you want to bring attention to.

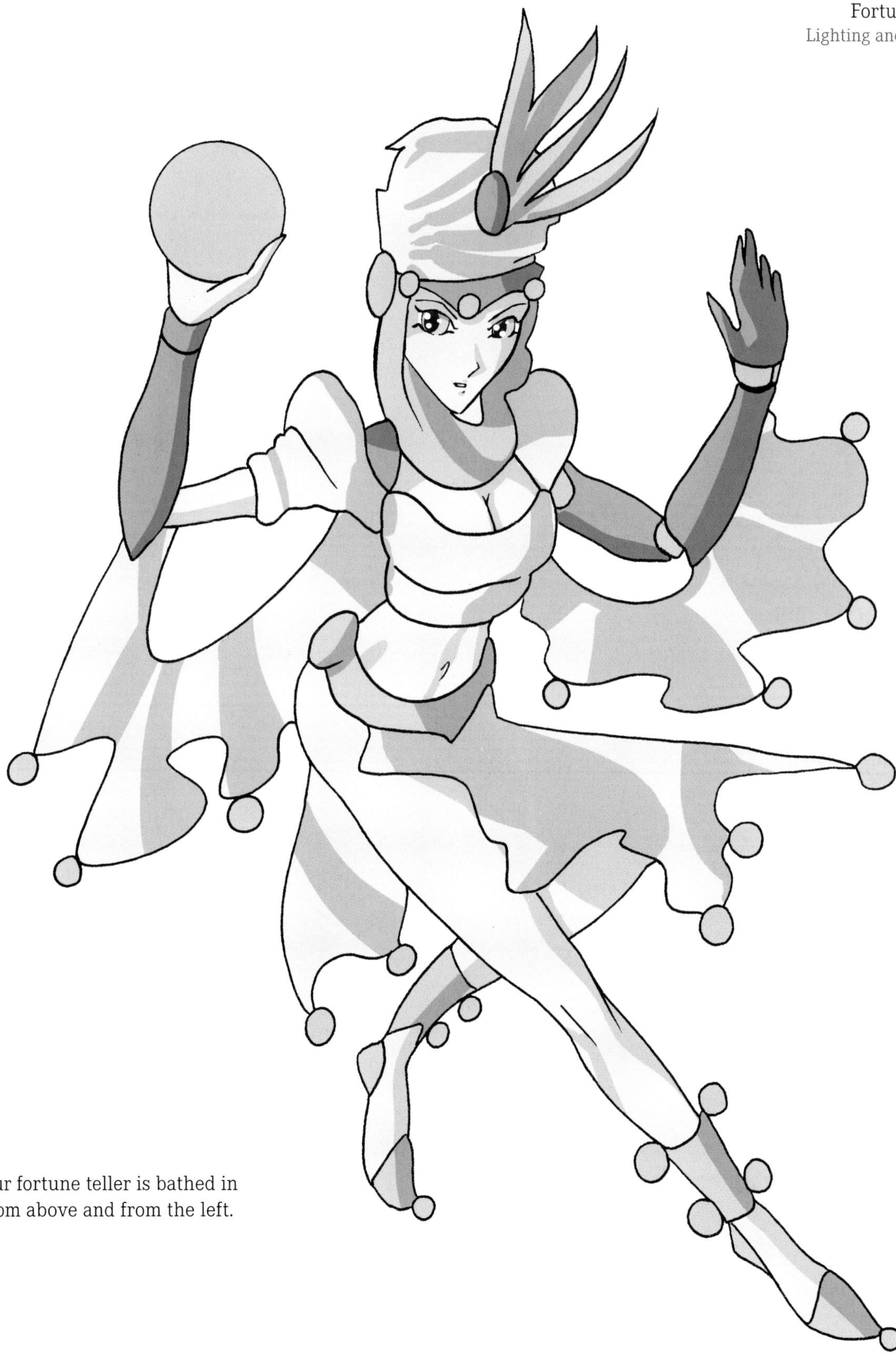

5

Here our fortune teller is bathed in light from above and from the left.

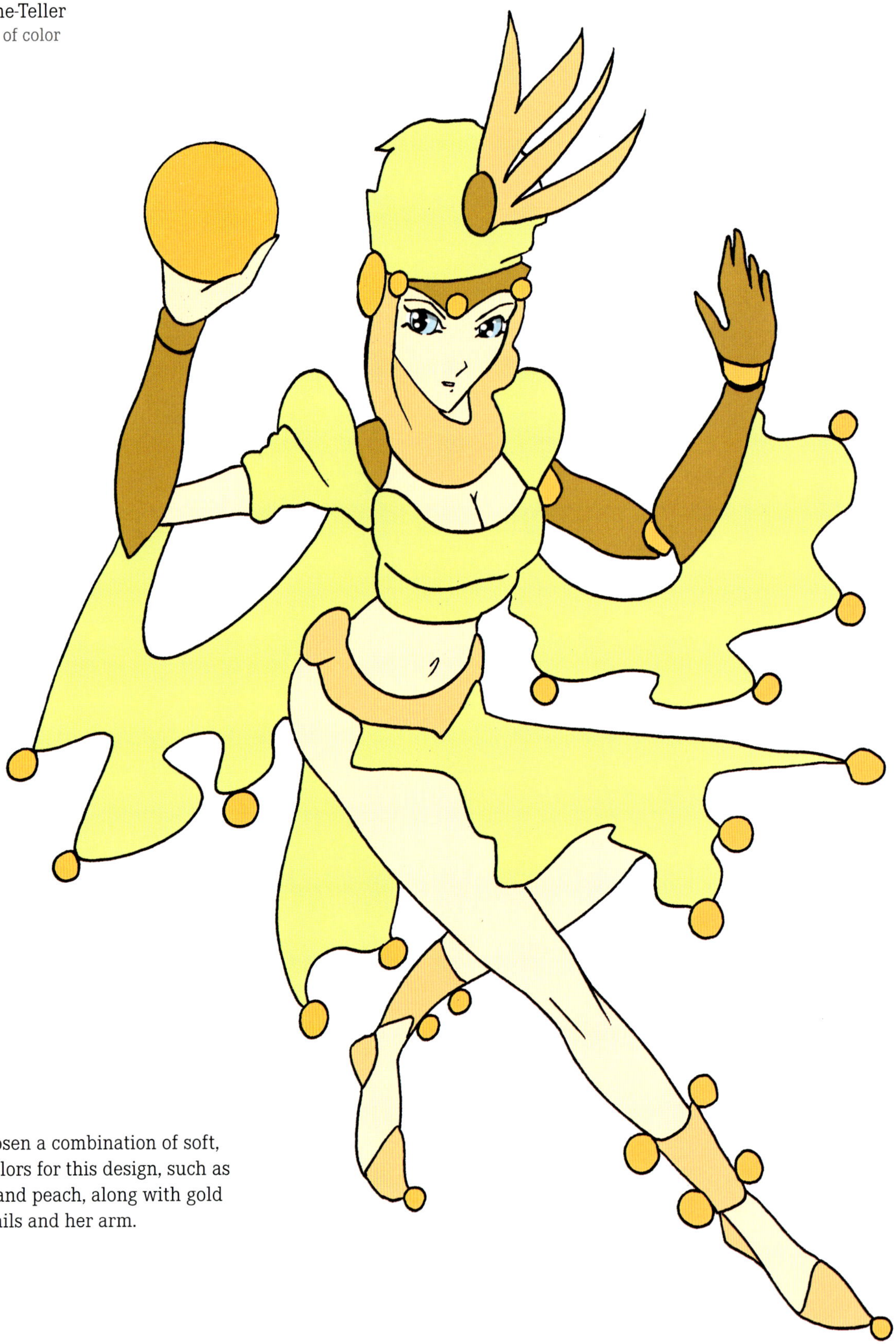

6

I've chosen a combination of soft, light colors for this design, such as lemon and peach, along with gold for details and her arm.

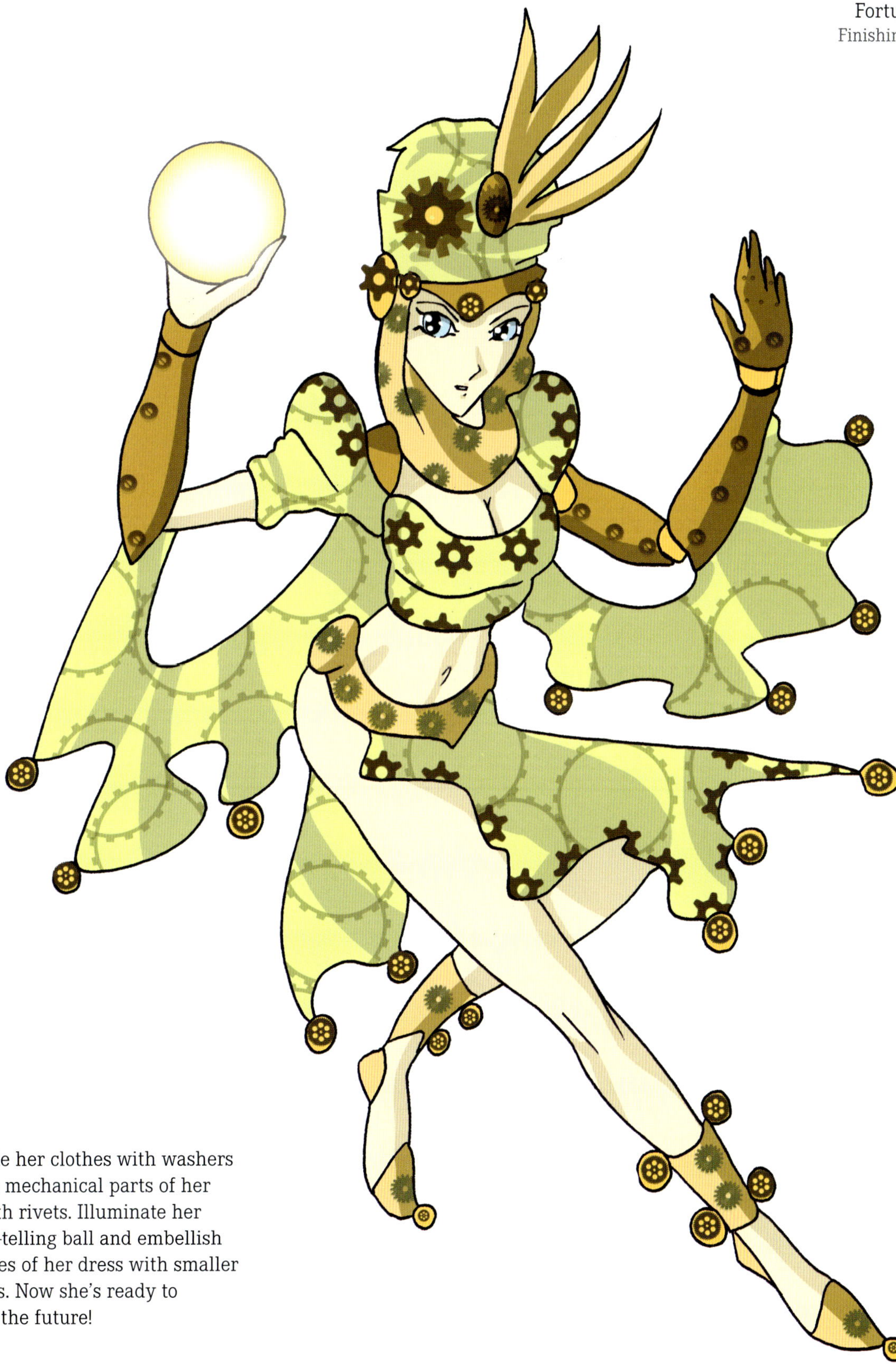

7

Decorate her clothes with washers and the mechanical parts of her arm with rivets. Illuminate her fortune-telling ball and embellish the edges of her dress with smaller washers. Now she's ready to predict the future!

NINJA

Suyuri Kane was a ruthless contract killer: he was a master of all fighting styles and was lethal in possession of any weapon. However, after falling in battle his clan turned their back on him. Suyuri spent years recovering from the wounds of that tragic day, but the wait has helped him realize all the damage that was done under the orders of the clan. Now he fights against his murderous brothers, determined to atone for his sins.

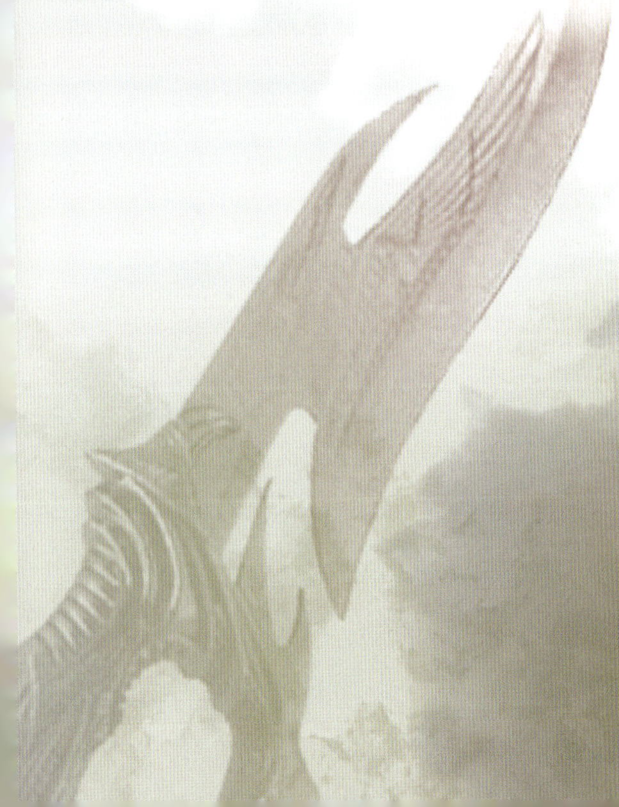

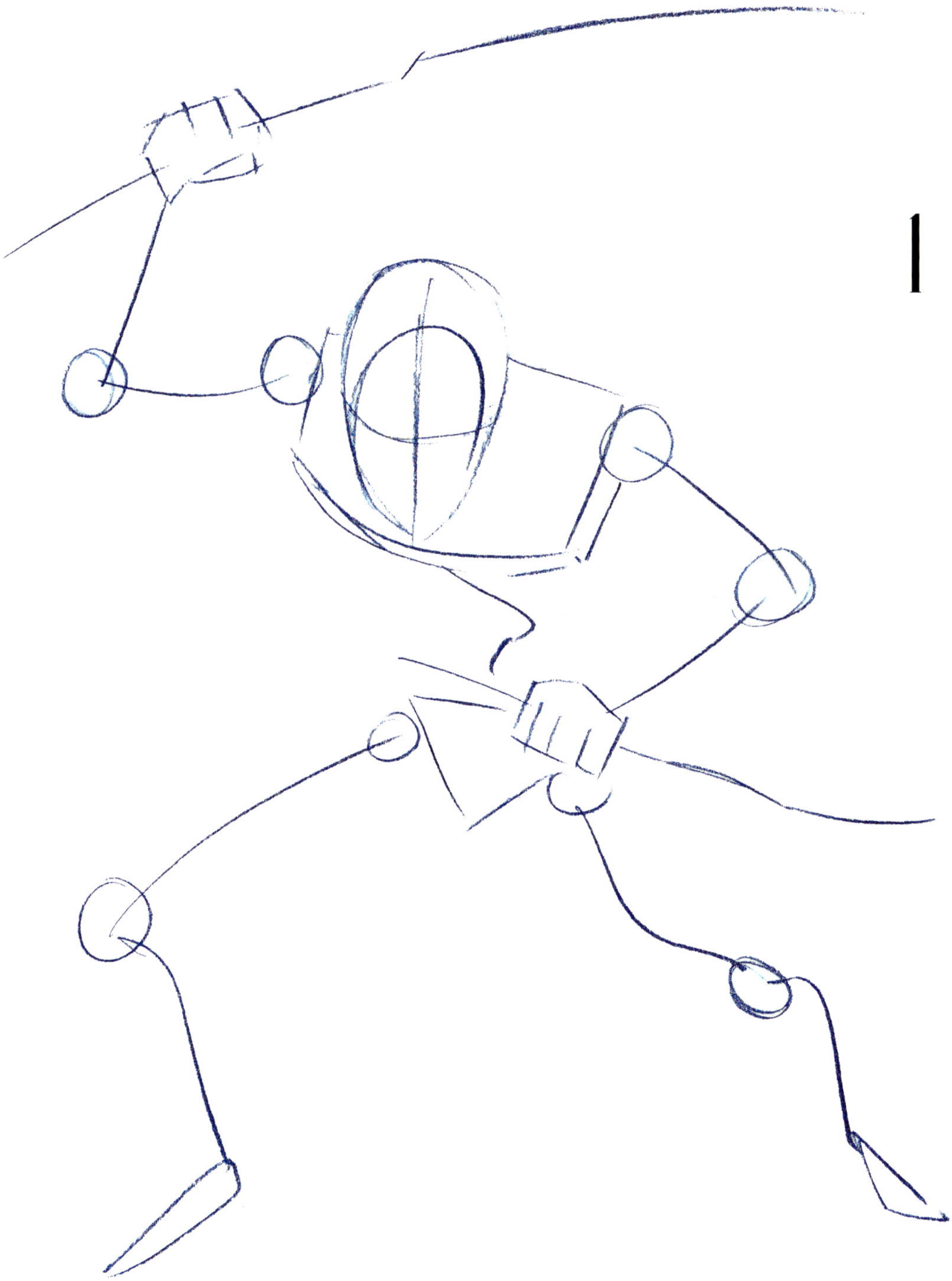

1

Begin by preparing the base of this inscrutable character in blue pencil.

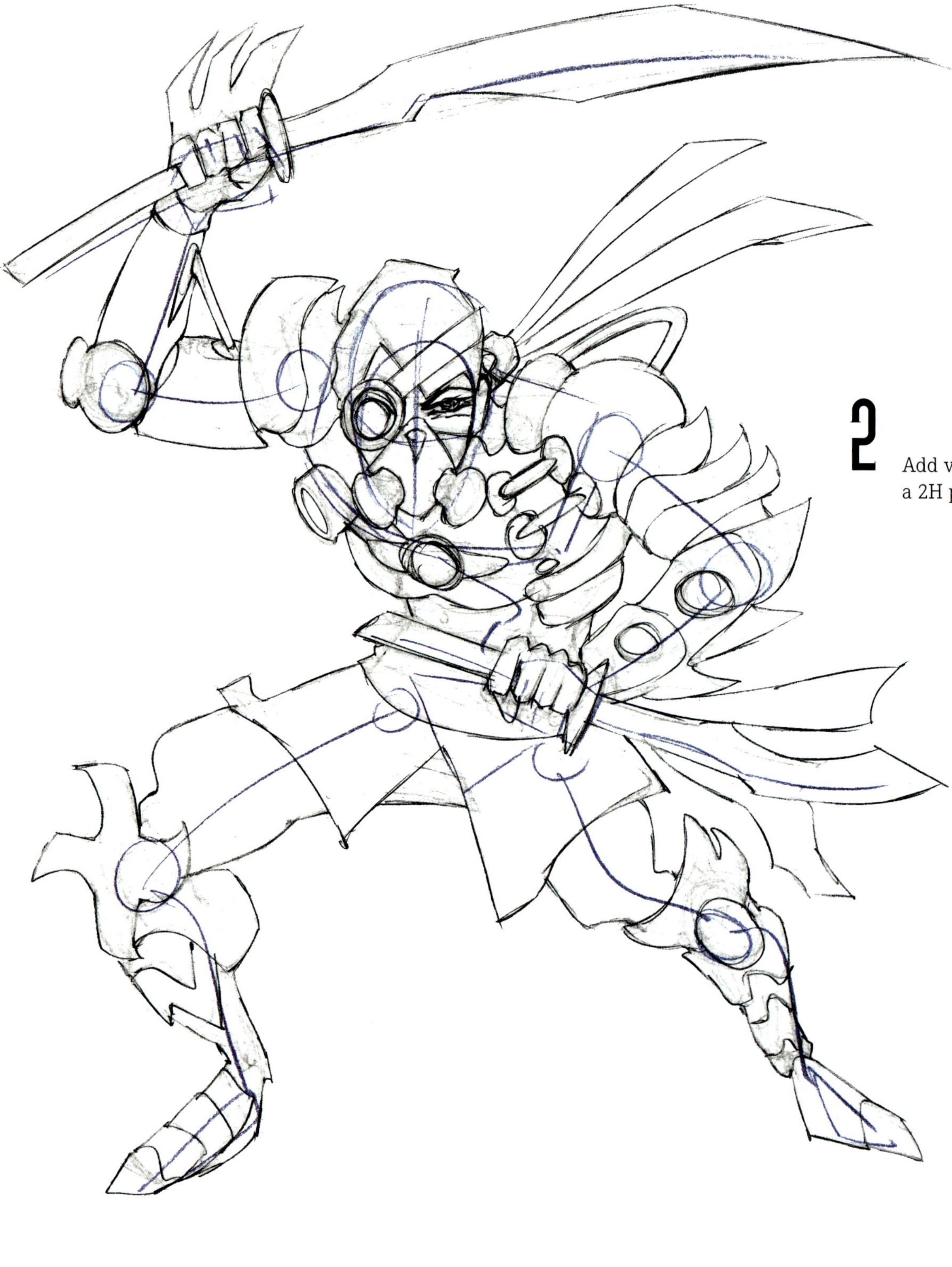

2

Add volume to the body with a 2H pencil.

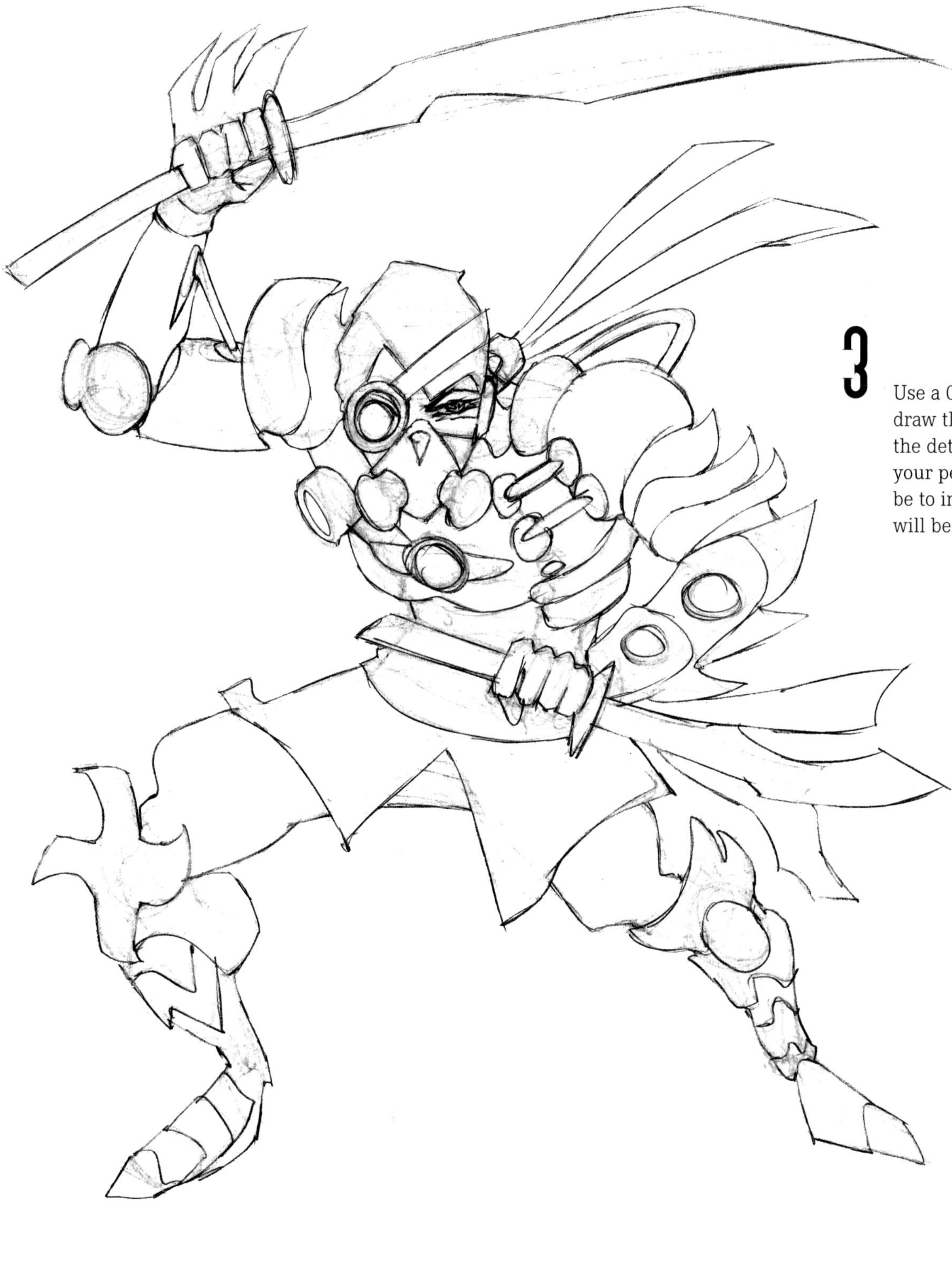

3

Use a 05-gauge pencil to completely draw the figure and give form to the detail. The better the finish of your pencil work, the easier it will be to ink and the better the finish will be.

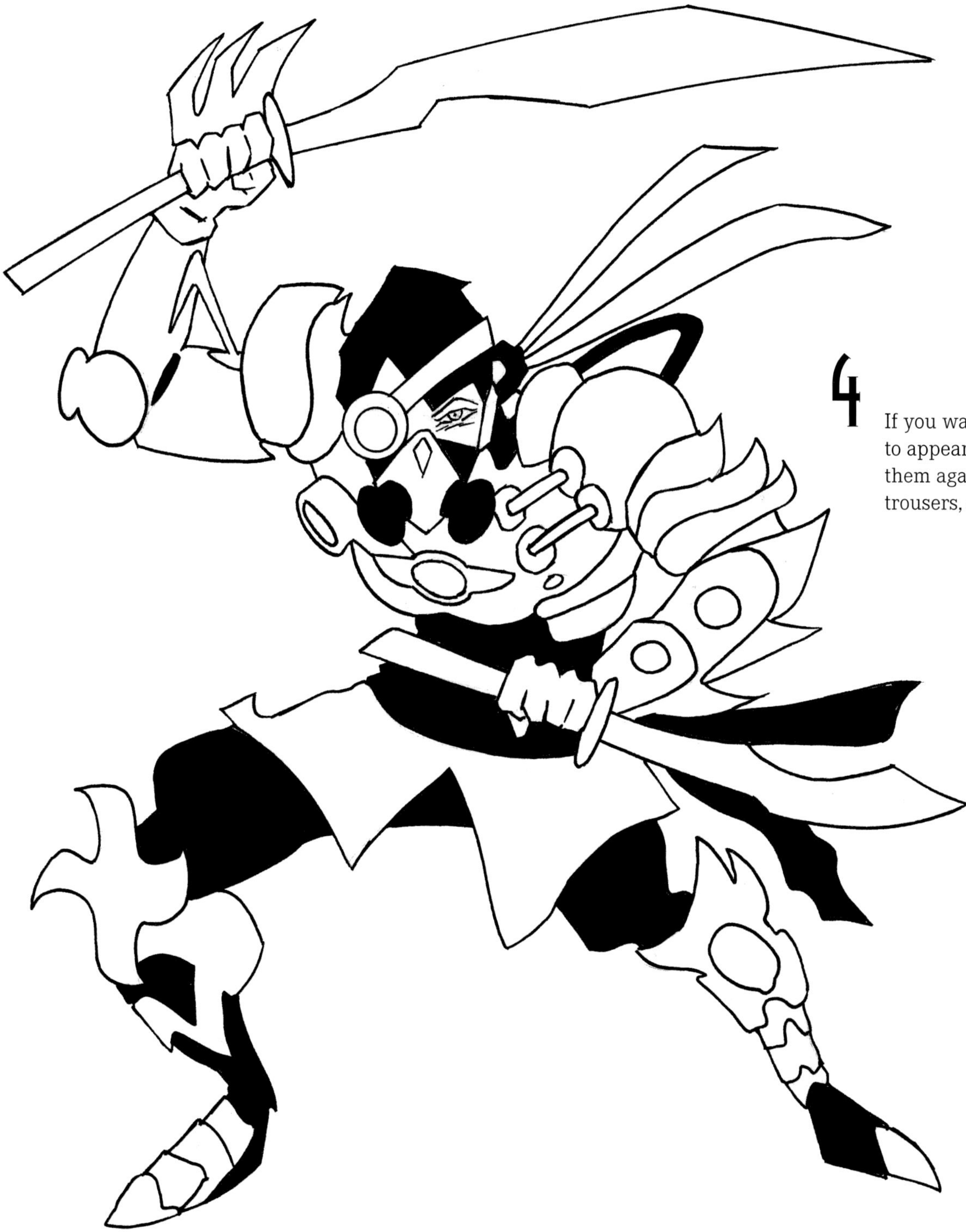

4

If you want any of the edging lines to appear more intense, draw over them again. Finally, color the mask, trousers, and sash in black.

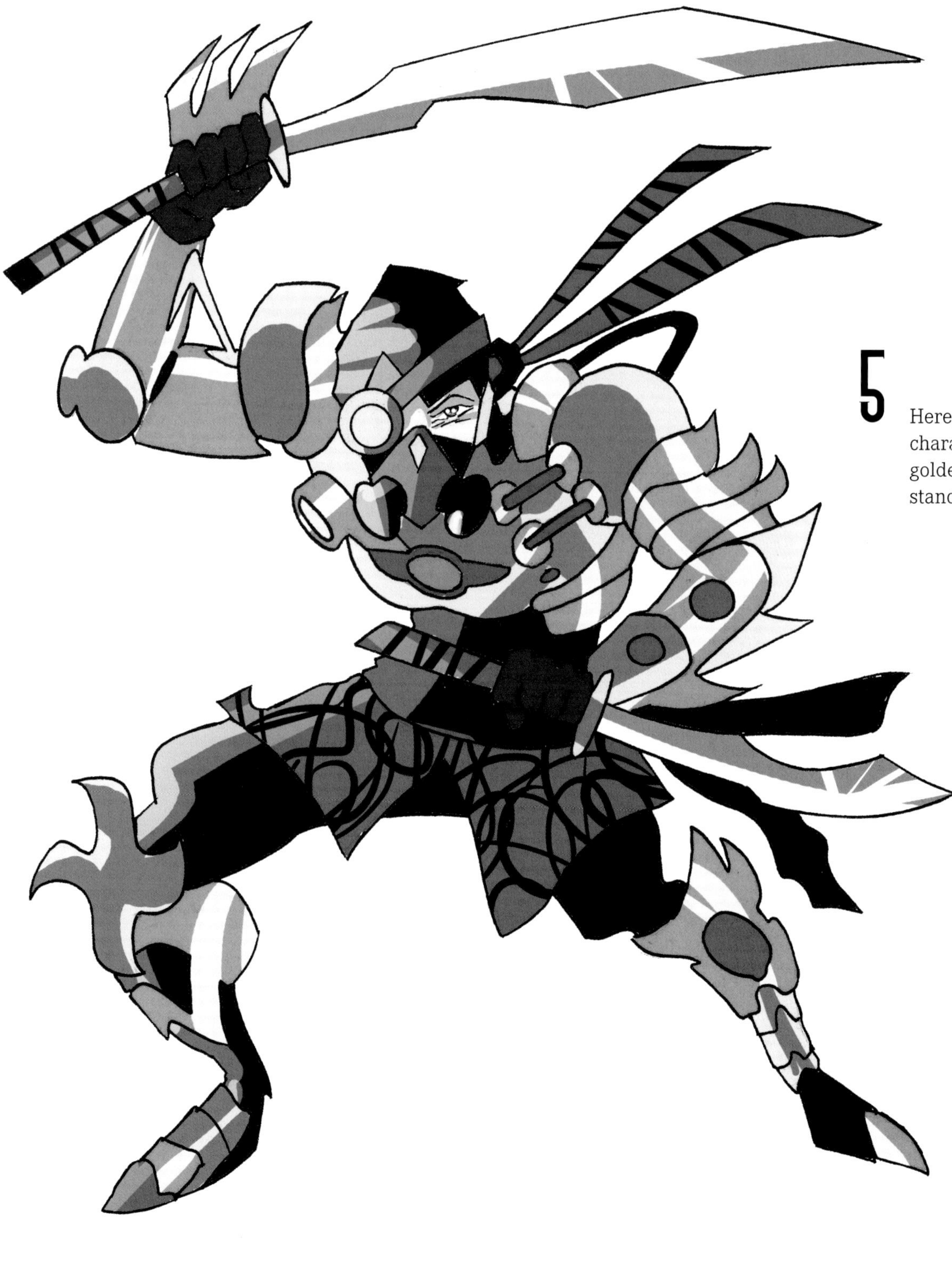

5

Here, the light is above the character, making the ninja's golden armor and two swords stand out.

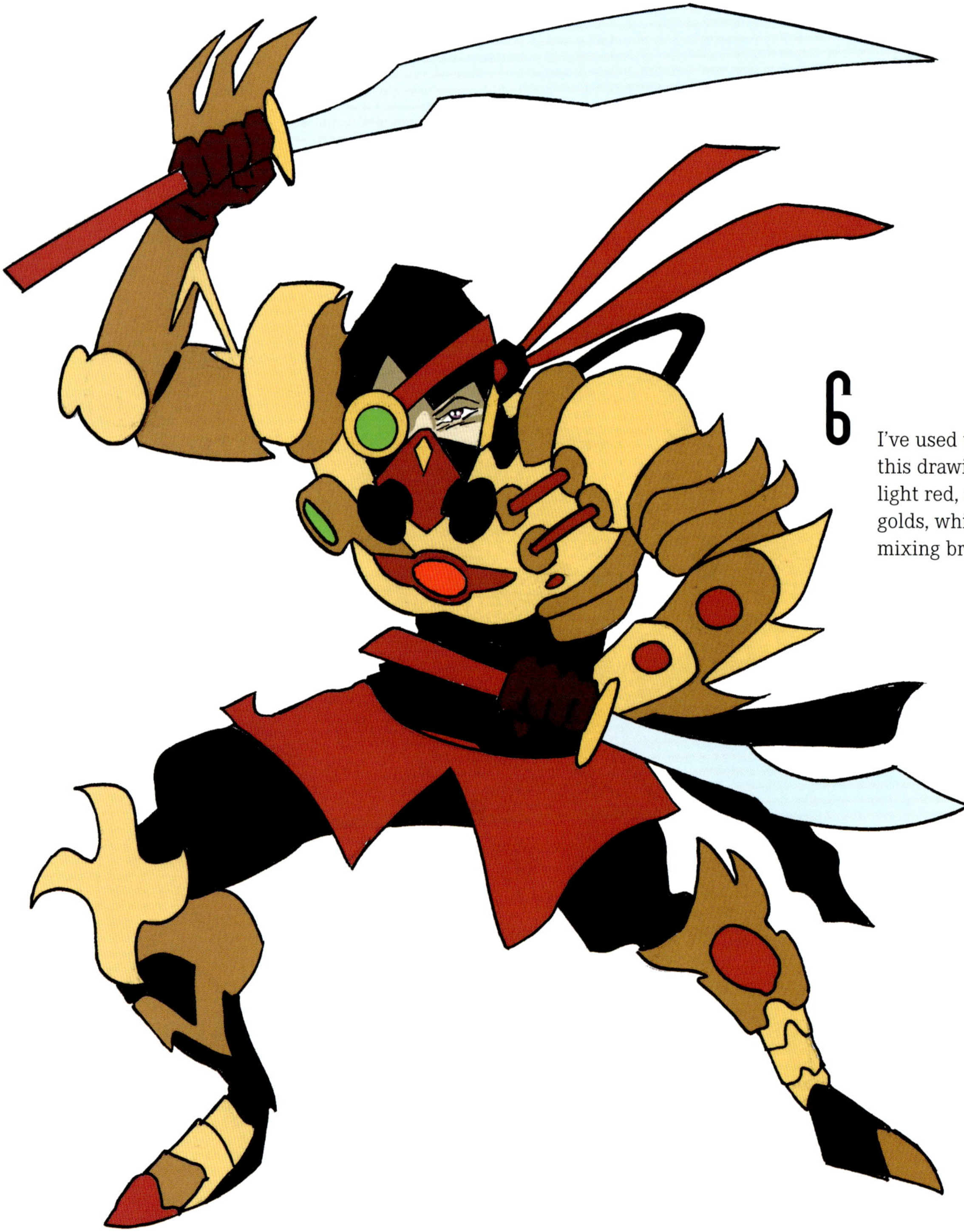

6

I've used the following colors for this drawing: green, blue, red, very light red, and, of course, a range of golds, which can be achieved by mixing brown with yellow.

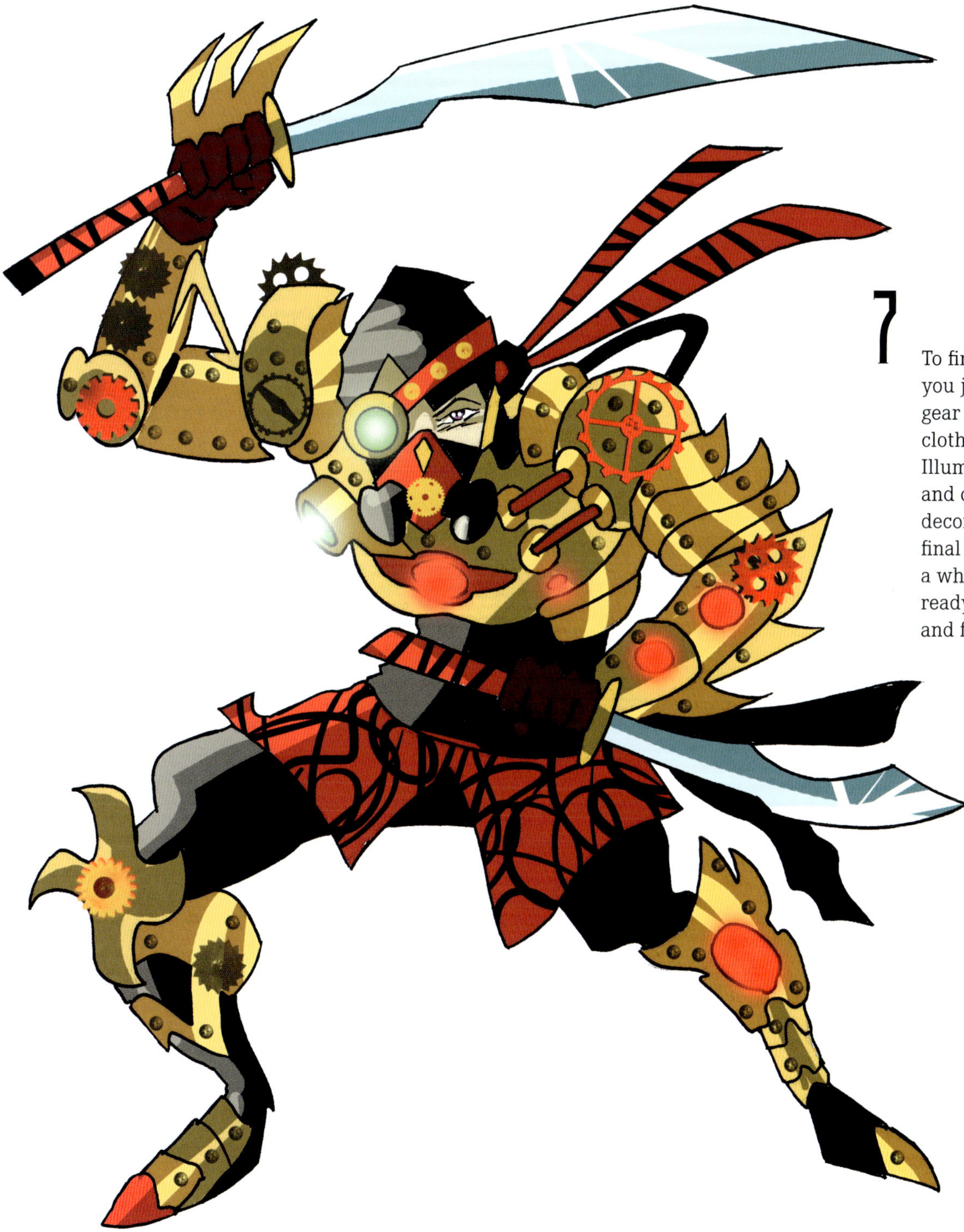

7

To finish this ninja drawing you just need to add tacks and gear wheels to the armor and clothes using a gold colored pen. Illuminate the red energy spheres and devices on the costume, decorate the swords, and add the final glimmers and touches with a white colored pencil. Now it's ready! This ninja looks fierce and formidable!

DOCTOR TERROR

Mortymer Scalpin was a great surgeon whose single obsession seemed to be healing the sick and giving them a healthy life. However, something must have gone wrong in his search for ancient ancestral remedies because overnight his aspirations changed from curing the living to resurrecting the dead. Now the doctor has had to go underground in order to unleash his sinister and dangerous experiments. Beware of passing him on your travels!

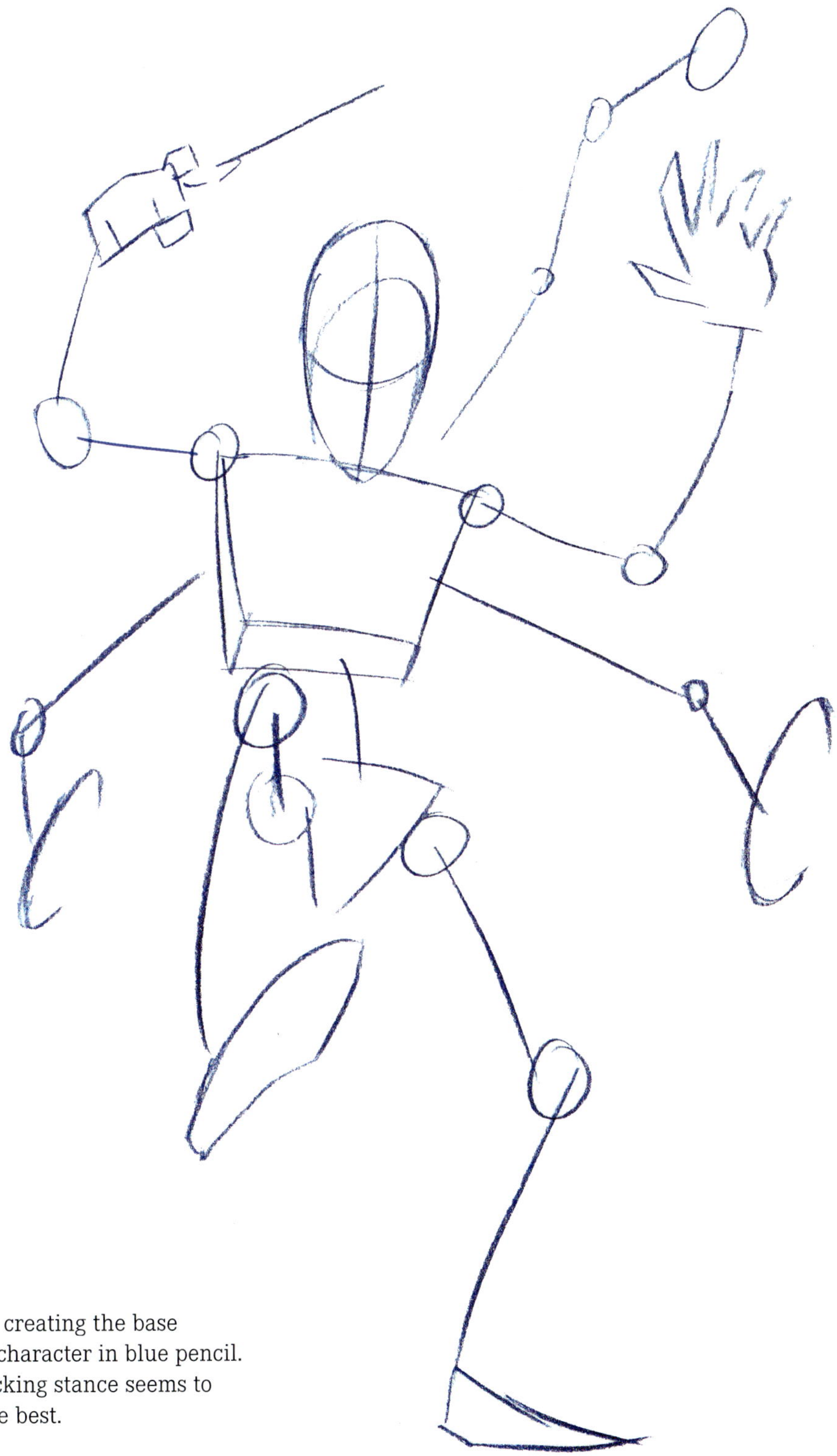

1

Start by creating the base of your character in blue pencil. An attacking stance seems to work the best.

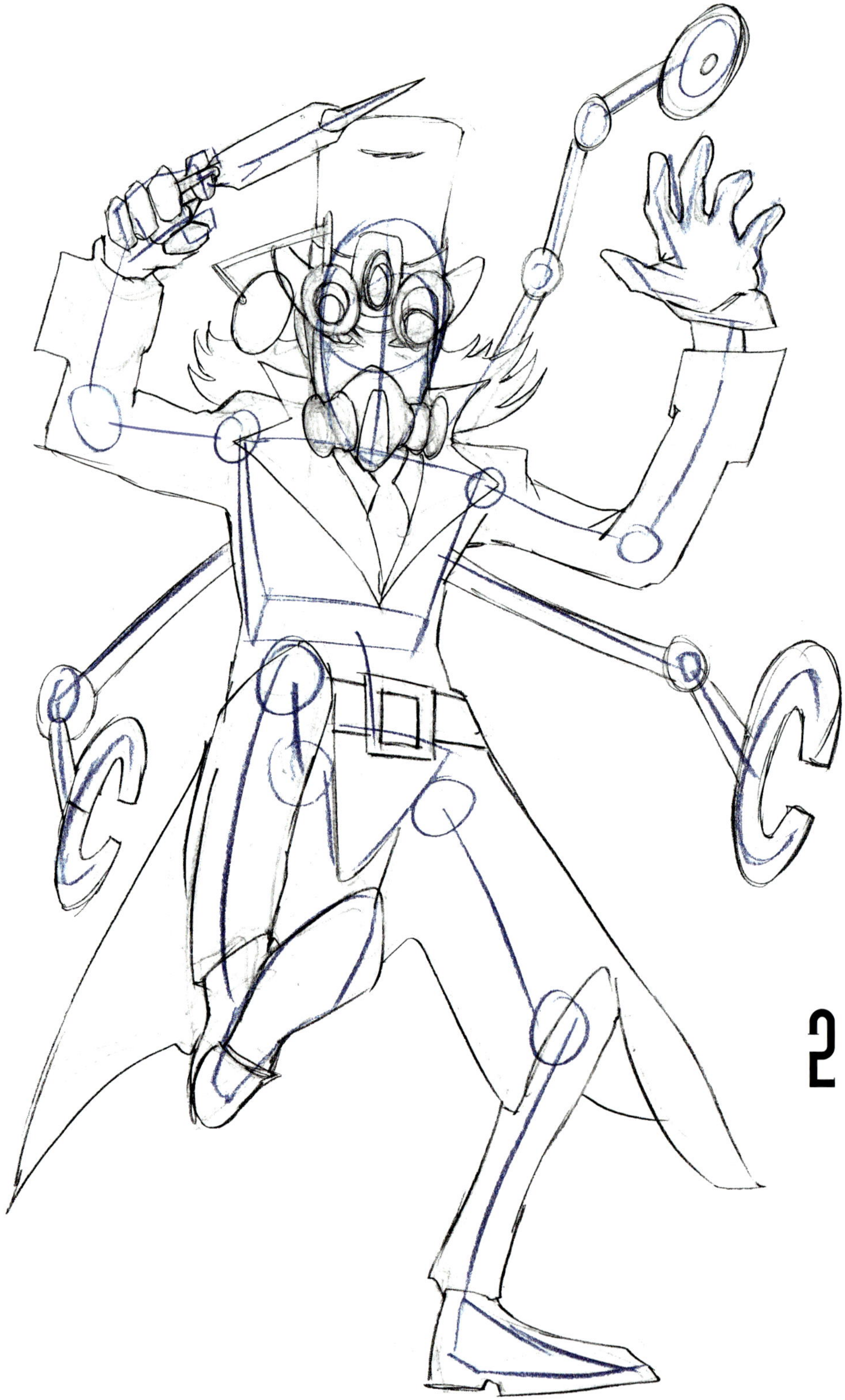

2

Add volume to the body with a 2H pencil, then perfect the details with a harder pencil, such as a 4H.

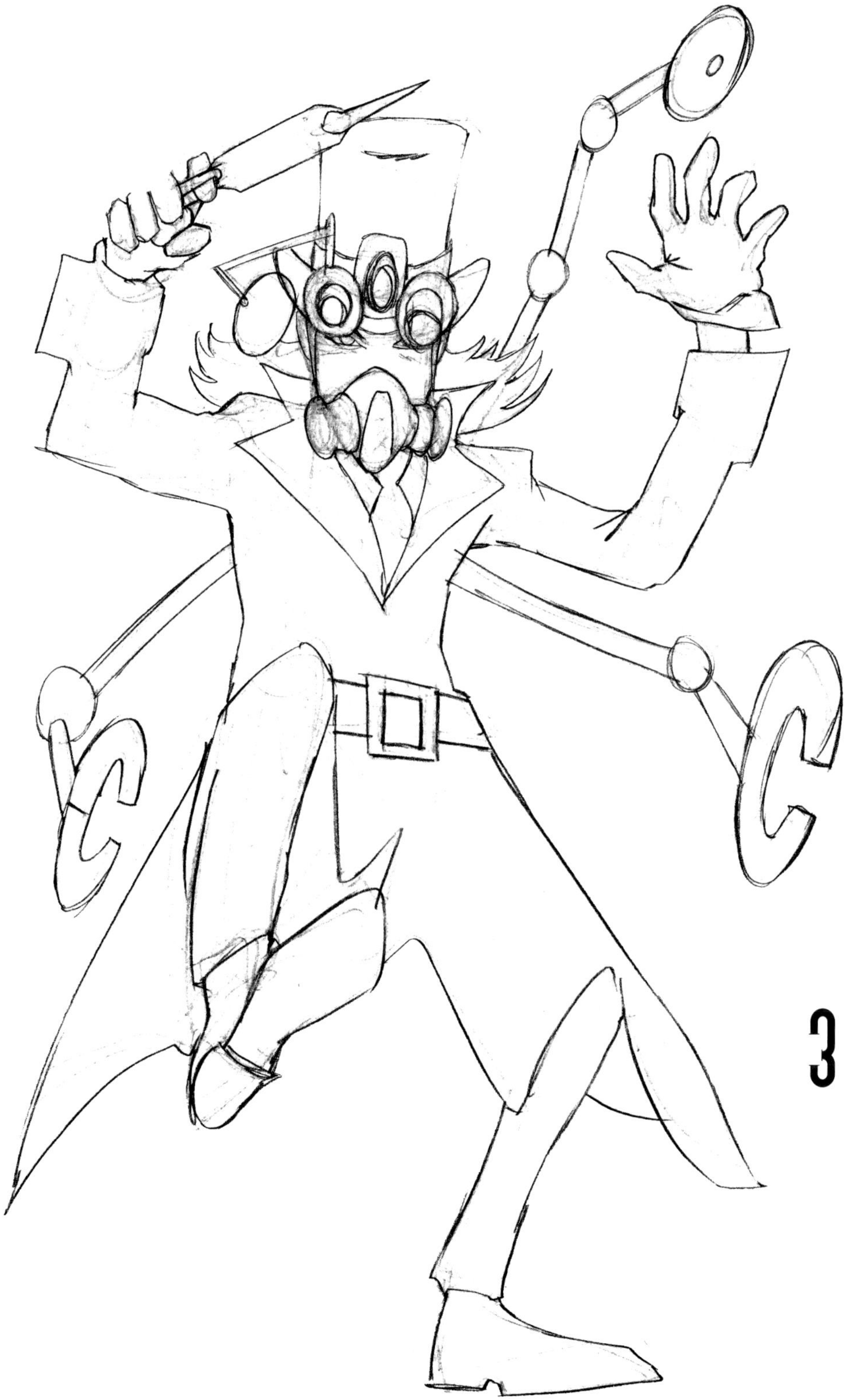

3

Use a 05-gauge pencil to completely draw the figure and give form to the detail. The better you carry out this stage, the easier it will be to ink the drawing.

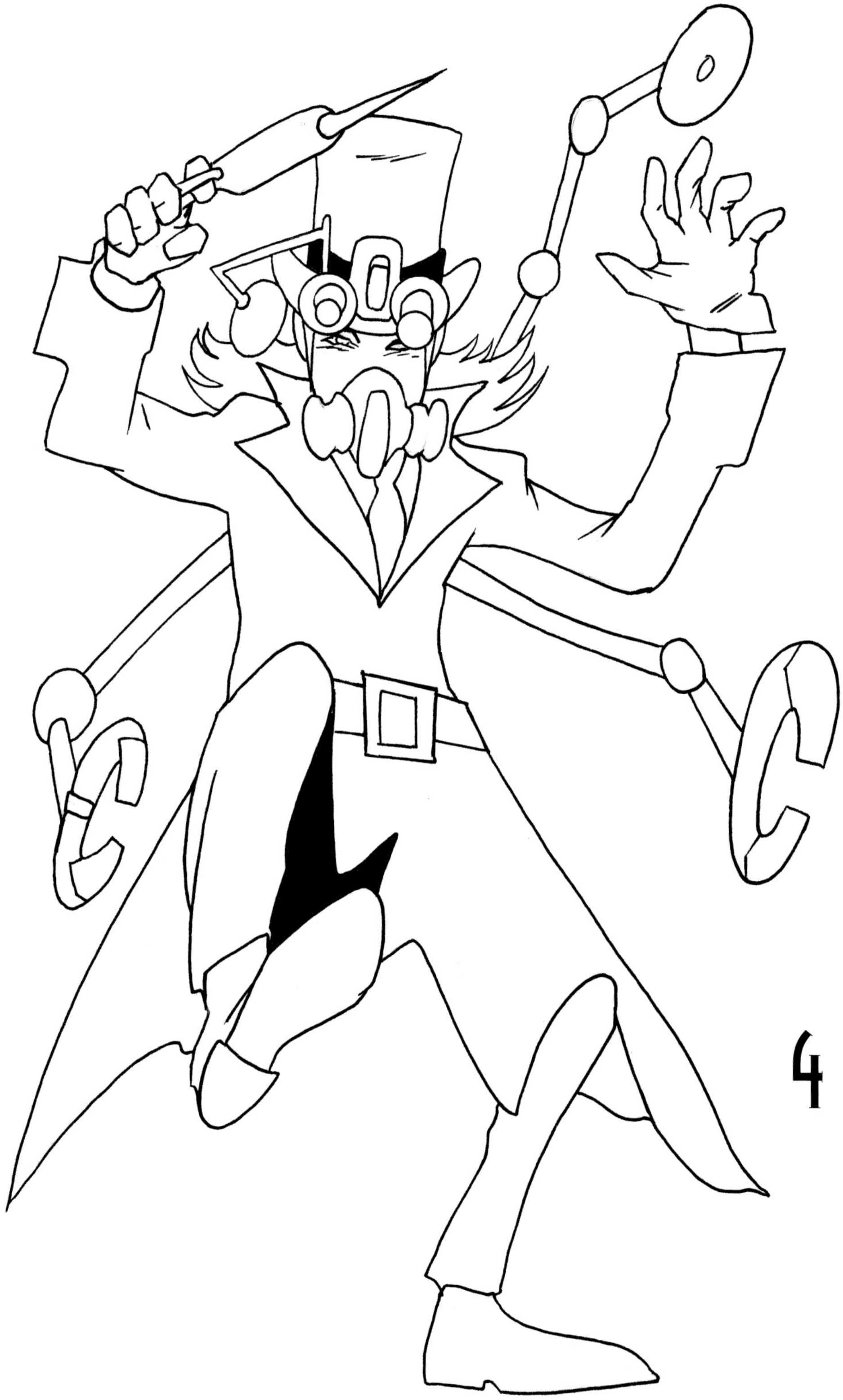

4

Go over your drawing with different calibre pens. I use a 0.2 for detail, a 0.4 for the figure, and an 0.8 just for the contour and to highlight the lines that I want to stand out. Color the base of the overcoat and the hatband in black.

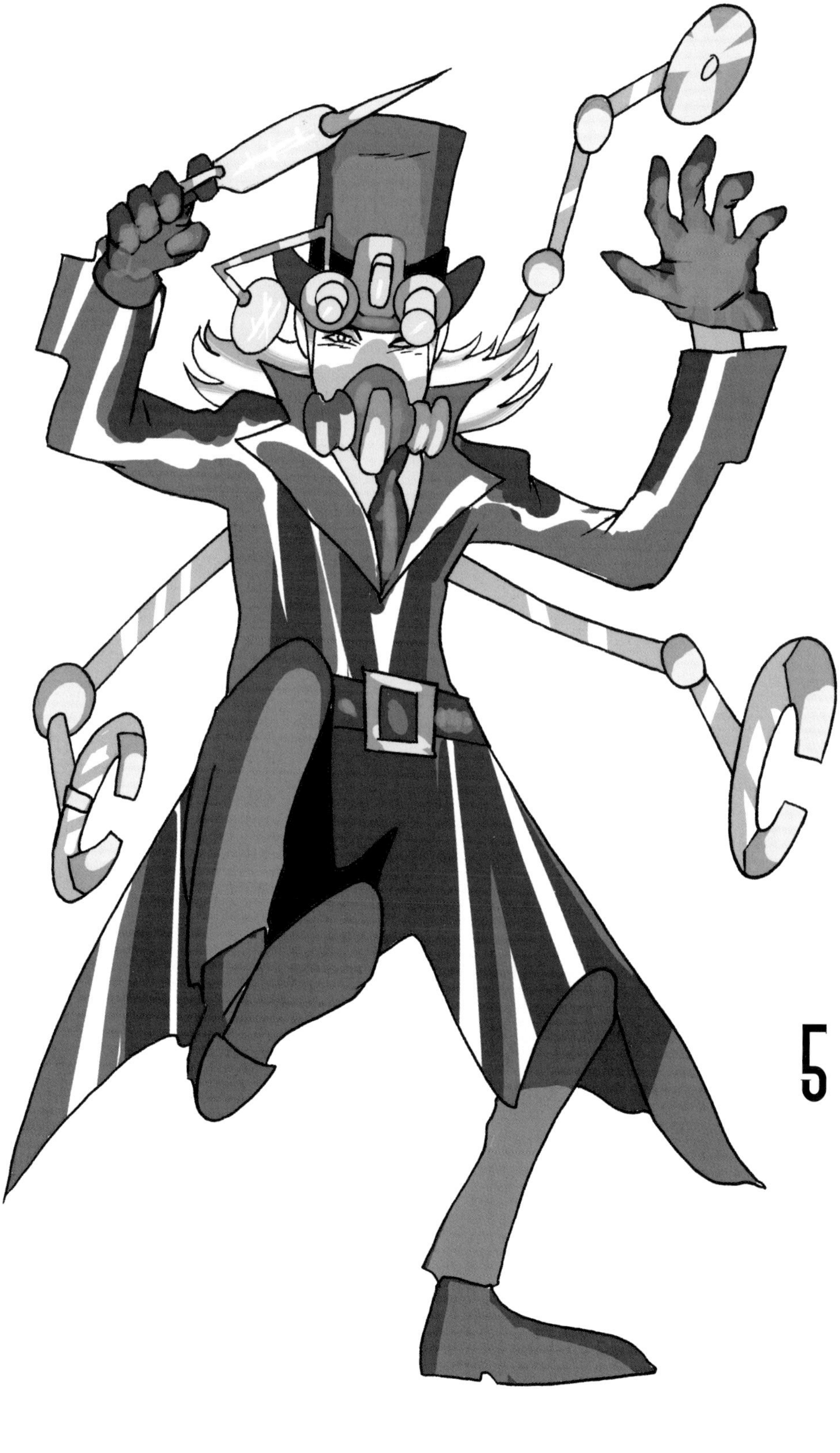

5

Now try a different effect: we are in the tunnels beneath the city where toxic waters create a diabolical light from below, giving your doctor a gloomy appearance.

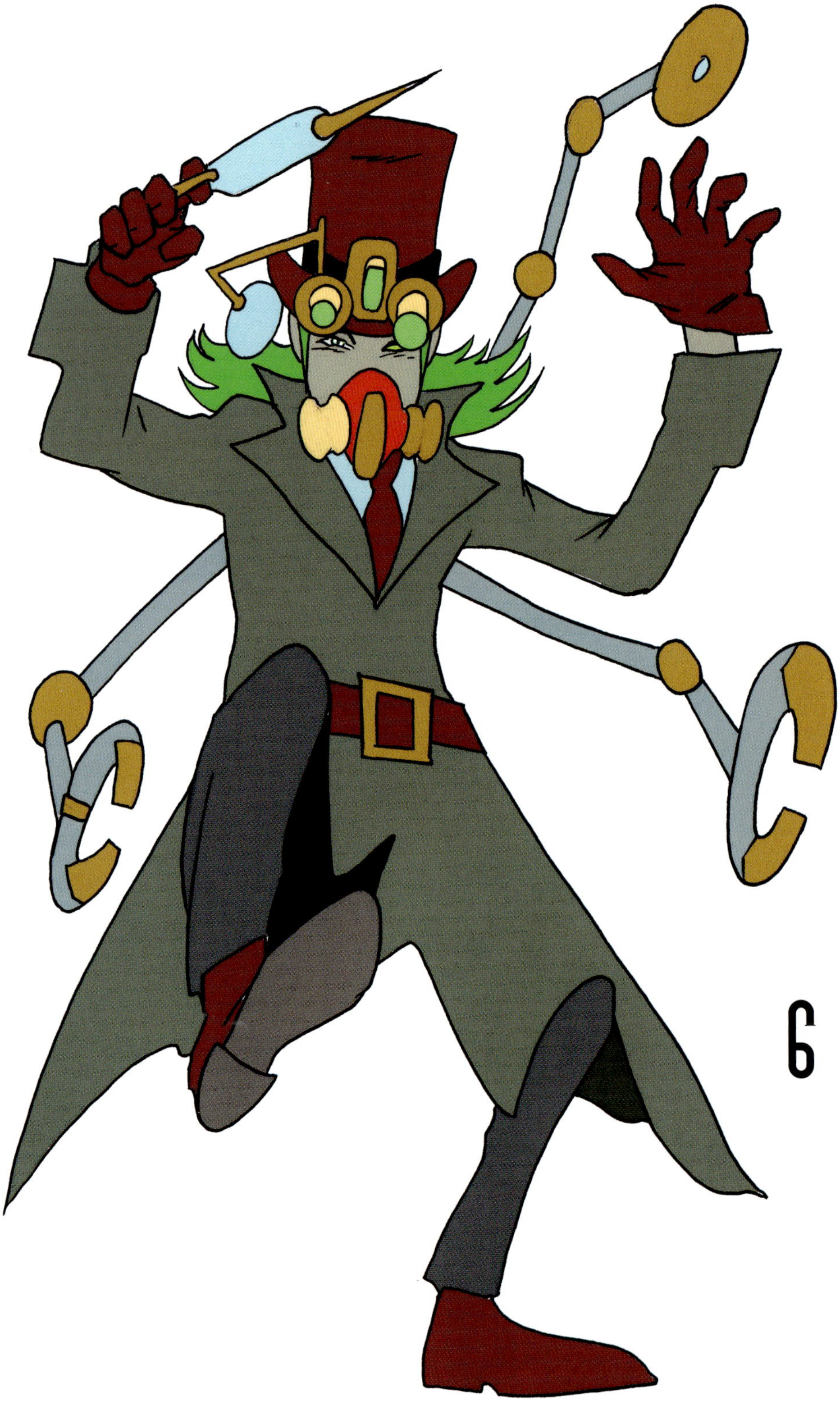

6

I've used the following colors: shades of green and gray with reddish brown tones. Using darker tones makes it easier to highlight them later with lighter ones. I've also used blue for the mechanical arms, gold tones for the rivets or joints, and red for the gas mask.

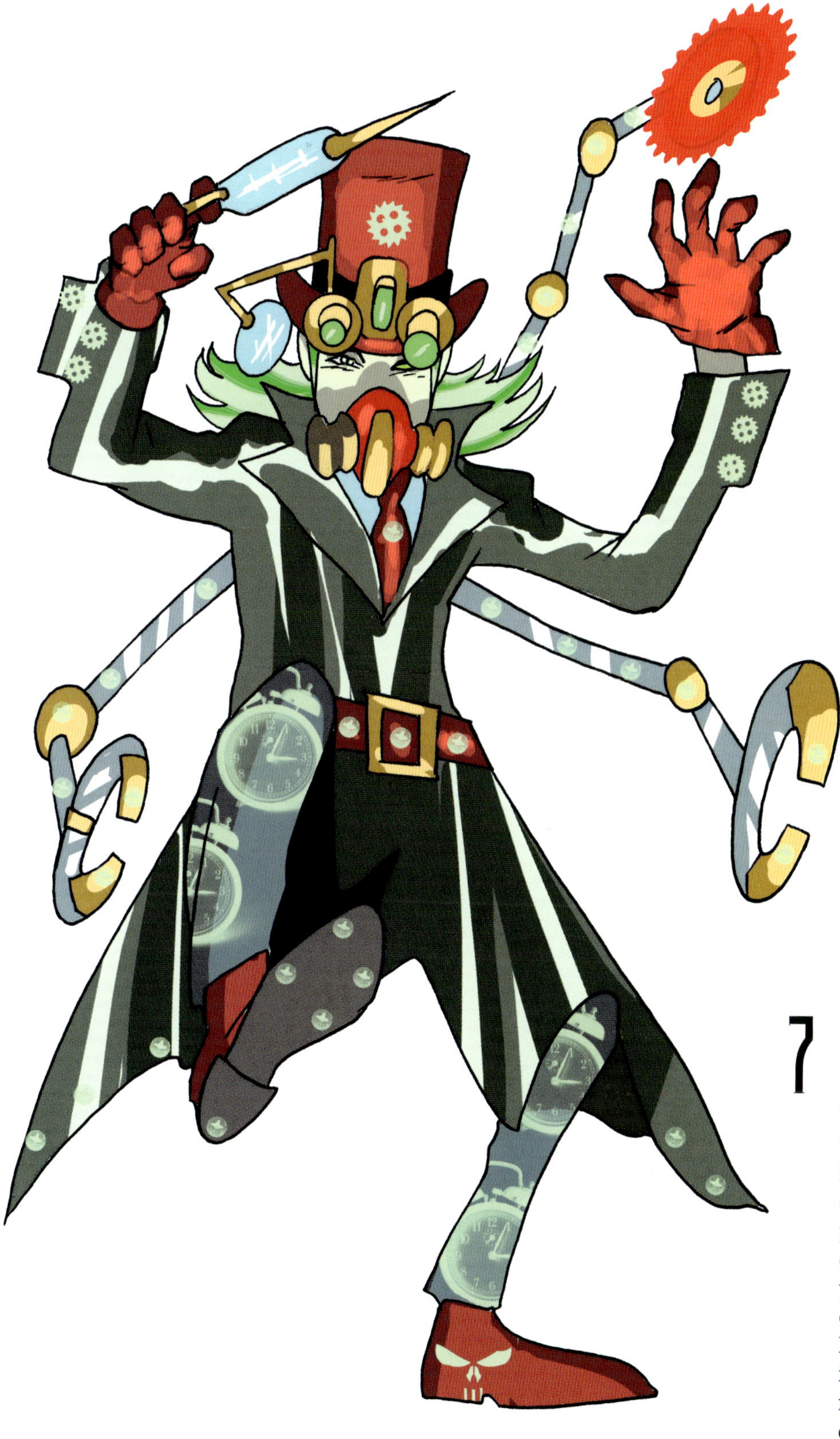

7

This is the part I like best. Highlight the whole character in green and fluorescent green. Decorate him with screws or rivets and draw clocks on the trousers. Be patient! If you're after something different, color in whatever you prefer. Finally, add a touch of lighter gold to the arms and highlight the folds in white. The icing on the cake would be to add a nice circular saw in red. Now your doctor is ready to terrify!

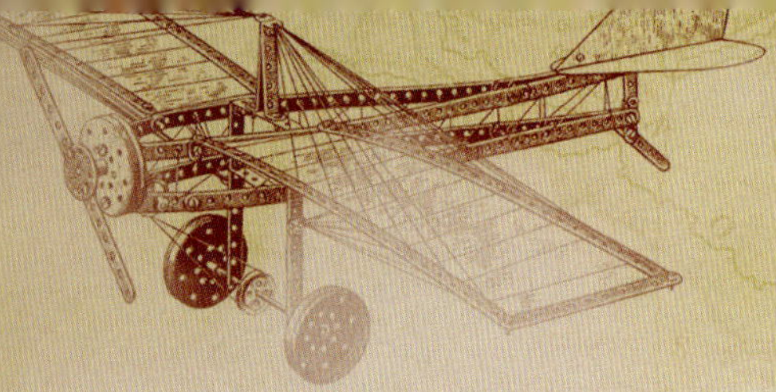

DYNAMITER

Bacus Balin is the rocket engineer for the Queen of Needles. This man's relentless curiosity has led him to develop a mobile rocket launcher: now all that remains is to prove its effectiveness in combat. Hopefully the rocket carrier will not leap into the air at the press of the button!

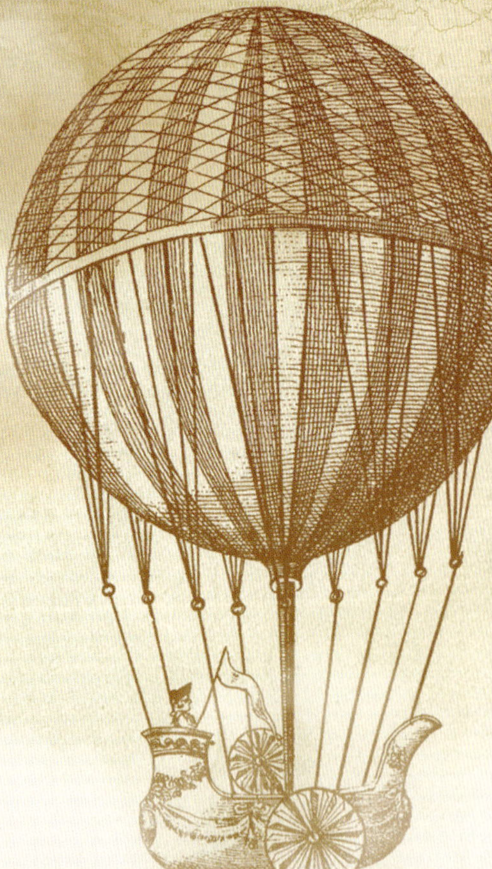

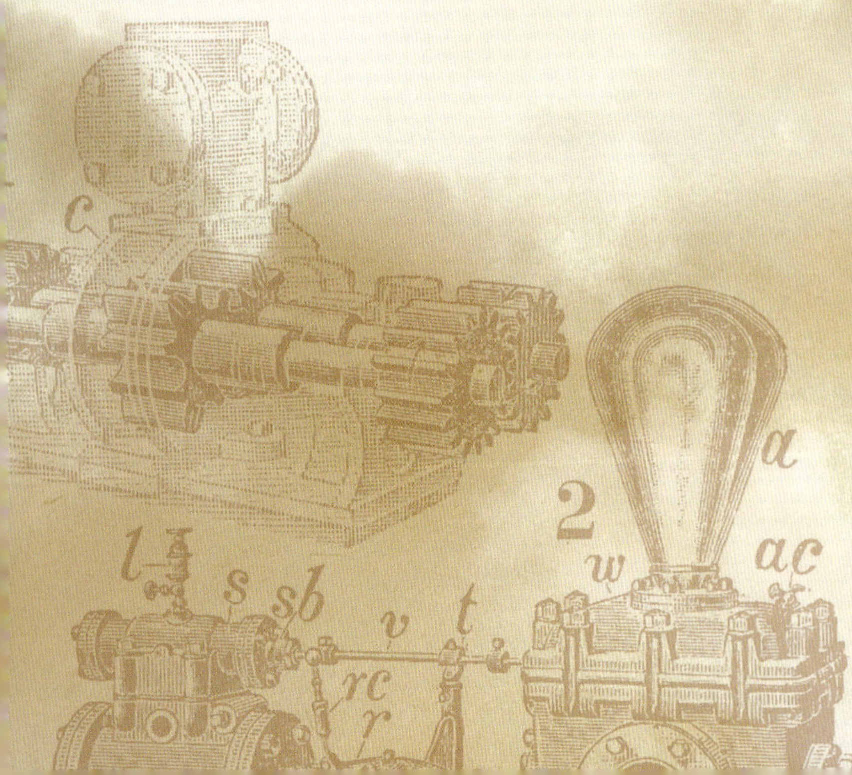

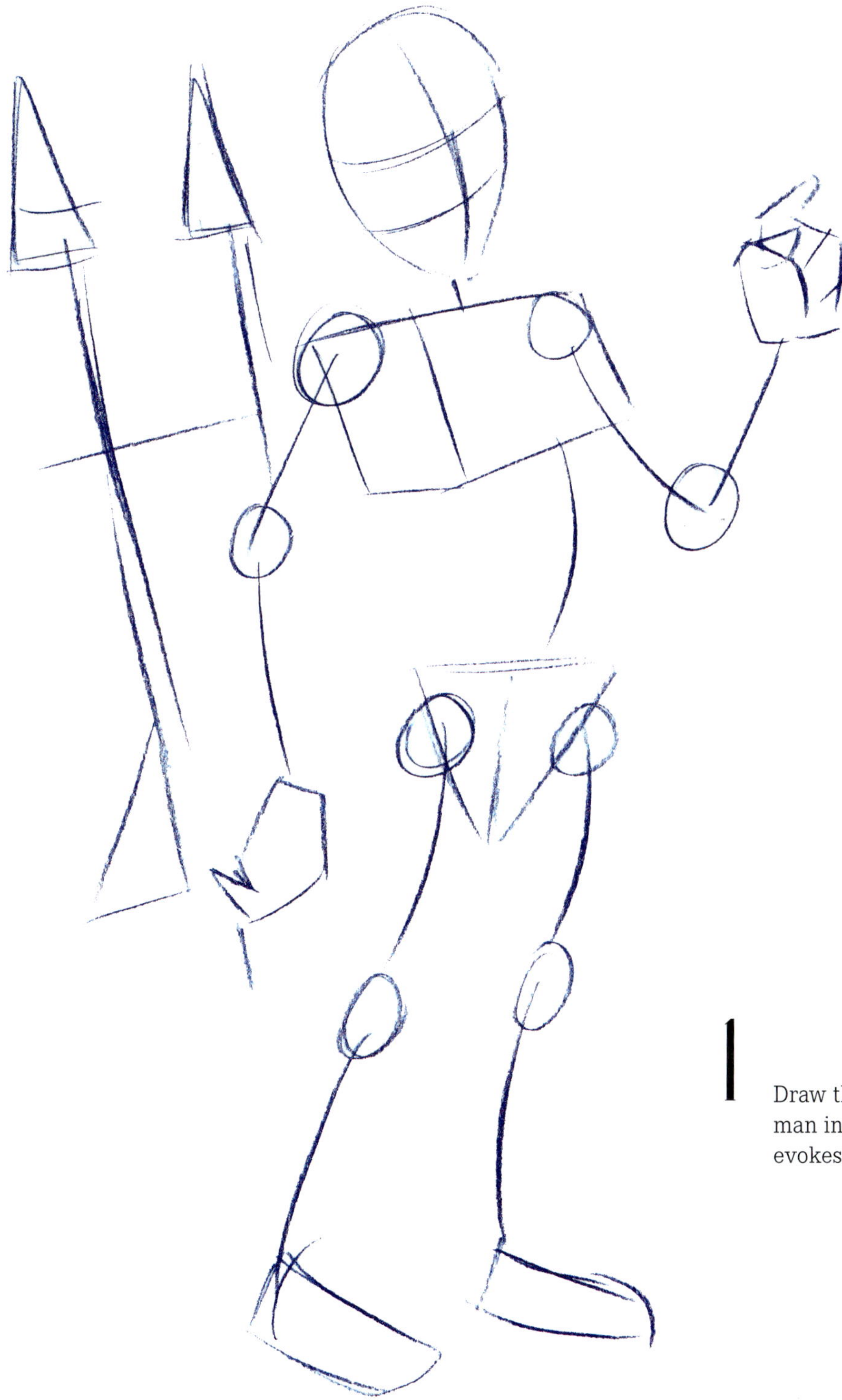

1

Draw the basis of your rocket man in blue pencil, in a pose that evokes a feeling of insecurity.

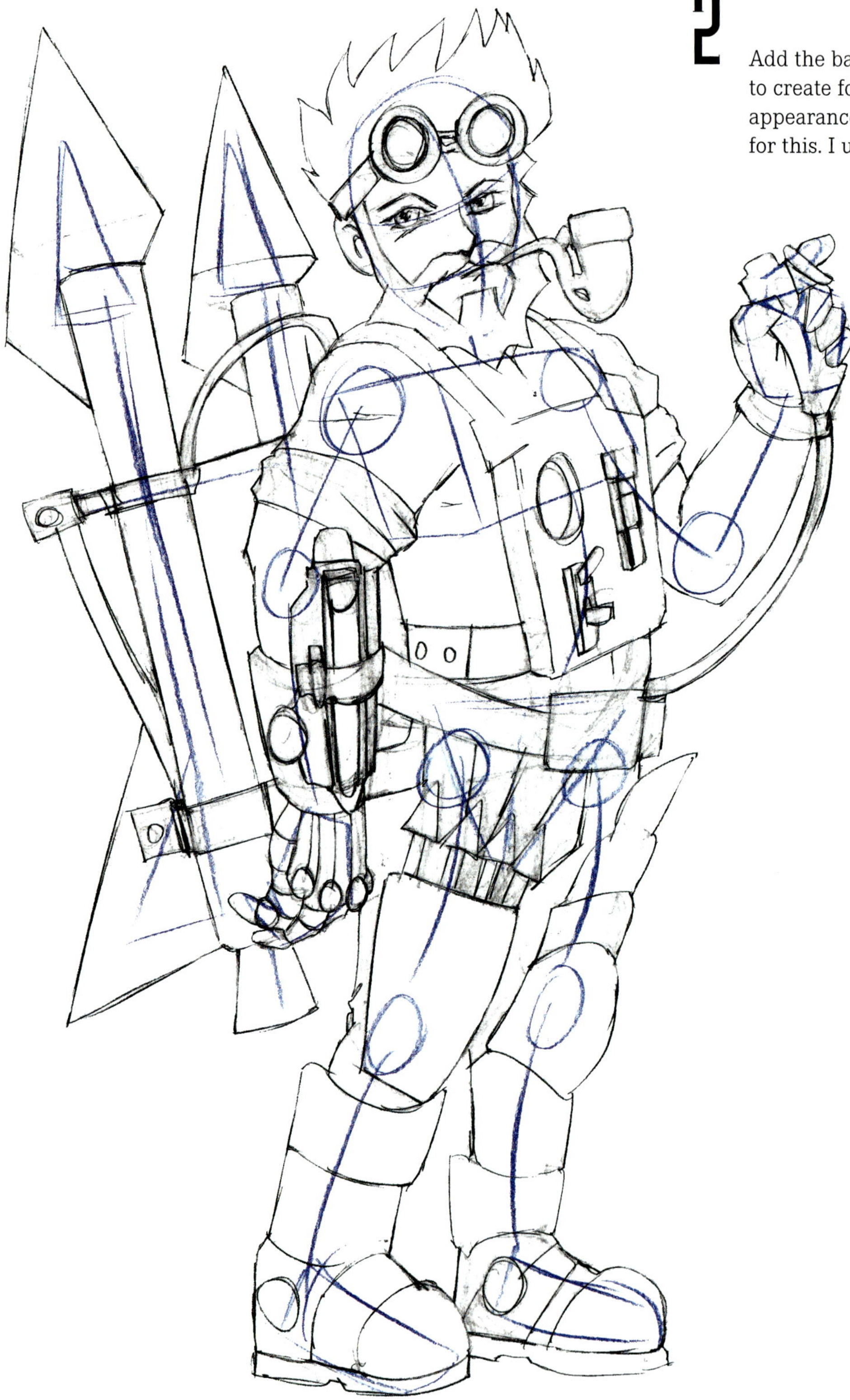

2

Add the base contour to the figure to create form and develop its appearance. A hard pencil is best for this. I use a 2H.

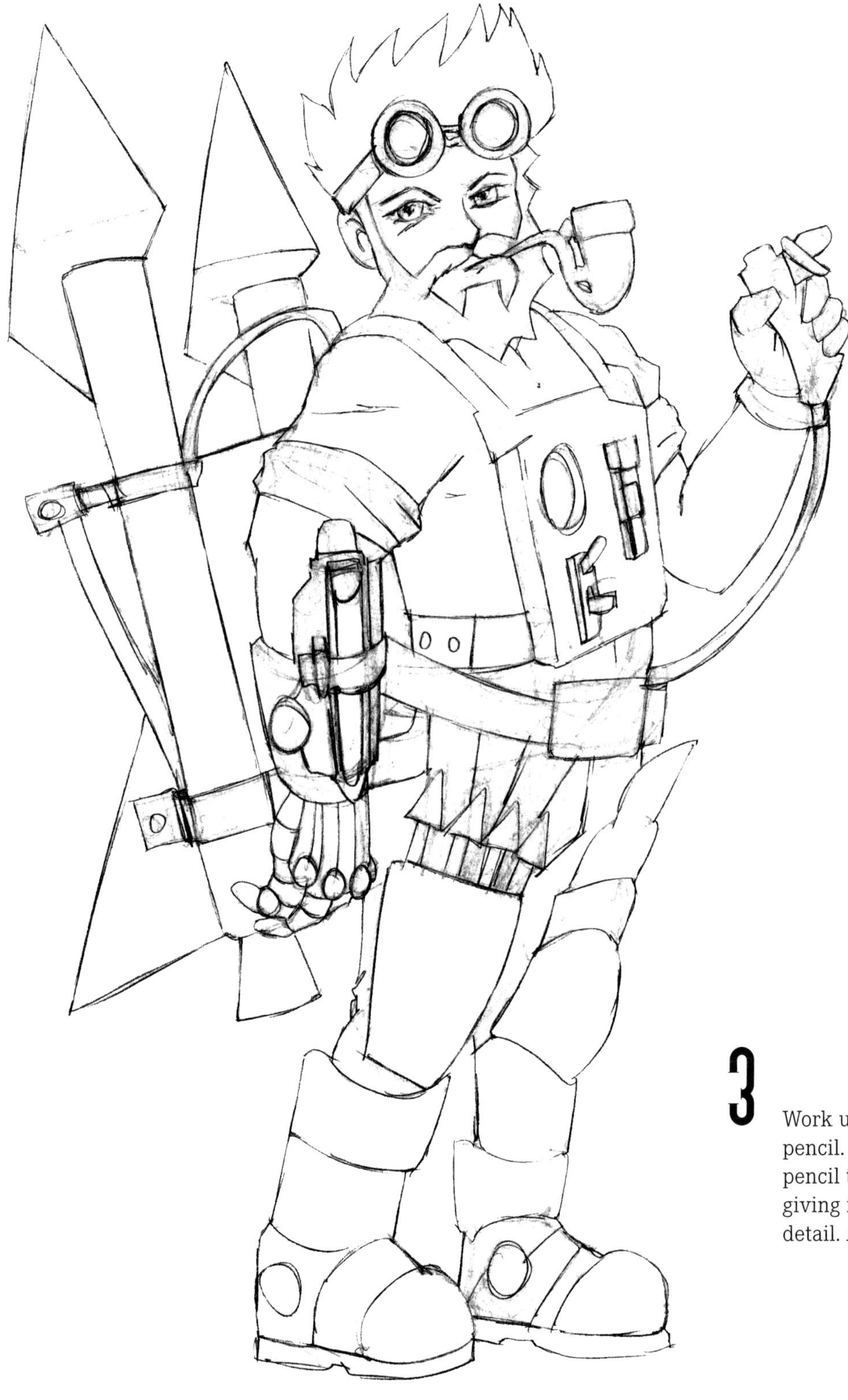

3

Work up the image with your pencil. Use a 05-calibre mechanical pencil to trace over the figure, giving it volume and adding in detail. Add shape to the character.

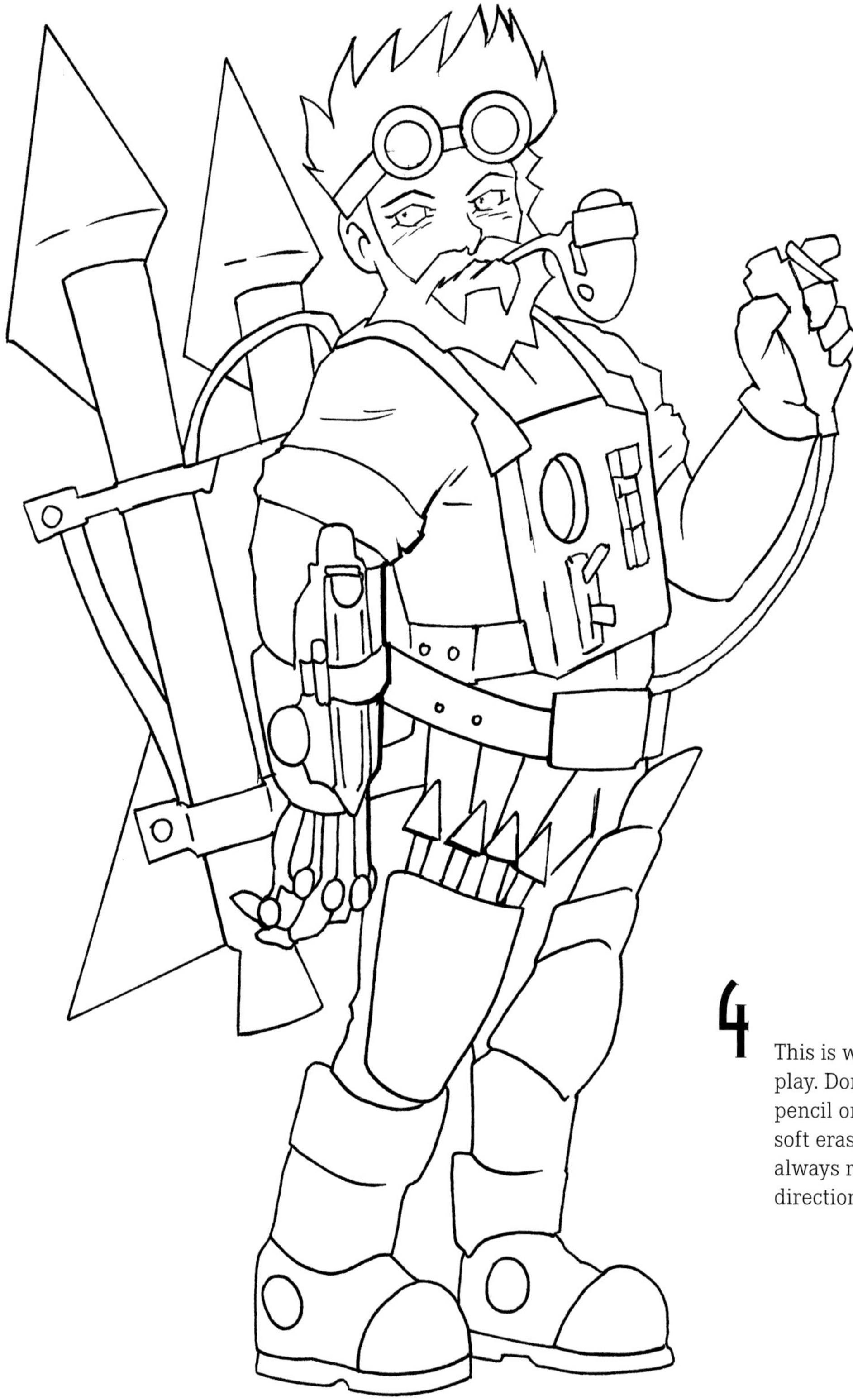

4

This is where the pens come into play. Don't forget to remove the pencil once the ink is dry. Use a soft eraser to rub out the pencil, always rubbing in the same direction.

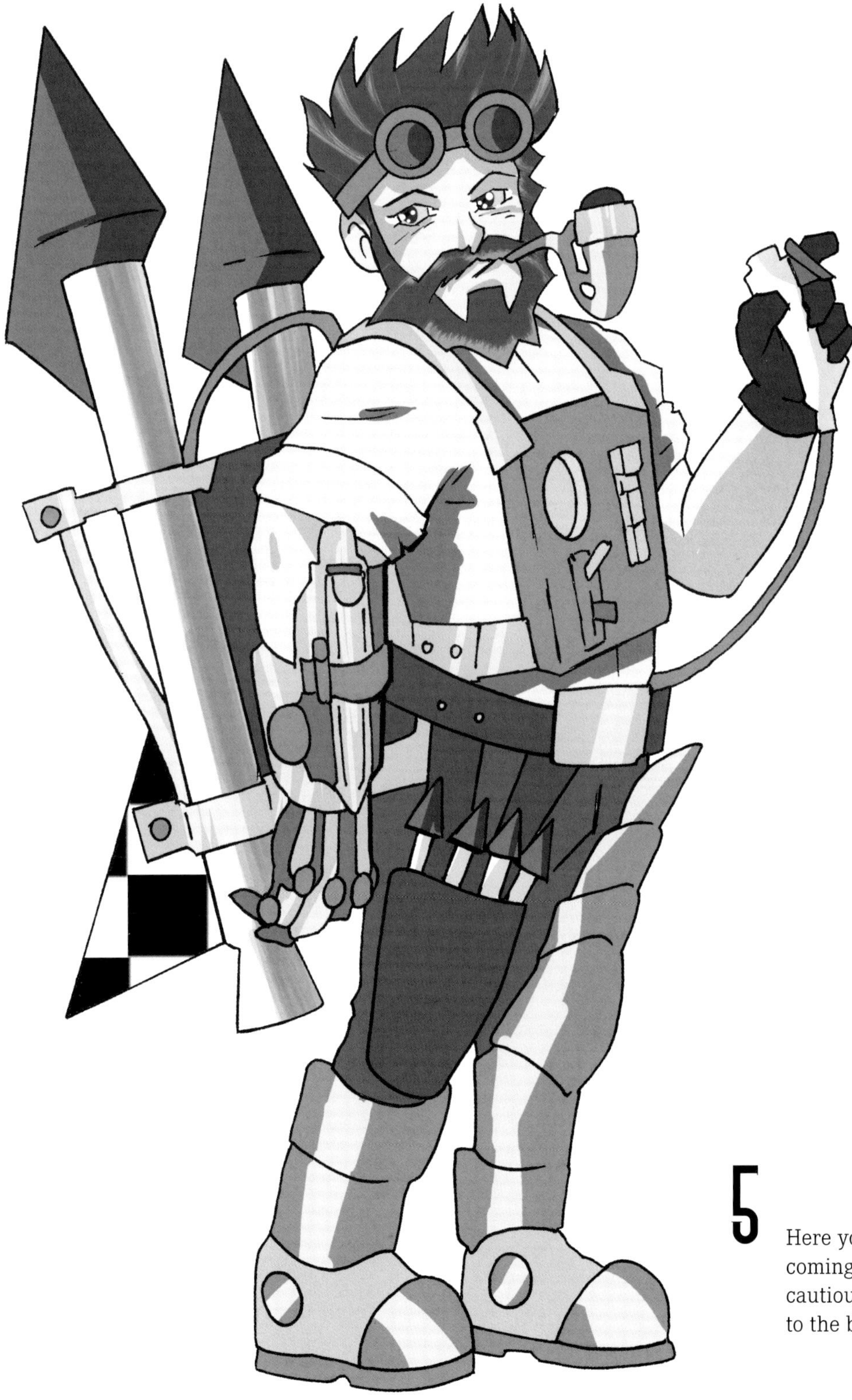

5

Here you can see the light is coming from the right of this cautious engineer, giving form to the body and the rocket frame.

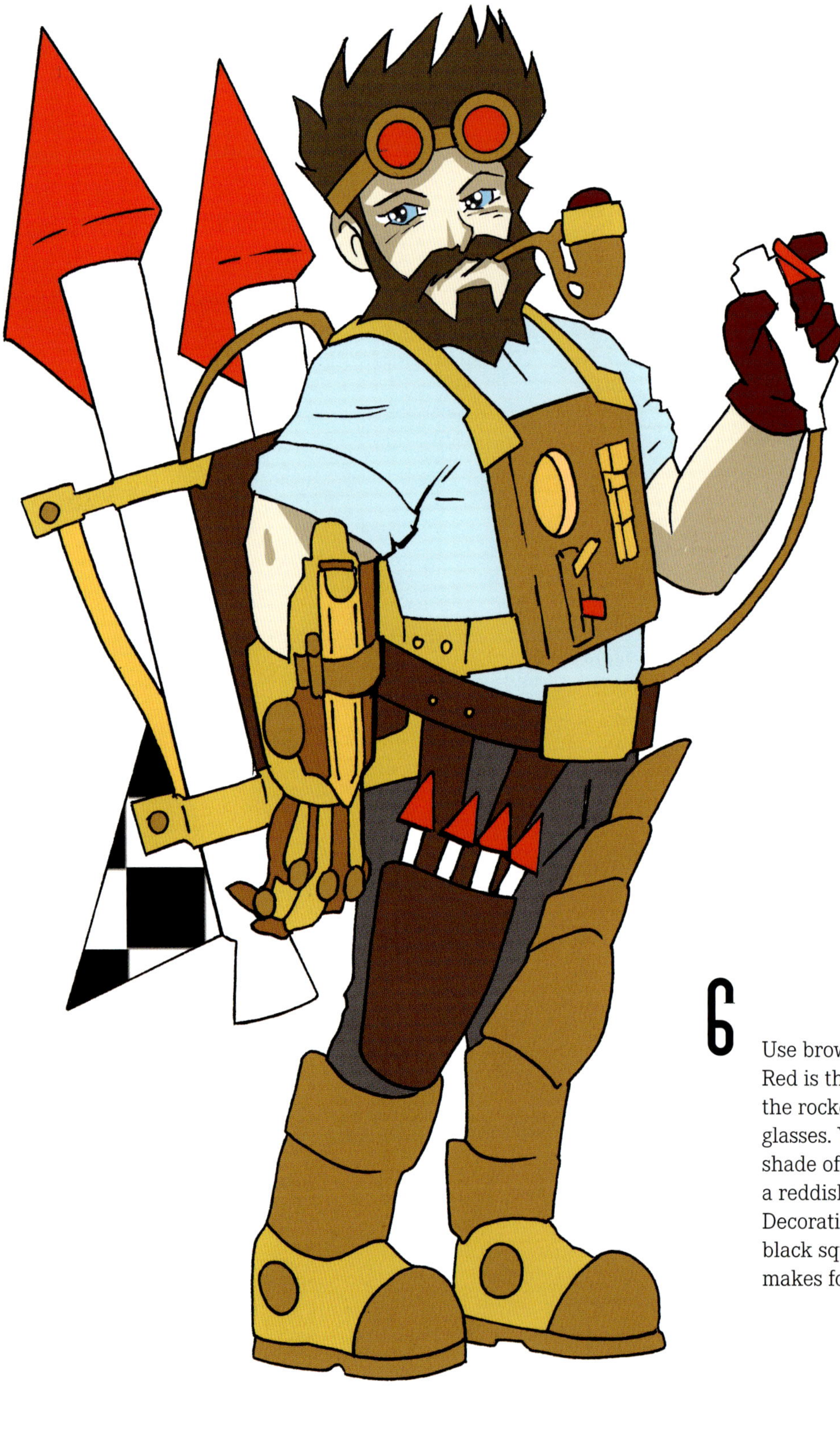

6

Use brown, blue, and gold colors. Red is the best choice for coloring the rocket heads and Bacus's glasses. You can use a different shade of gold for the details and a reddish brown for the glove. Decorating the rocket fins with black squares is a nice idea – it makes for a touch of humor!

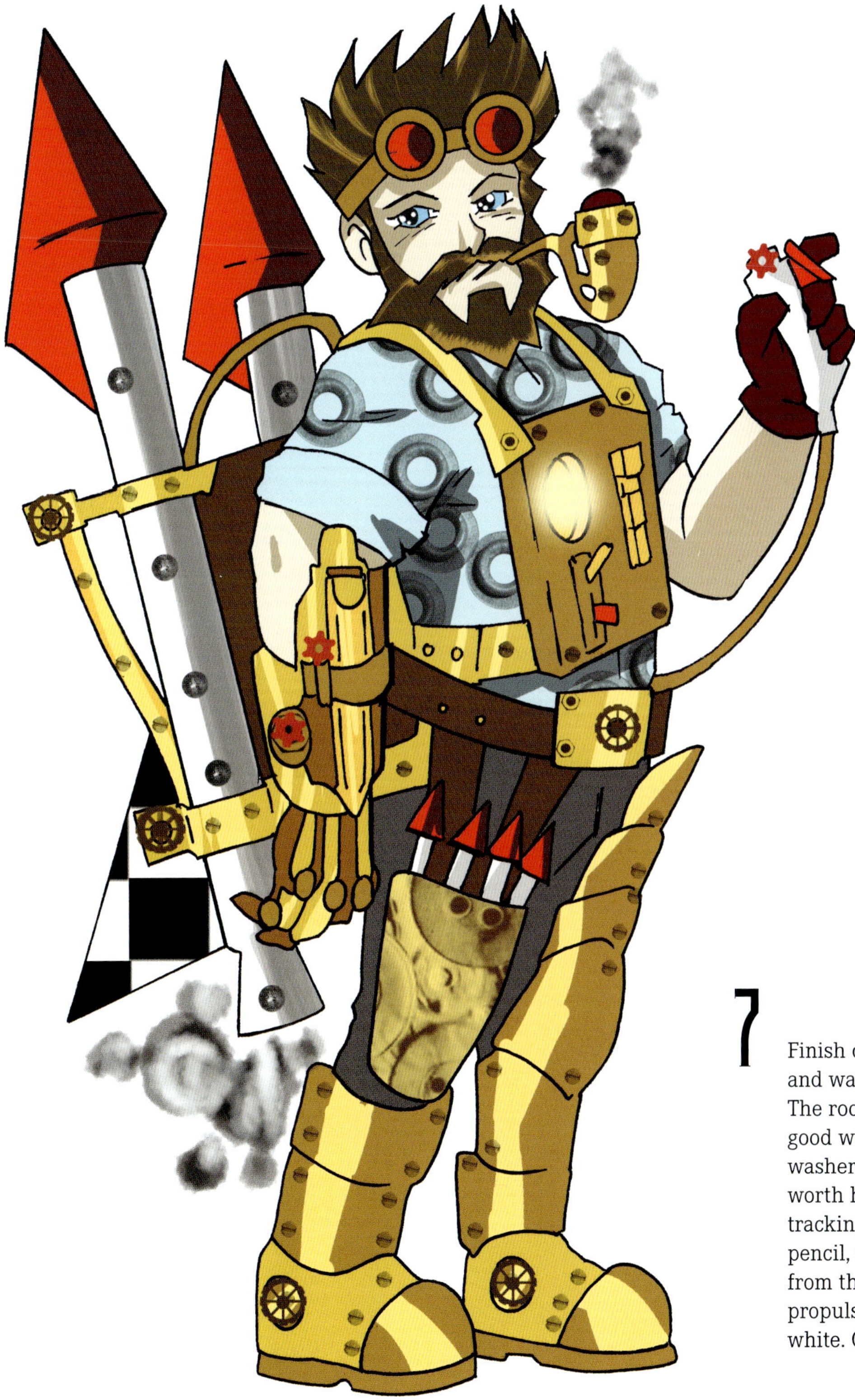

7

Finish off by adding rivets and washers to your liking. The rocketeer's blue shirt looks good with gray or dark blue washers. As a final touch, it is worth highlighting the rocket-tracking spheres in white or yellow pencil, and coloring the smoke from the pipe and the rocket propulsion system in black and white. Good luck, Mr. Rocketeer!

FIREMAN

Flynt Morrison is captain of the firefighters in the kingdom's cities. Fierce and brave (some would say foolhardy), he is always willing to risk his neck to put out a fire or save anyone who is in trouble.

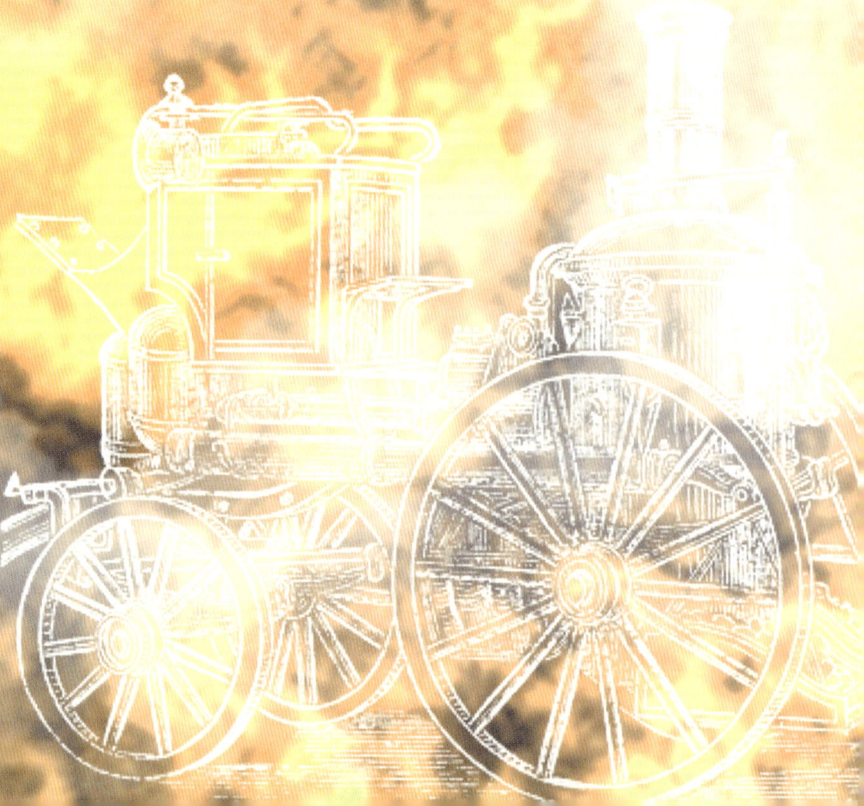

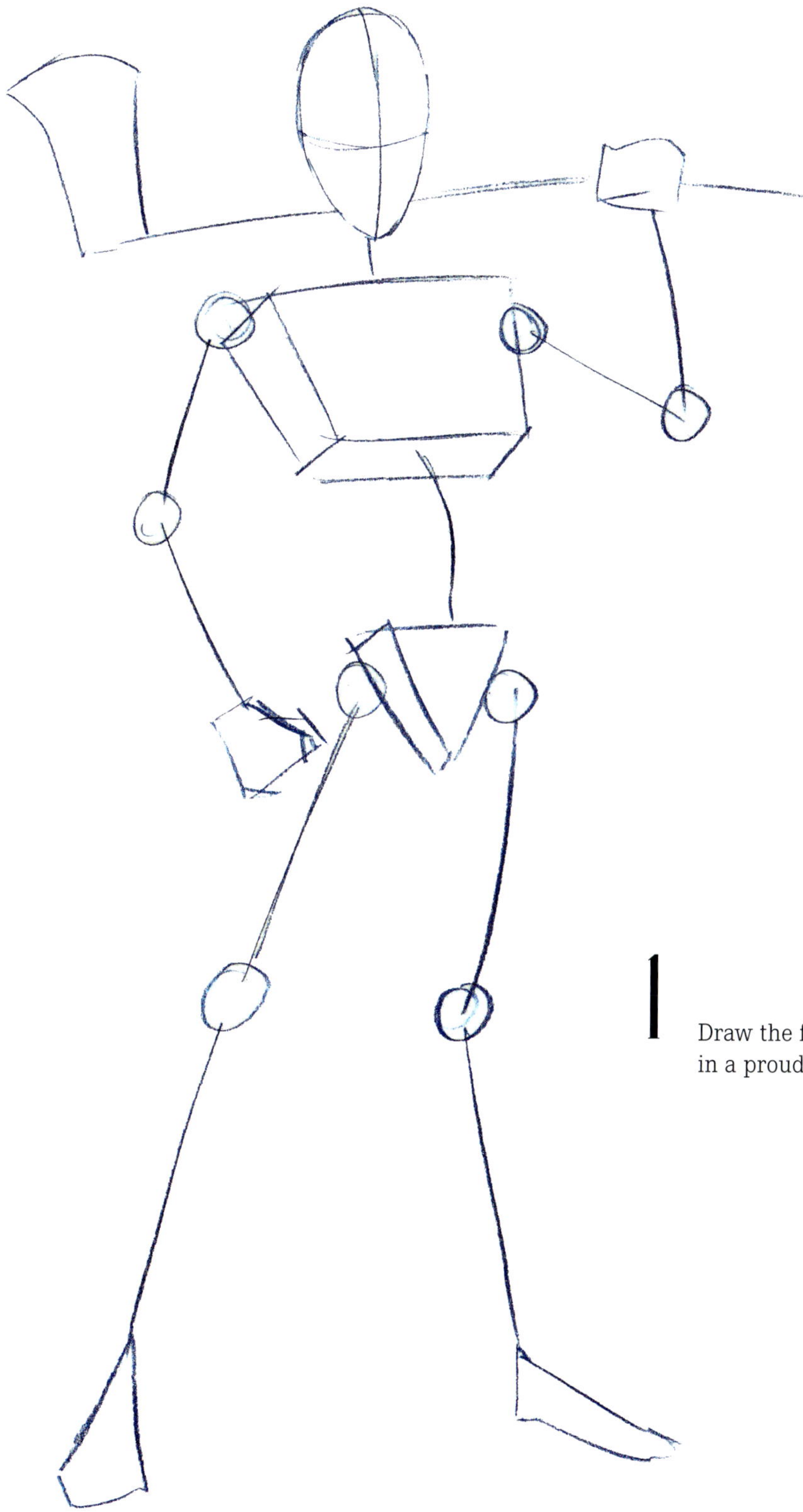

1

Draw the figure in blue pencil in a proud and fearless pose.

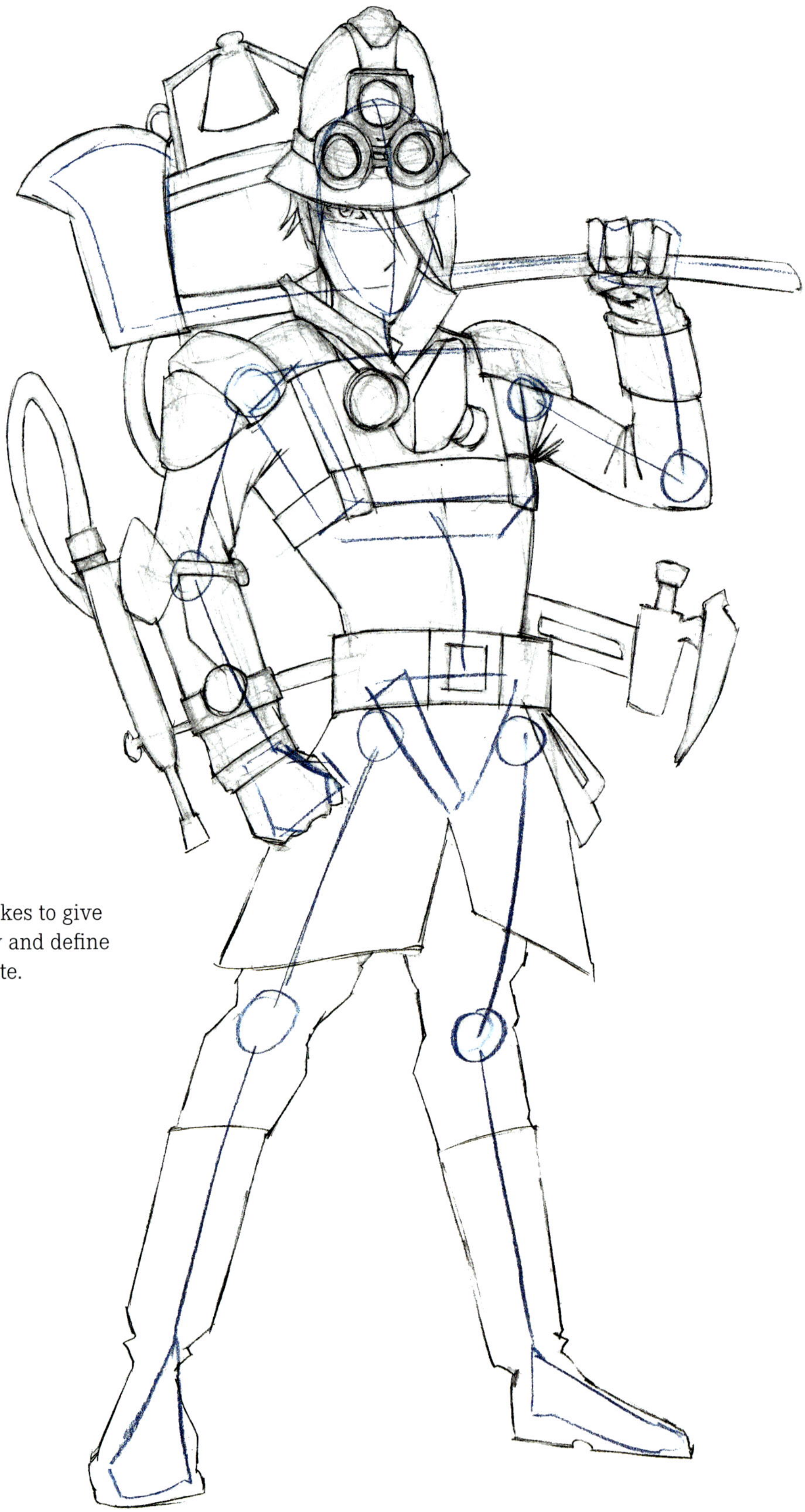

2

Add your 2H pencil strokes to give the drawing consistency and define the firefighter's silhouette.

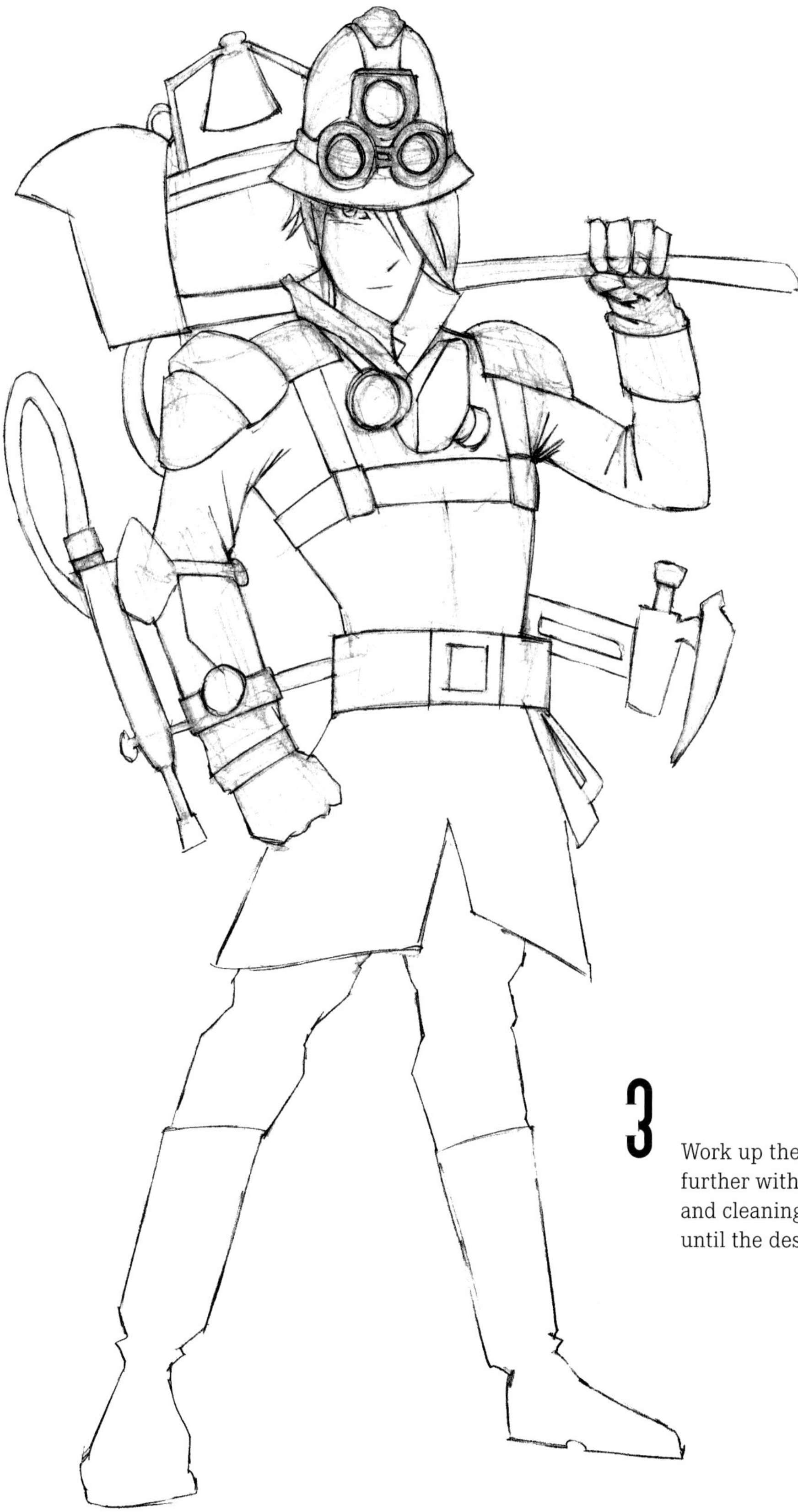

3

Work up the figure and details further with the pencil, removing and cleaning up leftover strokes until the design is ready for inking.

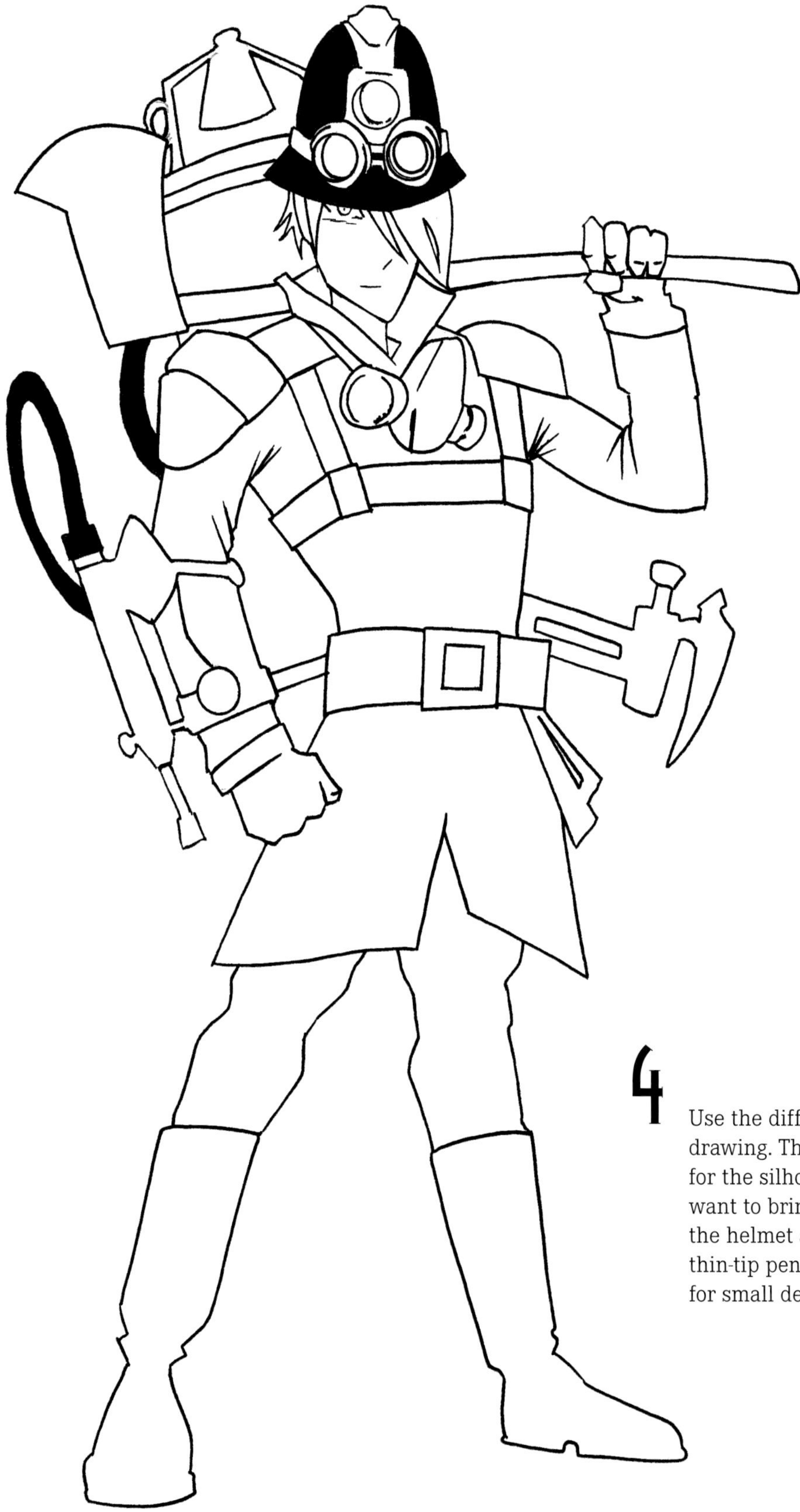

4

Use the different pens to ink the drawing. The thick-tip pen (0.8 mm) for the silhouette and parts you want to bring attention to such as the helmet and the hose, and the thin-tip pens (0.2 mm and 0.4 mm) for small details.

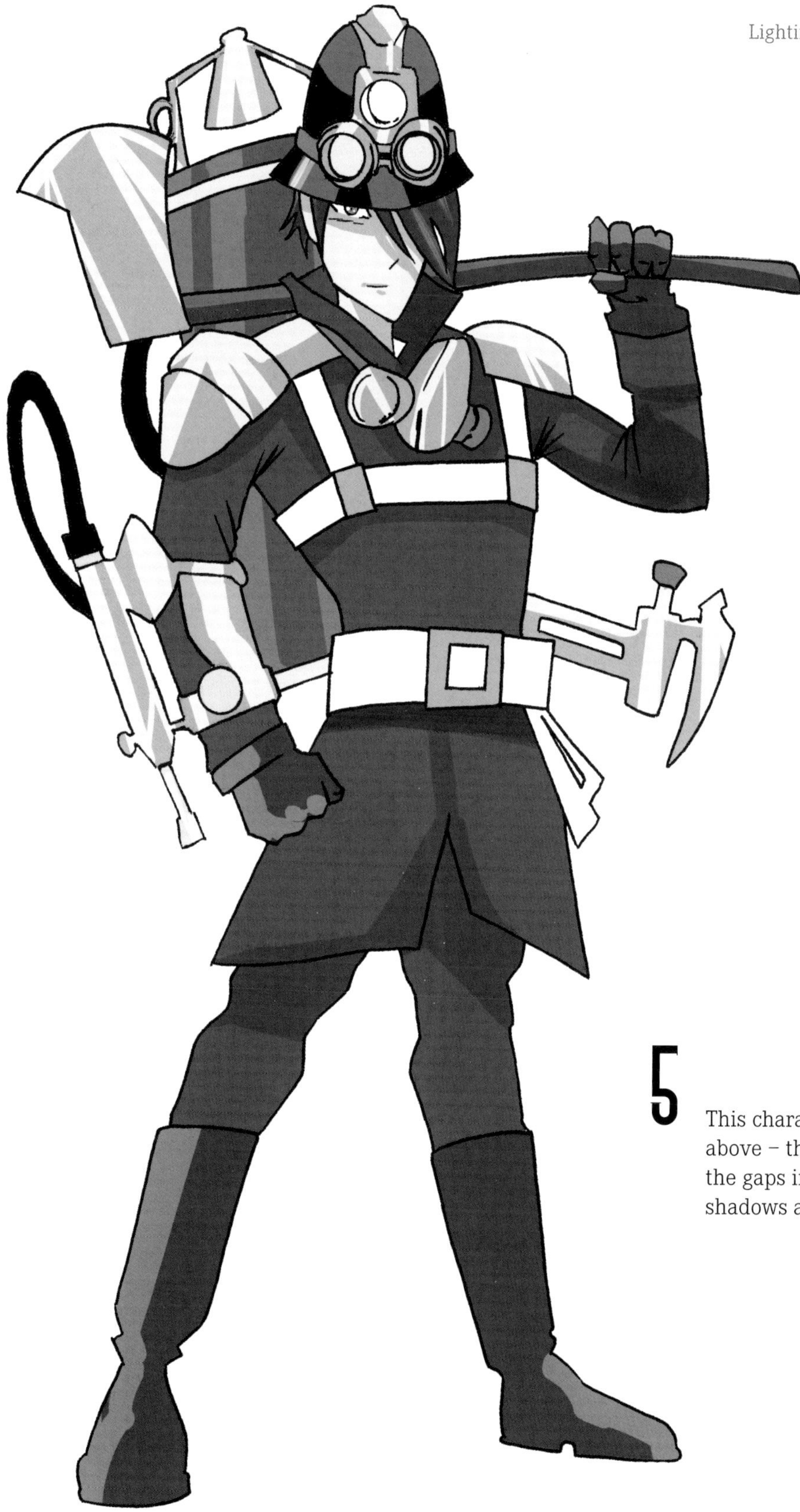

5

This character is lit from above – the light filters through the gaps in his uniform, creating shadows and volume.

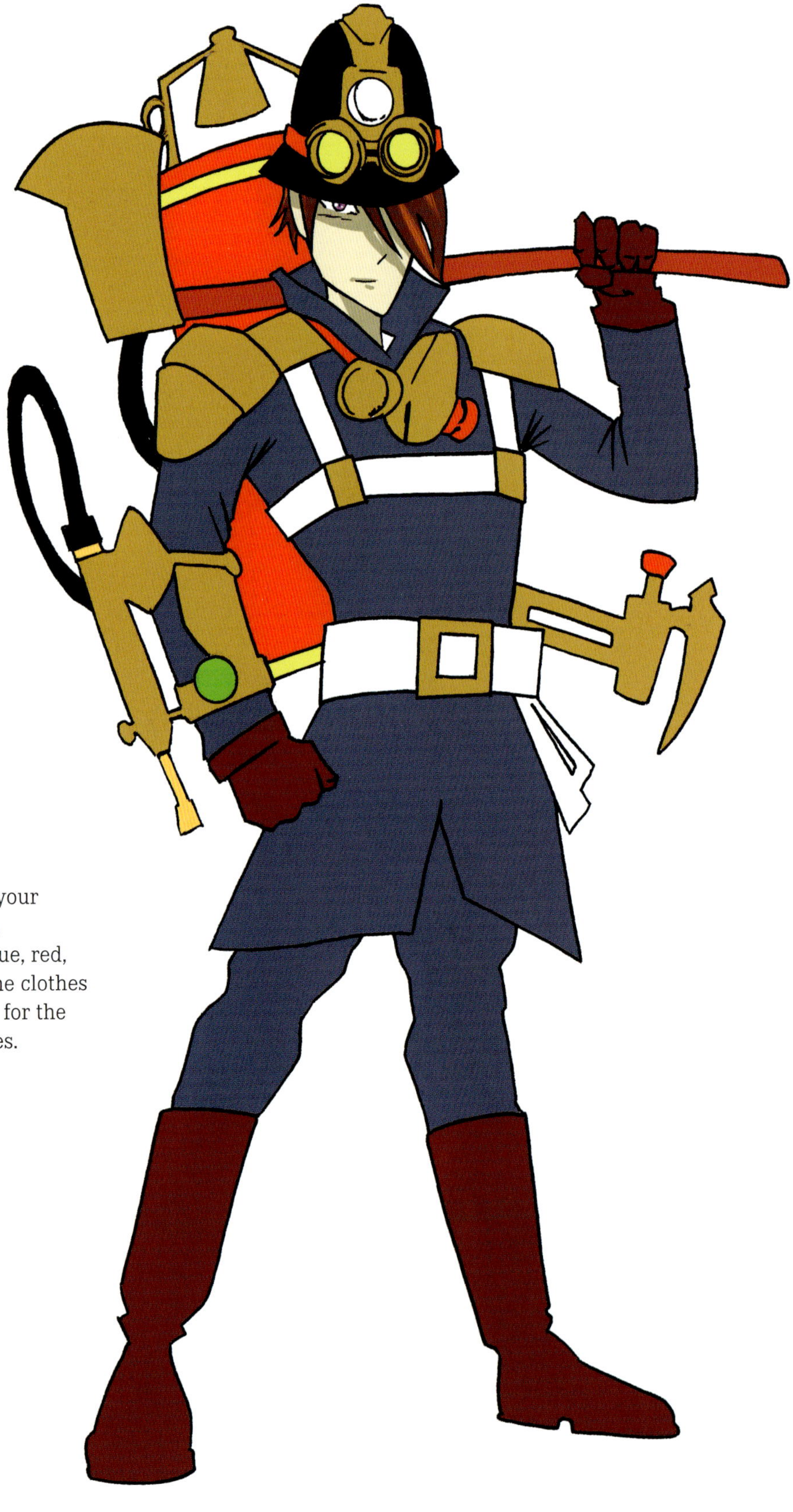

6

Add the base colors to your character. I've chosen a combination of navy blue, red, yellow, and white for the clothes – and an array of golds for the epaulets and accessories.

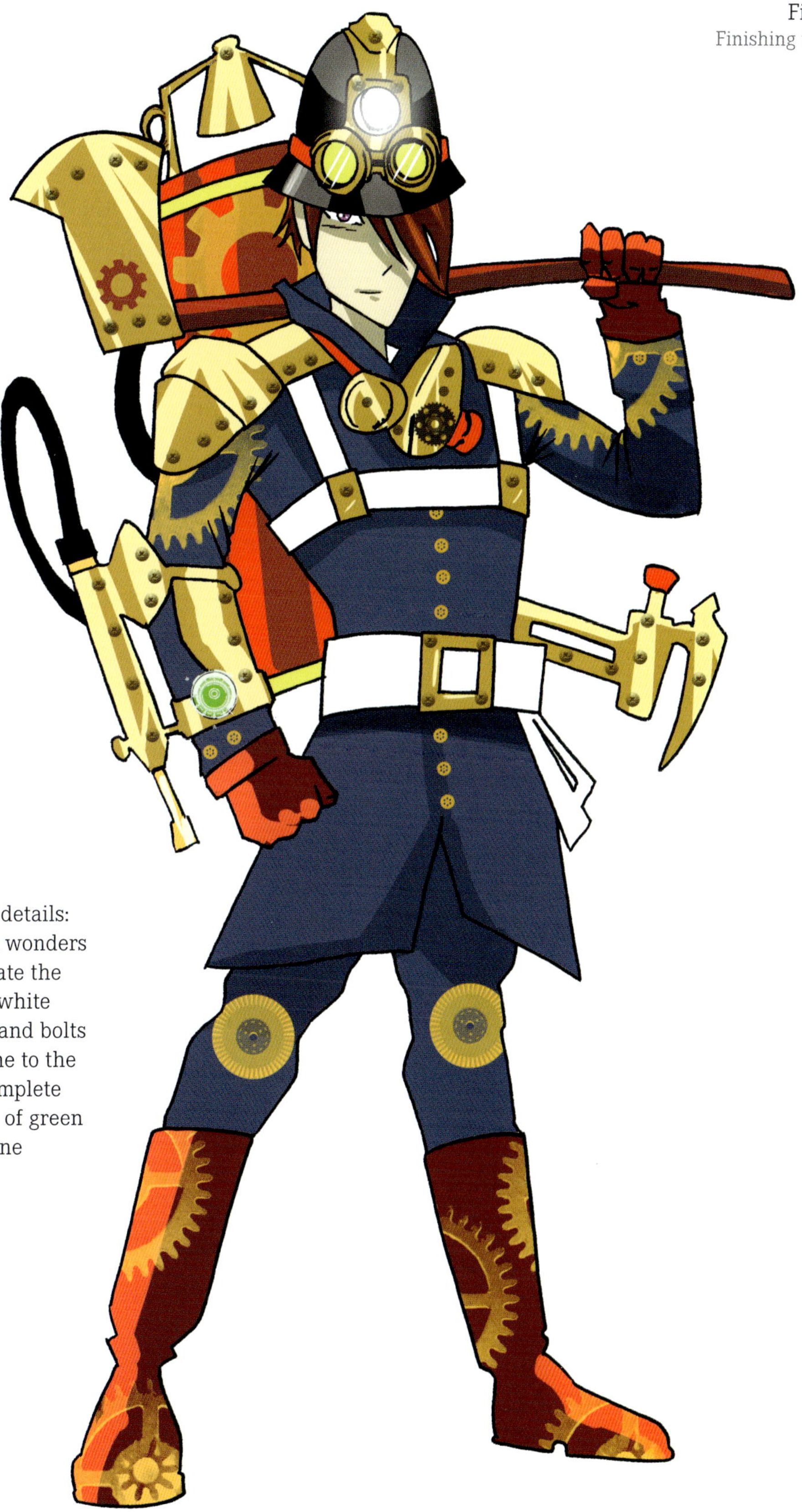

7

Finish off by adding the details: a few washers will work wonders for this fireman. Illuminate the light of his helmet with white pencil. Add a few rivets and bolts to his suit and some shine to the golden elements, and complete your image with a touch of green on the gauge. Did someone shout, "Fire!"?

SPY

Gretta "La Discreta" is a famous spy, highly sought after, who will do whatever it takes to complete a mission ... but only the rich can afford her. She has sold great secrets all over the kingdom, but now she is rumored to be working together with another lady – a lady of great beauty who has infiltrated the court of the Queen of Needles.

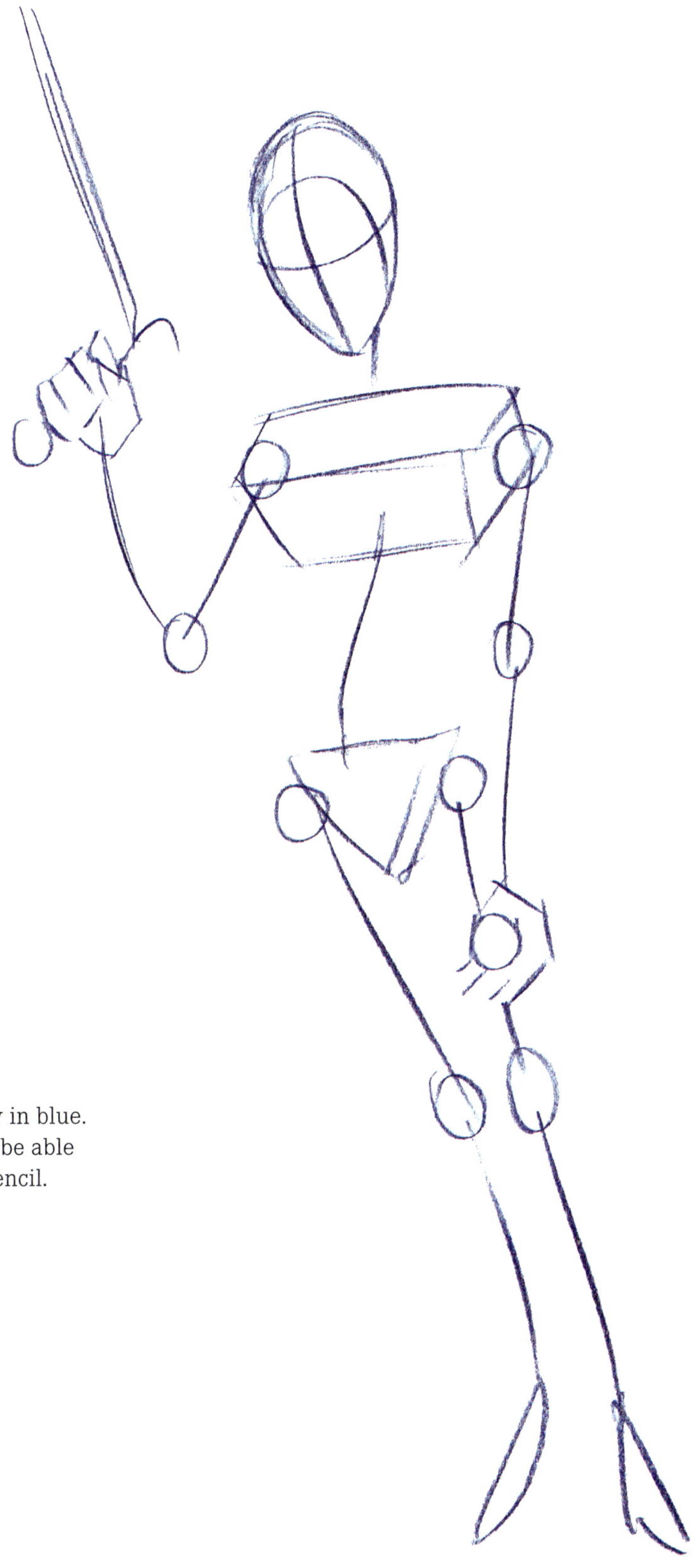

1

Draw the base of your spy in blue. With practice you should be able to draw this using a 2H pencil. Practice makes perfect!

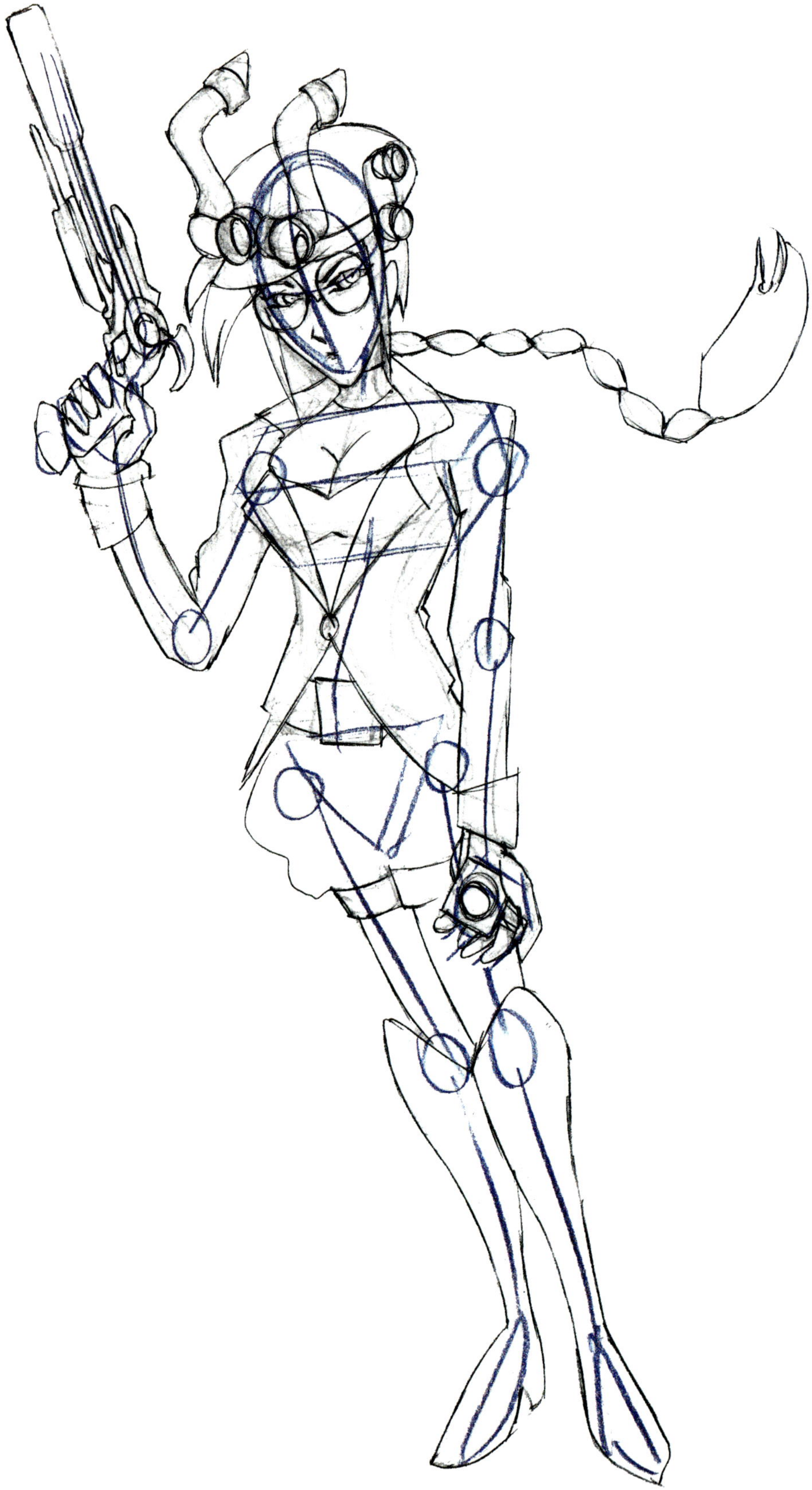

2

Use the 2H pencil in your blue draft to design the figure.

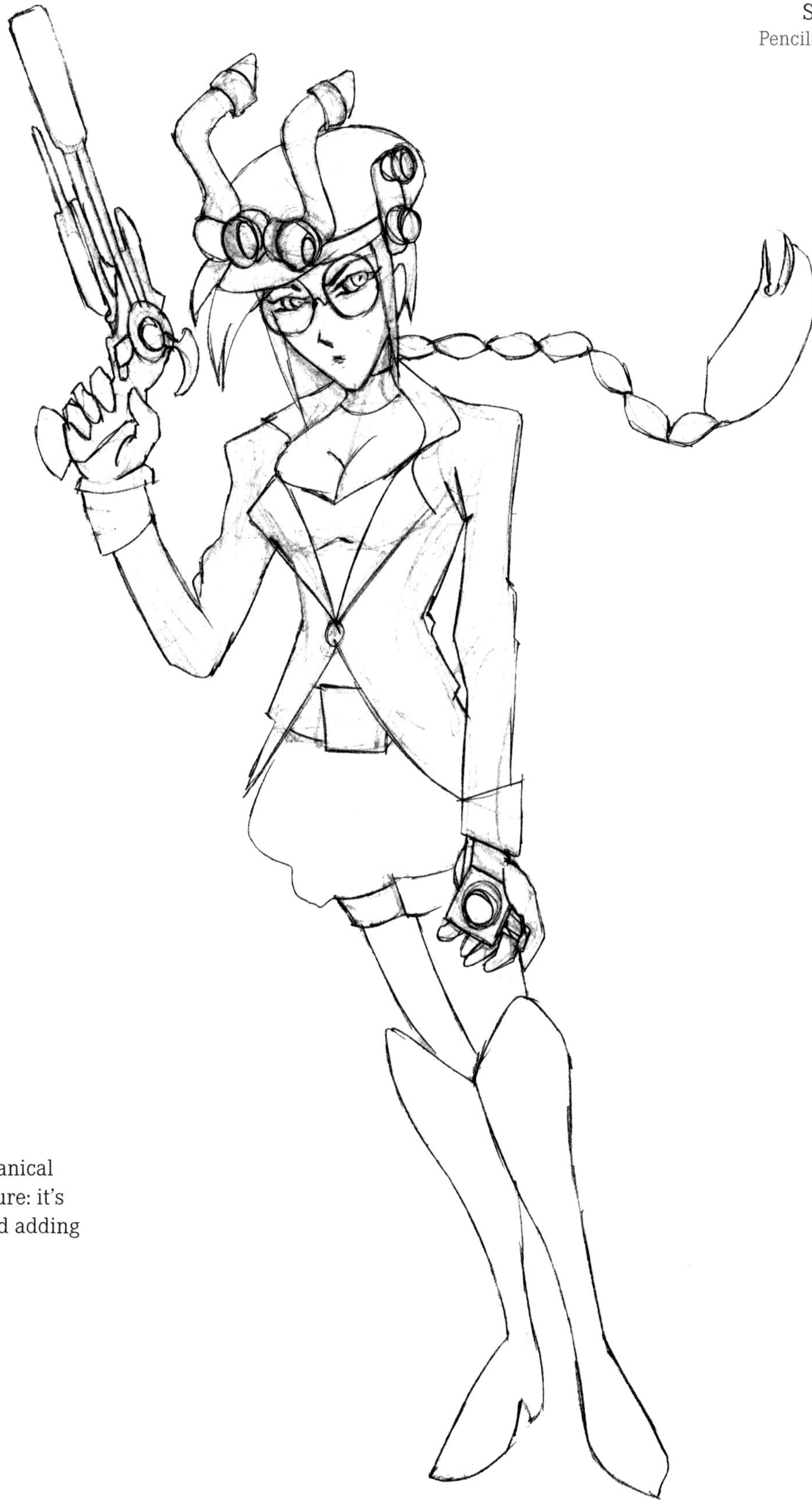

3

Using a 05-calibre mechanical pencil trace over the figure: it's all about giving form and adding the necessary details.

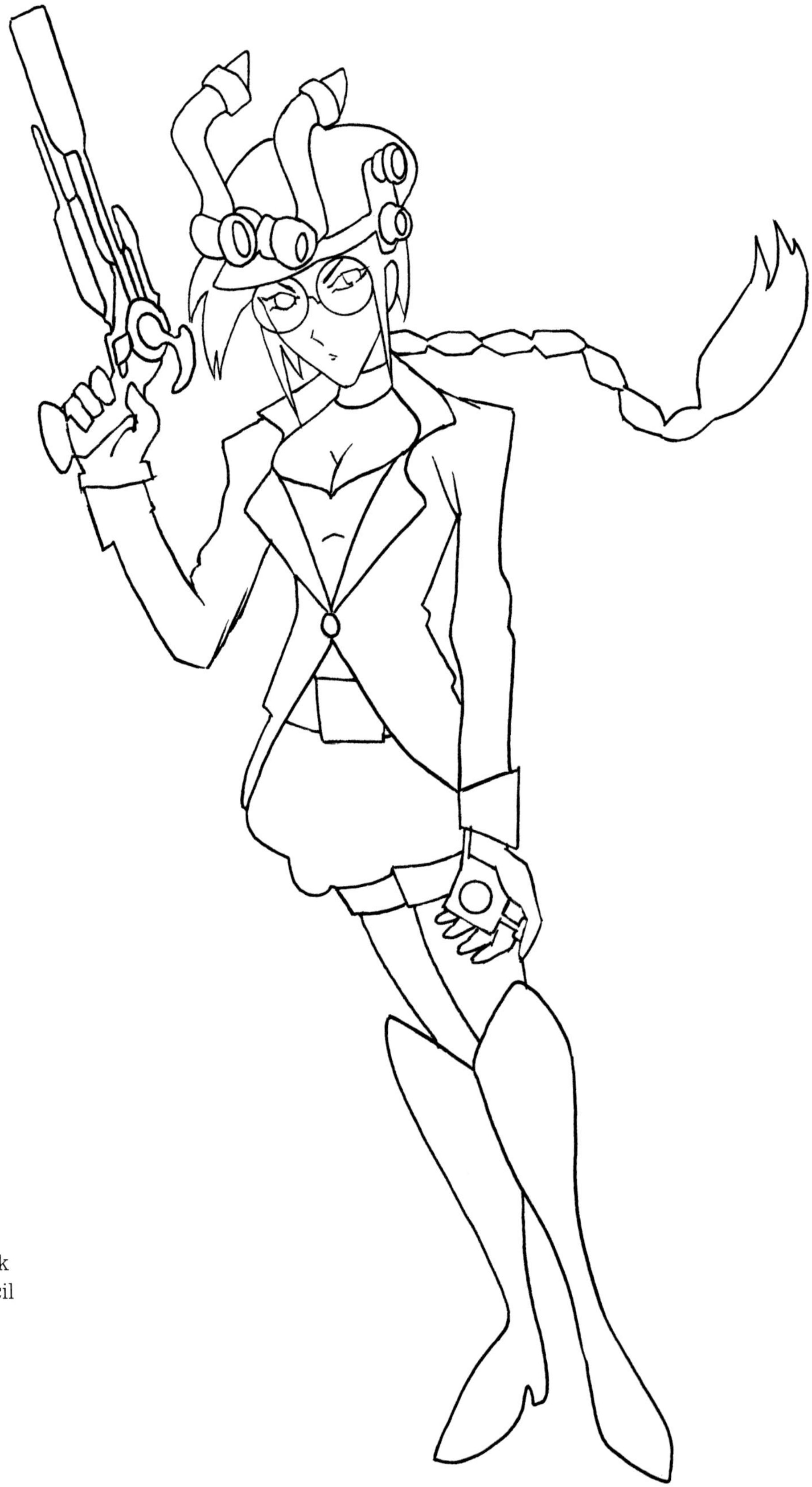

4

Use different calibre pens. As I have said before, use a 0.2 for detail, 0.4 for the figure, and 0.8 for the contour. Once the ink is dry you can remove the pencil with a soft eraser.

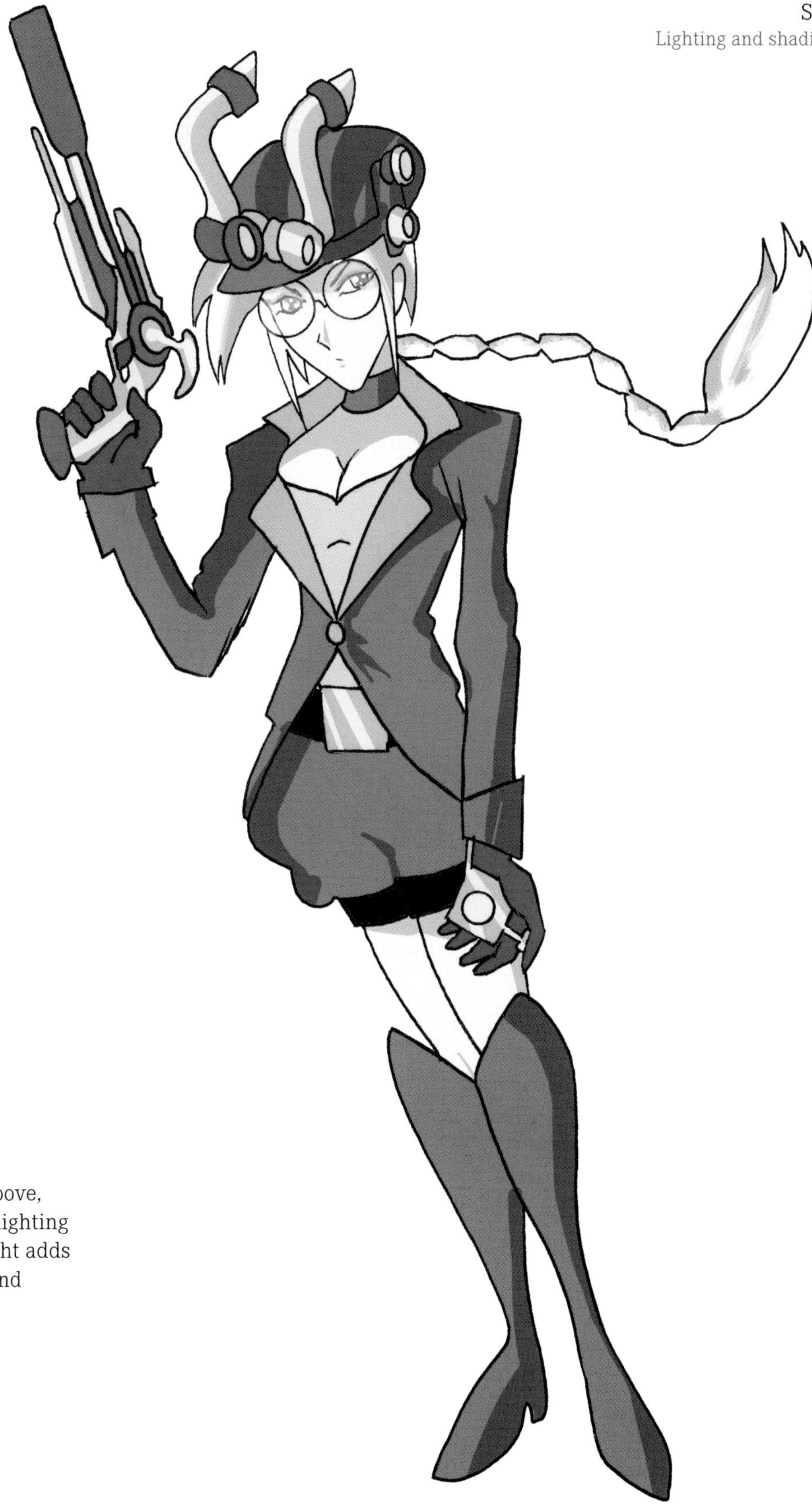

5

This figure is lit from above, as though from a lamp lighting up a large room. The light adds volume to her clothes and accessories.

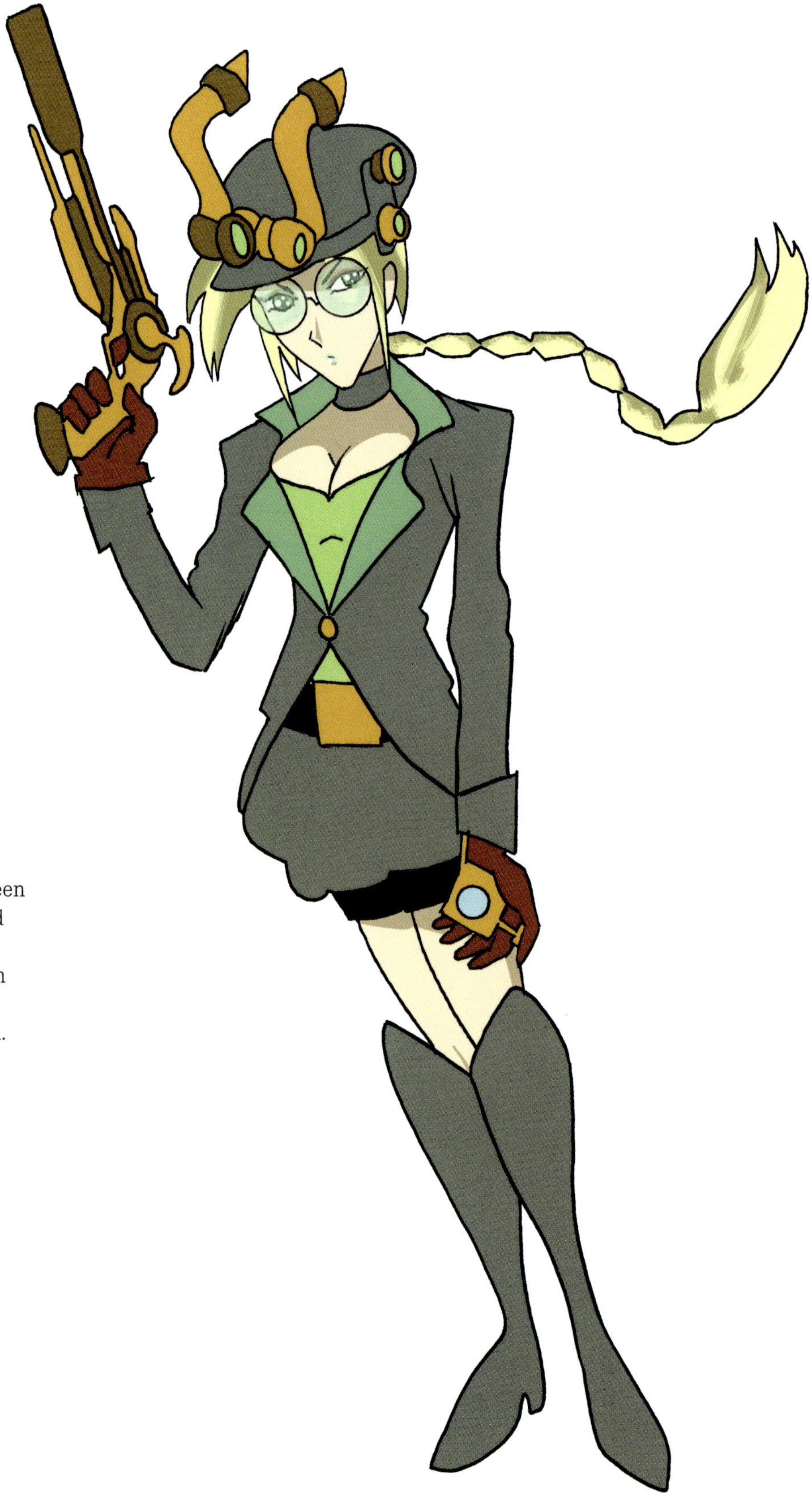

6

Use a general palette of light green tones. Use gold for the pistol and accessories such as the camera and buckle, and a reddish brown for the gloves. Your spy's hair is blond so use yellow to color it in.

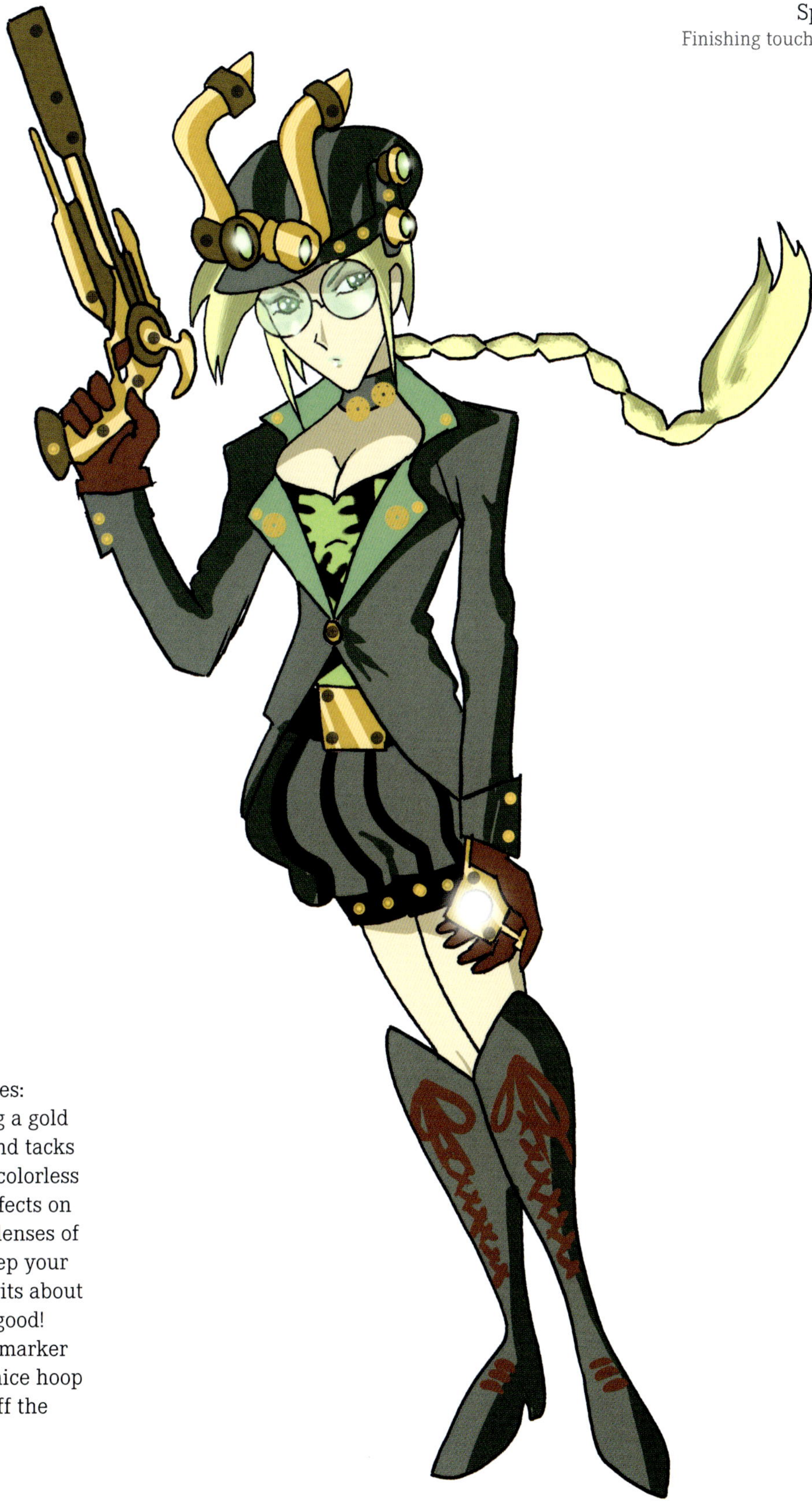

7

Add the finishing touches: shimmering glints using a gold pencil on the buttons and tacks of her outfit, and use a colorless marker for reflection effects on the camera and on the lenses of her hat. You need to keep your eyes peeled and your wits about you when a spy is this good! Using a reddish brown marker with a fine tip, draw a nice hoop on the boots to round off the attire. Ready!

TIME TRAVELER

Dick Kindred is the final descendant of a great family of scientists specializing in quantum physics. Dick is a great student of all the advances taking place in this field and discovered the whereabouts of another great inventor who had gone missing. The inventor confided in Dick, shared his secret, and left in his custody his most valuable achievement: a time machine. Now every mystery and secret in the world is at his fingertips. Let's hope Dick can protect them!

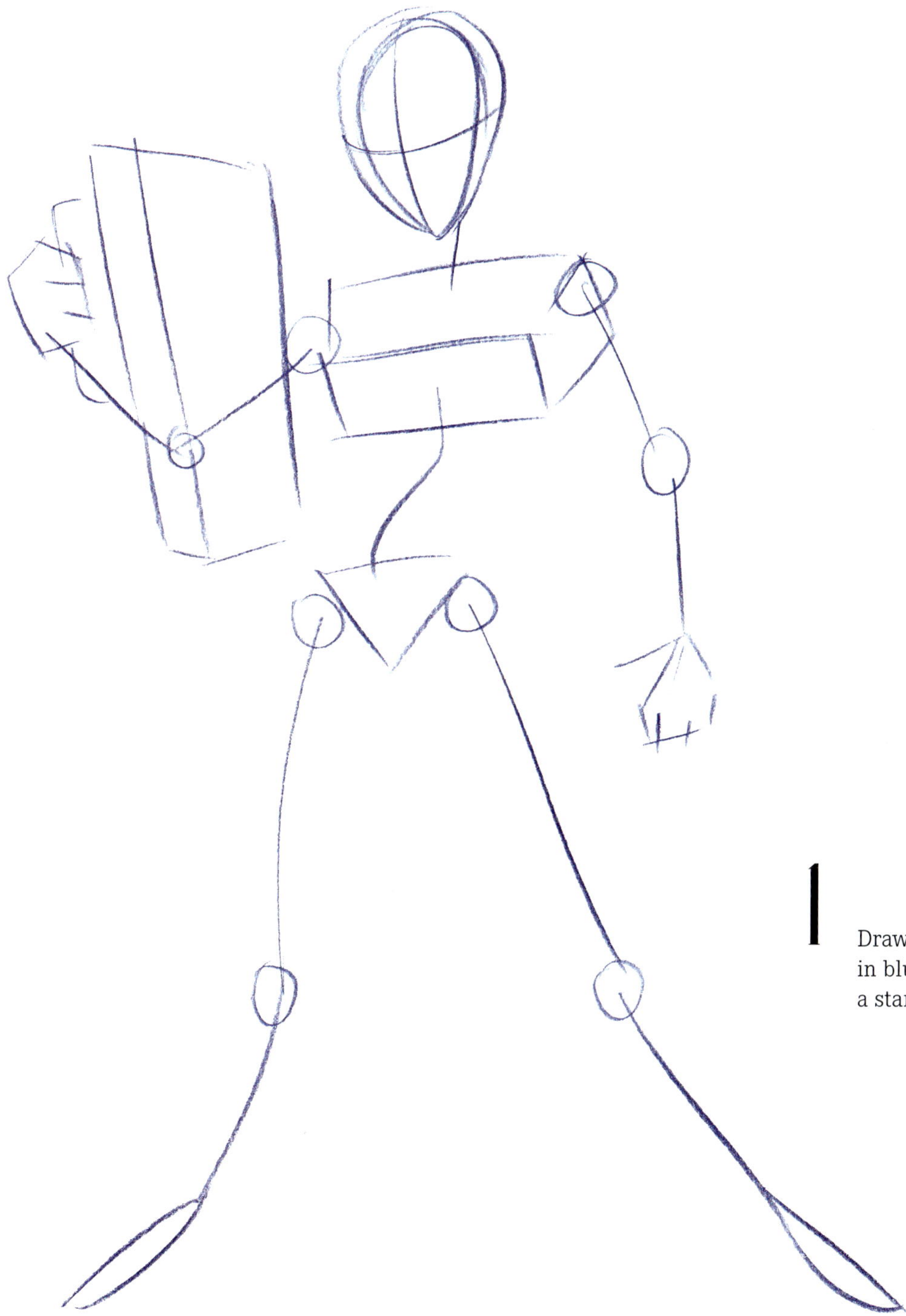

1

Draw the base of your traveler in blue pencil, giving him a stance that exudes class.

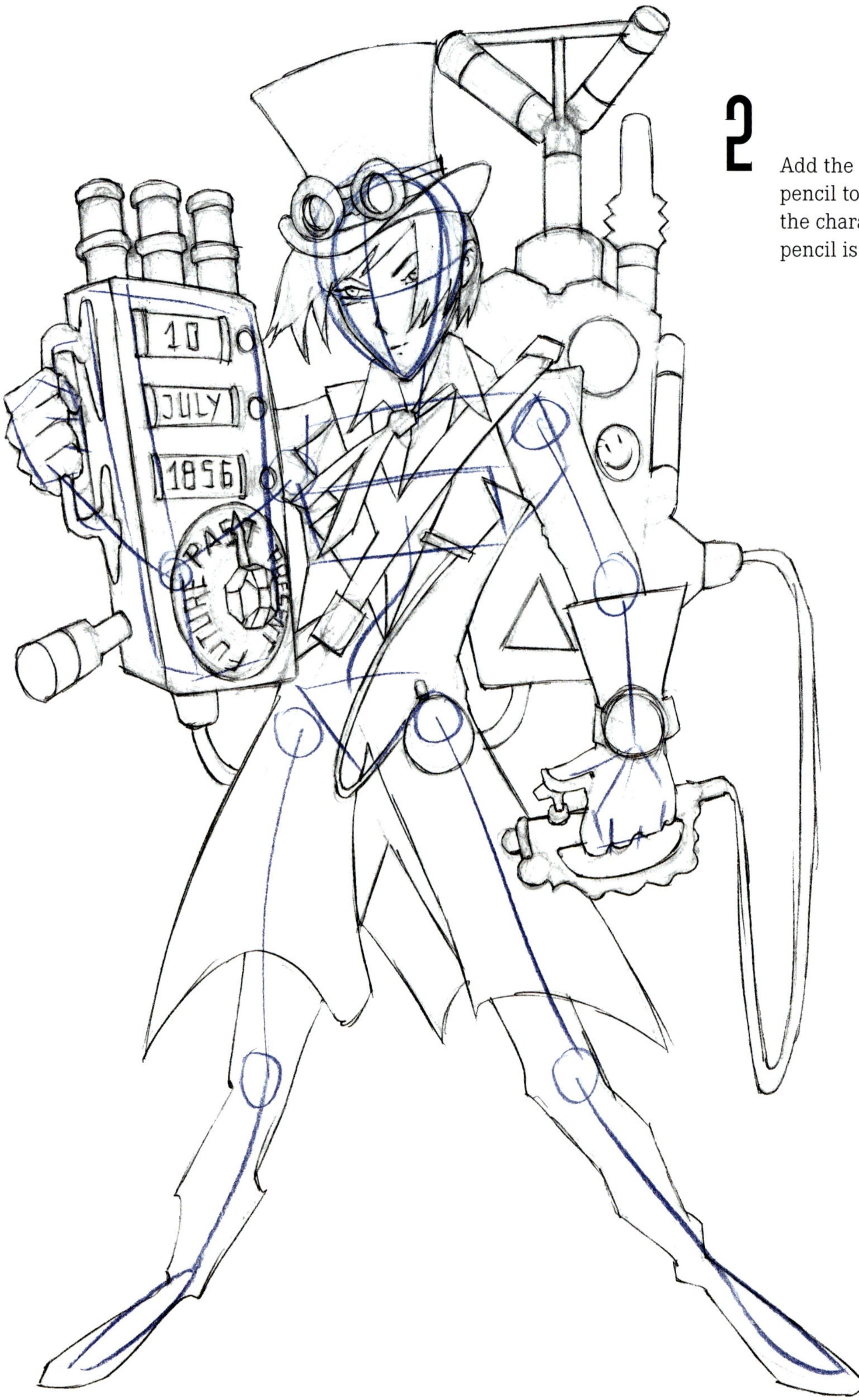

2

Add the outline to the base in pencil to create volume and define the character's appearance. A hard pencil is best for this. I use a 2H.

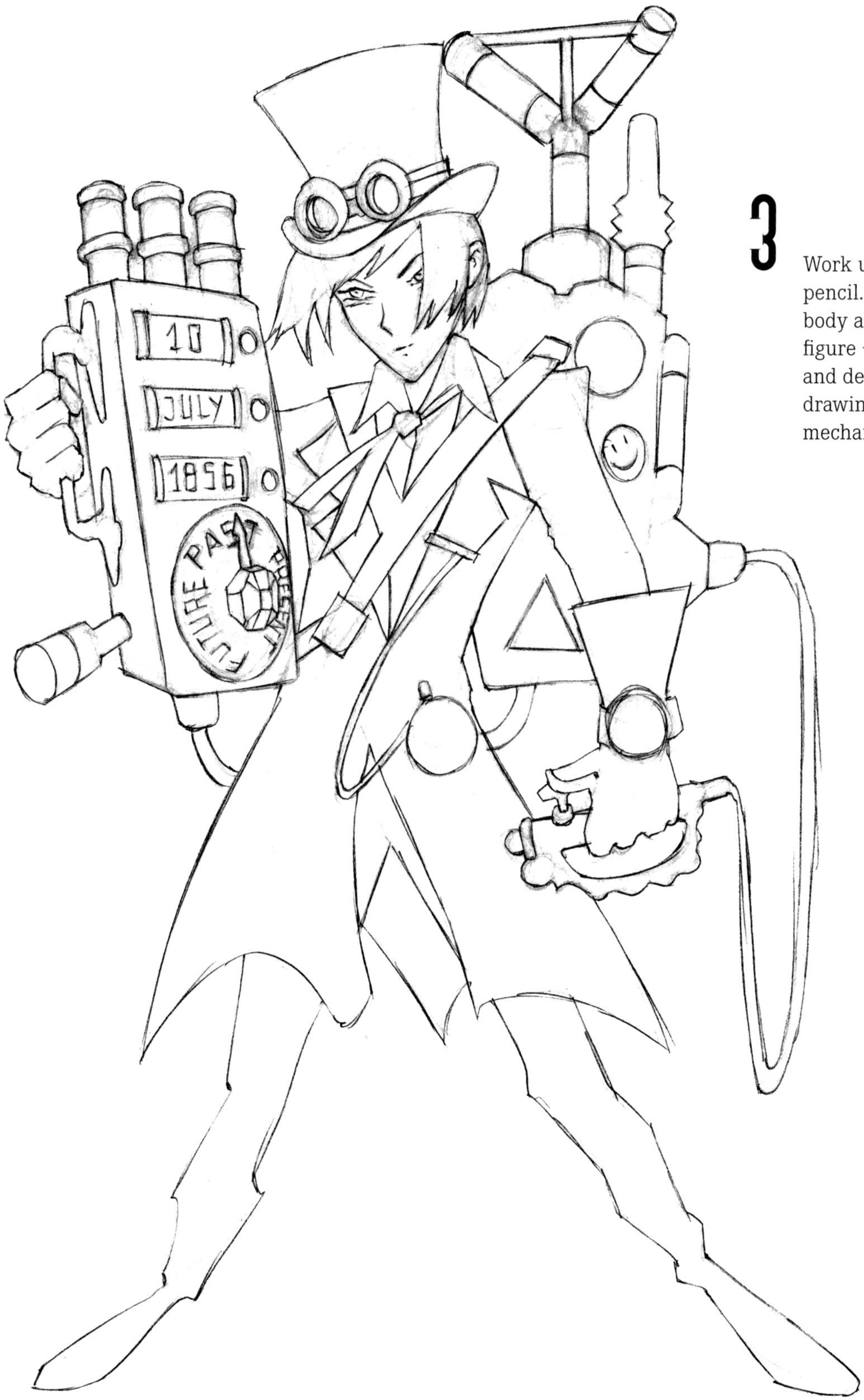

3

Work up the image with your pencil. Develop the character's body and add details to the figure – this will add volume and define the outline of the drawing. I use a Pilot 05-calibre mechanical pencil.

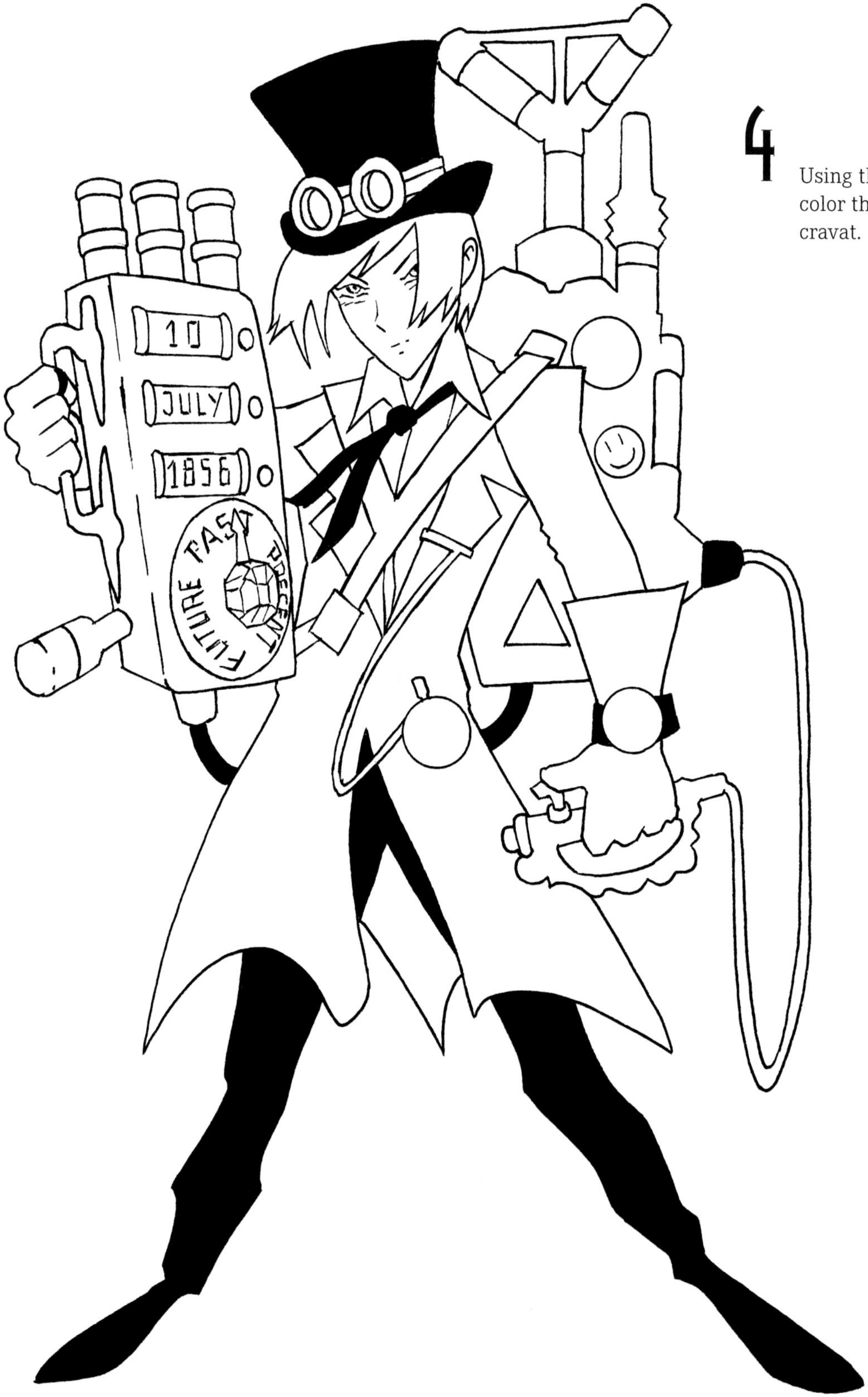

4

Using the thickest black pen, color the hat, trousers, and cravat.

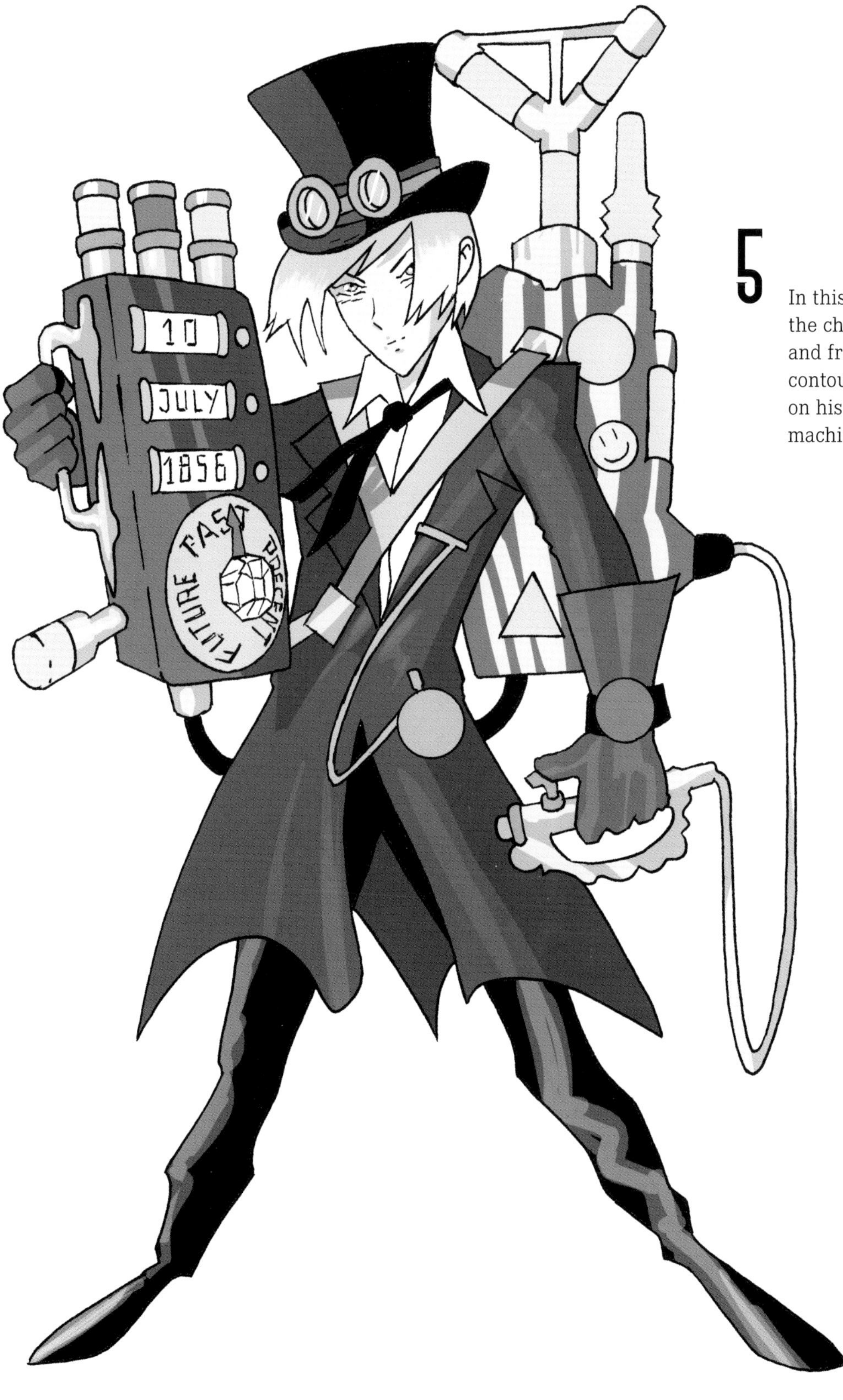

5

In this example the light crosses the character from left to right and from top to bottom, creating contours of light and shade both on his clothing and on the time machine.

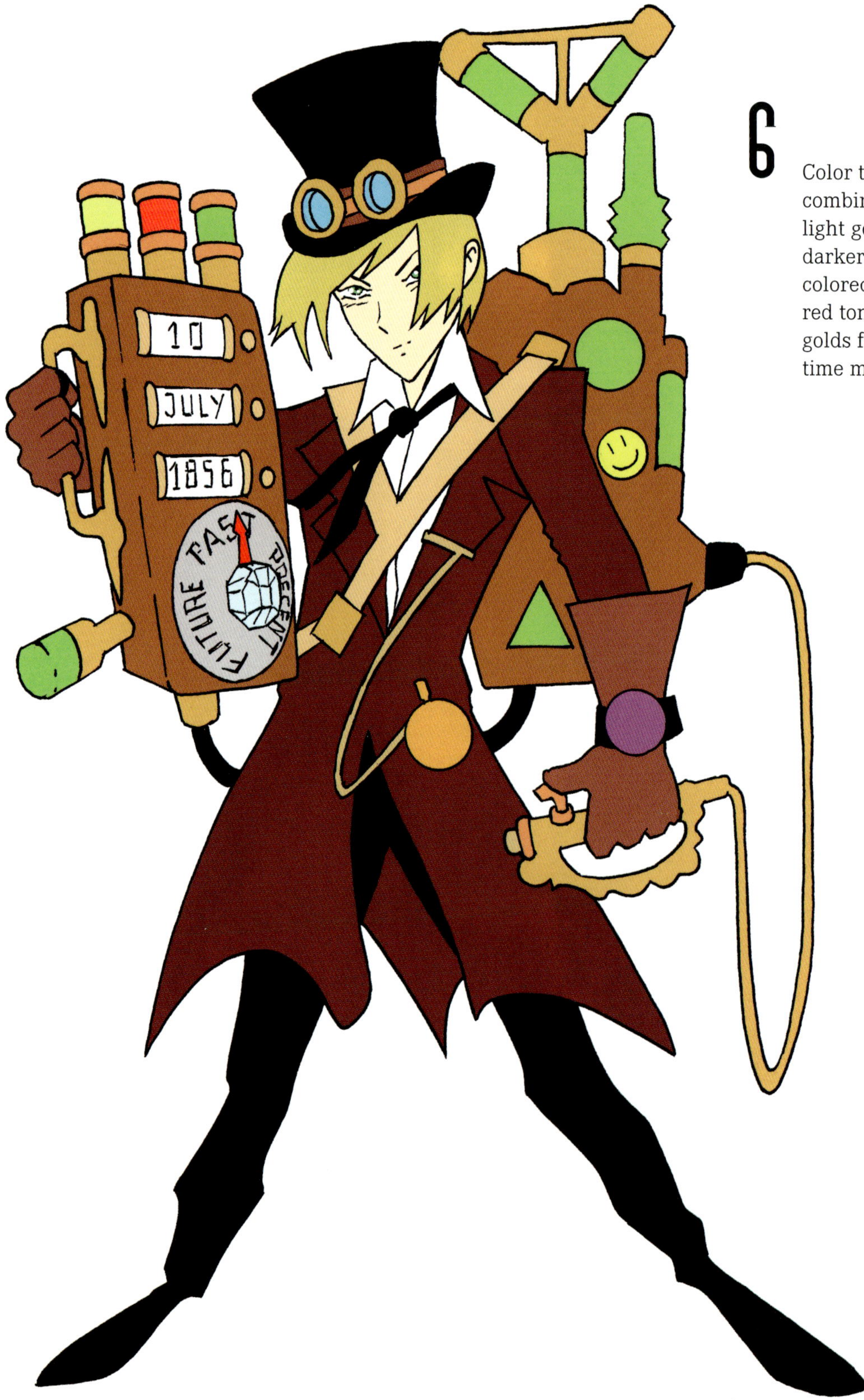

6

Color the drawing with a combination of burgundy, light gold, a more intense darker gold, and deep green colored pencils. Use russet red tones for the gloves, and golds for the impressive time machine.

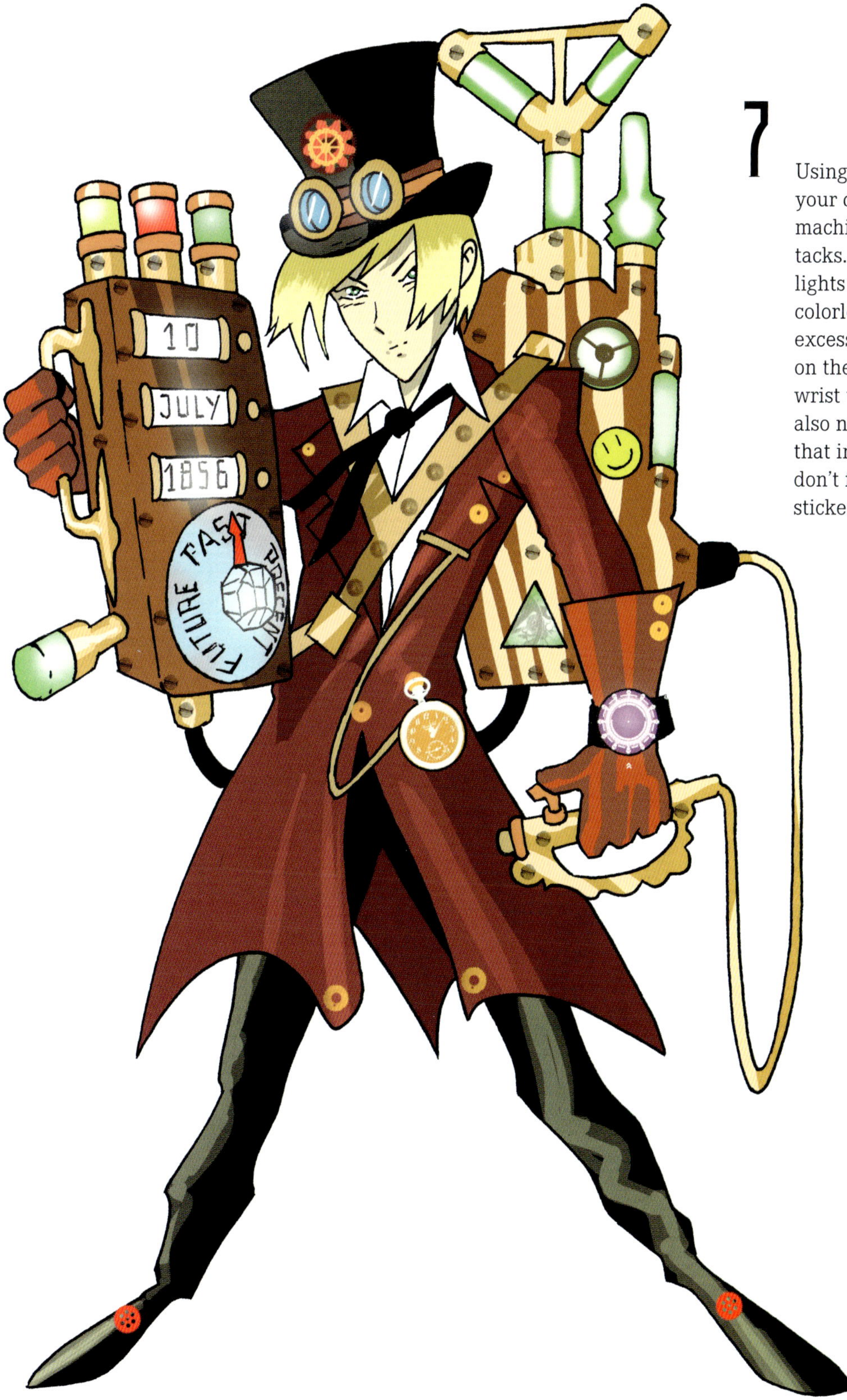

7

Using brush pens, decorate your character's clothes and his machine with gear wheels and tacks. Highlight the red and yellow lights on the machine with a colorless blender pen that removes excess of ink. Add the watches, one on the pocket and one on Dick's wrist using the same tools. You will also need to highlight the diamond that indicates the destination. And don't forget to color the smiley sticker in yellow!